FIRE MUSIC

Recent Titles in
the Music Reference Collection

The Classical Reproducing Piano Roll: A Catalogue-Index
Volume I: Composers
Larry Sitsky, compiler

The Classical Reproducing Piano Roll: A Catalogue-Index
Volume II: Pianists
Larry Sitsky, compiler

Woodwind Music of Black Composers
Aaron Horne, compiler

An Eighteenth-Century Musical Chronicle: Events 1750-1799
Charles J. Hall, compiler

Jazz Performers: An Annotated Bibliogaphy of Biographical Materials
Gary Carner, compiler

Songs, Odes, Glees and Ballads: A Bibliography of American Presidential Campaign Songsters
William Miles

Music History during the Renaissance Period, 1425-1520: A Documented Chronology
Blanche M. Gangwere

Music for Two or More Players at Clavichord, Harpsichord, Organ: An Annotated Bibliography
Sally Jo Sloane, compiler

Organ and Harpsichord Music by Women Composers: An Annotated Catalog
Adel Heinrich, compiler

Catalog of the Musical Works of William Billings
Karl Kroeger, compiler

FIRE MUSIC

A Bibliography of the New Jazz, 1959–1990

Compiled by
JOHN GRAY

Foreword by Val Wilmer

Music Reference Collection, Number 31

GREENWOOD PRESS
New York • Westport, Connecticut • London

Library of Congress Cataloging-in-Publication Data

Gray, John.
Fire music : a bibliography of the new jazz, 1959-1990 / compiled by John Gray ; foreword by Val Wilmer.
p. cm.—(Music reference collection, ISSN 0736-7740 ; no. 31)
Includes bibliographical references and indexes.
ISBN 0-313-27892-X (alk. paper)
1. Jazz—Bibliography. I. Title. II. Series.
ML128.J3G7 1991
016.78165'5—dc20 91-20601

British Library Cataloguing in Publication Data is available.

Library of Congress Catalog Card Number: 91-20601
ISBN: 0-313-27892-X
ISSN: 0736-7740

First published in 1991

Greenwood Press, 88 Post Road West, Westport, CT 06881
An imprint of Greenwood Publishing Group, Inc.

Printed in the United States of America

The paper used in this book complies with the Permanent Paper Standard issued by the National Information Standards Organization (Z39.48—1984).

10 9 8 7 6 5 4 3 2 1

Don't expect the answers to come to you. Don't wait for a leader to rise up and take you someplace. If you want information, and we have plenty, come and take it from us. It's on you. If you want to go out and begin something, you have to organize and study. You have to try many things before you may find some success. We are here to give you the help of our experience and knowledge, but now is the time of your generation and only you can make the choices.

Cleveland Sellers - SNCC

...I think I can truthfully say that in music I make or I have tried to make a conscious attempt to change what I've found, in music. In other words, I've tried to say, "Well, **this** I feel, could be better, in my opinion, so I will try to do this to make it better." This is what I feel that we feel in any situation that we find in our lives, when there's something we think could be better, we must make an effort to try and make it better. So it's the same socially, musically, politically, and in any department of our lives.

- John Coltrane

I think music is an instrument. It can create the initial thought patterns that can change the thinking of the people.

- John Coltrane

Contents

Foreword

The first Fire Music I heard was played by the King of the Zulus.* Bright, bold and burnished, King Louis's sound was unmistakable. No one, it seemed to me at the time, could play the horn with such fire. And although it would be some years before saxophonist Archie Shepp gave the title to one of his compositions, 'Fire Music,' I feel on reflection, is a most apposite term for the vehicle which has provided the means for the playing out of the drama of the African people in the Americas. Fire analogies permeate the music: instrumentalists are said to be 'burning' when they are inspired, to 'smoke' each other when playing competitively. Saxophonist Marion Brown described John Coltrane's Ascension as 'the kind of record you could use to warm up the apartment on a cold winter's day.'

Born out of tumult, revolt and the struggle for self-determination, African-American music is as life-enhancing in its most recent manifestations as it was in the days when Louis Armstrong picked up his first cornet and ran alongside a New Orleans parade. Its spiritual qualities are self-evident, its universal appeal reflected in a worldwide coterie of improvising musicians inspired by innovations rooted in Black Belt America. 'Great Black Music!' proclaims the members of Chicago's AACM (Association for the Advancement of Creative Musicians): 'Power stronger than itself!'

* * * * *

As a teenager growing up in the 1950s in London, a city that still showed the ravages of wartime, I found an antidote to the prevailing national mood of austerity in the music of Louis Armstrong and the 'bloods' of his day. In the most literal sense, Armstrong's 'day' was not mine, but like other outsiders of my generation I began my jazz journey by listening to the music of the 'classic' age: the Hot Fives and Sevens, Bessie Smith, Ma Rainey and Sidney Bechet. As time went by and my record collection expanded, so I became aware

* The King of the Zulus is a key figure in New Orleans' Mardi Gras parade. When the city paid tribute to its most distinguished musical son by crowning Louis Armstrong king in 1949, the trumpeter realized a lifelong ambition.

of the way in which the music had developed. Struggling against the limited horizons of the period, my existence was brightened by the continual discovery of artists who brought a unique individual and collective experience to bear on their music, stamping their work with what the New Orleans writer Kalamu ya Salaam has termed 'the African signature.'[1]

Long before I had any inkling of the way in which black music operated among its constituents as a force for 'regeneration and elevation'[2] I absorbed its legends. The life stories of its protagonists became as familiar to me as the music itself. My own rites of passage into adulthood were accompanied by the sounds of Afro-America, as a succession of visiting artists carried their musical wares across the Atlantic and converted people like me to something far more profound than rock 'n' roll. Big Bill Broonzy brought the Mississippi blues to an antiseptic concert hall where he was cheered to the echo; Clara Ward and Sister Rosetta Tharpe introduced the sanctified sound of the Holiness church into sweaty, smoke-filled clubs where jazz was played. We were graced by visits from royalty too: Duke Ellington and Count Basie seducing audiences with urbane and effortless charm. The musicians were friendly and I got to speak to some of them along the way. It was only a short step from there for me to becoming a writer.

Looking back at the ease with which I managed to establish myself as a commentator on music, I am sometimes surprised that the climate of the day enabled the views of one so young to be taken seriously. The story of African-American music is, after all, a drama of heroic proportions, the significance of which lies a little outside the ken of a 17 year old schoolgirl. Talking with the musicians was what enabled me to grasp that there was a great deal more to the music than that which met the ear.

The American visitors in their spotless band uniforms and mohair suits, were glamorous by comparison with the drabness that clung like a shroud around the shoulders of postwar Britain. Not surprisingly, we 'hip' enthusiasts hung on their every word as they handed round bottles of whiskey and menthol cigarettes--new to us then--and offered liberal splashes of cologne. Among them was a man who gave me my earliest clue to understanding the politics of culture. He was Joe Gordon, a marvelous trumpeter from Boston whose blistering playing epitomized his belief that the music had crucial significance for black people. There was no way you could argue with horn-playing like that, and the lessons I learnt from him will stay with me always.

When it came to the new wave of 'freedom' music that was emerging at the tail-end of bebop, there were two other people who helped me towards its appreciation. One was a musician, Art Davis, who came from Harrisburg, Pa., and worked on the two double-basses concept with John Coltrane. He sent me advance copies of the albums he cut with the saxophonist, <u>Ole</u> and <u>Ascension</u>, and through conversation and correspondence, made me aware of the politics and philosophy behind the music. His guidance in this respect was vital, for enormous changes were taking place in the structure of daily life in the United States and these were having repercussions among those who documented the music. With the racial status quo under attack and black people throughout society growing more outspoken, many critics were developing an antipathy towards the new music which was clearly shored up by the demands for black liberation and racial justice. Some writers expressed overt hostility towards progressives on the bandstand, and found their anger returned.

In Britain the mood was more relaxed. My other 'spirit guide' of those days was a Trinidadian named Johnny Millington. He was a devout jazz devotee who worked as a cook by day and contrived to meet the touring musicians--and supplement his income--by providing an essential service: cutting their hair.

When Coltrane came to London in 1961 with Eric Dolphy in tow, my acquaintance with Art Davis helped facilitate interviews with the two reedmen. Backstage, though, Johnny's hairclippers and his personable manner enabled us both to indulge in some easy socializing with Dolphy and the rest of the group. These snapshot meetings are indelibly printed on my memory, brief encounters that established the musicians as far more than names on a record. Our conversations were inconsequential, I am certain, yet to sit down and share a meal with Coltrane's serious young pianist, McCoy Tyner, enabled me to witness what manner of man played this demanding new music.

And 'demanding' is the appropriate word for, in common with other jazz enthusiasts of my generation, I resisted some manifestations of the 'new thing' initially. By comparison with what had gone before, it sounded harsh and unrelenting and could be uncomfortable to listen to. Getting to know musicians like Tyner was inspirational, the experience causing me to listen again, to weigh up and consider. The pianist was clearly dedicated, a responsible custodian of an enormous legacy. Another decade would pass before he would tell me, 'Music's not a play thing; it's as serious as your life,'[3] and give me the title for a book, but sitting in a Caribbean restaurant with him and his wife, eating rice-and-peas after hours, I already knew this, instinctively.

Not long after our encounter with Coltrane, Johnny Millington acquired some highly-prized American imports. Among these records were Ornette Coleman's <u>Change of the Century</u> and Eric Dolphy's first album on Prestige. These two names still created controversy in jazz circles, but playing these sides for me one evening, Johnny made little distinction between them and other current sounds popular in local Caribbean circles. It was saxophonist Marion Brown who pointed out that 'music is the thread that binds black people' and nowhere was this more clearly illustrated for me than that night at Johnny's. His acceptance of sounds regarded as 'far-out' by the mainstream jazz community, his unselfconscious featuring of them alongside the vocal duets of Dinah Washington and Brook Benton, guided me towards an appreciation of the universality of black music. I began to leave my listening prejudices behind.

I became a convert to the ways of the 'freedom' musicians, not least because I was inspired by the music's profound aesthetic and because I could see what the music represented for individuals far removed from each other in lifestyle and experience. As Kalamu ya Salaam has said, 'our music is no accident.'[4] And it was from people such as Johnny and Joe Gordon, Art Davis and McCoy, that I learnt the way in which the music had, in fact, been designed. I grew to believe that it was an essential part of a ritual which helped create reassurance and uplift among a people who were often under siege, and to foster a spirit of communality as well. And every time I heard Louis Armstrong play, I felt this, too.

African-American music goes beyond any Eurocentric notion of it as 'cultural phenomenon.' That it has continually inspired the lives and creativity of others from outside the culture only serves to reflect the extent to which, America is, as one writer put it, 'saturated with African modes of expression.'[5] For many outsiders who came upon the Fire Music of the 1960s, the black aesthetic became their goal, just as it had been for white Chicagoans like saxophonist Bud Freeman, hanging out to listen to King Oliver at the Lincoln Gardens in the 1920s, and the Lester Young soundalikes of a generation later.

The core belief I absorbed from my early mentors has coloured my documentation of the music. Years later it was best expressed for me in the course of a conversation with percussionist Jerome Cooper: 'Black music is how our lives are, and how we are looking at, and relating to, the outside world. It's just a state of mind.'[6]

Val Wilmer
London, July 1991

1. Kalamu ya Salaam, Keith Calhoun and Chandra McCormick. Our Music is No Accident. New Orleans Cultural Foundation Inc., 1988, p. 2.

2. Ibid. p. 14.

3. Valerie Wilmer. As Serious As Your Life. Westport, CT: Lawrence Hill, 1981, p. 258.

4. Salaam. Op. cit. p. 2.

5. Kevin Whitehead in Cadence, June 1991, p. 21.

6. Wilmer. Op. cit. p. 9.

Acknowledgments

Although all of the research for this project was carried out by myself I would like to thank the following people for their many valuable additions and contributions to the final work: Pheeroan akLaff, Jane Ira Bloom, Karen Burdick, Dave Burrell, Andrew Cyrille, Art Davis, Bill Dixon, Gunter Hampel, Gerry Hemingway, Cynthia B. Herbst (for Julius Hemphill), Steve Lacy, Richard Leigh, Wilber Morris, Kunle Mwanga (for Ed Blackwell), Bobby Naughton, Corine Parker (for Horace Tapscott), Errol Parker, Mario Pavone, Jeff Schwartz, Bill Smith, Norman Weinstein and Andrew White.

Jazz writer Val Wilmer occupies a niche of her own in this small pantheon and deserves all the kudos I can muster, for supplying the initial inspiration for Fire Music and providing assistance beyond the call of duty in turning up new citations on her own work as well as a plethora of other sources. I only hope that the result honors her contribution.

Finally, there are two figures who can truly be called responsible for this work: John Coltrane and my mother. Over the last decade they have supplied the essential resources--spiritual, mental, physical and financial--necessary to complete this work. For them, I say, MUCHO ACHE!

Introduction

In the fall of 1959 saxophonist Ornette Coleman arrived on the New York jazz scene and promptly set it on its head. Playing a music shorn of the traditional jazz structures--reliance on a single key, a set pattern of chord changes, a regular meter or bar lines--Coleman opened the door to a whole new era in jazz improvisation. In his wake would follow the innovations of John Coltrane, Cecil Taylor, Sun Ra, Albert Ayler, and a score of other improvisors intent on expanding the New Jazz vocabulary. Their legacy, known variously as "the jazz avant-garde," "the New Music," "free jazz," "the New Thing," "anti-jazz," "outside playing," "Great Black Music," "Creative Music," "Improvised Music," or, my preferred term, "the New Jazz," is Fire Music's subject.

While a number of works have been written on the New Jazz, most notably Ekkehard Jost's Free Jazz (# 61), Frank Kofsky's Black Nationalism and the Revolution in Music (# 62), John Litweiler's The Freedom Principle (# 64), and Valerie Wilmer's essential As Serious As Your Life (# 71), none has yet attempted to cover the music in its entirety. With this in mind I thought that now, a little more than three decades after the music's beginnings, might be a good time to take stock. What I have tried to do in these pages is to provide as complete a record as possible of the New Jazz and its many developments from 1959 to the present. Now, for the first time, users can find information on both the New Jazz's big names--Coleman, Coltrane, and Taylor--**and** such oft-overlooked topics as the jazz collectives and co-operative record labels of the 60s, 70s, and 80s, New York's jazz lofts of the 1970s, New Jazz activity around and outside of the United States, and much more.

To achieve this I have gathered a wide array of sources--books, dissertations, periodical and newspaper articles, films, videos, and audiotapes--in all the major Western languages. While the majority of these works are in English and French, users will also find a fair number of entries in Italian, German, Dutch, and Swedish. It is my hope that these additional entries will increase the book's usefulness for European researchers.

The number of individual performers and ensembles assembled is equally broad. Types of materials included for them emphasize biographical and critical works, although a selection of record and concert reviews may also be found. Those reviews that are included are primarily on major artists--such as Ornette Coleman, John Coltrane, and Cecil Taylor--to give users an indication of the critical sentiments of the time, pro and con. Album liner notes and works that contain only brief references to the New Jazz or that are less than two pages in length have been excluded.

Also, in a small number of cases in which an artist's career has had only a limited connection to the New Jazz--Chick Corea, Jayne Cortez, Steve Davis, Steve Kuhn, Abbey Lincoln, Jimmy Owens, Max Roach, Sonny Rollins, and Warren Smith--I have included only works pertaining to that period in their careers. This accounts for the brevity of their sections.

Research for Fire Music began nearly a decade ago as part of a Junior Field project of mine at the State University of New York at Purchase. In the years since that brief early work has been made unrecognizable by the literally thousands of additions and revisions made to it. The result is the behemoth now before you. To assist in this transformation I have gone through the Music Index (1959-Feb. 1990), Jazz Index (1977-1983), complete or near complete runs of thirty-six different journals and newspapers, the computerized library catalogue of the New York Public Library (CATNYP), and the 30,000,000 item RLIN (Research Libraries Information Network) database. Supplemental searches were conducted in most, if not all, of the currently available CD ROMs--Magazine Index, Academic Index, Reader's Guide to Periodical Literature, MLA International Bibliography, and Biography Index, as well as my own Black Arts Database, a bibliographic resource containing more than 35,000 entries on arts activity in Africa and the African Diaspora. (For a more complete list of sources consulted, see Appendix I.)

Accuracy was achieved by checking each of the book-length entries against the Library of Congress's National Union Catalogue and/or the RLIN and OCLC library databases. For journal articles, an attempt was made to view as large a number as possible; however, due to the wide dispersal of jazz periodicals across the United States and Europe, I was unable to verify each one.

In the case of performers included I have tried, whenever possible, to supply birth and death dates and countries of origin for each. Information on artists for whom I have been unable to locate this information or corrections of inaccurate data will be most appreciated.

Due to the extremely unpredictable availability of jazz recordings and the dearth of libraries and archives with large New Jazz holdings I have decided not to include a discography here. However I have included numerous citations to relevant discographies both in the Reference Works section (# 7076-7081) and in the sections on individual artists. I think that these works should fulfill most discographical needs.

Organization

Fire Music is organized into six basic sections followed by four appendixes and three indexes. The first section offers a chronology of important social, political and musical events that have helped shape the jazz world of the past three decades, while Section Two covers works on African American cultural history and the arts. Section Three lists general works and country/regional studies of the New Jazz. Section Four focuses on the various jazz collectives and co-operative record labels of the 60s, 70s, and 80s, while Section Five chronicles their stepchildren, the jazz lofts of the 1970s. The sixth and largest section is devoted to biographical and critical studies of more than 400 individual artists and ensembles. Four appendixes follow dealing with, respectively, Reference Works utilized in Fire Music's compilation; Archives and Research Centers with large jazz collections; and two lists, by country and instrument, of New Jazz artists. Three indexes--Artist, Subject, and Author--conclude the work.

Materials in each of these sections are broken down into the following categories: books, book sections, dissertations and theses, journals, articles, concert and record reviews, discographies, and media materials. A brief glance at some of the book's opening sections should make this system clear.

To assist users interested in finding related subjects and artists in Fire Music, I have also incorporated extensive cross referencing. However, the most complete information on a given artist, subject or author, will be found in the book's indexes.

Availability of Works

Because the bulk of the research for this project was carried out at three of the New York Public Library's Research Divisions I can safely say that a majority of the works included here may be found in those collections:

New York Public Library - Music Research Division of the Performing Arts Research Center at Lincoln Center (111 Amsterdam Ave., New York, NY 10023. Tel. 212/870-1650).

New York Public Library - Rodgers & Hammerstein Collection (same address as above. Tel. 212/870-1663).

New York Public Library - Schomburg Center for Research in Black Culture (515 Lenox Ave., New York, NY 10037. Tel. 212/862-4000).

For those who don't have access to these collections, or others listed in Appendix II, the best alternative is the Inter Library Loan department of your university or public library.

Conclusion

This work completes a decade-long odyssey inititated by a chance encounter with Val Wilmer's pioneering study As Serious As Your Life (# 71). It was there that I got my first real glimpse into the lives and music of African America's jazz vanguard and the fierce and exciting music they produced. This was also one of the, if not **the**, sources responsible for my decision to start documenting the lives and creative contributions of people of African descent, a journey that has now spawned six books, several articles, and a research center devoted to African and African Diaspora performance culture.

However, as Wilmer points out in her autobiography (# 70, p. xiii):

> It is hard to decide at what point something that has been a hobby becomes a part of life. Like many Whites caught up in the diversity of [the] African Diaspora, I've been challenged for attempting to document something outside my own experience. But I've been out here learning...and proximity has taught respect. I have always felt that those white people admitted as guests in the culture had a responsibility to support Black endeavour and make the information we gathered as well as the history as widely available as possible. There has been a pressing need for this, given the paucity of information available until lately. It has been my privilege to live with the constant realisation that the people I was meeting were part of history, or might very soon be.

I only hope that <u>Fire Music's</u> more than 7,100 entries will assist future generations of students, scholars, and listeners as much as <u>As Serious As Your Life</u> has assisted me.

Finally, despite nearly ten years of effort, I know, as does any researcher, that there is always more information out there, buried in a hundred small journals, little-known or unthought of monographs, as well as in the ever-increasing flood of new sources. Thus I urge any and all users to write to me care of the publisher or the Black Arts Research Center (# 7085) to alert me to any items I may have missed.

1

New Jazz Chronology

1954 Landmark "Brown v. Board of Education" decision handed down by Supreme Court ruling segregation of schools to be unconstitutional. Symbolic beginning to a new era.

1955/56 Death of Charlie Parker.

Fourteen year old Emmett Till lynched in Mississippi.

Montgomery (Alabama) Bus Boycott kicked off by Rosa Parks and led by Martin Luther King, Jr.

Cecil Taylor records first lp "Jazz Advance" for the Transition label.

Bassist Charles Mingus records his extended composition "Pithecanthropus Erectus" describing the metaphorical rise and fall of the white man.

1957 Ghana becomes first African nation to gain its independence. Followed by Guinea in 1958.

Civil Rights Act of 1957 passed--first since 1875. Allows Justice Department to bring suits on behalf of African Americans denied the right to vote.

Showdown at Little Rock (Arkansas) Central High School over school desegregation decree. President Eisenhower forced to send in federal troops to enforce the decree over the vociferous objections of Governor Orval Faubus. Signal for the coming era of massive white resistance to integration.

Cecil Taylor makes Newport Jazz Festival appearance.

1958 Charles Mingus records his "Faubus Fables" **without** its controversial lyrics.

Sonny Rollins's extended composition "Freedom Suite" released. However, due to some controversial personal thoughts by Rollins included in the liner notes, the record is pulled from the market after only a few weeks. Soon though it is re-released under the new title "Shadow Waltz" **without** Rollins's notes, inducing Rollins to switch record labels.

Ornette Coleman's first lp, Something Else!!! The Music of Ornette Coleman, recorded for the Contemporary label.

1959 The Shape of Jazz to Come, Ornette Coleman's first major recording, is released. In the Fall of this year Ornette also makes his epochal New York debut kicking off the largest controversy in the jazz world since the emergence of Charlie Parker and the Bebop era of the '40s.

Tenorman John Coltrane records his important Giant Steps album, indicating another of the major directions for jazz in the 60s.

Whites riot in New Orleans in attempt to stop the integration of local schools.

1960 First "sit-in" staged by four black college students at a Greensboro, North Carolina, lunch counter. In less than ten days their efforts would see echoes in fifteen Southern cities in five states.

Twelve former African colonies--the Congo, Somalia, Dahomey, Niger, Upper Volta, Ivory Coast, Chad, Congo Brazzaville, Gabon, Senegal, Mali and Nigeria--gain their independence. Soon thereafter Sierra Leone and Tanzania (1961), Uganda (1962), Kenya (1963), Malawi and Zambia (1964) also become independent. These newly liberated African states emerge as a major source of inspiration for African Americans seeking equal rights in the United States.

Civil Rights Act of 1960 passed allowing Justice Department to bring suit against states who withhold voting rights from blacks.

Newport Rebel Festival held. Guerrilla festival organized by Max Roach and Charles Mingus to protest the shoddy treatment of older players and the commercial exploitation of jazz music in general by George Wein's Newport Jazz Festival. Produces the first self-determination organization in jazz history, the short-lived Jazz Artists Guild.

Charles Mingus re-records his "Faubus Fables" for the Candid label, this time **with** the controversial lyrics left off of the original Columbia lp.

John Coltrane leaves Miles Davis to form own group.

Release of Ornette Coleman's Free Jazz, a 36-minute collective improvisation by a double quartet of two drummers, two bassists, two trumpeters and two horn players. The model for such later works as New York Eye and Ear Control and John Coltrane's epochal Ascension lp.

1961 Burning of Negro churches across the South as part of white intimidation campaign to squelch growing black resistance to racial discrimination.

First "Freedom Riders" embark on a bus trip through the Deep South to challenge segregation in Inter-State transportation. There they are met with fire bombs and armed white mobs. After repeated incidents, President Kennedy is finally forced to respond by sending federal marshals and federalized Alabama National Guardsman to protect riders in Montgomery. Despite summary beatings and jailings the rides continue and spread to other states.

Pianist Richard Abrams founds the Experimental Band, precursor to the Association for the Advancement of Creative Musicians, in Chicago.

Charlayne Hunter and Hamilton E. Holmes become first black students to attend the University of Georgia resulting in a white riot.

Release of three "protest" lps by Max Roach and Abbey Lincoln titled We Insist: Freedom Now Suite, It's Time and Percussion Bittersweet, touching off a major controversy in down beat magazine over the propriety of mixing jazz and politics.

Alto saxophonist/bass clarinetist Eric Dolphy joins tenorman John Coltrane in a combination that would put them at the forefront of New Jazz innovations in the 1960s. Their ensemble soon emerges as a focal point for the "anti-jazz" criticism being propagated at the time.

1962 White riot precipitated at the University of Mississippi after segregationist Governor Ross Barnett's appeals to mobs to prevent James Meredith from enrolling as "Ole Miss's" first black student. Results in injury of 375 federal marshalls and rioters and two deaths. Stopped by J.F.K.'s belated commitment of Federal troops and Mississippi National Guard.

West Coast pianist Horace Tapscott forms the Underground Musicians and Artists Association (UGMAA) to take control of, and disseminate, the black jazz heritage to Los Angeles's Watts community.

Cecil Taylor makes first major overseas tour of Scandinavian countries.

1963 Massive voter registration efforts undertaken by Dr. Martin Luther King, the Southern Christian Leadership Conference, and the Student Non-Violent Coordinating Committee.

Mississippi NAACP field secretary Medgar Evers is shot to death outside his home.

Alabama Governor George Wallace makes his famous doorway stand at the University of Alabama to prohibit the admission of Vivian Malone and James A. Hood as that university's first black students.

Police Chief Eugene "Bull" Connor looses attack dogs and water hoses on black children protesting segregation and job discrimination in Birmingham, Alabama.

Four black girls are killed in a racist bombing of a Birmingham church.

John Coltrane records his composition "Alabama" as memorial for the girls.

March on Washington at which Martin Luther King makes his now famous "I Have a Dream" speech.

President John F. Kennedy assassinated in Dallas.

LeRoi Jones initiates Black Arts program in Harlem (1963-1965) providing first community-based exposure for members of the Black Arts Movement.

1964 Civil Rights Act of 1964 passed barring discrimination in public accommodations, schools, hiring and voter registration. Also requires that federal funds be denied to any federally supported program which practices discrimination.

Mississippi Freedom Summer. The summer in which nearly a thousand young men and women - mostly white - went to Mississippi to live and work with Black Mississippi families. Their job--to help set up voter registration drives, to teach in Freedom Schools, and help work the fields.

Three civil rights workers--Michael Schwerner, Andrew Goodman and James Chaney--found murdered in Philadelphia, Mississippi.

Riots in black communities of Harlem, Brooklyn, and Rochester (New York), Philadelphia (Pennsylvania), New Jersey and Dixmoor, Illinois. The first of many "long, hot summers" of the 1960s.

Martin Luther King receives Nobel Peace Prize.

John Coltrane records A Love Supreme.

Eric Dolphy dies while on tour in Berlin.

Trumpeter Bill Dixon organizes two four-day concert series, the "October Revolution in Jazz" and "Four Days in December" to illustrate the fact that there is an audience for the New Jazz, despite the music industry's claims to the contrary.

1965 As an outgrowth of these concerts, Dixon, along with pianist Cecil Taylor, organizes the short-lived Jazz Composer's Guild with Archie Shepp, Sun Ra, Carla and Paul Bley, Burton Greene, Mike Mantler, Roswell Rudd and John Tchicai. Due to internal conflicts the Guild dissolves after only a few months.

Malcolm X shot and killed during a speech at Harlem's Audubon Ballroom.

Martin Luther King organizes the now famous march from Selma, Alabama, to the state capital, Montgomery, to demonstrate against discrimination in voter registration.

Voting Rights Act of 1965 passed providing for direct federal action to assure blacks the right to register and vote. Outlaws poll taxes, literacy tests and other impediments created to ensure black disenfranchisement.

Riot in Watts section of Los Angeles in which 34 are killed, 1,032 injured, 3,952 arrested.

Pharoah Sanders joins John Coltrane group. Epochal <u>Ascension</u> recording made for Impulse Records.

Association for the Advancement of Creative Musicians (AACM) founded by Muhal Richard Abrams, Jodie Christian, Steve McCall and Phil Cohran as a home for Chicago's musical experimentalists. Eventually establishes its own school to teach the concepts, history and techniques of the black musical heritage. The only black music self-help group still alive today.

1966 Stokely Carmichael becomes chairman of SNCC, launches Black Power movement.

Race riot in Chicago. Second major riot in a year which would see uprisings in 43 different U.S. cities.

Black Panther Party founded in Oakland, California by Huey Newton and Bobby Seale. Signals the emergence of the Black Power and Black Nationalism movements, the more radical, confrontational wings of the civil rights movement.

Pianist Carla Bley resurrects the Jazz Composers Guild under the new name Jazz Composers Orchestra Association. Sponsors series of concerts in New York.

1967 Newark riot.

First Black Power Conference held in Newark, New Jersey.

John Coltrane dies of cancer of the liver.

1968 Black Artists Group founded in St. Louis with Hamiet Bluiett, Baikida Carroll, Marty Ehrlich, Julius Hemphill, Oliver Lake, Floyd LeFlore, James Marshall, J.D. Parran, George Sams, Charles Bobo Shaw and Luther Thomas.

Martin Luther King initiates his Poor People's Campaign in order to highlight the need for greater job and pay equity in U.S. society.

Martin Luther King assassinated. Precipitates riots in more than 100 U.S. cities.

United States Attorney General Robert F. Kennedy assassinated.

Civil Rights Act of 1968 (also known as the Fair Housing Act) passed barring discrimination in the sale and rental of housing based on racial or religious background.

Richard M. Nixon elected president of the United States.

1969 First Paris Actuel Festival of Jazz, Rock and New Music held in Amougies, Belgium. First major European forum for New Jazz artists pushed out of the United States by rock music's take-over of the music industry.

Black Panthers Fred Hampton and Mark Clark shot to death in their beds during a Chicago police raid.

Ornette Coleman opens his Prince Street loft, Artist House, as a performance space.

1970 Multi-instrumentalist Roland Kirk founds the Jazz and People's Movement in an attempt to get more black musicians and music on television.

Albert Ayler found dead in New York's East River.

Sam Rivers opens Studio Rivbea, one of the first and most important of the New York loft jazz spaces of the 1970s.

1971 George Jackson killed in uprising at San Quentin prison.

Uprising at Attica State Correctional Facility.

Collective Black Artists group formed. Active from 1971 to the late 1970s in sponsoring concerts in the New York area.

1972 President Richard Nixon re-elected to a second term on the basis of his promise to shut the Pandora's Box of problems and disorder opened during the 1960s.

First Black Political Convention held in Gary, Indiana.

First New York Musicians Festival organized by Noah Howard, James Du Boise, Sam Rivers, and others, as an alternative for musicians locked out of George Wein's Newport in New York festival.

1973 Second New York Musicians Festival.

1975 Mozambique and Angola gain their independence.

1976 Jimmy Carter elected president of the United States.

First Loft Jazz Celebration.

1977 Second Loft Jazz Celebration.

1978/79 Decline of loft scene as more New York clubs begin to book New Jazz artists.

1980 Ronald Reagan elected president. Begins major roll back of civil rights gains of the 1950s and 60s.

1984 President Ronald Reagan re-elected to second term. First Sound Unity Festival. Four-day festival of black and white New Jazz improvisors organized by bassists Peter Kowald and William Parker. Similar in concept to the "October Revolution in Jazz" series organized by Bill Dixon in 1964.

Artists Alliance collective founded by bassist Reggie Workman. Responsible for a series of concerts and multi-media presentations at New York's Village Gate.

1986 First "Music Is an Open Sky" festival held at the New York club Sweet Basil.

1987 Second "Music Is an Open Sky" festival.

1988 Second Sound Unity Festival.

Knitting Factory opens in New York. Most important New York forum for New Jazz artists of the late 1980s and early 90s.

2

African American Cultural History and the Arts

A. GENERAL WORKS

1. Baldwin, James. "A Negro Assays the Negro Mood." New York Times Magazine (March 12 1961).

2. Barbour, Floyd B., ed. The Black Power Revolt: A Collection of Essays. Boston, MA: Porter Sargent Publisher, 1968. 287p.

3. Bennett, Lerone. Before the Mayflower: a history of black America. 5th revised ed. Chicago: Johnson Pub. Co., 1982. 681p.

4. Bracey, John H., August Meier and Elliott Rudwick, eds. Black Nationalism in America. Indianapolis: Bobbs-Merrill, 1970. 568p. Anthology of Black nationalist writings from the 1700s to the 1960s.

5. Brisbane, Robert. Black Activism: Black Revolution in the U.S., 1954-1970. Valley Forge, PA: Judson Press, 1974. 332p.

6. Carmichael, Stokely. Stokely Speaks; Black Power to Pan-Africanism. New York: Random House, 1971. 229p.

7. ________, and Charles V. Hamilton. Black Power: The Politics of Liberation in America. New York: Random House, 1967. 198p.

8. Eyes on the Prize: America's Civil Rights Years: a reader and guide. General editors, Clayborne Carson, David J. Garrow, Vincent Harding and Darlene Clark Hine. New York: Penguin Books, 1987. 355p.

9. Greer, Edward, comp. Black Liberation Politics: a reader. Boston: Allyn and Bacon, 1971. 398p.

10. Hampton, Henry, and Steve Fayer, with Sarah Flynn. Voices of Freedom: an oral history of the civil rights movement from the 1950s through the 1980s. New York: Bantam Books, 1990. 692p.

11. Herskovits, Melville J. The Myth of the Negro Past. Boston: Beacon Press, 1990. 368p. (Orig. 1941)

12. Isaacs, Harold R. The New World of Negro Americans. New York: John Day Company, 1963. 366p.

13. Lewis, Anthony, and The New York Times. Portrait of a Decade: The Second American Revolution. New York: Bantam Books, 1965. 273p.

14. Lincoln, C. Eric. The Black Muslims in America. Rev. ed. Boston: Beacon Press, 1973. 302p.

15. Lomax, Louis E. The Negro Revolt. New York: Signet Books, 1962. 288p.

16. Malcolm X, with Alex Haley. The Autobiography of Malcolm X. New York: Grove Press, 1965. 460p.

17. Marine, Gene. The Black Panthers. New York: New American Library, 1969. 224p.

18. Muse, Benjamin. The American Negro Revolution: From Non-Violence to Black Power, 1963-1967. Bloomington: Indiana University Press, 1968. 345p.

19. Report of the National Advisory Commission on Civil Disorders. New York: Bantam Books, 1968. 608p.

20. Weisbrot, Robert. Freedom Bound: A History of America's Civil Rights Movement. New York: W.W. Norton, 1989. 350p.

21. Williams, Juan. Eyes on the Prize: America's Civil Rights Years, 1954-1965. New York: Viking Penguin, 1987. 300p.

Media Materials

22. Eyes on the Prize: America's Civil Rights Years [video]. Alexandria, VA: PBS Video, 1986. 6 videocassettes (360 min.). Six part series on the southern civil rights struggle from 1954-1964. Part 1: Awakenings (1954-1956); Part 2: Fighting Back (1957-1962); Part 3: Ain't Scared of Your Jails (1960-1961); Part 4: No Easy Walk (1962-1966); Part 5: Mississippi: Is This America? (1962-1964); Part 6: Bridge to Freedom (1965). [A copy of this series is held by the Schomburg Collection - Sc Visual VRA-1]

23. Eyes on the Prize II: America at the Racial Crossroads [video]. 8 videocassettes (480 min.). Part 1: The Time Has Come (1964-65); Part 2: Two Societies (1965-68); Part 3: Power! (1967-68); Part 4: The Promised Land (1967-68); Part 5: Ain't Gonna Shuffle No More (1964-72); Part 6: A Nation of Law? (1968-71); Part 7: The Keys to the Kingdom (1974-80); Part 8: Back to the Movement (1979-1983). [Both of these series are available from PBS Video, 1320 Braddock Place, Alexandria, VA 22314-1698. Tel. 800/344-3337; or, Blackside, Inc., 486 Shawmut Ave., Boston, MA 02118. A copy of Eyes on the Prize II is also held by the Black Arts Research Center]

B. CULTURAL HISTORY AND THE ARTS

24. Blauner, Robert. "Black Culture: Myth or Reality?" In Afro-American Anthropology, eds. Norman E. Whitten and John F. Szwed. New York: The Free Press, 1970, pp. 347-365.

25. ________. "The Question of Black Culture." In Black America, ed. John F. Szwed. New York: Basic Books, 1970, pp. 110-120.

26. Cruse, Harold. "An Afro-American's Cultural Views." In Rebellion or Revolution? New York: William Morrow, 1968, pp. 48-67.

27. ________. The Crisis of the Negro Intellectual: A Historical Analysis of the Failure of Black Leadership. New York: Quill/Morrow, 1984. 696p. (Orig. 1967)

28. Gay, Geneva, and Willie L. Baber, eds. Expressively Black: The Cultural Basis of Ethnic Identity. New York: Praeger Publishers, 1987. 394p.

29. Gayle, Addison, ed. The Black Aesthetic. Garden City, NY: Doubleday, 1971. 432p.

30. Kochman, Thomas, ed. Rappin' and Stylin' Out: Communication in Urban Black America. Chicago: University of Chicago Press, 1972. 424p.

31. Pasteur, Alfred B., and Ivory L. Toldson. Roots of Soul: The Psychology of Black Expressiveness. New York: Anchor Press/Doubleday, 1982. 324p.

Articles

32. Gayle, Addison. "Blueprint for Black Criticism." First World (January-February 1977): 41-45.

33. George, Nelson. "Fort to the Future." Village Voice (January 16 1990): 38. Profile of the Black arts community in Fort Greene, Brooklyn.

34. Shipp, E. R. "Fort Greene: New Cultural Mecca." American Visions, Vol. 5, No. 1 (February 1990): 30-34.

35. ________. "Their Muse is Malcolm X; A new generation of creative artists, based in Brooklyn, is exploring what it means to be black in the 80's." New York Times (December 4 1988): Sec. 2, pp. 22-23.

36. Tate, Greg. "The Return of the Black Aesthetic: Cult-Nats Meet Freaky-Deke." Village Voice/Voice Literary Supplement (December 1986): 5-8.

37. Toldson, Ivory L., and Alfred B. Pasteur. "Therapeutic Dimensions of the Black Aesthetic." Journal of Non-White Concerns in Personnel and Guidance, Vol. 4, No. 4 (April 1976).

Media Materials

38. [Black arts criticism conference. Columbia University, Feb. 23, 1973. Part I] (Audiotape). New York, 1973. Duration: 59′ 56". [Held by the Schomburg Center - Sc Audio C-157 (Side 1-Side 2)] Discussion of prejudice and white criticism directed at black artists, musicians, and writers.

39. Contemporary Black Culture (Motion picture) WCBS-TV and Columbia University. Black Heritage: a history of Afro-Americans. Section 22: The Cultural Scene: from 1954 to the current mood. Released by Holt, Rinehart and Winston, 1969. 30 min. b&w. Roundtable discussion with Larry Neal (moderator), Charlie L. Russell, A. B. Spellman, and Barbara Ann Teer on the role of the Black artist in the struggle for self determination. [Held by the Schomburg Center - Sc Visual MPB-82]

40. It's Nation Time (1970) (film). 21 min. "At the Congress of African People in Atlanta, Georgia, Rev. Jesse Jackson, Rep. Julian Bond, LeRoi Jones, Minister Louis Farrakhan, and others speak on the themes of nationalism and Pan-Africanism. The conference was conceived as a means to create unity in order to establish the basis for a Black nation. The film's narrator talks with members of four workshops on political liberation, creativity, education and history. There are performances by the Challengers of Philadelphia, the Pharoah Sanders Quartet, and the Last Poets." [Catalogue description] [Available from the University of Illinois Film Center, 1325 South Oak St., Champaign, IL 61820. Tel. 217/333-1360]

The Black Arts Movement

41. Baraka, Amiri. "The Black Arts [Harlem, Politics, Search for a New Life]." In The Autobiography of LeRoi Jones. New York: Freundlich Books, 1984, pp. 202-229. Recollections of the Black Arts Movement by one its leading voices.

42. Davis, Charles T. "The American Scholar, the Black Arts, and/or Black Power." In Black is the Color of the Cosmos: essays on Afro-American literature and culture, 1942-1981, ed. Henry Louis Gates, Jr. New York: Garland Publishers, 1982, pp. 29-47.

43. Neal, Larry. "The Black Arts Movement." In The Black Aesthetic, ed. Addison Gayle. New York: Doubleday, 1972, pp. 272-290; Also in The Black American Writer. Volume II: Poetry and Drama, ed. C. W. E. Bigsby (Baltimore, MD: Penguin Books, 1971), pp. 187-202; and Five Black Writers, ed. Donald B. Gibson (New York: New York University Press, 1970), pp. 215-221. [Reprinted from The Drama Review (Summer 1968)].

44. ________. Visions of a Liberated Future: Black Arts Movement Writings. Includes commentaries by Amiri Baraka, Sonia Sanchez, et al. New York: Thunder's Mouth Press, 1989. 218p.

45. Perkins, Eugene. "The Black Arts Movement: Its Challenge and Responsibity." In The Black Seventies, ed. Floyd B. Barbour. Boston: P. Sargent, 1970, pp. 85-97.

Articles

46. Ford, Clebert. "Black Nationalism and the Arts." Liberator (New York), Vol. IV, No. 2 (February 1964): 14-16.

47. Neal, Larry. "Any Day Now: Black Art and Black Liberation." Ebony (August 1969): 54-58, 62.

48. _________. "The Social Background of the Black Arts Movement." Black Scholar, Vol. 18, No. 1 (January/February 1987): 11-22.

49. Turner, Sherry. "An Overview of the New Black Arts." Freedomways, Vol. 9, No. 2 (Spring 1969): 156-163.

3

The New Jazz: 1959-1990

GENERAL WORKS

Works in English

50. Backus, Rob. Fire Music: A Political History of Jazz. Chicago: Vanguard Books, 1977. 104p.

51. Balliett, Whitney. Dinosaurs in the Morning. New York: J.B. Lippincott, 1962. 224p. Collection of previously published criticism.

52. _________. Such Sweet Thunder. Indianapolis: Bobbs-Merrill Co, 1966. 366p. Collection of previously published criticism.

53. Budds, Michael J. Jazz in the Sixties: The Expansion of Musical Resources and Techniques. New Expanded Ed. Iowa City: University of Iowa Press, 1990. 216p. (Orig. 1978)

54. Davis, Francis. In the Moment: Jazz in the 1980s. New York: Oxford University Press, 1986. 258p. Collection of previously published profiles, interviews and criticism.

55. _________. Outcats: Jazz Composers, Instrumentalists, and Singers. New York: Oxford University Press, 1990. 261p. Collection of previously published writings.

56. Giddins, Gary. Rhythm-a-Ning: Jazz Tradition and Innovation in the '80s. New York: Oxford University Press, 1985. 291p. Collection of previously published criticism.

57. _________. Riding on a Blue Note: Jazz and American Pop. New York: Oxford University Press, 1981. 313p. Collection of previously published criticism.

58. Grime, Kitty. Jazz at Ronnie Scott's. Photography by Val Wilmer. London: Robert Hale, 1979. 192p. Includes excerpts from many published interviews by Valerie Wilmer as well as substantial material from unpublished Wilmer interviews with Archie Shepp.

59. Jones, LeRoi. Black Music. New York: Morrow, 1967. 221p. Collection of previously published writings.

60. __________. Blues People; Negro Music in White America. New York: William Morrow, 1963. 244p.

61. Jost, Ekkehard. Free Jazz. Graz: Universal Edition, 1974; New York: Da Capo Press, 1981. 214p.

62. Kofsky, Frank. Black Nationalism and the Revolution in Music. New York: Pathfinder Press, 1970. 280p.

63. Larkin, Phillip. All What Jazz; A Record Diary 1961-71. Rev. ed. New York: Farrar, Strauss and Giroux, 1985. 316p. (Orig. 1970) Collection of previously published criticism by a British poet laureate/jazz critic.

64. Litweiler, John. The Freedom Principle: Jazz After 1958. New York: Morrow, 1984. 324p. General history of the New Jazz.

65. Rivelli, Pauline, and Robert Levin, eds. The Black Giants. New York: The World Publishing Co., 1970. 126p. Collection of interviews previously published in Jazz & Pop magazine.

66. Sidran, Ben. Black Talk: How The Music of Black America Created a Radical Alternative to the Values of Western Literary Tradition. New Foreword by Archie Shepp. New York: Da Capo, 1981. 201p. (Reprint of 1971 ed.)

67. Sinclair, John, and Robert Levin. Music and Politics. New York: The World Publishing Co., 1971. 133p. Collection of interviews previously published in Jazz & Pop.

68. Williams, Martin. Jazz Masters in Transition, 1957-1969. New York: Macmillan, 1970. 288p. Collection of previously published writings.

69. Wilmer, Valerie. The Face of Black Music; photographs. Introduction by Archie Shepp. New York: Da Capo, 1976. 118p. Photo album including images of a number of New Jazz artists--Rashied Ali, Ed Blackwell, Roger Blank, Dennis Charles, Ornette Coleman, Andrew Cyrille, Richard Davis, Milford Graves, Billy Higgins, Hakim Jami, Art Lewis, Frank Lowe, Cal Massey, Dudu Pukwana, Dewey Redman, Revolutionary Ensemble, Archie Shepp, Cecil Taylor and Kenneth Terroade.

70. __________. Mama Said There'd Be Days Like This: My Life in the Jazz World. London: The Women's Press, 1989. 337p. Autobiography of the New Jazz's most prolific and perceptive chronicler.

71. __________. As Serious As Your Life: The Story of the New Jazz. London: Allison & Busby; London: Quartet, 1977; Westport, CT: Lawrence Hill & Co., 1981; London: Pluto Press, 1987. General history of the New Jazz. See also # 201.

Books with Sections on the New Jazz

72. Berendt, Joachim-Ernst. "Free." In Jazz: A Photo History. Translated by William Odom. New York: Schirmer Books, 1979, pp. 239-265.

73. Carr, Ian. "Energy/High-energy Music." In Jazz: The Essential Companion. New York: Prentice Hall Press, 1988. See also "Free Jazz (Improvised Music/Abstraction/Avant-garde)" in this same volume.

74. Clayton, Peter, and Peter Gammond. Jazz A-Z. London: Guinness Books, 1986. See the following entries: Energy Music (91-92), Far Out (93) and Free Jazz (99).

75. Fox, Charles. "New Innovators" and "Free and Far Out." In The Jazz Scene. London: Hamlyn, 1972, pp. 34-37, 100-105. Includes numerous photos by Valerie Wilmer.

76. Jost, Ekkehard. "Free Jazz." In The Story of Jazz, ed. Joachim-Ernst Berendt. Englewood Cliffs, NJ: Prentice-Hall; London: Barrie & Jenkins, 1978, pp. 116-133.

77. Miller, Lloyd, and James K. Skipper, Jr. "Sounds of Black Protest in Avant-Garde Jazz." In The Sounds of Social Change: Studies in Popular Culture, eds. R. Serge Denisoff and Richard A. Peterson. Chicago: Rand McNally, 1972, pp. 26-37. [Reprinted from Approaches to Deviance: Theories, Concepts and Research Findings, eds. Mark Lefton, James K. Skipper, Jr. and Charles H. McCaghy. New York: Appleton Century Crofts, 1968].

78. The New Grove Dictionary of Jazz. London: Macmillan Press, 1988. See the following terms: Action Jazz; Avant-garde jazz; Collective Improvisation; Free Jazz; Improvised Music; New Thing; Outside.

79. Tanner, Paul O.W., and Maurice Gerow. "The Eclectic Era: Free Form." In A Study of Jazz. 6th ed. Dubuque, IA: Wm. C. Brown, 1988.

80. Willener, Alfred. "Free Jazz." In The Action-Image of Society: On Cultural Politicization. New York: Pantheon Books, 1970, pp. 230-260.

Dissertations and Theses

81. Kofsky, Frank. "Black Nationalism and the Revolution in Music: Social change and stylistic development in the art of John Coltrane and others, 1954-1967." Dissertation (Ph.D.) University of Pittsburgh, 1973. 959p.

82. Radano, Ronald M. "A Cultural and Musical Analysis of Avant-Garde Jazz." Thesis (M.A.) University of Michigan, 1981. 255p.

Journals

83. Change (Detroit). 1965-1966. 2 issues.

84. The Cricket: Black Music in Evolution (Newark, NJ). Jihad Productions. 1968?-1971? 4 issues.

85. The Grackle: Improvised Music in Transition (Brooklyn, NY). 1977?-1979. 6 issues.

86. Impetus: New Music (London). 1977-1979. 9 issues.

87. Jazz 360o (Sierre, Switzerland). 1978?- .

88. Musics (London). 197?- .

89. Sounds & Fury (Utica, NY). Vol. 1-Vol. 2, No. 3 (July-August 1965-August 1966).

90. The Wire (London). No. 1- (Summer 1982-).

Articles

91. Bass, Milton. "Non-Jazz Jazz." Atlantic Monthly (October 1962): 130+.

92. "Bob Thiele digs 'new thing' jazz." Variety (April 21 1965): 51.

93. Clark, C. "Notes on the New Thing." Library Journal, Vol. 93 (April 15 1968): 61-64.

94. Cole, Bill. "The New Music." down beat (December 23 1971): 11+.

95. Cooke, Jack. "The Avant-Garde." Jazz Monthly (June 1966): 2-9.

96. Curnow, Wystan. "The Jazz Avant-Garde." Comment (Wellington), Vol. 9, No. 2 (April 1968): 41-43.

97. da Silva, Stewart. "The New Thing." Jazz News (February 21 1962): 9.

98. Dance, Stanley. "Lightly and Politely." Jazz Journal (April 1971): 27. See also # 200.

99. Dawbarn, Bob. "The New Wave!" Melody Maker (January 12 1963): 6.

100. __________, and Ross Russell. "For and Against Avant-Garde." Melody Maker (September 14 1968): 14.

101. Dixon, Bill. "Contemporary Jazz: An Assessment." Jazz & Pop (November 1967): 31-32.

102. __________. "Some Explanations of the Materials Thus Far Used in Contemporary Improvisation." Silo [Bennington College] (Fall 1987): 36-39.

103. __________. Book Reviews: Encyclopedia of Jazz in the Sixties / Four Lives in the Bebop Business. Freedomways (Summer 1967): 253-257.

104. D'Lugoff, Art. "Experimentation in Public: The Clubowners Viewpoint." down beat (April 8 1965): 14.

105. "down beat In Review: 1960-69." down beat (July 15 1976): 21-22.

106. Easter, Gilbert. "So What is Jazz?: A Mainstream View of the Avant-Garde." Jazz & Blues (June 1972): 25.

107. Ellis, Don. "The Avant-Garde is Not Avant-Garde!" down beat (June 30 1966): 21.

108. Ericsson, M. H. "Experimentation in Public: The Artist's Viewpoint." down beat (April 8 1965): 15.

109. Feather, Leonard. "Feather's Nest." down beat (February 15 1962): 40. Column in which Feather applauds John Tynan's "anti-jazz" assessment of John Coltrane and Eric Dolphy (db, Nov. 23 1961), and asserts that the leaders of the New Jazz are "outward bound with no destination," the contemporary equivalents of the emperor with no clothes. See also # 195.

110. _________. "Feather's Nest." down beat (September 23 1965): 44.

111. _________. "Feather's Nest: A Plea for Less Critical Infighting, More Attention to the Music Itself." down beat (December 16 1965): 13. See also # 159.

112. _________. "Hierarchy of the Jazz Anarchy; Symposium." Esquire (September 1965): 123-125.

113. _________. "Is Jazz Committing Suicide?" Melody Maker (September 15 1962): 20-21.

114. _________. "Jazz: Going Nowhere." Show (January 1962): 12-14. Infamous attack on "anti-jazz" developments in the jazz world.

115. _________. "Revolution in Rhythm." Melody Maker (January 21 1961): 12.

116. Fine, Milo. "Social Aspects of Free Jazz." Jazz Forum, No. 35 (June 1975): 46-48.

117. Flender, H. "A Comment on Social Protest Jazz." Variety (January 4 1967): 170.

118. Fox, Charles. "The New Wave in Jazz." Philips Music Herald (Spring 1966): 30-32.

119. "From Down Beat/The 60s: Tomorrow is the Question." down beat (July 2 1964): 50+.

120. Gitler, Ira. "Chords and Discords: To Hentoff from Gitler." down beat (September 9 1965): 8. Vitriolic attack on Nat Hentoff by critic Ira Gitler for his proposal of a potential Newport Jazz Festival program in which leading New Jazz players would be offered an evening slot instead of the traditionally less well attended afternoon session. For Hentoff's response see # 138.

121. Goodman, John. "On Music: Looking for the Black Message." The New Leader (January 1 1968): 26-28. Critical discussion of the "Black Power" jazz critics, Amiri Baraka and Archie Shepp, and their writings.

122. Green, Benny. "A Matter of Form." Jazz Journal (June 1962): 11-12. Critical discussion of the early 60s avant-garde with special emphasis on Coltrane/Dolphy and Ornette Coleman.

123. Halperin, Daniel. "Where Does the End Begin?" Jazz News and Review, Vol. 7, No. 21 (? 1963): 18-19.

124. Heckman, Don. "Breakthrough: A survey of the advances the avant-garde made during 1966 toward wider audience acceptance." Down Beat's Music '67, Vol. 12 (1967): 14+.

125. ________. "The New Jazz: A Matter of Doing." down beat (February 9 1967): 24-25.

126. ________. "Way Out There." Down Beat's Music '63, Vol. 8 (1963): 44-50.

127. Hennessey, Mike. "Avant Garde: A Plea for Sanity." Melody Maker (June 4 1966): 21.

128. Hentoff, Nat. "Jacobins of Jazz." Mademoiselle (August 1963): 268-269.

129. ________. "Jazz Revolution." Reporter (May 20 1965): 42+.

130. ________. "Learning to Listen to Avant-Garde - A Basic Problem." down beat (December 2 1965): 13.

131. ________. "The Life Perspectives of the New Jazz." Down Beat's Music '67, Vol. 12 (1967): 22-25.

132. ________. "A New Breed of Jazzman." Hi Fi/Stereo Review (January 1961): 38-40.

133. ________. "New Directions in Jazz." International Musician (September 1960): 14+.

134. ________. "The New Jazz." International Musician (October 1967): 5+.

135. ________. "The New Jazz." Vogue (February 1 1966): 177+.

136. _________. "New Jazz--Black, Angry and Hard to Understand." New York Times Magazine (December 25 1966): 36-39.

137. _________. "Paying New Jazz Dues." The Nation (June 22 1964): 635-637.

138. _________. "Second Chorus." down beat (October 21 1965): 39-40. Response to Ira Gitler attack above (# 120). Provides an interesting glimpse into the kind of critical warfare inspired by the New Music.

139. _________, et al. "Jazz Today, Where It Is and Where It Is Going." Billboard (June 29 1959): 24+.

140. Hicock, L. "The New Jazz, why you don't know about it and why you should." Coda, Vol. 10, No. 6 (1972): 31.

141. Hobson, Wilder. "Another Abstract Art." Saturday Review (October 28 1961): 50.

142. Hodeir, Andre. "Free Jazz." The World of Music, Vol. 10, No. 3 (1968): 20-29.

143. "Is the New Wave Just a Passing Fad?" Melody Maker (January 22 1966): 6.

144. "Jazz and Revolutionary Black Nationalism." Jazz (New York), Vol. 5 (April 1966): 28-30; (May 1966): 27-29; (June 1966): 28-30; (July 1966): 34-35; (August 1966): 28-29; (September 1966): 29-30; (October 1966): 39-41; (November 1966): 37-38; (December 1966): 43-45; Vol. 6 (January 1967): 38; (April 1967): 30; (May 1967): 38; (June 1967): 30; (July 1967): 37-38. The preceding pieces are from a New York panel discussion on the New Jazz with Archie Shepp, Frank Kofsky, Steve Kuhn, George Wein, LeRoi Jones, Robert Farris Thompson, Nat Hentoff, and Father Norman O' Connor.

145. "The Jazz Avant Garde: Pro & Con - A Discussion." Down Beat's Music '65, Vol. 10 (1965): 87-95. Discussion between jazz critics Dan Morgenstern, Ira Gitler, Martin Williams, Don Heckman and Don Schlitten on the jazz avant garde.

146. "Jazz Forum: Is "The New Thing" Anything?" Jazz (New York), Vol. 2, No. 5 (June 1963): 15. Roundtable discussion with record producer Dick Bock and critics Don Heckman, LeRoi Jones, Dave Kidd, John Norris and Nat Shapiro.

147. "Jazz Ideology in the '80s and Beyond." New Observations, No. 65 (March 1989). Special issue on the New Jazz edited by Roger Riggins.

148. "Jazz is Mugged by 'New Thing'." Jazz (New York), Vol. 4, No. 7 (July 1965): 22, 33. Responses to (# 186) by Bob Thiele, Frank Kofsky and Martin Williams.

149. Jones, LeRoi. "Jazz: The Avant-Garde." African Revolution, Vol. 1, No. 1 (May 1963): 130-133.

150. __________. "The Jazz Avant-Garde." Metronome (September 1961): 9-12, 39.

151. __________. "White Critics, Black Musicians, New Music." African Revolution, Vol. 1, No. 6 (October 1963): 143-152.

152. __________, and Milford Graves. "Position Paper." The Cricket: Black Music in Evolution (Newark, NJ), No. 4 (1971?): 12-19. From a paper presented at the Black Aesthetic and Black Artist Workshop conducted by LeRoi Jones and Milford Graves at the 3rd International Conference on Black Power in Philadelphia, August 29-September 1, 1971.

153. Kart, Larry. "Notes and Memories of the New Music." Down Beat's Music '69, Vol. 14 (1969): 34.

154. Kennard, D. "It Do Mean A Thing." Jazz Journal (June 1967): 18-19.

155. __________. "The Jazz Reformers." Jazz Journal (November 1967): 11.

156. Knox, Keith. "Sounds from the Avant Garde: the Aesthetic Problem." Jazz Monthly (February 1967): 10-12.

157. Kofsky, Frank. "The Avant-Garde Revolution: Origins and Directions." Jazz (New York), Vol. 5, No. 1 (January 1966): 14-19.

158. __________. "Black Nationalism in Jazz: The Forerunners Resist Establishment Repression, 1958-1963." The Journal of Ethnic Studies, Vol. 10, No. 2 (Summer 1982): 1-27; Reprinted in Jazz Research/Jazzforschung, Vol. 15 (1983): 9-35.

159. __________. "Frank Kofsky replies to Leonard Feather." Jazz (New York), Vol. 5, No. 2 (February 1966): 20, 30. Reply to Feather's down beat column above (# 111).

160. __________. "Music of Militancy; A New Breed Assumes Dominance." Commonweal, Vol. 89 (March 14 1969): 733-734.

161. Levin, Robert. "The New Jazz and the Nature of its Enemy." Sounds & Fury (April 1966): 40-42.

162. __________. "The Third World." Jazz and Pop (February 1971): 10-11.

163. Martin, T. E. "Notes on the New Wave." Jazz Monthly (January 1964): 58-62+.

164. Mathieu, Bill. "Inner Ear." down beat (April 23 1964): 41.

165. Matzorkis, Gus. "Down Where We All Live: Today's avant-garde revolution as seen in light of jazz' long history of internal strife." down beat (April 7 1966): 21-22; (April 21 1966): 16-17.

166. Miles, B. "Avant-Garde Defined." Music Journal (December 1964): 37+.

167. Miles, Robert. "Understanding the New Thing." Pieces of Jazz, No. 4 (Autumn 1968): 23-24.

168. "Music Men's New Movement Would 'Bring Jazz Out of its Narrow Shell.'" Variety (August 22 1962): 43.

169. "The New Jazz." BMI (March 1967): 23.

170. "The New Jazz." Newsweek (December 12 1966): 101-104, 106-106D.

171. "The New Jazz, a panel discussion with Marion Brown, John Norris, Ted O'Reilly and John Sinclair." Coda, Vol. 7, No. 7 (April/May 1966): 2-8.

172. "The New Thing." Time (April 6 1970): 87-88.

173. "The 'New Thing' According to Professor McSiegel." down beat (August 29 1963): 11+. [Satire]

174. Norris, John. "The New Jazz." Jazz Journal (December 1965): 16-17.

175. Owens, Jimmy. "Monies Due to the Creative Musician." Expansions (Winter 1975): 3-5.

176. Palmer, Bob. "Respect." down beat (January 31 1974): 29. Column calling for respect for the New Jazz. See also (# 185).

177. Pekar, Harvey. "The Critical Cult of Personality, Or, Stop That War--Them Cats Are Killing Themselves." down beat (January 13 1966): 19, 39. Discussion of the critical furor surrounding the New Jazz.

178. ________. "Experimental Collective Improvisation." Jazz Journal (November 1963): 8-9.

179. Peterson, Owen. "3rd Thoughts on the 'New Thing.'" Jazz Monthly (June 1968): 2-6.

180. Pinelli, Joe. "Joy in the New Music." Sounds & Fury (April 1966): 42-44.

181. "Point of Contact: A Discussion." Down Beat's Music '66, Vol. 11 (1966): 19-21, 24-26, 28-31, 110. Heated discussion on the jazz avant-garde between Archie Shepp, Cannonball Adderley, Art D'Lugoff, Roland Kirk, Sonny Murray, Cecil Taylor and Dan Morgenstern.

182. "Point of Departure." Down Beat's Music '66, Vol. 11 (1966): 32-34, 37, 106. Discussion between critic Bill Mathieu and composer Ralph Shapey about the aesthetics of the New Jazz.

183. Postgate, John. "The Black and White Show 1970-80: A Speculation on the Future of Jazz." Jazz Monthly (December 1970): 2-6.

184. Radano, Ronald M. "The Jazz Avant-Garde and the Jazz Community: Action and Reaction." Annual Review of Jazz Studies, Vol. 3 (1985): 71-79.

185. Ramsey, Doug. "With Respect to 'Respect'." down beat (March 14 1974): 38. Response to # 176.

186. Schoenfeld, Herm. "Jazz Mugged by 'New Thing': Latest Idiom Poisons at B.O." Variety (April 14 1965): 49. See also # 148.

187. Snowden, Don. "The Frontline of the Avant-Garde; While many who stretch the limits of jazz rely on foreign labels, some are landing U.S. recording contracts." Los Angeles Times/Calendar (July 22 1990): 7, 62-63. Includes comments from Don Cherry, Horace Tapscott, Don Pullen, Greg Osby and Vinny Golia.

188. Spellman, A. B. "Revoltion in Sound: Black Genius Creates a New Music in Western Sound." Ebony (August 1969): 84-89.

189. Stearns, Marshall. "New Directions in Jazz." Yale Review (September 1959): 154-160.

190. Stewart, James T. "Just Intonation and the New Black Revolutionary Music." The Cricket: Black Music in Evolution (Newark, NJ), No. 2 (1969?): 11-15.

191. "10 to 1." Down Beat's Music '66, Vol. 11 (1966): 14-18, 109. Ten critics (Bill Mathieu, Gilbert M. Erkine, Harvey Pekar, John S. Wilson, Pete Welding, Harvey Siders, Don DeMichael, Kenny Dorham, Don Nelson and Dan Morgenstern) review "The New Wave in Jazz" lp.

192. Tiegel, Eliot. "'Extended Energy' Jazz Energies New Wave of Enthusiasm: Youth Respond to Blend of Melodic Complexities and Contemporary Rhythms." Billboard (April 29 1972): 13-14+.

193. Traill, Sinclair. Editorial on 'the New Thing.' Jazz Journal (September 1965): 3.

194. Tynan, John. "Take Five." down beat (November 23 1961): 40. First of the many "anti-jazz" salvos to be leveled at the then emerging jazz avant-garde.

195. Williams, Martin. "The Bystander." down beat (March 10 1962): 39. Open letter to Leonard Feather in response to one of his down beat columns (# 109). Another example of Williams's standard critical stance during the 1960s in which he points out his critical support for the work of Ornette Coleman while denigrating the music of John Coltrane.

196. _________. "The Jazz Avant Garde: Who's in Charge Here?" Evergreen Review, Vol. 10, No. 41 (June 1966): 64-68.

197. _________. "New Thing in Jazz; with a selective list of key records by new musical pioneers." Harpers (October 1961): 68D-75.

198. Wilmer, Valerie. "African Beat." Jazz News and Review, Vol. 7, No. 19 (June 13-26 1963): 22-23. Discussion of the increasing use of African themes and rhythms in jazz of the early 1960s.

199. _________. "Great Black Music; Personal Opinion." Melody Maker (July 18 1970): 12.

200. _________. "One Sweet Letter to You." Jazz Journal (June 1971): 15. Response to an earlier column by Stanley Dance (# 98). Dance's reply may be found in this same issue, (p. 24).

201. _________, et al. "The Construction of Social Division and Music Practice." Musics (London), No. 15 (December 1977): 14-15; No. 16 (February 1978); No. 17 (May 1978): 4-6; No. 18 (July 1978): 6. The first installment in this saga is an extremely negative review of Wilmer's As Serious As Your Life (# 71) by British jazz writer Steve Lake, followed by responses from Wilmer and others, further correspondence from Richard Leigh, Talcott Belbin, Evan Parker and Peter Riley, and finally more responses from Wilmer and Alvin Curran along with a pro-Wilmer letter from drummer Dennis Charles.

202. Wilson, John S. "Who's Carrying the Jazz Banner Now?" New York Times (November 28 1965): Sec. 13, p. 8. Current state of jazz discussed.

203. Woodfin, Henry. "The New Jazz: 1. The Beginning." Sounds & Fury (February 1966): 18-19.

204. _________. "The New Jazz: 2. The Breakthrough." Sounds & Fury (April 1966): 16, 18; followed by an attack by Sounds & Fury's executive editor, Ralph Berton, on the honesty, critical abilities, etc. of Woodfin.

Works in French, German, Dutch and Italian

205. Bolelli, Franco. Musica Creativa: forme, espressioni e problematiche del nuovo jazz. Milano: Squilibri, 1978. 138p.

206. Buchter-Romer, Ute. New Vocal Jazz: Untersuchungen zur Zeitgenossichen improvisierten Musik mit der Stimme anhand ausgewahlter Beispiele. [Duisburg?: n.p., 1989] (Darmstadt: Copy Shop). 616p. [Thesis (doctoral)--Universitat-Gesamthochschule-Duisburg, 1989]

207. Cane, Giampiero. Canto Nero: Il Free Jazz degli Anni Sessanta. Rimini: Guaraldi, 1973. 297p.

208. Carles, Philippe, and Jean-Louis Comolli. Free Jazz, Black Power. 2nd ed. Paris: Editions Galilee, 1979. 478p. (Orig. 1971)

209. Jost, Ekkehard. Free Jazz; stilkritische Untersuchungen zum Jazz der 60er Jahre. Mainz: B. Schott, 1975. 256p.

210. Kumpf, Hans. Postserielle Musik und Free Jazz: Wechselwirkungen und Parallelen: Berichte, Analysen, Werkstattgesprache. 2nd ed. Rohrdorf: Rohrdorfer Musikverlag, 1981. 186p. (Orig. 1976)

211. Luzzi, Mario. Uomini e Avanguardie Jazz. Milan: Gammalibri, 1980. 290p.

212. Roggeman, Willy. Free en Andere Jazz-Essays. The Hague: Van Ditmar, 1969. 216p. [Dutch text]

213. Sportis, Yves. Free Jazz. Paris: Instant, 1990. 121p. (Encyclopedie Jazz Hot; 7)

214. Viera, Joe. Der Free Jazz: Formen und Modelle. Wien: Universal Edition, 1974. 60p. (Reihe Jazz, Nr. 7)

215. Vuijsje, Bert. De Nieuwe Jazz. Baarn: Bosch & Keuning, 1978. 224p. [Dutch text]

Books with Sections on the New Jazz

216. Berendt, Joachim-Ernst. "Free." In Photo-Story des Jazz. Frankfurt am Main: Kruger, 1978.

217. ________. "Free Jazz: Die Jazzentwicklung seit 1955." In Jazz Aktuell, ed. Claus Schreiner. Mainz: B. Schott's Soehne, 1968, pp. 8-23.

218. Carl Gregor, Duke of Mecklenburg. "Free Jazz." In Stilformen des Modernen Jazz: vom Swing zum Free Jazz. Baden-Baden: Koerner, 1979, pp. 153-171. (Collection d'etudes musicologiques, Bd. 63) [German text]

219. Carles, Philippe. "Le Free Jazz; and Post Free." In Le Jazz. Paris: Librairie Larousse, 1977, pp. 63-69, 70-78.

220. "Free Jazz." In Dictionnaire du Jazz, eds. Philippe Carles, et al. Paris: Laffont, 1988.

221. Piras, Marcello. "L'Avanguardia Americana." In Il Jazz degli anni Settanta. Milano: Gammalibri, 1980, pp. 39-84.

222. Polillo, Arrigo. "Rivolta: Il Free Jazz." In Jazz: la vicenda e i protagonisti della musica afro-americana. Milano: A. Mondadori, 1983, pp. 255-282.

Articles

223. Batel, G. "Free Jazz als intensive Form soziomusikalischer Kommunikation." Melos/NZ; Neue Zeitschrift fur Musik, Vol. 4, No. 6 (1978): 507-511.

224. Berendt, Joachim-Ernst. "Free Jazz--der neue Jazz der sechziger Jahre." Melos; Zeitschrift fur Neue Musik (October 1967): 345-351.

225. Binchet, J. P. "Le Face du Free." Jazz Magazine, No. 125 (December 1965): 82-83.

226. "Black Power et New Thing." Jazz Magazine, No. 150 (January 1968): 19+.

227. Comolli, Jean Louis. "Voyage au Bout de la New Thing." Jazz Magazine, No. 129 (April 1966): 24-29.

228. Dongala, E. "Le New Jazz: Une Interpretation." Presence Africaine, No. 68, 4e trim. (1968): 141-148.

229. "Free Jazz ohne Publikum?" Jazz Podium (September 1972): 15-17. Transcript from a Radio Bremen studio discussion between critic Siegfried Schmidt-Joos, saxophonist Peter Brotzmann, and record producer Manfred Eicher.

230. Gerber, Alain. "Notes sur la Nouvelle Chose." Jazz Magazine, No. 133 (August 1966): 42-45.

231. Jost, Ekkehard. "Free Jazz und die Musik der Dritten Welt." Jazz Research/Jazzforschung, Nr. 3/4 (1971-1972): 141-154.

232. ________. "Ist der Free Jazz tot? Anmerkungen zu einer windigen parole." Jazz Podium (January 1989): 16-19.

233. ________. "Musikalisches Theater und Free Jazz." Musik und Bildung (March 1976): 160-161.

234. ________. "Zum Problem des Politischen Engagements im Jazz." Jazz Research/Jazzforschung, Nr. 5 (1973): 33-43.

235. Koechlin, P. "Free Jazz." Musica (Chaix), No. 144 (March 1966): 53-55.

236. Kopelowicz, Guy. "Le Nouveau Jazz et la Realite Americain." Jazz Hot, No. 231 (May 1967): 18-23.

237. Lere, Pierre. "Free Jazz: Evolution ou Revolution." Revue d'Esthetique, Vol. 23, No. 3/4 (1970): 313-325.

238. Liefland, W. E. "Free Jazz--nur eine Geschichtsdelle?" Jazz Podium (June 1976): 10-12.

239. Malson, Lucien, and Andre Hodeir. "Des tentatives a l'ecart du free jazz." Jazz Magazine, No. 176 (March 1970): xvii-xix.

240. Maletto, Gian Mario. "Il Jazz della Rivolta Nera." Musica Jazz (April 1982).

241. Merceron, G. "Face a la New Thing." Jazz Hot, No. 209 (May 1965): 22-24.

242. Miller, Manfred. "Free Jazz: Eine New Thing Analyse." Jazz Podium (May 1966): 128-130; (June 1966): 156-159; (July 1966): 182-184.

243. Moussaron, Jean-Pierre. "Feu le Free?" Jazz Magazine, No. 371 (May 1988): 18-20.

244. Pecori, Franco. "Le ragioni del 'free.'" Musica Jazz (February 1967): 22-26.

245. Peynet, M. "Les Musiciens ont la Parole: le free." Jazz Hot, No. 259 (March 1970): 12-14.

246. "Du Primitivisme Africain au Jazz d'Avant Garde." Revue Musicale de Suisse Romande, Vol. 18, No. 3 (1965): 24.

247. "Releve des articles concernant la nouvelle chose." Jazz Hot, No. 231 (May 1967): 8+.

248. Rodriguez, Alberto. "Capire La 'Free Music': Il problema della valutazione e del giudizio critico alla luce della nuova musica." Musica Jazz (March 1967): 8-14; (April 1967): 8-14; (May 1967): 8-14.

249. Rutter, Larry. "Avantgarde: Perspektive einer revolution." Jazz Podium (October 1966): 266-268, 270.

250. Santamaria, Freddy. "Qu'en Pensent-ils?" Jazz Magazine, No. 148 (November 1967): 30-35. 17 jazz musicians express their opinions on "new things" in jazz.

251. Schaal, H. J. "Ist der Free Jazz noch zu Retten." Jazz Podium (August 1987): 15-17.

252. Schmidt-Joos, Siegfried. "Fortschritt ins Abseits? Zur situation des Free Jazz." Musik und Bildung (April 1973): 170-173.

253. Suppan, Wolfgang. "Free Jazz: Negation aesthetischer Kategorien--Rueckkehr zur funktionalen musik." Musikerziehung (Vienna), Vol. 26, No. 5 (1973): 206-208.

254. _________. "Free Jazz und seine anthropologischen Hintergruende." Jazz Podium (November 1973): 16-17.

255. Weyer, R. D. "Frei improvisierte musik und die sehnsucht nach ideologischer Harmonisierung." Jazz Podium (June 1984): 14-15.

COUNTRY AND REGIONAL STUDIES

A. UNITED STATES

CALIFORNIA

See also # 187, 1462, 1592, 1854, 2694, 2986, 3000, 3348-3356, 4115, 4877, 4953, 5091, 5625-5638, 6282-6308, 6697-6699

256. Carles, Philippe. "Los Angeles." Jazz Magazine, No. 212 (June 1973): 4-5.

257. Cohen, Elaine. "Caught: New Jazz Festival of California Musicians." down beat (July 1981): 56.

258. Crouch, Stanley. "Black Song West." Cricket, No. 2, pp. 2-8. Review of the New Art Jazz Ensemble and the jazz scene in Los Angeles.

259. Feather, Leonard. "Watts Apres la Crise." Jazz Magazine, No. 135 (October 1966): 15-16.

260. Franklin, A. David. "Los Angeles: incubator of jazz talent." Jazz Educators Journal, Vol. 18, No. 2 (1986): 12-14. Includes brief profiles of Don Cherry and Eric Dolphy.

261. Ginibre, Jean-Louis. "Los Angeles 68 de A a Z." Jazz Magazine, No. 156/57 (July/August 1968): 18-30.

262. "Jazz and Watts Youth." down beat (April 7 1966): 12-13.

263. "Lurning in Watts." down beat (December 1 1966): 12. On Henry Grant's Music Center, a community music center created in the wake of the Watts riot.

264. "Westward Ho! The Jazz Cry of the Sixties." Melody Maker (March 26 1966): 8.

265. Williams, Richard. "Jazz Cities, USA." Melody Maker (March 31 1973): 18.

DISTRICT OF COLUMBIA

266. Brower, W. A. "The 'space' is the place." Radio Free Jazz (July 1978): 24-25.

267. Weintraub, B. "'Loft Jazz' doing OK for D.C. space club." Billboard (April 8 1979): 33.

ILLINOIS

See also # 388-440, 756, 770, 900, 914-965, 1604, 1686, 2013-2017, 3088-3089, 3094-3104, 3113-3120, 3156, 3205-3207, 3880-3882, 3935, 3948, 3953-3957, 4112-4114, 4378-4379, 4556-4571, 4628-4633, 4774, 4796, 4799, 4801-4805, 5995, 6016, 6549, 6553, 6884-6894

268. Gifford, B. "Chicago: the 'new' music." Jazz & Pop (January 1969): 40-41.

269. Martin, Terry. "The Chicago Avant-Garde." Jazz Monthly (March 1968): 12-18.

MISSOURI

See # 443-454, 3671, 3674-3675, 3824-3826, 4336, 4405-4406, 5210

NEW YORK

See also # 626-693

270. Baraka, Amiri. The Autobiography of LeRoi Jones. New York: Freundlich Books, 1984, pp. 172-195. Recollections of the early years of the New Jazz scene in New York.

271. Jones, Hettie. How I Became Hettie Jones. New York: E.P. Dutton, 1990. 239p. Autobiography of Amiri Baraka's first wife which describes their life and the New York jazz scene during the late 1950s and early 1960s.

Dissertations

272. Such, David Glen. "Music, Metaphor and Values Among Avant-Garde Jazz Musicians Living in New York City." Dissertation (Ph.D.) University of California, Los Angeles, 1985.

Articles

273. Carl Gregor Herzog zu Mecklenburg. "Die New Yorker Schule des Free Jazz." Jazz Podium, Vol. 8 (1969): 260-263.

274. Heckman, Don. "Caught in the Act: A Perspective in Revolution." down beat (October 20 1966): 20-22. Review of a festival of leading free jazz musicians held at New York's Village Theatre.

275. Kofsky, Frank. "The Jazz Scene." Jazz [New York] (May 1967): 26. Review of a benefit concert for the civil rights organization SNCC held at the Village Theatre and organized by saxophonist Jackie McLean.

276. Kopelowicz, Guy. "Autumn in New York II." Jazz Hot, No. 215 (December 1965): 38-43. Report on New Jazz activities in New York. Includes a discussion of Albert Ayler, Marion Brown, Sun Ra, Paul Bley and ESP-Disk owner, Bernard Stollman.

277. Levin, Robert. "Some Observations on the State of the Scene." Sounds & Fury (July-August 1965): 5-6. Survey of the New York New Jazz scene with comments on Bernard Stollman's ESP record label, the Jazz Composers Guild, and more.

278. "New Thing, New York 1966." Jazz Hot, No. 274 (July 1971): 16-19.

279. "Strictly Ad Lib: New York." down beat (January 14 1965): 11. Brief report on New Jazz activity in New York.

280. Such, David G. "'Out There': A Metaphor of Transcendence among New York City Avant-Garde Jazz Musicians." New York Folklore, Vol. 7 (1981): 83-95.

281. Van der Mei, Elizabeth. "The New Music Scene." Coda (March 1967): 25-26. Review of a concert series at the Village Theatre.

282. ________. "The New Music Scene." Coda (August/September 1966): 29-30. Report on various New Jazz happenings in New York including Cecil Taylor's 1966 Town Hall concert, a Bill Dixon concert series and more.

283. Wilmer, Valerie. "Is the Avant Garde Alive and Kicking? A Report on the New York Scene." Music Maker [London] (February 1967): 32-33.

284. ________. "New York is Alive!" Jazz Forum, No. 23 (June 1973): 47-49. Report on the New Jazz scene in New York.

Bernard Stollman and ESP Records

See also # 276-277

285. "ESP." In Dictionnaire du Jazz, eds. Philippe Carles, et al. Paris: Laffont, 1988. Sketch of the important New York free jazz label.

286. Gardner, Mark. "ESP-disk." In The New Grove Dictionary of Jazz. London: Macmillan Press, 1980. Profile of the seminal New York label responsible for the early recordings of Albert Ayler, Marion Brown, Pharoah Sanders, Frank Wright, Milford Graves, et al.

287. Wilmer, Valerie. As Serious As As Your Life. Westport, CT: Lawrence Hill & Co., 1981, pp. 231-233.

Articles

288. Beckett, Alan. "E.S.P. Music." New Left Review, No. 42 (March-April 1967): 71-74. Review of lps by Byron Allen, Giuseppi Logan, Albert Ayler and Sunny Murray.

289. Berton, Ralph. "Conversations with Bernard Stollman." Sounds & Fury (April 1966): 36-38. Interview in which Stollman attempts to rebut, point by point, the charges made against him in Robert Levin's article above (# 277).

290. Noames, Jean Louis. "Du Cote Free." Jazz Magazine, No. 123 (October 1965): 12. Interview with Bernard Stollman.

291. "Qui etes-vous, Bernard Stollman?" Jazz Hot, No. 230 (April 1967): 13-17. [Interview]

292. Smith, Frank. "The New Music." East Village Other, Vol. 1, No. 3 (December 1965): 10. Review of ESP discs.

293. Williams, Richard. "Stollman and ESP: a label without myopia." Melody Maker (June 5 1971): 32.

PENNSYLVANIA

294. Crouch, Stanley. "The Other Philly Sound." Village Voice (January 5 1976): 58.

295. "Jazz Academy." Billboard (February 21 1981): 49. Brief note on Philadelphia's Long March Jazz Academy directed by Bill Lewis.

296. Woessner, Russell. "Philly's Long March Jazz School." down beat (November 1979): 16.

B. EUROPE AND BEYOND

297. Jost, Ekkehard. Europas Jazz 1960-1980. Frankfurt am Main: Fischer Taschenbuch Verlag, 1987. 470p. Survey of free jazz and its leading exponents in Europe (East and West Germany, Great Britain, the Netherlands and France).

298. Litweiler, John. "Free Jazz in Europe: American, National, International." In The Freedom Principle: Jazz After 1958. New York: William Morrow, 1984.

299. Noglik, Bert. Jazzwerkstatt International. Berlin: Verlag Neue Musik, 1981. 490p. Interviews with 24 of Europe's leading New Jazz artists.

Articles

300. Jost, Ekkehard. "Europaeische Jazz-Avantgarde: Emanzipation wohin?" Jazz Research/Jazzforschung, Vol. 11 (1979): 165-195. [English summary]

301. _________. "Tendenzen des Europaeischen Free Jazz der 70er Jahre." Musikforschung, Vol. 36, No. 2 (1983): 207-209.

302. Noglik, Bert. "Aktuelle Aspekte der Identitat von Jazz und 'Improvisierter Musik' in Europa: Differenziertes Selbstverstandnis und Internationalisierung." Jazzforschung, Vol. 19 (1987): 177-186.

AUSTRIA

303. Lange, Art. "Ad Lib: Cool Noir." down beat (March 1989): 60. On the efforts of Austrian concert producer Ingrid Karl to establish 'Creative Improvised Music' on the Vienna music scene.

BELGIUM

304. "Actuel Festival called a moderate success." Billboard (November 15 1969): 93.

305. Alessandrini, Paul. "Freepop...du cote d'ailleurs." Jazz Magazine, No. 173 (December 1969): 26-31.

306. Gras, Philippe. "Amougies: l'Europe, le 'free jazz' et la 'pop music.'" Chroniques de L'Art Vivant, No. 6 (December 1969): 2-7.

307. Welch, Jane. "Europe's Answer to Woodstock: The First Actuel Paris Music Festival." down beat (January 22 1970): 16-17, 31. Report on the Actuel Music Festival held in Amougies, Belgium.

CANADA

308. Miller, Mark. "Jazz 7. Avant Garde." In Encyclopedia of Music in Canada, eds. Helmut Kallmann, et al. Toronto/ Buffalo: University of Toronto Press, 1981, pp. 470-471.

Articles

309. Glassman, Marc, and Vernon Frazer. "The Avant Garde in Toronto; concert reviews." Coda, No. 217 (December '87/ January '88): 28-29.

310. Miller, Mark. "The New Jazz: A National Survey." The Canadian Composer (April 1982): 24-31. [French and English text]

311. Norris, John. "Jazz in Canada." International Musician (January 1967): 12, 26-27.

312. Smith, Bill. "The Avant Garde in Toronto." Coda, No. 219 (April/May 1988): 12-13.

313. Vickery, Stephen, and Marc Chenard. "The New Music in Canada; reviews from Toronto and Victoriaville." Coda, No. 223 (December '88/January '89): 10-13.

DENMARK

314. Slumstrup, Finn. "Free Jazz and Denmark." Jazz Forum, No. 13/14 (Autumn/Winter 1971): 67, 84.

FRANCE

315. "Free Jazz sur Seine." Jazz Magazine, No. 169-170 (September 1969): 18-23.

316. "Les Nuits de la Fondation Maeght." Chroniques de L'Art Vivant, No. 4 (September-October 1969): 6-7.

GERMANY

317. Berendt, Joachim Ernst. "Der deutsche Jazz und die Emanzipation (1961-1973)." In Ein Fenster aus Jazz. Frankfurt am Main: S. Fischer, 1977, pp. 222-234, 243-246.

318. Noglik, Bert, and Heinz-Jurgen Lindner. Jazz im Gesprach. Berlin: Verlag Neue Musik, 1978. 184p. Collection of interviews with several of East Germany's leading jazz artists.

319. Noll, Dietrich J. Zur Improvisation im Deutschen Free Jazz: Unters, zur Asthetik frei improvisierter Klangflachen. Hamburg: Verlag der Musikalienhandlung Wagner, 1977. 151p.

Articles

320. Andre, Jo. "Jazz-Brief: Wird Ornette Coleman doch siegen? Die junge Avantgarde auf dem 10. Deutschen Jazz-Festival in Frankfurt." Gottesdienst und Kirchenmusik (Munchen), No. 4-5 (1966): 174-175.

321. Bachmann, K. R. "New Jazz Meeting Baden-Baden." Jazz Podium (January 1975): 15.

322. Berendt, Joachim E. "West Germany: the jazz scene in the seventies." Jazz Forum, No. 38 (1975): 38-39.

323. Cuscuna, Michael. "A New Front; the creative reservoir of German jazz artists." Jazz & Pop (July 1969): 25-26. Brief survey of the German jazz avant-garde. Artists discussed include Karl Berger, Albert Mangelsdorff, Rolf and Joachim Kuhn, Gunter Hampel, Alexander von Schlippenbach and Wolfgang Dauner.

324. Jaenichen, Lothar. "12. Workshop Freie Musik in Berlin." Jazz Podium (May 1980): 14-15.

325. Jost, Ekkehard. "Ueber den Anfang vom Ende des Epigonentums und ueber die Ueberwindung der Kaputtspielphase im Westdeutschen Free Jazz." Neue Zeitschrift fur Musik, No. 3 (May-June 1979): 237-241.

326. "Kooperative New Jazz in Wiesbaden: Szenen aus der Provinz." Jazz Podium (January 1981): 22-23.

327. Liefland, W., and Werner Panke. "5 Tage des 9. Workshop Freie Musik in Berlin." Jazz Podium (June 1977): 22-24.

328. Panke, Werner. "Free Jazz Meeting in Baden-Baden." Neue Musikzeitung, Vol. 20, No. 1 (1971): 9.

329. Pluemper, H. D. "Workshop Freie Musik in Berlin." Jazz Podium (May 1973): 15-16.

330. Wilmer, Valerie. "Baden-Baden Free Jazz Meeting." Jazz Forum, No. 13/14 (1971): 68-69.

331. ________. "Baden-Baden Free Jazz Meeting." Swing Journal (March 1971): 54-63. Report on German free jazz festival.

332. ________. "Rap and Blow in Baden-Baden." Melody Maker (December 26 1970): 14. Review and photographs of the Baden-Baden Free Jazz Meeting.

Moers Music

333. Internationales Festival New Jazz. Presseschau. Moers, Germany: Stadt Moers Kulturamt. Annual. Compilation of press materials from the annual Moers New Jazz Festival. Copies of Numbers 6-15 (1977-1986) are held by the Music Research Division of the Performing Arts Library at Lincoln Center (# 7097).

334. "Moers Music." In The New Grove Dictionary of Jazz. London: Macmillan Press, 1988.

335. Smith, Bill. "Moers Festival." Coda, No. 156 (July-August 1977): 26-27.

GREAT BRITAIN

336. Atkins, Ronald. "Burbles and Squeaks - reflections on the British avant garde." In Jazz Now: the Jazz Centre Society Guide, ed. Roger Cotterrell. London: Quartet, 1976, pp. 39-47.

337. Carr, Ian. Music Outside: Contemporary Jazz in Britain. London: Latimer New Dimensions, 1973; New York: Da Capo, 1977. 179p.

338. Cerutti, Gustave, and Philippe Renaud. Five British Independent Labels 1968-1987. Sierre: G. Cerutti (avenue du Marche 8, CH-3960, Sierre, Switzerland), 1989(?). Complete discography of the five most important British free jazz labels--Bead, Incus, Matchless, Leo and Ogun.

Articles

339. Ansell, Kenneth. "Free Jazz in Britain." The Wire, No. 14 (April 1985): 26-27, 29.

340. Bird, Christopher. "Britain's jazz scene loosens up; many modern players are forming their own labels." Billboard (April 10 1976): 24.

341. "The British Avante-Garde." down beat (July 11 1968): 24-25, 32.

342. Lake, Steve. "Breaking down the barriers." Melody Maker (December 14 1974): 40.

343. ________. "Welcome to Europe!" Melody Maker (January 19 1974): 16. Preview of the Co-Op Festival of Improvised Music. Includes brief profiles of AMM, Peter Broetzmann, Albert Mangelsdorff, Frank Perry and Alexander von Schlippenbach.

344. ________, and Chris Welch. "Free for All!--Are We Ignoring a Musical Revolution or Is It Undisciplined Anarchy?" Melody Maker (December 15 1973): 40-42. Roundtable discussion between three of Britain's leading free jazz artists--John Stevens, Derek Bailey and Keith Tippett, and one of its more traditional denizens--Bruce Turner, about the musical value of free improvisation.

345. McRae, Barry. "The British Free Jazz Movement." Jazz Forum, No. 81 (1983): 40-44.

346. Riley, Peter. "Jazz in Britain: Eleven Improvisors Wigmore Hall London." Jazz Journal (June 1975): 24.

347. Rose, Cynthia. "New Wave Jazzers." New Statesman & Society (November 25 1988): 13-15.

348. Rusenberg, Michael. "Off Limits: Jazz-Avantgarde in England." Jazz Podium, Vol. 21, No. 6 (1972): 194-195.

349. Schonfield, Victor. "Rule Brittania? Britain taking avant-garde lead." down beat (July 11 1968): 24+.

Incus Records

See also # 338

350. Carr, Ian. "Incus Records." In Jazz: The Essential Companion. New York: Prentice Hall Press, 1988.

351. "Incus." In Dictionnaire du Jazz, eds. Philippe Carles, et al. Paris: Laffont, 1988.

352. "Incus." In The New Grove Dictionary of Jazz. London: Macmillan Press, 1988.

Articles

353. Ansell, Kenneth. "Incus for the Record." Wire, No. 15 (May 1985): 42-43.

354. Fox, Charles. "Incus Festival of Improvised Music." New Statesman (May 16 1986): 32-33.

355. Riley, Peter. "Incus Records." Coda, No. 167 (June 1979): 3-8.

356. Rouy, Gerard. "Incus; ou, la force tranquille." Jazz Magazine, No. 254 (May 1977): 20-21.

Ogun

See also # 338

357. Adams, Simon. "Ogun." In The New Grove Dictionary of Jazz. London: Macmillan Press, 1988.

ITALY

358. Soutif, Daniel. "Black Saint Story." Jazz Magazine, No. 358 (February 1987): 40. Profile of the Italian record label most responsible for documenting American New Jazz artists of the 1970s and '80s and its owner, Giovanni Bonandrini.

NETHERLANDS

359. "The Amsterdam October Meeting." Coda, No. 218 (February/March 1988): 10-11.

360. Koopmans, Rudy. "Jazzmusiker gehen neue Wege des Musiktheaters." Jazz Podium (January 1977): 7-10. Discussion of the music-theater works of Willem Breuker, Instant Composers Pool, Misha Mengelberg, et al.

361. "The Moving Spirits in Dutch Jazz." Jazz Forum, No. 15 (1972): 32.

362. Schoemaker, Bill. "Jazz in Holland." Coda, No. 211 (Dec 86/ Jan 87): 22-23. Survey of recent New Jazz lps from Holland.

POLAND

363. Kowal, Roman. "New Jazz and Some Problems of its Notations; Exemplified in the scores of Polish jazz composers." Jazzforschung, Bd. 3/4 (1971-72): 180-193.

RUSSIA

364. Feigin, Leo, ed. Russian Jazz, New Identity. London: Quartet Books, 1985. 217p.

Articles

365. Ciaffardini, David. "Russian Jazz: Red and Hot New Music." Sound Choice, No. 14 (Spring 1990): 47-49.

366. Collier, James Lincoln. "Jazz's Future: A Soviet View." New York Times (November 6 1989): Sec. 2, pp. 1, 19. Comments by Russia's 'leading jazz critic', Alexey Batashev, on the state of jazz in Russia and Eastern Europe.

367. Fuller, Jack. "Jazz: It's Red and it's hot." Chicago Tribune (May 7 1989): Sec. 13, pp. 26-27.

368. Kumpf, Hans. "Soviet Avantgarde Jazz Festival in Zuerich." Jazz Podium (August 1989): 24.

369. Mandel, Howard. "Ad Lib: The State of Jazz in the USSR." down beat (September 1988): 56, 63.

370. Mathieson, Kenny. "Outlines." Wire, No. 75 (May 1990): 63. Review of Leo Feigin's eight-CD set "Document: New Music from Russia - The 1980s."

371. Rowland, Mark. "Paradoxical Freedom Back in the U.S.S.R.: Russian jazz." Musician, No. 68 (June 1984): 36+.

372. Vikharieff, Yuri. "The 'New Thing' in Russia." down beat (September 10 1964): 16-18.

Leo Records

373. "Leo (ii)." In The New Grove Dictionary of Jazz. London: Macmillan Press, 1988.

Articles

374. Ciaffardini, David. Leo Feigin interview. Sound Choice, No. 14 (Spring 1990): 50-52.

375. Davis, Francis. "Ad Lib: The fight for freedom." down beat (April 1984): 70, 69. Profile of Leo Records and its releases of Soviet new jazz artists.

376. Feigin, Leo. "An Open Letter to New Music Community." Jazzthetik, Vol. 4, No. 11 (November 1990): 43; Also in Option, No. 36 (January/February 1991): 10. Describes the difficulties facing Leo Records after the demise of the US-based New Music Distribution Service along with a plea to record buyers to buy Leo product in order to save the label.

377. Lee, David. "Leo Records: out of the USSR." Coda, No. 212 (February-March 1987): 15-17.

378. Reed, Joan. "Leo Feigin: jazz cosmonaut." Ear, Vol. 12, No. 7 (October 1987): 14-15. Interview with the owner of Leo Records and indefatigable promoter of Russian new jazz.

379. Turner, Andrew. "Leo Records." The Wire, No. 1 (Summer 1982): 26-27. Interview with Leo Feigin on his Leo record label, the label responsible for introducing Russian New Jazz to the West.

SWITZERLAND

380. "Hat Art." In The Penguin Encyclopedia of Popular Music, ed. Donald Clarke. New York: Viking, 1989.

381. "Hat Hut." In The New Grove Dictionary of Jazz. London: Macmillan Press, 1988. Brief sketch of the Swiss record label.

Articles

382. Carles, Philippe. "Deux Faces du Disque: Timeless, Hat Hut." Jazz Magazine, No. 338 (1985).

383. ________, and Serge Loupien. "Hat Hut de A a Z." Jazz Magazine, No. 275 (1979).

384. Solothurnmann, Jurg. "Free Jazz in Switzerland." Jazz Forum, No. 13/14 (Autumn/Winter 1971): 75-76.

4

The Jazz Collectives

385. Baker, Malcolm Lynn. "Black Nationalism and Free Jazz Collectives: the black musician's approach to economic self-determinism." Jazz Research Papers, Vol. 6 (1986): 24-29.

386. Fox, Ted. "Success Story: Self-Made Records." Jazz Magazine (New York), Vol. 2, No. 4 (1978): 48-55. Discussion of independent, artist-produced record labels.

387. Hunt, David C. "Black Voice Lost in White Superstructure." Coda, Vol. 11, No. 6 (February 1974): 12-14.

ASSOCIATION FOR THE ADVANCEMENT OF CREATIVE MUSICIANS [AACM]
Founded 1965. Chicago.

388. Berendt, Joachim Ernst. "The AACM." In The Jazz Book: from ragtime to fusion and beyond. Completely rev. Westport, CT: Lawrence Hill, 1982, pp. 359-361.

389. Jost, Ekkehard. "The Chicagoans." In Free Jazz. Graz: Universal Edition, 1974, pp. 163-179. Musical analysis of the work of various AACM artists.

390. Litweiler, John. The Freedom Principle: Jazz After 1958. New York: William Morrow, 1984, pp. 172-187, 189-199, 265-286.

391. Wilmer, Valerie. "The AACM - Chicago's Alternative Society." In As Serious As Your Life. Westport, CT: Lawrence Hill & Co., 1981, pp. 112-126. See also, p. 259.

Biographical Dictionaries

392. "AACM." In Dictionnaire du Jazz, eds. Philippe Carles, et al. Paris: Laffont, 1988.

393. "AACM." In The Penguin Encyclopedia of Popular Music, ed. Donald Clarke. New York: Viking, 1989, p. 1.

394. Carles, Philippe, and Jean-Louis Comolli. Free Jazz, Black Power. 2nd ed. Paris: Editions Galilee, 1979, pp. 363-364.

395. Claghorn, Charles Eugene. "AACM." In Biographical Dictionary of Jazz. Englewood Cliffs, NJ: Prentice-Hall, 1982, p. 329.

396. Feather, Leonard, and Ira Gitler. The Encyclopedia of Jazz in the Seventies. New York: Horizon, 1976.

397. Kernfeld, Barry. "Association for the Advancement of Creative Musicians." In The New Grove Dictionary of American Music. London: Macmillan Press, 1986.

398. _________. "Association for the Advancement of Creative Musicians." In The New Grove Dictionary of Jazz. London: Macmillan Press, 1988.

399. Southern, Eileen. Biographical Dictionary of Afro-American and African Musicians. Westport, CT: Greenwood Press, 1982.

Journals

400. The New Regime. 196?- . House publication of the AACM. 3 issues? [No. 1 held by the Black Arts Research Center (# 7085)]

Articles

401. "A.A.C.M." Swing Journal (Japan), Vol. 29, No. 8 (1975): 231+.

402. "AACM celebrates." down beat (November 20 1975): 8. Report on the AACM's celebration of its 11th anniversary.

403. Abrams, Muhal Richards, and John Shenoy Jackson. "The Association for the Advancement of Creative Musicians." Black World, Vol. XXII, No. 1 (November 1973): 72-74.

404. Balliett, Whitney. "Jazz; Association for the Advancement of Creative Language." New Yorker (June 20 1977): 92-97.

405. Bourget, Jean-Loup. "L'A.A.C.M. a Douze Ans." Jazz Magazine, No. 258 (October 1977): 6-7.

406. Bowie, Lester. "A.A.C.M." Jazz Hot, No. 256 (December 1969): 24-25.

407. Case, Brian. "Like Hi Man, I's Yo New Neighbor." New Musical Express (January 11 1975): 30.

408. Caux, Daniel, et al. "A.A.C.M. Chicago." Jazz Hot, No. 254 (October 1969): 16-19.

409. "Chicago Exodus; AACM Members Off to Paris." down beat (June 26 1969): 14.

410. "Chicago's AACM Gets Weekly Radio Program." down beat (March 6 1969): 10.

411. Corbett, John. "The Music's Still Happenin'." Down Beat (December 1990): 61, 66. Assessment of the AACM as it approaches its 25th anniversary.

412. Cuscuna, Michael. "Blowing in the Windy City: a look at the Chicago scene." down beat (December 12 1968): 19, 41.

413. DeMuth, Jerry. "15 Years of the AACM." Jazz Forum, No. 68 (1980): 28-32.

414. Dold, R. Bruce. "AACM School on the Upswing." down beat (June 1983): 12.

415. Dutilh, Alex. "L'AACM ou l'Ardeur Collective." Jazz Hot, No. 356/357 (Dec 1978-Jan 1979): 12-16.

416. Emenari, Lofton A., III. "The AACM School of Music: Fulfilling a Promise." Arts Midwest Jazzletter, Vol. 7, No. 3 (Fall 1989): 1-2.

417. Giddins, Gary. "AACM--Free to Be; Abrams, Mitchell, Threadgill." Village Voice (March 1 1988): 80, 50.

418. ________. "Inside Free Jazz: The AACM in New York." Village Voice (May 30 1977): 46-48.

419. Gifford, B. "Chicago: The 'New' Music." Jazz & Pop, No. 8 (January 1969): 40-41.

420. Goodman, Alan. "The AACM and The BAG: in and out of the tradition." Crawdaddy (October 1975): 74-75.

421. Jackson, John Shenoy. "The AACM: An Overview." Jazz Forum, No. 68 (1980): 27.

422. "Jazz Musicians Group in Chicago Growing." Down Beat (July 28 1966): 11.

423. Kopulos, Gordon. "A.A.C.M." Jazz Journal (November 1976): 6-8.

424. Lee, David. "AACM." Coda, No. 156 (July/August 1977): 33-34.

425. Levi, Titus. "AACM: 20 Years and Beyond." OPtion (March/April 1985): 27.

426. Litweiler, John. "Chicago's AACM." Sounds & Fury (August 1966): 45.

427. Martin, Terry. "The Chicago Avant-garde." Jazz Monthly (March 1968): 12-18.

428. Muni, Kai. "AACM: Continuing the Tradition; twenty-one years of great black music." Be-Bop And Beyond, Vol. 4, No. 2 (March/April 1986): 8-10.

429. Paige, E. "Avante-Garde Assn. Has Strong Overseas Support." Billboard (June 23 1973): 58.

430. "Profile." down beat (August 15 1974): 34-35.

431. Quinn, Bill. "The AACM: A Promise." Down Beat's Music '68, Vol. 13 (1968): 46-50.

432. Rockwell, John. "2 Concerts for 'Creative Musicians.'" New York Times (September 17 1982).

433. Schmoller, Gail. "Black Music at Columbia College Chicago." American Music Teacher (June/July 1988): 58-59.

434. Tesser, Neil. "The AACM: Ancient to the Future." Musician, Player and Listener, No. 31 (March 1981): 34, 108, 112.

Concert Reviews

435. Litweiler, John. "Caught in the Act: Various Artists." down beat (October 19 1967): 44. AACM concert.

436. _________. "Heard & Seen: Altoists and Other Chicagoans." Coda (March 1967): 28-29. [Braxton/Jarman/Mitchell]

437. _________. "Three to Europe." Jazz Monthly (November 1969): 20-22. [Braxton, Jarman, et al.]

438. Smith, Bill. "The Creative Arts Collective with members of the AACM." Coda, No. 140 (August 1975): 6-7.

439. Townley, Ray. "Jazz Showcase - Chicago." Coda, No. 11 (1973): 40-42.

Discographies

440. Tepperman, Barry. "The New Music from Chicago: A Discography of the AACM." Pieces of Jazz (1970): 52-54.

BLACK ARTISTS FOR COMMUNITY ACTION (New York)

441. "Guggenheim to Mingus; Protest at Foundation." down beat (May 27 1971): 8. Report on protest by the BAFCA, led by Charles Mingus, of the Guggenheim Foundation.

442. Levin, Robert. "The Third World." Jazz & Pop (June 1971): 10-11.

BLACK ARTISTS GROUP (St. Louis)

443. "Black Artists Group." In Dictionnaire du Jazz, eds. Philippe Carles, et al. Paris: Laffont, 1988.

444. Carles, Philippe, and Jean-Louis Comolli. Free Jazz, Black Power. 2nd ed. Paris: Editions Galilee, 1979, p. 368.

445. Case, Brian, and Stan Britt. The Harmony Illustrated Encyclopedia of Jazz. 3rd ed. New York: Harmony Books, 1987.

446. Hazell, Ed. "Black Artists Group." In The New Grove Dictionary of Jazz. London: Macmillan Press, 1988.

447. Litweiler, John. The Freedom Principle: Jazz After 1958. New York: William Morrow, 1984, pp. 187-189.

448. Wilmer, Valerie. As Serious As Your Life. Westport, CT: Lawrence Hill & Co., 1981, p. 260.

Articles

449. Cullaz, Maurice. "Black Artists Group of St. Louis." Jazz Hot, No. 296 (July/August 1973): 22-23. [Interview]

450. Goodman, Alan. "The AACM and The BAG: In and Out of the Tradition." Crawdaddy (October 1975): 74-75.

Concert Reviews

451. Goddet, Laurence. "Black Artists Group et Portal au Palace." Jazz Hot, No. 294 (May 1973): 23.

452. "Jazz en Direct." Jazz Magazine, No. 211 (May 1973): 30-31.

453. "Jazz en Direct: Paris." Jazz Magazine, No. 207 (January 1973): 10.

454. "Salon d'Automne." Jazz Magazine, No. 206 (December 1972): 48.

CANADIAN CREATIVE MUSIC COLLECTIVE

455. Miller, Mark. "CCMC." In Encyclopedia of Music in Canada, eds. Helmut Kallmann, et al. Toronto/Buffalo: University of Toronto, 1981, p. 170.

Articles

456. Boucher, Max. "Canadian Improvised Music: CCMC and the Music Gallery." Musics (London), No. 18 (July 1978): 21.

457. Smith, Bill. "The Creative Arts Collective with members of the AACM." Coda, No. 140 (August 1975): 6-7.

458. Snider, Norman. "Call it Frontier Music." Toronto Globe and Mail (June 22 1977).

COLLECTIVE BLACK ARTISTS (New York)

459. Claghorn, Charles Eugene. "CBA Ensemble." In Biographical Dictionary of Jazz. Englewood Cliffs, NJ: Prentice-Hall, 1982, p. 335.

Journals

460. Expansions (New York). 1971- . CBA journal.

Articles

461. "CBA Conference Seeks Unity of Black Artists." Down Beat (July 20 1972): 10-11.

462. "New York's Jazz Organizations." Jazz Forum, No. 44 (1976): 25-26.

463. "Odds And." Coda, Vol. 12, No. (April 1975): 32. Brief note on the CBA and its Ensemble.

464. Patterson, P. "Black Musicians." Black Enterprise, Vol. 2 (February 1972): 8.

465. Salaam, Yusef A. "Money, Management, and All That Jazz: Collective Black Artists, Inc." Black Enterprise, Vol. 9 (December 1978): 45+.

466. Weathers, Diane. "The CBA: A Grass Roots Movement." Black Creation, Vol. 5, No. 1 (Fall 1973): 34.

467. _________. "The Collective Black Artists." Black World, Vol. XXII, No. 1 (November 1973): 74-77.

468. "What is the CBAE? Down Beat (February 28 1974): 10.

Concert Reviews

469. "CBA Explosion." Down Beat (July 15 1976): 10.

470. "Carter Joins Collective." Down Beat (May 18 1978): 11. Note on the appearance of Ron Carter with the CBA Ensemble.

471. Keepnews, Peter. "Worth a Trip to Queens." Village Voice (April 4 1974).

472. Wilson, John S. "Jazz: Black Artists Group." New York Times (February 22 1979): C26.

473. _________. "Many Take a Turn as Leader in Collective Black Artists Band." New York Times (July 11 1974): 24.

474. _________. "Pharoah Sanders and an Ensemble." New York Times (January 28 1978): 11.

CREATIVE ARTS COLLECTIVE (Detroit)

475. Bryant, Steve. "Creative Arts Collective." Arts Midwest Jazzletter, Vol. 7, No. 3 (Fall 1989): 4-5. Detroit-based organization founded in 1978 by guitarist Spencer Barefield.

CREATIVE MUSIC STUDIO (Woodstock, NY)

See also Berger, Karl

476. "Creative Music Flick." down beat (July 13 1978): 14. Review of a documentary film on the Creative Music Studio.

477. "A Creative Spring in Woodstock." Jazz Forum, No. 53 (1978): 16.

478. Jost, Ekkehard. "Karl Berger's Creative Music Studio." Jazz Podium (December 1976): 9-11.

479. "Karl Berger's Creative Music Foundation." Jazz Forum, No. 27 (February 1974): 27-28.

480. Landri, Carla de. "CMS Slates New Ideas, Reaches Towards Public." down beat (November 1979): 17.

481. Negre, Marie-Paule, and Christian Gauffre. "Karl Berger: L'Ecole de Woodstock." Jazz Magazine, No. 280 (November 1979): 28-29, 64, 66.

482. Occhiogrosso, Peter. "Karl Berger: Music Universe c/o Woodstock, NY." down beat (June 3 1976): 18+.

483. "On the Scene: U.S.A. - The Woodstock School." Jazz Forum, No. 86 (1984): 27-28.

484. Panke, W. "Zentrum der Weltmusik: Creative Music Studio in Woodstock." Jazz Podium (September 1983): 4-5.

485. Plakias, M. "Where Teaching Meets Jamming." Jazz Magazine (Northport, NY), Vol. 3, No. 1 (Fall 1978): 28-29.

486. Rusch, Kea. "Creative Music Studio." Cadence (September 1977): 20-21.

487. _________. "Creative Music Studio: Fall Session." Cadence (December 1976): 10-11.

488. Smith, Arnold Jay. "Traditions Upheld and Broken at Jazz School near Woodstock." Billboard (April 10 1982): 58.

489. Solothurnmann, Jurg. "Karl and Ingrid Berger: 'Music Universe' in Woodstock." Jazz Forum, No. 66 (1980): 34-37.

490. "Swinging News: USA - Creative Music Studio Autumn and Winter Sessions." Jazz Forum, No. 45 (1977): 15-16.

491. Zabor, Rafi. "Creative Music Studio." Musician, Player & Listener, No. 40 (February 1982): 66-68, 71, 90.

CREATIVE MUSICIANS IMPROVISORS FORUM (New Haven, CT)

492. McNally, Owen. "Music Has Message for the World." Hartford Courant (October 23 1981): D1, D10.

493. Motavalli, Jim. "Meet the CMIF Composers." New Haven Advocate (January 31 1979).

494. Waz, Joe. "Creative Music Forum." New Haven Advocate (January 25 1978).

Concert Reviews

495. Frazer, Vernon. "CMIF/AACM." Coda, No. 188 (February 1983): 34-35. Review of a performance by the Creative Improvisors Orchestra and an AACM big band.

496. ________. "In Performance: Creative Improvisors Orchestra." Coda, No. 194 (February 1984): 24-25.

FREE MUSIC PRODUCTION (Berlin)

497. "FMP." In The New Grove Dictionary of Jazz. London: Macmillan Press, 1988.

498. Forst, Achim, ed. Free Music Production: Records, Informations. Berlin: Free Music Production (Luebecker Str. 19, 1000 Berlin 21, Germany), 1982. 48p.

499. Improvised Music: Free Music Production; eine Jahresubersicht-unser Live-Programm 1988... und ein biBchen mehr [An overview of our 1988 Live Concerts...plus a little more]. Berlin: Free Music Production, 1988. 64p.

500. "New Artists Guild." In The New Grove Dictionary of Jazz. London: Macmillan Press, 1988. Sketch of the precursor to Free Music Production.

Articles

501. Brauer, C. "Still More FMP." Cadence (March 1978): 24-25.

502. "Free Music Production." Coda, No. 201 (April/May 1985): 22-23. Survey of FMP releases.

503. Froese, D. H. "Das Platten-Programm der FMP: Free Music in Beispielen." Jazz Podium (July-August 1973): 17.

504. Gebers, Jost. "Free Music Production." Neue Zeitschrift fuer Musik, Nr. 3 (May-June 1979): 250-251.

505. Jaenichen, Lothar. "10 Jahre Free Music Production in Berlin." Jazz Podium (October 1979): 15-17. Interview with Jost Gebers.

506. Keefer, J., and Gerard Rouy. "FMP Story." Jazz Magazine, No. 265 (June 1978): 22-23.

507. Lake, Steve. "Einundzwanzig Jahre FMP." Jazzthetik, Vol. 4, No. 3 (March 1990): 12-17.

508. Margull, G. "Konsequenz." Jazz Podium (July-August 1973): 13-16. Interview with Jost Gebers re: FMP.

509. "On the Scene--West Berlin: FMP: Troubled Times." Jazz Forum, No. 88 (1984): 24-25.

510. Quinke, R. "Die Berliner Free Music Production." Musik und Bildung, Bd. 9 (October 1977): 556-559.

511. Rouy, Gerard. "Berlin: Free Music Production." Jazz Magazine, No. 238 (November 1975): 12-15. Interview with Peter Kowald and Alexander von Schlippenbach re: FMP.

512. Rusch, Bob. "FMP Music Production summer releases." Cadence, Vol. 2, No. 6/7 (July 1977): 12+.

513. Wood, Anthony. "FMP." The Wire, No. 4 (Summer 1983): 30-32, 42.

JAZZ AND PEOPLE'S MOVEMENT (New York)

514. "Jazz and People's Movement." In The New Grove Dictionary of Jazz. London: Macmillan Press, 1988.

515. Wilmer, Valerie. "Politics, The Media and Collectivism." In As Serious As Your Life. Westport, CT: Lawrence Hill & Co., 1981, pp. 215-217.

Articles

516. Bruer, J. "Musikerprotest mot USA-TV." Orkester Journalen (October 1970): 8-9+.

517. Cuscuna, Michael. "Rahsaan Roland Kirk." Jazz & Pop (April 1971): 32-38. [Interview]

518. Feather, Leonard. "TV Soundings." down beat (April 1 1971): 13. Report on a performance by Rahsaan Roland Kirk, Archie Shepp, et al. on the Ed Sullivan Show brought about as a result of J&PM pressure.

519. "Grass Roots Jazz Protest Hits TV." down beat (October 15 1970): 12.

520. "Jazz & People's Movement Promised NBC Action." down beat (November 12 1970): 11.

521. "Jazz Avant Garde Wants on Tube." Rolling Stone (November 26 1970): 8.

522. "Jazz, Cavett and the JPM: An Exchange." down beat (January 21 1971). Exchange between J&PM member Andrew Cyrille and down beat editor Dan Morgenstern re: Morgenstern's criticisms below (# 525) of a J&PM panel discussion on the October 17 1970 Dick Cavett Show.

523. "The Jazz Protest." BMI (December 1970): 15.

524. "Jazz Protesters do Cavett Show, Push On." down beat (November 26 1970): 8.

525. Morgenstern, Dan. "It Don't Mean A Thing..." Down Beat (December 10 1970): 13. See also # 522.

526. Spitzer, David. "Rahsaan-Philosopher of Sound." Crescendo International (December 1971): 6.

527. Wilmer, Valerie. "Cyrille-ism." Melody Maker (May 29 1971): 16.

JAZZ ARTISTS GUILD (New York)

528. Balliett, Whitney. "David and Goliath." In Dinosaurs in the Morning. New York: J.B. Lippincott, 1962.

529. Hentoff, Nat. "Bringing Dignity to Jazz." In The Jazz Life. New York: Dial Press, 1961.

530. Priestley, Brian. "Jazz Artists Guild." In The New Grove Dictionary of Jazz. London: Macmillan Press, 1988.

Articles

531. Cuscuna, Michael. "The Newport Rebel Festival." Coda, No. 206 (February/March 1986): 6-7. (Reprinted from the liner notes to "The Complete Candid Recordings of Charles Mingus" Mosaic Records.)

532. Heckman, Don. "Record Reviews: Jazz Artists Guild." Metronome (October 1961): 37. Review of the "Newport Rebels" lp done by members of the Charles Mingus/Max Roach founded Jazz Artists Guild.

533. Lees, Gene. "Newport the Trouble." down beat (August 18 1960): 20-23, 44. Report on the Rebel Festival at the Newport Jazz Festival.

534. Lyttelton, Humphrey. "Will This Mean a Brighter Jazz Scene." Melody Maker (December 10 1960): 8. Reflection by a British musician on the creation of the Jazz Artists Guild.

535. "Special Report: Newport." Metronome (September 1960): 5. Report by critic Robert A. Perlongo on the riots at the 1960 Newport Jazz Festival.

JAZZ COMPOSERS GUILD (New York)

See also Dixon, Bill

536. "Jazz Composers Guild." In Dictionnaire du Jazz, eds. Philippe Carles, et al. Paris: Laffont, 1988.

537. "Jazz Composers Guild." In The New Grove Dictionary of Jazz. London: Macmillan Press, 1988.

538. McRae, Barry. The Jazz Cataclysm. London: J. M. Dent, 1967, pp. 160-162. Brief discussion of the October Revolution concert series and the Jazz Composers Guild.

539. "October Revolution in Jazz." In The New Grove Dictionary of Jazz. London: Macmillan Press, 1988.

540. Wilmer, Valerie. "Bill Dixon and the Jazz Composers Guild." In As Serious As Your Life. Westport, CT: Lawrence Hill & Co., 1981, pp. 213-215.

Articles

541. "Avant-Garde: After the Revolution, Reaction Sets In." Melody Maker (July 24 1965): 6.

542. "Avant-Garde Organizes, To Present Concert Series." down beat (December 31 1964): 10.

543. Beckett, Alan. "The New Wave in Jazz. 3: The October Revolution." New Left Review, No. 34 (November-October 1965): 92. Discusses the recorded works of some of the best known members of the New York jazz avant-garde and the Jazz Composers Guild--Cecil Taylor, Archie Shepp, Don Cherry, John Tchicai, and Sunny Murray.

544. Hentoff, Nat. "The Persistent Challenge of Cecil Taylor." down beat (February 25 1965): 18, 40. Interview with Taylor re: the Jazz Composers Guild.

545. Levin, Robert. "The Jazz Composer's Guild: An Assertion of Dignity." down beat (May 6 1965): 17-18.

546. Morgenstern, Dan, and Martin Williams. "The October Revolution: 2 Views of the Avant-Garde in Action." down beat (November 19 1964): 15, 33.

547. "Quelques Hommes en Colere." Jazz Magazine, No. 120 (July 1965): 16.

548. "Strictly Ad Lib: New York." down beat (March 11 1965): 12. Brief report on the activities of the JCG.

549. "Strictly Ad Lib: New York." down beat (May 20 1965): 11. Report on a Jazz Composers Guild concert series.

550. "26 Jazzmen Nouveaux e la Question." Jazz Magazine, No. 125 (December 1965): 42-3.

Concert Reviews

551. Heckman, Don. "Caught in the Act: The Jazz Composers Guild." down beat (February 11 1965): 37-38.

552. Kopelowicz, Guy. "Autumn in New York." Jazz Hot, No. 214 (November 1965): 31.

553. Spellman, A. B. "Jazz at the Judson: Jazz Composers Guild." The Nation (February 8 1965): 149-151.

554. Wilson, John S. "Avant-Garde Series Offers Cecil Taylor and Dixon Quintet." New York Times (December 29 1964): 21. Describes the program for the "Four Days in December" series.

555. ________. "Dig That Free Form Jazz." New York Times (January 24 1965): Sec. 2, p. 13.

556. ________. "Judson Hall Program." New York Times (December 30 1964): 14.

JAZZ COMPOSERS ORCHESTRA ASSOCIATION (New York)

557. Claghorn, Charles Eugene. Biographical Dictionary of American Music. West Nyack, NY: Parker Pub. Co., 1973.

558. ________. "Jazz Composers Orchestra." In Biographical Dictionary of Jazz. Englewood Cliffs, NJ: Prentice-Hall, 1982, p. 348.

559. "Jazz Composers Orchestra Association." In Dictionnaire du Jazz, eds. Philippe Carles, et al. Paris: Laffont, 1988.

560. "Jazz Composers Orchestra Association." In The New Grove Dictionary of Jazz. London: Macmillan Press, 1988.

Articles

561. Dister, A. "The Jazz Composers Orchestra." Jazz Hot, No. 281 (March 1972): 4-9.

562. Fox, Ted. "Success Story: Self-Made Records." Jazz Magazine (Northport, NY), Vol. 2, No. 4 (1978): 48-55. Profile of the JCOA, and others.

563. Gourgues, Maurice. "'Communications' ou les Libertes de 68." Jazz Magazine, No. 296 (April 1981): 30-31. Discussion of the Jazz Composers Orchestra's 1968 debut recording.

564. Hentoff, Nat. "Don't Mourn--Organize." down beat (May 18 1967): 15.

565. Hodeir, Andre, et al. "La New Thing et le Jazz Composers Orchestra." Jazz Magazine, No. 176 (March 1970): XV-XVII.

566. "Jazz Composer's Band to Issue Own Albums." down beat (August 8 1968): 11.

567. "Jazz Composers Orchestra." Coda, Vol. 9, No. 12 (1971): 41.

568. "Jazz Composers Orchestra Continues." Jazz & Pop (January 1968): 10.

569. "Jazz Composers Orchestra Plans New Extended Activities." Jazz & Pop (May 1970): 10.

570. "The Jazz Composers Orchestra." Jazz Monthly (July 1968): 6-8.

571. "JCOA Seeks Musicians for Workshop Series." down beat (February 15 1973): 9.

572. Knox, Keith. "Jazz Composers Orchestra: Experimentorkester foer Idealister." Orkester Journalen (January 1969): 10-11.

573. Rusch, Robert D. "JCOA." Jazz Journal (September 1972): 5.

574. "Service Set to Spur Avant-Garde Jazz." Billboard (July 1 1972): 3.

575. Van der Mei, Elizabeth. "The JCOA: Mike Mantler talks with Elizabeth van der Mei." Coda, Vol. 8, No. 10 (November/December 1968): 2-11.

576. Watson, Ron. "Special Review: The Jazz Composers Orchestra." Pieces of Jazz, No. 6 (1969): 5-8. Review of the JCO's 1968 debut recording.

577. Williams, Martin. "New Jazz Big Band/but..." Saturday Review (December 28 1968): 56.

Concert Reviews

578. Berton, Ralph. "Caught in the Act." down beat (September 9 1965): 22.

579. Heckman, Don. "Caught in the Act: Jazz Composers Orchestra." down beat (July 24 1969): 29-30.

580. Klee, Joe H. "Caught in the Act: Don Cherry and the Jazz Composers Orchestra." down beat (May 10 1973): 33.

581. "New Series of Workshops with the Jazz Composers Orchestra." Jazz Forum, No. 18 (August 1972): 37-38.

582. "New Works Heard in JCOA Free Concerts." down beat (April 1 1971): 11.

583. Powers, W. "Heard and Seen." Coda, Vol. 11, No. 1 (1973): 43.

M-BASE (Macro-Basic Array of Structured Extemporizations)

584. George, Nelson. "Fort to the Future." Village Voice (January 16 1990): 38. Profile of the Fort Greene, Brooklyn neighborhood which is home to the M-BASE collective.

585. Louis, Errol T. "Jazz Makes a New Sound with Soul, Pop and Computers; a Brooklyn collective of young musical upstarts finds inspiration in anything from bebop to kung fu movies and Motown." Smithsonian (October 1989): 176+. Includes comments from Greg Osby, Steve Coleman, Geri Allen and Robin Eubanks.

586. Milkowski, Bill. "Caught: M-BASE, Brooklyn Academy of Music." down beat (March 1989): 50-51. [Concert review]

587. Shipp, E. R. "Their Muse is Malcolm X." New York Times (December 4 1988): Sec. 2, pp. 1, 22-23. Brooklyn-based jazz collective founded by Steve Coleman. Other members include Greg Osby, Robin Eubanks, Cassandra Wilson and Geri Allen.

588. Snowden, Don. "The Front Line of the Avant-Garde." Los Angeles Times/Calendar (July 22 1990): 62. Includes comments by Greg Osby re: M-BASE.

MUSICIANS OF BROOKLYN INITIATIVE (M.O.B.I.)

589. Laskin, David L. "Big Bands and New Music: Musicians of Brooklyn Initiative." Ear, Vol. 13, No. 1 (1988): 33.

590. Mandel, Howard. "Musicians of Brooklyn Initiative: Infant Steps." Village Voice (October 8 1985): 73, 79.

NEW MUSIC DISTRIBUTION SERVICE

591. Fox, Ted. "Success Story: Self-Made Records." Jazz Magazine (Northport, NY), Vol. 2, No. 4 (1978): 48-55. Profile of NMDS, and others.

592. "NMDS: To Be Or Not to Be." Ear, Vol. 15, No. 6 (October 1990): 11. Report on the NMDS's suspension of operations.

593. "Open Letter to NMDS and the New Music Community." Jazzthetik, Vol. 4, No. 2 (February 1990): 4. Letter from European independent record label owners Leo Feigin (Leo Records), Chris Cutler (Recommended Records), George Coppens (Osmosis), Burkhard Hennen (Moers) and Didier Petit (Leo/France) re: monies owed to them by NMDS for unreturned recordings.

594. Rosenbluth, Jean. "Grass Route: New Music nabs an audience for the offbeat." Billboard (February 20 1988): 49-50.

595. Somer, Jack. "The Survival of the Avant Garde." Stereo Review (January 1976): 70.

NEW YORK CITY ARTISTS' COLLECTIVE

See also # 1965

596. Levi, Titus. "Some Assembly Required: New York City Artists' Collective." Option (July/August 1986): 46-47.

597. Szwed, John. "New York City Artists' Collective: Free on Third." Village Voice (May 8 1990): 81.

NEW YORK MUSICIANS ORGANIZATION

598. Caux, Daniel. "Black Music: New York Musician's Organization." L'Art Vivant, No. 36 (Fevrier 1973): 26-27. Profile of the organizers behind the New York Musician's Jazz Festival--James du Boise, director of the New York loft Studio We and saxophonist Noah Howard.

599. Flicker, Chris. "The New York Musicians Organization." Jazz Hot, No. 299 (November 1973): 12-14.

600. Howard, Noah. "New York for You." Jazz Hot, No. 294 (May 1973): 19.

601. ________. "New York pour Vous." Jazz Hot, No. 295 (June 1973): 16-17.

New York Musicians Festival

602. Cole, Bill. "1972 New York Musicians Festival." Coda, Vol. 10, No. 8 (1972): 45-46.

603. "New York Musicians Stage Own Festival." down beat (September 14 1972): 9.

604. Wilmer, Valerie. "Sam Rivers, L'Autre New York." Jazz Magazine, No. 204 (October 1972): 38-39. Interview with one of the producers of New York Musicians Festival.

2nd New York Musicians Festival

605. Ledbetter, Les. "It's Jazz's Turn Now - For Next 10 Days." New York Times (June 29 1973): 11.

606. "New York Musicians Set Summer Festival." down beat (May 24 1973): 12.

607. Phillips, McCandlish. "Musicians' Group Plans Jazz Fete." The New York Times (March 19 1973): 47.

608. Wilson, John S. "When Does a Lot of Jazz Become Just Too Much?" New York Times (July 10 1973): 48. Remarks on both the Newport Jazz and New York Musicians Festival.

Concert Reviews

609. Goodman, George. "Jazz for the Dawn Patrol Gets 5-Borough Event Off." New York Times (July 1 1973): 30. Review of a performance by Eddie Gail (sic) and Kuntu and Aubrey Welsh at Ornette Coleman's Prince Street loft, Artist House.

610. Ledbetter, Les. "Buffs Find New Hero to Emulate." New York Times (July 9 1973): 42. Review of Alice Tully Hall concert with Milford Graves and the Dave Burrell Quintet.

611. ________. "Mixon Trio's Zesty Pace Begins a Sparkling Bill." New York Times (July 6 1973): 11. Review of the third night of concerts presented by the New York Musicians Organization at Alice Tully Hall. Danny Mixon Trio, Ted Daniel Sextet, Clifford Jordan Quartet, Caravan and the Earl Cross Nonette.

612. ________. "Wilson Sings Stand Out." New York Times (July 3 1973): 10. Review of a concert by Joe Lee Wilson, the Rene McLean Sextet, Ken McIntyre Quintet and the Aboriginal Music Society, presented as part of the New York Musicians' Five Borough Jazz Festival.

613. Wilmer, Valerie. "Caught in the Act: NY Musicians Fest." Melody Maker (July 21 1973): 48.

SOUND UNITY (New York)

Sound Unity Festival (1984)

See also # 4153, 5205

614. Jaenichen, Lothar. "Peter Kowald ueber Aktivitaeten seines New Yorker Aufenthaltes." Jazz Podium (April 1984): 14-15. Interview with bassist Peter Kowald, one of the co-producers of the Sound Unity Festival.

615. "On the Scene--U.S.A.: Sound Unity Festival." Jazz Forum, No. 88 (1984): 23.

616. "Peter Kowald fuehrt Sound Unity Festival in New York durch." Jazz Podium (June 1984): 33.

Concert Reviews

617. Kennedy, David. "Sound Unity Festival." Cadence (August 1984): 31-32, 72.

618. Mandel, Howard. "All Together Now." Village Voice (June 19 1984): 62, 87, 89.

619. Sugiyama, Kazunori. "On the Scene." Coda, No. 197 (August 1984): 29.

2nd International Sound Unity Festival (1988)

620. Bratton, Elliot and Noble. "The Second International Sound Unity Festival." Coda, No. 221 (August/September 1988): 36-39.

STRATA CORPORATION (Detroit)

621. Chadbourne, Eugene. "Strata-East." Coda, No. 135 (January 1975): 7-12.

622. Hunt, David C. "Black Voice Lost in White Superstructure." Coda, Vol. 11, No. 6 (February 1974): 14.

STRATA-EAST (New York)

623. Chadbourne, Eugene. "Strata-East." Coda, No. 135 (January 1975): 7-12.

624. Fishel, Jim. "'Condominium' idea behind NY label." Billboard (April 24 1976): 6.

625. Parks, Carole A. "Strata-East Records, Inc." Black World, Vol. XXII, No. 1 (November 1973): 77-78.

5

The New York Loft and Club Scene

626. "Loft." In Dictionnaire du Jazz, eds. Philippe Carles, et al. Paris: Laffont, 1988.

Articles

627. Albertson, Chris. "Loft Jazz." Stereo Review (May 1978): 80-83.

628. Gilmore, Mikal S. "Jazz Sizzles into the 70s." Music Journal [New York] (May 1971): 18-21.

629. Jost, Ekkehard. "Pop-Information: Loft-Szene New York City." Musik und Bildung (September 1976): 475-476; Also in Jazz Podium (September 1977): 10-11.

630. McRae, Barry. "Loft Horizon." Jazz Journal International (September 1977): 32.

631. _________. "Tommorrow is Now." Jazz Journal International (July 1990): 9.

632. "New York's Cerebral Trip: Loft Jazz." Billboard (July 9 1977): 62, 68.

633. Occhiogrosso, Peter. "Jazzscene: Out from the Lofts." Melody Maker (November 5 1977): 48.

634. _________. "Lofty Heights." Melody Maker (April 16 1977): 6.

635. Panke, Werner. "New York Loft Scene." Jazz Forum, No. 52 (1978): 56-59.

636. "Qu'est-ce que la loft generation?" Jazz Magazine, No. 255 (June 1977): 13-23.

637. Rivers, Sam. "La Musique dans les Greniers de New York." Musique en Jeu, No. 32 (September 1978): 105-108.

638. Smith, Arnold Jay. "Players Move to New Venues - New York's Loft Scene." Billboard (August 19 1978): 53, 72.

639. Welburn, Ron. "The Soho Loft Jazz." Music Journal [New York] (March 1977): 26-28.

640. Wilmer, Valerie. "New York Downtown Musics (Lower East Side)." Jazz Magazine, No. 237 (October 1975): 24-27.

Newspaper Articles

641. Crouch, Stanley. "Jazz Lofts: A Walk Through the Wild Sounds." New York Times Magazine (April 17 1977): 40, 42, 46.

642. Mannheimer, Susan. "Jazz Lofts." Soho Weekly News (April 18 1974): 16-17.

643. Occhiogrosso, Peter. "Living "Loft" Jazz on Record." Soho Weekly News (November 18 1976): 38, 46.

644. _________. "New Sounds in New York [Back in the Apple Again]." Soho Weekly News Supplement - 1976 Newport Jazz Festival in New York (June 24 1976): 15.

645. _________. "Papp's Jazz Cabaret." Soho Weekly News (March 9 1978): 17-18. Article on the precursor to the Public Theater's New Jazz at the Public series with reminiscences of the loft jazz scene of the mid-70s.

646. Palmer, Robert. "Loft Jazz Shifts to a Different Scene." New York Times (January 26 1979): C19. Article on decline of loft scene as club and concert opportunities grow.

647. _________. "The Pop Life." New York Times (July 22 1977): C17. General discussion of the loft jazz scene.

New York Loft Jazz Celebration

648. Giddins, Gary. "Jazz: Up from Saloons; The new music incubated in lofts and cellars 15 years ago; now they signal their success with a 63-hour New York Loft Jazz celebration." Village Voice (June 7 1976): 82.

649. "Loft Weekend." down beat (August 12 1976): 20.

650. Palmer, Robert. "Loft Jazz Goes on a Three-Day Toot." New York Times (June 4 1976): C1, C17.

651. Wilson, John S. "3-Day Loft Jazz Festival Veers to the Avant-Garde." New York Times (June 6 1976).

652. _________, and Robert Palmer. "Jazz of Jankry Group and Monty Waters, In Loft Festival, Adheres to Mainstream." New York Times (June 7 1976).

2nd New York Loft Jazz Celebration

653. "Lofty Celebration." down beat (July 14 1977): 13.

654. Occhiogrosso, Peter. "I Was Sitting On My Patio One Afternoon and I Hallucinated a Loft Jazz Concert." Soho Weekly News (June 2 1977): 41. [Preview]

655. Palmer, Robert. "A Jazz Festival in the Lofts." The New York Times (June 3 1977): C18. [Preview]

656. Rosovsky, P. "Jazz Festival in N.Y. Lofts." Variety (June 8 1977): 60.

657. Wilson, John S., and Robert Palmer. "Loft Jazz Celebration Livens New York." New York Times (June 6 1977): 37. [Concert reviews]

658. ________. "Loft Jazz Festival Ends on a Popular Note." New York Times (June 7 1977): 31. [Concert reviews]

INDIVIDUAL CLUB AND LOFT SPACES

ALI'S ALLEY (77 Greene Street) (founded 1974) - Rashied Ali

659. Crouch, Stanley. "Rashied Ali - the Lofts: Up from Slavery." Soho Weekly News Supplement - 1976 Newport Jazz Festival in New York (June 24 1976): 5.

660. Howland, Harold. "Rashied Ali: The Will to Survive." Modern Drummer (July 1984): 28-31, 94-98. [Interview] Includes a discussion of Ali's loft, Ali's Alley.

AXIS IN SOHO/M. Elson Gallery (463 West Broadway)

661. "Jazz at the Axis." down beat (December 1 1977): 10.

662. Johnson, Tom. "New Outlets for New Music." Village Voice (February 10 1978).

THE BROOK (40 W. 17th Street, 8th Fl.) - Charles Tyler

663. Johnson, Tom. "New Outlets for New Music." Village Voice (February 10 1978).

ENVIRON (476 Broadway, 11th Floor) - John Fischer

664. Berg, Chuck. "Caught: Loft Jazz Grand Party, Environ." down beat (January 13 1977): 38-39.

665. Crouch, Stanley. "Jazz in the Lofts: New Directions." Soho Weekly News (January 15 1976): 35, 38. Review of a performance by saxophonist David Ware. Includes a description of Environ.

666. "New Environ for New York." down beat (January 29 1976): 8. On the opening of this jazz loft.

667. Safane, Cliff. "John Fischer: face to INTERface." Jazz Forum, No. 71 (1981): 45-49. Interview with one of the founders of Environ.

JAZZMANIA (14 East 23rd Street, 4th Fl.) - Mike Morgenstern

668. Occhiogrosso, Peter. "Up From Under." Soho Weekly News (March 11 1976): 36. Review of a David Eyges performance. Includes a description of Jazzmania and its music policy.

KNITTING FACTORY (Houston Street)

669. Hoban, Phoebe. "Knit Wits: All That Downtown Jazz." New York (July 31 1989): 46-49. Profile of the Knitting Factory's co-owners, Michael Dorf and Bob Appel.

670. Sinker, Mark. "Remnants of the Avant-Garde." New Statesman & Society (March 30 1990): 44, 46. Profile of the leading New York new jazz forum of the late 1980s.

THE LADIES FORT (2 Bond Street) - Joe Lee Wilson

671. Goodman, Alan. "Two Jazzmen Open House in SOHO." Crawdaddy, No. 47 (April 1975): 74.

672. Kastin, David. "Profile: Joe Lee Wilson." down beat (February 24 1977): 34-36. Profile of singer and Ladies Fort owner Joe Lee Wilson.

673. Taylor, J. R. "Notes: The Lofts." Jazz Magazine (Northport, NY), Vol. 2, No. 1 (Fall 1977): 23. Discussion of scheduling conflicts and tension between Stanley Crouch's programming of the Ladies Fort and Sam Rivers' Studio Rivbea during the annual Newport in New York jazz festival.

674. Tomkins, Les. "Joe Lee Travels Hopefully." Crescendo International (August 1978): 15-16.

675. "U.S.A.: Joe Lee Wilson Leaves the Fort." Jazz Forum, No. 53 (1978): 16.

676. Wilmer, Valerie. "Joe Lee - 'Space' Singer." Melody Maker (August 28 1976): 28. [Interview]

STUDIO RIVBEA (24 Bond Street) (1970-1979) - Sam Rivers

677. Atherton, J. "Jazz News: Rivers' Summer Festival." Melody Maker (July 13 1974): 20.

678. Brower, W. A. "Sam Rivers: Warlord of the Lofts." down beat (November 16 1978): 21-22, 39, 47-49.

679. Gans, Charles J. "Sam Rivers: A Determined Survivor." Jazz Forum, No. 54 (1978): 29-32, 42.

680. Goodman, Alan. "Two Jazzman Open House in SOHO." Crawdaddy, No. 47 (April 1975): 74.

681. "News: Rivers Speaks Out." down beat (April 20 1978): 10. Report on meeting between Rivers and down beat editors in which he criticizes them for having ignored the loft scene.

682. Palmer, Bob. "Sam Rivers: An Artist on an Empty Stage." down beat (February 13 1975): 12-13, 33. [Interview]

683. _________. "Sam Rivers, Father Radical." Rolling Stone (August 10 1978): 26. Feature article on Studio Rivbea.

684. Rava, Graciela. "Le Rivbea de Bea Rivers." Jazz Magazine, No. 262 (February 1978): 24-26.

685. Taylor, J. R. "Notes: The Lofts." Jazz Magazine (Northport, NY), Vol. 2, No. 1 (Fall 1977): 23. Discussion of scheduling conflicts and tension between Stanley Crouch's programming of the Ladies Fort and Sam Rivers' Studio Rivbea during the annual Newport in New York jazz festival.

Concert Reviews

686. Hutton, Randy. "Heard and Seen: Studio Rivbea." Coda, Vol. 11, No. 11 (1974): 31-34. [Festival review]

687. Occhiogrosso, Peter. "Rivbea: An Historic Festival." Soho Weekly News (May 20 1976): 35.

688. _________. "Rivbea Festival: New Moments." Village Voice (July 21 1975): 96.

689. Simosko, Vladimir. "Studio Rivbea Spring Festival." Coda, No. 149 (July 1976): 8-10. [Festival review]

SWEET BASIL

690. Mandel, Howard. "The Liberal Bias." Village Voice (March 10 1987): 77. Review of Sweet Basil's new jazz festival "Music is an Open Sky."

691. Watrous, Peter. "Establishing the Fringe." Village Voice (March 4 1986): 70. Review of the "Music is an Open Sky" festival.

TIN PALACE (Bowery and E. 2nd Street)

692. "Critic Crouch Books a Hip Palace." down beat (March 22 1979): 9.

693. Occhiogrosso, Peter. "Up from Under." Soho Weekly News (March 11 1976): 36. Review of a Charles Tyler concert at the Tin Palace. Includes a description of the club and its history.

6

Biographical and Critical Studies

GENERAL WORKS

694. Dahl, Linda. Stormy Weather: The Music and Lives of a Century of Jazzwomen. New York: Pantheon Books, 1984. Includes brief sketches of Alice Coltrane (169); Amina Claudine Myers (170); Joanne Brackeen (170-172); Jane Ira Bloom (173-174); Barbara Donald (175); Monnette Sudler (176); Jeanne Lee (179-180); Jay Clayton (180-181); Linda Sharrock (181); Rita Warford (181) and the Feminist Improvising Group (184).

695. McRae, Barry. "Free Form." In The Jazz Cataclysm. London: J.M. Dent, 1967, pp. 152-170. Includes brief discussions of the work of Prince Lasha and Sonny Simmons (154-156), the New York Contemporary 5 and John Tchicai (157), Archie Shepp (157-159), Bill Dixon (159-160), Jimmy Giuffre (160-161), Roswell Rudd (161-162), Cecil Taylor (162-164), Andrew Hill (164-165), Bobby Hutcherson (165-166), Sun Ra (166-168), Pharoah Sanders (168-169), Byron Allen (169), Giuseppi Logan (169) and Albert Ayler (169-170).

Articles

696. "Declaration by the Avant Garde." Down Beat's Music '64, Vol. 9 (1964): 65-70. Includes statements from Bill Barron, Carla Bley, Paul Bley, Don Cherry, Ted Curson, Joe Daly, Bill Dixon, Don Ellis, Don Friedman, Jimmy Giuffre, Joe Harriott, Don Heckman, Prince Lasha, Ken McIntyre, Sonny Simmons, John Tchicai, and Jimmy Woods on the jazz avant-garde.

697. Giddins, Gary. "Weatherbird: The trombone's connected to the..." Village Voice (September 3 1980): 56-57. Survey of jazz trombonists including Ray Anderson, George Lewis, Albert Mangelsdorff and Roswell Rudd.

698. Harrison, Max. "Over the Hills and Faraway: Further American Avant-Garde Releases." Jazz Monthly (January 1967): 14-17. Review of lps by Albert Ayler (Spirits Rejoice); Milford Graves (Milford Graves Percussion Ensemble); Giuseppi Logan (More Giuseppi Logan); Don Pullen/Milford Graves (Live at Yale); Sun Ra (Heliocentric Worlds of Sun Ra); and Frank Wright (Frank Wright Trio).

699. Jones, LeRoi. "Apple Cores 4: New Voices in Newark." down beat (March 10 1966): 13+. Some of the artists discussed include Pharoah Sanders, Marion Brown and Rashied Ali. [Reprinted in # 59]

700. ________. "Apple Cores 3: Strong Voices in Today's Black Music." down beat (February 10 1966): 15, 48. Discusses the music of some of the New Jazz's leading voices--Albert Ayler, Sonny Murray, Sun Ra, et al. [Reprinted in # 59]

701. McElfresh, Suzanne. "New York Improvisers: A Woman's Work is Never Done." Ear (March 1990): 18-22. Profiles of five of New York's women improvisers: Marion Brandis (flute), Marilyn Crispell (piano), Shelley Hirsch (vocal), Terry Jenoure (violin) and Myra Melford (piano).

702. Mulhern, Tom. "Improvisational Avant-Garde Guitar, its history, its proponents, its future." Guitar Player (April 1979): 36+. Among the dozen or so guitarists included here are Sonny Sharrock, Derek Bailey, Hans Reichel and Michael Gregory Jackson.

703. Osterman, Robert. "The Moody Men Who Play the New Music." National Observer (June 7 1965): 22. Includes comments from Byron Allen, Albert Ayler, Ornette Coleman, Milford Graves, Gary Peacock, and Cecil Taylor.

704. Porter, Lewis. "Jazzwomen Part II: 'You Can't Get Up There Timidly'." Music Educators Journal (October 1984): 42-51. Includes comments from Alice Coltrane, Carla Bley, Joanne Brackeen and Barbara Donald.

705. Reeve, Stephen. "The New Piano in the New Jazz." Jazz Journal (September 1969): 25, 40. Survey of recordings by Cecil Taylor, Don Pullen, Sun Ra, Andrew Hill, Paul Bley and Chris McGregor.

706. Tepperman, Barry. "Rudd, Moncur and some other stuff." Coda (July/August 1971): 8-11. Survey of trombonists affiliated in some way with the avant-garde. Among those discussed are Roswell Rudd, Grachan Moncur, Lester Lashley, Paul Rutherford, Malcolm Griffiths, et al.

707. Zabor, Rafi. "Funny, You Look Like a Musician." Village Voice (July 2 1979): 72-73. Responses of Anthony Braxton, Anthony Davis, George Lewis, Roscoe Mitchell and James Newton to the frequent criticism of the "Europeanness" of their work.

INDIVIDUAL ARTISTS

AALTONEN, JUHANI (1935-) (Finland) - Tenor/Alto Sax

708. Gronow, Pekka. "Aaltonen, Juhani." In The New Grove Dictionary of Jazz. London: Macmillan Press, 1988.

709. Vuorela, Jari-Pekka. "Juhani Aaltonen." In Finnish Jazz. 3rd rev. ed. Helsinki: Foundation for the Promotion of Finnish Music Information Centre, 1986, p. 8.

Articles

710. "Eurojazz personalities, Finland." Jazz Forum, No. 11 (Spring 1971): 100.

711. Sermila, Jarmo. "Juhani Aaltonen." Jazz Forum, No. 42 (1976): 52-53.

ABDULLAH, AHMED [Leroy Bland] (1946-) - Trumpet

712. Carles, Philippe, and Jean-Louis Comolli. Free Jazz, Black Power. 2nd ed. Paris: Editions Galilee, 1979, p. 364.

713. Dictionnaire du Jazz, eds. Philippe Carles, et al. Paris: Laffont, 1988.

714. Wilmer, Valerie. As Serious As Your Life. Westport, CT: Lawrence Hill & Co., 1981, p. 259.

Articles

715. Rusch, Bob. "Ahmed Abdullah: interview." Cadence, Vol. 7, No. 9 (September 1981): 5-8, 95.

716. Smith, Arnold Jay. "Profile: Ahmed Abdullah." down beat (April 20 1978): 36-37.

ABORIGINAL MUSIC SOCIETY

See # 612

ABRAMS, MUHAL RICHARD (1930-) - Piano

See also # 417

717. Jost, Ekkehard. "Muhal Richard Abrams." In Jazzmusiker: Materialen zur Soziologie der Afro-Amerikanischen Musik. Frankfurt am Main: Ullstein, 1982, pp. 188-203.

718. Vuijsje, Bert. De Nieuwe Jazz. Baarn: Bosch & Keuning, 1978, pp. 191-202. [Interview]

Biographical Dictionaries

719. Berry, Lemuel, Jr. Biographical Dictionary of Black Musicians and Music Educators. Guthrie, OK: Educational Book Publishers, 1978.

720. Carles, Philippe, and Jean-Louis Comolli. Free Jazz, Black Power. 2nd ed. Paris: Editions Galilee, 1979, pp. 364-365.

721. Carr, Ian. "Abrams, Muhal Richard." In Jazz: The Essential Companion. New York: Prentice Hall Press, 1988.

722. Case, Brian, and Stan Britt. The Harmony Illustrated Encyclopedia of Jazz. 3rd ed. New York: Harmony Books, 1987.

723. Claghorn, Charles Eugene. Biographical Dictionary of Jazz. Englewood Cliffs, NJ: Prentice-Hall, 1982.

724. Dictionnaire du Jazz, eds. Philippe Carles, et al. Paris: Laffont, 1988.

725. Feather, Leonard, and Ira Gitler. The Encyclopedia of Jazz in the Seventies. New York: Horizon Press, 1976.

726. Jeske, Lee. "Abrams, Muhal Richard." In The New Grove Dictionary of Jazz. London: Macmillan Press, 1988.

727. McRae, Barry. "Muhal Richard Abrams." In The Jazz Handbook. Harlow, Essex, Eng.: Longman, 1987, p. 180.

728. The Penguin Encyclopedia of Popular Music, ed. Donald Clarke. New York: Viking, 1989.

729. Southern, Eileen. Biographical Dictionary of Afro-American and African Musicians. Westport, CT: Greenwood Press, 1982.

730. Who's Who in Entertainment. 1st ed. 1989-1990.

731. Wilmer, Valerie. As Serious As Your Life. Westport, CT: Lawrence Hill & Co., 1981, p. 259.

Articles

732. Bernard, M. "Richard Abrams et l'A.A.C.M." Jazz Magazine, No. 209 (March 1973): 20-21.

733. Bourget, Jean-Loup. "Muhal Richard Abrams: vers la musique." Jazz Magazine, No. 256 (July/August 1977): 22-25, 42. [Interview]

734. De Muth, Jerry. "Muhal Richard Abrams: jazz innovator, founder of the AACM." Contemporary Keyboard (May 1978): 20, 48-49.

735. "Dico Disco & Co." Jazz Magazine, No. 298 (June 1981): 33. Biographical sketch.

736. Giddins, Gary. "Muhal Richard Abrams and the AACM." Radio Free Jazz (June 1978): 7-10. [Interview]

737. ________. "Muhal Richard Abrams: Meet This Composer." Village Voice (June 20 1989): 104; Repr. in Jazz Forum, No. 120 (1989): 4-6.

738. Goddet, Laurent, and Alex Dutilh. "Le Pere." Jazz Hot, No. 356/357 (Dec 1978/Jan 1979): 17-21, 88. [Interview]

739. Kart, Larry. "Record Reviews: Levels and Degrees of Light." down beat (November 14 1968): 20.

740. Lake, Steve. "Muhal Richard Abrams/Leo Smith/Roscoe Mitchell." Melody Maker (January 1 1977): 22.

741. _________. "Number One Man." Melody Maker (December 22 1973): 43.

742. Levi, Titus. "Muhal Abrams: Into the Palace of Music." OPtion (March/April 1985): 26-27.

743. Litweiler, John B. "AACM's 20th Anniversary - An Interview with Muhal Richard Abrams, Founder and Father Figure." (Chicago) Reader (May 9 1975).

744. _________. "A Man with an Idea." down beat (October 5 1967): 23+.

745. Macnie, Jim. "Muhal Richard Abrams' Abstract Blues." Musician (November 1990): 30, 32, 34.

746. McRae, Barry. "Muhal Richard Abrams." Jazz Journal International (April 1980): 25-26.

747. Mandel, Howard. "Laureate for Our Time." Village Voice (October 23 1990): 90.

748. "Muhal Richard Abrams wins Jazzpar award." Variety (October 11 1989): 200.

749. Palmer, Robert. "Muhal Richard Abrams." Rolling Stone (September 7 1978): 19.

750. Silverman, L., and Larry Birnbaum. "The World According to Muhal." Ear: New Music News, Vol. 13, No. 4 (June 1988): 18-19, 21. [Interview]

751. Smith, Will. "Record Reviews: Young at Heart/Wise in Time." down beat (December 9 1971): 18.

752. "La Terre Promise selon Abrams." Jazz Magazine, No. 212 (June 1973): 10-12. [Interview]

753. Tinder, Cliff. "Faces: Muhal Richard Abrams." Musician, No. 51 (January 1983): 40-41.

754. Townley, Ray. "Profile: Muhal Richard Abrams." down beat (August 15 1974): 34-35.

755. Watrous, Peter. "A Jazz Fixture of No Fixed Style." New York Times (October 11 1990).

756. Williams, Richard. "Who's Blowin' in the Windy City." Melody Maker (April 21 1973): 51. [Concert review]

ACKLEY, BRUCE - Reeds

See also # 5625-5638

757. Szigeti, P. "Bruce Ackley: interview." Cadence, Vol. 10, No. 6 (June 1984): 19-21.

AEBI, IRENE (1939-) (Switzerland) - Vocal

758. Dictionnaire du Jazz, eds. Philippe Carles, et al. Paris: Laffont, 1988.

759. Loupien, Serge. "Les cordes d'Irene." Jazz Magazine, No. 250 (December 1976): 18-19. [Interview]

AIR

760. Claghorn, Charles Eugene. Biographical Dictionary of Jazz. Englewood Cliffs, NJ: Prentice-Hall, 1982, p. 327.

761. Dictionnaire du Jazz, eds. Philippe Carles, et al. Paris: Laffont, 1988.

762. Mandel, Howard. "Air." In The New Grove Dictionary of Jazz. London: Macmillan Press, 1988.

763. The Penguin Encyclopedia of Popular Music, ed. Donald Clarke. New York: Viking, 1989, p. 12.

Articles

764. "Dico Disco & Co." Jazz Magazine, No. 298 (June 1981): 33. Biographical sketch.

765. Giddins, Gary. "Air: Heirs." Village Voice (November 12 1979): 94.

766. ________. "Riffs: Air is an Equal Opportunity Trio." Village Voice (October 17 1977): 65.

767. Levi, Titus. "Air: Always Fresh." Option (March/April 1985): 27.

768. Litweiler, John. "Air: Impossible to Pigeonhole." down beat (December 16 1976): 22, 50-51. [Interview]

769. McRae, Barry. "Avant Courier: Air." Jazz Journal International (June 1983): 6-7.

770. Mitchell, Charles. "Caught: Air, N.A.M.E. Gallery, Chicago." down beat (March 25 1976): 39-41. [Concert review]

771. Palmer, Robert. "Air - Democracy in Action." New York Times (June 11 1978).

772. ________. "Time for Air's Improvisational Three-for-All." Rolling Stone (February 8 1979): 30.

773. Zabor, Rafi. "Air." Musician, Player and Listener, No. 32 (April-May 1981): 54-58, 68.

AKLAFF, PHEEROAN [Paul Maddox] (1955-) - Drums

774. Dictionnaire du Jazz, eds. Philippe Carles, et al. Paris: Laffont, 1988.

Articles

775. Drozdowski, Ted. "Pheeroan ak Laff: Cosmic Consciousness from the Sparkplug of New Jazz." Musician (June 1989): 83+.

776. Riggins, Roger. "Pheeroan AkLaff." Coda, No. 186 (October 1982): 8-9. [Interview]

777. Rusch, Bob. "Pheeroan ak Laff." Cadence, Vol. 14, No. 7 (July 1988): 5-17, 26; No. 8 (August 1988): 27-33, 92. [Interview]

ALI, MUHAMMAD [Raymond Patterson] (1936-) - Drums

778. Carles, Philippe, and Jean-Louis Comolli. Free Jazz, Black Power. 2nd ed. Paris: Editions Galilee, 1979, p. 365.

779. Dictionnaire du Jazz, eds. Philippe Carles. Paris: Laffont, 1988.

780. Wilmer, Valerie. As Serious As Your Life. Westport, CT: Lawrence Hill & Co., 1981, p. 259.

ALI, RASHIED [Robert Patterson, Jr.] (1935-) - Drums

See also # 69, 659-660, 699

781. Berry, Lemuel, Jr. Biographical Dictionary of Black Musicians and Music Educators. Guthrie, OK: Educational Book Publishers, 1978.

782. Carles, Philippe, and Jean-Louis Comolli. Free Jazz, Black Power. 2nd ed. Paris: Editions Galilee, 1979, p. 365.

783. Carr, Ian. "Ali, Rashied." In Jazz: The Essential Companion. New York: Prentice Hall Press, 1988.

784. Claghorn, Charles Eugene. "Ali, Rashied." In Biographical Dictionary of Jazz. Englewood Cliffs, NJ: Prentice-Hall, 1982. See also entry on "Ali's Alley Orchestra," p. 327.

785. ________. Biographical Dictionary of American Music. West Nyack, NY: Parker Pub. Co., 1973.

786. Dictionnaire du Jazz, eds. Philippe Carles, et al. Paris: Laffont, 1988.

787. Feather, Leonard. The Encyclopedia of Jazz in the Sixties. New York: Horizon Press, 1966.

788. ________, and Ira Gitler. The Encyclopedia of Jazz in the Seventies. New York: Horizon Press, 1976.

789. The Penguin Encyclopedia of Popular Music, ed. Donald Clarke. New York: Viking, 1989.

790. Reclams Jazzfuhrer. 2nd, rev. ed. Stuttgart: Reclam, 1977.

791. Ullman, Michael. "Ali, Rashied." In The New Grove Dictionary of American Music. London: Macmillan Press, 1986.

792. ________. "Ali, Rashied." In The New Grove Dictionary of Jazz. London: Macmillan Press, 1988.

793. Who's Who Among Black Americans. 6th ed. 1990/91. Detroit: Gale Research, 1990.

794. Wilmer, Valerie. As Serious As Your Life. Westport, CT: Lawrence Hill & Co., 1981, pp. 170-172, 259.

Articles

795. Ali, Rashied. "'Ce que j'ai appris chez Coltrane.'" Jazz Magazine, No. 218 (January 1974): 18-19.

796. Cressant, P. "Rashied Ali et 'Rashied Ali'." Jazz Hot, No. 260 (April 1970): 7.

797. "Dico Disco and Co." Jazz Magazine, No. 298 (June 1981): 33. Biographical sketch.

798. Fox, Ted. "Success Story: Self-Made Records." Jazz Magazine (New York), Vol. 2, No. 4 (1978): 51-52. Includes a discussion of Ali's record label Survival.

799. Gans, Charles J. "Rashied Ali." Jazz Forum, No. 75 (1982): 25-26. [Profile]

800. Howland, Harold. "Rashied Ali: The Will to Survive." Modern Drummer (July 1984): 28-31, 94-98. [Interview]

801. "Lettre de Rashied." Jazz Magazine, No. 187 (March 1971): 13+.

802. Welburn, Ron. "Rashied Ali's Survival Recording Company." Black World, Vol. 24 (November 1974): 22-23.

803. Wilmer, Valerie. "Ali: the ubiquitous gigger." Melody Maker (December 4 1971): 28.

804. ________. "Dialogue of the Drummers." Coda, No. 131 (September 1974): 2-5. [Interview]

805. ________. "Rashied, the other drummer with Trane." Melody Maker (April 6 1968): 8.

806. ________. "Rashied's Survival." Melody Maker (June 8 1974): 63.

807. ________. "Trois Jeunes Tambours." Jazz Magazine, No. 202 (July 1972): 10+.

Concert Reviews

808. Davidson, Martin. "Jazz caught in the act." Melody Maker (May 20 1972): 30.

809. Welch, Jane. "Caught in the Act: Clifford Thornton New Art Ensemble/Jayne Cortez/Rashied Ali Quartet." down beat (October 1 1970): 27-28.

810. Wilmer, Valerie. "Caught in the Act: Dialogue of the Drums." down beat (November 25 1971): 26-27. Review of a trio performance by Ali, Andrew Cyrille and Milford Graves at New York's Cami Hall.

ALLEN, BYRON (1940-) - Alto Saxophone

See also # 288, 695, 703

811. Carles, Philippe, and Jean-Louis Comolli. Free Jazz, Black Power. 2nd ed. Paris: Editions Galilee, 1979, p. 365.

812. Claghorn, Charles Eugene. Biographical Dictionary of American Music. West Nyack, NY: Parker Pub. Co., 1973.

813. ________. Biographical Dictionary of Jazz. Englewood Cliffs, NJ: Prentice-Hall, 1982.

814. Dictionnaire du Jazz, eds. Philippe Carles, et al. Paris: Laffont, 1988.

815. Feather, Leonard. The Encyclopedia of Jazz in the Sixties. New York: Horizon Press, 1966.

816. Wilmer, Valerie. As Serious As Your Life. Westport, CT: Lawrence Hill & Co., 1981, p. 259.

Articles

817. "Dictionnaire de l'Alto." Jazz Magazine, No. 137 (December 1966): 39. Biographical sketch.

818. Morgenstern, Dan. "Caught in the Act." down beat (July 15 1965): 12. [Concert review]

819. "News." Cadence (November 1977): 52. Update on Allen's whereabouts.

820. Rusch, Bob. "Byron Allen: interview." Cadence, Vol. 4, No. 2/3 (May 1978): 8+.

ALLEN, GERI (1957-) - Piano

See also # 585, 587

821. Dictionnaire du Jazz, eds. Philippe Carles, et al. Paris: Laffont, 1988.

822. Handy, D. Antoinette. Black Women in American Bands and Orchestras. Metuchen, NJ: Scarecrow Press, 1981, pp. 237-238.

Articles

823. Gribetz, Sid. "Geri Allen." Jazz Times (November 1989): 16, 28.

824. Kevorkian, Kyle. "Back to Africa." Mother Jones (November 1989): 15.

825. ________, and Ed Hazell. "Profile: Geri Allen's Reign: renaissance of rhythm." Keyboard Magazine (June 1987): 24.

826. "Les Musiques en Allen." Jazz Magazine, No. 373 (July-August 1988): 40-41. [Interview]

827. Palmer, Don. "Geri Allen: Real-Life Music Comes to Town." down beat (July 1988): 24-25.

828. Urpeth, Peter. "Allen Keys." The Wire, No. 67 (September 1989): 40-41, 43.

829. Watrous, Peter. "She Plays with Fire." Vogue (October 1985): 110.

ALLEN, MARSHALL (1924-) - Alto Saxophone

830. Carles, Philippe, and Jean-Louis Comolli. Free Jazz, Black Power. 2nd ed. Paris: Editions Galilee, 1979, p. 366.

831. Claghorn, Charles Eugene. Biographical Dictionary of American Music. West Nyack, NY: Parker Pub. Co., 1973.

832. ________. Biographical Dictionary of Jazz. Englewood Cliffs, NJ: Prentice-Hall, 1982.

833. Dictionnaire du Jazz, eds. Philippe Carles, et al. Paris: Laffont, 1988.

834. Feather, Leonard. The Encyclopedia of Jazz in the Sixties. New York: Horizon Press, 1966.

835. The New Grove Dictionary of Jazz. London: Macmillan Press, 1988.

836. Wilmer, Valerie. As Serious As Your Life. Westport, CT: Lawrence Hill & Co., 1981, p. 259.

Articles

837. Fiofori, Tam. "Right Sound at the Right Time." Melody Maker (March 27 1971): 24.

838. ________. "Les Premiers Satellites." Jazz Magazine, No. 196 (January 1972): 21.

839. "L'Impossible Liberte; Entretien avec Sun Ra, John Gilmore, Marshall Allen, et Pat Patrick." Jazz Magazine, No. 196 (January 1972): 10-13. [Interview]

ALTENA, MAARTEN (1943-) (Netherlands) - Bass

840. Carles, Philippe, and Jean-Louis Comolli. Free Jazz, Black Power. 2nd ed. Paris: Editions Galilee, 1979, p. 453.

841. Dictionnaire du Jazz, eds. Philippe Carles, et al. Paris: Laffont, 1988.

842. Eyle, Wim van. "Altena, Maarten." In The New Grove Dictionary of Jazz. London: Macmillan Press, 1988.

843. Vuijsje, Bert. Jazzportretten. Amsterdam: Van Gennep, 1983, pp. 101-109. [Dutch text]

Articles

844. Ansell, Kenneth. "Maarten van Regteren Altena." Impetus (London), No. 6 (1977): 262-264. [Interview]

845. Chenard, Marc. "The Composer's Touch: A Profile of Dutch Bassist Maarten Altena." Coda, No. 229 (Dec 1989-Jan 1990): 10-12.

846. Rouy, Gerard. "Maarten Altena: 'vers l'independance'." Jazz Magazine, No. 295 (March 1981): 32-34. [Interview]

847. Schoemaker, Bill. "Maarten Altena." down beat (March 1989): 46-47.

848. Summers, Russ. "The Jazz Fest Circuit: Barre Phillips, Maarten Altena and Pierre Dorge in Vancouver." Option, No. 36 (January/February 1991): 44-49.

ALTSCHUL, BARRY (1943-) - Drums

See also # 1977-1981

849. Carles, Philippe, and Jean-Louis Comolli. Free Jazz, Black Power. 2nd ed. Paris: Editions Galilee, 1979, p. 366.

850. Carr, Ian. "Altschul, Barry." In Jazz: The Essential Companion. New York: Prentice Hall Press, 1988.

851. Claghorn, Charles Eugene. Biographical Dictionary of Jazz. Englewood Cliffs, NJ: Prentice-Hall, 1982.

852. Dictionnaire du Jazz, eds. Philippe Carles, et al. Paris: Laffont, 1988.

853. Feather, Leonard, and Ira Gitler. The Encyclopedia of Jazz in the Seventies. New York: Horizon Press, 1976.

854. The Penguin Encyclopedia of Popular Music, ed. Donald Clarke. New York: Viking, 1989.

855. Wild, David. "Altschul, Barry." In The New Grove Dictionary of Jazz. London: Macmillan Press, 1988.

856. Wilmer, Valerie. As Serious As Your Life. Westport, CT: Lawrence Hill & Co., 1981, p. 283.

Articles

857. Altschul, Barry. "The Music of the Drums." Modern Drummer, Vol. 5, No. 2 (1981): 42-43.

858. Carles, Philippe. "Les Paris de Barry." Jazz Magazine, No. 298 (June 1981): 34-36. [Interview]

859. Cuscuna, Michael. "Barry Altschul: Mister Joy." Jazz & Pop (April 1968): 16-17.

860. Goddet, Laurent, and Alex Dutilh. "Mr. Joy." Jazz Hot, No. 342 (October 1977): 32-37, 52-53. [Interview]

861. Jeske, Lee. "Barry Altschul's Drum Role." down beat (February 1982): 17-19, 64.

862. Keepnews, Peter. "Barry Altschul: Traps in the South Bronx." down beat (February 13 1975): 14+.

863. Lindenmaier, H. Lukas. "Barry Altschul: interview." Cadence, Vol. 6, No. 6 (June 1980): 5-8, 28.

864. Mattingly, Rick. "The Artistic Integrity of Barry Altschul." Modern Drummer (November 1982): 12-15, 64-68. [Interview]

865. Safane, Clifford Jay. "Barry Altschul." Coda, No. 168 (August 1979): 11-13. [Interview]

866. Wilmer, Valerie. "Altschul in a Nutshell." Melody Maker (January 30 1981): 32.

AMALGAM (formed 1967) (Great Britain)

867. "On the Scene: Amalgam." Jazz Forum, No. 32 (December 1974): 23.

868. Schonfield, Victor. "Amalgam." Melody Maker (July 8 1967): 4.

Concert Reviews

869. "Caught in the Act." Melody Maker (January 27 1979): 29.

870. "Caught in the Act." Melody Maker (June 25 1977): 42.

871. "Caught in the Act." Melody Maker (January 5 1974): 19.

872. Hyder, Ken. "Caught in the Act." Melody Maker (February 3 1973): 49.

873. McRae, Barry. "Jazz in Britain." Jazz Journal (September 1967): 22. Review of the debut performance of Amalgam at London's Little Theatre Club.

874. Schonfield, Victor. "Caught in the Act." Melody Maker (September 23 1967): 4.

875. Williams, Richard. "Caught in the Act." Melody Maker (November 29 1969): 6.

AMM (Great Britain)

See also # 343

876. The Penguin Encyclopedia of Popular Music, ed. Donald Clarke. New York: Viking, 1989, pp. 25-26.

Articles

877. "AMM: Eddie Prevost, Keith Rowe." Perspectives of New Music, Vol. 21, No. 1-2 (1982-83): 34+. Interview with two members of the British new jazz ensemble.

878. "AMM Music London." Jazz Podium (April 1972): 120.

879. Ansell, Kenneth. "AMM: The Sound as Music." Wire, No. 11 (January 1985): 21-27.

880. Charlton, Hannah. "AMMmusic." Collusion (London), No. 3 (June/September 1982): 28-32.

881. Jack, Adrian. "The Group Scene." Music and Musicians (March 1972): 23-24.

882. Lake, Steve. "AMM: only beginners." Melody Maker (February 15 1975): 45.

883. Miles. "London Report." East Village Other, Vol. 1, No. 9 (April 1-15 1966): 10. Report on the British new jazz ensemble AMM.

884. Parsons, Michael. "Sounds of Discovery." Musical Times (May 1968): 430.

885. Schonfield, Victor. "Cornelius Cardew, AMM and the path to perfect hearing." Jazz Monthly (May 1968): 10-11.

Concert Reviews

886. Morgan, Alun. "On Stage." Jazz & Blues (May 1973): 33.

887. "On the Bandstand." Jazz Forum, No. 36 (August 1975): 20.

888. Williams, Richard. "Caught in the Act." Melody Maker (December 18 1971): 26.

889. ________. "Caught in the Act." Melody Maker (March 25 1972): 18.

ANDERSON, FRED (1929-) - Tenor Saxophone

890. Carles, Philippe, and Jean-Louis Comolli. Free Jazz, Black Power. 2nd ed. Paris: Editions Galilee, 1979, p. 366.

891. Dictionnaire du Jazz, eds. Philippe Carles, et al. Paris: Laffont, 1988.

892. Jost, Ekkehard. "Fred Anderson." In Jazzmusiker: Materialen zur Soziologie der Afro-Amerikanischen Musik. Frankfurt am Main: Ullstein, 1982, pp. 203-212.

893. The Penguin Encyclopedia of Popular Music, ed. Donald Clarke. New York: Viking, 1989, p. 29.

894. Such, David G. "Anderson, Fred." The New Grove Dictionary of Jazz. London: Macmillan Press, 1988.

895. Wilmer, Valerie. As Serious As Your Life. Westport, CT: Lawrence Hill & Co., 1981, p. 260.

Articles

896. Cohen, Elaine. "Fred Anderson." Coda, No. 197 (August 1984): 18-20. [Interview]

897. Friedman, Sharon, and Larry Birnbaum. "Fred Anderson: AACM's Biggest Secret." down beat (March 8 1979): 20-21, 40. [Interview]

898. Jost, Ekkehard. "Neighbors mit Fred Anderson und William Brimfield." Jazz Podium, Vol. 26, No. 2 (1977): 19-20.

899. Mandel, Howard. "Fred Anderson's Great Hope." Musician, Player and Listener, No. 38 (December 1981): 26, 28, 33, 114.

900. Mitchell, Charles. "Caught: Fred Anderson Sextet, Museum of Contemporary Art, Chicago." down beat (June 3 1976): 35-36. [Concert review]

901. Self, Wayne K. "Guarding the Old Guard." Arts Midwest Jazzletter, Vol. 6, No. 1 (Fall 1988): 7-9.

902. Solothurnmann, Jurg. "Fred Anderson." Jazz Forum, No. 68 (1980): 38-43.

ANDERSON, RAY (1952-) - Trombone

See also # 697

903. Carr, Ian. "Anderson, Ray." In Jazz: The Essential Companion. New York: Prentice Hall Press, 1988.

904. Case, Brian, and Stan Britt. The Harmony Illustrated Encyclopedia of Jazz. 3rd ed. New York: Harmony Books, 1987.

905. _Dictionnaire du Jazz_, eds. Philippe Carles, et al. Paris: Laffont, 1988.

906. McRae, Barry. "Ray Anderson." In _The Jazz Handbook_. Harlow, Essex, Eng.: Longman, 1987, p. 226.

907. Wild, David. "Anderson, Ray." In _The New Grove Dictionary of Jazz_. London: Macmillan Press, 1988.

Articles

908. Levenson, Jeff. "Ray Anderson: slidin' into first." _down beat_ (August 1989): 27+.

909. Lewis, David. "Ray Anderson." _Coda_, No. 212 (February-March 1987): 18-19. [Interview]

910. Loupien, Serge, and Gerard Rouy. "Ray Andersen [sic]." _Jazz Magazine_, No. 266-267 (July-August 1978): 42-43. [Interview]

911. Mathieson, Kenny. "Ray Anderson: Romancing the Bone." _Wire_, No. 79 (September 1990): 10-12.

912. Schoemaker, Bill. "Ray Anderson: 'Boning Up for the Future." _down beat_ (July 1982): 21-23. [Interview]

913. Smith, Arnold Jay. "Ray Anderson: Talking His Own Truths." _Jazz Times_ (June 1990): 13.

ART ENSEMBLE OF CHICAGO (formed 1968)

914. McRae, Barry. "Art Ensemble of Chicago." In _The Jazz Handbook_. Harlow, Essex, Eng.: Longman, 1987, pp. 181-183.

915. Rockwell, John. "Jazz, Group Improvisation, Race and Racism." In _All American Music: Composition in the Late Twentieth Century_. New York: Alfred A. Knopf, 1983, pp. 164-175.

Biographical Dictionaries

916. Carr, Ian. "Art Ensemble of Chicago." In _Jazz: The Essential Companion_. New York: Prentice Hall Press, 1988.

917. Case, Brian, and Stan Britt. _The Harmony Illustrated Encyclopedia of Jazz_. 3rd ed. New York: Harmony Books, 1987.

918. Claghorn, Charles Eugene. _Biographical Dictionary of Jazz_. Englewood Cliffs, NJ: Prentice-Hall, 1982, p. 329.

919. _Dictionnaire du Jazz_, eds. Philippe Carles, et al. Paris: Laffont, 1988.

920. Feather, Leonard, and Ira Gitler. _The Encyclopedia of Jazz in the Seventies_. New York: Horizon Press, 1976.

921. Kernfeld, Barry. "Art Ensemble of Chicago." In The New Grove Dictionary of American Music. London: Macmillan Press, 1986.

922. ________. "Art Ensemble of Chicago." In The New Grove Dictionary of Jazz. London: Macmillan Press, 1988.

923. The Penguin Encyclopedia of Popular Music, ed. Donald Clarke. New York: Viking, 1989, pp. 43-44.

924. Southern, Eileen. Biographical Dictionary of Afro-American and African Musicians. Westport, CT: Greenwood Press, 1982.

Articles

925. Birnbaum, Larry. "Art Ensemble of Chicago: 15 Years of Great Black Music." down beat (May 3 1979): 15+. [Interview]

926. Carles, Philippe. "De l'AACM a ECM: l'Art Ensemble." Jazz Magazine, No. 320 (July/August 1983): 52-53. [Interview]

927. Case, Brian. "Like Hi Man, I's Yo New Neighbor." New Musical Express (January 11 1975): 30. [Interview]

928. Conley, G. W. "A Fresh New Art is Born, and the Message is Impact." Melody Maker (August 30 1969): 10.

929. Dumetz, G. "Brigitte et l'Art Ensemble." Jazz Monthly, No. 177 (April 1970): 13.

930. Franceschi, B. "Art Ensemble of Chicago." Jazz Magazine, No. 286 (May 1980): 15-16.

931. Gans, Charles. "Art Ensemble of Chicago: Nice Guys Finish First." Jazz Forum, No. 68 (1980).

932. Giddins, Gary. "Nice Guys are So Much Fun." Village Voice (May 14 1979): 57.

933. Goddet, Laurent, and Alex Dutilh. "L'Art, Ensemble." Jazz Hot, No. 356/357 (Dec 1978/Jan 1979): 23-28. Interview with Joseph Jarman and Roscoe Mitchell re: the Art Ensemble.

934. "Jarman and Mitchell Cut New Wax." down beat (April 21 1977): 9. Brief report on the founding of the Art Ensemble's own label AECO Records.

935. Keepnews, Peter. "Art Ensemble's tour celebrates 'Third Decade.'" Billboard (October 6 1984).

936. Kemper, Peter. "Zur funktion des Mythos im Jazz der 70er Jahre: Soziokulturelle Aspekte eines musikalischen Phanomens dargestellt an der aesthetischen konzeption des Art Ensemble of Chicago." Jazz Research/Jazzforschung, Vol. 13 (1981): 45-78. [English summary]

937. _________. "Das Programm der Great Black Music: ein Gesprach mit den Mitgliedern des Art Ensemble of Chicago." Jazz Podium (August 1980): 3-8. [Interview]

938. Kostakis, Peter. "A Primer for the Gradual Understanding of the Art Ensemble of Chicago (AEC)." Brilliant Corners: A Magazine of the Arts (Chicago), No. 3 (Spring 1976): 68-76.

939. Levi, Titus. "The Art Ensemble." OPtion (March/April 1985): 24, 26.

940. Litweiler, John. "Art Ensemble of Chicago: Adventures in the Urban Bush." down beat (June 1982): 19-22, 60.

941. Lock, Graham. "Windy City Warriors." Wire, No. 9 (November 1984).

942. McRae, Barry. "Avant Courier." Jazz Journal (December 1972): 20-21.

943. Millroth, Thomas. "Great Black Music." Nutida Musik (Stockholm), Vol. 16 (1972-1973): 43-50.

944. Palmer, Don. "20th Anniversary for an Unusual Jazz Ensemble." New York Times (April 14 1985): Sec. 2, p. 24.

945. Palmer, Robert. "Art Ensemble of Chicago takes jazz to the stage." Rolling Stone (November 1 1979): 9, 29-30.

946. _________. "Playing or Clowning, They Work Together." New York Times (July 29 1977).

947. Salaam, Kalamu ya. "Full Force: From the Ancient to the Future." Black Collegian, No. 35 (1980/81): 24-26, 28, 31-32.

948. Solothurnmann, Jurg. "Insights and Views of the Art Ensemble of Chicago." Jazz Forum, No. 49 (1977): 28-33. [Interview]

949. Spitzer, David D. "Art Ensemble of Chicago." Different Drummer, Vol. 1, No. 12 (October 1974): 26-29.

950. Ware, Celestine, and Al Auster. "Art Ensemble of Chicago: Making Music Out of Self-Determination." The American Rag, Vol. 1, No. 2/3 (1980).

951. Zabor, Rafi. "Art Ensemble of Chicago." Musician, No. 100 (February 1987): 78+. [Interview]

952. _________. "Profile: The Art Ensemble." Musician, Player and Listener, No. 17 (March-April 1979): 39-44.

Concert Reviews

953. Albin, Scott. "Caught... Art Ensemble of Chicago, Five Spot, New York." down beat (December 4 1975): 34.

954. Caux, Daniel. "Le delire et la rigeur de 'l'art ensemble' de Chicago." Jazz Hot, No. 252 (July-August 1969): 8.

955. "L'AACM a Paris." Jazz Hot, No. 303 (March 1974): 25-26.

956. Paige, E. "Talent in Action." Billboard (December 25 1971): 16.

957. Rand, Richard. "Caught in the Act: Art Ensemble of Chicago, University of Wisconsin." down beat (September 14 1972): 38.

958. Wilmer, Valerie. "Caught in the Act: Art Ensemble of Chicago, Paris." down beat (June 25 1970): 26.

Record Reviews

959. Bourne, Mike. "Record Reviews: Les Stances a Sophie." down beat (December 9 1971): 18, 21.

960. Litweiler, John. "Record Reviews: People in Sorrow." down beat (April 30 1970): 22, 24.

961. Mandel, Howard. "Record Reviews: The Paris Session." down beat (February 12 1976): 25-26.

Discographies

962. Bolelli, Franco. "Together/Alone: Discografia Art Ensemble of Chicago." Almanacco Musica (Milano), No. 2 (Winter 1979): 57-60.

963. Janssens, Eddy, and Hugo de Craen. Art Ensemble of Chicago: discography, unit and members. Brussels: New Think! (E. Jacquemain-laan 54a, B-1000 Brussels), 1983. 114p.

Media Materials

964. Art Ensemble of Chicago (1983). Producer: Bright Thoughts Company. Documentary.

965. The Art Ensemble of Chicago: Live from the Jazz Showcase (1981). 50 min. [Available from Rhapsody Films, P.O. Box 179, New York, NY 10014. Tel. 212/243-0152; Or, Stash Records, 611 Broadway, Suite 411, New York, NY 10012. Tel. 1-800-666-JASS]

ARTISTS' JAZZ BAND (formed 1962) (Canada)

966. Encyclopedia of Music in Canada, eds. Helmut Kallmann, et al. Toronto/Buffalo: University of Toronto Press, 1981, p. 36.

Articles

967. Baker, Richard. "Canadian New Music." Coda, No. 153 (January/February 1977): 16. [Record review]

968. Gallagher, Greg. "The Artists' Jazz Band: Musical Mind-benders in Jazz." The Canadian Composer, No. 108 (February 1976): 22+.

969. Norris, John. "Heard and Seen." Coda, Vol. 11, No. 10 (June/July 1974): 34. [Concert review]

AVENEL, JEAN-JACQUES (1948-) (France) - Bass

970. Dictionnaire du Jazz, eds. Philippe Carles, et al. Paris: Laffont, 1988.

Articles

971. Goddet, Laurent. "L'Avenir d'Avenel." Jazz Hot, No. 316 (May 1975): 30.

972. Loupien, Serge. "Voix Nouvelles: Jean-Jacques Avenel; toutes les cordes." Jazz Magazine, No. 263 (March-April 1978): 37-38. [Interview]

973. "Paris Bass Revolution." Jazz Hot, No. 295 (June 1973): 21.

974. Soutif, Daniel. "Open Jazz." Jazz Magazine, No. 242 (March 1976): 5-6.

AYLER, ALBERT (1936-1970) - Tenor Saxophone

See also # 276, 286, 288, 695, 698, 700, 703, 2508, 2535, 6433, 6596

Works in English

975. Gleason, Ralph J. "The Death of Albert Ayler." In Celebrating the Duke, and Louis, Bessie, Billie, Bird, Carmen, Miles, Dizzy, and other heroes. Boston: Little, Brown, 1975, pp. 148-151.

976. Jost, Ekkehard. "Albert Ayler." In Free Jazz. Graz: Universal Editions, 1974, pp. 121-132.

977. Litweiler, John. "Albert Ayler." In The Freedom Principle: Jazz After 1958. New York: Morrow, 1984, pp. 151-171.

978. Wilmer, Valerie. "Albert Ayler - Spiritual Unity." In As Serious As Your Life. Westport, CT: Lawrence Hill & Co., 1981, pp. 92-111, 260.

Biographical Dictionaries

979. Baker's Biographical Dictionary of Musicians. 7th ed. rev. by Nicolas Slonimsky. New York: Schirmer Books, 1984.

980. Berry, Lemuel, Jr. Biographical Dictionary of Black Musicians and Music Educators. Guthrie, OK: Educational Book Publishers, 1978, p. 213.

981. Carr, Ian. "Ayler, Albert." In *Jazz: The Essential Companion*. New York: Prentice Hall Press, 1988.

982. Case, Brian, and Stan Britt. *The Harmony Illustrated Encyclopedia of Jazz*. 3rd ed. New York: Harmony Books, 1987.

983. Claghorn, Charles Eugene. *Biographical Dictionary of American Music*. West Nyack, NY: Parker Pub. Co., 1973.

984. _________. *Biographical Dictionary of Jazz*. Englewood Cliffs, NJ: Prentice-Hall, 1982.

985. Feather, Leonard. *The Encyclopedia of Jazz in the Sixties*. New York: Horizon Press, 1966.

986. _________, and Ira Gitler. *The Encyclopedia of Jazz in the Seventies*. New York: Horizon Press, 1976.

987. James, Michael. "Ayler, Albert." In *The New Grove Dictionary of Music and Musicians*. London: Macmillan Press, 1980, Vol. 1, pp. 754-755.

988. Kernfeld, Barry. "Ayler, Albert." In *The New Grove Dictionary of American Music*. London: Macmillan Press, 1986.

989. _________. "Ayler, Albert." In *The New Grove Dictionary of Jazz*. London: Macmillan Press, 1988.

990. McRae, Barry. "Albert Ayler." In *The Jazz Handbook*. Harlow, Essex, Eng.: Longman, 1987, pp. 183-184.

991. *The Penguin Encyclopedia of Popular Music*, ed. Donald Clarke. New York: Viking, 1989, p. 55.

992. Southern, Eileen. *Biographical Dictionary of Afro-American and African Musicians*. Westport, CT: Greenwood Press, 1982.

Articles

993. "Albert Ayler." *International Times* (London), No. 12 (March 13-26, 1967): 9. Personal statement by Ayler.

994. Barton, A. "The Ayler Enigma." *Jazz Journal* (February 1967): 10-11.

995. Beckett, Alan. "The New Wave in Jazz. 4. Free Music." *New Left Review*, No. 35 (January-February 1966): 93-96.

996. Case, Brian. "The Holy Ghost." *New Musical Express* (July 6 1974): 40.

997. Cook, Richard. "My Name is Albert Ayler." *Wire*, No. 58/59 (December 1988-January 1989): 60-63.

998. Crouch, Stanley. "Albert Ayler: Talking in Tongues." *Soho Weekly News* (February 5 1976): 36, 40-41.

999. Goldman, Jon, and Martin Davidson. "Albert Ayler, Life and Recordings." Cadence, Vol. 1, No. 4 (April 1976): 8-10.

1000. Hames, Mike. "The Death of Albert Ayler [and] Other Matters." The Wire (London), No. 6 (Spring 1984): 27-28.

1001. Heckman, Don. "Albert Ayler." BMI (March 1968): 17.

1002. Hentoff, Nat. "The Truth is Marching In." down beat (November 17 1966): 16-18, 40. [Interview]

1003. Jones, LeRoi. "Strong Voices in Today's Black Music." down beat (February 10 1966): 15.

1004. Kofsky, Frank. "An Interview with Albert and Donald Ayler." Jazz & Pop (September 1968): 21-24. [Interview]

1005. ________. "John Coltrane and the Jazz Revolution: the Case of Albert Ayler." Jazz (New York), Vol. 5, No. 9 (1966): 24-5; and Vol. 5, No. 10 (1966): 20-22. [Reprinted in # 62]

1006. Lange, Art. "Hall of Fame." down beat (August 1983): 14.

1007. Litweiler, John. "Albert Ayler." down beat (1982): 45+.

1008. ________. "The Legacy of Albert Ayler." down beat (April 1 1971): 14-15, 29.

1009. Lock, Don. "The New Conservatism." Jazz Monthly (May 1968): 3-5.

1010. Mortifoglio, Richard. "Riffs: Albert Ayler as Angel of History." Village Voice (August 7 1978): 43-44.

1011. "Seven Steps to Jazz." Melody Maker (May 14 1966): 8. Brief biographical sketch.

1012. Shadwick, Keith. "The Rise and Fall of Albert Ayler." Music Maker (December 1971): 7-9.

1013. Simpson, Frank. "Pop Saves the Avant-Garde!" Melody Maker (April 13 1968): 8.

1014. Smith, Bill, and Brian Case. "The Truth is Marching In." The Wire, No. 3 (Spring 1983): 12-13.

1015. Smith, Frank. "His Name Is Albert Ayler." Jazz (New York), Vol. 4, No. 11 (December 1965): 11-14.

1016. Vestergaard, Ole. "Spirited Reply to Ayler." down beat (February 9 1967): 8. Letter from Ayler's producer at the Swedish Debut Records label disputing his claim in an earlier db interview (# 1002) that Debut had neglected to pay him royalties for his Debut recordings.

1017. Williams, Martin. "Albert Ayler for Example." Saturday Review (November 27 1965): 69-70.

1018. Williams, Richard. "Ayler--Beyond This World." Melody Maker (December 12 1970): 25. [Tribute]

1019. Wilmer, Valerie. "Ayler: Mystic Tenor With A Direct Hotline to Heaven?." Melody Maker (October 15 1966): 6.

1020. ________. "Albert and Don Ayler." Jazz Monthly (December 1966): 11-13. [Interview]

1021. Woodfin, Henry. "Whither Albert Ayler?" down beat (November 17 1966): 19.

Works in French, German, Dutch and Swedish

1022. Dulfer, Hans. "Albert Ayler." In Jazz in China. Amsterdam: Bakker, 1980, pp. 138-142. [Dutch text]

1023. Roggeman, Willy. "Albert Ayler." In Free en Andere Jazz-Essays. The Hague: Van Ditmar, 1969, pp. 103-107. [Dutch text]

Biographical Dictionaries

1024. Carles, Philippe, and Jean-Louis Comolli. Free Jazz, Black Power. 2nd ed. Paris: Editions Galilee, 1979, pp. 366-368.

1025. Dictionnaire du Jazz, eds. Philippe Carles, et al. Paris: Laffont, 1988.

1026. Reclams Jazzfuhrer. 2nd, rev. ed. Stuttgart: Reclam, 1977.

1027. Reda, Jacques. Anthologie des Musiciens de Jazz. Paris: Stock, 1981, pp. 329-331.

1028. Tenot, Frank. Dictionnaire du Jazz. Paris: Larousse, 1967.

Articles

1029. Carles, Philippe. "La Bataille d'Ayler n'est pas Finie." Jazz Magazine, No. 185 (January 1971): 36-41.

1030. Caux, Daniel. "Free Jazz." Chroniques de l'Art Vivant (Paris), No. 7 (janvier 1970): 30. Includes a brief personal statement by Ayler.

1031. Caux, Jacqueline, and Daniel Caux. "My Name is Albert Ayler." Chroniques de l'Art Vivant (Paris), No. 17 (February 1971): 24-25.

1032. Endress, Gudrun. "Albert Ayler Interview." Jazz Podium (October 1966): 254-256.

1033. Jarvis, Edward. "Albert Ayler." Orkester Journalen (July-August 1987): 8-11. [Swedish text]

1034. Jazz 360o (Sierre, Switzerland), No. 32 (November 1980). Special issue devoted to Ayler.

1035. Le Bris, M. "L'Artiste Vole Par Son Art." Jazz Hot, No. 229 (March 1967): 16-19.

1036. "Les Secrets d'Albert le Grand." Jazz Magazine, No. 142 (May 1967): 34-39+.

1037. Millroth, Thomas. "Aylers Dilemma; Reflexioner kring Albert Ayler och hans musik." Orkester Journalen (November 1972): 6-7. [Swedish text]

1038. Positif, Francois. "Albert Ayler, le Magicien." Jazz Hot, No. 213 (October 1965): 20-22.

1039. Quersin, Benoit. "Ayler et l'Avant-Garde." Jazz Magazine, No. 115 (February 1965): 13.

Obituaries

1040. "Albert Ayler dead." Melody Maker (December 12 1970): 1.

1041. "Albert Ayler Dead: Drowning." Rolling Stone, No. 73 (December 24 1970): 6.

1042. "Albert Ayler Dies." down beat (January 7 1971): 8.

1043. "Albert Ayler 1936-1970." Jazz & Pop (February 1971): 27.

1044. "Albert Ayler, 36, Jazz Saxophonist." New York Times (December 4 1970): 50.

1045. "Ayler's death still a mystery." Melody Maker (January 9 1971): 6.

1046. Black Perspective in Music, Vol. 1, No. 2 (1973): 197.

1047. Jazz Forum, No. 11 (Spring 1971): 30.

1048. Jazz Journal (August 1971): 28.

1049. Jazz Magazine, No. 186 (February 1971): 14.

1050. Joans, Ted. "Spiritual Unity - Albert Ayler - Mister AA of Grade Double A Sounds." Coda, Vol. 10, No. 2 (August 1971): 2-4.

1051. McRae, Barry. "Albert Ayler - an obituary." Jazz Journal (February 1971): 2.

1052. Shepp, Archie. "Albert Ayler 1934-1970." New York Times (December 20 1970): Sec. 2, p. 33. Memorial.

1053. Tercinet, Alain, et al. "Albert Ayler." Jazz Hot, No. 268 (January 1971): 20-26.

Concert Reviews

1054. Atkins, Ronald. "Albert Ayler at L.S.E." Jazz Monthly (January 1967): 12-13.

1055. Burke, Patrick. "Albert Ayler: A Preliminary Checklist of Concert/Club, etc. Appearances..." Discographical Forum, Nos. 12-15 (May-November 1969).

1056. Hoefer, George. "Caught in the Act: Albert Ayler, Village Theater." down beat (May 18 1967): 24-25.

1057. Kettle, Rupert. "The New Jazz." East Village Other, Vol. 1, No. 8 (March 15-April 1 1966): 5.

1058. Morgenstern, Dan. "Caught in the Act: Bud Powell/Byron Allen/Albert Ayler/Giuseppi Logan." down beat (July 15 1965): 12.

1059. Norris, John. "Three Notes with Albert Ayler." Coda (April/May 1966): 9-11. Review of Ayler's performance at the "Titans of the Tenor" concert.

1060. Staaram, P. "Jazz Libre en Quebec." Jazz Magazine, No. 148 (November 1967): 12-13.

1061. Van Der Mei, Elizabeth. "Caught in the Act." down beat (July 14 1966): 30-31. Review of a Village Vanguard concert.

1062. Zwerin, Michael. "Jazz Journal." Village Voice (May 19 1966).

Record Reviews

1063. Baldwin, W. A. "Albert Ayler -- Conservative Revolution?" Jazz Monthly (January 1968): 10-13.

1064. Dorham, Kenny, and Bill Mathieu. "Record Reviews: Spiritual Unity." down beat (July 15 1965): 29-31. Dual review.

1065. Goldman, Jon, and Martin Davidson. "Albert Ayler, Life and Recordings." Cadence, Vol. 1, No. 4 (April 1976): 8-10.

1066. Heineman, Alan. "Record Reviews: New Grass." down beat (July 24 1969): 18.

1067. Kart, Larry. "Record Reviews: Music is the Healing Force of the Universe." down beat (October 15 1970): 20.

1068. Litweiler, John. "Record Reviews: Albert Ayler Vol. 1 & 2." down beat (June 22 1972): 18, 21. Review of Shandar lps recorded live at Nuits de la Fondation Maeght.

1069. McRae, Barry. "Avant Courier No. 8: Message from Albert." Jazz Journal (September 1972): 10-11.

1070. Maizlish, Mort. "The Sound Spreads When You Hear It..." Sounds & Fury (April 1966): 45-46. Review of "Spiritual Unity."

1071. Martin, Terry. "Record Reviews: My Name is Albert Ayler." Jazz Monthly (March 1966): 20.

1072. Mathieu, Bill. "Record Reviews: My Name is Albert Ayler." down beat (November 18 1965): 24.

1073. Pekar, Harvey. "Record Reviews: Spirits Rejoice." down beat (September 8 1966): 28.

1074. Priestley, Brian. "Record Reviews: Ghosts." Jazz Monthly (March 1966): 20.

1075. Quinn, Bill. "Four Modernists." down beat (June 13 1968): 28-29. Review of "Love Cry."

1076. Rouda, R. "Record Reviews: Music is the Healing Force of the Universe." Coda, Vol. 9, No. 11 (1971): 21.

1077. Shadoian, J. "Record Reviews: The Further Adventures of Albert Ayler--New Grass." Journal of Popular Culture, Vol. 4, No. 4 (1971): 994-998.

1078. Steingroot, Ira. "Record Reviews: Vibrations." down beat (August 14 1975): 22-23.

1079. Welding, Pete. "Record Reviews: Albert Ayler in Greenwich Village." down beat (July 11 1968): 26.

1080. ________. "Record Reviews: Bells." down beat (September 23 1965): 34.

Discographies

1081. Hames, Mike. Albert Ayler, Sunny Murray, Cecil Taylor, Byard Lancaster, Kenneth Terroade on Disc and Tape. Ferndown, Eng.: Hames (16 Pinewood Road, Ferndown, Dorset BH22 9RW), 1983. 61p.

1082. Rissi, Mathias. Albert Ayler: Discography. Adliswil, Switzerland: M. Rissi (Haldenstr. 23, CH-8134 Adliswil), 1977. 9p.

AYLER, DONALD (1942-) - Trumpet

1083. Berry, Lemuel, Jr. Biographical Dictionary of Black Musicians and Music Educators. Guthrie, OK: Educational Book Publishers, 1978, p. 213.

1084. Claghorn, Charles Eugene. Biographical Dictionary of American Music. West Nyack, NY: Parker Pub. Co., 1973.

1085. ________. Biographical Dictionary of Jazz. Englewood Cliffs, NJ: Prentice-Hall, 1982.

1086. Dictionnaire du Jazz, eds. Philippe Carles, et al. Paris: Laffont, 1988.

1087. Feather, Leonard. The Encyclopedia of Jazz in the Sixties. New York: Horizon Press, 1966.

1088. The New Grove Dictionary of Jazz. London: Macmillan Press, 1988.

1089. Reclams Jazzfuhrer. 2nd, rev. ed. Stuttgart: Reclam, 1977.

1090. Wilmer, Valerie. As Serious As Your Life. Westport, CT: Lawrence Hill & Co., 1981, p. 260.

Articles

1091. Kofsky, Frank. "An Interview with Albert and Donald Ayler." Jazz & Pop, No. 7 (September 1968): 21-24. [Interview]

1092. Rusch, Bob. "Don Ayler: interview." Cadence, Vol. 5, No. 2 (February 1979): 14-17.

1093. Wilmer, Valerie. "Albert and Don Ayler." Jazz Monthly (December 1966): 11-13. [Interview]

BAILEY, DEREK (1930-) (Great Britain) - Guitar

See also # 344, 702, 2593-2608

1094. Bailey, Derek. Musical Improvisation. Englewood Cliffs, NJ: Prentice-Hall, 1980. 154p.

Biographical Dictionaries

1095. Carles, Philippe, and Jean-Louis Comolli. Free Jazz, Black Power. 2nd ed. Paris: Editions Galilee, 1979, pp. 368-369.

1096. Carr, Ian. "Bailey, Derek." In Jazz: The Essential Companion. New York: Prentice Hall Press, 1988.

1097. Case, Brian, and Stan Britt. The Harmony Illustrated Encyclopedia of Jazz. 3rd ed. New York: Harmony Books, 1987.

1098. Claghorn, Charles Eugene. Biographical Dictionary of Jazz. Englewood Cliffs, NJ: Prentice-Hall, 1982.

1099. Dean, Roger T. "Bailey, Derek." In The New Grove Dictionary of Jazz. London: Macmillan Press, 1988.

1100. Dictionnaire du Jazz, eds. Philippe Carles, et al. Paris: Laffont, 1988.

1101. Feather, Leonard, and Ira Gitler. The Encyclopedia of Jazz in the Seventies. New York: Horizon Press, 1976.

1102. International Who's Who in Music and Musicians' Directory. 12th ed. 1990/91.

1103. Jazz Now: the Jazz Centre Society Guide, ed. Roger Cotterrell. London: Quartet Books, 1976, pp. 109-110.

1104. McRae, Barry. "Derek Bailey." In The Jazz Handbook. Harlow, Essex, Eng.: Longman, 1987, pp. 184-185.

1105. The Penguin Encyclopedia of Popular Music, ed. Donald Clarke. New York: Viking, 1989, pp. 61-62.

Articles

1106. Ansell, Kenneth. "Derek Bailey." Impetus (London), No. 6 (1977): 242-244. [Interview]

1107. ________. "Derek Bailey and Company." The Wire, No. 15 (May 1985): 33-35.

1108. Case, Brian. "Living on the Brink." Melody Maker (August 2 1980): 15. [Interview]

1109. Cook, Richard. "The Guy Who Found the Lost Chord." New Musical Express (October 13 1984): 6-7. [Interview]

1110. Dallas, Karl. "Improvisations." Melody Maker (June 26 1976): 41. [Interview]

1111. "Derek Bailey." Jazz Hot, No. 321 (November 1975): 22.

1112. "Derek Bailey." Jazz Hot, No. 296 (July-August 1973): 26.

1113. "Derek Bailey." Jazz Hot, No. 283 (May 1972): 54.

1114. Dery, Mark. "Improvisation Pioneer Derek Bailey." Guitar Player (April 1988): 70+.

1115. Drozdowski, Ted. "Derek Bailey: Triumph of the Free Will." Musician, No. 114 (April 1988): 10.

1116. "Forum: Improvisation." Perspectives of New Music, Vol. 21, No. 1/2 (1982-83): 46+. [Interview]

1117. Gaudynski, Thomas. "Derek Bailey: interview." Cadence, Vol. 10, No. 7 (July 1984): 11-14.

1118. Goddet, Laurent. "La Compagnie Bailey." Jazz Hot, No. 360 (April 1979): 16-20, 52.

1119. Hyder, Ken. "Bailey: a step forward." Melody Maker (March 24 1973): 41.

1120. Lockett, Mark. "Derek Bailey: CEO of Free Music." Ear (April 1990): 22-25.

1121. McRae, Barry. "Best of British. - No. 2: Derek Bailey." Jazz Journal International (March 1978): 19-20, 24.

1122. ________. "Braxton, Bailey and Company--the art of ad hoc ad lib." Jazz Journal International (July 1977): 22-23.

1123. Pareles, Jon. "A British Improviser Who Likes the Word Free." New York Times (December 17 1982).

1124. Riggins, Roger. "Derek Bailey: musician at work." Jazz Forum, No. 88 (1984): 44+. [Interview]

1125. Rouy, Gerard. "Bailey et Compagnie." Jazz Magazine, No. 269 (October 1978): 46-49. [Interview]

1126. Sandow, Gregory. "The Limits of Freedom." Village Voice (May 17 1983): 83.

1127. Schonfield, Victor. "Caught in the Act: Spontaneous Music Ensemble/Derek Bailey, Little Theatre Club." down beat (January 11 1968): 41. [Concert review]

1128. ________. "Derek Bailey and total improvisation." Melody Maker (January 31 1970): 22.

1129. van den Berg, Erik. "Ear Mail: Derek Bailey, extemporisations of a Dutch-phile." Key Notes (Amsterdam), No. 22 (1985): 32-34.

1130. Williams, Richard. "Derek Bailey: feeding the post-Cage ear." Melody Maker (July 10 1971): 14.

1131. Wilmer, Val. "Themes on Improvisation." Time Out (August 1-7 1980): 19.

BANG, BILLY [William Vincent Walker] (1947-) - Violin

See also # 6107

1132. Dictionnaire du Jazz, eds. Philippe Carles, et al. Paris: Laffont, 1988.

1133. McRae, Barry. "Billy Bang." In The Jazz Handbook. Harlow, Essex, Eng.: Longman, 1987, pp. 226-227.

Articles

1134. Case, Brian. "Jazzscene: Heartstrings." Melody Maker (October 20 1979): 40. [Profile]

1135. Davis, Francis. "Playing for Keeps: violinists Billy Bang and John Blake fiddle around with jazz." High Fidelity (May 1985): 73+. [Interview]

1136. Jeske, Lee. "Billy Bang." down beat (September 1981): 26-28, 71, 74. [Interview]

1137. Levi, Titus. "Billy Bang: Hearing Things His Own Way." Option (May/June 1985): 35. [Interview]

1138. Lock, Graham. "Billy Bang." Wire, No. 57 (November 1988): 26-28.

1139. Macnie, Jim. "Billy Bang: Scratchin' at the Avant-Garde Hoedown." Musician, No. 126 (April 1989): 20, 22, 24.

1140. McRae, Barry. "Avant Courier." Jazz Journal International (July 1982): 20-21. [Profile]

1141. Rusch, Bob. "Billy Bang: interview." Cadence, Vol. 6, No. 11 (November 1980): 5-9, 81.

BARBIERI, GATO [Leandro] (1935-) (Argentina) - Tenor Sax

1142. Gullo, Lillo, and Angelo Leonardi. ...Visintin: Gato Barbieri. Milano: Ottaviano, 1979. 96p.

Biographical Dictionaries

1143. Carles, Philippe, and Jean-Louis Comolli. Free Jazz, Black Power. 2nd ed. Paris: Editions Galilee, 1979, pp. 369-370.

1144. Carr, Ian. "Barbieri, Gato." In Jazz: The Essential Companion. New York: Prentice Hall Press, 1988.

1145. Case, Brian, and Stan Britt. The Harmony Illustrated Encyclopedia of Jazz. 3rd ed. New York: Harmony Books, 1987.

1146. Claghorn, Charles Eugene. Biographical Dictionary of American Music. West Nyack, NY: Parker Pub. Co., 1973.

1147. _________. Biographical Dictionary of Jazz. Englewood Cliffs, NJ: Prentice-Hall, 1982.

1148. Collins, Catherine. "Barbieri, Gato." In The New Grove Dictionary of Jazz. London: Macmillan Press, 1988.

1149. Dictionnaire du Jazz, eds. Philippe Carles, et al. Paris: Laffont, 1988.

1150. Feather, Leonard. The Encyclopedia of Jazz in the Sixties. New York: Horizon Press, 1966.

1151. _________, and Ira Gitler. The Encyclopedia of Jazz in the Seventies. New York: Horizon Press, 1976.

1152. McRae, Barry. "Gato Barbieri." In The Jazz Handbook. Harlow, Essex, Eng.: Longman, 1987, p. 186.

1153. The Penguin Encyclopedia of Popular Music, ed. Donald Clarke. New York: Viking, 1989.

1154. Reclams Jazzfuhrer. 2nd, rev. ed. Stuttgart: Reclam, 1977.

1155. Wilmer, Valerie. As Serious As Your Life. Westport, CT: Lawrence Hill & Co., 1981, p. 260.

Articles

1156. Allen, Bonnie. "Musicmakers: Gato Barbieri." Essence (August 1978): 28, 30.

1157. Arnoldi, N. "Un entretien avec Gato Barbieri." Jazz Hot, No. 262 (June 1970): 18-19.

1158. ________. "La part de Gato." Jazz Hot, No. 242 (August-September 1968): 17-19.

1159. Birnbaum, Larry. "Gato Barbieri: the Argentine Eclectic." down beat (April 21 1977): 15+.

1160. Carles, Philippe. "Gato Barbieri." Jazz Magazine, No. 215 (September 1973): 41-43. [Interview]

1161. ________. "Gato Barbieri: l'autre Amerique." Jazz Magazine, No. 197 (February 1972): 26+. [Interview]

1162. ________. "'Il Pacato Gato.'" Jazz Magazine, No. 155 (June 1968): 10-11.

1163. Case, Brian. "Ey, Gringo--You Wan' Hot Tango?" New Musical Express (July 20 1974): 37. [Interview]

1164. Feather, Leonard. "Blindfold Test." down beat (January 171 1974): 27.

1165. Garztecki, M. "The Cat that Walks by Himself." Jazz Forum, No. 36 (August 1975): 34-38. [Interview]

1166. Hentoff, Nat. "Gato Barbieri: Music from the Third World." Jazz & Pop (March 1970): 41-43.

1167. Levy, A. "Gato Barbieri: Tango to the Top." down beat (May 10 1973): 13-14.

1168. McRae, Barry. "Avant Courier; El Gato." Jazz Journal (October 1976): 22-24.

1169. Nemko, Frankie. "Last Tango in the Third World." Melody Maker (March 23 1974): 48.

1170. Palmer, Robert. "Gato: 'I Need a Lot of Rest.'" down beat (June 20 1974): 14+. [Interview]

1171. Pinckney, Warren R. "Gato's Trane-ing." Jazz Forum, No. 108 (1987): 33-37.

1172. Vance, Joel. "Meet Gato Barbieri." Stereo Review (January 1975): 68-69.

BARKER, THURMAN (1948-) - Drums

1173. Carles, Philippe, and Jean-Louis Comolli. Free Jazz, Black Power. 2nd ed. Paris: Editions Galilee, 1979, p. 370.

1174. Dictionnaire du Jazz, eds. Philippe Carles, et al. Paris: Laffont, 1988.

1175. The New Grove Dictionary of Jazz. London: Macmillan Press, 1988.

1176. The Penguin Encyclopedia of Popular Music, ed. Donald Clarke. New York: Viking, 1989, p. 72.

1177. Wilmer, Valerie. As Serious As Your Life. Westport, CT: Lawrence Hill & Co., 1981, p. 260.

Articles

1178. Hazell, Ed. "Portraits: Thurman Barker." Modern Drummer (November 1987): 36+. [Interview]

1179. Mandel, Howard. "Thurman Barker: A Drummer for All Seasons." down beat (March 1986): 26-29. [Interview]

BATISTE, ALVIN (1932-) - Clarinet

1180. Dictionnaire du Jazz, eds. Philippe Carles, et al. Paris: Laffont, 1988.

1181. Fairweather, Digby. "Batiste, Alvin." In Jazz: The Essential Companion. New York: Prentice Hall Press, 1988.

1182. Horne, Aaron. Woodwind Music of Black Composers. New York: Greenwood Press, 1990, pp. 12-13.

1183. Jacobi, Hugh William. Contemporary American Composers: based at American Colleges and universities. Paradise, CA: Paradise Arts Publisher, 1975.

1184. The New Grove Dictionary of Jazz. London: Macmillan Press, 1988.

Articles

1185. Birnbaum, Larry. "Profile: Alvin Batiste." down beat (October 1982): 54-55.

1186. Wilmer, Valerie. "Alvin Batiste: New Thing a New Orleans." Jazz Magazine, No. 322 (October 1983): 44-45. [Interview]

1187. ________. "Alvin Batiste and Ellis Marsalis." Coda, No. 173 (June 1980): 8-12. [Interview]

BAUER, CONRAD (E. Germany) (1943-) - Trombone

1188. Noglik, Bert. "Bauer, Conrad." In The New Grove Dictionary of Jazz. London: Macmillan Press, 1988.

1189. ________, and Heinz-Jurgen Lindner. "Conrad Bauer." In Jazz im Gesprach. Berlin: Verlag Neue Musik, 1978, pp. 10-21.

Articles

1190. Koehl, R. "Conny Bauer und Joe Sachse." Jazz Podium (January 1990): 36-37.

1191. Noglik, Bert. "Conrad Bauer." Jazz Podium (October 1978): 11-14. [Interview]

1192. _________. "Die Posaunisten Conrad und Johannes Bauer." Brass Bulletin, No. 60 (1987): 38-40. [Also in English and French]

1193. _________. "The Trombone Brothers--Conrad Bauer: music that communicates with the listener." Jazz Forum, No. 109 (1987): 40-43.

1194. "Plattentest mit Conny Bauer." Jazz Podium (August 1984): 8-9.

BECKETT, HARRY (1935-) (Barbados/Great Britain) - Trumpet

1195. Carr, Ian. "Beckett, Harry." In Jazz: The Essential Companion. New York: Prentice Hall Press, 1988.

1196. Dean, Roger T. "Beckett, Harry." In The New Grove Dictionary of Jazz. London: Macmillan Press, 1988.

1197. Jazz Now: the Jazz Centre Society Guide, ed. Roger Cotterrell. London: Quartet Books, p. 113.

Articles

1198. Dawbarn, Bob. "Salvation Army to the Collier Band." Melody Maker (February 8 1969): 12.

1199. de Ledesma, Charles. "Got It Made." The Wire, No. 14 (April 1985): 24-25.

1200. "Harry turns promoter." Melody Maker (December 2 1972): 20.

1201. Hyder, Ken. "Beckett's where it's at." Melody Maker (April 20 1974): 54. [Interview]

1202. King, M. C. "British Jazzmen, No. 11: Harry Beckett." Jazz Journal, Vol. 24, No. 9 (1971).

1203. Williams, Richard. "Beckett on top." Melody Maker (March 4 1972): 12.

1204. _________. "Harry, sideman supreme." Melody Maker (June 20 1970): 18.

1205. Wilmer, Val. "Top Brass." Wire, No. 70/71 (Dec 1989-Jan 1990): Supplement X.

BEER, RONNIE (1941-) (South Africa) - Alto/Tenor Sax

1206. Carles, Philippe, and Jean-Louis Comolli. Free Jazz, Black Power. 2nd ed. Paris: Editions Galilee, 1979, p. 370.

Articles

1207. de Ledesma, Charles. "Ronnie Beer." The Wire, No. 12 (February 1985): 35.

1208. Dumetz, G. "Beer dans la galere." Jazz Magazine, No. 176 (March 1970): 11-12.

1209. Gras, Philippe. "Ronnie Beer." Jazz Hot, No. 251 (June 1969): 25-27. [Interview]

BENNINK, HAN (1942-) (Netherlands) - Percussion

1210. Vuijsje, Bert. De Nieuwe Jazz. Baarn: Bosch & Keuning, 1978, pp. 155-165. [Interview]

Biographical Dictionaries

1211. Carles, Philippe, and Jean-Louis Comolli. Free Jazz, Black Power. 2nd ed. Paris: Editions Galilee, 1979, p. 370.

1212. Carr, Ian. "Bennink, Han." In Jazz: The Essential Companion. New York: Prentice Hall Press, 1988.

1213. Dictionnaire du Jazz, eds. Philippe Carles, et al. Paris: Laffont, 1988.

1214. Iannapollo, Robert J. "Bennink, Han." In The New Grove Dictionary of Jazz. London: Macmillan Press, 1988.

1215. The Penguin Encyclopedia of Popular Music, ed. Donald Clarke. New York: Viking, 1989.

Articles

1216. Ansell, Kenneth. "Han Bennink." Impetus (London), No. 6 (1977): 253-254, 270. [Interview]

1217. Cook, Richard. "Han Bennink: Turning Lots of Buttons." The Wire, No. 29 (July 1986): 30-31, 48.

1218. "Dico Disco & Co." Jazz Magazine, No. 298 (June 1981): 37. Biographical sketch.

1219. Goddet, Laurent. "Han Bennink: autopsie d'un batteur." Jazz Hot, No. 291 (February 1973): 26-27. [Interview]

1220. Hemingway, Gerry. "Percussion Discussion: Han Bennink, Milford Graves, and Joey Baron." Ear (March 1989): 36-42.

1221. Hyder, Ken. "Bennink: music and comedy." Melody Maker (October 6 1973): 20.

1222. Lagerwerff, Frits. "Han Bennink." Jazz Nu [Amsterdam] (May 1981): 340-346. [Interview]

1223. Panke, Wolfgang. "Han Bennink." Jazz Podium (April 1972): 98-99.

1224. Rouy, Gerard. "Han Bennink parle." Jazz Magazine, No. 195 (December 1971): 7-8. [Interview]

1225. Schoemaker, Bill. "Han Bennink/Peter Brotzmann: first entrances and Last Exits." down beat (January 1987): 24-26. [Interview]

1226. Thiem, Michael. "The Bizarre World of Han Bennink." Jazz Forum, No. 47 (1977): 50-53. [Interview]

1227. Williams, Richard. "Bennink and the 'do it yourself' league." Melody Maker (January 10 1970): 8.

Discographies

1228. Eyle, Wim van. "Han Bennink disco." Jazz/Press (Holland), No. 31 (February 1977): 8-9.

BERESFORD/COOMBES/HAUGE/RUSSELL/SOLOMON (Great Britain)

1229. Lake, Steve. "Pool Players." Melody Maker (January 11 1975): 32. Profile of the British free jazz quintet.

BERESFORD, STEVE (1950-) (Great Britain) - Piano

See also # 1229

1230. Carles, Philippe, and Jean-Louis Comolli. Free Jazz, Black Power. 2nd ed. Paris: Editions Galilee, 1979, pp. 370.

Articles

1231. Ansell, Kenneth. "Steve Beresford." Impetus (London), No. 6 (1977): 261-262. [Interview]

1232. Case, Brian. "Murdering Popular Song." Melody Maker (September 29 1979): 28+. [Interview]

BERGER, KARL-HANNS (1935-) (Germany/US) - Vibraphone

See also # 323, 476-491

1233. Jost, Ekkehard. "Karl Berger." In Jazzmusiker: Materialen zur Soziologie der Afro-Amerikanischen Musik. Frankfurt am Main: Ullstein, 1982, pp. 168-174.

1234. Ullman, Michael. "Karl Berger." In Jazz Lives. Washington, D.C.: New Republic Books, 1980, pp. 163-173.

Biographical Dictionaries

1235. Carles, Philippe, and Jean-Louis Comolli. Free Jazz, Black Power. 2nd ed. Paris: Editions Galilee, 1979, p. 371.

1236. Carr, Ian. "Berger, Karl Hans." In Jazz: The Essential Companion. New York: Prentice Hall Press, 1988.

1237. Claghorn, Charles Eugene. Biographical Dictionary of Jazz. Englewood Cliffs, NJ: Prentice-Hall, 1982.

1238. Dictionnaire du Jazz, eds. Philippe Carles, et al. Paris: Laffont, 1988.

1239. Feather, Leonard, and Ira Gitler. The Encyclopedia of Jazz in the Seventies. New York: Horizon Press, 1976.

1240. Kernfeld, Barry. "Berger, Karl." In The New Grove Dictionary of American Music. London: Macmillan Press, 1986.

1241. ________. "Berger, Karl." In The New Grove Dictionary of Jazz. London: Macmillan Press, 1988.

1242. Reclams Jazzfuhrer. 2nd, rev. ed. Stuttgart: Reclam, 1977.

1243. Wilmer, Valerie. As Serious As Your Life. Westport, CT: Lawrence Hill & Co., 1981, p. 260.

Articles

1244. Blum, Joe. "Karl Berger." Echology (Buffalo, NY), No. 1 (1987).

1245. ________. "Karl Berger: Beyond the Creative Music Studio." Jazz Times (June 1986): 13.

1246. DiNardo, R. "Karl Berger." Coda, Vol. 11, No. 12 (1974): 2-6. [Interview]

1247. Leigh, Stuart. "Interview: Karl Berger and Aiyb Diengh." Ear Magazine East (June-August 1981): 4-6.

1248. Negre, Marie-Paule, and Christian Gauffre. "Karl Berger: L'Ecole de Woodstock." Jazz Magazine, No. 280 (November 1979): 28-29, 64, 66.

1249. "New Gotham Jazz Venue." Variety (May 31 1978): 81. Review of the documentary, "A Berger to Go," a 23 min. portrait of Berger's life and music by Robert Mickelson.

1250. Occhiogrosso, Peter. "Karl Berger: Music Universe c/o Woodstock, NY." down beat (June 3 1976): 18-19+.

1251. Solothurnmann, Jurg. "Karl and Ingrid Berger: "Music Universe" in Woodstock." Jazz Forum, No. 66 (1980): 34-37.

BERGMAN, BORAH - Piano

1252. Davis, Francis. "Circles, Whirls, and Eights." In Outcats: Jazz Composers, Instrumentalists, and Singers. New York: Oxford University Press, 1990, pp. 117-122.

Articles

1253. Camier, Marcel. "D'une seule main." Jazz Magazine, No. 270 (November/December 1978): 20. [Profile]

1254. Sandow, Gregory. "Borah Bergman Thinks, Thinks, Thinks." Village Voice (March 18 1981): 70.

1255. Wagner, C. "Borah Bergman." Jazz Podium (March 1986): 14-15.

BERNE, TIM (1954-) - Alto Saxophone

1256. Dictionnaire du Jazz, eds. Philippe Carles, et al. Paris: Laffont, 1988.

Articles

1257. Endress, Gudrun. "Sounds und Strukturen: Tim Berne." Jazz Podium (February 1988): 3+. [Interview]

1258. Garnier, J. L. "La route de Berne." Jazz Magazine, No. 326 (February 1984): 40-41. [Interview]

1259. Hahn, Steve. "Tim Berne." OPtion (March/April 1989): 66-69.

1260. Lobko, Sonia. "Interview: Tim Berne." Jazz 360o (Sierre, Switzerland), No. 57 (March 1983): 2-10.

1261. Lock, Graham. "Tim Berne." Wire, No. 58/59 (December 1988/January 1989): 28-30.

1262. Moon, Tom. "Tim Berne Gets Fractured; Jazz saxophonist 'Berne's' the rules but saves the spirit." Musician (December 1989): 21-22, 24.

1263. Riggins, Roger. "Tim Berne: man in the middle." Jazz Forum, No. 92 (1985): 42-45. [Interview]

1264. Rusch, Bob. "Tim Berne: interview." Cadence, Vol. 9, No. 10 (October 1983): 5-12.

1265. Santoro, Gene. "Music: Tim Berne, Bill Frisell, Hank Roberts." The Nation (April 2 1988): 474-476. Discussion of recent recordings by Berne, guitarist Bill Frisell and cellist Hank Roberts.

1266. ________. "Tim Berne." Interview (April 1988): 24.

1267. Silsbee, Kirk. "Profile: Tim Berne." down beat (November 1982): 53-54.

1268. Watrous, Peter. "Indescribably Eclectic." Musician, No. 100 (February 1987): 11.

1269. Whitehead, Kevin. "Tim Berne: beyond the five-year plan." down beat (July 1987): 23+.

BLACK MUSIC INFINITY

1270. Claghorn, Charles Eugene. Biographical Dictionary of Jazz. Englewood Cliffs, NJ: Prentice-Hall, 1982, p. 331. Sketch of "Black Music Infinity," the West Coast ensemble founded by Stanley Crouch.

BLACKWELL, ED (1929-) - Drums

See also # 69, 1187, 5111-5116

1271. Wilmer, Valerie. "A Family of Rhythms." In As Serious As Your Life. Westport, CT: Lawrence Hill & Co., 1981, pp. 178-188, 261.

Biographical Dictionaries

1272. Carles, Philippe, and Jean-Louis Comolli. Free Jazz, Black Power. 2nd ed. Paris: Editions Galilee, 1979, p. 372.

1273. Case, Brian, and Stan Britt. The Harmony Illustrated Encyclopedia of Jazz. 3rd ed. New York: Harmony Books, 1987.

1274. Claghorn, Charles Eugene. Biographical Dictionary of Jazz. Englewood Cliffs, NJ: Prentice-Hall, 1982.

1275. Dictionnaire du Jazz, eds. Philippe Carles, et al. Paris: Laffont, 1988.

1276. Feather, Leonard, and Ira Gitler. The Encyclopedia of Jazz in the Seventies. New York: Horizon Press, 1976.

1277. The Penguin Encyclopedia of Popular Music, ed. Donald Clarke. New York: Viking, 1989.

1278. Priestley, Brian. "Blackwell, Ed." In Jazz: The Essential Companion. New York: Prentice Hall Press, 1988.

1279. Tenot, Frank. Dictionnaire du Jazz. Paris: Larousse, 1967.

1280. Ullman, Michael. "Blackwell, Ed." In The New Grove Dictionary of American Music. London: Macmillan Press, 1986.

1281. ________. "Blackwell, Ed." In The New Grove Dictionary of Jazz. London: Macmillan Press, 1988.

Articles

1282. "Blackwell faces money, medical woes." down beat (June 6 1974): 10.

1283. Fish, Scott Kevin. "Ed Blackwell: Singin' on the Set." Modern Drummer (November 1981): 14+. [Interview]

1284. Goddet, Laurent, and Alex Dutilh. "Ed Blackwell: l'homme de Nouvelle Orleans." Jazz Hot, No. 372 (April 1980): 13-19. [Interview]

1285. Jakobs, C. "Ed Blackwell: le partage du plaisir." Jazz Magazine, No. 213 (July 1973): 12-13. [Interview]

1286. Mandel, Howard. "Blindfold Test: Ed Blackwell." down beat (July 1980): 51, 67.

1287. Mathieson, Kenny. "Ed Blackwell: Tap, March and Dance." Wire, No. 52 (June 1988): 28-29, 31.

1288. Palmer, Robert. "Ed Blackwell: Crescent City Thumper." down beat (June 16 1977): 17+. [Interview]

1289. Romano, Aldo. "Drum Conversation: Ed Blackwell par Aldo Romano." Jazz Magazine, No. 388 (December 1989): 12-16. [Interview]

1290. Salaam, Kalamu ya. "Edward Blackwell - The Rhythm King." Coda, No. 218 (February/March 1988): 4-6. [Interview]

1291. _________. "Give the Drummer Some." Wavelength (April 1988): 35-37.

1292. Su, Alice. "Ed Blackwell." Jazz (Basel), No. 4 (1983).

1293. Suhor, Charles. "New Jazz in the Cradle." down beat (August 31 1961): 16. [Profile]

1294. Vries, Renze de. "Ed Blackwell." Jazz Nu, No. 55 (May 1983): 311-313. [Interview] [Dutch text]

1295. Wilmer, Valerie. "Ed Blackwell--alive and kicking." Melody Maker (May 29 1976): 48. [Interview]

1296. _________. "Ed Blackwell; a question of survival." Melody Maker (November 13 1971): 26.

1297. _________. "Ed Blackwell: Well-tempered Drummer." down beat (October 3 1968): 18-19, 38.

1298. _________. "Street Parade Fan." Melody Maker (March 9 1968): 10.

BLAND, LEROY

See Abdullah, Ahmed

BLANK, ROGER (1938-) - Drums

See also # 69

1299. Carles, Philippe, and Jean-Louis Comolli. Free Jazz, Black Power. 2nd ed. Paris: Editions Galilee, 1979, p. 373.

1300. Dictionnaire du Jazz, eds. Philippe Carles, et al. Paris: Laffont, 1988.

1301. Wilmer, Valerie. As Serious As Your Life. Westport, CT: Lawrence Hill & Co., 1981, p. 261.

1302. ________. "Blank Expression." Melody Maker (January 6 1973): 30.

BLEY, CARLA (1938-) - Piano/Arranger/Bandleader

See also # 696, 704

Works in English

1303. Dahl, Linda. "Carla Bley." In Stormy Weather: The Music and Lives of a Century of Jazzwomen. New York: Pantheon Books, 1984, pp. 202-210.

1304. Feather, Leonard. The Passion for Jazz. New York: Horizon Press, 1980, pp. 123-126.

1305. Placksin, Sally. American Women in Jazz. New York: Wideview Books, 1982, pp. 251-254.

Biographical Dictionaries

1306. Anderson, Ruth. Contemporary American Composers: a biographical dictionary. 2nd ed. Boston, MA: G.K. Hall, 1982.

1307. Carles, Philippe, and Jean-Louis Comolli. Free Jazz, Black Power. 2nd ed. Paris: Editions Galilee, 1979, p. 373.

1308. Carr, Ian. "Bley, Carla." In Jazz: The Essential Companion. New York: Prentice Hall Press, 1988.

1309. Case, Brian, and Stan Britt. The Harmony Illustrated Encyclopedia of Jazz. 3rd ed. New York: Harmony Books, 1987.

1310. Claghorn, Charles Eugene. Biographical Dictionary of American Music. West Nyack, NY: Parker Pub. Co., 1973.

1311. ________. Biographical Dictionary of Jazz. Englewood Cliffs, NJ: Prentice-Hall, 1982.

1312. Cohen, Aaron I. International Encyclopedia of Women Composers. 2nd ed. Revised and Enlarged. New York: Books & Music (USA), 1987.

1313. Dictionnaire du Jazz, eds. Philippe Carles, et al. Paris: Laffont, 1988.

1314. Feather, Leonard. The Encyclopedia of Jazz in the Sixties. New York: Horizon Press, 1966.

1315. ________, and Ira Gitler. The Encyclopedia of Jazz in the Seventies. New York: Horizon Press, 1976.

1316. McRae, Barry. "Carla Bley." In The Jazz Handbook. Harlow, Essex, Eng.: Longman, 1987, pp. 187-188.

1317. The Penguin Encyclopedia of Popular Music, ed. Donald Clarke. New York: Viking, 1989, p. 119.

1318. Reclams Jazzfuhrer. 2nd, rev. ed. Stuttgart: Reclam, 1977.

1319. Robinson, J. Bradford. "Bley, Carla." In The New Grove Dictionary of Jazz. London: Macmillan Press, 1988.

1320. Who's Who in Entertainment. 1st ed. 1989-1990.

1321. Wilmer, Valerie. As Serious As Your Life. Westport, CT: Lawrence Hill & Co., 1981, p. 261.

Articles

1322. "And Now, the Emerging Wacko Countess - Carla Bley!!!" Jazz Magazine (Northport, NY), Vol. 2, No. 3 (1978): 36-43. [Interview]

1323. Blumenthal, Bob. "Carla Bley's Avant Garde Good Humor." Rolling Stone (May 3 1979): 26+. [Interview]

1324. Britt, Stan. "Carla Bley." The Wire, No. 2 (Winter 1982/83): 16-18. [Interview]

1325. Christopherson, J. "Carla Bley." Jazz Journal International, Vol. 35 (June 1982): 20+.

1326. Cooke, Jack. "Carla Bley: The Lone Arranger." Wire, No. 56 (October 1988): 28-30.

1327. Cuscuna, Michael. "Carla Bley's New Opera: Worth the Toil and Trouble." down beat (March 30 1972): 16-17. Discussion of Bley's opera "Escalator Over the Hill."

1328. Geracimos, Ann. "Blonde Who Joined Man's Jazz World." New York Herald Tribune (April 6 1965). [Profile]

1329. Hentoff, Nat. "Carla Bley." BMI (December 1970): 17. [Profile]

1330. "High Speed Raps." Melody Maker (March 13 1976): 35. [Interview]

1331. Hinely, W. Patrick. "Carla Bley: Musical Mystique." Jazz Times (August 1990): 13.

1332. Jefferson, M. "Crossing the Borders." Newsweek (September 2 1974): 61.

1333. Knox, Keith. "Mantler/Bley Quintet." Jazz Monthly (February 1967): 8-9.

1334. Levi, Titus. "Under the Volcano: a conversation with Carla Bley, Steve Swallow, Mike Mantler and Jack Cumming." Coda, No. 212 (February/March 1987): 4-5.

1335. Mandel, Howard. "Carla Bley: Independent Ringleader." down beat (June 1 1978): 18+. [Interview]

1336. Palmer, Don. "My Dinner with Carla." down beat (August 1984): 24-26.

1337. Palmer, Robert. "Carla Bley and Her Band in Village." New York Times (July 31 1981). [Profile]

1338. Paton, Maureen. "Bley Time." Melody Maker (September 10 1977): 39.

1339. Primack, Bret. "Carla Bley: First Lady of the Avant-Garde." Contemporary Keyboard (February 1979): 9-11. [Interview]

1340. Smith, Bill. "An Interview with Carla Bley and Mike Mantler." Coda, Vol. 10, No. 9 (1972): 11-14.

1341. Thompson, Keith G. "Carla Bley and Mike Mantler--A Unique Condition." Pieces of Jazz (1970): 41-44.

1342. Trzaskowski, Andrzej. "Carla Bley-Mike Mantler." Jazz Forum, No. 55 (1978): 37-40. Survey of Bley/Mantler's Watt recordings.

1343. Weller, S. "Carla Bley...and all her jazz." Ms., Vol. 4 (August 1975): 35-37. [Interview]

1344. Wise, D. "Carla: Female of the Free Jazz Species." Melody Maker (November 26 1966): 8.

1345. Zabor, Rafi. "Carla Bley: The Toast of the Continent." Musician, No. 35 (August 1981): 64-72.

Works in French and German

1346. "L'Album Anniversaire." Jazz Magazine, No. 334 (December 1984): 41.

1347. Buhles, Gunter. "Die Jazzkomponisten Carla Bley: Kurzbiographie, Werkanalyse, Wurdigung." Jazzforschung, Nr. 8 (1976): 11-39.

1348. "Carla Bley." Jazz Magazine, No. 235 (August 1975): 18-19. [Interview]

1349. Dister, A. "The Jazz Composers Orchestra." Jazz Hot, No. 281 (March 1972): 4-7.

1350. Gauffre, Christian. "Carla Bley sauve les meubles." Jazz Magazine, No. 360 (1987): 24-25. [Interview]

1351. Haller, P. "Carla Bley." Jazz Magazine, No. 303 (January 1982): 54-5.

1352. Merceron, G. "L'Art Multiforme de Carla Bley." Jazz Hot, No. 258 (February 1970): 21-3; and No. 259 (March 1970): 21.

1353. Schneider, R. D. "Die Muzik von Carla Bley und Michael Mantler." Jazz Podium (November 1980): 10-11.

1354. Vincent, F. "Carla Bley." Jazz Magazine, No. 282 (January 1980): 14.

BLEY, PAUL (1932-) - Piano

See also # 276, 696, 705

1355. Endress, Gudrun. "Paul Bley." In Jazz Podium. Stuttgart: Deutsche Verlags-Anstalt, 1980, pp. 190-195.

1356. "IAI." In Dictionnaire du Jazz, eds. Philippe Carles, et al. Paris: Laffont, 1988. Profile of Bley's record label Improvising Artist Inc.

1357. Lyons, Leonard. "Paul Bley." In The Great Jazz Pianists. New York: Morrow, 1983, pp. 158-166.

1358. Miller, Mark. "Paul Bley." In Boogie, Pete & the Senator: Canadian Musicians in Jazz: the Eighties. Toronto: Nightwood Editions, 1987, pp. 56-67.

1359. Roggeman, Willy. "Paul Bley." In Free en Andere Jazz-Essays. The Hague: Van Ditmar, 1969, pp. 81-87. [Dutch text]

Biographical Dictionaries

1360. Blake, Ran. "Bley, Paul." In The New Grove Dictionary of Jazz. London: Macmillan Press, 1988.

1361. Carles, Philippe, and Jean-Louis Comolli. Free Jazz, Black Power. 2nd ed. Paris: Editions Galilee, 1979, p. 374.

1362. Carr, Ian. "Bley, Paul." In Jazz: The Essential Companion. New York: Prentice Hall Press, 1988.

1363. Case, Brian, and Stan Britt. The Harmony Illustrated Encyclopedia of Jazz. 3rd ed. New York: Harmony Books, 1987.

1364. Claghorn, Charles Eugene. Biographical Dictionary of American Music. West Nyack, NY: Parker Pub. Co., 1973.

1365. _________. Biographical Dictionary of Jazz. Englewood Cliffs, NJ: Prentice-Hall, 1982.

1366. Dictionnaire du Jazz, eds. Philippe Carles, et al. Paris: Laffont, 1988.

1367. Feather, Leonard. The Encyclopedia of Jazz. Rev. ed. New York: Horizon Press, 1960.

1368. _________. The Encyclopedia of Jazz in the Sixties. New York: Horizon Press, 1966.

1369. _________, and Ira Gitler. The Encyclopedia of Jazz in the Seventies. New York: Horizon Press, 1976.

1370. Miller, Mark. "Bley, Paul." In Encyclopedia of Music in Canada, eds. Helmut Kallmann, et al. Toronto/Buffalo: University of Toronto Press, 1981, p. 93.

1371. The Penguin Encyclopedia of Popular Music, ed. Donald Clarke. New York: Viking, 1989, pp. 119-120.

1372. Reclams Jazzfuhrer. 2nd, rev. ed. Stuttgart: Reclam, 1977.

1373. Tenot, Frank. Dictionnaire du Jazz. Paris: Larousse, 1967.

1374. Who's Who in Entertainment. 1st ed. 1989-1990.

1375. Wilmer, Valerie. As Serious As Your Life. Westport, CT: Lawrence Hill & Co., 1981, p. 261.

Articles

1376. "Abroad." BMI (October 1966): 18-19.

1377. Anders, J. "Paul Bley." Jazz Podium (May 1981): 28.

1378. "Banlieues Bleues." Jazz Magazine, No. 339 (May 1985): 15.

1379. "Bley Talks." BMI (November-December 1968): 35.

1380. Case, Brian. "Presenting, on keyboards, briar pipe and chuckles: Mr. Paul Bley." New Musical Express (January 3 1976): 20, 33. [Interview]

1381. Cuscuna, Michael. "Paul Bley: Being Together." down beat (October 17 1968): 20-21. [Interview]

1382. Dobbin, Len. "Paul Bley." Coda (June/July 1965): 2-4. [Profile]

1383. Ginibre, Jean-Louis. "Du Ble Pour Bley." Jazz Magazine, No. 126 (January 1966): 16-17. [Interview]

1384. Goddet, Laurent. "Un Canadian bien Tranquille." Jazz Hot, No. 276 (October 1971): 6-12. [Interview]

1385. Heckman, Don. "Paul Bley." down beat (March 12 1964): 16-17.

1386. Hentoff, Nat. "Paul Bley." BMI (January 1972): 18.

1387. Klee, Joe, and Will Smith. "Focus on Paul Bley." down beat (January 14 1974): 12-13.

1388. Knox, Keith. "Paul Bley: An Introduction." Jazz Monthly (December 1966): 7-10.

1389. Lake, Steve. "Bley School." Melody Maker (October 9 1976): 50. [Interview]

1390. Levin, E. "Paul Bley: Avant-gardist in Mellow Years." Jazz Magazine (Northport, NY), Vol. 1, No. 4 (1977): 46-47. [Interview]

1391. Lyons, Len. "Paul Bley: Improvising Artist." Contemporary Keyboard (May 1977): 8-9+. [Interview]

1392. ________. "Perspective: IAI-Paul Bley's Bold Experiment." down beat (May 19 1977): 50-52. [Interview]

1393. Merceron, G. "Pudique Bley." Jazz Hot, No. 219 (April 1966): 16+. [Interview]

1394. "Paul Bley-Gene Perla." Jazz Forum, No. 52 (1978): 26-28. [Interview]

1395. Smith, Bill. "Paul Bley." Coda, No. 116 (April 1 1979): 2-11. [Interview w/ discography]

1396. Zwerin, Mike. "Paul Bley: Ramblin' with the Disappearing Man." Wire, No. 24 (February 1986): 7.

Discographies

1397. Peterson, I. S., and Laurent Goddet. "Discographie de Paul Bley." Jazz Hot, No. 332 (November 1976): 26-8.

Media Materials

1398. Imagine the Sound (1981). 91 min. Directed by Ron Mann. Documentary featuring the music and thoughts of Paul Bley, Bill Dixon, Archie Shepp and Cecil Taylor. [For distribution information contact: Bill Smith, c/o Coda Publications, Box 87, Station J, Toronto, Ontario M4J 4X8, Canada]

BLOOM, JANE IRA (1955-) - Soprano Sax

See also # 694

1399. Davis, Francis. "Outchicks." In Outcats: Jazz Composers, Instrumentalists, and Singers. New York: Oxford University Press, 1990, pp. 122-128. Discussion of Bloom's "Modern Drama" lp.

1400. Placksin, Sally. American Women in Jazz. New York: Wideview Press, 1982, pp. 281-285.

Biographical Dictionaries

1401. Case, Brian, and Stan Britt. The Harmony Illustrated Encyclopedia of Jazz. 3rd ed. New York: Harmony Books, 1987.

1402. Cohen, Aaron I. International Encyclopedia of Women Composers. 2nd ed. Revised and Enlarged. New York: Books & Music (USA), 1987.

1403. Dictionnaire du Jazz, eds. Philippe Carles, et al. Paris: Laffont, 1988.

1404. Who's Who in Entertainment. 1st ed. 1989-1990.

Articles

1405. Bouchard, Fred. "Profile: Jane Ira Bloom." down beat (December 1981): 64-65.

1406. Cole, Wendy. "To Each Her Own: Jane Ira Bloom." Time, Vol. 136, No. 19 (Fall 1990): 49. [Profile]

1407. Gauffre, Christian. "Jane Ira Bloom." Jazz Magazine, No. 303 (January 1982): 50-51. [Interview]

1408. Gourse, Leslie. "Jane Ira Bloom." Jazz Times (November 1987): 7. [Interview]

1409. Houtchens, C. J. "A Discovery in Jazz." Final Frontier; The Magazine of Space Exploration, Vol. 1, No. 3 (July/August 1988): 41-42, 61. [Profile]

1410. King, Bill. "Interview: Jane Ira Bloom Up to the Challenge." The Jazz Report (Toronto), Vol. 2, No. 4 (February/March 1989): 1-2, 26.

1411. Kinnally, William. "Jane Ira Bloom; NASA commissions avant saxist for sonic impressions." Jazziz (January 1989): 59.

1412. Klotz, Irene. "Sax in Space." Space World (November 1988): 5.

1413. Mandel, Howard. "Riffs: Jane Ira Bloom." down beat (July 1986): 14.

1414. Price, Tim. "Jane Ira Bloom." Saxophone Journal (November/December 1989): 12-16. [Interview]

1415. Van Trikt, Ludwig. "Jane Ira Bloom: short talk." Cadence, Vol. 12, No. 2 (February 1986): 20-21.

1416. Woodard, Josef. "A female saxist updates tradition." Musician, No. 109 (November 1987): 12.

Newspaper Articles

1417. Cordle, Owen. "Finding Her Own Sound." The News and Observer/The Raleigh Times (March 3 1989).

1418. Holden, Stephen. "The Pop Life: Saxophone Improviser." New York Times (December 23 1987).

1419. Korall, Burt. "Jane Ira Bloom: Finessing the Soprano." International Musician (November 1988): 6+.

1420. Snowden, Don. "Jane Bloom: A Live Wire in Electronic Jazz." Los Angeles Times (April 19 1989).

BLUIETT, HAMIET (1940-) - Baritone Saxophone

See also # 6943-6957

1421. Carles, Philippe, and Jean-Louis Comolli. Free Jazz, Black Power. 2nd ed. Paris: Editions Galilee, 1979, p. 375.

1422. Dictionnaire du Jazz, eds. Philippe Carles, et al. Paris: Laffont, 1988.

1423. McRae, Barry. "Hamiet Bluiett." In The Jazz Handbook. Harlow, Essex, Eng.: Longman, 1987, pp. 229-230.

1424. The Penguin Encyclopedia of Popular Music, ed. Donald Clarke. New York: Viking, 1989.

1425. Wild, David. "Bluiett, Hamiet." In The New Grove Dictionary of Jazz. London: Macmillan Press, 1988.

1426. Wilmer, Valerie. As Serious As Your Life. Westport, CT: Lawrence Hill & Co., 1981, p. 283.

Articles

1427. Alexandre, Veronique. "Hamiet Bluiett." Jazz Magazine, No. 291 (November 1980): 14-15. [Interview]

1428. Case, Brian. "De-Subdued Baritone." Melody Maker (January 24 1981): 26. [Interview]

1429. Goddett, Laurent. "Interview: Bluiett's Blues." Jazz Hot, No. 361 (May 1979): 21-24.

1430. McRae, Barry. "Avant Courier: Hamiet Bluiett." Jazz Journal International (November 1983): 10-11.

1431. Stern, Chip. "Stars on the Rise: Hamiet Bluiett." down beat (September 7 1978): 24. [Interview]

1432. Van Trikt, Ludwig. "Hamiet Bluiett: a short talk." Cadence, Vol. 12, No. 5 (May 1986): 5-7.

1433. Welburn, Ron. "A Conversation with Hamiett Bluiett." The Grackle, No. 5 (1979): 11-13.

BLYTHE, ARTHUR (1940-) - Alto Saxophone

See also # 4381-4386

1434. Carles, Philippe, and Jean-Louis Comolli. Free Jazz, Black Power. 2nd ed. Paris: Editions Galilee, 1979, p. 375.

1435. Carr, Ian. "Blythe, Arthur." In Jazz: The Essential Companion. New York: Prentice Hall Press, 1988.

1436. Case, Brian, and Stan Britt. The Harmony Illustrated Encyclopedia of Jazz. 3rd ed. New York: Harmony Books, 1987.

1437. Claghorn, Charles Eugene. Biographical Dictionary of Jazz. Englewood Cliffs, NJ: Prentice-Hall, 1982.

1438. Dictionnaire du Jazz, eds. Philippe Carles, et al. Paris: Laffont, 1988.

1439. Feather, Leonard, and Ira Gitler. "Black Arthur." In The Encyclopedia of Jazz in the Seventies. New York: Horizon Press, 1976.

1440. Hazell, Ed. "Blythe, Arthur." In The New Grove Dictionary of Jazz. London: Macmillan Press, 1988.

1441. McRae, Barry. "Arthur Blythe." In The Jazz Handbook. Harlow, Essex, Eng.: Longman, 1987, pp. 230-231.

1442. The Penguin Encyclopedia of Popular Music, ed. Donald Clarke. New York: Viking, 1989.

1443. Wilmer, Valerie. As Serious As Your Life. Westport, CT: Lawrence Hill & Co., 1981, p. 283.

Articles

1444. Albin, Scott. "Caught: Arthur Blythe Quartet, The Brook, New York." down beat (December 2 1976): 33. [Concert review]

1445. "Arthur Blythe." Jazz Echo, Vol. 9, No. 42 (1979): 1+. [Interview]

1446. "Black is Blythe." Jazz Magazine, No. 285 (April 1980): 30+.

1447. Blumenthal, Bob. "Arthur Blythe: Refreshing Traditions." down beat (April 1980): 25-26, 64.

1448. Brodacki, Krystian, and Charles J. Gans. "Arthur Blythe: Awakening Giant." Jazz Forum, No. 71 (1981): 36-41, 49. [Interview]

1449. Case, Brian. "Another Music for a Different Loft." New Musical Express (April 29 1978): 22-23. [Interview]

1450. _________. "Arthur Blythe: In the Tradition." Black Music and Jazz Review [London] (November 1982): 26-27.

1451. Caux, Beatrice. "Black Arthur." Jazz Hot, No. 378/9 (December 1980/January 1981): 34-36.

1452. Cook, Richard. "Blowing with Mr. Blythe." New Musical Express (September 19 1981): 31. [Interview]

1453. Coppens, George. "Black is Blythe." Jazz Magazine, No. 285 (April 1980): 30-31, 62-63.

1454. Davis, Francis. "Apples, Oranges and Arthur Blythe." Jazz Times (February 1982): 10-11.

1455. _________. "Blindfold Test: Arthur Blythe." down beat (August 1982): 51.

1456. Flaherty, Liam. "King Arthur's Court." Option (March/April 1990): 54-57.

1457. Kamins, Richard B. "Arthur Blythe." Coda, No. 168 (August 1979): 36-37.

1458. Larsen, Peter H. "Arthur Blythe." Melody Maker (December 1981): 13-14. [Interview]

1459. Levenson, Jeff. "Arthur Blythe's Creative Challenge." down beat (October 1987): 23-25. [Interview]

1460. McRae, Barry. "Avant Courier: the work of altoist Arthur Blythe." Jazz Journal International (January 1983): 16-17.

1461. Mieses, Stanley. "The Intuitive Vision." Melody Maker (April 21 1979): 24. [Profile]

1462. Occhiogrosso, Peter. "U.S. News: Blythe, Hot from the Coast." Melody Maker (February 18 1978): 6.

1463. Palmer, Robert. "Jazz: Arthur Blythe's Spirits Soar in New York." Rolling Stone (May 3 1979): 35. [Interview]

1464. Pareles, Jon. "Arthur Blythe's Spirit: Take the Coltrane." Feature (New York), No. 96 (May 1979): 26-27. [Interview]

1465. Reidinger, B. "Arthur Blythe: extending the basics." Jazz Times (June 1988): 25+. [Interview]

1466. Rock, Henry. "Arthur Blythe: Interview." Cadence, Vol. 3, No. 11/12 (March 1978): 7-8.

1467. Safane, Clifford Jay. "Arthur Blythe." Jazz Echo, No. 42 (October 1979): 1, 20.

1468. Stern, Chip. "Arthur Blythe." Musician, Player & Listener, No. 19 (July-August 1979): 44-48.

Newspaper Articles

1469. Giddins, Gary. "Blythe and [Sunny] Murray Tower Over the Loft Underground." Village Voice (June 20 1977): 58.

1470. ________. "Weatherbird: Float Like a Jelly Roll, Sting Like the Blues." Village Voice (May 7 1979): 86-87. [Reprinted in # 57]

1471. Occhiogrosso, Peter. "Arthur Blythe/Tin Palace." Soho Weekly News (April 8 1976): 37.

1472. Stern, Chip. "Arthur Blythe: The Long Road to Greatness." Soho Weekly News (August 24 1978).

BONI, RAYMOND (1947-) (France) - Guitar

1473. Carles, Philippe, and Jean-Louis Comolli. Free Jazz, Black Power. 2nd ed. Paris: Editions Galilee, 1979, pp. 375-376.

1474. Dictionnaire du Jazz, eds. Philippe Carles, et al. Paris: Laffont, 1988.

Articles

1475. "Dico Disco & Co." Jazz Magazine, No. 298 (June 1981): 37. Biographical sketch.

1476. Gerber, Alain. "Association Vivante." Jazz Magazine, No. 201 (June 1972): 6+.

1477. Goddet, Laurent. "La Bande a Boni." Jazz Hot, No. 274 (July 1971): 23.

1478. "Raymond Boni." Jazz Hot, No. 283 (May 1972): 56.

1479. Ruda, M. "Raymond Boni--du cote des inconnus." Jazz Magazine, No. 246 (August 1976): 4.

1480. Rusch, Bob. "Raymond Boni: Interview." Cadence, Vol. 12, No. 7 (July 1986): 16-20, 28.

BORCA, KAREN - Bassoon

1481. Demetz, Bettina. "New Faces: Karen Borca." Ear, Vol. 12, No. 7 (October 1987): 22.

BOURELLY, JEAN-PAUL - Guitar

1482. Milkowski, Bill. "Guitarists All Around: Jean Paul Bourelly." down beat (May 1988): 25-26.

1483. Palmer, Don. "Jean-Paul Bourelly: Blues to the Future." Village Voice (May 2 1989): 90.

BOWIE, JOSEPH (1953-) - Trombone

1484. Carles, Philippe, and Jean-Louis Comolli. Free Jazz, Black Power. 2nd ed. Paris: Editions Galilee, 1979, p. 376.

1485. Dictionnaire du Jazz, eds. Philippe Carles, et al. Paris: Laffont, 1988.

1486. The New Grove Dictionary of Jazz. London: Macmillan Press, 1988.

1487. Wilmer, Valerie. As Serious As Your Life. Westport, CT: Lawrence Hill & Co., 1981, p. 261.

Articles

1488. Bloom, Steve. "Jazz-Punk-Funk: Defunkt." down beat (June 1981): 25-26.

1489. Brennan, M. "On the Edge." Melody Maker (July 30 1983): 6+. [Interview]

1490. Cook, Richard. "Defunkt: the life and death of romance." New Musical Express (May 29 1982): 28-29. [Interview]

1491. Goldstein, Daniel. "Defunkt: Le Retour a la Danse." Jazz Hot, No. 386/387 (July-August 1981): 29-31. [Interview]

1492. Hewitt, Paulo. "Debunking the Funk." Melody Maker (June 13 1981): 18. [Interview]

1493. McElfresh, Suzanne. "Afunk-Garde: genre bashing." Ear, Vol. 12, No. 2 (April 1987): 22-23.

1494. Mandel, Howard. "Riffs: De Funktion of Irony." Village Voice (October 5 1982): 86.

1495. Simper, P. "The Funk Commando." Melody Maker (July 17 1982): 6. [Interview]

1496. Thrills, Adrian. "The Thin Black Thermonuclear Threats." New Musical Express (June 27 1981): 26-27. [Interview]

1497. Toakin, R. "Funky, Punky and Chic." Melody Maker (March 15 1980): 19-20.

BOWIE, LESTER (1941-) - Trumpet

See also # 914-965, 4381-4386

1498. Fruhaulf, Helmut. Lester Bowie's Brass Fantasy: European Tour, Oct./Nov. 86; eine Tournee-Dokumentation. Burghausen: Blick-Punkt, 1988. 47p.

Biographical Dictionaries

1499. Carles, Philippe, and Jean-Louis Comolli. Free Jazz, Black Power. 2nd ed. Paris: Editions Galilee, 1979, p. 376.

1500. Carr, Ian. "Bowie, Lester." In Jazz: The Essential Companion. New York: Prentice Hall Press, 1988.

1501. Claghorn, Charles Eugene. Biographical Dictionary of Jazz. Englewood Cliffs, NJ: Prentice-Hall, 1982.

1502. Dictionnaire du Jazz, eds. Philippe Carles, et al. Paris: Laffont, 1988.

1503. Feather, Leonard, and Ira Gitler. The Encyclopedia of Jazz in the Seventies. New York: Horizon Press, 1976.

1504. Jeske, Lee. "Bowie, Lester." In The New Grove Dictionary of American Music. London: Macmillan Press, 1986.

1505. ________. "Bowie, Lester." In The New Grove Dictionary of Jazz. London: Macmillan Press, 1988.

1506. The Penguin Encyclopedia of Popular Music, ed. Donald Clarke. New York: Viking, 1989, pp. 139-140.

1507. Who's Who in Entertainment. 1st ed. 1989-1990.

1508. Wilmer, Valerie. As Serious As Your Life. Westport, CT: Lawrence Hill & Co., 1981, p. 261-262.

Articles

1509. Arnold, T. K. "Lester Bowie: Jazz is Jazz." Billboard (February 23 1985): 40. [Interview]

1510. "The Art of Lester Bowie." Jazz Echo, Vol. 9, No. 39 (1979): 7.

1511. Be-Bop and Beyond, Vol. 2, No. 1 (January/February 1984). [Interview]

1512. Bouchard, Fred. "Blindfold Test." down beat (September 1984): 41.

1513. Bradshaw, Paul. "Blowing Out the Tradition." Wire, No. 34/35 (December 1986/January 1987): 43-45.

1514. Branker, Anthony D. J. "The Free Thinking Don Cherry and Lester Bowie: trumpeters in the tradition?" Jazz Research Papers, Vol. 9 (1989): 25-32.

1515. Case, Brian. "Gittin' to Know y'All." Melody Maker (February 24 1979): 23, 38. [Interview]

1516. Coppens, George, and Frits Lagerwerff. "Lester Bowie." Coda, No. 164/65 (February 1979): 12-15. [Interview]

1517. Endress, Gudrun. "Lester Bowie." Jazz Podium (May 1983): 4-9.

1518. Henderson, Bill. "Lester Bowie's Trumpet Voluntary." Black Music and Jazz Review (London), Vol. 2, No. 2 (May 1979): 10-12. [Interview]

1519. Levi, Titus. "Lester Speaks Out." OPtion (March/April 1985): 24-25.

1520. Litweiler, John B. "There Won't Be Any More Music." Down Beat's Music '72, Vol. 17 (1972): 23-26, 37. [Interview]

1521. McRae, Barry. "Avant Courier: Lester Bowie." Jazz Journal (December 1980): 12-13. [Profile]

1522. Mandel, Howard. "Lester Bowie, M.D.: Magical Dimensions." down beat (March 1984): 14-17.

1523. Mathieu, Bill. "Record Reviews: Numbers 1 & 2." down beat (May 2 1968): 26.

1524. O'Hagan, Sean. "Miles Davis Meets Donald Duck." New Musical Express (November 1 1986): 22-23. [Interview]

1525. Primack, Bret. "Blindfold Test." down beat (May 17 1979): 33.

1526. Reidinger, B. "Lester Bowie." Jazz Times (August 1988): 9. [Interview]

1527. Rendle, P., and Rafi Zabor. "Lester Bowie: Roots, Research, and the Carnival Chef." Musician, Player & Listener, No. 44 (June 1982): 64-71.

1528. Rusch, Bob. "Lester Bowie." Cadence, Vol. 5, No. 12 (December 1979): 3-6+. [Interview]

1529. Shand, John. "Lester Bowie: tying it all up." Jazz (Sydney), No. 3 (May/June 1981): 18-20. [Interview]

1530. Stokes, W. Royal. "Lester Bowie: The Realities of Jazz." Jazz Times (July 1985): 12-13. [Interview]

1531. Swenson, John. "Saturday Review talks to Lester Bowie." Saturday Review (November/December 1985): 86.

1532. Townley, Ray. "Lester - Who?" down beat (January 31 1974): 11-12.

1533. Wilmer, Valerie. "Bowie--The Bright Star." Melody Maker (April 25 1970): 14.

1534. _________. "Lester Bowie: Extending the Tradition." down beat (April 29 1971): 13+.

1535. _________. "A Maverick at the Mouthpiece." Time Out [London] (February 9-15 1979).

1536. Yagoda, B. "Lester Bowie." Esquire (December 1982): 118-120.

Newspaper Articles

1537. Crouch, Stanley. "Lester Bowie: Beyond Bohemia." Village Voice (May 18 1982): 66.

1538. _________. "Telescoping the Tradition." Soho Weekly News (January 8 1976): 38.

1539. "The RW Interview: Lester Bowie." Revolutionary Worker (June 17 1985): 8-9, 13-15.

1540. Washington Post (October 11 1986): G4. [Interview]

BOYKINS, RONNIE (1935-1980) - Bass

1541. Carles, Philippe, and Jean-Louis Comolli. Free Jazz, Black Power. 2nd ed. Paris: Editions Galilee, 1979, p. 377.

1542. Dictionnaire du Jazz, eds. Philippe Carles, et al. Paris: Laffont, 1988.

1543. The New Grove Dictionary of Jazz. London: Macmillan Press, 1988.

1544. Wilmer, Valerie. As Serious As Your Life. Westport, CT: Lawrence Hill & Co., 1981, p. 262.

Articles

1545. Caux, Jacqueline, and Caux, Daniel. "Ronnie Boykins." Jazz Magazine, No. 223 (June 1974). [Interview]

1546. Welburn, Ron. "Ronnie Boykins." The Grackle, Vol. 1, No. 4 (1977-78): 37-43; Reprinted in Jazz Spotlite News (April/May 1980): 6-7.

Obituaries

1547. Coda (June 1980): 38.
1548. down beat (July 1980): 12.
1549. Jazz Magazine, No. 288 (July-August 1980): 10.

BRACKEEN, CHARLES (1940-) - Tenor Saxophone

1550. Carles, Philippe, and Jean-Louis Comolli. Free Jazz, Black Power. 2nd ed. Paris: Editions Galilee, 1979, p. 377.

1551. Dictionnaire du Jazz, eds. Philippe Carles, et al. Paris: Laffont, 1988.

1552. Wilmer, Valerie. As Serious As Your Life. Westport, CT: Lawrence Hill & Co., 1981, p. 262.

Articles

1553. Cuscuna, Michael. "Profile: Charles Brackeen." down beat (August 15 1974): 34-35.

1554. Riggins, Roger. "Charles Brackeen." Coda, No. 174 (August 1980): 14-15. [Profile]

BRACKEEN, JOANNE (1938-) - Piano

See also # 694, 704

1555. Feather, Leonard. The Passion for Jazz. New York: Horizon Press, 1980, pp. 144-148.

1556. Placksin, Sally. American Women in Jazz. New York: Wideview Press, 1982, pp. 273-276.

Biographical Dictionaries

1557. Carr, Ian. "Brackeen, Joanne." In Jazz: The Essential Companion. New York: Prentice Hall Prentice, 1988.

1558. Case, Brian, and Stan Britt. The Harmony Illustrated Encyclopedia of Jazz. 3rd ed. New York: Harmony Books, 1987.

1559. Claghorn, Charles Eugene. Biographical Dictionary of Jazz. Englewood Cliffs, NJ: Prentice-Hall, 1982.

1560. Dictionnaire du Jazz, eds. Philippe Carles, et al. Paris: Laffont, 1988.

1561. Dobbins, Bill. "Brackeen, JoAnne." In The New Grove Dictionary of American Music. London: Macmillan Press, 1986.

1562. ________. "Brackeen, JoAnne." In The New Grove Dictionary of Jazz. London: Macmillan Press, 1988.

1563. Feather, Leonard, and Ira Gitler. The Encyclopedia of Jazz in the Seventies. New York: Horizon Press, 1976.

1564. The Penguin Encyclopedia of Popular Music, ed. Donald Clarke. New York: Viking, 1989.

Articles

1565. Blumenthal, Bob. "The Arrival of JoAnne Brackeen." Rolling Stone (March 6 1980): 35.

1566. ________. "JoAnne Brackeen: First Comes the Sound." down beat (August 1982): 26-27, 55.

1567. Feather, Leonard. "Blindfold Test: Joanne Brackeen." down beat (February 1980): 50.

1568. George, Nelson. "JoAnne Brackeen: Pianist for a New Era." down beat (July 1980): 22-23, 59. [Interview]

1569. Gourse, Leslie. "Joanne Brackeen: Free to Explore." Jazz Times (August 1990): 15.

1570. ________. "Joanne Brackeen: Swinging Dissonance." down beat (November 1988): 26-28. [Interview]

1571. Hill, Hal. "Joanne Brackeen." Coda, No. 200 (February 1985): 11-12. [Interview]

1572. Nelsen, Don. "Joann [sic] Brackeen." Jazz Times (April/May 1981): 10-12. [Interview]

1573. "On the Bandstand: Joanne Brackeen." Jazz Forum, No. 46 (1977): 26-27.

1574. Safane, Clifford Jay. "Joanne Brackeen: profile of an emerging jazz piano headliner." Contemporary Keyboard (November 1979): 18-20, 22.

1575. Smith, Arnold Jay. "Profile: Joanne Brackeen." down beat (March 10 1977): 16+. [Interview]

1576. Tomkins, Les. "A New Girl on the Jazz Piano Scene: Joanne Brackeen." Crescendo International (March 1979): 16-17. [Interview]

1577. Weinreich, R. "Play it Momma." Village Voice (July 3 1978): 64-65.

Media Materials

1578. Marian McPartland's Piano Jazz, No. 12: Joanne Brackeen. Duration: 60 min. Pianist Joanne Brackeen discusses her career with interviewer Marian McPartland, and also plays selected songs. [Held by the Rodgers & Hammerstein Collection at Lincoln Center (# 7097)]

BRADFORD, BOBBY LEE (1934-) - Trumpet

1579. Jones, LeRoi. "Introducing Bobby Bradford." In Black Music. New York: Morrow, 1967, pp. 99-103.

1580. Kofsky, Frank. "John Carter and Bobby Bradford." In The Black Giants. New York: The World Publishing Co., 1970, pp. 41-46.

Biographical Dictionaries

1581. Berry, Lemuel, Jr. Biographical Dictionary of Black Musicians and Music Educators. Guthrie, OK: Educational Book Publishers, 1978.

1582. Carles, Philippe, and Jean-Louis Comolli. Free Jazz, Black Power. 2nd ed. Paris: Editions Galilee, 1979, pp. 377-378.

1583. Case, Brian, and Stan Britt. The Harmony Illustrated Encyclopedia of Jazz. 3rd ed. New York: Harmony Books, 1987.

1584. Claghorn, Charles Eugene. Biographical Dictionary of Jazz. Englewood Cliffs, NJ: Prentice-Hall, 1982.

1585. Dictionnaire du Jazz, eds. Philippe Carles, et al. Paris: Laffont, 1988.

1586. Feather, Leonard, and Ira Gitler. The Encyclopedia of Jazz in the Seventies. New York: Horizon Press, 1976.

1587. Hazell, Ed. "Bradford, Bobby." In The New Grove Dictionary of Jazz. London: Macmillan Press, 1988.

1588. The Penguin Encyclopedia of Popular Music, ed. Donald Clarke. New York: Viking, 1989.

1589. Priestley, Brian. "Bradford, Bobby." In Jazz: The Essential Companion. New York: Prentice Hall Press, 1988.

1590. Wilmer, Valerie. As Serious As Your Life. Westport, CT: Lawrence Hill & Co., 1981, p. 262.

Articles

1591. Be-Bop And Beyond, Vol. 3, No. 3 (May/June 1985). [Interview]

1592. Crouch, Stanley. "Black Song West." The Cricket: Black Music in Evolution (Newark, NJ), No. 2 (1968?): 3-8. Profile of Bobby Bradford and John Carter.

1593. James, Michael. "Order and Feeling, Discipline and Fire; An Introduction to the John Carter and Bobby Bradford Quartet." Jazz & Blues (April 1973): 6-9. [Record review]

1594. Jones, LeRoi. "Introducing Bobby Bradford." Kulchur, No. 7 (Autumn 1962): 53-56. [Repr. in # 1579]

1595. Page, Les. "Bobby Bradford." Melody Maker (July 9 1977): 44.

1596. Raether, K. "Ornette: Bobby Bradford's Portrait of an Emerging Giant." Jazz Magazine (Northport, NY), Vol. 1, No. 3 (1977): 43-46. [Interview w/ discography]

1597. Ramanan, Roland. "Earful Symmetry." Wire, No. 70/71 (Dec 1989-Jan 1990): 60-61, 63, 88. [Interview]

1598. Weber, Mark. "Bobby Bradford." Coda, No. 157 (October 1977). [Interview]

1599. Williams, Richard. "Bradford-No Secrets." Melody Maker (August 25 1973): 39. [Interview]

1600. _________. "Memories of Ornette." Melody Maker (July 17 1971): 28. Interview with Bradford focusing on his relationship with Ornette Coleman.

Media Materials

1601. The New Music. Directed by Peter Bull and Alex Gibney. 29 min., color. Brief documentary portrait of two of the new music's unsung masters, John Carter and Bobby Bradford. [Available from Rhapsody Films, P.O. Box 179, New York, NY 10014. Tel. 212/243-0152]

BRAXTON, ANTHONY (1945-) - Reeds

See also # 436-437, 707, 1977-1981

Works in English

1602. Braxton, Anthony. Composition Notes, Books A-E. Oakland, CA: Synthesis Music (Mills College, Music Dept., 5000 MacArthur Blvd., Oakland 94613), 1985. 5 vols.

1603. _________. Tri-Axium Writings. Oakland, CA: Synthesis Music, 1985. 3 vols.

1604. Litweiler, John. "Leo Smith, Anthony Braxton, Joseph Jarman, and Roscoe Mitchell." In The Freedom Principle: Jazz After 1958. New York: William Morrow, 1984, pp. 265-286.

1605. Lock, Graham. Forces in Motion: Anthony Braxton and the Meta-reality of Creative Music. Interviews and Tour Notes, England 1985. London: Quartet Books, 1988; New York: Da Capo, 1989. 432p.

1606. Ullman, Michael. "Anthony Braxton." In Jazz Lives. Washington, D.C.: New Republic Books, 1980, pp. 199-214.

Biographical Dictionaries

1607. Carr, Ian. "Braxton, Anthony." In Jazz: The Essential Companion. New York: Prentice Hall Press, 1988.

1608. Case, Brian, and Stan Britt. The Harmony Illustrated Encyclopedia of Jazz. 3rd ed. New York: Harmony Books, 1987.

1609. Claghorn, Charles Eugene. Biographical Dictionary of Jazz. Englewood Cliffs, NJ: Prentice-Hall, 1982.

1610. Feather, Leonard, and Ira Gitler. The Encyclopedia of Jazz in the Seventies. New York: Horizon Press, 1976.

1611. Kernfeld, Barry. "Braxton, Anthony." In The New Grove Dictionary of American Music. London: Macmillan Press, 1986.

1612. _________. "Braxton, Anthony." In The New Grove Dictionary of Jazz. London: Macmillan Press, 1988.

1613. McRae, Barry. "Anthony Braxton." In The Jazz Handbook. Harlow, Essex, Eng.: Longman, 1987, pp. 188-189.

1614. The Penguin Encyclopedia of Popular Music, ed. Donald Clarke. New York: Viking, 1989.

1615. Southern, Eileen. Biographical Dictionary of Afro-American and African Musicians. Westport, CT: Greenwood Press, 1982.

1616. Who's Who in Entertainment. 1st ed. 1989-1990.

1617. Wilmer, Valerie. As Serious As Your Life. Westport, CT: Lawrence Hill & Co., 1981, p. 262.

Dissertations

1618. Radano, Ronald Michael. "Anthony Braxton and His Two Musical Traditions, The Meeting of Concert Music and Jazz." Dissertation (Ph.D., Ethnomusicology) University of Michigan, 1985. 2 vols.

Articles

1619. Ansell, Kenneth, and Stuart MacDonald. "Anthony Braxton." Impetus (London), No. 6 (1977): 248-252. [Interview]

1620. Balliett, Whitney. "Jazz." New Yorker (April 4 1977): 84-86.

1621. Blumenthal, Bob. "Reedman Anthony Braxton plays by his own rules." Rolling Stone (June 2 1977): 30-31. [Interview]

1622. Braxton, Anthony. "8KN- (J-6) I R10." Source, issue 10, Vol. 5, No. 2 (1971): 40-45. Transcription of a Braxton composition.

1623. Carey, Joe. "Anthony Braxton: Interview." Cadence, Vol. 10, No. 3 (March 1984): 5-10, 21.

1624. Case, Brian. "Highs 'n' Lows." New Musical Express (January 29 1977): 18. [Interview]

1625. Demierre, J. "Bale: The Composed Music of Anthony Braxton." Dissonanz/Dissonance, No. 19 (February 1989): 26.

1626. De Muth, Jerry. "Anthony Braxton--George Lewis." Cadence, Vol. 2, No. 2 (December 1976): 3+.

1627. Gazzoli, Guido. "Anthony Braxton." Jazz Forum, No. 62 (1979): 32-35, 41. [Interview]

1628. Henschen, Bob. "Anthony Braxton: Alternative Creativity in This Time Zone." down beat (February 22 1979): 18-20. [Interview]

1629. Kehler, Elizabeth. "Wesleyan University - Broadening Horizons." Down Beat (October 1990): 23. On Braxton's appointment to head Wesleyan U's jazz program.

1630. Kostakis, Peter, and Art Lange. "Conversation with Anthony Braxton." Brilliant Corners: A Magazine of the Arts (Chicago), No. 4 (Fall 1976): 53-99.

1631. Lake, Steve. "'I make more money at chess than at music.'" Melody Maker (October 11 1975): 48. [Interview]

1632. _________. "There's God on a Chessboard." Musics (London), No. 13 (August 1977): 19-23. [Interview]

1633. Laskin, David LL. "Anthony Braxton: Play or Die." Ear (May 1989): 40-46.

1634. Levin, Robert. "Anthony Braxton and the Third Generation." Jazz & Pop (October 1970): 12-14. [Reprinted in # 67]

1635. Lock, Graham. "Let 100 Orchestras Blow." The Wire, No. 16 (June 1985): 19-22.

1636. McRae, Barry. "Avant Courier." Jazz Journal (December 1972): 20-21.

1637. _________. "Avant Courier: Lookout Form." Jazz Journal (August 1974): 19.

1638. _________. "Braxton, Bailey and Company--the art of ad hoc ad lib." Jazz Journal International (July 1977): 22-23.

1639. Morton, Brian. "Anthony Braxton: Rite Angles." The Wire, No. 65 (July 1989): 30-32. [Interview]

1640. Occhiogrosso, Peter. "Anthony Braxton explains himself." down beat (August 12 1976): 15+. [Interview]

1641. Radano, Ronald M. "Braxton's Reputation." Musical Quarterly (Fall 1986): 503+.

1642. Rothbart, Peter. "Play or Die: Anthony Braxton interview." down beat (February 1982): 20-23.

1643. Saal, Hubert. "Two Free Spirits." Newsweek (August 8 1977): 52-53.

1644. Shoemaker, Bill. "Anthony Braxton: The Dynamics of Creativity." down beat (March 1989): 20-22.

1645. ________. "Braxton on Braxton." Jazz Times (November 1982): 10-11.

1646. Smith, Bill. "The Anthony Braxton Interview." Coda, Vol. 11, No. 8 (April 1974): 2-8, 10-11.

1647. Tepperman, Barry. "Further Soundings from the A.A.C.M. - Some Notes." Pieces of Jazz (1971): 19-22.

1648. ________. "Perspectives on Anthony Braxton." Jazz Forum, No. 45 (1977): 34-37.

1649. Townley, Ray. "Anthony Braxton." down beat (February 14 1974): 12-13.

1650. Vickery, Steve. "Anthony Braxton: Forces in Motion; An Overview." Coda, No. 222 (October-November 1988): 4-7. Lengthy review of Graham Lock's Forces in Motion (# 1605).

1651. Whitehead, Kevin. "Book Look." Cadence (November 1990): 27-29. Review of Braxton's five volume Composition Notes (# 1602).

1652. Wilmer, Valerie. "Anthony Braxton." Jazz & Blues, Vol. 1, No. 2 (1971). [Interview]

1653. ________. "Anthony Braxton and the Tools of Tommorrow's Music." Melody Maker (February 6 1971): 12.

1654. ________. "Braxton's Next Move." Melody Maker (December 30 1972): 30.

1655. Woodard, Josef. "Structure, Vocabulary and Tradition: Saxophonist Anthony Braxton." Option, No. 23 (November/ December 1988): 61-63.

Newspaper Articles

1656. Ahlgren, C. "Anthony Braxton: He Puts an Analytic Mind to His Musical Matters." San Francisco Examiner (October 13 1985).

1657. Litweiler, John B. "Anthony Braxton: Music for Interplanetary Travel." (Chicago) Reader (January 26 1979).

1658. ________. "The Future of Jazz." Chicago Tribune (August 25 1989): Sec. 5, p. 3. [Profile]

1659. Tate, Greg. "Grooves of Academe: Anthony Braxton's Grace Notes." Village Voice/Voice Literary Supplement (November 7 1989): 26. [Review of # 1605]

Works in French, German and Italian

1660. Bolelli, Franco. "La Scienza dell'Utopia: Conversazione con Anthony Braxton." In Musica Creativa. Milano: Squilibri, 1978, pp. 107-121.

1661. Carles, Philippe, and Jean-Louis Comolli. Free Jazz, Black Power. 2nd ed. Paris: Editions Galilee, 1979, p. 378.

1662. Cerchiari, Luca. "Anthony Braxton." In Il Jazz degli Settanta. Milano: Gammalibri, 1980, pp. 9-35.

1663. Dictionnaire du Jazz, eds. Philippe Carles, et al. Paris: Laffont, 1988.

1664. Reda, Jacques. Anthologie des Musiciens de Jazz. Paris: Stock, 1981, pp. 342-343.

Articles

1665. "Anthony Braxton." Jazz Magazine, No. 234 (July 1975): 32-33. [Interview]

1666. Bougardier, G. "Anthony Braxton." Jazz Magazine, No. 283 (February 1980): 9-10.

1667. "Braxton at Home." Jazz Magazine, No. 276 (June 1979): 28-31. Photo essay.

1668. Carles, Philippe. "Braxton: le jazz est une musique dangereuse." Jazz Magazine, No. 205 (November 1972): 12-17; No. 206 (December 1972): 18-21.

1669. Caux, Daniel. "A Propos du Groupe d'Anthony Braxton." Jazz Hot, No. 255 (November 1969): 8-9.

1670. Cerchiari, Luca. "La Carriera e la Musica di Anthony Braxton." Musica Jazz (January 1980): 5-10; (February 1980): 16-20.

1671. Coudert, Francoise Marie. "Bilan de Braxton." Jazz Magazine, No. 334 (December 1984): 69+. [Interview]

1672. Dutilh, Alex. "Anthony Braxton solitaire et sublime." Jazz Hot, No. 318 (July/August 1975): 26.

1673. Echenoz, J., and Bernard Loupias. "Anthony Braxton." Jazz Hot, No. 282 (April 1972): 4+.

1674. Goddet, Laurent. "Braxton's Back." Jazz Hot, No. 318 (July/August 1975): 21+. [Interview]

1675. ________, and Alex Dutilh. "Anthony Braxton; ou, L'art de la surprise." Jazz Hot, No. 349 (May 1978): 6-14; No. 350 (June 1978): 14-17.

1676. Kleinert, G. "Disziplin der Improvisation: Anthony Braxton und Rova." Jazz Podium (March 1989): 12-15. [Interview]

1677. Le Bec, Jean-Yves. "Braxton et la regle de 3." Jazz Magazine, No. 386 (October 1989): 54-55. [Interview]

1678. Moussaron, Jean-Pierre. "L'aube de Braxton." Jazz Magazine, No. 255 (June 1977): 28+.

1679. Ogan, Bernd. "Anthony Braxton." Jazz Podium (June 1979): 22-23.

1680. Pellicciotti, Giacomo. "Braxton et Roach: ensemble a Alassio." Jazz Magazine, No. 270 (November-December 1978): 32-35.

1681. Soutif, Daniel. "L'esprit de la musique selon Braxton." Jazz Magazine, No. 289 (September 1980): 62.

1682. Tagliaferri, Enrico. "Anthony Braxton e la Cultura Nera." Musica Jazz (December 1979): 8-12.

1683. Wilson, Peter Niklas. "Zur Kompositionstechnik von Anthony Braxton." Jazz Podium (August 1982): 4-7.

1684. _________. "Kreativitaet als Kategorischer Imperativ: Ornette Coleman und Anthony Braxton komponierten fuer das 'Ensemble Modern'." Neue Zeitschrift fuer Musik (January 1990): 31-32.

Concert Reviews

1685. Klee, Joe H. "Caught in the Act: Anthony Braxton, Town Hall, New York." down beat (September 14 1972): 36.

1686. Litweiler, John. "Caught in the Act: Alvin Fielder-Anthony Braxton, University of Chicago." down beat (May 18 1967): 25-26.

Record Reviews

1687. Kart, Larry. "Record Reviews: Three Compositions of New Jazz." down beat (November 14 1968): 20.

1688. Klee, Joe. "Record Reviews: For Alto." down beat (June 24 1971): 18.

1689. Mitchell, Charles. "Record Reviews: Creative Music Orchestra Music 1976." down beat (October 7 1976): 20.

1690. Occhiogrosso, Peter. "Spotlight Review: Creative Music Orchestra Music 1976." Radio Free Jazz (July 1976): 11.

1691. Schoemaker, Bill. "Eddying Figures." Down Beat (November 1990): 47. Survey of recent releases and reissues of Braxton material.

Discographies

1692. Bollelli, Franco. "Braxtography." Almanacco Musica (Milano), No. 1 (Summer 1979): 83-88.

1693. De Craen, Hugo, and Eddy Janssens. Anthony Braxton discography. Brussels: New Think (Dalialaan, B-2500 Lier, Belgium), 1982.

1694. Dutilh, Alex. "Discographie d'Anthony Braxton." Jazz Hot, No. 329 (July/August 1969): 46-49.

1695. Rissi, Mathias. Anthony Braxton: A Discography. Adliswil, Switzerland: Mathias Rissi (Haldenstr. 23, CH-8134 Adliswil), 1977. 16p.

1696. Wachtmeister, Hans. A Discography and Bibliography of Anthony Braxton. Stocksund, Sweden: Blue Anchor (Radjursvagen 18, S-182 75, Stocksund), 1982. 119p.

BREUKER, WILLEM (1944-) (Netherlands) - Reeds/Bandleader

See also # 360

1697. Giddins, Gary. "Breuker Battles the Bourgeoisie." In Riding on a Blue Note. New York: Oxford University Press, 1987, pp. 205-210.

1698. Noglik, Bert. "Willem Breuker." In Jazzwerkstatt International. Berlin: Verlag Neue Musik, 1981, pp. 226-251. [Interview]

1699. Vuijsje, Bert. De Nieuwe Jazz. Baarn: Bosch & Keuning, 1978, pp. 148-154. [Interview]

Biographical Dictionaries

1700. Berendt, Joachim E. "Breuker, Willem." In The New Grove Dictionary of Music and Musicians. London: Macmillan Press, 1980, Vol. 3, p. 266.

1701. Carles, Philippe, and Jean-Louis Comolli. Free Jazz, Black Power. 2nd ed. Paris: Editions Galilee, 1979, pp. 378-379.

1702. Dictionnaire du Jazz, eds. Philippe Carles, et al. Paris: Laffont, 1988.

1703. Eyle, Wim van. "Breuker, Willem." In The New Grove Dictionary of Jazz. London: Macmillan Press, 1988.

Articles

1704. Besecker, Bill. "Willem Breuker (Kollektief) Profile." Coda, No. 230 (February/March 1990): 26-27.

1705. Bourne, Michael. "Willem Breuker, & Kompany: Euro-Bop, With a Twist." down beat (May 1989): 28-30.

1706. Buzelin, Jean. "Willem Breuker Kollectif." Jazz Hot, No. 329 (July-August 1976): 55.

1707. ________, et Francoise Buzelin. "Le Theatre fou de Willem Breuker." Jazz Hot, No. 347 (March 1978): 14-19.

1708. "Dico Disco & Co." Jazz Magazine, No. 298 (June 1981): 37. Biographical sketch.

1709. Giddins, Gary. "Willem Breuker in Amerika." Jazzjaarboek (Amsterdam), Vol. 5 (1986): 61-67.

1710. Hofstein, F. "Willem Breuker." Jazz Magazine, No. 290 (October 1980): 17.

1711. Koopmans, Rudy. "The Retarded Clockmaker." Key Notes (Amsterdam), No. 1 (1975): 19-31. Analysis of the musics of Willem Breuker and Misha Mengelberg.

1712. Millroth, Thomas. "Willem Breuker." Coda, Vol. 11, No. 4 (1973): 37-38.

1713. Pareles, Jon. "Willem Breuker Band Delivers a European Jazz." New York Times (October 28 1983): C26.

1714. Rouy, Gerard. "Willem Breuker." Jazz Magazine, No. 295 (March 1981): 34-35. [Interview]

1715. Smith, Bill. "The Willem Breuker Interview." Coda, No. 160 (April 1978): 4-7.

1716. Thiem, Michael. "Willem Breuker: music with its feet on the ground." Jazz Forum, No. 58 (1979): 37-39, 42. [Interview]

1717. Watson, Ben. "Kollektief Calls." Wire (November 1989): 43-44.

BRIMFIELD, WILLIAM (1938-) - Trumpet

1718. Carles, Philippe, and Jean-Louis Comolli. Free Jazz, Black Power. 2nd ed. Paris: Editions Galilee, 1979, p. 379.

1719. Jost, Ekkehard. "Neighbors mit Fred Anderson und William Brimfield." Jazz Podium, Vol. 26, No. 2 (1977): 19-20.

1720. Wilmer, Valerie. As Serious As Your Life. Westport, CT: Lawrence Hill & Co., 1981, p. 262.

BROETZMANN, PETER (1941-) (W. Germany) - Tenor Saxophone

See also # 343, 4380

1721. Noglik, Bert. "Peter Brotzmann." In Jazzwerkstatt International. Berlin: Verlag Neue Musik, 1981, pp. 190-211. [Interview]

Biographical Dictionaries

1722. Carles, Philippe, and Jean-Louis Comolli. Free Jazz, Black Power. 2nd ed. Paris: Editions Galilee, 1979, p. 379.

1723. Carr, Ian. "Brotzmann, Peter." In Jazz: The Essential Companion. New York: Prentice Hall Press, 1988.

1724. Claghorn, Charles Eugene. Biographical Dictionary of Jazz. Englewood Cliffs, NJ: Prentice-Hall, 1982.

1725. Dictionnaire du Jazz, eds. Philippe Carles, et al. Paris: Laffont, 1988.

1726. Feather, Leonard, and Ira Gitler. The Encyclopedia of Jazz in the Seventies. New York: Horizon Press, 1976.

1727. Iannapollo, Robert J. "Brotzmann, Peter." In The New Grove Dictionary of Jazz. London: Macmillan Press, 1988.

1728. Reclams Jazzfuhrer. 2nd, rev. ed. Stuttgart: Reclam, 1977.

Articles

1729. Gruenfeld, H. D. "Interview mit Peter Broetzmann: zu Kurz gekommen: die Klarinette." Jazz Podium (November 1984): 7-8.

1730. Jost, Ekkehard. "Peter Broetzmann." Jazz Podium (October 1987): 16-18.

1731. Knox, Keith. "Peter Brotzmann." Jazz Monthly (January 1968): 15. [Record review]

1732. Lindenmaier, H. Lukas. "Peter Broetzmann: interview." Cadence, Vol. 4, No. 10 (October 1978): 3, 5-7, 20, 22.

1733. Panke, Werner. "A Portrait of Peter Broetzmann." Jazz Forum, No. 38 (1975): 46-48.

1734. Schoemaker, Bill. "Han Bennink/Peter Brotzmann: first entrances and Last Exits." down beat (January 1987): 24-26. [Interview]

1735. Turi, G. "Peter Broetzmann: Music from the Stomach." Jazz Forum, No. 115 (1988): 46-49. [Interview]

1736. Witherden, Barry. "Peter Brotzmann: Low Life Giant." Wire, No. 73 (March 1990): 38, 41.

BROOKS, ARTHUR (1946-) - Trumpet

1737. Rusch, Bob. "Art Brooks: Interview." Cadence, Vol. 5, No. 7 (July 1979): 12-16.

BROOMER, STUART (1947-) (Canada) - Piano/bass

1738. Miller, Mark. "Broomer, Stuart." In Encyclopedia of Music in Canada, eds. Helmut Kallmann, et al. Toronto/Buffalo: University of Toronto Press, 1981, p. 122.

Articles

1739. Garber, Lloyd. "Stuart Broomer." Coda, No. 156 (July-August 1977): 14-15.

1740. Miller, Mark. "Profile: Stuart Broomer." down beat (May 18 1978): 38-39. [Interview]

BROTHERHOOD OF BREATH (Great Britain)

1741. "Brotherhood of Breath." In Dictionnaire du Jazz, eds. Philippe Carles, et al. Paris: Laffont, 1988.

1742. Carr, Ian. "Chris MacGregor - The Brotherhood of Breath." In Music Outside: Contemporary Jazz in Britain. London: Latimer New Dimensions, 1973, pp. 90-103, 162.

Articles

1743. McRae, Barry. "Avant Courier: The Brotherhood." Jazz Journal, Vol. 28 (November 1975): 10+.

1744. "New Band for Chris." Melody Maker (May 16 1970): 8. Brief note on the formation of the Brotherhood of Breath.

1745. Schade, Horst. "Chris McGregor's Brotherhood of Breath." Hi Fi-Stereophone (December 1971): 1160, 1162, 1164. [German text]

1746. Wilmer, Valerie. "Caught in the Act: Brotherhood of Breath." Melody Maker (July 4 1970): 8. [Concert review]

1747. _________. "Chris McGregor--the Brotherhood of Breath." Jazz Forum, No. 10 (1970): 68-70.

BROWN, MARION (1935-) - Alto Saxophone

See also # 171, 276, 286, 699

Works in English

1748. Brown, Marion. Notes to Afternoon of a Georgia Faun: Views and Reviews. Northampton, MA: NIA Music, 1973. 61p.

1749. _________. Recollections. Frankfurt: JAS Publications, 1984. 285p.

Biographical Dictionaries

1750. Carr, Ian. "Brown, Marion." In Jazz: The Essential Companion. New York: Prentice Hall Press, 1988.

1751. Case, Brian, and Stan Britt. The Harmony Illustrated Encyclopedia of Jazz. 3rd ed. New York: Harmony Books, 1987.

1752. Claghorn, Charles Eugene. Biographical Dictionary of American Music. West Nyack, NY: Parker Pub. Co., 1973.

1753. ________. Biographical Dictionary of Jazz. Englewood Cliffs, NJ: Prentice-Hall, 1982.

1754. Feather, Leonard. The Encyclopedia of Jazz in the Sixties. New York: Horizon Press, 1966.

1755. ________, and Ira Gitler. The Encyclopedia of Jazz in the Seventies. New York: Horizon Press, 1976.

1756. The Penguin Encyclopedia of Popular Music, ed. Donald Clarke. New York: Viking, 1989.

1757. Southern, Eileen. Biographical Dictionary of Afro-American and African Musicians. Westport, CT: Greenwood Press, 1982.

1758. Such, David G. "Brown, Marion." In The New Grove Dictionary of Jazz. London: Macmillan Press, 1988.

1759. Wilmer, Valerie. As Serious As Your Life. Westport, CT: Lawrence Hill & Co., 1981, p. 262.

Dissertations and Theses

1760. Brown, Marion. "Faces and Places: The Music and Travels of a Contemporary Jazz Musician." Thesis (M.A.) Wesleyan University, 1976. 2 vols.

1761. Hardin, Christopher L. "Black Professional Musicians in Higher Education: A Study Based on in-depth interviews." Dissertation (Ed.D.) University of Massachusetts, 1987.

Articles

1762. Be-Bop and Beyond, Vol. 3, No. 3 (May/June 1985). [Interview]

1763. Brown, Marion. "Improvisation and the Aural Tradition in Afro-American Music." Black World (November 1973): 14-19.

1764. Frazer, Vernon. "Marion Brown." Coda (July 1976): 2-5. [Interview]

1765. Kelley, William Melvin. "Two Black Browns from Georgia." Jazz & Pop (June 1968): 12-14. Profile of soul star James Brown and saxophonist Marion Brown.

1766. McNally, Owen. "Saxophonist Seeks New Horizons in World Music." Hartford Courant Magazine (September 14 1975): 2-4, 6-7.

1767. Maizlish, Mort. "Marion Brown." Jazz & Pop (October 1967): 13-16.

1768. "Marion Brown." International Times (London), No. 12 (March 13-26, 1967): 8-9. [Interview]

1769. "'Music is the Thread that binds Black People.'" Soul (March 31 1975): 11.

1770. Nieves, Felipe. "Treasuring Marion Brown." (Northampton, Mass.) Daily News Weekend (May 30 1985): W-1, W-6.

1771. Palmer, Bob. "Marion Brown; 'Geechee Recollections in New England.'" down beat (February 28 1974): 12-13. [Interview]

1772. Quinn, Bill. "Marion Brown: Topside Underground." down beat (February 9 1967): 14-15, 38, 40.

1773. Spellman, A. B. "Marion Brown: Growing Into Gianthood." Liberator (New York), Vol. 6, No. 9 (September 1966): 20.

1774. Tucci, Linda. "With Marion Brown: The Artist in Maine." The Black Perspective in Music, Vol. 1, No. 1 (Spring 1973): 60-63. [Reprinted from the Maine Times [Topsham, Maine] (November 17 1972)]

1775. Wilmer, Valerie. "Marion Brown--back to the Southland." Melody Maker (July 4 1970): 12.

Works in French and German

1776. Carles, Philippe, and Jean-Louis Comolli. Free Jazz, Black Power. 2nd ed. Paris: Editions Galilee, 1979, p. 380.

1777. Dictionnaire du Jazz, eds. Philippe Carles, et al. Paris: Laffont, 1988.

1778. Reclams Jazzfuhrer. 2nd, rev. ed. Stuttgart: Reclam, 1977.

1779. Roggeman, Willy. "Marion Brown." In Free en Andere Jazz-Essays. The Hague: Van Ditmar, 1969, pp. 113-116.

Articles

1780. Berger, Daniel. "Marion Brown par lui meme." Jazz Hot, No. 242 (August-September 1968): 21-22. [Interview]

1781. "Black, Brown and Free." Jazz Magazine, No. 133 (August 1966): 26-33. [Interview]

1782. Carles, Philippe. "Marion Brown: un splendide isolement." Jazz Magazine, No. 213 (July 1973): 14+. [Interview]

1783. ________. "Sous l'Oeil du Maitre." Jazz Magazine, No. 151 (February 1968): 13.

1784. ________, and M. C. Ramonet. "Un Autre Brown." Jazz Magazine, No. 148 (November 1967): 13.

1785. Constant, Denis. "Le petit maitre du nouveau jazz." Jazz Magazine, No. 174 (January 1970): 32+.

1786. Constantin, P. "Naissance d'un Musicien." Jazz Hot, No. 240 (April 1968): 25-26.

1787. "Dictionnaire de l'Alto." Jazz Magazine, No. 137 (December 1966): 40. Biographical sketch.

1788. Kofulla, Theodore. "Jazz im Film: Marion Brown." Jazz Podium (August 1972): 23.

1789. Le Bris, M., and B. Vincent. "Marion Brown: l'afrique a vaincu." Jazz Hot, No. 235 (October 1967): 17-21; No. 236 (November 1967): 13-15.

1790. Levitt, Al. "Suite Georgia Brown." Jazz Magazine, No. 326 (February 1984): 22-24; No. 327 (March 1984): 22-23; No. 328 (April 1984): 24+; No. 330 (June 1984): 50-51. [Interview]

1791. "Marion Brown Interview." Jazz Podium (September 1966): 228-230.

1792. Mark, G. "Marion Brown." Jazz Hot, No. 246 (January 1969): 12.

1793. "Pieges pour Marion." Jazz Magazine, No. 148 (November 1967): 26-27.

1794. Schmidt-Joos, Siegfried. "Free Jazz Gallery III: Marion Brown." Neue Musikzeitung, Vol. 18, No. 2 (1969): 9.

1795. Schmitt, Jurgen Abi. "'Ich Will Mich Auf Nichts Festlegen!': Gesprach mit dem musiker, komponisten, lehrer, schriftsteller und maler Marion Brown." Jazz (Basel), Nr. 3 (1984).

Discographies

1796. De Craen, Hugo, and Eddy Janssens. Marion Brown Discography. Brussels: New Think! Publications (E. Jacquemainlaan 54a, 15, 1000 Brussels), 1985. 52p.

1797. Tepperman, Barry. "Marion Brown discography." Jazz Monthly (September 1970): 19-21.

Media Materials

1798. Do You Hear What I'm Trying to Say? Documentary on Brown by Henry English done as a Master's thesis for the New York University Film Institute.

1799. See the Music. Dir. Theodore Kofulla. West German documentary.

BURRELL, DAVE (1940-) - Piano

See also # 610

1800. Carles, Philippe, and Jean-Louis Comolli. Free Jazz, Black Power. 2nd ed. Paris: Editions Galilee, 1979, pp. 380-381.

1801. Feather, Leonard, and Ira Gitler. The Encyclopedia of Jazz in the Seventies. New York: Horizon Press, 1976.

1802. Hazell, Ed. "Burrell, Dave." In The New Grove Dictionary of Jazz. London: Macmillan Press, 1988.

1803. The Penguin Encyclopedia of Popular Music, ed. Donald Clarke. New York: Viking, 1989.

1804. Wilmer, Valerie. As Serious As Your Life. Westport, CT: Lawrence Hill & Co., 1981, p. 262-263.

Articles

1805. Jeske, Lee. "Dave Burrell: Candy Girl's son makes good." down beat (February 1981): 26+. [Interview]

1806. Ley, E. M. "Dave Burrell: Ich male dit den klaengen der Welt." Jazz Podium (November 1985): 12-14. [Interview]

1807. Primack, Bret. "Dave Burrell: a jazz piano odyssey from Hawaii to Harlem." Keyboard Magazine (September 1981): 22+.

1808. Riggins, Roger. "Dave Burrell." Coda (October 1 1980): 16-18. [Interview]

1809. Van Trikt, Ludwig. "Dave Burrell." Cadence (July 1988): 18-26. [Interview]

BUTLER, FRANK (1928-1984) - Drums

1810. Dictionnaire du Jazz, eds. Philippe Carles, et al. Paris: Laffont, 1988.

1811. Feather, Leonard. The Encyclopedia of Jazz in the Sixties. New York: Horizon Press, 1966.

1812. ________, and Ira Gitler. The Encyclopedia of Jazz in the Seventies. New York: Horizon Press, 1976.

1813. Williams, J. Kent. "Butler, Frank." In The New Grove Dictionary of Jazz. London: Macmillan Press, 1988.

Articles

1814. Gerber, Alain. "Butler, a l'ouest le meilleur." Jazz Magazine, No. 131 (June 1966): 48-52.

1815. Wilmer, Valerie. "Frank Butler, l'autre batteur de Coltrane." Jazz Magazine, No. 271 (January 1979): 30, 35, 60.

1816. ________. "What the Butler Plays." Melody Maker (September 4 1976): 35. [Interview]

Obituaries

1817. Cadence (September 1984): 78.
1818. Coda, No. 199 (December 1984): 39.
1819. down beat (November 1984): 14.
1820. Jazz Forum, No. 90 (1984): 22.
1821. Jazz Magazine, No. 332 (Sept-Oct 1984): 5.
1822. Jazz Times (September 1984): 10.

CARL, RUEDIGER (W. Germany) - Saxophone

1823. Brun, Jean-Paul. "A Short Portrait of Rudiger Carl, discographie." Jazz 360o (Sierre, Switzerland), No. 63 (November 1983): 6-9; No. 64 (December 1983): 15-16.

1824. Buzelin, Jean, and Francoise. "Hans Reichel, Rudiger Carl: deux nouvelles voix de la N.M.E." Jazz Hot, No. 359 (March 1979): 22-25. [Interview]

1825. Froese, D. H. "Neuer start nach dem grossen Unbehagen: der saxophonist Ruediger Carl." Jazz Podium (April 1973): 17-19.

CARROLL, BAIKIDA (1947-) - Trumpet

1826. Anderson, Ruth. Contemporary American Composers: a biographical dictionary. 2nd ed. Boston, MA: G.K. Hall, 1982.

1827. Carles, Philippe, and Jean-Louis Comolli. Free Jazz, Black Power. 2nd ed. Paris: Editions Galilee, 1979, p. 381.

1828. Dictionnaire du Jazz, eds. Philippe Carles, et al. Paris: Laffont, 1988.

1829. The New Grove Dictionary of Jazz. London: Macmillan Press, 1988.

1830. Wilmer, Valerie. As Serious As Your Life. Westport, CT: Lawrence Hill & Co., 1981, p. 263.

Articles

1831. Danson, Peter. "Baikida Carroll." Coda, No. 192 (October 1983): 12-16. [Interview]

CARTER, JOHN (1929-) - Clarinet

1832. Kofsky, Frank. "John Carter and Bobby Bradford." In The Black Giants. New York: The World Publishing Co., 1970, pp. 41-46.

1833. Weinstein, Norman. A Night in Tunisia: Imaginations of Africa in Jazz. Metuchen, NJ: Scarecrow Press, 1991. Includes a chapter on John Carter.

Biographical Dictionaries

1834. ASCAP Biographical Dictionary. 4th ed. New York: R.R. Bowker, 1980.

1835. Carles, Philippe, and Jean-Louis Comolli. Free Jazz, Black Power. 2nd ed. Paris: Editions Galilee, 1979, p. 381.

1836. Claghorn, Charles Eugene. Biographical Dictionary of Jazz. Englewood Cliffs, NJ: Prentice-Hall, 1982.

1837. Dictionnaire du Jazz, eds. Philippe Carles, et al. Paris: Laffont, 1988.

1838. Feather, Leonard, and Ira Gitler. The Encyclopedia of Jazz in the Seventies. New York: Horizon Press, 1976.

1839. Hazell, Ed. "Carter, John." In The New Grove Dictionary of Jazz. London: Macmillan Press, 1988.

1840. The Penguin Encyclopedia of Popular Music, ed. Donald Clarke. New York: Viking, 1989.

1841. Priestley, Brian. "Carter, John." In Jazz: The Essential Companion. New York: Prentice Hall Press, 1988.

1842. Wilmer, Valerie. As Serious As Your Life. Westport, CT: Lawrence Hill & Co., 1981, p. 263.

Articles

1843. Be-Bop And Beyond, Vol. 3, No. 3 (May/June 1985). [Interview]

1844. "Dico Disco & Co." Jazz Magazine, No. 298 (June 1981): 37. Biographical sketch.

1845. Endress, Gudrun. "John Carter." Jazz Podium (May 1985): 4-6, 8-9. [Interview]

1846. Giddins, Gary. "John Carter: Bumper Crop." Village Voice (March 21 1989): 86.

1847. James, Michael. "Order and Feeling, Discipline and Fire; An Introduction to the John Carter and Bobby Bradford Quartet." Jazz & Blues (April 1973): 6-9. [Record review]

1848. Jeske, Lee. "John Carter: Clarinet Liberation." down beat (November 1982): 18-20.

1849. Keller, David. "The Carter Years: John Carter - Jazz and America." Jazz Times (July 1984): 12+.

1850. Kern, R. "John Carter." Jazz Podium (June 1981): 34-35.

1851. Levi, Titus. "John Carter's Clarinet: 'Where I Should Have Been All Along.'" Option (March/April 1986): 42-43. [Interview]

1852. Lindenmaier, H. Lukas. "John Carter: Interview." Cadence, Vol. 6, No. 2 (February 1980): 11-12, 43.

1853. Palmer, Robert. "John Carter's Case for the Clarinet." New York Times (June/July ? 1985).

1854. Rouy, Gerard. "John Carter, Californie, Coleman, et Clarinette." Jazz Magazine, No. 279 (October 1979): 38-41, 63, 65.

1855. Weber, Mark. "John Carter." Coda, No. 157 (September/October 1977): 8-10.

Media Materials

1856. The New Music. Directed by Peter Bull and Alex Gibney. 29 min., color. Brief documentary portrait on two of the new music's unsung masters, John Carter and Bobby Bradford. [Available from Rhapsody Films, P.O. Box 179, New York, NY 10014. Tel. 212/243-0152]

CARTER, KENT (1939-) - Bass

See also # 867-875

1857. Carles, Philippe, and Jean-Louis Comolli. Free Jazz, Black Power. 2nd ed. Paris: Editions Galilee, 1979, p. 382.

1858. Dictionnaire du Jazz, eds. Philippe Carles. Paris: Laffont, 1988.

1859. The New Grove Dictionary of Jazz. London: Macmillan Press, 1988.

1860. Wilmer, Valerie. As Serious As Your Life. Westport, CT: Lawrence Hill & Co., 1981, p. 263.

Articles

1861. Case, Brian. "Kent Carter: Interview." Into Jazz (London), Vol. 1, No. 3 (1974).

1862. Loupien, Serge. "Kent Carter: La Beaute de la Basse." Jazz Magazine, No. 262 (February 1978): 29-31. [Interview]

1863. "Les Paradoxes de TOK." Jazz Magazine, No. 283 (February 1980): 50, 68. Includes a brief biography.

CHANCEY, VINCENT (1950-) - French Horn

1864. Van Trikt, Ludwig. "Vincent Chancey." Cadence, Vol. 13, No. 9 (September 1987): 15-20, 24.

1865. Who's Who in Entertainment. 1st ed. 1989-1990.

CHARLES, DENNIS (1933-) (St. Croix/U.S.) - Drums

See also # 69

1866. Jones, LeRoi. "Introducing Dennis Charles." In Black Music. New York: William Morrow, 1967, pp. 87-91.

Biographical Dictionaries

1867. Carles, Philippe, and Jean-Louis Comolli. Free Jazz, Black Power. 2nd ed. Paris: Editions Galilee, 1979, pp. 382-383.

1868. Dictionnaire du Jazz, eds. Philippe Carles, et al. Paris: Laffont, 1988.

1869. Feather, Leonard. The Encyclopedia of Jazz. New ed. New York: Horizon Press, 1960.

1870. The New Grove Dictionary of Jazz. London: Macmillan Press, 1988.

1871. Priestley, Brian. "Charles, Dennis." In Jazz: The Essential Companion. New York: Prentice Hall Press, 1988.

1872. Reclams Jazzfuhrer. 2nd, rev. ed. Stuttgart: Reclam, 1977.

1873. Wilmer, Valerie. As Serious As Your Life. Westport, CT: Lawrence Hill & Co., 1981, p. 263.

Articles

1874. Van Trikt, Ludwig. "Dennis Charles." Cadence, Vol. 13, No. 10 (October 1987): 5-10, 28.

1875. Wilmer, Valerie. "Dennis Charles." Jazz Magazine, No. 223 (1974).

1876. _________. "Looking Back with Charles." Melody Maker (December 25 1971): 22.

CHAUTEMPS, JEAN LOUIS (1931-) (France) - Tenor Saxophone

1877. Carles, Philippe, and Jean-Louis Comolli. Free Jazz, Black Power. 2nd ed. Paris: Editions Galilee, 1979, p. 383.

1878. Dictionnaire du Jazz, eds. Philippe Carles, et al. Paris: Laffont, 1988.

1879. Laplace, Michel. "Chautemps, Jean Louis." In The New Grove Dictionary of Jazz. London: Macmillan Press, 1988.

1880. Roggeman, Willy. "Jean Louis Chautemps." In Free en Andere Jazz-Essays. The Hague: Van Ditmar, 1969, pp. 129-133. [Dutch text]

Articles

1881. "A la recherche du Chautemps perdu." Jazz Magazine, No. 316 (March 1983): 18-21. Photo essay.

1882. Carles, Philippe. "L'Afrique de l'ONJ par Chautemps." Jazz Magazine, No. 351 (June 1986): 30-33. [Interview]

1883. ________, and Francis Marmande. "L'avis a quartre." Jazz Magazine, No. 326 (February 1984): 26-29. [Interview]

1884. "Chautemps chaud devant." Jazz Magazine, No. 376 (November 1988): 22-23. Photo essay.

1885. Chautemps, Jean Louis. "Choisir un Saxophone." Jazz Magazine, No. 279 (October 1979): 52-54.

1886. ________. "La crise de boeuf." Jazz Magazine, No. 249 (November 1976): 10-11.

1887. ________. "Mixture pour un Tombeau de l'Anatole." Musique en Jeu, No. 32 (September 1978): 93-97.

1888. ________. "Sur Coltrane." Jazz Hot, No. 265 (October 1970): 16.

1889. ________, and P. Mefano. "Chautemps au Cirque Mefano." Jazz Magazine, No. 302 (December 1981): 26+. [Dialogue]

1890. "Chautemps suspend ton fol." Jazz Magazine, No. 120 (July 1965): 16-17.

1891. "Dico Disco & Co." Jazz Magazine, No. 298 (June 1981): 38. Biographical sketch.

1892. Gerber, Alain. "Quand Jean-Louis Chautemps cuisine Alain Gerber." Jazz Magazine, No. 254 (May 1977): 28-30; No. 255 (June 1977): 24+. [Interview]

1893. Ginibre, Jean-Louis. "Le Libertaire Controverse." Jazz Magazine, No. 119 (June 1965): 56-61. [Interview]

1894. Loupien, Serge. "Les collages et les colles de Chautemps." Jazz Magazine, No. 282 (January 1980): 52-55, 68. Fourteen musicians comment on Chautemps and his music.

CHEKASIN, VLADIMIR (1947-) (Russia) - Reeds

See also # 3210-3238

1895. Mihaiu, V. "Vladimir Chekasin: the art of absurd." Jazz Forum, No. 115 (1988): 50-52. [Interview]

1896. Ojakaar, Walter. "Chekasin, Vladimir." In The New Grove Dictionary of Jazz. London: Macmillan Press, 1988.

CHERRY, DON (1936-) - Trumpet

See also # 187, 543, 580, 696, 5065-5067, 5111-5116

Works in English

1897. Jones, LeRoi. "Don Cherry." In Black Music. New York: Morrow Paperback Editions, 1967, pp. 162-171.

1898. Jost, Ekkehard. "Don Cherry." In Free Jazz. Graz: Universal Edition, 1974, pp. 133-162. Formal analysis of Cherry's recordings.

1899. Taylor, Arthur. "Don Cherry." In Notes and Tones: Musician to Musician Interviews. New York: Perigee Books, 1982, pp. 175-178. Transcript of an interview conducted in 1971.

Biographical Dictionaries

1900. Baker's Biographical Dictionary of Musicians. 7th ed. revised by Nicolas Slonimsky. New York: Schirmer Books, 1984.

1901. Berry, Lemuel, Jr. Biographical Dictionary of Black Musicians and Music Educators. Guthrie, OK: Educational Book Publishers, 1978.

1902. Carr, Ian. "Cherry, Don." In Jazz: The Essential Companion. New York: Prentice Hall Press, 1988.

1903. Case, Brian, and Stan Britt. The Harmony Illustrated Encyclopedia of Jazz. 3rd ed. New York: Harmony Books, 1987.

1904. Claghorn, Charles Eugene. Biographical Dictionary of American Music. West Nyack, NY: Parker Pub. Co., 1973.

1905. _________. Biographical Dictionary of Jazz. Englewood Cliffs, NJ: Prentice-Hall, 1982.

1906. Feather, Leonard. The Encyclopedia of Jazz. New ed. New York: Horizon Press, 1960.

1907. _________. The Encyclopedia of Jazz in the Sixties. New York: Horizon Press, 1966.

1908. _________, and Ira Gitler. The Encyclopedia of Jazz in the Seventies. New York: Horizon Press, 1976.

1909. Gridley, Mark C. "Cherry, Don." In The New Grove Dictionary of American Music. London: Macmillan Press, 1986.

1910. _________. "Cherry, Don." In The New Grove Dictionary of Jazz. London: Macmillan Press, 1988.

1911. McRae, Barry. "Don Cherry." In The Jazz Handbook. Harlow, Essex, Eng.: Longman, 1987, pp. 189-190.

1912. The Penguin Encyclopedia of Popular Music, ed. Donald Clarke. New York: Viking, 1989.

1913. Southern, Eileen. Biographical Dictionary of Afro-American and African Musicians. Westport, CT: Greenwood Press, 1982.

1914. Wilmer, Valerie. As Serious As Your Life. Westport, CT: Lawrence Hill & Co., 1981, p. 263.

Articles

1915. Appleton, J. "The Making of 'Human Music.'" Music Journal (July 1971): 30+.

1916. Branker, Anthony D. J. "The Free Thinking Don Cherry and Lester Bowie: trumpeters in the tradition?" Jazz Research Papers, Vol. 9 (1989): 25-32.

1917. Brodowski, Pawel. "Don Cherry: Sound Voyager." Jazz Echo, Vol. 9, No. 40 (1979): 1+.

1918. Clark, Ron. "An Interview with Don Cherry on March 17, 1985." Artist and Influence (1986): 11-21.

1919. Cook, Richard. "Don Cherry: A Man and His Communion." The Wire (London), No. 4 (Summer 1983): 12-14.

1920. Davis, Francis. "Don Cherry: A Jazz Gypsy Comes Home." Musician, No. 53 (March 1983): 52-55, 91.

1921. "Don Cherry." BMI (November 1971): 9.

1922. Durfee, Roy. "Don Cherry." Coda, No. 209 (August/September 1986): 11-13.

1923. Goldman, Vivien. "Black Gypsy, Folk Dreams." Melody Maker (September 22 1979): 23. [Interview]

1924. "Good News: Coleman, Don Cherry reunite." down beat (March 20 1969): 14.

1925. Harrison, Max. "Symphony for Improvisors." Jazz Monthly (December 1967): 22+.

1926. Hennessey, Mike. "Cherry's Catholicity: the kaleidoscopic view of jazz." down beat (July 28 1966): 14-15.

1927. _________. "Don Cherry." Melody Maker (April 22 1967): 12.

1928. Houston, Bob. "An Amplifier for the Spirit." Melody Maker (November 23 1968): 10.

1929. Jeske, Lee. "Don Cherry: The Cherry Variations." down beat (June 1983): 18-20.

1930. Johnson, Martin. "Music as a Part of Life." Pulse! (May 1989): 47.

1931. Jones, Andrew. "Global Villager: Don Cherry's Musical Journey." Option, No. 35 (November/December 1990): 64-67, 161. [Interview]

1932. Jones, LeRoi. "Don Cherry: Making It the Hard Way." down beat (November 21 1963): 16+.

1933. _________. "Don Cherry: Trumpet of the Year." African Revolution, Vol. 1, No. 9 (January 1964): 137-141.

1934. Kalbacher, Gene. "Freedom in His Pocket: Don Cherry and the Leaders." Hot House, Vol. 5, No. 5 (May 1986): 14-15.

1935. Knox, Keith. "Don Cherry's Symphony of the Improvisers." Jazz Monthly (August 1967): 5-10. [Interview]

1936. _________. "Whole Earth Jazz." Jazz & Blues (July 1972): 6+.

1937. Lake, Steve. "Don Cherry: Trumpet to Timbuktu." Wire, No. 79 (September 1990): 18-21. [Interview]

1938. McRae, Barry. "Avant Courier: Don Cherry--a disappearing giant?" Jazz Journal (October 1975): 8-9.

1939. Mandel, Howard. "The World in His Pocket: Don Cherry." down beat (July 13 1978): 20+. [Interview]

1940. Occhiogrosso, Peter. "Emissary of the Global Muse: Don Cherry." down beat (October 9 1975): 14+.

1941. Wilmer, Valerie. "Cherry Blossoms Out." Melody Maker (January 2 1971): 14.

1942. _________. "Cherry Chat." Melody Maker (February 12 1972): 12.

1943. Woodard, Josef. "Don Cherry: Globetrotter in the Mainstream." down beat (November 1989): 23-25. [Interview]

Newspaper Articles

1944. Hooper, Joseph. "Not Your Average Family; Three Talented Cherrys--Don, Neneh and Eagle-Eye--and how they grew." New York Times Magazine (December 10 1989): 48-50, 54, 58-59, 122.

1945. Occhiogrosso, Peter. "Getting in Tune with Planet Earth." Soho Weekly News (June 5 1975): 18, 37. [Interview]

1946. Snowden, Don. "Don Cherry's Expedition." Los Angeles Times Calendar (March 10 1985).

Works in French, German and Dutch

1947. Roggeman, Willy. "Don Cherry." In Free en Andere Jazz-Essays. The Hague: Van Ditmar, 1969, pp. 67-72. [Dutch text]

Biographical Dictionaries

1948. Carles, Philippe, and Jean-Louis Comolli. Free Jazz, Black Power. 2nd ed. Paris: Editions Galilee, 1979, p. 383.

1949. Dictionnaire du Jazz, eds. Philippe Carles, et al. Paris: Laffont, 1988.

1950. Reclams Jazzfuhrer. 2nd, rev. ed. Stuttgart: Reclam, 1977.

1951. Tenot, Frank. Dictionnaire du Jazz. Paris: Larousse, 1967.

Articles

1952. Carles, Philippe. "Le Don Paisible." Jazz Magazine, No. 119 (June 1965): 24-29.

1953. _________, and Francis Marmande. "Don Cherry: de la nuit au jour." Jazz Magazine, No. 269 (October 1978): 34-37.

1954. Coudert, Francoise Marie. "Cherry: un nouveau Don?" Jazz Magazine, No. 343 (October 1985): 22-23. [Interview]

1955. "Don Cherry a Notre Dame." Jazz Hot, No. 230 (April 1967): 22-26.

1956. "Don Cherry's Drei Monologe." Jazz Podium (February 1966): 122-126.

1957. Gerber, Alain. "Cherry: pas si free." Jazz Magazine, No. 136 (November 1966): 64-67.

1958. Ioakimidis, Demetre. "Trois Trompettistes de la Nouvelle Vague." Jazz Hot, No. 169 (October 1961): 20-21. [Don Cherry/Freddie Hubbard/Richard Williams]

1959. Le Bec, Jean Yves. "Don Cherry: Complete Communion." Jazz Magazine, No. 365 (1987): 22-23. [Interview]

1960. Pellicciotti, Giacomo. "Don Cherry." Jazz Magazine, No. 247 (September 1976): 29-30. [Interview]

Concert Reviews

1961. "Caught in the Act." down beat (May 15 1969): 30.

1962. "Caught in the Act." down beat (December 12 1968): 33.

1963. Van der Mei, Elizabeth. "Caught in the Act." down beat (November 3 1966): 26.

Discography

1964. Hames, Mike, and Roy Wilbraham. The Music of Don Cherry on Disc and Tape. Ferndown: Hames (16 Pinewood Road, Ferndown, Wimborne, Dorset BH22 9RW, England), 1980-82. 41p.

CHRISTI, ELLEN - Vocals

1965. Christi, Ellen. "Ideological Dimensions of Postmodernist Resistance to Improvised Music." New Observations, No. 65 (March 1989): 18-19. Includes a brief discussion of the New York City Artists' Collective.

1966. Riggins, Roger. "Ellen Christi: Star of Destiny." Coda, No. 224 (February/March 1989): 23-25. [Interview]

CHRISTMANN, GUNTER (1942-) (W. Germany) - Trombone

1967. Dictionnaire du Jazz, eds. Philippe Carles, et al. Paris: Laffont, 1988.

1968. Iannapollo, Robert J. "Christmann, Gunter." In The New Grove Dictionary of Jazz. London: Macmillan Press, 1988.

1969. Noglik, Bert. "Gunter Christmann." In Jazzwerkstatt International. Berlin: Verlag Neue Musik, 1981, pp. 279-297. [Interview]

Articles

1970. Christmann, Gunter. "Free Improvisation." Journal of the International Trombone Association, Vol. 10, No. 2 (1982): 32-34.

1971. _________, and Detlef Schoenenberg. "Nur alte Ahnungen von einer freien Musik." Neue Musikzeitung, Vol. 27, No. 2 (1978): 12.

1972. Froese, D. H. "Das Free Jazz Duo Schoenenberg-Christmann: We Play." Jazz Podium (May 1973): 22-23.

1973. "Guenther Christmann." Newsletter of the International Trombone Association, Vol. 8, No. 3 (1981): 7.

1974. Panke, Werner. "Christmann-Schoenenberg duo." Coda, No. 154 (March-April 1977): 10-11.

1975. _________. "Gunter Christman and Detlef Schonenberg: plunged into musical risks." Jazz Forum, No. 48 (1977): 43-45. [Profile]

1976. Schipper, E. "Wie heisst das Stueck? Christmann-Schoenenberg Duo." Jazz Podium (May 1977): 12-14.

CIRCLE

1977. Claghorn, Charles Eugene. Biographical Dictionary of Jazz. Englewood Cliffs, NJ: Prentice-Hall, 1982, p. 335.

Articles

1978. Constant, Denis. "La Quadrature du Cercle." Jazz Magazine, No. 187 (March 1971): 7.

1979. "Dave Holland forms Circle." Jazz & Pop (February 1971): 25-26.

1980. Smith, Bill. "Song for the Newborn." Coda (March/April 1973): 2-4. Interview with Dave Holland re: Circle.

1981. Wilmer, Valerie. "Caught in the Act: Circle." Melody Maker (May 15 1971): 30. [Concert review]

CLARK, CHARLES E. (1945-1969) - Bass

1982. Carles, Philippe, and Jean-Louis Comolli. Free Jazz, Black Power. 2nd ed. Paris: Editions Galilee, 1979, p. 384.

1983. Claghorn, Charles Eugene. Biographical Dictionary of Jazz. Englewood Cliffs, NJ: Prentice-Hall, 1982.

1984. Feather, Leonard, and Ira Gitler. The Encyclopedia of Jazz in the Seventies. New York: Horizon Press, 1976.

1985. The New Grove Dictionary of Jazz. London: Macmillan Press, 1988.

1986. The Penguin Encyclopedia of Popular Music, ed. Donald Clarke. New York: Viking, 1989.

1987. Wilmer, Valerie. As Serious As Your Life. Westport, CT: Lawrence Hill & Co., 1981, p. 263-264.

Obituaries

1988. down beat (May 29 1969): 10-11.
1989. Jazz Magazine, No. 167 (June 1969): 14.

CLAY, JAMES (1935-) - Tenor Saxophone

1990. Dictionnaire du Jazz, eds. Philippe Carles, et al. Paris: Laffont, 1988.

1991. Feather, Leonard. The Encyclopedia of Jazz. Rev. ed. New York: Horizon Press, 1960.

Articles

1992. Atkins, Jerry. "James Clay: interview." Cadence, Vol. 6, No. 5 (May 1980): 11-14, 83.

1993. Giddins, Gary. "James Clay: Origin of a Tenor." Village Voice (September 19 1989): 82.

1994. Schuller, Tim. "James Clay." Coda, No. 178 (April 1981): 10-12. [Interview]

CLAYTON, JAY - Vocals

See # 694

CLINE, ALEX (1956-) - Percussion

1995. Underwood, Lee. "Profile: Alex and Nels Cline." down beat (July 1981): 52-53.

CLINE, NELS (1956-) - Guitar

1996. Underwood, Lee. "Profile: Alex and Nels Cline." down beat (July 1981): 52-53.

COBBS, CALL, Jr. (1911?-1971) - Piano

1997. Dictionnaire du Jazz, eds. Philippe Carles, et al. Paris: Laffont, 1988.

1998. Wilmer, Valerie. "Conversation with Call." Melody Maker (August 21 1971): 12. [Interview]

Obituaries

1999. down beat (November 11 1971): 9.
2000. Jazz Forum, No. 16 (March-April 1972): 43.
2001. Jazz Hot, No. 279 (January 1972): 28.
2002. Jazz Magazine, No. 195 (December 1971): 9.

COE, TONY (1934-) (Great Britain) - Alto Sax/Clarinet

2003. Carr, Ian. "Coe, Tony." In Jazz: The Essential Companion. New York: Prentice Hall Press, 1988.

2004. Claghorn, Charles Eugene. Biographical Dictionary of Jazz. Englewood Cliffs, NJ: Prentice-Hall, 1982.

2005. Dictionnaire du Jazz, eds. Philippe Carles, et al. Paris: Laffont, 1988.

2006. Fairweather, Digby. "Coe, Tony." In The New Grove Dictionary of Jazz. London: Macmillan Press, 1988.

2007. Feather, Leonard. The Encyclopedia of Jazz. Rev. ed. New York: Horizon Press, 1960.

2008. _________. The Encyclopedia of Jazz in the Sixties. New York: Horizon Press, 1966.

2009. _________, and Ira Gitler. The Encyclopedia of Jazz in the Seventies. New York: Horizon Press, 1976.

2010. Jazz Now: the Jazz Society Centre Guide, ed. Roger Cotterrell. London: Quartet Books, 1976, pp. 121-122.

2011. The Penguin Encyclopedia of Popular Music, ed. Donald Clarke. New York: Viking, 1989.

Articles

2012. Charlton, Hannah. "Tony Coe: existence pacifique." Jazz Magazine, No. 315 (February 1983): 32-33. [Interview]

COHRAN, PHIL (1927-) - Trumpet

2013. Dictionnaire du Jazz, eds. Philippe Carles, et al. Paris: Laffont, 1988.

Articles

2014. Baraka, Imamu Amiri. "Phil Cohran: Affro-Arts Theater." The Cricket: Black Music in Evolution (Newark, NJ), No. 2 (1969): 55-56. Brief discussion of Cohran and his activities in Chicago.

2015. Cohran, Philip. "The Spiritual Musician." Change (Detroit), No. 2 (Spring/Summer 1966): 35-36.

2016. Figi, J. B. "Phil Cohran." down beat (December 1984): 54-55. [Profile]

2017. Quinn, Bill. "Caught in the Act: Philip Cohran." down beat (March 23 1967): 30. [Concert review]

COLEMAN, DENARDO - Drums

See also # 2277-2278, 2287, 2296

2018. Stern, Chip. "Drums." Musician, Player and Listener, No. 40 (February 1982): 59. [Interview]

2019. Williams, Al. "Caught in the Act." down beat (May 15 1969): 30. [Concert review]

COLEMAN, ORNETTE (1930-) - Alto Sax/Violin/Trumpet

See also # 69, 122, 195, 260, 703, 1187, 1596, 1600, 1854, 2508, 2550, 3869, 5113

Works in English

2020. A Collection of [26] Compositions by Ornette Coleman. Preface by Gunther Schuller. New York, 1961. 32p.

2021. An Evening with Ornette Coleman. Live New Departures: programme. London: New Departures, 1965. Souvenir program from Coleman's August 29, 1965 British debut. Includes biographies of Coleman, David Izenson and Charles Moffett. [Held by the Black Arts Research Center (# 7085)]

2022. Litweiler, John. Ornette Coleman: a critical biography. London: Quartet, 1990.

2023. McRae, Barry. Ornette Coleman. London: Apollo Press, 1988. 96p. (Jazz masters series; 14)

Books with Sections on Ornette Coleman

2024. Coleman, Ornette. "Something to Think About." In Free Spirits: Annals of the Insurgent Imagination, eds. Paul Buhle, et al. San Francisco: City Lights Books, 1982.

2025. Collier, Graham. Jazz; a student and teacher's guide. Cambridge: Cambridge University Press, 1975, pp. 69-76.

2026. Giddins, Gary. "Harmolodic Hoedown." In Rhythm-A-Ning: Jazz and Innovation in the 80s. New York: Oxford University Press, 1985, pp. 235-249.

2027. _________. "Ornette Coleman, Continued." In Riding On A Blue Note. New York: Oxford Unversity Press, 1981, pp. 179-189.

2028. Goldberg, Joe. "Ornette Coleman." In Jazz Masters of the Fifties. New York: Da Capo Press, 1983, pp. 228-246. (Reprint of 1965 ed.)

2029. _________. "The Symposium." In Jazz Panorama, ed. Martin Williams. New York: Crowell-Collier, 1962, pp. 292-298. [Satire]

2030. Hentoff, Nat. "Ornette Coleman." In The Jazz Life. New York: The Dial Press, 1961, pp. 222-248.

2031. Jones, Quincy, Martin Williams, Hsio Wen Shih. "Ornette Coleman." In Jazz Panorama, ed. Martin Williams. New York: Crowell-Collier, 1962, pp. 284-298.

2032. Jost, Ekkehard. "Ornette Coleman." In Free Jazz. Graz: Universal Edition, 1974, pp. 44-65.

2033. Kernfeld, Barry. "Harmolodic Theory." In The New Grove Dictionary of Jazz. London: Macmillan Press, 1988.

2034. Litweiler, John. "Ornette Coleman: The Birth of Freedom." In The Freedom Principle: Jazz After 1958. New York: Morrow, 1985, pp. 31-58.

2035. McRae, Barry. "Ornette Coleman." In The Jazz Cataclysm. London: J.M. Dent, 1967, pp. 122-133.

2036. Porter, Lewis. "The 'Blues Connotation' in Ornette Coleman's Music: with some general thoughts on the relation of Blues and Jazz." In Proceedings of the First International Conference on Jazz Studies, ed. Francesco Gerosa. Bologna: Nuova Alfa, 1989.

2037. Rockwell, John. "Free Jazz, Body Music and Symphonic Dreams." In All American Music: Composition in the Late Twentieth Century. New York: Alfred A. Knopf, 1983, pp. 185-197.

2038. Spellman, A. B. "Ornette Coleman." In Four Lives in the Bebop Business. New York: Pantheon Books, 1966, pp. 79-150.

2039. Taylor, Arthur. "Ornette Coleman." In Notes and Tones: Musician to Musician Interviews. New York: Perigee Books, 1982, pp. 32-41. Transcript of a 1969 interview.

2040. Williams, Martin. "Ornette Coleman: Innovation from the Source." In The Jazz Tradition. New and rev. ed. New York: Oxford University Press, 1983, pp. 235-248. Reprint of # 2298.

2041. Wilmer, Valerie. "Ornette Coleman - The Art of the Improvisor." In As Serious As Your Life. Westport, CT: Lawrence Hill & Co., 1981, pp. 60-74. See also, p. 264.

Biographical Dictionaries

2042. ASCAP Biographical Dictionary. 4th ed. New York: R.R. Bowker, 1980.

2043. Baker's Biographical Dictionary of Musicians. 7th ed. revised by Nicolas Slonimsky. New York: Schirmer Books, 1984.

2044. Berry, Lemuel, Jr. Biographical Dictionary of Black Musicians and Music Educators. Guthrie, OK: Educational Book Publishers, 1978.

2045. Carr, Ian. "Coleman, Ornette." In Jazz: The Essential Companion. New York: Prentice Hall Press, 1988.

2046. Case, Brian, and Stan Britt. The Harmony Illustrated Encyclopedia of Jazz. 3rd ed. New York: Harmony Books, 1987.

2047. Claghorn, Charles Eugene. Biographical Dictionary of American Music. West Nyack, NY: Parker Pub. Co., 1973.

2048. _________. Biographical Dictionary of Jazz. Englewood Cliffs, NJ: Prentice-Hall, 1982.

2049. Feather, Leonard. The Encyclopedia of Jazz. Rev. ed. New York: Horizon Press, 1960.

2050. _________. The Encyclopedia of Jazz in the Sixties. New York: Horizon Press, 1966.

2051. _________, and Ira Gitler. The Encyclopedia of Jazz in the Seventies. New York: Horizon Press, 1976.

2052. The Penguin Encyclopedia of Popular Music, ed. Donald Clarke. New York: Viking, 1989.

2053. Roach, Hildred. Black American Music: Past and Present. Malabar, FL: Krieger Pub. Co., 1985, Vol. 1, p. 142.

2054. Schuller, Gunther. "Coleman, Ornette." In The New Grove Dictionary of American Music. London: Macmillan Press, 1986.

2055. _________. "Coleman, Ornette." In The New Grove Dictionary of Jazz. London: Macmillan Press, 1988.

2056. Southern, Eileen. Biographical Dictionary of Afro-American and African Musicians. Westport, CT: Greenwood Press, 1982.

2057. Who's Who Among Black Americans. 6th ed. 1990/91. Detroit: Gale Research, 1990.

2058. Who's Who in Entertainment. 1st ed. 1989-1990.

2059. Williams, Martin. "Coleman, Ornette." In The New Grove Dictionary of Music and Musicians. London: Macmillan Press, 1980, Vol. 4, pp. 526-527.

Interviews

2060. Allen, Gordon F. X. "The Coleman Manifesto." Black Music and Jazz Review [London] (June 1982): 26-27.

2061. Blumenthal, Bob. "Dancing in Our Heads: A Conversation with Ornette Coleman." Boston Phoenix (December 1 1981): 2, 16.

2062. Bourne, Michael. "Ornette's Innerview." down beat (November 22 1973): 16-17.

2063. Bresnick, Adam, and Russell Fine. "Ornette Coleman: interview." Cadence, Vol. 8, No. 9 (September 1982): 5-7, 51.

2064. Case, Brian. "Focus on Sanity." Melody Maker (June 27 1981): 22-23.

2065. Dawbarn, Bob. "Coleman: it's all still over the ridge." Melody Maker (August 14 1965): 6.

2066. ________. "Ornette Stirs It Up Again." Melody Maker (March 2 1968): 10. Interview focusing on Coleman's Royal Albert Hall concert and his difficulties with the British Musicians Union.

2067. DiMartino, Dave. "Ornette Coleman: the symphony continues for legendary player/composer back in spotlight." Billboard (June 25 1988): 33+.

2068. Feather, Leonard. "The Blindfold Test: Ornette Coleman." down beat (January 7 1960): 39-40.

2069. ________. "Interview: Ornette Coleman." down beat (July 1981): 16-19, 62-63.

2070. Goldman, Vivien. "Ornette Coleman: On Feeling Human." New Musical Express (July 10 1982): 16-17, 45.

2071. Hamilton, Andy. "Harmolody Without Tears: Ornette Explains." Wire (London), No. 40 (June 1987): 11.

2072. Hennessey, Mike. "Ornette: there is no bad music, only bad musicians." Melody Maker (December 18 1965): 8.

2073. Korall, Burt. "I've Talked Enough; interviews with Sonny Rollins, John Coltrane and Ornette Coleman." Melody Maker (September 15 1962): 8-9.

2074. Lake, Steve. "Prime Time and Motion." The Wire (London), No. 19 (September 1985): 31-35.

2075. _________. "Stirring Up Ornette's Nest." Melody Maker (August 17 1974): 24.

2076. Lange, Art. "Ornette Coleman and Pat Metheny: Songs of Innocence and Experience." down beat (June 1986): 16+.

2077. Litweiler, John. "...What do you play after you play the melody?" Disc'ribe, No. 3 (Fall 1982): 5-8, 20.

2078. Mandel, Howard. "Ornette Coleman: The Color of Music." down beat (August 1987): 16-19.

2079. _________. "Ornette Coleman: The Creator as Harmolodic Magician." down beat (October 5 1978): 17-19, 75.

2080. Morgenstern, Dan. "Ornette Coleman from the heart." down beat (April 8 1965): 16-18.

2081. Morthland, John. "Roots and Branches." High Fidelity/Musical America (October 1984): 104+.

2082. "Ornette-talk: a 1971 interview." Disc'ribe, No. 1 (Fall 1980): 5.

2083. Robinson, Winston C., Jr. "Ornette Coleman: An Interview with the Guru of Improvisation." East Village Eye (December 1985/January 1986): 29, 66.

2084. Russell, Charlie L. "Ornette Coleman Sounds Off." Liberator (New York), Vol. V, No. 7 (July 1965): 12-15.

2085. "Triple Play." Metronome (September 1960): 38-40. Discussion between O.C. and critics Bill Coss and Robert A. Perlongo concerning recordings by the Ornette Coleman Quartet and others involved in the New Music.

2086. Troupe, Quincy, et al. "Ornette Coleman." Musician, No. 100 (February 1987): 34+.

2087. Wilmer, Valerie. "The Art of Insecurity." Melody Maker (October 30 1971): 18; (November 6 1971): 12.

2088. _________. "Ornette Coleman." Jazz Monthly (May 1966): 13-15.

2089. _________. "Ornette Tells It Like It Is." Jazzbeat, Vol. 2, No. 11 (November 1965): 16-17.

Articles

2090. Abel, Bob. "The Man with the White Plastic Sax." Hi-Fi/ Stereo Review (August 1960): 40-44.

2091. Adderley, Julian. "Cannonball looks at Ornette Coleman." down beat (May 26 1960): 20-21.

2092. "Back From Exile." Time (January 22 1965): 43.

2093. Balliett, Whitney. "Jazz: Ornette." New Yorker, Vol. 58 (August 30 1982): 62-67. Profile of Ornette and Prime Time.

2094. _________. "Jazz: Ornette Coleman's Music." New Yorker (January 16 1965): 117-118+.

2095. _________. "The True Essence." New Yorker (June 4 1960): 33-34.

2096. Batten, J. H. "The Morning Line on Ornette Coleman: Some Critical Motives." Jazz Monthly (May 1960): 12.

2097. Beckett, Alan. "The New Wave in Jazz: Ornette Coleman." New Left Review, No. 31 (May-June 1965): 90-94.

2098. Blumenthal, Bob. "Ornette: An Experimental Music That Has Aged Gracefully." Jazz Magazine (Northport, NY), Vol. 1, No. 3 (Spring 1977): 39-42.

2099. Brown, Marion. "Ornette Revisited." African Revolution, Vol. 1, No. 8 (December 1963): 137-140.

2100. Clay, Carolyn. "Unfinished Symphonies." Esquire (May 1987): 109. Discussion of O.C.'s unfinished symphony "The Oldest Language."

2101. Close, Al. "Ornette Coleman and feeling." Jazz Monthly (January 1961): 9.

2102. Coleman, Ornette. "Ornette Coleman: Harmolodics and the Oldest Language." Musician, Player and Listener, No. 12 (May 1-June 15 1978): 8-10.

2103. _________. "Pro Session: Prime Time for Harmolodics." down beat (July 1983): 54-55.

2104. _________. "To Whom It May Concern." down beat (June 1 1967): 19.

2105. "Coleman, Ornette." Current Biography 1961.

2106. Collier, James Lincoln. "Ornette Coleman." Esquire (December 1981): 90-92.

2107. Cooke, Jack. "Ornette Coleman Revisited." Jazz Monthly (July 1966): 9-11.

2108. Coss, Bill, and Dave Solomon. "A Visit to the King in Queens: an interview with Dizzy Gillespie." Metronome (February 1961): 16. Includes a discussion of Gillespie's reactions to Ornette's music.

2109. Dance, Stanley. "Lightly and Politely: Ornette Ennobled." Jazz Journal (February 1963): 22-24. Column focusing on critical reactions to Ornette Coleman's music.

2110. Davis, Francis. "Ornette's Permanent Revolution." Atlantic (September 1985): 99-102.

2111. Dawbarn, Bob. "The Controversy, Jazz or Concert Artist?" Melody Maker (March 9 1968): 10.

2112. Feather, Leonard. "Naked--that's Ornette Coleman." Melody Maker (September 14 1963): 7.

2113. ________. "Ornette Coleman: From Martyrdom to Freedom." Sepia (September 1981): 47-54.

2114. Fordham, John. "The Enfant Terrible and the Revolutionary Baptist." Time Out [London] (July 7-13 1978): 16.

2115. Fricke, David. "Ornette Coleman's time: with a little help from the Grateful Dead, jazz's eternal iconoclast is finding a new audience." Rolling Stone (March 9 1989): 88+.

2116. Gaskell, P. "Can you follow Ornette?" Jazz Monthly (February 1963): 6-7.

2117. Gleason, Ralph J. "Perspectives." down beat (January 21 1960): 44.

2118. "Good News: Coleman, Don Cherry reunite." down beat (March 20 1969): 14.

2119. Grogan, David. "Ornette Coleman; shunned, scorned and often misunderstood, he remains a restless free spirit on the frontiers of jazz." People (October 13 1986): 108+.

2120. Halperin, Daniel. "Two New Boys." Jazz News, Vol. 5, No. 1 (January 7 1961): 2. Profile of O.C. and Eric Dolphy.

2121. Heckman, Don. "Beyond the Cool." Time (June 27 1960): 56.

2122. ________. "Inside Ornette Coleman." down beat (September 9 1965): 13-15; (December 16 1965): 20-21. Formal analysis of Coleman's music.

2123. ________. "Ornette and the Sixties." down beat (July 2 1964): 58+.

2124. ________. "Ornette Coleman and the Quiet Revolution." Saturday Review (January 12 1963): 78-79.

2125. ________. "Ornette Coleman: the new questions." Jazz Monthly (July 1960): 13+.

2126. ________, and Al Cohn. "Jazzman as Serious Composer: Two Views of Ornette Coleman." American Record Guide (September 1968): 24-25.

2127. Hentoff, Nat. "Ornette Coleman: Biggest Noise in Jazz." Esquire (March 1961): 82-87.

2128. Hoefer, George. "The Hot Box." *down beat* (January 21 1960): 42. Notes on the furor over Coleman's New York debut.

2129. Houston, Bob. "Ornette; the new wave, resident in London." *Melody Maker* (April 16 1966): 6.

2130. Hunt, David C. "Coleman, Coltrane and Shepp: the need for an educated audience." *Jazz & Pop* (October 1968): 18-21.

2131. "Impressive preview of Coleman's magnum opus." *down beat* (August 17 1972): 10-11. Discussion of harmolodic theory.

2132. Jezer, Marty. "Ornette Coleman on the Frontiers of Jazz." *Music Journal* (March 1963): 77-80.

2133. Kofsky, Frank. "Ornette Coleman: 'Jazz' Musician." *Jazz & Pop* (November 1970): 34-35.

2134. Korall, Burt. "Coleman finally wins through." *Melody Maker* (August 6 1960): 13.

2135. Kozak, R. "N.Y. concert dates, film deal for Ornette Coleman." *Billboard* (July 4 1981): 51+.

2136. Maher, Jack. "The School of Jazz; Amazing talent marks third year." *Metronome* (October 1959): 15.

2137. Mandel, Howard. "Ornette Coleman: Return of the Native in His Prime: Caravan of Dreams' Cowtown Debut." *Musician*, No. 64 (February 1984): 28, 30, 32.

2138. _________. "Ornette Coleman and Charlie Haden: Still Something Else!!" *Wire*, No. 40 (June 1987): 31-35.

2139. _________. "Ornette Coleman's Prime Time: Primeval Update." *Down Beat* (November 1990): 30-31.

2140. Mingus, Charlie. "Another View of Coleman." *down beat* (May 26 1960): 21.

2141. Morgenstern, Dan. "Dionysus in New York." *Jazz Journal* (July 1960): 17-19.

2142. _________. "New York Scene." *Jazz Journal* (January 1960): 22-23. Appraisal of Coleman's New York debut and the attendant critical furor.

2143. "Ornette gets grant." *down beat* (May 18 1967): 13. Note on Coleman's receipt of a Guggenheim Foundation grant.

2144. "Ornette in London, plans extended stay out of U.S." *down beat* (September 23 1965): 17.

2145. "Ornette: justification for the faithful." *Melody Maker* (September 4 1965): 6. Report on Coleman's British debut at Fairfield Hall in Croydon, England.

2146. "Ornette, noise or music--the controversy continues." Melody Maker (May 7 1966): 6. Round up of British critical opinion on O.C.'s music.

2147. Palmer, Robert. "Ornette Coleman: A True Original Who Did It His Way." Rolling Stone (May 15 1980): 26.

2148. _________. "Ornette Coleman and the Circle with a Hole in the Middle." Atlantic (December 1972): 91-93.

2149. _________. "Ornette Coleman makes new waves." Rolling Stone (August 25 1977): 17.

2150. Pekar, Harvey. "Tomorrow is the Question." Jazz Journal (November 1962): 8+.

2151. "Play Sincere." Newsweek (January 25 1965): 84.

2152. Point, Michael. "Ornette Coleman." down beat (January 1984): 50.

2153. Postgate, John. "Between you and me." Jazz Monthly (February 1961): 16. Brief dismissal of Coleman's music.

2154. "Readers' Profiles: Ornette Coleman." Jazz Forum, No. 27 (February 1974): 5.

2155. Russell, George, and Martin Williams. "Ornette Coleman and Tonality." Jazz Review, Vol. 3 (June 1960): 6-10.

2156. Seidenberg, R. "Made in America." Horizon (November 1986): 14-16.

2157. "Seven Steps to Jazz." Melody Maker (May 7 1966): 8. Biographical sketch.

2158. Sheridan, Chris. "Aeolus Examined: Ornette Coleman as influence." Jazz Journal International (January 1981): 16-17.

2159. Smith, Frank. "Music and Internal Activities; contacting greatness in art and the music of Ornette Coleman." Jazz (New York), Vol. 5, No. 4 (April 1966): 13-15; No. 5 (May 1966): 22-23, 30; No. 6 (June 1966): 18-20.

2160. Snowden, Don. "Ornette Coleman." Jazz Times (September 1987): 21.

2161. Spellman, A. B. "Genesis of the New Music--III: Ornette Coleman." Evergreen Review (June 1967): 78-80.

2162. Summers, Russ. "Elements of Style: Composer, Musician and Living Legend Ornette Coleman." Option, No. 21 (July/August 1988): 37-40.

2163. Thompson, Vern. "Ornette Coleman." Different Drummer, Vol. 1, No. 15 (January 1975): 25-27.

2164. Troupe, Quincy. "Ornette Coleman: Going Beyond Outside." Musician, Player and Listener, No. 37 (November 1981): 72-77, 80.

2165. Tynan, John. "Ornette: The First Beginning." down beat (July 21 1960): 32, 58.

2166. "U.S. jazzman's permit irks British musicians because of 'concert' tag." Variety (September 15 1965): 65.

2167. Voce, Steve. "No, No Ornette." Jazz Journal (August 1962): 15.

2168. ________. "Put Down That Bamboo Saxophone." Jazz Journal (October 1967): 13. A British critic vents his shock and dismay at jazz critics for naming Coleman to the top alto spot in the 1967 down beat Critics' Poll.

2169. White, Ted. "Ornette Coleman: too much too soon?" Metronome (June 1960): 41.

2170. Whitworth, B. "Ornette Coleman: Innovator or Incompetent?" Holiday (September 1965): 81-82+.

2171. Wild, David. "Ornette Coleman and Prime Time." down beat (August 1982): 56.

2172. Williams, Martin. "No work in U.S. for Ornette?" down beat (June 30 1966): 12, 28.

2173. ________. "Ornette Coleman." ASCAP Today, Vol. 3, No. 2 (1969): 14-16.

2174. ________. "Ornette Coleman - First Impressions." Kulchur, No. 2 (1960): 49-53.

2175. ________. "Ornette Coleman: A New Kind of Improvising." Jazz (New York), Vol. 2, No. 9 (November-December 1963): 24-25. Revised version of an article originally published in International Musician (January 1962): 20+.

2176. ________. "Ornette Coleman: ten years after." down beat (December 25 1969): 24-25; (January 8 1970): 11+.

2177. ________. "Rehearsing with Ornette." Metronome (December 1961): 19+.

2178. Williams, Richard. "Ornette and the Pipes of Joujouka." Melody Maker (March 17 1973): 22-23.

2179. Wilmer, Valerie. "Ornette Coleman: Second Opinion." Melody Maker (September 27 1969): 14.

2180. Zabor, Rafi. "Ornette Coleman." Musician, Player and Listener, Vol. 1, No. 9 (1977): 6+.

Newspaper Articles

2181. Cohen, Debra Rae. "Ornette in Neon." Village Voice (April 6 1982): 69.

2182. Crouch, Stanley. "Ornette Coleman's Jet-Age Jump Band." Village Voice (July 1 1981): 68-69.

2183. Figi, J. B. "Ornette Coleman: A Surviving Elder in the Universal Brotherhood of Those Who Make Music." Chicago Reader (June 22 1973).

2184. Keepnews, Peter. "It's Prime Time for Coleman." New York Post (June 30 1977).

2185. ________. "Ornette Coleman: Aging Revolutionary as Mystery Man." Village Voice (May 26 1975): 114-115.

2186. Palmer, Robert. "Coleman's Jazz-Rock: Pacesetter for the 80's." New York Times (June 24 1981): C17.

2187. ________. "A Revolutionary Returns." New York Times (June 30 1977): C15.

2188. Pareles, Jon. "Hartford Salutes a Jazz Maverick in Ornette Coleman Week." New York Times (June 30 1985): 44.

2189. Rohter, Larry. "Ornette Coleman's Original Quartet Goes Home." New York Times (September 10 1990): C15, C22.

2190. Wilson, John S. "Ornette Coleman is Back After 2 Years; His Repertory Includes Pieces on the Violin." New York Times (January 13 1965).

2191. Zwerin, Michael. "Breaking the Sound Barriers of Jazz." International Herald Tribune (November 7 1984).

Works in French, German, Italian, Dutch and Swedish

2192. Carles, Philippe. "Ornette Coleman." In Le Jazz. Paris: Librairie Larousse, 1977, pp. 90-92.

2193. Endress, Gudrun. "Ornette Coleman." In Jazz Podium. Stuttgart: Deutsche Verlags-Anstalt, 1980, pp. 182-189.

2194. Polillo, Arrigo. "Ornette Coleman." In Jazz: la vicenda e i protagonisti della musica afro-americana. Milano: A. Mondadori, 1983, pp. 743-758.

2195. Roggeman, Willy. "Ornette Coleman." In Free en Andere Jazz-Essays. The Hague: Van Ditmar, 1969, pp. 55-66. [Dutch text]

2196. ________. "De Romantiek van de Free Jazz." In Jazzologie: 1940-1965. Brugge: De Galge, 1965, pp. 193-202. Analysis of Coleman's "Free Jazz" recording. [Dutch text]

Biographical Dictionaries

2197. Carles, Philippe, and Jean-Louis Comolli. Free Jazz, Black Power. 2nd ed. Paris: Editions Galilee, 1979, pp. 384-386.

2198. Dictionnaire du Jazz, eds. Philippe Carles, et al. Paris: Laffont, 1988.

2199. Reclams Jazzfuhrer. 2nd, rev. ed. Stuttgart: Reclam, 1977.

2200. Reda, Jacques. Anthologie des Musiciens de Jazz. Paris: Stock, 1981, pp. 307-310.

2201. Tenot, Frank. Dictionnaire du Jazz. Paris: Larousse, 1967.

Articles

2202. "Alors faut-il le mettre au poteau ou sur un piedestal ce fameux Ornette Coleman?" Comp. by J. R. Masson. Jazz Magazine, No. 6 (November 1960): 26-29.

2203. Arrigoni, A. "Il nuovo jazz di Ornette Coleman." Musica Jazz (January 1961): 14-17.

2204. ________. "Qualcosa sta cambiando." Musica Jazz (June 1960): 17-21.

2205. Binchet, J. P. "Honnette Ornette." Jazz Magazine, No. 119 (June 1965): 20-23.

2206. Carles, Philippe. "Ornette: musique non temperee." Jazz Magazine, No. 212 (June 1973): 16-17. [Interview]

2207. ________. "Ornette Coleman et la centrifugeuse." Jazz Magazine, No. 171 (October 1969): 15.

2208. Cressant, P. "Ornette Coleman." Jazz Hot, No. 254 (October 1969): 6-7.

2209. Dahlgren, C. "Amerikanska Nyheter." Orkester Journalen (December 1959): 10+. [Profile]

2210. ________. "Ornette Coleman, Man Med Problem." Orkester Journalen (February 1963): 10-11.

2211. Delorme, Michel. "Ornette prophete en son pays?" Jazz Hot, No. 224 (octobre 1966): 3.

2212. ________, et al. "Consecration d'Ornette." Jazz Hot, No. 219 (April 1966): 5-6.

2213. "Dictionnaire de l'Alto." Jazz Magazine, No. 137 (December 1966): 41. Biographical sketch.

2214. Endress, Gudrun. "Ornette Coleman." Jazz Podium (September 1978): 10-15. [Interview]

2215. "Les Faces d'Ornette." Jazz Magazine, No. 250 (December 1976): 20-22.

2216. Jost, Ekkehard. "Zur Musik Ornette Colemans." Jazz Research/Jazzforschung, Nr. 2 (1970): 105-124.

2217. Kumpf, Hans. "Skies of America: Ornette Coleman." Jazz Podium (November 1974): 18+.

2218. Le Bec, Jean-Yves. "Ornette Coleman: today is the question." Jazz Magazine, No. 365 (1987): 20-21. [Interview]

2219. Loupien, Serge, and Gerard Rouy. "Ornette au Net." Jazz Magazine, No. 299 (July-August 1981): 56-57. [Interview]

2220. Marmande, Francis. "Ornette Coleman." Jazz Magazine, No. 195 (December 1971): 28-29.

2221. ________. "Retour sur Ornette." Jazz Magazine, No. 207 (January 1973): 14-17.

2222. Mortara, A. "Ancora su Coleman e Giuffre." Musica Jazz (August-September 1960): 17-18.

2223. ________. "Giuffre, Coleman e la rivoluzione." Musica Jazz (June 1960): 14-16.

2224. Nahman, P. "En Angleterre, premier triomphe europeen pour Ornette Coleman." Jazz Hot, No. 213 (October 1965): 7-8.

2225. "Ornette a la Mutualite." Jazz Magazine, No. 129 (April 1966): 13-14.

2226. "Ornette Coleman." Jazz Hot, No. 281 (March 1972): 12-15. Montage of journal excerpts.

2227. Pailhe, J. "1965: the Ornette Coleman trio." Jazz Hot, No. 302 (February 1974): 20-23.

2228. Paudras, Francis. "Nouvelle Dimension: Ornette." Jazz Hot, No. 205 (January 1965): 16-23. [Interview]

2229. Polillo, Arrigo. "Tiro al Piccione." Musica Jazz (July 1960): 20-22.

2230. Quersin, Benoit. "L'homme au plastique entre les dents." Jazz Magazine, No. 8 (December 1962): 48-49.

2231. Reda, Jacques. "Du free jazz prisonnier." Jazz Magazine, No. 128 (March 1966): 9.

2232. "Il ritorno di Coleman." Musica Jazz (March 1965): 13.

2233. Van Peebles, Melvin. "Tete a Tete avec Ornette." Jazz Magazine, No. 125 (December 1965): 26-31.

2234. Williams, Martin. "Ornette Coleman." Jazz Magazine, No. 6 (January 1960): 26-29.

2235. _________. "Ornette, le coupable no. 1?" Jazz Hot (December 1963): 39-41.

2236. Wilson, Peter Niklas. "Kreativitaet als Kategorischer Imperativ: Ornette Coleman und Anthony Braxton komponierten fuer das 'Ensemble Modern'." Neue Zeitschrift fuer Musik (January 1990): 31-32.

2237. _________. "Ornette Coleman: Exkurs 4: Harmolodics--das unbekannte Wesen." Jazz Podium (September 1989): 10-15.

Concert Reviews

2238. Balliett, Whitney. "Jazz Concerts: Composer of the New Thing." New Yorker (February 27 1965): 122-124.

2239. _________. "Jazz Concerts: Haymaker." New Yorker (April 16 1960): 169-170.

2240. _________. "Jazz Concerts: Ornette Coleman at Town Hall." New Yorker (January 5 1963): 80-82.

2241. _________. "Jazz Concerts: Quartet and the Philadelphia Woodwind Quintet at the Village Theatre." New Yorker (March 25 1967): 125-126.

2242. _________. "Jazz Concerts: Victory." The New Yorker (February 6 1960): 116-118.

2243. Cole, Bill. "Caught in the Act." down beat (February 18 1971): 31. Review of a concert at Wesleyan University.

2244. "Combo reviews." Variety (July 26 1961): 55.

2245. Cooke, Jack. "Ornette Coleman at Croydon." Jazz Monthly (October 1965): 22-24.

2246. Coss, Bill. "Caught in the Act." down beat (January 31 1963): 32. Review of a concert at New York's Town Hall.

2247. Craddock, J. "Ornette Coleman at the Five Spot." Jazz Journal (April 1960): 25+.

2248. Cuscuna, Michael. "Caught in the Act: Ornette Coleman Quartet, Town Hall, Philadelphia." down beat (September 5 1968): 30.

2249. Dance, Stanley. "First Time in New York." Jazz Journal (February 1960): 23. Review of the debut performance of the O.C. Quartet at New York's Five Spot club.

2250. Fiofori, Tam. "Response: Performances - "An Evening with Ornette Coleman." Change (Detroit), No. 1 (Fall/Winter 1965): 21-23. Review of O.C.'s Croydon concert in Great Britain.

2251. Harrison, Max. "Ornette Coleman in Paris." Melody Maker (February 26 1966): 23.

2252. Heckman, Don. "Ornette '65." Jazz (New York), Vol. 4, No. 3 (March 1965): 24. Report on Coleman's return to the New York jazz scene with a Village Vanguard appearance.

2253. Hoefer, George. "Caught in the Act." down beat (January 7 1960): 40-41. Review of Coleman's New York debut performance at the Five Spot club.

2254. Klee, Joe. "Caught in the Act." down beat (February 1 1973): 30.

2255. Kofsky, Frank. "It Happened in Monterey." Jazz Journal (November 1960): 2-3. Review of a Monterey Jazz Festival performance.

2256. McRae, Barry. "Emotion Modulation: Ornette Coleman in Concert." Jazz Journal (April 1968): 5.

2257. ________. "Ornette Coleman live." Jazz Journal (October 1965): 8-9.

2258. ________. "The Ornette Coleman trio at Ronnie Scott's club." Jazz Journal (June 1966): 9.

2259. Mitchell, S. "Caught in the Act: Ornette Coleman." down beat (November 12 1970): 34.

2260. Morgenstern, Dan. "Caught in the Act." down beat (February 25 1965): 15.

2261. ________. "Caught in the Act: Ornette Coleman-Philadelphia Woodwind Quintet." down beat (May 18 1967): 24.

2262. ________. "Heard and Seen." Metronome (October 1961): 7.

2263. ________. "Jazz by Schuller." Metronome (August 1960): 43-45. Review of a performance by Coleman and Eric Dolphy on a program organized by Gunther Schuller.

2264. ________. "News and Views: Ornette's concert." Jazz (New York), Vol. 2, No. 2 (Feb 1963): 14-15.

2265. ________. "Ornette Meets Dizzy." Metronome (March 1961): 24-25. Report on a December 1960 concert at New York's Jazz Gallery at which O.C. played with Dizzy Gillespie.

2266. Norris, John. "Heard and Seen: Ornette Coleman, Town Tavern, Toronto." Coda, Vol. 9, No. 11 (1971): 41-42.

2267. Occhiogrosso, Peter. "Ornette - Miles of the Eighties." Melody Maker (July 30 1977): 32-33. Review of a Newport Jazz Festival appearance.

2268. "Ornette to premiere string quartet, R & B trio." down beat (January 3 1963): 11-12. Preview of Coleman's Town Hall concert.

2269. Schonfield, Victor. "Caught in the Act." down beat (July 14 1966): 31+.

2270. White, Ted. "Ornette and Jimmy." Metronome (September 1960): 44. Review of a Five Spot performance by Coleman and Jimmy Giuffre.

2271. Williams, Martin. "Caught in the Act." down beat (May 15 1969): 30.

2272. Wilmer, Valerie. "Caught in the Act: Ornette Coleman, Royal Albert Hall." down beat (May 2 1968): 32-33.

2273. Wilson, John S. "Ornette Coleman Heard in Concert." New York Times (April 5 1960): 45. Review of a concert at New York's Circle in the Square theatre.

2274. Zwerin, Michael. "A State of Mind; the excellence of Ornette." down beat (March 9 1967): 16. Discussion of an O.C. performance at the Village Theater in New York.

Record Reviews

See also # 2085, 2196

2275. Balliett, Whitney. "Jazz Records." New Yorker (October 28 1961): 164-168.

2276. Broomer, Stuart. "Ornette Coleman: Outlook of the Sixties." Coda (October/November 1966): 2-5.

2277. Coleman, Ornette, Pete Welding, Shelly Manne and Cannonball Adderley. "'Round 'The Empty Foxhole.'" down beat (November 2 1967): 16-17. Comments by Coleman, critic Pete Welding and musicians Manne and Adderley on Coleman's lp "The Empty Foxhole", the recorded debut for Coleman's son, Denardo.

2278. Cooke, Jack. "Ornette and Son." Jazz Monthly, Vol. 13 (July 1967): 13-15.

2279. DeMichael, Don. "In Review: This Is Our Music." down beat (May 11 1961): 25.

2280. Farmer, Art. "Something Else!!!" Jazz Review, Vol. 2 (July 1959): 18.

2281. Gleason, Ralph G. "In Review: Change of the Century." down beat (August 18 1960): 25.

2282. Harrison, Max. "Coleman and the Consequences." Jazz Monthly (June 1966): 10-15. Review of 6 ESP lps.

2283. ________. "Two from Coleman." Jazz Monthly (February 1969): 17+.

2284. Heckman, Don. "Ornette Coleman's Legacy to Black Rock." High Fidelity (January 1983): 84-85. Review of Coleman's lp "Broken Shadows."

2285. James, Michael. "Some Interesting Contemporaries." Jazz & Blues (January 1973): 13. Discussion of O.C.'s Contemporary lps.

2286. Jones, Quincy. "Something Else!!!" Jazz Review, Vol. 2 (May 1959): 29.

2287. Kart, Larry. "Record Reviews: Ornette at 12." down beat (June 12 1969): 21.

2288. Litweiler, John. "Record Reviews: New York is Now!" down beat (January 23 1969): 21.

2289. McRae, Barry. "Avant Courier: Kaleidoscope." Jazz Journal (February 1973): 10. Survey of Coleman's recorded work.

2290. Martin, Terry. "Ornette Coleman on Atlantic." Jazz Monthly (May 1965): 21-22.

2291. ________. "The Plastic Muse." Jazz Monthly, Vol. 10 (May 1964): 13-15; (June 1964): 14-18; (August 1964): 20-21; (September 1964): 5-6; Vol. 11 (May 1965): 21+.

2292. Mathieu, Bill. "Record Reviews: At the 'Golden Circle' Stockholm, Vol. 1." down beat (March 23 1966): 31.

2293. "Two Views of Ornette Coleman." American Record Guide (August 1960): 1017.

2294. Tynan, John. "Record Reviews: Free Jazz." down beat (January 18 1962): 28.

2295. Welding, Pete. "Record Reviews: At Town Hall." down beat (January 27 1966): 30.

2296. Williams, Martin. "Ornette Coleman: Father and Son." Saturday Review (July 29 1967): 45. Review of "The Empty Foxhole."

2297. ________. "Ornette Coleman in Stockholm." Saturday Review (June 11 1966): 83+.

2298. ________. "Ornette Coleman: The Meaning of Innovation." Evergreen Review (November-December 1960): 123-133.

2299. Williams, Richard. "Ornette in the Studio." Melody Maker (April 22 1972): 21. Report from the studio on the recording of Coleman's "Skies of America" with the London Symphony Orchestra.

Discographies

2300. Ruppli, Michael. "Discographie d'Ornette Coleman." Jazz Hot, No. 334 (February 1977): 24-25.

2301. Wild, David, and Michael Cuscuna. Ornette Coleman, 1958-1979: A Discography. Ann Arbor, MI: Wildmusic, 1980. 76p.

Bibliographies

2302. Wolfe, Alain, comp. Ornette Coleman: periodical articles [1959-1977]. Chicago: Chicago Public Library, Fine Arts Division, Music Section (78 East Washington St., Chicago, IL 60602), 1979. 7p. Typescript.

Media Materials

2303. David, Moffett, & Ornette: The Ornette Coleman Trio 1966. 26 min., b&w. Dir. Dick Fontaine. Portrait of the Ornette Coleman Trio of the mid-60s--David Izenson, Charles Moffett and Ornette Coleman. [Available from Rhapsody Films, P.O. Box 179, New York, NY 10014. Tel. 212/243-0152.]

2304. Ornette: Made in America. Dir. Shirley Clarke.

2305. Giddins, Gary. "Film: Ornate Coleman." Village Voice (February 25 1986): 62.

2306. Maslin, Janet. "Film: "Ornette," portrait of musician." New York Times (February 21 1986): C8.

2307. Snowden, Don. "Jazz Portrait 'Ornette' 20 Years in the Making." Los Angeles Times (January 22 1986): Part IV, p. 2.

COLEMAN, STEVE (1956-   ) - Alto Saxophone

See also # 585, 587

2308. Davis, Francis. "Bronx Cheer." In Outcats: Jazz Composers, Instrumentalists, and Singers. New York: Oxford University Press, 1990, pp. 238-241. [Profile]

2309. Dictionnaire du Jazz, eds. Philippe Carles, et al. Paris: Laffont, 1988.

2310. McRae, Barry. "Steve Coleman." In The Jazz Handbook. Harlow, Essex, Eng.: Longman, 1987, p. 234.

Articles

2311. Bennett, Karen. "Steve Coleman: Rhythm-A-Lingo." Wire, No. 81 (November 1990): 28-31. [Interview]

2312. Goatty, F., and D. Michel. "Un Nomme Coleman." Jazz Magazine, No. 377 (Decembre 1988): 22-23. [Interview]

2313. Gratzer, W. "Steve Coleman." Jazz Podium (November 1985): 8-9. [Interview]

2314. Lewis, Steve. "Steve Coleman: A Single Mind." Wire, No. 41 (July 1987): 26-29.

2315. McElfresh, Suzanne. "Afunk-Garde: genre bashing." Ear, Vol. 12, No. 2 (April 1987): 22-23.

2316. Macnie, Jim. "Greg Osby and Steve Coleman." Musician (January 1989): 18, 20, 24.

2317. Mandel, Howard. "Steve Coleman: music for life." down beat (February 1988): 20-22.

2318. Van Trikt, Ludwig. "Steve Coleman." Cadence, Vol. 12, No. 8 (August 1986): 20-23. [Interview]

COLSON, ADEGOKE STEVE (1949-) - Piano

2319. "Adegoke Steve Colson and Iqua Colson." Jazz World Index, No. 52 (April 1982): 3.

2320. International Who's Who in Music and Musicians' Directory. 12th ed. 1990/91.

COLSON, IQUA [Kristine Browne] - Vocals

2321. "Adegoke Steve Colson and Iqua Colson." Jazz World Index, No. 52 (April 1982): 3.

COLTRANE, ALICE [Alice McLeod] (1937-) - Piano/Harp

See also # 694, 704

2322. Rivelli, Pauline. "Alice Coltrane." In The Black Giants. New York: World Publishing Co., 1970, pp. 122-126. [Interview] [Reprint of # 2350]

Biographical Dictionaries

2323. Case, Brian, and Stan Britt. The Harmony Illustrated Encyclopedia of Jazz. 3rd ed. New York: Harmony Books, 1987.

2324. Claghorn, Charles Eugene. Biographical Dictionary of Jazz. Englewood Cliffs, NJ: Prentice-Hall, 1982.

2325. _________. "McLeod, Alice." In Biographical Dictionary of American Music. West Nyack, NY: Parker Pub. Co., 1973.

2326. Cohen, Aaron I. International Encyclopedia of Women Composers. 2nd ed. Revised and Enlarged. New York: Books & Music (USA), 1987.

2327. Dictionnaire du Jazz, eds. Philippe Carles, et al. Paris: Laffont, 1988.

2328. Feather, Leonard. The Encyclopedia of Jazz in the Sixties. New York: Horizon Press, 1966.

2329. ________, and Ira Gitler. The Encyclopedia of Jazz in the Seventies. New York: Horizon Press, 1976.

2330. Handy, D. Antoinette. Black Women in American Bands and Orchestras. Metuchen, NJ: Scarecrow Press, 1981, pp. 192-193.

2331. Hazell, Ed. "Coltrane, Alice." In The New Grove Dictionary of Jazz. London: Macmillan Press, 1988.

2332. "McLeod, Alice (Coltrane)." In Reclams Jazzfuhrer. 2nd, rev. ed. Stuttgart: Reclam, 1977.

2333. Priestley, Brian. "Coltrane, Alice." In Jazz: The Essential Companion. New York: Prentice Hall Press, 1988.

2334. Southern, Eileen. Biographical Dictionary of Afro-American and African Musicians. Westport, CT: Greenwood Press, 1982.

2335. Who's Who Among Black Americans. 6th ed. 1990/91. Detroit: Gale Research, 1990.

2336. Wilmer, Valerie. As Serious As Your Life. Westport, CT: Lawrence Hill & Co., 1981, p. 264.

Articles

2337. "Alice Coltrane sues church." Melody Maker (November 21 1981): 4. See also # 2348.

2338. Berendt, Joachim Ernst. "Alice Coltrane." Jazz Forum, No. 17 (June 1972): 54-56.

2339. Bernard, M. "Le Chemin d'Alice." Jazz Magazine, No. 218 (January 1974): 14+.

2340. Dews, Angela. "Alice Coltrane." Essence (December 1971): 42.

2341. Endress, Gudrun. "Lady Trane." Jazz Podium (February 1973): 16-19.

2342. "Impulse, Mrs. Coltrane in Legacy Agreement." down beat (September 5 1968): 13.

2343. "Impulse Records inks John Coltrane's widow to exclusive disk deal." Variety (July 24 1968): 44.

2344. "Impulse Records signs Alice Coltrane." Jazz & Pop, Vol. 7 (September 1968): 14.

2345. "John's spirit lives on in Alice." Soul, Vol. 8 (June 11 1973): 11.

2346. Lerner, D. "Alice Coltrane: Jazz Pianist, Inspirational Organist." Keyboard, Vol. 8, No. 11 (1982).

2347. Nickerson, R. "Alice Coltrane." Soul Illustrated, Vol. 3, No. 5 (1972): 46-49.

2348. "Notes on People. Coltrane's Widow Sues." New York Times (October 24 1981). Report on Alice Coltrane's suit against the San Francisco-based One Mind Temple Evolutionary Transitional Church of Christ for using the Coltrane name without authorization. See also # 2337.

2349. "The Results of My Music I Leave to God." Soul, Vol. 8 (January 7 1974): 10.

2350. Rivelli, Pauline. "Alice Coltrane." Jazz & Pop, Vol. 7, No. 9 (September 1968): 26-30. [Reprinted in # 2322]

Media Materials

2351. Marian McPartland's Piano Jazz, No. 30: Alice Coltrane. 59 min. Pianist Alice Coltrane discusses her career with interviewer Marian McPartland and plays selected songs. [Held by the Rodgers & Hammerstein Collection at Lincoln Center (# 7097)]

COLTRANE, JOHN (1926-1967) - Tenor/Soprano Saxophone

See also # 109, 122, 195, 795, 805, 1815, 1888, 2345, 3330, 4088, 4103, 4179, 4243, 6663, 6665, 6864

Works in English

2352. Aebersold, Jamey. John Coltrane: play-a-long book and record sets, Volumes 27 & 28. New Albany, IN: J. Aebersold (P.O. Box 1244-D, New Albany, IN 47151-1244), 1983. 2 books and lps.

2353. Baker, David. The Jazz Style of John Coltrane: a musical and historical perspective. Lebanon, IN: Studio P/R, 1980.

2354. Cole, Bill. John Coltrane. New York: Schirmer Books, 1976. 264p.

2355. Gellat, Tim. About John Coltrane; a profile of his life and music. New York: New York Jazz Museum, 1974. 23p.

2356. Harper, Michael S. Dear John, Dear Coltrane: poems. Urbana: University of Illinois Press, 1985. 88p. (Repr. of 1970 ed.)

2357. Priestley, Brian. John Coltrane. London: Apollo, 1987. 96p.

2358. Simpkins, C. O. Coltrane: A Biography. Baltimore, MD: Black Classic Press, 1989. 287p. (Reprint of 1975 ed.)

2359. Thomas, J. C. Chasin' The Trane: The Music and Mystique of John Coltrane. New York: Doubleday, 1975. 252p.

2360. White, Andrew. Trane 'n Me: A Semi-Autobiography. A Treatise on the Music of John Coltrane. Washington, D.C.: Andrew's Musical Enterprises, 1981. 64p.

2361. ________. The Works of John Coltrane. Washington, D.C.: Andrew's Music (4830 South Dakota Ave., N.E., Washington, D.C. 20017), n.d. 10 vols. Transcriptions of 421 of Coltrane's solos.

Books with Sections on John Coltrane

2362. Berendt, Joachim-Ernst. "Coltrane and After." In Jazz: A Photo History. Translated by William Odom. New York: Schirmer Books, 1979, pp. 217-225.

2363. Goldberg, Joe. "John Coltrane." In Jazz Masters of the Fifties. New York: Da Capo Press, 1983, pp. 189-212. (Reprint of 1965 ed.)

2364. Jost, Ekkehard. Free Jazz. Graz: Universal Edition, 1974, pp. 17-34, 84-104.

2365. Kofsky, Frank. Black Nationalism and the Revolution in Music. Revised ed. New York: Pathfinder Press, 1983. (Orig. 1970)

2366. Lenz, Gunter H. "Black Poetry and Black Music: History and Tradition: Michael Harper and John Coltrane." In History and Tradition in Afro-American Culture, ed. Gunter H. Lenz. Frankfurt: Campus, 1984, pp. 277-326.

2367. Litweiler, John. "John Coltrane: The Passion for Freedom." In The Freedom Principle: Jazz After 1958. New York: Morrow, 1984, pp. 80-104.

2368. McRae, Barry. "John Coltrane." In The Jazz Cataclysm. London: J.M. Dent, 1967, pp. 100-110.

2369. Weinstein, Norman. A Night in Tunisia: Imaginations of Africa in Jazz. Metuchen, NJ: Scarecrow Press, 1991. Includes a chapter on John Coltrane.

2370. Williams, Martin. "John Coltrane: A Man in the Middle." In The Jazz Tradition. New and rev. ed. New York: Oxford University Press, 1983, pp. 225-234. Reprint of # below.

2371. Wilmer, Valerie. "John Coltrane - A Love Supreme." In As Serious As Your Life. Westport, CT: Lawrence Hill & Co., 1981, pp. 31-45. See also, p. 264.

Biographical Dictionaries

2372. Baker's Biographical Dictionary of Musicians. 7th ed. revised by Nicolas Slonimsky. New York: Schirmer Books, 1984.

2373. Berry, Lemuel, Jr. Biographical Dictionary of Black Musicians and Music Educators. Guthrie, OK: Educational Book Publishers, 1978.

2374. Case, Brian, and Stan Britt. The Harmony Illustrated Encyclopedia of Jazz. 3rd ed. New York: Harmony Books, 1987.

2375. Claghorn, Charles Eugene. Biographical Dictionary of American Music. West Nyack, NY: Parker Pub. Co., 1973.

2376. ________. Biographical Dictionary of Jazz. Englewood Cliffs, NJ: Prentice-Hall, 1982.

2377. Feather, Leonard. The Encyclopedia of Jazz. Rev. ed. New York: Horizon Press, 1960.

2378. ________. The Encyclopedia of Jazz in the Sixties. New York: Horizon Press, 1966.

2379. ________, and Ira Gitler. The Encyclopedia of Jazz in the Seventies. New York: Horizon Press, 1976.

2380. Kernfeld, Barry. "Coltrane, John." In The New Grove Dictionary of American Music. London: Macmillan Press, 1986.

2381. ________. "Coltrane, John." In The New Grove Dictionary of Jazz. London: Macmillan Press, 1988.

2382. The Penguin Encyclopedia of Popular Music, ed. Donald Clarke. New York: Viking, 1989.

2383. Priestley, Brian. "Coltrane, John." In Jazz: The Essential Companion. New York: Prentice Hall Press, 1988.

2384. Southern, Eileen. Biographical Dictionary of Afro-American and African Musicians. Westport, CT: Greenwood Press, 1982.

Dissertations and Theses

2385. Cole, William Shadrack. "The Style of John Coltrane, 1955-1967." Dissertation (Ph.D.) Wesleyan University, 1974.

2386. Grey, De Sayles R. "John Coltrane and the 'Avant-Garde' Movement in Jazz History." Dissertation (Ph.D.) University of Pittsburgh, 1986. 175p.

2387. Kelly, Michael P. "Harmonic Formulae and Other Compositional Devices Found in the Music of John Coltrane Before 1961." Thesis (M.A.) S.U.N.Y. at Buffalo, 1987.

2388. Kernfeld, Barry Dean. "Adderley, Coltrane and Davis at the Twilight of Bop: The Search for Melodic Coherence (1958-1959)." Dissertation (Ph.D.) Cornell, 1981. 340p.

2389. Kofsky, Frank. "Black Nationalism and the Revolution in Music: Social change and stylistic development in the art of John Coltrane and others, 1954-1967." Dissertation (Ph.D.) University of Pittsburgh, 1973. 959p.

2390. Porter, Lewis R. "John Coltrane's Music of 1960 through 1967: Jazz Improvisation as Composition." Dissertation (Ph.D.) Brandeis University, 1983. 329p.

Interviews

2391. Blume, A. "An Interview with John Coltrane." Jazz Review, Vol. 2 (January 1959): 25+.

2392. Coleman, Ray. "Coltrane: 'Next thing for me--African rhythms'." Melody Maker (July 11 1964): 6.

2393. Coltrane, John, and Don DeMichael. "Coltrane on Coltrane." down beat (September 29 1960): 26-27. [Reprinted in down beat (July 20 1972): 30-31; and (July 12 1979): 17, 53].

2394. Dawbarn, Bob. "I'd like to play your clubs; interview with John Coltrane." Melody Maker (November 25 1961): 8.

2395. Delorme, Michael, and Claude Lenissois. "Interview with John Coltrane." Trans. by David Sinclair. Change (Detroit), No. 2 (Spring/Summer 1966): 67-69. [Translation of # 2480]

2396. DeMichael, Don. "John Coltrane and Eric Dolphy Answer the Jazz Critics." down beat (April 12 1962): 20-23. [Reprinted down beat (July 12 1979): 16, 52-53].

2397. Feather, Leonard. "For Coltrane the Time is Now." Melody Maker (December 19 1964): 10.

2398. ________. "Honest John." down beat (February 19 1959): 39. [Blindfold Test]

2399. Hennessey, Mike. "Coltrane: dropping the ball and chain from jazz." Melody Maker (August 14 1965): 6.

2400. Kofsky, Frank. "Brief interview with John Coltrane." Jazz & Pop, Vol. 7 (March 1968): 22-23. Excerpt from an interview done in Japan.

2401. ________. "John Coltrane." Jazz & Pop, Vol. 6 (September 1967): 23-31.

2402. Korall, Burt. "I've Talked Enough; interviews with Sonny Rollins, John Coltrane and Ornette Coleman." Melody Maker (September 15 1962): 8-9.

2403. Wilmer, Valerie. "Conversation with Coltrane." Jazz Journal (January 1962): 1-2.

Articles

2404. "About John Coltrane (as viewed by Bob Thiele)." Jazz (New York), Vol. 5, No. 8 (August 1966): 22.

2405. Baker, David. "Pro Session: Woodwinds: Analysis of the Music of John Coltrane." down beat (October 1979): 70-72.

2406. _________. "Profile of a Giant." Educator, Vol. 11, No. 3 (1979): 10-13.

2407. Benston, Kimberly W. "Late Coltrane: A Remembering of Orpheus." Massachusetts Review (Winter 1977): 770-781.

2408. Blumenthal, Bob. "John Coltrane." New Republic (February 12 1977): 26-28.

2409. Carno, Zita. "The Style of John Coltrane." Jazz Review, Vol. 2 (October 1959): 17-21; (November 1959): 13-17.

2410. Case, Brian. "The Trane now waiting on p. 30..." New Musical Express (January 25 1975): 30. Career overview.

2411. Chapman, Abraham. "An Interview with Michael S. Harper." Arts in Society, Vol. 11, No. 3 (Fall/Winter 1974): 466-470. In depth discussion of the influence of Coltrane's music on poet Michael Harper's writings.

2412. Coda (May/June 1968). Special Coltrane issue.

2413. Coltrane, Alice. "Remembering...John Coltrane." Essence (November 1987): 73.

2414. "Coltrane--anti-jazz or the wave of the future?" Melody Maker (September 28 1963): 11.

2415. Coltrane, John. "A Love Supreme." Jazz (New York), Vol. 4, No. 3 (1965): 16-17. [Poem]

2416. Cook, Richard. "John Coltrane: Everytime I Hear a Sound." Wire, No. 22 (December 1985): 30-33.

2417. _________. "John Coltrane: A Spiritual 'Trane Ride from the Birdland Blues to A Love Supreme; Tribute to a Jazz Giant." New Musical Express (December 25 1982): 60-62, 77.

2418. Cooke, Jack. "Late Coltrane." Jazz Monthly (January 1970): 2-6.

2419. Cordle, Owen. "The Soprano Saxophone: from Bechet to Coltrane to Shorter." down beat (July 20 1972): 14-15.

2420. Crowder, Ralph L. "The Legacy of a Jazz Giant: John Coltrane." Black Collegian (January-February 1985): 216-228.

2421. Dawbarn, Bob. "Coltrane: Following Sonny's Steps?" Melody Maker (October 15 1966): 8. On rumors that Coltrane had taken a hiatus from the jazz scene, a la Sonny Rollins, to reassess his musical options.

2422. Douglas, Robert L. "From Blues to Protest/ Assertiveness: The Art of Romare Bearden and John Coltrane." International Review of African American Art, Vol. 8, No. 2 (1988): 28-43.

2423. Edey, Mait. "John Coltrane." Jazz Review, Vol. 3 (May 1960): 22+.

2424. Feather, Leonard. "Coltrane; does it now mean a thing, if it ain't got that swing?" Melody Maker (April 16 1966): 6. Report on the personnel changes taking place in Coltrane's ensemble.

2425. Ficarra, Frank. "Coltrane, Rollins, and the Ulysses Spirit." Jazz Research Papers, Vol. 6 (1986): 92-95.

2426. "Finally Made." Newsweek (July 24 1961): 64.

2427. Gibson, J. "John Coltrane: the formative years." Jazz Journal (June 1960): 9-10.

2428. Gitler, Ira. "'Trane on the Track." down beat (October 16 1958): 16-17. Biographical portrait.

2429. Hentoff, Nat. "John Coltrane: challenges without end." International Musician (March 1962): 12-13.

2430. Hultin, Randi. "I Remember 'Trane." Down Beat's Music '68, Vol. 13 (1968): 104-105.

2431. Hunt, David C. "Coleman, Coltrane and Shepp: the need for an educated audience." Jazz & Pop (October 1968): 18-21.

2432. Kernfeld, Barry. "Two Coltranes." Annual Review of Jazz Studies, Vol. 2 (1983): 7-66.

2433. Kofsky, Frank. "Bob Thiele talks to Frank Kofsky about John Coltrane." Coda (May/June 1968): 2-10.

2434. ________. "Revolution, Coltrane and the Avant-Garde." Jazz (New York), Vol. 4, No. 7 (1965): 13-16; No. 8 (1965): 18-22.

2435. Kopulos, Gordon. "John Coltrane: retrospective perspective." down beat (July 22 1971): 14+.

2436. Lees, Gene. "Coltrane--Man and Music." Jazz News (September 27 1961): 5-6.

2437. ________. "Consider Coltrane." Jazz (New York), Vol. 2, No. 2 (February 1963): 7.

2438. Lenz, Guenter H. "The Politics of Black Music and the Tradition of Poetry: Amiri Baraka and John Coltrane." Jazz Research/Jazzforschung, Vol. 18 (1986): 193-231.

2439. Liebman, Dave. "A look at John Coltrane groups." Educator, Vol. 11, No. 3 (1979): 14-16.

2440. Loftus, Alistair. "Thoughts of 'Trane." Jazz Journal International (March 1978): 14-15.

2441. Logan, Wendell. "The Case of Mr. John Coltrane: a compositional view." Numus West, Vol. 2, No. 2 (1975): 40-45.

2442. Palmer, Bob. "From the Inside Out: Bob Palmer interviews Bob Thiele." Coda, Vol. 10, No. 1 (June 1971): 31-34. Includes a detailed discussion of the relationship between Coltrane and his ABC-Impulse producer Bob Thiele.

2443. Pinckney, Warren R., Jr. "Rhythmic Structuralism in the Music of John Coltrane." Jazz Research Papers, Vol. 4 (1984): 88-97.

2444. Schoemaker, Bill. "Ad Lib: The Coltrane Legacy." down beat (September 1986): 63, 61.

2445. "Seven Steps to Jazz." Melody Maker (May 14 1966): 8. Biographical sketch.

2446. Simpkins, Cuthbert O. "Last Chord." Coda, No. 151 (October 1976): 10-11. Response to a review of Simpkins' Coltrane: A Biography (# 2358) by Ron Welburn.

2447. Spellman, A. B. "Genesis of the New Music--I: Coltrane." Evergreen Review (February 1967): 81-83.

2448. Stepto, Robert B. "Michael Harper's Extended Tree: John Coltrane and Sterling Brown." The Hollins Critic, Vol. XIII, No. 3 (June 1976). 16p.

2449. "Still a force in '79: musicians talk about John Coltrane." down beat (July 12 1979): 20+.

2450. Stone, Reppard. "The Harmonic Symmetry in John Coltrane's Giant Steps." Jazz Research Papers, Vol. 8 (1988): 97-102.

2451. Strickland, Edward. "What Coltrane Wanted: The Legendary Saxophonist Forsook Lyricism for the Quest for Ecstasy." The Atlantic (December 1987): 100-102.

2452. Tepperman, Barry. "John Coltrane - An Overview." Coda, No. 201 (April/May 1985): 4-6.

2453. Toperoff, Sam. "Remembering the Great 'Trane." Newsday (July 17 1977): 15, 23.

2454. Turner, Richard. "John Coltrane: a biographical sketch." The Black Perspective in Music, Vol. 3, No. 1 (1975): 3-16.

2455. Watrous, Peter. "John Coltrane: a life supreme." Musician, No. 105 (July 1987): 102+.

2456. White, Andrew. "Ad Lib: The Coltrane Legacy." down beat (September 1986): 63, 61, 48.

2457. ________. "The Coltrane Context." Jazz Forum, No. 106 (1987): 4-6.

2458. ________. "Coltrane transcribed." down beat (July 12 1979): 45-47.

2459. _________. "Coltrane's Saxophonic Technique." Saxophone Journal (Summer 1981).

2460. _________. "Pro Session: John Coltrane's Solo on Countdown--A Tenor Saxophone Transcription." down beat (September 1986): 56-59.

2461. "Who's On First?" down beat (March 10 1966): 8. Report on the departures of Elvin Jones and McCoy Tyner from the ensemble due to aesthetic differences with Coltrane.

2462. Wilson, John S. "Coltrane's 'Sheets of Sound'." New York Times (August 13 1967).

Works in French, German, Dutch and Italian

2463. Berendt, Joachim-Ernst. "Coltrane und Danach." In Photo-Story des Jazz. Frankfurt am Main: Kruger, 1978. [See Chapter 11]

2464. Carles, Philippe. "John Coltrane." In Le Jazz. Paris: Librairie Larousse, 1977, pp. 93-97.

2465. Filtgen, Gerd, and Michael Ausserbauer. John Coltrane: sein Leben, seine Musik, seine Schallplatten. Gauting-Buchendorf: Oreos, 1983. 220p.

2466. Gerber, Alain. Le Cas Coltrane. Marseille, France: Editions Parentheses, 1985. 158p.

2467. Polillo, Arrigo. "John Coltrane." In Jazz: la vicenda e i protagonisti della musica afro-americana. Milano: A. Mondadori, 1983, pp. 727-742.

2468. Roggeman, Willy. Jazzologie: 1940-1965. Brugge: De Galge, 1965, pp. 118-138, 203-209. The first set of pages here (118-138) offer a general discussion of Coltrane's work while the second provides a detailed analysis of his recording "A Love Supreme."

Biographical Dictionaries

2469. Carles, Philippe, and Jean-Louis Comolli. Free Jazz, Black Power. 2nd ed. Paris: Editions Galilee, 1979, pp. 386-389.

2470. Dictionnaire du Jazz, eds. Philippe Carles, et al. Paris: Laffont, 1988.

2471. Reclams Jazzfuhrer. 2nd, rev. ed. Stuttgart: Reclam, 1977.

2472. Reda, Jacques. Anthologie des Musiciens de Jazz. Paris: Stock, 1981, pp. 273-276.

2473. Tenot, Frank. Dictionnaire du Jazz. Paris: Larousse, 1967.

Articles

2474. "Autour de Coltrane." Jazz Magazine, No. 218 (January 1974): 13-19.

2475. Bolognani, M. "John Coltrane; sensibilita o transformismo?" Musica Jazz, Vol. 18 (November 1962): 37-38.

2476. "Cinq personnages en quete de 'Trane'." Jazz Hot, No. 172 (January 1962): 16-21.

2477. "Coltrane par Amiri Baraka (LeRoi Jones)." Jazz Magazine, No. 275 (May 1979): 30+. [poems]

2478. "Controverse autour de Coltrane." Jazz Hot, No. 26 (May 1960): 28-29.

2479. Delorme, Michael. "Coltrane 1963: vers la composition." Jazz Hot, No. 193 (December 1963): 10-11. [Interview]

2480. ________, and Claude Lenissois. "Coltrane, Vedette d'Antibes." Jazz Hot, No. 212 (September 1965): 5-6. [Interview] [See also # 2395]

2481. "Le Dossier Coltrane." Jazz Magazine, No. 6 (May 1960): 22-27.

2482. Dutilh, Alex. "Trane vu par Jeanneau." Jazz Hot, No. 339-340 (July-August 1977): 44-50. Comments on Coltrane by the 'Trane-influenced tenor saxophonist Francois Jeanneau.

2483. Horenstein, Stephen. "L'Offrande Musicale de Coltrane." Jazz Magazine, No. 283 (February 1980): 32-33. Musical analysis of the Coltrane composition "Offering."

2484. Ioakimidis, Demetre. "Sonny Rollins et John Coltrane en Parallele." Jazz Hot, No. 179 (September 1962): 24+; No. 180 (October 1962): 22-25; No. 181 (November 1962): 22-24; No. 182 (December 1962): 30-34.

2485. "John Coltrane 1926-1967." Jazz Magazine, No. 145 (August 1967): 16-23. Photo essay.

2486. Koechlin, P. "Coltrane a Paris." Jazz Hot, No. 212 (September 1965): 10.

2487. ________. "L'Ombre de Coltrane sous le Soleil de Parker." Jazz Hot, No. 194 (January 1964): 10.

2488. Kowski, Franck. "John Coltrane: une interview inedite." Le Jazzophone, No. 16 (1983): 34-40.

2489. Kriegel, Volker. "John Coltrane: Ein Personliches Portraet." Rock Session, Vol. 7 (1983): 44-56.

2490. Lees, Gene. "L'Homme Coltrane." Jazz Magazine, No. 7 (November 1961): 34-35.

2491. Lemery, Denis. "Comme un seul homme." Jazz Magazine, No. 115 (February 1965): 30-34. Interview and analysis of the function and contribution of Elvin Jones, McCoy Tyner and Jimmy Garrison to Coltrane's music.

2492. "Lettere al Direttore: Pro e Contro Coltrane." Musica Jazz (July 1960): 10-12.

2493. Marmande, Francois. "Vingt ans apres J.C.: A Supreme Love." Jazz Magazine, No. 362 (1987): 17-20.

2494. Masson, Jean-Robert. "La nuit des magiciens." Jazz Magazine, No. 9 (January 1963): 22-29. Discussion of French critical perspectives on Coltrane's music.

2495. Mortara, A. "Coltrane (e altri); la crisi del parkerismo." Musica Jazz, Vol. 17 (March 1961): 18-22.

2496. ________. "John Coltrane; la maturazione di uno stile." Musica Jazz, Vol. 17 (May 1961): 10-14.

2497. Pailhe, J. "Coltrane 1967/1977." Jazz Hot, No. 339-340 (July-August 1977): 52-56.

2498. Positif, Francois. "John Coltrane: une interview." Jazz Hot, No. 172 (January 1962): 12+.

2499. ________. "New York in Jazz Time." Jazz Hot, No. 26 (December 1960): 25.

2500. Quersin, Benoit. "La Passe Dangereuse." Jazz Magazine, No. 9 (January 1963): 39-40. [Interview]

2501. Santucci, U. "Jazz + Microstruttura + John = Coltrane." Musica Jazz (July-August 1963): 12-17.

2502. "Special Coltrane." Jazz Hot, No. 265 (Octobre 1970): 6-25.

2503. Tenot, Frank, M. Poulain, and J. C. Dargenpierre. "John Coltrane." Jazz Magazine, No. 8 (January 1962): 18-19.

2504. Testoni, Gian Carlo, and Arrigo Polillo. "Impressioni su Coltrane." Musica Jazz, Vol. 19 (January 1963): 10-14.

2505. "E Tornato John Coltrane." Musica Jazz, Vol. 19 (December 1963): 16-17.

2506. "Trane et Woody a Paris." Jazz Magazine, No. 122 (September 1965): 7-8.

Obituaries/Memorials

2507. Anthony, Paul. "John Coltrane: Beyond Genius, Night Trane." Liberator (New York), Vol. 7, No. 9 (September 1967): 18-19.

2508. "Ayler, Coleman quartets play for Trane funeral." Melody Maker (August 5 1967): 3.

2509. "Coltrane dead of a liver ailment." Billboard (July 29 1967): 12.

2510. "Coltrane dies in New York." Melody Maker (July 22 1967): 1.

2511. "Coltrane is Given a Jazz Man's Funeral Here." New York Times (July 22 1967): 13.

2512. Cooke, Jack. "In Memoriam." Jazz Monthly (September 1967): 2.

2513. Dance, Stanley. "Jazz." Music Journal (September 1967): 92.

2514. Delorme, Michel. "John Coltrane est mort." Jazz Hot, No. 234 (August 1967): 15-16.

2515. Garland, Phyl. "Requiem for 'Trane. Avant-garde giant leaves musical legacy." Ebony (November 1967): 66-68, 70, 72, 74.

2516. High Fidelity and Musical America (October 1967): MA13.

2517. "Hommage a Coltrane." Jazz Magazine, No. 146 (Septembre 1967): 12-15.

2518. Houston, Bob. "Always Expect the Unexpected." Melody Maker (July 29 1967): 6. Tribute to Trane with a recap of British perspectives on his music.

2519. "In Memoriam." BMI (October 1967): 26-27.

2520. International Musician (August 1967): 17.

2521. Jazz & Pop, Vol. 6 (Sept. 1967): 7.

2522. "John Coltrane." Variety (July 19 1967): 63.

2523. "John Coltrane dies." down beat (August 24 1967): 12-13.

2524. "John William Coltrane, 1926-1967: tributes." down beat (September 7 1967): 15-17.

2525. "John Coltrane, Jazz Star, Dies; Inventive Saxophone Player, 40." New York Times (July 18 1967): 37.

2526. New York Times (July 19 1967): 39. Funeral announcement.

2527. Spellman, A. B. "John Coltrane: 1926-1967." The Nation (August 14 1967): 119-120.

2528. "Tributes to John Coltrane--From Readers...and Musicians." down beat (September 7 1967): 16-17. Memorial tributes to Coltrane.

2529. Williams, Martin. "Legacy of John Coltrane." Saturday Review (September 16 1967): 69, 72.

2530. Zimmerman, P. D. "Death of a Jazzman." Newsweek (July 31 1967): 78-79.

Concert Reviews

2531. Atkins, Ronald. "John Coltrane and Dizzy Gillespie in Britain." Jazz Monthly (February 1962): 11-12.

2532. "Combo Reviews." Variety (July 26 1961): 55.

2533. Dawbarn, Bob. "What Happened?" Melody Maker (November 18 1961): 15. A British critic's "baffled, bothered, and bewildered" response to a performance by the Coltrane Quintet, then on tour in Britain as part of a Norman Granz JATP package with Dizzy Gillespie.

2534. "Le 17 [dix-sept] juillet 1967--disparaissait John Coltrane." Jazz Hot, No. 280 (February 1972): 16-17. Photo essay.

2535. Giddins, Gary. "The Night Coltrane Terrorized Philharmonic Hall." Village Voice (December 1 1975): 90-91. Remembrance of the epochal February 1966 "Titans of the Tenor" concert with 'Trane, Ayler, et al.

2536. Grime, Kitty. "Gillespie Coltrane Opening Show." Jazz News, Vol. 5, No. 46 (November 15 1961): 3.

2537. Hennessey, Mike. "Forty seven minutes of magnificent Coltrane." Melody Maker (July 31 1965): 8. Report on an appearance by the John Coltrane Quartet at the Sixth International Jazz Festival in Antibes, France.

2538. Jacka, Phillip. "Coltrane and Monk at Stamford [sic]." Coda (April/May 1966): 12-13. Review of concert at Stanford University.

2539. James, Michael. "The John Coltrane Quartet in Amsterdam." Jazz Monthly (December 1963): 16-17.

2540. "Jazz Gallery, N.Y." Variety (May 25 1960): 66.

2541. Jones, LeRoi. "Caught in the Act: John Coltrane-Cecil Taylor-Art Blakey." down beat (February 27 1964): 34. Review of a New Year's eve concert at Philharmonic Hall in New York.

2542. Lenissois, Claude, and Jef Gilson. "Concerts: Les fabuleux demons Coltraniens sont revenus le 1er novembre." Jazz Hot, No. 193 (December 1963): 9-10.

2543. Morgenstern, Dan. "Titans of the Tenor Sax." down beat (April 7 1966): 36-37. Review of concert held at New York's Philharmonic Hall.

2544. "The New Coltrane." down beat (May 5 1966): 8. Letters in response to # 2543.

2545. "Plugged Nickel, Chi." Variety (March 16 1966): 65.

2546. Qamar, Nadi. "Titans of the Saxophone." Liberator (New York), Vol. VI, No. 4 (April 1966): 21. Review of the "Titans of the Tenor" concert.

2547. Sinclair, John. "Cecil Taylor, John Coltrane, and Archie Shepp at the Down Beat Festival, Chicago, 8/15/65." Change (Detroit), No. 1 (Fall/Winter 1965): 34-38.

2548. Spellman, A. B. "Heard and Seen: John Coltrane Sextet, Village Gate." Metronome (November 1961): 8.

2549. _________. "Trane + 7 = A Wild Night at the Gate." down beat (December 30 1965): 15+. [Reprinted down beat (July 12 1979): 19].

2550. "Strictly Ad Lib." down beat (March 12 1964): 8. Report on an unscheduled appearance by Ornette Coleman with the John Coltrane Quartet at New York's Half Note club.

2551. Tynan, John. "Take Five." down beat (November 23 1961): 40. [Reprinted down beat (July 12 1979)]. The first salvo of the "anti-jazz" jeremiads of the 1960s.

Record Reviews

2552. "Ascension - An Afternoon with Coltrane." Jazz (New York), Vol. 4, No. 11 (December 1965): 16-17. Photos from the Coltrane's "Ascension" session taken by Charles Stewart.

2553. Beckett, Alan. "The New Wave in Jazz: The Older Avant-Garde." New Left Review, No. 32 (July-August 1965): 87. Discussion of the recorded works of Coltrane and Sonny Rollins.

2554. Borromeo, Filippo. "Lettre: su 'Ascension.'" Musica Jazz (July 1978): 47-48. Response to # 2559.

2555. DeMichael, Don. "Record Reviews: Coltrane Plays the Blues and Coltrane." down beat (October 11 1962): 32, 34.

2556. _________. "Record Reviews: Expression." down beat (March 7 1968): 26.

2557. _________. "Record Reviews: A Love Supreme." down beat (April 8 1965): 27.

2558. _________, and William Russo. "Record Reviews: Meditations." down beat (December 1 1966): 28. Dual review of Coltrane's "Meditations" lp. See also # 2564.

2559. Gianolio, Aldo and Paolio. "Un Capolvoro di Coltrane: Ascension." Musica Jazz (March 1978): 12-16. Analysis of Coltrane's "Ascension." See also # 2553.

2560. Gitler, Ira, and Pete Welding. "Record Reviews: Double View of Coltrane 'Live'." down beat (April 26 1962): 29. Dual review of Coltrane's "Live at the Village Vanguard" lp.

2561. Gourgues, Maurice. "Guide pour 'Ascension': pour ecouter un des chefs d'oeuvre du free-jazz." Jazz Magazine, No. 219 (February 1974): 14-15.

2562. Hadlock, Richard B. "Record Reviews: Ole Coltrane." down beat (February 1 1962): 24.

2563. Jones, LeRoi. "A Coltrane Trilogy." Metronome (December 1961): 34-36. Review of Giant Steps, Coltrane Jazz and My Favorite Things. [Reprinted in African Revolution, Vol. 1, No. 4-5 (August-September 1963): 228-232].

2564. "Letters: Those Coltrane Reviews." down beat (January 12 1967): 8. Responses to # 2558.

2565. McPartland, Marian. "Record Reviews: New Thing at Newport." down beat (April 21 1966): 32. Review of the recording from a live Coltrane/Shepp performance recorded at the Newport Jazz Festival.

2566. McRae, Barry. "Arena: Ascension." Jazz Journal (August 1976): 10. Discussion of "Ascension" and its influence on other free jazz players and ensembles.

2567. _________. "John Coltrane - the Impulse years." Jazz Journal (July 1971): 2-6.

2568. Mathieu, Bill. "Record Reviews: Ascension." down beat (May 5 1966): 25.

2569. _________. "Record Reviews: Coltrane Live at Birdland." down beat (April 9 1964): 26.

2570. _________. "Record Reviews: Kulu Se Mama." down beat (June 15 1967): 32-33.

2571. Miles, Robert. "A Love Supreme: an analysis and appreciation." Pieces of Jazz, No. 3 (Summer 1968): 33-36.

2572. "Odyssey, Om and Ohnedaruth." IT (London), No. 61 (August 1-14 1969): 12. Survey of Coltrane's recorded works.

2573. Pekar, Harvey. "Record Reviews: Om." down beat (May 2 1968): 26.

2574. Porter, Lewis. "John Coltrane's A Love Supreme: jazz improvisation as composition." Journal of the American Musicological Society, Vol. 38, No. 3 (1985): 593+.

2575. Spellman, A. B. "Jazz: Coltrane Live at the Village Vanguard." Kulchur, No. 7 (Autumn 1962): 97-99.

2576. Taylor, Cecil. "John Coltrane: Soultrane." Jazz Review, Vol. 2 (January 1959): 34.

2577. Voce, Steve. "Basic Trane-ing." Jazz Journal (August 1967): 10. British critic's perspective on several late Coltrane recordings.

2578. Welding, Pete. "Record Reviews: Live at the Village Vanguard Again." down beat (February 23 1967): 26.

2579. Whitehead, Kevin. "Trane Wrecks." Down Beat (November 1990): 49, 52-53. Survey of recent reissues.

2580. Williams, Martin. "Coltrane Triumphant." Saturday Review (January 16 1965): 73-74. Review of Coltrane's "Crescent" lp.

2581. ________. "Coltrane Up to Date." Saturday Review (April 30 1966): 67.

2582. ________. "John Coltrane: man in the middle." down beat (December 14 1967): 15-17. Review essay on Coltrane's career and recordings.

2583. ________. "Record Reviews: Africa/Brass." down beat (January 18 1962): 29, 32.

2584. Wilson, John S. "Jazz and the Anarchy of the Avant Garde." New York Times (April 24 1966). Review of "Ascension."

2585. Woodfin, Henry. "Coltrane's Progress." Sounds & Fury (September/October 1965): 6-7.

Discographies

2586. Davis, Brian. John Coltrane Discography. 2nd ed. London: Brian Davis and Ray Smith, 1976. 50p.

2587. Jepsen, Jorgen G. A Discography of John Coltrane. Rev. ed. Copenhagen: Knudsen, 1969(?). 35p.

2588. John Coltrane discography, ed. Jazz Spot Intro. Tokyo: Jazz Spot Intro., 1976. 27p.

2589. Rissi, Mathias. John Coltrane; discography. Adliswil, Switzerland: M. Rissi (Haldenstr. 23, CH-8134, Adliswil), 1977. 39p.

2590. Wild, David. The Recordings of John Coltrane: A Discography. Ann Arbor, MI: Wildmusic (PO Box 2138, Ann Arbor, MI 48106), 1979.

Bibliographies

2591. Dick, Ellen A., comp. John Coltrane: periodical articles [1958-1978]. Chicago: Chicago Public Library, Fine Arts Division, Music Section (78 East Washington St., Chicago, IL 60602), 1979. 8p. Xerox copy.

Media Materials

2592. The Coltrane Legacy. 60 min. Video documentary featuring interviews with former Coltrane sidemen (Elvin Jones, McCoy Tyner, Reggie Workman) and live tv performance footage from the early 1960's with the classic quartet and Eric Dolphy. [Available from Video Artists International, Inc., Box 153, Ansonia Station, Dept. J2, New York, NY 10023].

COMPANY

2593. Adams, Simon. "Company." In The New Grove Dictionary of Jazz. London: Macmillan Press, 1988.

2594. Riley, Peter. The Musicians, The Instruments. London: Vanessa The Many Press, 1978. 36p. Companion booklet to a "Company Week" concert series.

Articles

2595. Ansell, Kenneth. "Company." Impetus, No. 6 (1977): 240-241.

2596. ________. "Derek Bailey and Company." The Wire, No. 15 (May 1985): 33-35.

2597. ________. "Eight's Company." Melody Maker (May 5 1979): 47. Report on a British tour by Company.

2598. Charlton, Hannah. "Welcome to the Company." Melody Maker (June 6 1981): 31.

2599. Lake, Steve. "In Mixed Company..." Melody Maker (January 29 1977): 38.

2600. McRae, Barry. "Arena: Three or More's Company." Jazz Journal (August 1976): 10. Report on the founding of Company.

2601. ________. "Braxton, Bailey and Company--the art of ad hoc ad lib." Jazz Journal International (July 1977): 22-23.

Concert Reviews

2602. "Caught in the Act." Melody Maker (August 28 1976): 37.

2603. "Caught in the Act." Melody Maker (February 19 1977): 48; (April 23 1977): 18; (June 4 1977): 46; (October 29 1977): 69.

2604. "Caught in the Act." Melody Maker (February 25 1978): 62.

2605. "Caught in the Act." Melody Maker (March 10 1979): 45; (August 11 1979): 22; (August 25 1979): 31; (September 1 1979): 30.

2606. Charlton, Hannah. "Caught in the Act: Company." Melody Maker (February 28 1981): 37.

2607. "Jazz Live!" Jazz Journal International (August 1977): 22-24; (December 1977): 26-27.

Discographies

2608. Bergerone, Riccardo. Company 1976-1983 (radio broadcasts, records, concerts). Sierre: Jazz 360o (c/o G. Cerutti, 8, ave du Marche, CH-3960, Sierre, Switzerland), 1983. 12p.

COOK, MARTY (1947-) - Trombone

2609. Fitterling, Thomas. "New York Sound Explosion: Marty Cook." Jazz Podium (September 1980): 23.

2610. Gschwendner, Willie. "Marty Cook's New Jazz and Jim Pepper." Jazz Podium (May 1986): 24-25.

2611. Laages, M. "Marty Cook." Jazz Podium (January 1981): 26.

2612. Ogan, Bernd. "Marty Cook Group." Jazz Podium (April 1985): 25.

2613. Weber, Horst. "Marty Cook." Jazz Podium (February 1982). [Profile]

COOMBES, NIGEL (Great Britain) - Violin

See also # 1229

2614. Case, Brian. "Let's Hear it from the Cool Front Room." New Musical Express (March 11 1978): 34-35. [Interview]

COOPER, JEROME (1946-) - Drums

2615. Carles, Philippe, and Jean-Louis Comolli. Free Jazz, Black Power. 2nd ed. Paris: Editions Galilee, 1979, p. 389.

2616. Claghorn, Charles Eugene. Biographical Dictionary of Jazz. Englewood Cliffs, NJ: Prentice-Hall, 1982.

2617. Dictionnaire du Jazz, eds. Philippe Carles, et al. Paris: Laffont, 1988.

2618. Feather, Leonard, and Ira Gitler. The Encyclopedia of Jazz in the Seventies. New York: Horizon Press, 1976.

2619. Hazell, Ed. "Cooper, Jerome." In The New Grove Dictionary of Jazz. London: Macmillan Press, 1988.

2620. Southern, Eileen. Biographical Dictionary of Afro-American and African Musicians. Westport, CT: Greenwood Press, 1982.

2621. Wilmer, Valerie. As Serious As Your Life. Westport, CT: Lawrence Hill & Co., 1981, p. 265.

Articles

2622. Hazell, Ed. "Jerome Cooper: the music of the drums." Modern Drummer (April 1986): 26+. [Interview]

2623. Riggins, Roger. "The Jerome Cooper Interview." The Grackle, No. 5 (1975): 19-20.

2624. Stern, Chip. "Jerome Cooper." Musician, Player and Listener, No. 22 (January 1980): 32-33.

2625. Wilmer, Valerie. "The Drummer as Artist." Melody Maker (February 3 1973): 34.

COOPER, LINDSAY (1940-) (Great Britain) - Bassoon/oboe

See also # 3131-3133

2626. Carles, Philippe, and Jean-Louis Comolli. Free Jazz, Black Power. 2nd ed. Paris: Editions Galilee, 1979, p. 389.

Articles

2627. "The Henry Cow File." Melody Maker (February 9 1974): 20. Biographical sketch.

2628. Wilmer, Val. "Breaking Down the Status Quo." City Limits (September 10-16 1982): 43.

2629. _________. "Caught in the Act: Lindsay Cooper." Melody Maker (January 14 1978): 14. [Concert review]

2630. _________. "La musique des femmes a une fonction politique differente." Jazz Magazine (March 1979): 28-29, 70.

COREA, CHICK [Armando Anthony] (1941-) - Piano

See also # 1977-1981

2631. Wilmer, Valerie. "Chick Corea and his Scientology." Melody Maker (February 27 1971): 12. [Interview]

CORTEZ, JAYNE - Poet

2632. Richmond, Norman. "Jayne Cortez." Fuse (Toronto), Vol. 6, No. 1-2 (May-June 1982): 72-74.

2633. Wilmer, Val. "From the Fire." City Limits (January 24-30 1986): 17.

2634. _________. "Jayne Cortez - The Unsubmissive Blues." Coda, No. 230 (February/March 1990): 16-19. [Interview]

2635. _________. "Jayne Cortez and the Unsubmissive Blues." Wire, No. 18 (August 1985): 18-19, 21. [Interview]

COURSIL, JACQUES (1939-) (France) - Trumpet

2636. Carles, Philippe, and Jean-Louis Comolli. Free Jazz, Black Power. 2nd ed. Paris: Editions Galilee, 1979, p. 390.

2637. Kopelowicz, Guy. "Un Americain de Montmartre: Jacques Coursil." Jazz Hot, No. 249 (April 1969): 32-33.

2638. Wilmer, Valerie. As Serious As Your Life. Westport, CT: Lawrence Hill & Co., 1981, p. 265.

COWELL, STANLEY (1941-) - Piano

2639. Claghorn, Charles Eugene. Biographical Dictionary of Jazz. Englewood Cliffs, NJ: Prentice-Hall, 1982.

2640. Dictionnaire du Jazz, eds. Philippe Carles, et al. Paris: Laffont, 1988.

2641. Feather, Leonard. The Encyclopedia of Jazz in the Seventies. New York: Horizon Press, 1976.

2642. Hazell, Ed. "Cowell, Stanley." In The New Grove Dictionary of Jazz. London: Macmillan Press, 1988.

2643. Southern, Eileen. Biographical Dictionary of Afro-American and African Musicians. Westport, CT: Greenwood Press, 1982.

Articles

2644. Brower, W. A. "Stanley Cowell's 'Ancestral Streams.'" Jazz Times (July 1981): 10-12.

2645. Cuscuna, Michael. "Stanley Cowell: More to Come." down beat (October 16 1969): 18.

2646. "Feature Interview: Stanley Cowell." Expansions, Vol. 1, No. 3 (1971): 4.

2647. Lyons, Len. "Stanley Cowell: Versatile Jazz Pianist and Multi-Keyboardist." Contemporary Keyboard (June 1979): 30+. [Interview]

2648. Styx, John. "Stanley Cowell." Radio Free Jazz, Vol. 18, No. 2 (1977): 16, 19.

COXHILL, LOL (1932-) (Great Britain) - Alto Saxophone

2649. Nuttall, Jeff. The Bald Soprano: A Portrait of Lol Coxhill. Nottingham: Tak Tak Tak, 1989. 108p.

Biographical Dictionaries

2650. Carles, Philippe, and Jean-Louis Comolli. Free Jazz, Black Power. 2nd ed. Paris: Editions Galilee, 1979, p. 390.

2651. Carr, Ian. "Coxhill, Lol." In Jazz: The Essential Companion. New York: Prentice Hall Press, 1988.

2652. Dictionnaire du Jazz, eds. Philippe Carles, et al. Paris: Laffont, 1988.

2653. Gilbert, Mark. "Coxhill, Lol." In The New Grove Dictionary of Jazz. London: Macmillan Press, 1988.

2654. Jazz Now: the Jazz Centre Society Guide, ed. Roger Cotterrell. London: Quartet Books, 1976, pp. 124-125.

2655. The Penguin Encyclopedia of Popular Music, ed. Donald Clarke. New York: Viking, 1989.

Articles

2656. Ansell, Kenneth. "Lol Coxhill." Impetus (London), No. 4 (1977): 188-190; No. 5 (1977): 222-225; No. 6 (1977): 246-247. [Interview]

2657. Bussy, Pascal. "Entretien avec Lol Coxhill." Jazz Hot, No. 396 (September/October 1982): 7.

2658. Coxhill, Lol. "Premiere Apparence et au dela." Jazz Ensuite, No. 1 (1983).

2659. Hyder, Ken. "Street Playing Man." Melody Maker (May 26 1973): 57.

2660. Ilic, Dave. "Lol Coxhill: just a bald headed busker?" The Wire, No. 5 (Autumn 1983): 28-29. [Interview]

2661. "Making Waves: iced Lol." Melody Maker (June 19 1976): 12. [Interview]

2662. Rouy, Gerard. "Lol Coxhill: 'avec un parfum tres anglais'." Jazz Magazine, No. 274 (April 1979): 43-44. [Interview]

2663. Smith, Bill. "Lol Coxhill." Coda, No. 189 (April 1983): 14-17. [Interview]

2664. Watson, Ben. "Lol Coxhill: Up to the Ears." The Wire, No. 67 (September 1989): 24-26, 60.

2665. Williams, Richard. "Buster who came in from the cold." Melody Maker (June 6 1970): 22.

2666. ________. "Lol: here there and everywhere." Melody Maker (June 24 1972): 47.

Media Materials

2667. Frog Dance (1983). Arts Council of Great Britain documentary.

CREATIVE CONSTRUCTION COMPANY

2668. Berg, Chuck. "Record Reviews: CCC." down beat (May 20 1976): 29.

2669. Claghorn, Charles Eugene. Biographical Dictionary of Jazz. Englewood Cliffs, NJ: Prentice-Hall, 1982, p. 337.

CRISPELL, MARILYN (1947-) - Piano

See also # 701

2670. American Keyboard Artists, eds. Stephen Husarik and Marilyn J. Joyce. Chicago, IL: Chicago Biographical Center, 1989.

2671. Crispell, Marilyn. "Some Information on My Compositions." In Untitled Mss. Woodstock, NY: Crispell Publishing (P.O. Box 499, Woodstock, NY 12498), 1986.

2672. Dictionnaire du Jazz, eds. Philippe Carles, et al. Paris: Laffont, 1988.

2673. Lock, Graham. "Marilyn Crispell, piano." In Forces in Motion: The Music and Thoughts of Anthony Braxton. New York: Da Capo Press, 1989, pp. 179-188. [Interview]

Articles

2674. Chapin, Gary Parker. "Spontaneous Combustion: Marilyn Crispell's Keyboard Epiphanies." Option, No. 35 (November/December 1990): 46-50. [Interview]

2675. Lock, Graham. "Singing Furiously in Delicate Tongues." Wire, No. 51 (May 1988): 32-35, 59.

2676. "Les Musiques de Marilyn Crispell." Jazz Magazine, No. 295 (March 1981): 15.

2677. Mandel, Howard. "Profile: Marilyn Crispell." down beat (September 1984): 42-43.

2678. Pareles, Jon. "Two Who Are Playing New Jazz Piano Styles." New York Times (January 14 1983).

2679. Riggins, Roger. "Marilyn Crispell: pianist for the future." Jazz Forum, No. 79 (1982): 37-41. [Interview]

2680. Rusch, Bob. "Marilyn Crispell: interview." Cadence, Vol. 10, No. 2 (February 1984): 9-12.

2681. Smith, Bill. "Marilyn Crispell: Rhythms Hung in Undrawn Sky." Coda, No. 216 (October/November 1987): 6-7. [Interview]

CROSS, EARL (1933-) - Trumpet

See also # 611

2682. Carles, Philippe, and Jean-Louis Comolli. Free Jazz, Black Power. 2nd ed. Paris: Editions Galilee, 1979, p. 391.

2683. Wilmer, Valerie. As Serious As Your Life. Westport, CT: Lawrence Hill & Co., 1981, p. 265.

Articles

2684. Knox, Keith. "Earl Cross: interview." Cadence, Vol. 9, No. 7 (July 1983): 5-7, 28.

2685. Wilmer, Valerie. "Cross Words." Melody Maker (January 5 1974): 33.

CROUCH, STANLEY (1945-) - Drums/Critic

See also # 673, 692, 1270

2686. Jost, Ekkehard. "Stanley Crouch." In Jazzmusiker: Materialen zur Soziologie der Afro-Amerikanischen Musik. Frankfurt am Main: Ullstein, 1982, pp. 72-77.

Biographical Dictionaries

2687. Barnett, Anthony. "Crouch, Stanley." In The New Grove Dictionary of Jazz. London: Macmillan Press, 1988.

2688. Carles, Philippe, and Jean-Louis Comolli. Free Jazz, Black Power. 2nd ed. Paris: Editions Galilee, 1979, p. 391.

2689. Claghorn, Charles Eugene. Biographical Dictionary of Jazz. Englewood Cliffs, NJ: Prentice-Hall, 1982.

2690. Feather, Leonard, and Ira Gitler. The Encyclopedia of Jazz in the Seventies. New York: Horizon Press, 1976.

2691. The Penguin Encyclopedia of Popular Music, ed. Donald Clarke. New York: Viking, 1989.

2692. Priestley, Brian. "Crouch, Stanley." In Jazz: The Essential Companion. New York: Prentice Hall Press, 1988.

Articles

2693. "Caught." Down Beat (March 11 1976): 34+. [Concert review]

2694. Occhiogrosso, Peter. "Profiles: Stanley Crouch and David Murray." Down Beat (March 25 1976): 38-39.

2695. Riggins, Roger. "Subtraction is the Name of the Game." Soho Weekly News (March 24 1977): 43-44.

CUYPERS, LEO (1947-) (The Netherlands) - Piano

2696. Vuijsje, Bert. De Nieuwe Jazz. Baarn: Bosch & Keuning, 1978, pp. 166-174. [Interview]

Articles

2697. "Cuypers: down with purism." Melody Maker (June 17 1978): 46.

2698. "Leo Cuypers wins 1973 Ilcken award." Jazz Forum, No. 28 (April 1974): 21-22.

2699. Pan, Max. "Leo Cuypers: lone wolf of the improvised music scene." Key Notes (Amsterdam), No. 11 (1980): 8-13. [Interview]

CYRILLE, ANDREW (1939-) - Percussion

See also # 69, 522

2700. ASCAP Biographical Dictionary. 4th ed. New York: R.R. Bowker, 1980.

2701. Carles, Philippe, and Jean-Louis Comolli. Free Jazz, Black Power. 2nd ed. Paris: Editions Galilee, 1979, pp. 391-392.

2702. Carr, Ian. "Cyrille, Andrew." In Jazz: The Essential Companion. New York: Prentice Hall Press, 1988.

2703. Claghorn, Charles Eugene. Biographical Dictionary of Jazz. Englewood Cliffs, NJ: Prentice-Hall, 1982.

2704. Dictionnaire du Jazz, eds. Philippe Carles, et al. Paris: Laffont, 1988.

2705. Feather, Leonard, and Ira Gitler. The Encyclopedia of Jazz in the Seventies. New York: Horizon Press, 1976.

2706. The Penguin Encyclopedia of Popular Music, ed. Donald Clarke. New York: Viking, 1989.

2707. Ullman, Michael. "Cyrille, Andrew." In The New Grove Dictionary of American Music. London: Macmillan Press, 1986.

2708. _________. "Cyrille, Andrew." In The New Grove Dictionary of Jazz. London: Macmillan Press, 1988.

2709. Wilmer, Valerie. As Serious As Your Life. Westport, CT: Lawrence Hill & Co., 1981, p. 265.

Articles

2710. "Andrew Cyrille." Percussive Notes, Vol. 18, No. 1 (1979): 21.

2711. Case, Brian. "Make like a chimp (or choose your own alternative)." New Musical Express (October 4 1975): 28-29. [Interview]

2712. Davis, Francis. "Other Musicians March to His Beat." Philadelphia Inquirer (December 27 1986): C3.

2713. Giddins, Gary. "Note: Andrew Cyrille Has a New Band." Village Voice (August 5 1981): 56, 58.

2714. Gray, John. "Andrew Cyrille." Coda, No. 199 (December 1984): 13-17. [Interview]

2715. Henderson, Bill. "Cyrille-ism." Black Music and Jazz Review, Vol. 2, No. 3 (June 1979): 16-17. [Interview]

2716. Howland, Harold. "Andrew Cyrille: an aesthetic endeavor." Modern Drummer (Dec 1981/Jan 1982): 22+. [Interview]

2717. "Institute of Percussive Studies." Jazz Magazine (Northport, NY), Vol. 3, No. 4 (Fall 1979): 103.

2718. Jeske, Lee. "Blindfold Test: Andrew Cyrille." down beat (March 1982): 54.

2719. Lattanzi, Guglielmo, and Dino Giannasi. "Due chiacchiere con Andrew Cyrille e Jimmy Lyons." Musica Jazz (December 1975): 18-19, 48. [Interview]

2720. Loupien, Serge, and Gerard Rouy. "Andrew Cyrille: tambour, danse et parole." Jazz Magazine, No. 290 (October 1980): 44-45, 64. [Interview]

2721. Mandel, Howard. "Andrew Cyrille: Passion for Percussion." down beat (August 1984): 28-30.

2722. Pullman, Peter. "Andrew Cyrille: Everything Has a Sound." Village Voice/Voice Jazz Special (August 30 1988): 16-17.

2723. Stephenson, Gene. "Conversation with Andrew Cyrille: dialogue of the drums." The Black Perspective in Music, Vol. 3, No. 1 (1975): 53-57. [Interview]

2724. Welburn, Ron. "Andrew Cyrille: A Different Drummer." Jazz Forum, No. 55 (1978): 24-27, 36. [Interview]

2725. Welch, Jane. "Different Drummers: a composite profile." down beat (March 19 1970): 18.

2726. Wilmer, Valerie. "Andrew Cyrille." The Wire, No. 9 (1984).

2727. _________. "Cyrille-ism." Melody Maker (May 29 1971): 16.

2728. _________. "Dialogue of the Drummers." Coda, No. 131 (September 1974): 2-5.

2729. _________. "Skintight." Time Out (September 15-21 1978).

2730. _________. "Talking Drums." Melody Maker (May 27 1972): 30.

2731. _________. "Trois Jeunes Tambours." Jazz Magazine, No. 202 (July 1972): 10+.

Concert Reviews

2732. Cole, Bill. "Caught in the Act: Andrew Cyrille and the Ensemble Plus." down beat (January 21 1971): 30-31.

2733. Hollenberg, David. "Caught: Maono." down beat (May 19 1977): 42-43.

2734. Wilmer, Valerie. "Caught in the Act: Dialogue of the Drums, Cami Hall, New York." down beat (November 25 1971): 26-27. Review of a trio performance by Cyrille, Milford Graves and Rashied Ali.

DANIEL, TED (1943-) - Trumpet

See also # 611

2735. Carles, Philippe, and Jean-Louis Comolli. Free Jazz, Black Power. 2nd ed. Paris: Editions Galilee, 1979, p. 392.

2736. Wilmer, Valerie. As Serious As Your Life. Westport, CT: Lawrence Hill & Co., 1981, p. 265-266.

Articles

2737. Carles, Philippe. "'Jouer quelque chose qui ait un sens...' Ted Daniel." Jazz Magazine, No. 217 (December 1973): 26-28. [Interview]

2738. Case, Brian. "As Quiet as its Kept..." New Musical Express (November 4 1978): 41. [Interview]

2739. Wilmer, Valerie. "Rare Daniel." Melody Maker (February 10 1973): 42.

DARA, OLU [Charles Jones III] (1941-) - Trumpet

2740. Dictionnaire du Jazz, eds. Philippe Carles, et al. Paris: Laffont, 1988.

2741. Mandel, Howard. "Olu Dara." In The New Grove Dictionary of Jazz. London: Macmillan Press, 1988.

Articles

2742. Coppens, George. "Olu Dara." Coda, No. 170 (December 1979): 4-8. [Interview]

2743. McElfresh, Suzanne. "A Taste of Okra Every Day." Ear: Magazine of New Music, Vol. 11, No. 3 (November 1986): 14+.

2744. Palmer, Don. "Faces: Olu Dara." Musician, Player and Listener, No. 37 (November 1981): 38.

2745. Stern, Chip. "Olu Dara." Musician, No. 63 (January 1984): 24, 26, 28, 30.

2746. Woessner, Russell. "Profile: Olu Dara." down beat (August 1982): 52-53.

DAUNER, WOLFGANG (1935-) (W. Germany) - Piano

See also # 323

2747. Berendt, Joachim-Ernst, and Wolfram Knauer. "Dauner, Wolfgang." In The New Grove Dictionary of Jazz. London: Macmillan Press, 1988.

2748. Carr, Ian. "Dauner, Wolfgang." In Jazz: The Essential Companion. New York: Prentice Hall Press, 1988.

2749. Feather, Leonard. The Encyclopedia of Jazz in the Sixties. New York: Horizon Press, 1966.

2750. ________, and Ira Gitler. The Encyclopedia of Jazz in the Seventies. New York: Horizon Press, 1976.

2751. Reclams Jazzfuhrer. 2nd, rev. ed. Stuttgart: Reclam, 1977.

Articles

2752. Berendt, Joachim-Ernst. "Profile: Wolfgang Dauner." down beat (March 1980): 55-56.

2753. Endress, Gudrun. "Weitgespanntes Musikalisches Schaffen: Wolfgang Dauner." Jazz Podium (September 1973): 12-16.

2754. Zimmerle, D. "The Wide Musical World of Wolfgang Dauner." Jazz Forum, No. 38 (1975): 44+.

DAVIS, ANTHONY (1951-) - Piano

See also # 707

2755. Carr, Ian. "Davis, Anthony." In Jazz: The Essential Companion. New York: Prentice Hall Press, 1988.

2756. Dictionnaire du Jazz, eds. Philippe Carles, et al. Paris: Laffont, 1988.

2757. Kernfeld, Barry. "Davis, Anthony." In The New Grove Dictionary of American Music. London: Macmillan Press, 1986.

2758. ________. "Davis, Anthony." In The New Grove Dictionary of Jazz. London: Macmillan Press, 1988.

2759. Who's Who in America. 46th ed. 1990/91.

2760. Who's Who in Entertainment. 1st ed. 1989-1990.

Articles

2761. Case, Brian. "Form and the Connecticut Yankee." Melody Maker (September 1 1979): 32. [Interview]

2762. "Connecticut Journal." New York Times (December 27 1981): Sec. 23, p.3. Discussion of Davis's interest in Duke Ellington and his Yale University class on the subject.

2763. "Davis, Anthony." Current Biography 1990.

2764. Davis, Francis. "Anthony Davis: New Music Traditionalist." down beat (January 1982): 21-23, 68.

2765. "Dico Disco & Co." Jazz Magazine, No. 298 (June 1981): 40. Biographical sketch.

2766. Giddins, Gary. "Jazz Out of School: in search of a text." Village Voice (February 19 1979): 58.

2767. Goddet, Laurent. "Anthony Davis: L'Apres-Taylor." Jazz Hot, No. 367 (November 1979): 15-18. [Interview]

2768. Kalbacher, Gene. "Anthony Davis Episteme." Jazz (Basel), Nr. 4 (1984). [Interview]

2769. Mandel, Howard. "Blindfold Test." down beat (June 1984): 56.

2770. Miller, Jim. "Playing with Fire; A New Generation of Jazz Experimentalists is Bringing Formal Complexity and Daredevil Energy to its Music." Newsweek (November 28 1983): 99-101.

2771. Palmer, Robert. "Jazz: Mindspeech Music--Anthony Davis' New Musical Language." Rolling Stone (May 1 1980): 26.

2772. Primack, Bret. "Anthony Davis." Contemporary Keyboard (November 1980): 48, 52-60. [Interview]

2773. Riggins, Roger. "Modern Gothic: an interview with Anthony Davis." The Grackle, No. 5 (1979): 15-16.

2774. Safane, Clifford Jay. "Profile: Anthony Davis." down beat (December 1979): 64, 66.

2775. Smith, Bill. "An Interview with Anthony Davis." Coda, No. 175 (October 1980): 4-9.

2776. Solothurnmann, Jurg. "Anthony Davis." Jazz Forum, No. 74 (1982): 38-43. [Interview]

2777. Tinder, Cliff. "Anthony Davis." Musician, No. 46 (August 1982): 64, 68-72. [Interview]

2778. Van Trikt, Ludwig. "Anthony Davis: interview." Cadence, Vol. 12, No. 10 (October 1986): 15-19.

DAVIS, ART [Arthur David] (1934-   ) - Bass

2779. Davis, Arthur. The Arthur Davis System for Double Bass. Corona del Mar, CA: Arkimu (3535 East Coast Highway, Suite 50, Corona del Mar, CA 92625), 1976.

2780. Walton, Ortiz. "Arthur Davis, a Suit Against the New York Philharmonic." In Music: Black, White and Blue. New York: William Morrow, 1972, pp. 73-91.

Biographical Dictionaries

2781. Carles, Philippe, and Jean-Louis Comolli. Free Jazz, Black Power. 2nd ed. Paris: Editions Galilee, 1979, p. 393.

2782. Carr, Ian. "Davis, Art." In Jazz: The Essential Companion. New York: Prentice Hall Press, 1988.

2783. Claghorn, Charles Eugene. Biographical Dictionary of American Music. West Nyack, NY: Parker Pub. Co., 1973.

2784. _________. Biographical Dictionary of Jazz. Englewood Cliffs, NJ: Prentice-Hall, 1982.

2785. Dictionnaire du Jazz, eds. Philippe Carles, et al. Paris: Laffont, 1988.

2786. Feather, Leonard. The Encyclopedia of Jazz. New ed. New York: Horizon Press, 1960.

2787. _________. The Encyclopedia of Jazz in the Sixties. New York: Horizon Press, 1966.

2788. Reclams Jazzfuhrer. 2nd, rev. ed. Stuttgart: Reclam, 1977.

2789. Southern, Eileen. Biographical Dictionary of Afro-American and African Musicians. Westport, CT: Greenwood Press, 1982.

2790. Ullman, Michael. "Davis, Art." In The New Grove Dictionary of Jazz. London: Macmillan Press, 1988.

2791. Who's Who Among Black Americans. 6th ed. 1990/91. Detroit: Gale Research, 1990.

2792. Who's Who in America. 46th ed. 1990-1991.

2793. Who's Who in American Music: Classical, ed. Jacques Cattell Press. 2nd ed. New York: R.R. Bowker, 1985.

2794. Who's Who in the East. 17th ed. 1979-1980.

2795. Who's Who in the West. 22nd ed. 1989-1990.

2796. Wilmer, Valerie. As Serious As Your Life. Westport, CT: Lawrence Hill & Co., 1981, p. 266.

Articles

2797. "Annuaire biographique de la contrebasse." Jazz Magazine, No. 9 (May 1963): 24. Biographical sketch.

2798. Bratton, Elliot, and Ted Panken. "Art Davis." Cadence, Vol. 12, No. 9 (September 1986): 12-19, 76. [Interview]

2799. Coss, Bill. "The Emergence of Art Davis." down beat (September 28 1961): 24.

2800. Ioakimidis, Demetre. "Art Davis." Jazz Hot, No. 184 (February 1963): 24-25.

2801. Kohlhaase, Bill. "This Musician Cooks; Bassist Art Davis, Man of Many Parts, Plays Costa Mesa Tonight." Los Angeles Times/Calendar (October 21 1989): F-1.

2802. Lee, David. "Art Davis." Coda, No. 183 (April 1982): 16-19. [Interview]

2803. Ubiles, Joe. "Music: An Interview with Art Davis." Black Creation, Vol. 4, No. 1 (Fall 1972): 22-24.

2804. Wilmer, Valerie. "Art Davis--a struggle for recognition." Jazz Monthly (February 1962): 6-9.

2805. ________. "Davis--a martyr to his art." Melody Maker (October 7 1972): 40.

2806. ________. "Interview: Art Davis." Jazz News (June 21 1961): 9.

DAVIS, CHARLES (1933-) - Baritone Saxophone

2807. Berry, Lemuel, Jr. Biographical Dictionary of Black Musicians and Music Educators. Guthrie, OK: Educational Book Publishers, 1978, p. 232.

2808. Carles, Philippe, and Jean-Louis Comolli. Free Jazz, Black Power. 2nd ed. Paris: Editions Galilee, 1979, p. 393.

2809. Claghorn, Charles Eugene. Biographical Dictionary of American Music. West Nyack, NY: Parker Pub. Co., 1973.

2810. ________. Biographical Dictionary of Jazz. Englewood Cliffs, NJ: Prentice-Hall, 1982.

2811. Dictionnaire du Jazz, eds. Philippe Carles, et al. Paris: Laffont, 1988.

2812. Feather, Leonard. The Encyclopedia of Jazz in the Sixties. New York: Horizon Press, 1966.

2813. ________, and Ira Gitler. The Encyclopedia of Jazz in the Seventies. New York: Horizon Press, 1976.

2814. Gardner, Mark. "Davis, Charles." In The New Grove Dictionary of Jazz. London: Macmillan Press, 1988.

2815. Reclams Jazzfuhrer. 2nd, rev. ed. Stuttgart: Reclam, 1977.

2816. Wilmer, Valerie. As Serious As Your Life. Westport, CT: Lawrence Hill & Co., 1981, p. 266.

Articles

2817. "Dictionnaire du Baryton." Jazz Magazine, No. 143 (June 1967): 33. Biographical sketch.

2818. Kronzek, Allan Zola. "Charles Davis: Baritone Saxophone as a Way of Life." down beat (May 20 1965): 18-19.

DAVIS, RICHARD (1930-) - Bass

See also # 69

2819. Taylor, Arthur. "Richard Davis." In Notes and Tones. New York: Perigee Books, 1982, pp. 208-218. [Interview]

Biographical Dictionaries

2820. Bennett, Bill. "Davis, Richard." In The New Grove Dictionary of Jazz. London: Macmillan Press, 1988.

2821. Berry, Lemuel, Jr. Biographical Dictionary of Black Musicians and Music Educators. Guthrie, OK: Educational Book Publishers, 1978.

2822. Claghorn, Charles Eugene. Biographical Dictionary of American Music. West Nyack, NY: Parker Pub. Co., 1973.

2823. _________. Biographical Dictionary of Jazz. Englewood Cliffs, NJ: Prentice-Hall, 1982.

2824. Dictionnaire du Jazz, eds. Philippe Carles, et al. Paris: Laffont, 1988.

2825. Feather, Leonard. The Encyclopedia of Jazz. Rev. ed. New York: Horizon Press, 1960.

2826. _________. The Encyclopedia of Jazz in the Sixties. New York: Horizon Press, 1966.

2827. _________, and Ira Gitler. The Encyclopedia of Jazz in the Seventies. New York: Horizon Press, 1976.

2828. Priestley, Brian. "Davis, Richard." In Jazz: The Essential Companion. New York: Prentice Hall Press, 1988.

2829. Reclams Jazzfuhrer. 2nd, rev. ed. Stuttgart: Reclam, 1977.

2830. Who's Who Among Black Americans. 6th ed. 1990/91.

2831. Who's Who in Entertainment. 1st ed. 1989-1990.

Articles

2832. Berle, A. "Bassist Richard Davis: From Bo Diddley to Stravinsky." Guitar Player (June 1978): 30+.

2833. Freedman, Samuel. "Richard Davis, bassist tenured in the Big Ten." down beat (November 1979): 16.

2834. Gerber, Alain. "Regards sur l'art du grand Richard." Jazz Magazine, No. 166 (May 1969): 18+.

2835. Horricks, Raymond. "A Portrait of Richard Davis." Crescendo International (March 1988): 17-19; (April 1988): 24+.

2836. Hunt, David C. "The Contemporary Approach to Jazz Bass." Jazz & Pop (August 1969): 18-20.

2837. Macnie, Jim. "A bass kingpin gets the itch to reclaim his turf." Musician, No. 111 (January 1988): 15+.

2838. Morgenstern, Dan. "Richard Davis: the complete musician." down beat (June 2 1966): 23-24.

2839. Primack, Bret. "Profile: Richard Davis." down beat (November 17 1977): 32-33.

2840. Tolnay, T. "Double Take: Ron Carter and Richard Davis." down beat (May 11 1972): 14+.

2841. Wilmer, Valerie. "Courts Change But Not Richard." Melody Maker (September 9 1967): 17.

2842. ________. "The Face of the Bass." Melody Maker (January 8 1972): 16.

2843. ________. "Learning to Live with the Electric Bass." Melody Maker (September 20 1969): 10.

DAVIS, STEVE (1929-1987) - Bass

2844. Carner, Gary. "Davis, Steve." In The New Grove Dictionary of Jazz. London: Macmillan Press, 1988.

Obituaries

2845. Billboard (September 19 1987): 82.
2846. Cadence (November 1987): 94.
2847. Variety (September 2 1987): 87.

DEAN, ELTON (1945-) (Great Britain) - Alto Saxophone

2848. Carr, Ian. "Dean, Elton." In Jazz: The Essential Companion. New York: Prentice Hall Press, 1988.

2849. Gilbert, Mark. "Dean, Elton." In The New Grove Dictionary of Jazz. London: Macmillan Press, 1988.

2850. Jazz Now: the Jazz Centre Society Guide, ed. Roger Cotterell. London: Quartet Books, 1976, p. 127.

Articles

2851. Ansell, Kenneth. "Elton Dean." Impetus (London), No. 3 (1976).

2852. Case, Brian. "On the Road with The Dean." New Musical Express (October 2 1976): 22-23.

2853. Henshaw, L. "Who likes brass!" Melody Maker (November 17 1973): 44.

2854. Loupien, Serge. "Elton Dean beaucoup de musique dans mes tiroirs." Jazz Magazine, No. 274 (April 1979): 47.

2855. Peacock, S. "Elton Dean: Two's Company." Sounds (June 26 1971): 7.

2856. Williams, Richard. "American Experience." Melody Maker (August 14 1971): 9.

DECODING SOCIETY

2857. Claghorn, Charles Eugene. Biographical Dictionary of Jazz. Englewood Cliffs, NJ: Prentice-Hall, 1982, p. 338.

DETROIT FREE JAZZ

2858. Claghorn, Charles Eugene. Biographical Dictionary of Jazz. Englewood Cliffs, NJ: Prentice-Hall, 1982, p. 339. Brief sketch of the late 60s Detroit group anchored by drummer Don Moye.

DICKERSON, WALT (1931-   ) - Vibraphone

2859. Carles, Philippe, and Jean-Louis Comolli. Free Jazz, Black Power. 2nd ed. Paris: Editions Galilee, 1979, p. 393.

2860. Claghorn, Charles Eugene. Biographical Dictionary of American Music. West Nyack, NY: Parker Pub. Co., 1973.

2861. _________. Biographical Dictionary of Jazz. Englewood Cliffs, NJ: Prentice-Hall, 1982.

2862. Dean, Roger T. "Dickerson, Walt." In The New Grove Dictionary of Jazz. London: Macmillan Press, 1988.

2863. Dictionnaire du Jazz, eds. Philippe Carles, et al. Paris: Laffont, 1988.

2864. Feather, Leonard. The Encyclopedia of Jazz in the Sixties. New York: Horizon Press, 1966.

2865. Wilmer, Valerie. As Serious As Your Life. Westport, CT: Lawrence Hill & Co., 1981, p. 266.

Articles

2866. DeMichael, Don. "Impressions of Walt Dickerson." down beat (October 25 1962): 19, 44.

2867. Diliberto, John. "Profile: Walt Dickerson." down beat (July 1980): 53.

2868. Durfee, Roy. "This is Walt Dickerson." Coda, No. 208 (June/July 1986): 24-26. [Interview]

2869. "Monsieur 100,000 Walt." Jazz Magazine, No. 119 (June 1965): 36-39.

2870. Sheridan, Chris. "Walt Dickerson." Jazz Journal International (May 1980): 29-30.

2871. Tepperman, Barry. "Vibes in Motion: Earl Griffith and Walt Dickerson." Coda (November/December 1971): 6-8.

Discographies

2872. Mulder, Jan. "Walt Dickerson discography." Jazz Freak, Vol. 8, No. 2 (November 1980): 17-18.

DIXON, BILL [William Robert] (1925-) - Trumpet

See also # 282, 536-556, 695-696, 1737

Works in English

2873. Dixon, Bill. L'Opera: a Collection of Letters, Writings, Musical Scores, Drawings, and Photographs (1967-1986) [Volume One]. North Bennington, VT: Metamorphosis Music, BMI (P.O. Box 215, North Bennington, VT 05257), 1986. 183p.

2874. Rusch, Robert. "Bill Dixon." In JazzTalk: The Cadence Interviews. Secaucus, NJ: Lyle Stuart, 1984, pp. 121-175. [Reprinted from Cadence, Vol. 8, Nos. 3, 4, 5]

Biographical Dictionaries

2875. Berry, Lemuel, Jr. "Dixon, William R." Biographical Dictionary of Black Musicians and Music Educators. Guthrie, OK: Educational Book Publishers, 1978.

2876. Carr, Ian. "Dixon, Bill." In Jazz: The Essential Companion. New York: Prentice Hall Press, 1988.

2877. Claghorn, Charles Eugene. Biographical Dictionary of Jazz. Englewood Cliffs, NJ: Prentice-Hall, 1982.

2878. ________. "Dixon, William Robert." In Biographical Dictionary of American Music. West Nyack, NY: Parker Pub. Co., 1973.

2879. "Dixon, William R." In Who's Who Among Black Americans. 6th ed. 1990/91. Detroit: Gale Research, 1990.

2880. "Dixon, William Robert." In Who's Who in America. 45th ed. 1988-89.

2881. "Dixon, William Robert." In Who's Who in Entertainment. 1st ed. 1989-1990.

2882. Feather, Leonard. The Encyclopedia of Jazz in the Sixties. New York: Horizon Press, 1966.

2883. Kernfeld, Barry. "Dixon, Bill." In The New Grove Dictionary of American Music. London: Macmillan Press, 1986.

2884. _________. "Dixon, Bill." In The New Grove Dictionary of Jazz. London: Macmillan Press, 1988.

2885. The Penguin Encyclopedia of Popular Music, ed. Donald Clarke. New York: Viking, 1989.

2886. Southern, Eileen. Biographical Dictionary of Afro-American and African Musicians. Westport, CT: Greenwood Press, 1982.

2887. Wilmer, Valerie. As Serious As Your Life. Westport, CT: Lawrence Hill & Co., 1981, p. 266.

Dissertations

2888. Hardin, Christopher L. "Black Professional Musicians in Higher Education: A Study Based on in-depth interviews." Dissertation (Ed.D.) University of Massachusetts, 1987.

Articles

2889. Anderson, Jack. "Judith Dunn and the Endless Quest." Dance Magazine (November 1967): 48-51, 66-67. Interview with Dunn and Bill Dixon on their collaborative dance/music works.

2890. Auerbach, Brian. "Bill Dixon: Return of the Man." Option (September/October 1985): 38-40.

2891. "Bill Dixon." BMI (March 1968): 15. [Profile]

2892. "Conversation in Manhattan." Impulse (1967): 57-64. Roundtable discussion with choreographers Jean Erdman, Trisha Brown, Judith Dunn, Deborah Hay, Meredith Monk, Constance Poster, Yvonne Rainer and the lone non-dancer Bill Dixon.

2893. Dixon, Bill. "Collaboration: 1965-1972." Contact Quarterly, Vol. X, No. 2 (Spring/Summer 1985): 7-12. Discussion of Dixon's collaboration with choreographer Judith Dunn.

2894. _________. "Contemporary Jazz: An Assessment." Jazz & Pop, Vol. 6 (November 1967): 31-32.

2895. _________. "Dixon Digs at Jones." down beat (January 2 1964): 6-7. Letter to LeRoi Jones in which Dixon takes him to task for neglecting to mention his contributions to the music of the New York Contemporary Five.

2896. _________. "To Whom It May Concern." Coda, Vol. 8, No. 4 (October/November 1967): 2-10.

2897. _________. "To Whom It May Concern Nineteen Years Later." Coda, No. 211 (Dec 86/Jan 87): 24.

2898. _________. "WINTER SONG, 1964." down beat (May 21 1964): 39-42. Musical score of a Bill Dixon composition.

2899. ________, and Taylor Castell. "Bill Dixon." Sounds & Fury (July/August 1965): 38-40. Exchange between Dixon and Sounds & Fury's publisher Taylor Castell.

2900. Dunn, Judith. "A Letter to Helen." Dance Perspectives, No. 38 (Summer 1969): 44-49. Letters to a friend describing Dunn's collaborative residency with Bill Dixon at The Ohio State University.

2901. "Esperantic Jazz for U.N. Fans." down beat (August 4 1960): 11-12. Report on a jazz concert series programmed by Dixon for the United Nations Jazz Society.

2902. Joans, Ted. "Bill Dixon: the intransigent black musician arrives very much alive in Paris." Coda, No. 152 (December 1976): 10-11.

2903. Levin, Robert. "The Jazz Composers Guild: An Assertion of Dignity." down beat (May 6 1964): 17-18.

2904. MacGregor, S. B. "Bill Dixon." Coda, No. 153 (January-February 1977): 33-34. Observations on Dixon's appearance at Paris' 'Festival de l'Automne'.

2905. Riggins, Robert. "Professor Bill Dixon: Intents of an Innovator." down beat (August 1980): 30-32.

2906. Thompson, Keith G. "Bill Dixon - Too Long in the Background." Pieces of Jazz (1970): 106-108.

2907. "United Nations Jazz." Metronome (August 1960): 8. Brief report on Dixon's United Nations Jazz Society.

2908. Wilmer, Valerie. "Bill Dixon the Loner." Melody Maker (January 13 1973): 30.

2909. ________. "Dixon: Keeping On Doing It." Time Out (London), No. 540 (August 22-28 1980): 17.

Newspaper Articles

2910. Harrington, Stephanie. "Choreographing a Rumble in Avant-Garde Storefront." Village Voice (November 17 1966): 14-15. Report on the Judson Arts Workshop, a New York arts workshop in which Dixon and choreographer Judith Dunn were active.

2911. Johnston, Jill. "Dance Journal: Interview with Judith Dunn." Village Voice (November 17 1966): 14-15. Includes a discussion of Dunn's collaborations with Bill Dixon.

2912. Robinson, Winston C., Jr. "Bill Dixon's October Revolution." East Village Eye (February 1985): 27.

2913. "U.N. Cats Dig Jazz." New York Times Magazine (June 12 1960): 54-55. Photos of a U.N. Jazz Society event.

2914. Zwerin, Michael. "Jazz Journal: Just Music?" Village Voice (March 2 1967).

Works in French, Italian, and German

2915. Carles, Philippe, and Jean-Louis Comolli. Free Jazz, Black Power. 2nd ed. Paris: Editions Galilee, 1979, pp. 393-394.

2916. Dictionnaire du Jazz, eds. Philippe Carles, et al. Paris: Laffont, 1988.

2917. Reclams Jazzfuhrer. 2nd, rev. ed. Stuttgart: Reclam, 1977.

2918. Tenot, Frank. Dictionnaire du Jazz. Paris: Larousse, 1967.

Articles

2919. "Bill Dixon." Jazz Podium (October 1968): 306-309. [Profile]

2920. "Bill Dixon: A Contre-Courant." Jazz Magazine, No. 219 (February 1974).

2921. "Bill Dixon de Bennington au Festival d'Automne." Jazz Magazine, No. 247 (September 1976): 36-37.

2922. Farne, Libero. "Bill Dixon: Dall'Onu All Rivoluzione d'Ottobre." Musica Jazz (July 1987): 20-23.

2923. _________. "Bill Dixon: La Liberta Organizzata." Musica Jazz (June 1989): 20-25.

2924. Goddet, Laurent. "Bill Dixon." Jazz Hot, No. 300 (December 1973): 6-11; No. 301 (January 1974): 15-17. [Interview]

2925. Horenstein, Steven H. "L'Enseignement de Bill Dixon a Bennington." Jazz Magazine, No. 219 (February 1974): 224.

2926. _________. "Les Lecons de Bill Dixon." Jazz Magazine, No. 238 (November 1975): 18-19; No. 239 (December 1975): 24-5; No. 240 (January 1976): 16-17; and No. 241 (February 1976): 14-15.

2927. Leonardi, Angelo. "Bill Dixon ha molte cose da dire." Musica Jazz (March 1981): 3-6. [Interview]

2928. Schumann, Heiner. "Plattentest mit Bill Dixon." Jazz Podium (May 1985): 12.

2929. Thebault, Yves. "Quand Bill Dixon Ecoute." Jazz Magazine, No. 253 (Avril 1977): 16-17, 41.

2930. Zufferey, Maurice. "Bill Dixon." Jazz 360o (Switzerland), No. 46 (March 1982): 5-8. [Interview]

Concert Reviews

2931. "L'Album Aniversaire." Jazz Magazine, No. 334 (December 1984): 45.

2932. Bethune, C. "Bill Dixon." Jazz Magazine, No. 289 (September 1980): 15.

2933. Frazer, Vernon. "Around the World: Hartford." Coda, No. 194 (February 1984): 32. Report on a concert at Wesleyan University.

2934. Hoefer, George. "Caught in the Act: Bill Dixon-Archie Shepp." down beat (March 14 1963): 36. Review of a Judson Hall concert.

2935. McDonagh, Don. "Dunn/Dixon Group Performs '1972-73', Hour-Long Dance." New York Times (December 8 1972): 35.

2936. Maskey, Jacqueline. "Judith Dunn and Bill Dixon, Judson Memorial Church." Dance Magazine (September 1966): 30-31. Review of a collaborative dance/music performance by Dunn and Dixon of "Dew Horse."

2937. Stodolsky, Ellen. "Judith Dunn and Bill Dixon, Theatre of the Riverside Church." Dance Magazine (February 1973): 33.

2938. Sundin, B. "Archie Shepp-Bill Dixon Quartet." Orkester Journalen (September 1962): 12-13.

2939. Tinder, Cliff. "Caught: Bill Dixon Trio; Third Street Music School, New York." down beat (October 1982): 57.

2940. Weiss, Jason. "Bill Dixon: Chapelle des Lombards, Paris, June 18-24, 1980." Coda, No. 174 (September 1980): 35.

Record Reviews

2941. Cooke, Jack. "New York Nouvelle Vague 2." Jazz Monthly (April 1965): 29-30. Review of Archie Shepp/Bill Dixon Quartet lp on Savoy Records.

2942. Davis, Francis. "Record Reviews: Bill Dixon In Italy, Vol. 1 & 2." down beat (December 1981): 54-55.

2943. Fero, Charles. "Sounds Recalled: Archie Shepp/Bill Dixon Quartet." Sounds & Fury (April 1966): 64. Review of Dixon's first Savoy lp.

2944. Fine, Milo. "Record Reviews: Bill Dixon in Italy, Vol. 1." Cadence (July 1981): 58-60.

2945. __________. "Record Reviews: Collection." Cadence (September 1985): 75. Review of Dixon's limited edition double lp on the Cadence Jazz Records label.

2946. Hentoff, Nat. "Record Reviews: Intents and Purposes." Hi Fi/Stereo Review (April 1968): 116.

2947. Kostakis, Peter. "Record Reviews: Collection." down beat (February 1986): 29-30. Review of Dixon's limited edition double album issued by Cadence Records.

2948. Lee, David. "Record Reviews: Bill Dixon In Italy, Vol. 1 & 2." Coda, No. 180 (October 1981): 25-26. Review of two Soul Note lps.

2949. Mathieu, Bill. "Record Reviews: Archie Shepp-Bill Dixon Quartet." down beat (September 26 1963): 35.

2950. Norris, John. "Record Reviews: Intents and Purposes." Coda (April 1970): 20-21.

2951. Riggins, Roger. "Trumpet Variations." Coda, No. 194 (February 1984): 37-38. Review of Dixon's Soul Note lp "November 1981."

2952. Rusch, Bob. "Globe Trotting." Cadence (November 1981): 44. Review of the Fore lp "Considerations 1 & 2."

2953. ________. "Record Reviews: November 1981." Cadence, Vol. 9, No. 1 (January 1983): 59.

2954. Smith, Tim. "Record Reviews: Thoughts." Cadence (December 1987): 77-78. Review of Dixon's Soul Note lp "Thoughts."

2955. Spellman, A. B. "Archie Shepp/Bill Dixon Quartet." Kulchur, No. 11 (Autumn 1963): 94-95. Review of Dixon's first recording for the Savoy label.

2956. Welding, Pete. "Record Reviews: Bill Dixon 7-tette/Archie Shepp and the New York Contemporary 5." down beat (October 8 1964): 27-28. Review of Dixon's Savoy lp.

2957. Whitehead, Kevin. "Steer Horns." down beat (April 1988): 32. Discussion of the Soul Note lp "Thoughts."

2958. Zwerin, Michael. "The Artistry of Bill Dixon." down beat (November 30 1967): 28-29. Review of Dixon's RCA lp "Intents and Purposes."

Discographies

2959. Cerutti, Gustave. "Discographie: Bill Dixon." Jazz 360o (Switzerland), No. 43 (December 1981): 12-14.

Media Materials

2960. Bill Dixon (Audiotape). New York: Duke Ellington Society, New York Chapter, 1967. 65 min. Recorded in New York City, 1967. Dixon speaks about his career and the state of jazz, in particular the jazz avant-garde, ca. the mid-60s. [Held by the Schomburg Center - Sc Audio C-491 (Side 1 & 2)]

2961. Imagine the Sound (1981). 91 min. Directed by Ron Mann. Documentary on the life and music of Bill Dixon, Archie Shepp, Paul Bley and Cecil Taylor. [For distribution information contact: Bill Smith, c/o Coda Publications, Box 87, Station J, Toronto, Ontario M4J 4X8, Canada]

2962. Index (Motion Picture) 1964-67. 4 min. Filmed by Gene Friedman. Colaborative dance/music performance by Dixon and dancer Judith Dunn. [Held by the Dance Collection - Lincoln Center (*MGZHB2-745)]

2963. Judson Dance Theatre Reconstructions (Videotape) 1982. Includes a reconstruction of the Dixon/Dunn work "Dewhorse" performed here by Dixon and dancer Cheryl Lilienstein. [Held by the Dance Collection - Lincoln Center (*MGZIC 9-559)]

DOERGE, PIERRE (1946-) (Denmark) - Guitar/Bandleader

2964. Wiedemann, Erik. "Dorge, Pierre." In The New Grove Dictionary of Jazz. London: Macmillan Press, 1988.

Articles

2965. Baggenaes, Roland. "The New Jungle Orchestra." Coda, No. 215 (August-September 1987): 18-19. Interview with Doerge re: his big band, The New Jungle Orchestra.

2966. Feldman, Mitchell. "Pierre Dorge and the New Jungle Orchestra: One World, Many Musics." down beat (November 1986): 26+. [Interview]

2967. Stanley, Larry. "Eareviews: New Jungle Orchestra." Ear, Vol. 12, No. 7 (October 1987): 26.

2968. Summers, Russ. "The Jazz Fest Circuit: Barre Phillips, Maarten Altena and Pierre Dorge in Vancouver." Option, No. 36 (January/February 1991): 44-49.

DOLPHY, ERIC ALLAN (1928-1964) - Alto Sax/Bass Clarinet

See also # 109, 122, 260, 2592

Works in English

2969. Horricks, Raymond. The Importance of Being Dolphy. Tunbridge Wells: Costello, 1988. 96p. (Jazz Avant-Garde Series)

2970. Simosko, Vladimir, and Barry Tepperman. Eric Dolphy: a musical biography and discography. New York: Da Capo Press, 1979. 132p. (Reprint of 1974 ed.)

2971. Williams, Martin. "Introducing Eric Dolphy." In Jazz Panorama; from the pages of the Jazz Review. New York: Crowell, 1962, pp. 281-283.

Biographical Dictionaries

2972. Berry, Lemuel, Jr. Biographical Dictionary of Black Musicians and Music Educators. Guthrie, OK: Educational Book Publishers, 1978.

2973. Case, Brian, and Stan Britt. The Harmony Illustrated Encyclopedia of Jazz. 3rd ed. New York: Harmony Books, 1987.

2974. Claghorn, Charles Eugene. Biographical Dictionary of American Music. West Nyack, NY: Parker Pub. Co., 1973.

2975. ________. Biographical Dictionary of Jazz. Englewood Cliffs, NJ: Prentice-Hall, 1982.

2976. Feather, Leonard. The Encyclopedia of Jazz. Rev. ed. New York: Horizon Press, 1960.

2977. ________. The Encyclopedia of Jazz in the Sixties. New York: Horizon Press, 1966.

2978. Kernfeld, Barry. "Dolphy, Eric." In The New Grove Dictionary of American Music. London: Macmillan Press, 1986.

2979. ________. "Dolphy, Eric." In The New Grove Dictionary of Jazz. London: Macmillan Press, 1988.

2980. The Penguin Encyclopedia of Popular Music, ed. Donald Clarke. New York: Viking, 1989.

2981. Priestley, Brian. "Dolphy, Eric." In Jazz: The Essential Companion. New York: Prentice Hall Press, 1988.

2982. Southern, Eileen. Biographical Dictionaries of Afro-American and African Musicians. Westport, CT: Greenwood Press, 1982.

2983. Wilmer, Valerie. As Serious As Your Life. Westport, CT: Lawrence Hill & Co., 1981, p. 266.

Articles

2984. Avakian, George. "Eric Dolphy - A Tribute." Jazz (New York), Vol. 3, No. 6 (October 1964): 14.

2985. Beckett, Alan. "Motifs: Eric Dolphy." New Left Review, No. 26 (Summer 1964): 69-71.

2986. "Benefit for Dolphy parents in Los Angeles nets $895." down beat (October 8 1964): 13.

2987. Cooke, Jack. "Eric Dolphy." Jazz Monthly (January 1966): 24-30.

2988. DeMichael, Don. "John Coltrane and Eric Dolphy answer the jazz critics." down beat (April 12 1962): 20-23.

2989. Downs, Clive G. "An Annotated Bibliography of Eric Dolphy Solo Transcriptions." Jazzforschung, Vol. 21 (1989): 49-54.

2990. ________. "Eric Dolphy--were the critics out to lunch?" Jazz Journal International (May 1978): 10-11.

2991. "Eric Dolphy." International Musician (August 1959): 19.

2992. Feather, Leonard. "Why Shouldn't I Imitate Birds?" Melody Maker (October 5 1963): 8.

2993. Green, Benny. "A Matter of Form." Jazz Journal (June 1962): 11-12.

2994. Halperin, Daniel. "Two New Boys." Jazz News, Vol. 5, No. 1 (January 7 1961): 2. Profile of Eric Dolphy and Ornette Coleman.

2995. Heckman, Don. "The Value of Eric Dolphy." down beat (October 8 1964): 17. [Tribute]

2996. Houston, Bob. "The dilemma that was Dolphy." Melody Maker (July 11 1964): 8.

2997. "In Tribute Eric Dolphy 1928-1964." down beat (August 27 1964): 12.

2998. "International Jazz Critic's Poll: the winners." down beat (August 3 1961): 16.

2999. Jannotta, Roger. "'God Bless the Child': an analysis of an unaccompanied bass clarinet solo by Eric Dolphy." Jazz Research/Jazzforschung, Nr. 9 (1977): 37-48.

3000. Kerr, David. "Eric Dolphy - The Los Angeles Years." Jazz Times (November 1981).

3001. Korall, Burt. "Freer Jazz from the 'New Wave'." Melody Maker (December 16 1961): 8.

3002. Kynaston, Trent. "Eric Dolphy's solo on Teenie's Blues - an alto sax transcription." down beat (December 1988): 64.

3003. Loveless, C. "Outward Bound with Eric Dolphy." Jazz Journal (July 1963): 16-18.

3004. "Seven Steps to Jazz." Melody Maker (May 7 1966): 8. Biographical sketch.

3005. Twelftree, Alan. "Second Opinion: Eric Dolphy." Melody Maker (June 14 1969): 17.

3006. Whent, C. "A Personal Note on Eric Dolphy." Jazz Monthly (September 1964): 15-16.

3007. Williams, Martin. "Introducing Eric Dolphy." The Jazz Review, Vol. 3 (June 1960): 16.

3008. Williams, Richard. "Straight Ahead--the early work of Oliver Nelson and Eric Dolphy." Jazz Journal (July 1967): 4+.

3009. Wilmer, Valerie. "Eric Dolphy." Jazz News (November 29 1961): 9-10.

Works in French, German, Dutch and Italian

3010. Roggeman, Willy. "Blues for Eric." In Jazzologie: 1940-1965. Brugge: De Galge, 1965, pp. 170-174. [Dutch text]

Biographical Dictionaries

3011. Carles, Philippe, and Jean-Louis Comolli. Free Jazz, Black Power. 2nd ed. Paris: Editions Galilee, 1979, pp. 394-395.

3012. Dictionnaire du Jazz, eds. Philippe Carles, et al. Paris: Laffont, 1988.

3013. Reclams Jazzfuhrer. 2nd, rev. ed. Stuttgart: Reclam, 1977.

3014. Reda, Jacques. Anthologie des Musiciens de Jazz. Paris: Stock, 1981, pp. 294-296.

3015. Tenot, Frank. Dictionnaire du Jazz. Paris: Larousse, 1967.

Articles

3016. "Dictionnaire de l'Alto." Jazz Magazine, No. 42 (December 1966): 42. Biographical sketch.

3017. "Eric Dolphy...le passeur." Jazz Magazine, No. 119 (June 1965): 40-49.

3018. Goddet, Laurent. "Eric Dolphy--une lutte contre l'ombre." Jazz Hot, No. 262 (June 1970): 11+.

3019. "I Remember Eric..." Jazz Hot, No. 310 (November 1974): 10-13. 1961 interview.

3020. Ioakimidis, Demetre. "Eric Dolphy." Jazz Hot, No. 167 (July-August 1961): 22-26.

3021. Lenissois, Claude, and Jef Gilson. "Adieu Eric." Jazz Hot, No. 201 (September 1964): 10-11.

3022. Maffei, Pino. "Eric Dolphy." Musica Jazz (January 1961): 25.

3023. Positif, Francois. "Pour Eric Dolphy, le meilleur contrebassiste c'est Charlie Mingus." Jazz Hot, No. 169 (October 1961): 14-17.

Obituaries

3024. "Eric Dolphy's Untimely Death at 35 Shocks Musical World." Sepia (June 1965): 53.

3025. Hentoff, Nat. "Second Chorus." down beat (August 27 1964): 40.

3026. International Musician (August 1964): 35.

3027. "Mort d'Eric." Jazz Magazine, No. 109 (August 1964): 1.

3028. Orkester Journalen (July-August 1964): 16.

3029. "Reed man Eric Dolphy dies in Berlin." down beat (August 13 1964): 8.

3030. Variety (July 15 1964): 63.

3031. White, C. "Eric Dolphy." Jazz Journal (August 1964): 28-29.

Concert Reviews

3032. Coss, Bill. "Eric Dolphy--Ree Dragonette." down beat (January 17 1963): 42-43.

3033. "Dolphy au Club (Saint-Germain, Paris)." Jazz Magazine, No. 7 (November 1961): 15.

3034. Morgenstern, Dan. "Jazz by Schuller." Metronome (August 1960): 43-45. Review of a performance by Ornette Coleman and Eric Dolphy on a program organized by composer Gunther Schuller.

3035. Tynan, John. "Take 5." down beat (November 23 1961): 40.

Record Reviews

3036. Brown, Marion. "Jazz: Eric Dolphy Conversations." Kulchur, No. 13 (Spring 1964): 99-100.

3037. DeMichael, Don. "Record Reviews: Out to Lunch." down beat (December 17 1964): 27-29.

3038. Mathieu, Bill. "Record Reviews: Conversation." down beat (January 16 1964): 26.

3039. Pekar, Harvey. "Record Reviews: Eric Dolphy at the Five Spot, Vol. II." down beat (February 13 1964): 30.

Discographies

See also # 2970

3040. Kraner, Dietrich Heinz. The Eric Dolphy Discography (1958-1964). Graz: Modern Jazz Series, 1967. 16p.

3041. Portaleoni, Sergio. "Discografia: Eric Dolphy." Musica Jazz, Vol. 33, No. 3 (1977): 46-48; No. 5 (1977): 46-48.

3042. Reichardt, Uwe. Like a Human Voice: The Eric Dolphy Discography. West Germany: Norbert Ruecker (Postfach 14, D-6384 Schmitten 1, GDR), 1986. 80p.

3043. Rissi, Mathias. Eric Dolphy; discography. Adliswil, Switzerland: M. Rissi (Haldenstr. 23, CH-8134 Adliswil), 1977. 29p.

DONALD, BARBARA (1942-) - Trumpet

See also # 694, 704

3044. Placksin, Sally. American Women in Jazz. New York: Wideview Press, 1982, pp. 255-258.

Biographical Dictionaries

3045. Claghorn, Charles Eugene. Biographical Dictionary of Jazz. Englewood Cliffs, NJ: Prentice-Hall, 1982.

3046. Dictionnaire du Jazz, eds. Philippe Carles, et al. Paris: Laffont, 1988.

3047. Feather, Leonard, and Ira Gitler. The Encyclopedia of Jazz in the Seventies. New York: Horizon Press, 1976.

3048. The New Grove Dictionary of Jazz. London: Macmillan Press, 1988.

Articles

3049. DeBarros, Paul. "Profile: Barbara Donald." down beat (May 1983): 47-48.

3050. Rusch, Bob. "Barbara Donald: interview." Cadence, Vol. 9, No. 6 (June 1983): 9-12.

DOYLE, ARTHUR (1944-) - Tenor Sax/Bass Clarinet/Flute

3051. Carles, Philippe, and Jean-Louis Comolli. Free Jazz, Black Power. 2nd ed. Paris: Editions Galilee, 1979, p. 395.

3052. Wilmer, Valerie. As Serious As Your Life. Westport, CT: Lawrence Hill & Co., 1981, p. 266-267.

Articles

3053. "Caught." down beat (June 3 1976): 37. [Concert review]

3054. Gauffre, Christian. "Arthur Doyle: Alabama feeling." Jazz Magazine, No. 330 (June 1984): 41+. [Interview]

DRESSER, MARK (1952-) - Bass

3055. Carles, Philippe, and Jean-Louis Comolli. Free Jazz, Black Power. 2nd ed. Paris: Editions Galilee, 1979, p. 395.

3056. Lock, Graham. "Mark Dresser, Bass." In Forces in Motion: The Music and Thoughts of Anthony Braxton. New York: Da Capo, 1989, pp. 117-123. [Interview]

DUBIN, LARRY (1931-1978) (Canada) - Drums

3057. Miller, Mark. "Dubin, Larry." In Encyclopedia of Music in Canada, eds. Helmut Kallmann, et al. Toronto/Buffalo: University of Toronto Press, 1981, p. 282.

3058. _________. "Larry Dubin." In Jazz in Canada. Toronto: Nightwood Editions, 1988, pp. 128-145. (Orig. 1982)

Articles

3059. Miller, Mark. "'Larry Dubin: either you play or you don't'." Coda, No. 166 (April-May 1979): 12-14. [Interview]

3060. Snow, Michael. "Larry Dubin's Music." Impulse, Vol. 7, No. 1 (1978).

Obituaries

3061. Coda, No. 161 (June 1978): 30.

3062. Jazz Journal International (August 1978): 37.

DUDEK, GERD (1938-) (Germany) - Reeds

3063. Carles, Philippe, and Jean-Louis Comolli. Free Jazz, Black Power. 2nd ed. Paris: Editions Galilee, 1979, p. 396.

3064. Carr, Ian. "Dudek, Gerd." In Jazz: The Essential Companion. New York: Prentice Hall Press, 1988.

3065. Claghorn, Charles Eugene. Biographical Dictionary of Jazz. Englewood Cliffs, NJ: Prentice-Hall, 1982.

3066. Iannapollo, Robert J. "Dudek, Gerd." In The New Grove Dictionary of Jazz. London: Macmillan Press, 1988.

3067. Reclams Jazzfuhrer. 2nd, rev. ed. Stuttgart: Reclam, 1977.

DYANI, JOHNNY (1945-1986) (South Africa) - Bass

3068. Carles, Philippe, and Jean-Louis Comolli. Free Jazz, Black Power. 2nd ed. Paris: Editions Galilee, 1979, p. 396.

3069. Carr, Ian. "Dyani, Johnny." In Jazz: The Essential Companion. New York: Prentice Hall Press, 1988.

3070. De Ledesma, Charles. "Dyani, Johnny." In The New Grove Dictionary of Jazz. London: Macmillan Press, 1988.

3071. Dictionnaire du Jazz, eds. Philippe Carles, et al. Paris: Laffont, 1988.

Articles

3072. Ansell, Kenneth. "Johnny Dyani." Impetus (London), No. 7 (1978): 279-280; No. 8 (1978): 329-330. [Interview]

3073. Collin, Leif. "Johnny Dyani." Orkester Journalen (March 1983): 7-9. [Interview]

3074. de Ledesma, Charles. "Johnny Dyani." Wire, No. 12 (February 1985): 35-36.

3075. Knox, Keith. "Johnny 'Mbizo' Dyani." Jazz Forum, No. 104 (1987): 20-22.

3076. Solothurnmann, Jurg. "'Ich bin eigentlich ein Volksmusiker': Ein gesprach mit dem sudafrikanischen Bassisten Johnny Dyani." Jazz (Basel), Nr. 4 (1984). [Interview]

3077. _________. "Johnny Dyani: Music is Like Medicine." Jazz Forum, No. 87 (1984): 42-47. [Interview]

3078. Wilmer, Valerie. "Johnny Dyani: Working for Africa." Melody Maker (February 13 1971): 26.

Obituaries

3079. Cadence (December 1986): 92.
3080. Coda (December 1986): 40; (February/March 1987): 6.
3081. down beat (February 1987): 13.
3082. Jazz Magazine, No. 356 (December 1986): 7.
3083. Jazz Podium (December 1986): 44.
3084. Wire, Nos. 34/35 (December 1986-January 1987): 9.

EHRLICH, MARTY (1955-) - Reeds

3085. Dictionnaire du Jazz, eds. Philippe Carles, et al. Paris: Laffont, 1988.

Articles

3086. Gill, Jonathan M. "Profile: Marty Ehrlich." down beat (July 1986): 51-52.

3087. Macnie, Jim. "Marty Ehrlich's Delicate Balance: NYC's most underrated reedman walks a jazz tightrope." Musician (January 1990): 16, 18, 35.

EL-ZABAR, KAHIL - Percussion

See also # 3094-3096

3088. Goddet, Laurent. "Kahil el-Zabar: The Preacher." Jazz Hot, No. 354 (October 1978): 26-28. [Interview]

3089. Sachs, Lloyd. "Bold Souls: a new generation is taking the reins at one of the country's most vital centers for jazz." Chicago (May 1989): 146, 151, 172, 176.

EMERY, JAMES (1951-) - Guitar

See also # 6107-6108

3090. Dictionnaire du Jazz, eds. Philippe Carles, et al. Paris: Laffont, 1988.

Articles

3091. Jeske, Lee. "Profile: James Emery." down beat (May 1983): 46.

3092. Sandow, Gregory. "Music: Minor Ideals." Village Voice (May 27 1981): 78-79.

3093. Woodard, Josef. "James Emery." Frets, Vol. 8 (June 1986): 41+. [Interview]

ETHNIC HERITAGE ENSEMBLE

3094. Claghorn, Charles Eugene. Biographical Dictionary of Jazz. Englewood Cliffs, NJ: Prentice-Hall, 1982, p. 340.

Articles

3095. "... if the TV change, the way of the people will change... : the Ethnic Heritage Ensemble." Jazz (Basel), No. 4 (1983).

3096. Tinder, Cliff. "Faces: Ethnic Heritage Ensemble." Musician, Player and Listener, No. 33 (June 1981): 32.

EWART, DOUGLAS (1946-) - Reeds

3097. Carles, Philippe, and Jean-Louis Comolli. Free Jazz, Black Power. 2nd ed. Paris: Editions Galilee, 1979, p. 397.

3098. Such, David G. "Ewart, Douglas." In The New Grove Dictionary of Jazz. London: Macmillan Press, 1988.

3099. Wilmer, Valerie. As Serious As Your Life. Westport, CT: Lawrence Hill & Co., 1981, p. 267.

Articles

3100. Hrynchuk, Halya. "Douglas Ewart, Un Enfant de l'AACM." Jazz Magazine, No. 268 (September 1978): 42-45.

3101. Lindenmaier, H. Lukas. "Doug Ewart: interview." Cadence, Vol. 5, No. 11 (November 1979): 3-4+.

3102. Litweiler, John. "Profile: Doug Ewart." down beat (July 14 1977): 22-23.

EXPERIMENTAL BAND (formed 1961)

3103. Claghorn, Charles Eugene. Biographical Dictionary of Jazz. Englewood Cliffs, NJ: Prentice-Hall, 1982, p. 341.

3104. The New Grove Dictionary of Jazz. London: Macmillan Press, 1988.

EYGES, DAVID (1950-) - Cello

3105. Dictionnaire du Jazz, eds. Philippe Carles, et al. Paris: Laffont, 1988.

Articles

3106. Bouchard, Fred. "David Eyges." down beat (October 5 1978): 46-47.

3107. "Caught!" down beat (October 5 1978): 51. [Concert review]

3108. "David Eyges." Jazz Magazine (Northport, NY), Vol. 3, No. 4 (Fall 1979): 104.

3109. Occhiogrosso, Peter. "Up From Under." Soho Weekly News (March 11 1976): 36. [Concert review]

3110. Rusch, Bob. "David Eyges: interview." Cadence, Vol. 6, No. 12 (December 1980): 5-10, 18.

FASTEAU, ZUSAAN KALI (1947-) - Reeds/Percussion/Piano/Voice

3111. Carles, Philippe, and Jean-Louis Comolli. Free Jazz, Black Power. 2nd ed. Paris: Editions Galilee, 1979, p. 397.

3112. "The Questionnaire." Cadence (December 1989): 63-64. Biographical sketch compiled from information supplied by Fasteau to Cadence editor Bob Rusch.

FAVORS, MALACHI (1937-) - Bass

See also # 914-965

3113. Carles, Philippe, and Jean-Louis Comolli. Free Jazz, Black Power. 2nd ed. Paris: Editions Galilee, 1979, p. 397.

3114. Claghorn, Charles Eugene. Biographical Dictionary of Jazz. Englewood Cliffs, NJ: Prentice-Hall, 1982.

3115. Dictionnaire du Jazz, eds. Philippe Carles, et al. Paris: Laffont, 1988.

3116. Feather, Leonard, and Ira Gitler. The Encyclopedia of Jazz in the Seventies. New York: Horizon Press, 1976.

3117. Kernfeld, Barry. "Favors, Malachi." In The New Grove Dictionary of Jazz. London: Macmillan Press, 1988.

3118. Who's Who in Entertainment. 1st ed. 1989-1990.

3119. Wilmer, Valerie. As Serious As Your Life. Westport, CT: Lawrence Hill & Co., 1981, p. 267.

Articles

3120. Case, Brian. "Favors: Bass Basic." Melody Maker (May 1979): 52+.

FAVRE, PIERRE (1937-) (Switzerland) - Drums

3121. Carles, Philippe, and Jean-Louis Comolli. Free Jazz, Black Power. 2nd ed. Paris: Editions Galilee, 1979, p. 398.

3122. Carr, Ian. "Favre, Pierre." In Jazz: The Essential Companion. New York: Prentice Hall Press, 1988.

3123. Dictionnaire du Jazz, eds. Philippe Carles, et al. Paris: Laffont, 1988.

3124. Iannapollo, Robert J. "Favre, Pierre." In The New Grove Dictionary of Jazz. London: Macmillan Press, 1988.

3125. Reclams Jazzfuhrer. 2nd, rev. ed. Stuttgart: Reclam, 1977.

Articles

3126. Carles, Philippe. "Pierre Favre." Jazz Magazine, No. 216 (October-November 1973): 27-29. [Interview]

3127. "Pierre Favre: European drummer/clinician." Jazz and Pop (November 1968): 46-47.

3128. Romano, Aldo. "'Pourquoi j'aime Pierre Favre.'" Jazz Magazine, Vol. 162, No. 2 (1969): 9.

3129. "Swiss drummer sees USA on cymbal ride." down beat (October 3 1968): 12.

3130. Terrones, G. "Pierre Favre parle a..." Jazz Hot, No. 270 (March 1971): 20-21.

FEMINIST IMPROVISING GROUP (Great Britain)

See also # 694

3131. Charlton, Hannah. "Jazzscene: No Apologies." Melody Maker (December 8 1979): 41. [Interview]

3132. "Feminist Improvisation Group." Musics (London), No. 20 (December 1978): 9-11. Round-table discussion between the members of the FIG.

3133. Merck, Mandy. "Arrival of the Prodigal Daughters." Time Out (London), No. 496 (October 19-25 1979): 23.

FEW, BOBBY (1935-) - Piano

3134. Carles, Philippe, and Jean-Louis Comolli. Free Jazz, Black Power. 2nd ed. Paris: Editions Galilee, 1979, p. 398.

3135. Dictionnaire du Jazz, eds. Philippe Carles, et al. Paris: Laffont, 1988.

3136. Wilmer, Valerie. As Serious As Your Life. Westport, CT: Lawrence Hill & Co., 1981, p. 267.

Articles

3137. Carles, Philippe. "Bobby Few: Ma Musique Classique Noire." Jazz Magazine, No. 262 (February 1978): 20-23, 52.

FEZA, MONGEZI (1945-1975) (South Africa/UK) - Trumpet

3138. Carr, Ian. "Feza, Mongezi." In Jazz: The Essential Companion. New York: Prentice Hall Press, 1988.

3139. De Ledesma, Charles. "Feza, Mongezi." In The New Grove Dictionary of Jazz. London: Macmillan Press, 1988.

3140. Dictionnaire du Jazz, eds. Pierre Carles, et al. Paris: Robert Laffont, 1988.

3141. Jazz Now: the Jazz Centre Society Guide, ed. Roger Cotterrell. London: Quartet Books, 1976, p. 131.

Articles

3142. de Ledesma, Charles. "Mongezi Feza: 1945-1975." Wire, No. 12 (February 1985): 32-33.

3143. Hyder, Ken. "Spear Heads." Melody Maker (February 23 1974): 45.

3144. Lake, Steve. "Mongs: Unique Stylist." Melody Maker (December 27 1975): 2+. [Tribute]

3145. Wilmer, Valerie. "Mongesi Feza and his pocket trumpet." Melody Maker (October 24 1970): 14. [Interview]

Obituaries

3146. Coda, No. 145 (March 1976): 32.
3147. Crescendo International, Vol. 14 (February 1976): 2.
3148. Jazz Forum, No. 39 (1976): 18.
3149. Jazz Magazine, No. 240 (Janvier 1976): 6.
3150. Jazz Podium, Vol. 25 (February 1976): 26-27.
3151. Performing Right, No. 65 (May 1976): 28.

FIELDER, ALVIN Jr. (1935-) - Drums

3152. Carles, Philippe, and Jean-Louis Comolli. Free Jazz, Black Power. 2nd ed. Paris: Editions Galilee, 1979, pp. 398-399.

3153. Claghorn, Charles Eugene. Biographical Dictionary of Jazz. Englewood Cliffs, NJ: Prentice-Hall, 1982.

3154. Dictionnaire du Jazz, eds. Philippe Carles, et al. Paris: Laffont, 1988.

3155. Feather, Leonard, and Ira Gitler. The Encyclopedia of Jazz in the Seventies. New York: Horizon Press, 1976.

Articles

3156. Litweiler, John. "Caught in the Act: Alvin Fielder-Anthony Braxton, University of Chicago." down beat (May 19 1967): 25-26. [Concert review]

3157. Wilmer, Valerie. "Taking Care of Business." Melody Maker (August 2 1975): 28.

FISCHER, JOHN (1930-) (Belgium/US) - Piano

See also # 664-667, 3852-3855

3158. Kumpf, Hans. "John Fischer: Interaktions-Musik." Jazz Podium (April 1977): 16-18. [Interview]

3159. "The Questionnaire." Cadence (January 1991): 28, 33, 91. Compilation of biographical information submitted by Fischer to Cadence editor Bob Rusch.

3160. Safane, Cliff. "John Fischer: face to INTERface." Jazz Forum, No. 71 (1981): 45-49. [Interview]

3161. Solothurnmann, Jurg. "Painter and Jazz Musician: two sides of John Fischer." Jazz Forum, No. 89 (1984): 32-40. [Interview]

FOLWELL, BILL - Bass

3162. Carles, Philippe, and Jean-Louis Comolli. Free Jazz, Black Power. 2nd ed. Paris: Editions Galilee, 1979, p. 399.

3163. Wilmer, Valerie. As Serious As Your Life. Westport, CT: Lawrence Hill & Co., 1981, p. 267.

FREEMAN, CHICO [Earl Lavon] (1949-) - Reeds

See also # 4381-4386

3164. Baraka, Amiri (LeRoi Jones), and Amina Baraka. The Music; reflections on jazz and blues. New York: Morrow, 1987, pp. 246-248. Reprint of the Baraka's liner notes to Freeman's India Navigation lp "The Outside Within."

Biographical Dictionaries

3165. Carles, Philippe, and Jean-Louis Comolli. Free Jazz, Black Power. 2nd ed. Paris: Editions Galilee, 1979, p. 400.

3166. Case, Brian, and Stan Britt. The Harmony Illustrated Encyclopedia of Jazz. 3rd ed. New York: Harmony Books, 1987.

3167. Dictionnaire du Jazz, eds. Philippe Carles, et al. Paris: Laffont, 1988.

3168. Hazell, Ed. "Freeman, Chico." In The New Grove Dictionary of Jazz. London: Macmillan Press, 1988.

3169. The Penguin Encyclopedia of Popular Music, ed. Donald Clarke. New York: Viking, 1989.

3170. Priestley, Brian. "Freeman, Chico." In Jazz: The Essential Companion. New York: Prentice Hall Press, 1988.

3171. Wilmer, Valerie. As Serious As Your Life. Westport, CT: Lawrence Hill & Co., 1981, p. 283.

Articles

3172. Aronson, David. "Chico Freeman." Jazz (Basel), Nr. 3 (1984). [Interview]

3173. Carles, Philippe. "Chico Freeman: Les Noms du Pere." Jazz Magazine, No. 280 (November 1979): 33-35+.

3174. Case, Brian. "Chico Freeman: The Outside Within." Black Music and Jazz Review [London] (October 1982): 24-25.

3175. ________. "Computing the Spirit Sensitive: Chico Freeman." The Wire (London), No. 30 (August 1986): 26-27, 29.

3176. ________. "The Tenor Sax Uri Geller: Neck Breaking a Speciality..." New Musical Express (September 24 1977): 50-51. [Interview]

3177. "Dico Disco & Co." Jazz Magazine, No. 298 (June 1981): 41-42. Biographical sketch.

3178. Dutilh, Alex, and Claude Baro. "Le Releve." Jazz Hot, No. 356/357 (Dec 1978/Jan 1979): 34-36. [Interview]

3179. Feather, Leonard. "Blindfold Test: Chico Freeman." down beat (May 1982): 47.

3180. Gans, Charles J. "Chico Freeman: new music from the source." Jazz Forum, No. 68 (1980): 44-49.

3181. Giddins, Gary. "Chico Freeman Arrives on Time." Village Voice (February 21 1977): 79, 81.

3182. Henkel, K. "Freemans Freiheit: Gespraech mit Chico Freeman." Jazz Podium (August 1989): 8-11.

3183. Irwin, P. "Profile: Chico Freeman." down beat (March 8 1979): 34-35.

3184. Israel, Stephen. "Freeman and Murray: New Jazz Wave Flows from Lofts." The Villager (December 22 1977): 19, 24.

3185. Kuhl, Chris. "Cecil McBee, Chico Freeman: interview." Cadence, Vol. 9, No. 6 (June 1983): 5-8, 12.

3186. Levi, Titus. "2nd Generation Sax: The Tenor Traditions of Chico and Von Freeman." OPtion, No. 20 (June 1988): 74-78.

3187. McRae, Barry. "A Freeman." Jazz Journal, Vol. 30, No. 12 (1977): 19.

3188. Marmande, Isabelle and Francis. "Chico Freeman: L'Esprit de Famille." Jazz Magazine, No. 259 (November 1977): 26-27. [Interview]

3189. Roberts, Jim. "Chico Freeman: Tradition in Transition." down beat (December 1983): 24-26.

3190. Sheridan, Chris. "Prometheus Observed: Chico Freeman." Jazz Journal International, Vol. 32, No. 11 (1979): 9.

3191. _________. "Young Men Ascending; Some Notes on Chico Freeman and George Adams." Jazz Journal International (October 1980): 26-27. [Profile]

3192. Stokes, W. Royal. "Chico Freeman: letting the music happen." Jazz Times (June 1987): 10. [Interview]

3193. Tesser, Neil. "Von and Chico Freeman: Tenor Dynasty." down beat (July 1980): 24-27.

3194. Wilmer, Valerie. "Chico the Free Man." Melody Maker, No. 52 (September 24 1977): 42.

FREEMAN, EARL (1939-) - Bass/Harp/Flute

3195. Carles, Philippe, and Jean-Louis Comolli. Free Jazz, Black Power. 2nd ed. Paris: Editions Galilee, 1979, p. 400.

3196. Wilmer, Valerie. As Serious As Your Life. Westport, CT: Lawrence Hill & Co., 1981, p. 268.

3197. _________. "Freeman Fighter." Melody Maker (May 13 1972): 26.

FRIEND, BECKY (1945-) - Flute

3198. Berg, Chuck. "Profile: Becky Friend." down beat (April 5 1979): 36-38.

Concert Reviews

3199. Caux, Daniel. "Alan Silva a Paris." Jazz Hot, No. 249 (April 1969): 9.

3200. _________. "La vieille Grille." Jazz Hot, No. 248 (March 1969): 9.

3201. Cressant, P. "A la cite Universitaire." Jazz Hot, No. 247 (February 1969): 8-9.

3202. Pinguet, Francis. "Et a Rouen." Jazz Hot, No. 247 (February 1969): 8-9.

FRISELL, BILL - Guitar

3203. Diliberto, John. "Bill Frisell: Guitars and Scatterations." Down Beat (May 1989): 16+.

3204. Watrous, Peter. "Bill Frisell's Progress in Music's Avant-Garde." New York Times (May 25 1990): C14.

GADDY, CHRISTOPHER (1943-1968) - Piano

3205. Carles, Philippe, and Jean-Louis Comolli. Free Jazz, Black Power. 2nd ed. Paris: Editions Galilee, 1979, pp. 400-401.

3206. "Final Bar." down beat (April 18 1968): 14. [Obituary]

3207. Wilmer, Valerie. As Serious As Your Life. Westport, CT: Lawrence Hill & Co., 1981, p. 268.

GALE, EDDIE (1941-) - Trumpet

See also # 609

3208. Levin, Robert. "The Third World." Jazz & Pop (June 1970): 12. [Profile]

3209. Rusch, Bob. "Eddie Gale interview." Cadence (October 1989): 13-18, 92.

GANELIN TRIO (Russia)

3210. Barban, Efim. "The Ganelin Trio: An Unguided Comet." In Russian Jazz, New Identity, ed. Leo Feigin. London: Quartet Books, 1985, pp. 30-38.

3211. Davis, Francis. "Avant-Garde Comrades." In Outcats: Jazz Composers, Instrumentalists, and Singers. New York: Oxford University Press, 1990, pp. 227-233. Reprint of # 3220.

3212. Fordham, John. "The Ganelin Trio in London." In Russian Jazz, New Identity, ed. Leo Feigin. London: Quartet Books, 1985, pp. 61-67.

3213. Noglik, Bert. "Ganelin Trio." In Jazzwerkstatt International. Berlin: Verlag Neue Musik, 1981, pp. 29-46. [Interview]

Biographical Dictionaries

3214. Carr, Ian. "Ganelin Trio." In Jazz: The Essential Companion. New York: Prentice Hall Press, 1988.

3215. Case, Brian, and Stan Britt. The Harmony Illustrated Encyclopedia of Jazz. 3rd. ed. New York: Harmony Books, 1987.

3216. The Penguin Encyclopedia of Popular Music, ed. Donald Clarke. New York: Viking, 1989.

Articles

3217. Barban. "From Russian Without Consent: Ganelin - Tarasov - Chekasin." Coda, No. 184 (June 1982): 12-14. [Interview trans. from the Russian]

3218. Boulay, S. "Soviet trio swings America." Jazz Forum, No. 103 (1986): 38-42.

3219. Cotterrell, Roger. "The Ganelin Trio." The Wire, No. 2 (Winter 1982/83): 7.

3220. Davis, Francis. "Music: Avant-Garde Comrades." The Atlantic (November 1986): 126+. [Reprinted in # 3211]

3221. Duncan, Amy. "Soviet Trio Takes Daring Liberties with Familiar Jazz Styles." Christian Science Monitor (June 30 1986): 29.

3222. Feigin, Leo. "New Sound from Behind the Iron Curtain." The Wire, No. 7 (Summer 1984): 9-12.

3223. Guregian, Elaine. "The Ganelin Trio." The Instrumentalist (September 1986): 111-112.

3224. Hennessey, Mike. "Europajazz: From Russia with jazz." Jazz Times (February 1984): 6.

3225. Le Bec, Jean-Yves. "Nouveaux Tableaux d'une Exposition." Jazz Magazine, No. 360 (1987): 36-37. [Interview]

3226. Lock, Graham. "A Hammer and Sickle Sonance." Wire, No. 20 (October 1985): 16-19.

3227. McRae, Barry. "Avant Courier." Jazz Journal International (May 1984): 12-13.

3228. Maino, Francesco. "Ganelin, Tarasov and Chekasin: interview." Cadence, Vol. 9, No. 1 (January 1983): 18-20.

3229. Mandel, Howard. "The Ganelin Trio: Jazz Detente." down beat (September 1986): 26+.

3230. Mihaiu, V. "Ganelin Trio: prophetic visions." Jazz Forum, No. 91 (1984): 30-36.

3231. Prevost, Eddie. "The Ganelin Trio: Reviewed." The Wire, No. 7 (Summer 1984): 14-16. [Record review]

3232. "Soviet Union: Braxton, Ganelin trio tops in critics' poll." Jazz Forum, No. 58 (1979): 14-15.

3233. Sutherland, S., and Peter Keepnews. "Iron Curtain sounds come west." Billboard (March 31 1984): 51.

3234. Testa, Bart. "Ambassadors of Jazz." Maclean's (July 14 1986): 45-46.

3235. "Vyacheslav Ganelin Trio." Jazz Forum, No. 49 (1977): 26.

3236. Whitney, Craig R. "Lithuania Is Home for Hottest Soviet Jazz Combo." New York Times (August 12 1979): 8.

3237. Yurchenkov, V. D. "Russian jazzmen play in Europe; Cologne radio concert is seen as major breakthrough." Billboard (October 31 1981): 96.

Media Materials

3238. Jazz Summit (1987). 28 min. Film/video. Directed by Jackie Ochs. Documentary on the Ganelin Trio's first trip to the U.S. [Available from First Run/Icarus Films, 200 Park Avenue South, Suite 1319, New York, NY 10003]

GANELIN, VYACHESLAV (1944-) (Russia) - Piano

See also # 3210-3238

3239. Dictionnaire du Jazz, eds. Philippe Carles, et al. Paris: Laffont, 1988.

3240. McRae, Barry. "Vyacheslav Ganelin." In The Jazz Handbook. Harlow, Essex, Eng.: Longman, 1987, pp. 235-236.

3241. Ojakaar, Walter. "Ganelin, Vyacheslav." In The New Grove Dictionary of Jazz. London: Macmillan Press, 1988.

Articles

3242. Doerschuk, Bob. "Vyacheslav Ganelin: Soviet Free Jazz." Keyboard Magazine (January 1987): 48.

3243. Lake, Steve. "Vyacheslav Ganelin." Jazzthetik, Vol. 2, No. 12 (December 1988): 12-18.

3244. "On the Bandstand." Jazz Forum, No. 49 (1977): 26.

GARE, LOU (Great Britain) - Tenor Saxophone

See also # 876-889

3245. Schonfield, Victor. "We're Not Interested in Music." Melody Maker (June 5 1971): 28. [Interview]

3246. Welch, Chris. "Caught in the Act." Melody Maker (March 4 1972): 42. [Concert review]

GARRETT, DONALD RAFAEL (1932-1989) - Bass/Bass Clarinet/Flute

3247. Carles, Philippe, and Jean-Louis Comolli. Free Jazz, Black Power. 2nd ed. Paris: Editions Galilee, 1979, p. 401.

3248. Dictionnaire du Jazz, eds. Philippe Carles, et al. Paris: Laffont, 1988.

3249. The New Grove Dictionary of Jazz. London: Macmillan Presss, 1988.

3250. Wilmer, Valerie. As Serious As Your Life. Westport, CT: Lawrence Hill & Co., 1981, p. 268.

Articles

3251. Carles, Philippe. "Rafael Garrett." Jazz Magazine, No. 216 (October-November 1973): 31-32. [Interview]

3252. Wilmer, Valerie. "It's Too Much of a Hassle--Rafael." Melody Maker (April 17 1971): 26.

Obituaries

3253. Coda, No. 229 (Dec 1989/Jan 1990): 24.
3254. Down Beat (December 1989): 62; (January 1990): 12.
3255. Jazz Magazine, No. 388 (December 1989): 7.
3256. Jazz Times (January 1990): 5.
3257. Orkester Journalen (December 1989): 44.
3258. Wire, No. 70/71 (Dec 1989/Jan 1990): 7.

GARRISON, JIMMY (1934-1976) - Bass

See also # 2491

3259. Berry, Lemuel, Jr. Biographical Dictionary of Black Musicians and Music Educators. Guthrie, OK: Educational Book Publishers, 1978.

3260. Carles, Philippe, and Jean-Louis Comolli. Free Jazz, Black Power. 2nd ed. Paris: Editions Galilee, 1979, pp. 401-402.

3261. Carr, Ian. "Garrison, Jimmy." In Jazz: The Essential Companion. New York: Prentice Hall Press, 1988.

3262. Claghorn, Charles Eugene. Biographical Dictionary of American Music. West Nyack, NY: Parker Pub. Co., 1973.

3263. ________. Biographical Dictionary of Jazz. Englewood Cliffs, NJ: Prentice-Hall, 1982.

3264. Dictionnaire du Jazz, eds. Philippe Carles, et al. Paris: Laffont, 1988

3265. Feather, Leonard. The Encyclopedia of Jazz. New ed. New York: Horizon Press, 1960.

3266. _________. The Encyclopedia of Jazz in the Sixties. New York: Horizon Press, 1966.

3267. _________, and Ira Gitler. The Encyclopedia of Jazz in the Seventies. New Yor: Horizon Press, 1976.

3268. Kernfeld, Barry. "Garrison, Jimmy." In The New Grove Dictionary of American Music. London: Macmillan Press, 1986.

3269. _________. "Garrison, Jimmy." In The New Grove Dictionary of Jazz. London: Macmillan Press, 1988.

3270. The Penguin Encyclopedia of Popular Music, ed. Donald Clarke. New York: Viking, 1989.

3271. Reclams Jazzfuhrer. 2nd, rev. ed. Stuttgart: Reclam, 1977.

3272. Tenot, Frank. Dictionnaire du Jazz. Paris: Larousse, 1967.

3273. Wilmer, Valerie. As Serious As Your Life. Westport, CT: Lawrence Hill & Co., 1981, p. 268.

Articles

3274. "Annuaire biographique de la contrebasse." Jazz Magazine, No. 9 (May 1963): 25. Biographical sketch.

3275. Flicker, Chris. "Jimmy Garrison." Jazz Magazine, No. 234 (July 1975): 20+. [Interview]

3276. "Garrison: Call it Art, not Jazz." Melody Maker (September 4 1965): 6.

3277. Garrison, Jimmy. "'Pourquoi je suis reste avec Coltrane.'" Jazz Magazine, No. 218 (June 1974): 16+.

3278. Heckman, Don. "Jimmy Garrison: After Coltrane." down beat (March 9 1967): 18-19, 40.

3279. Nolan, Herb. "Jimmy Garrison; bassist in the front line." down beat (June 6 1974): 18, 41. [Interview]

3280. Rava, Graciela. "La Musique en Mouvements de Roberta Garrison." Jazz Magazine, No. 263 (March-April 1978): 40-41, 52. Interview with Jimmy Garrison's wife.

3281. Russell, Charlie L. "The Evolution of a Jazz Musician." Liberator (New York), Vol. IV, No. 11 (November 1964): 14-15, 30. [Profile]

3282. Wallace, D. "Jimmy Garrison." Jazz Journal (June 1969): 2-3.

3283. Wilmer, Valerie. "Garrison liberating the bass." Melody Maker (February 5 1972): 14.

Obituaries

3284. Giddins, Gary. "Deaths in the Family." Village Voice (May 3 1976): 91.

3285. Cadence (May 1976): 32.
3286. Crescendo International (January 1977): 38.
3287. down beat (June 3 1976): 10.
3288. Jazz Forum, No. 42 (1976): 20-21.
3289. Jazz Journal (November 1976): 38.
3290. Jazz Magazine, No. 244 (May 1976): 4.
3291. Melody Maker (May 1 1976): 18.
3292. Orkester Journalen (May 1976): 7.

GASLINI, GIORGIO (1929-) (Italy) - Piano

3293. Bassi, Adriano. Giorgio Gaslini: Vita, lotte, opere di un protagonist della music contemporanea. Padova: Muzzio, 1986. 207p. (Gli strumenti della musica; 14)

3294. Gaslini, Giorgio. Musica Totale: intuizioni, vita ed esperienze musicali nello spirito del '68. Milano: Feltrinelli, 1975. 108p. (I Nuovi testi, 8)

3295. ________. Tecnica e Arte del Jazz. Milano: Ricordi, 1982. 216p.

Biographical Dictionaries

3296. Carles, Philippe, and Jean-Louis Comolli. Free Jazz, Black Power. 2nd ed. Paris: Editions Galilee, 1979, p. 402.

3297. Carr, Ian. "Gaslini, Giorgio." In Jazz: The Essential Companion. New York: Prentice Hall Press, 1988.

3298. Claghorn, Charles Eugene. Biographical Dictionary of Jazz. Englewood Cliffs, NJ: Prentice-Hall, 1982.

3299. Dictionnaire du Jazz, eds. Philippe Carles, et al. Paris: Laffont, 1988.

3300. Feather, Leonard. The Encyclopedia of Jazz in the Sixties. New York: Horizon Press, 1966.

3301. ________, and Ira Gitler. The Encyclopedia of Jazz in the Seventies. New York: Horizon Press, 1976.

3302. Reclams Jazzfuhrer. 2nd, rev. ed. Stuttgart: Reclam, 1977.

3303. Santi, Piero, and Adriano Mazzoletti. "Gaslini, Giorgio." In The New Grove Dictionary of Jazz. London: Macmillan Press, 1988.

Articles

3304. Carles, Philippe. "Gaslini experimente." Jazz Magazine, No. 134 (September 1966): 12.

3305. Gaslini, Giorgio. "Musique Totale." Musique en Jeu (Paris), No. 26 (February 1977): 48-61.

3306. Houston, Bob. "Spearhead of the European Avant Garde." Melody Maker (July 10 1965): 6.

3307. Jeske, Lee. "Profile: Giorgio Gaslini." down beat (March 1981): 51-52.

GAYLE, CHARLES (1939-) - Tenor Saxophone

See also # 597, 4157

3308. Davis, Francis. "Out There: Charles Gayle Keeps Free Jazz Alive." Village Voice (January 1 1991): 47, 73, 92.

3309. Kobe, Reiner. "Charles Gayle." Jazz Podium (April 1985): 33-34. [Interview]

GILMORE, JOHN (1931-) - Tenor Saxophone

3310. Berry, Lemuel, Jr. Biographical Dictionary of Black Musicians and Music Educators. Guthrie, OK: Educational Book Publishers, 1978, p. 240.

3311. Carles, Philippe, and Jean-Louis Comolli. Free Jazz, Black Power. 2nd ed. Paris: Editions Galilee, 1979, p. 402.

3312. Claghorn, Charles Eugene. Biographical Dictionary of American Music. West Nyack, NY: Parker Pub. Co., 1973.

3313. _________. Biographical Dictionary of Jazz. Englewood Cliffs, NJ: Prentice-Hall, 1982.

3314. Dictionnaire du Jazz, eds. Philippe Carles, et al. Paris: Laffont, 1988.

3315. Feather, Leonard. The Encyclopedia of Jazz in the Sixties. New York: Horizon Press, 1966.

3316. _________, and Ira Gitler. The Encyclopedia of Jazz in the Seventies. New York: Horizon Press, 1976.

3317. Kernfeld, Barry. "Gilmore, John." In The New Grove Dictionary of American Music. London: Macmillan Press, 1986.

3318. _________. "Gilmore, John." In The New Grove Dictionary of Jazz. London: Macmillan Press, 1988.

3319. Priestley, Brian. "Gilmore, John." In Jazz: The Essential Companion. New York: Prentice Hall Press, 1988.

3320. Reclams Jazzfuhrer. 2nd, rev. ed. Stuttgart: Reclam, 1977.

3321. Wilmer, Valerie. As Serious As Your Life. Westport, CT: Lawrence Hill & Co., 1981, p. 268.

Articles

3322. Diliberto, John. "John Gilmore: Three Decades in the Sun's Shadow." down beat (May 1984): 26-28, 62. [Interview]

3323. Fiofori, Tam. "Gilmore: A Tenor Spearhead." Melody Maker (April 3 1971): 24.

3324. ________. "Les Premiers Satellites." Jazz Magazine, No. 196 (January 1972): 18-21.

3325. "L'Impossible Liberte; Entretien avec Sun Ra, John Gilmore, Marshall Allen et Pat Patrick." Jazz Magazine, No. 196 (January 1972): 10-13. [Interview]

3326. Lock, Graham. "Big John's Special." Wire, No. 82/83 (Dec 1990/Jan 1991): 20-23. [Interview]

3327. Rusch, Bob. "John Gilmore: oral history/interview." Cadence, Vol. 4, No. 7 (August 1978): 18+.

3328. Sato, Art. "Interview...John Gilmore." Be-Bop And Beyond, Vol. 4, No. 2 (March/April 1986): 15-21.

3329. Simosko, Vladimir. "John Gilmore." Coda (June/July 1975): 12-16; preceded by a Gilmore discography, pp. 9-11.

3330. Wilmer, Valerie. "Gilmore and 'Trane: The Sun Ra Link." Melody Maker (December 27 1980): 16+.

3331. ________. "John Gilmore." The Wire, No. 17 (July 1985): 14-17, 19.

3332. ________. "John Gilmore a l'ombre de Sun Ra." Jazz Magazine, No. 283 (February 1980): 24+.

GLOBE UNITY ORCHESTRA (formed 1966)

3333. Carr, Ian. "Globe Unity Orchestra." In Jazz: The Essential Companion. New York: Prentice Hall Press, 1988.

3334. Dictionnaire du Jazz, eds. Philippe Carles, et al. Paris: Laffont, 1988.

3335. Giddins, Gary. "The Limits of Global Unity." In Rhythm-A-Ning: Jazz Tradition and Innovation in the 80's. New York: Oxford University Press, 1985, pp. 207-211. [Reprinted from the Village Voice (January 3 1984): 71]

3336. Iannapollo, Robert J. "Globe Unity Orchestra." In The New Grove Dictionary of Jazz. London: Macmillan Press, 1988.

Articles

3337. Bachmann, K. R. "Globe Unity Orchestra und das New Jazz Meeting Baden-Baden." Jazz Podium (January 1976): 16-17.

3338. Buzelin, Jean. "Les Sillons du Globe Unity." Jazz Hot, No. 329 (July-August 1976): 44-45.

3339. "Globe Unity sur le carreau de la mine." Jazz Magazine, No. 241 (February 1976): 16-19.

3340. Jaenichen, Lothar. "Globe Unity Orchestre." Jazz Podium (February 1985): 38-39.

3341. Jeske, Lee. "Free Players from Many Lands Form Globe Unity Orchestra." down beat (September 1980): 28, 31-33. Interview with three members of Globe Unity--Albert Mangelsdorff, Enrico Rava and Alexander von Schlippenbach.

3342. McRae, Barry. "Globe Unity: a fusion of stylistic contrasts." Jazz Journal International (March 1978): 38-39.

3343. Noglik, Bert. "Globe Unity Orchestra." Jazz Magazine [US] (June 1984): 22-23.

3344. Schlippenbach, Alexander von. "Potenzierung Musikalischer Energien: das Globe Unity Orchester." Jazz Podium (March 1975): 11-13.

Concert Reviews

3345. "Caught in the Act." Melody Maker (December 17 1977): 17.

3346. Schoemaker, Bill. "Caught." down beat (March 1984): 51.

Discographies

3347. Maertens, Guido. "Discographie: Globe Unity Orchestra." Jazz 360o (Sierre, Switzerland), No. 27 (April 1980): 6-9.

GOLIA, VINNY (1956-   ) - Reeds

See also # 187

3348. Claghorn, Charles Eugene. Biographical Dictionary of Jazz. Englewood Cliffs, NJ: Prentice-Hall, 1982.

3349. Dictionnaire du Jazz, eds. Philippe Carles, et al. Paris: Laffont, 1988.

Articles

3350. Hahn, Steve. "Vinny Golia." Option (May/June 1986): 42-44. [Interview]

3351. Levi, Titus. "Vinny Golia: With a painter's eye and a musician's ear, this multi-reedman/composer keeps exploring new directions." down beat (May 1987): 45-46.

3352. Rusch, Bob. "Vinny Golia: interview." Cadence, Vol. 9, No. 3 (March 1983): 17-19, 22.

3353. Stokes, W. Royal. "Vinny Golia." Jazz Times (October 1988): 22. [Interview]

3354. Underwood, Lee. "Profile: Vinny Golia." down beat (February 1981): 48-49.

3355. Weber, Mark. "Vinny Golia." Coda, No. 164/5 (February 1979): 33. [Profile]

3356. Werner, Hans-Ulrich, and Wolfgang Jenke. "Painting Music: Vinny Golia." Jazz Podium (November 1982): 8-10.

GOMEZ, EDDIE (1944-) (Puerto Rico/U.S.) - Bass

3357. Carles, Philippe, and Jean-Louis Comolli. Free Jazz, Black Power. 2nd ed. Paris: Editions Galilee, 1979, pp. 402-403.

3358. Claghorn, Charles Eugene. Biographical Dictionary of American Music. West Nyack, NY: Parker Pub. Co., 1973.

3359. ________. Biographical Dictionary of Jazz. Englewood Cliffs, NJ: Prentice-Hall, 1982.

3360. Feather, Leonard. The Encyclopedia of Jazz in the Sixties. New York: Horizon Press, 1966.

3361. Priestley, Brian. "Gomez, Eddie." In Jazz: The Essential Companion. New York: Prentice Hall Press, 1988.

3362. Reclams Jazzfuhrer. 2nd, rev. ed. Stuttgart: Reclam, 1977.

3363. Ullman, Michael. "Gomez, Eddie." In The New Grove Dictionary of Jazz. London: Macmillan Press, 1988.

3364. Wilmer, Valerie. As Serious As Your Life. Westport, CT: Lawrence Hill & Co., 1981, p. 268.

Articles

3365. Gourse, Leslie. "Eddie Gomez: the importance of being Eddie." Jazz Times (June 1988): 17. [Interview]

3366. McPartland, Marian. "Looking to the Future: Ron McLure, Eddie Gomez." down beat (June 2 1966): 20-22.

3367. Robson, B. "Eddie Gomez: interview." Cadence, Vol. 6, No. 11 (November 1980): 14+.

3368. Wilmer, Valerie. "Pocket Sized Giant of the Bass." Melody Maker (October 28 1967): 8.

GOODE, COLERIDGE (1914-) (Jamaica/UK) - Bass

3369. Massarik, Jack. "Coleridge Goode." Wire, No. 4 (Summer 1983): 17-19. Interview with the bassist who's work with Joe Harriott during the 1960s helped open the way for free jazz in Great Britain.

3370. Wilmer, Valerie. "Musicians of the Caribbean 5: The Master of the Bass." Flamingo (London), Vol. 3, No. 8 (May 1964): 36-37.

GRAVES, MILFORD (1941-) - Drums

See also # 69, 152, 286, 610, 698, 703, 5058-5064

3371. Jones, LeRoi. "Apple Cores # 6." In Black Music. New York: Morrow Paperback Editions, 1967, pp. 140-141.

3372. Vuijsje, Bert. De Nieuwe Jazz. Baarn: Bosch & Keuning, 1978, pp. 80-90. [Interview]

3373. Wilmer, Valerie. As Serious As Your Life. Westport, CT: Lawrence Hill & Co., 1981, pp. 164-170, 269.

Biographical Dictionaries

3374. Berry, Lemuel, Jr. Biographical Dictionary of Black Musicians and Music Educators. Guthrie, OK: Educational Book Publishers, 1978, p. 241.

3375. Carles, Philippe, and Jean-Louis Comolli. Free Jazz, Black Power. 2nd ed. Paris: Editions Galilee, 1979, p. 403.

3376. Case, Brian, and Stan Britt. The Harmony Illustrated Encyclopedia of Jazz. 3rd. ed. New York: Harmony Books, 1987.

3377. Claghorn, Charles Eugene. Biographical Dictionary of American Music. West Nyack, NY: Parker Pub. Co., 1973.

3378. ________. Biographical Dictionary of Jazz. Englewood Cliffs, NJ: Prentice-Hall, 1982.

3379. Dictionnaire du Jazz, eds. Philippe Carles, et al. Paris: Laffont, 1988.

3380. Feather, Leonard. The Encyclopedia of Jazz in the Sixties. New York: Horizon Press, 1966.

3381. ________, and Ira Gitler. The Encyclopedia of Jazz in the Seventies. New York: Horizon Press, 1976.

3382. James, Michael. "Graves, Milford." In The New Grove Dictionary of Music and Musicians. London: Macmillan Press, 1980, Vol. 7, p. 649.

3383. Priestley, Brian. "Graves, Milford." In Jazz: The Essential Companion. New York: Prentice Hall Press, 1988.

3384. Reclams Jazzfuhrer. 2nd, rev. ed. Stuttgart: Reclam, 1977.

3385. Ullman, Michael. "Graves, Milford." In The New Grove Dictionary of American Music. London: Macmillan Press, 1986.

3386. ________. "Graves, Milford." In The New Grove Dictionary of Jazz. London: Macmillan Press, 1988.

Articles

3387. "L'Art Vivant de Milford." Jazz Magazine, No. 218 (January 1974): 6.

3388. Burwell, Paul. "Babi Music." Collusion (London), No. 1 (August 1981): 30-33. [Interview]

3389. Caux, Daniel. "Black Music: New York Musician's Organization." L'Art Vivant, No. 36 (Fevrier 1973): 28-29.

3390. ________. "Free Jazz." Chroniques de l'Art Vivant, No. 7 (Janvier 1970): 30. Includes a brief personal statement by Graves.

3391. ________. "Milford Graves." Jazz Hot, No. 251 (June 1969): 14-17; No. 252 (July-August 1969): 18-20.

3392. ________. "Milford Graves: Une Discipline du Corps et de l'Esprit." L'Art Vivant, No. 45 (Dec 1973/Jan 1974): 32-37.

3393. Cooke, Jack. "Backwards, forwards, sideways; a study of Milford Graves." Jazz Monthly (August 1968): 4-8; (September 1968): 4-9.

3394. Gillis, Verna. "Milford Graves: interview." Cadence, Vol. 6, No. 5 (May 1980): 5-10; No. 6 (June 1980): 9-13.

3395. Graves, Milford, and Hugh Glover. "Examining Patients with Sound." Ear Magazine, Vol. 9, No. 3 (November/December 1984): 5.

3396. ________, and Don Pullen. "Black Music." Liberator (New York), Vol. 7, No. 1 (January 1967): 20. Personal statement by the drummer and pianist on their independent record label SRP (Self Reliance Program).

3397. Hemingway, Gerry. "Percussion Discussion: Han Bennink, Milford Graves, and Joey Baron." Ear (March 1989): 36-42.

3398. Marvin X. "Marvin X Interviews Milford Graves." Journal of Black Poetry, Vol. 1, No. 12 (Summer-Fall 1969): 46-55.

3399. Mathieu, Bill. "Milford Graves speaks words." down beat (November 3 1966): 22+. [Interview]

3400. "Milford Graves." The Cricket: Black Music in Evolution, No. 1 (1968?): 14-17.

3401. Neal, L. P. "Black Revolution in Music: a talk with drummer Milford Graves." Liberator (New York), Vol. V, No. 9 (September 1965): 14-15.

3402. Riggins, Roger. "Milford Graves: meditations among us." Coda, No. 183 (April 1982): 14-15. [Interview]

3403. Welch, Jane. "Different Drummers: a composite profile." down beat (March 19 1970): 37.

3404. Wilmer, Valerie. "Dialogue of the Drummers." Coda, No. 131 (September 1974): 2-5.

3405. ________. "Drumming Up a Storm." City Limits [London] (June 4-10 1982): 52.

3406. ________. "Milford Graves." Coda, No. 150 (July-August 1976): 8-11. [Interview]

3407. ________. "Milford Graves: Taking the Drum Back to its Origins." Melody Maker (November 5 1966): 10.

3408. ________. "Musicians Talking: Milford Graves." Jazz Monthly (July 1969): 8-10. [Interview]

3409. ________. "Talking Drums." Melody Maker (May 27 1972): 30.

3410. ________. "Trois Jeunes Tambours." Jazz Magazine, No. 202 (July 1972): 10+.

3411. ________. "Using the Music to Heal." Melody Maker (April 10 1976): 39.

Concert Reviews

3412. Albin, Scott. "Caught: Milford Graves Ensemble, WBAI Free Music Store, New York." down beat (June 3 1976): 37.

3413. Wilmer, Valerie. "Caught in the Act: Dialogue of the Drums." down beat (November 25 1971): 26-27. Trio performance by Graves, Andrew Cyrille and Rashied Ali.

3414. ________. "Caught in the Act: Milford Graves, Storefront Museum, Jamaica, New York." down beat (February 1 1973): 29-30.

Record Reviews

3415. Jones, LeRoi. "Apple Cores: A Few Notes on the Avant-Garde." down beat (January 26 1967): 10. Review of Graves-Don Pullen lp recorded live at Yale University. [Reprinted in # 3371]

3416. Mandel, Howard. "Record Reviews: Dialogue of the Drums." down beat (April 10 1975): 20, 22. Review of live performance lp by Graves and Andrew Cyrille recorded at Columbia University.

3417. Mathieu, Bill. "Record Reviews: Milford Graves-Don Pullen Duo." down beat (April 20 1967): 36, 38, 40. Review of SRP lp recorded live at Yale University.

3418. ________. "Record Reviews: Nommo." down beat (November 14 1968): 22.

3419. Quinn, Bill. "Record Reviews: Milford Graves-Sunny Morgan Percussion Ensemble." down beat (December 15 1966): 24.

GREENE, BURTON (1937-   ) - Piano

3420. Carles, Philippe, and Jean-Louis Comolli. Free Jazz, Black Power. 2nd ed. Paris: Editions Galilee, 1979, p. 403.

3421. Claghorn, Charles Eugene. Biographical Dictionary of Jazz. Englewood Cliffs, NJ: Prentice-Hall, 1982.

3422. Dictionnaire du Jazz, eds. Philippe Carles, et al. Paris: Laffont, 1988.

3423. Feather, Leonard, and Ira Gitler. The Encyclopedia of Jazz in the Seventies. New York: Horizon Press, 1976.

3424. Hazell, Ed. "Greene, Burton." In The New Grove Dictionary of Jazz. London: Macmillan Press, 1988.

3425. Wilmer, Valerie. As Serious As Your Life. Westport, CT: Lawrence Hill & Co., 1981, p. 269.

Articles

3426. Alessandrini, D. "Jazz on the Grass." Jazz Magazine, No. 169-170 (September 1969): 9.

3427. Balleras, John. "Burton Greene: Jazzing the European Heritage." down beat (June 1980): 28-29.

3428. "Burton Greene: Mieux Vaut Tard." Jazz Magazine, No. 126 (January 1966): 17-18.

3429. Carles, Philippe. "Les Faux Freres du Free." Jazz Magazine, No. 171 (October 1967): 11-12.

3430. Corneau, A., and Daniel Berger. "Burton Greene, ou le Partage de l'Energie." Jazz Hot, No. 231 (May 1967): 26-28. [Interview]

3431. "Du Cote Free." Jazz Magazine, No. 138 (January 1967): 18-19.

3432. Fine, Milo. "Burton Greene." Jazz Forum, No. 49 (1977): 24-25.

3433. Greene, Burton. "Commentary on the New Music." Sounds & Fury (April 1966): 44-45.

3434. Jones, LeRoi. "The Burton Greene Affair." down beat (August 25 1966): 13.

GREGORY, MICHAEL

See Jackson, Michael Gregory

GRIFFITH, EARL - Vibraphone

3435. Carles, Philippe, and Jean-Louis Comolli. Free Jazz, Black Power. 2nd ed. Paris: Editions Galilee, 1979, p. 403.

3436. Tepperman, Barry. "Vibes in Motion: Earl Griffith and Walt Dickerson." Coda (November/December 1971): 6-8.

GRIFFITHS, MALCOLM (1941-) (Great Britain) - Trombone

See also # 706

3437. Jazz Now: The Jazz Centre Society Guide, ed. Roger Cotterrell. London: Quartet Books, 1976.

3438. Norris, John, and Ted O'Reilly. "Bringing It All Back Home: Malcolm Griffiths." Coda (March/April 1970): 8-10. [Interview]

3439. Skrimshire, Nevil. "Griffiths, Malcolm." In The New Grove Dictionary of Jazz. London: Macmillan Press, 1988.

GRIMES, HENRY (1935-1984?) - Bass

3440. Carles, Philippe, and Jean-Louis Comolli. Free Jazz, Black Power. 2nd ed. Paris: Editions Galilee, 1979, p. 404.

3441. Claghorn, Charles Eugene. Biographical Dictionary of American Music. West Nyack, NY: Parker Pub. Co., 1973.

3442. ________. Biographical Dictionary of Jazz. Englewood Cliffs, NJ: Prentice-Hall, 1982.

3443. Dictionnaire du Jazz, eds. Philippe Carles, et al. Paris: Laffont, 1988.

3444. Feather, Leonard. The Encyclopedia of Jazz. Rev. ed. New York: Horizon Press, 1960.

3445. ________, and Ira Gitler. The Encyclopedia of Jazz in the Seventies. New York: Horizon Press, 1976.

3446. Priestley, Brian. "Grimes, Henry." In Jazz: The Essential Companion. New York: Prentice Hall Press, 1988.

3447. Reclams Jazzfuhrer. 2nd, rev. ed. Stuttgart: Reclam, 1977.

3448. Tenot, Frank. Dictionnaire du Jazz. Paris: Larousse, 1967.

3449. Voigt, John. "Grimes, Henry." In The New Grove Dictionary of Jazz. London: Macmillan Press, 1988.

3450. Wilmer, Valerie. As Serious As Your Life. Westport, CT: Lawrence Hill & Co., 1981, p. 269.

Articles

3451. "Annuaire biographique de la contrebasse." Jazz Magazine, No. 9 (May 1963): 25. Biographical sketch.

3452. Cadence (March 1986): 93. [Obituary]

3453. Jazz Magazine, No. 349 (April 1986): 9. [Obituary]

GUERIN, BEB [Bernard] (1941-1980) (France) - Bass

3454. Carles, Philippe, and Jean-Louis Comolli. Free Jazz, Black Power. 2nd ed. Paris: Editions Galilee, 1979, p. 404.

3455. Dictionnaire du Jazz, eds. Philippe Carles, et al. Paris: Laffont, 1988.

Articles

3456. Brown, Marion. "Blues pour Beb." Jazz Magazine, No. 296 (April 1981): 43, 52. [Tribute]

3457. Litterst, Gerhard. "Blick auf die Franzoesische Jazzszene: In Memoriam Beb Guerin." Jazz Podium (November 1982): 14-15.

3458. Marmande, Francis. "Beb Guerin: echos d'un silence." Jazz Magazine, No. 293 (January 1981): 30-31. [Tribute]

3459. ________. "Hommage a Beb Guerin." Jazz Magazine, No. 293 (January 1981): 31.

3460. "Paris Bass Revolution." Jazz Hot, No. 295 (June 1973): 21.

GUY, BARRY (1947-) (Great Britain) - Bass

See also # 4483-4488

3461. Carles, Philippe, and Jean-Louis Comolli. Free Jazz, Black Power. 2nd ed. Paris: Editions Galilee, 1979, p. 404.

3462. Carr, Ian. "Guy, Barry." In Jazz: The Essential Companion. New York: Prentice Hall Press, 1988.

3463. Dean, Roger T. "Guy, Barry." In The New Grove Dictionary of Jazz. London: Macmillan Press, 1988.

3464. International Who's Who in Music and Musicians' Directory. 12th ed. 1990/91.

3465. Jazz Now: the Jazz Centre Socety Guide, ed. Roger Cotterrell. London: Quartet Books, 1976, pp. 135-136.

Articles

3466. Ansell, Kenneth. "Barry Guy: a Most Ingenious Paradox." The Wire, No. 8 (1984): 20+.

3467. "Barry Guy." Music and Musicians (January 1972): 7-8.

3468. Charlton, Hannah. "Jazzscene: Guy Keeps Score." Melody Maker (March 15 1980): 39.

3469. Cole, Hugo. "Avant-Garde Bass." Composer (London), No. 59 (Winter 1976-77): 25-27.

3470. Lake, Steve. "How to be Spontaneous." Melody Maker (September 4 1976): 35.

3471. MacSweeney, Alix. "Barry Guy." The Strad (August 1978): 311, 313, 315.

3472. Williams, Richard. "Jazz Exposure and the Bass." Melody Maker (May 23 1970): 8.

3473. ________. "A Worried Guy." Melody Maker (April 15 1972): 20.

HADEN, CHARLIE (1937-) - Bass

See also # 5111-5116

3474. Vuijsje, Bert. De Nieuwe Jazz. Baarn: Bosch & Keuning, 1978, pp. 91-103. [Interview]

Biographical Dictionaries

3475. Carles, Philippe, and Jean-Louis Comolli. Free Jazz, Black Power. 2nd ed. Paris: Editions Galilee, 1979, p. 405.

3476. Case, Brian, and Stan Britt. The Harmony Illustrated Encyclopedia of Jazz. 3rd. ed. New York: Harmony Books, 1987.

3477. Claghorn, Charles Eugene. Biographical Dictionary of American Music. West Nyack, NY: Parker Pub. Co., 1973.

3478. ________. Biographical Dictionary of Jazz. Englewood Cliffs, NJ: Prentice-Hall, 1982.

3479. Dictionnaire du Jazz, eds. Philippe Carles, et al. Paris: Laffont, 1988.

3480. Feather, Leonard. The Encyclopedia of Jazz in the Sixties. New York: Horizon Press, 1966.

3481. ________, and Ira Gitler. The Encyclopedia of Jazz in the Seventies. New York: Horizon Press, 1976.

3482. Gridley, Mark C. "Haden, Charlie." In The New Grove Dictionary of American Music. London: Macmillan Press, 1986.

3483. _________. "Haden, Charlie." In The New Grove Dictionary of Jazz. London: Macmillan Press, 1988.

3484. McRae, Barry. "Charlie Haden." In The Jazz Handbook. Harlow, Essex, Eng.: Longman, 1987, pp. 195-196.

3485. The Penguin Encyclopedia of Popular Music, ed. Donald Clarke. New York: Viking, 1989.

3486. Priestley, Brian. "Haden, Charlie." In Jazz: The Essential Companion. New York: Prentice Hall Press, 1988.

3487. Reclams Jazzfuhrer. 2nd, rev. ed. Stuttgart: Reclam, 1977.

3488. Tenot, Frank. Dictionnaire du Jazz. Paris: Larousse, 1967.

3489. Who's Who in Entertainment. 1st ed. 1989-1990.

3490. Wilmer, Valerie. As Serious As Your Life. Westport, CT: Lawrence Hill & Co., 1981, p. 269.

Articles

3491. "Bassist Exclaims; Portugal Detains." Rolling Stone (December 23 1971): 24.

3492. Carey, Joe. "Charlie Haden revived the Liberation Music Orchestra." Jazz Times (March 1983): 7+.

3493. Carles, Philippe, and Francis Marmande. "Les Retours d'Haden." Jazz Magazine, No. 277 (July-August 1979): 40-43. [Interview]

3494. Cuscuna, Michael. "Charlie Haden's Protest Jazz." down beat (November 13 1969): 13.

3495. _________. "A New Music of Political Protest." Saturday Review (December 13 1969): 55-56.

3496. "Dico Disco & Co." Jazz Magazine, No. 298 (June 1981): 42. Biographical sketch.

3497. Feather, Leonard. "Blindfold Test." down beat (June 2 1966): 36.

3498. Flicker, Chris. "Charlie Haden." Jazz Hot, No. 279 (January 1972): 20-21. [Interview]

3499. Gilmore, Mikal. "Charlie Haden Battles Back." Rolling Stone (September 21 1978): 21. [Interview]

3500. Haden, Charlie, and Dan Morgenstern. "Echoes of Spain." down beat (March 19 1970): 8, 11. Exchange between Haden and Morgenstern re: Morgenstern's criticism of Haden's "Liberation Music Orchestra" lp.

3501. "Haden Gets Lesson in Portuguese Politics." down beat (January 20 1972): 9.

3502. Hunt, David C. "The Contemporary Approach to Jazz Bass." Jazz & Pop (August 1969): 18-20.

3503. "International Jazz Critics Poll: the winners." down beat (August 3 1961): 17.

3504. Lake, Steve. "Haden: Face of the bass." Melody Maker (May 29 1976): 48. [Interview]

3505. Levin, Robert. "The Third World." Jazz & Pop (July 1970): 14. Discussion of Liberation Music Orchestra's first lp.

3506. Lewis, Scott. "Charlie Haden's Liberation." Coda, No. 212 (February/March 1987): 8-9. [Interview]

3507. Litweiler, John. "First Bassman." Chicago Tribune (September 21 1989): Sec. 5, p. 3. [Profile]

3508. Lock, Graham. "Viva La Humans!" The Wire (London), No. 19 (September 1985): 37, 39. [Interview]

3509. McRae, Barry. "Avant Courier: Charlie Haden." Jazz Journal International (August 1984): 8-9.

3510. Mandel, Howard. "Charlie Haden's search for freedom." down beat (September 1987): 20+. [Interview]

3511. ________. "Ornette Coleman and Charlie Haden: Still Something Else!!." Wire (London), No. 40 (June 1987): 31-35.

3512. Morgenstern, Dan. "Charlie Haden--from Hillbilly to Avant-Garde--a rocky road." down beat (March 9 1967): 20-21, 42.

3513. O'Reilly, Ted. "Charlie Haden: Liberation Music." Coda (May/June 1971): 6-8. [Interview]

3514. Palmer, Bob. "Charlie Haden's Creed." down beat (July 20 1972): 16+.

3515. Pekar, Harvey. "The Development of Modern Bass." down beat (October 11 1962): 20-21.

3516. Rava, Graciela. "Charlie Haden: le son de sa voix." Jazz Magazine, No. 312 (November 1982): 38-39.

3517. Romano, Aldo, and Philippe Carles. "Les Idees d'Haden." Jazz Magazine, No. 176 (March 1970): 27-31. [Interview]

3518. Williams, Martin. "Caught in the Act." down beat (May 15 1969): 30. [Concert review - Liberation Music Orchestra]

3519. Williams, Richard. "Charlie: off the record." Melody Maker (November 20 1971): 14.

3520. Wilmer, Valerie. "The bassist you can hear round corners." Melody Maker (October 14 1967): 19.

3521. _________. "Haden Presents a Song for Che." Melody Maker (January 31 1970): 8.

3522. _________. "A Song for Che and Charlie." IT (London), No. 74 (February 22-March 13 1970): 13.

3523. Woodard, Josef. "The Charlie Haden Story." Jazz Times (July 1988): 18-20. [Interview]

3524. _________. "Present at the Creation: Bassist Charlie Haden." Option, No. 21 (July/August 1988): 41-43.

3525. Zabor, Rafi. "Charlie Haden Liberation and Revelation: the Probing Essence of Modern Bass." Musician, No. 66 (April 1984): 42-46, 48, 50, 52.

3526. Zipkin, Michael. "Charlie Haden: Struggling Idealist." down beat (July 13 1978): 27+. [Interview]

Media Materials

3527. Charlie Haden, Jazz Bassist (Audiocassette). 30 minutes. Haden describes his music and experiences--from singing country and western songs to leading his own Liberation Music Orchestra. [Available from National Public Radio, Cassette Publishing, 2025 M Street, N.W., Washington, D.C. 20036. Cassette # FA-85-11-26]

HAMPEL, GUNTER (1937-) (W. Germany/U.S.) - Vibraphone/Reeds

See also # 323

3528. Berendt, Joachim Ernst. Ein Fenster aus Jazz. Frankfurt am Main: S. Fischer, 1977, pp. 228-232.

3529. Hampel, Gunter. Schriften, Publikationen, Interviews, Antworten: deutsche Veroffentlichungen. Goettingen: Birth, 1979(?). 32p.

3530. _________. Verbal Introduction. Goettingen/New York: Birth (211 E. 11th St., #2, New York, NY 10003), 198?. [English/German text]

3531. Noglik, Bert. "Gunter Hampel." In Jazzwerkstatt International. Berlin: Verlag Neue Musik, 1981, pp. 383-398. [Interview]

3532. Noll, Dietrich J. "Aspekte der Klangflachenimprovisation I: Gunter Hampel." In Zur Improvisation im Deutschen Free Jazz. Hamburg: Verlag der Musikalienhandlung Wagner, 1977, pp. 33-54.

Biographical Dictionaries

3533. Carles, Philippe, and Jean-Louis Comolli. Free Jazz, Black Power. 2nd ed. Paris: Editions Galilee, 1979, p. 405.

3534. Carr, Ian. "Hampel, Gunter." In Jazz: The Essential Companion. New York: Prentice Hall Press, 1988.

3535. Claghorn, Charles Eugene. Biographical Dictionary of Jazz. Englewood Cliffs, NJ: Prentice-Hall, 1982.

3536. Dean, Roger T. "Hampel, Gunter." In The New Grove Dictionary of Jazz. London: Macmillan Press, 1988.

3537. Dictionnaire du Jazz, eds. Philippe Carles, et al. Paris: Laffont, 1988.

3538. Feather, Leonard, and Ira Gitler. The Encyclopedia of Jazz in the Seventies. New York: Horizon Press, 1976.

3539. Reclams Jazzfuhrer. 2nd, rev. ed. Stuttgart: Reclam, 1977.

Articles

3540. "Gunter Hampel: histoire de Birth." Jazz Magazine, No. 281 (December 1979): 63+. [Interview]

3541. Hampel, Gunter. "Transformation." Musik und Bildung (Mainz), Vol. 9, No. 10 (1977): 526-532.

3542. Hentoff, Nat. "Gunter Hampel: an introduction." Jazz & Pop (July 1970): 25-27.

3543. Lange, Art. "Interview with Gunter Hampel." Brilliant Corners: A Magazine of the Arts, No. 9 (Summer 1978): 83-95.

3544. Riggins, Roger. "Jeanne Lee and Gunter Hampel." Coda, No. 164/165 (February 1979): 6-9. [Interview]

3545. Tepperman, Barry. "Birth." Coda, Vol. 11, No. 3 (September/October 1973): 11-14.

Media Materials

3546. Gunter Hampel Trio. Live at New York's Macrobiotic Center, April 3, 1989.

3547. Coming Age Orchestra Live at the Gasteig Jazz Festival, Munich, December 23, 1988.

3548. Gunter Hampel Coming Age Orchestra. Gottingen jazz festival performance, November 28, 1987.

3549. Galaxie Dream Band: The Next Generation. Video of a performance in Stuttgart, W. Germany, May 13, 1987.

3550. Gunter Hampel All Star Orchestra. New York concert at Columbia University's Wollman Auditorium, April 24, 1983.

All of the above videos are available from Gunter Hampel. For more information contact: Gunter Hampel, 211 E. 11th Street, #2, New York, NY 10003. Tel. 212/477-1695; Or, Birth Records, Phil. Reis Strasse 10, D-3400 Goettingen, Germany.

HANNIBAL

See Peterson, Hannibal Marvin

HARPER, BILLY (1943-) - Tenor Saxophone

3551. ASCAP Biographical Dictionary. 4th ed. New York: R.R. Bowker, 1980.

3552. Carr, Ian. "Harper, Billy." In Jazz: The Essential Companion. New York: Prentice Hall Press, 1988.

3553. Case, Brian, and Stan Britt. The Harmony Illustrated Encyclopedia of Jazz. 3rd. ed. New York: Harmony Books, 1987.

3554. Claghorn, Charles Eugene. Biographical Dictionary of Jazz. Englewood Cliffs, NJ: Prentice-Hall, 1982.

3555. Dictionnaire du Jazz, eds. Philippe Carles, et al. Paris: Laffont, 1988.

3556. Feather, Leonard, and Ira Gitler. The Encyclopedia of Jazz in the Seventies. New York: Horizon Press, 1976.

3557. Rusch, Robert D. "Billy Harper." In JazzTalk: the Cadence interviews. Secaucus, NJ: Lyle Stuart, 1984, pp. 93-103.

3558. Who's Who in Entertainment. 1st ed. 1989-1990.

3559. Wild, David. "Harper, Billy." In The New Grove Dictionary of Jazz. London: Macmillan Press, 1988.

3560. Wilmer, Valerie. As Serious As Your Life. Westport, CT: Lawrence Hill & Co., 1981, p. 269.

Articles

3561. Gans, Charles J. "Billy Harper: a spiritual messenger." Jazz Forum, No. 70 (1981): 41-45. [Interview]

3562. Griffith, Pat. "Caught in the Act." down beat (February 3 1972): 28. [Concert review]

3563. Harper, Billy. "L'Electricite, l'argent et la verite." Jazz Magazine, No. 246 (August 1976): 18-19.

3564. Keepnews, Peter. "Billy Harper's Search for Truth." down beat (June 20 1974): 13, 37. [Interview]

3565. Meadow, Elliott. "Billy Harper." Different Drummer, Vol. 1, No. 11 (April 1974): 19.

3566. ________. "Make Room for Billy Harper." down beat (June 24 1971): 16-17.

3567. Occhiogrosso, Peter. "Billy Harper; Now's the Time." Soho Weekly News (May 11 1975): 29.

3568. Olsson, J. "'Att ova ar en ritual'--Billy Harper." Orkester Journalen (October 1974): 6-8. [Interview]

3569. Rouy, Gerard, and Philippe Carles. "Billy Harper; ou, Le Futur Anterieur." Jazz Magazine, No. 239 (December 1975): 36-37. [Interview]

3570. Rusch, Bob. "Billy Harper: interview." Cadence, Vol. 5, No. 8 (August 1979): 3-7, 22.

3571. Sermila, Jarmo. "Billy Harper, a big man from Texas." Jazz Forum, No. 37 (1975): 32-35. [Interview]

3572. Tomkins, Les. "Introducing Billy Harper." Crescendo International (November 1973): 14-15.

3573. Wilmer, Valerie. "Billy's Bag." Melody Maker (April 29 1972): 38.

3574. _________. "Billy Harper." Jazz Magazine, No. 215 (September 1973): 43-44.

HARRIOTT, JOE [Arthurlin] (1928-1972) (Jamaica/G. Britain) - Alto Saxophone

See also # 696, 3761

3575. Cotterrell, Roger. Joe Harriott - A Bio-Discography. N.p.: the Author (16 Bentley Drive, Gants Hill, Ilford, Essex, England IG2 2QD), n.d. (ca. 1974).

Biographical Dictionaries

3576. Carr, Ian. "Harriott, Joe." In Jazz: The Essential Companion. New York: Prentice Hall Press, 1988.

3577. Case, Brian, and Stan Britt. The Harmony Illustrated Encyclopedia of Jazz. 3rd. ed. New York: Harmony Books, 1987.

3578. Claghorn, Charles Eugene. Biographical Dictionary of American Music. West Nyack, NY: Parker Pub. Co., 1973.

3579. _________. Biographical Dictionary of Jazz. Englewood Cliffs, NJ: Prentice-Hall, 1982.

3580. Dictionnaire du Jazz, eds. Philippe Carles, et al. Paris: Laffont, 1988.

3581. Feather, Leonard. The Encyclopedia of Jazz. New ed. New York: Horizon Press, 1960.

3582. _________. The Encyclopedia of Jazz in the Sixties. New York: Horizon Press, 1966.

3583. _________, and Ira Gitler. The Encyclopedia of Jazz in the Seventies. New York: Horizon Press, 1976.

3584. The Penguin Encyclopedia of Popular Music, ed. Donald Clarke. New York: Viking, 1989.

3585. Reclams Jazzfuhrer. 2nd, rev. ed. Stuttgart: Reclam, 1977.

3586. Sheridan, Chris. "Harriott, Joe." In The New Grove Dictionary of Jazz. London: Macmillan Press, 1988.

Articles

3587. Cotterrell, Roger. "Joe Harriott." The Wire, No. 4 (Summer 1983): 15-16.

3588. Dawbarn, Bob. "The Next Step?" Melody Maker (September 10 1960): 12.

3589. "Dictionnaire de l'Alto." Jazz Magazine, No. 137 (December 1966): 44. Biographical sketch.

3590. Grime, Kitty. "In Review: Joe Harriott at the Ronnie Scott Club." Jazz News, Vol. 5, No. 38 (September 20 1961): 10. [Concert review]

3591. Halperin, Daniel. "Abstraction or Distraction." Jazz News, Vol. 5, No. 6 (February 11 1961): 2. Essay on Harriott.

3592. Harriott, Joe. "The Truth About Free Form Jazz." The Jazz Scene (London), Vol. 2, No. 2 (February 1963): 23-25.

3593. Jazz News (May 20 1960). Cover photo of Harriott.

3594. Jones, Max. "East still meeting West." Melody Maker (October 14 1967): 21.

3595. ________. "Joe Harriott: Ten Years After." Melody Maker (February 6 1971).

3596. Martin, T. E. "Joe Harriott." Jazz Monthly (January 1965): 2-4.

3597. Merrydown, John. "Harriott is Paving the Way to Real Originality." Jazz News (August 19 1960): 3.

3598. "Personal Appearance: The Joe Harriott Quintet." Jazz News, Vol. 5, No. 9 (March 1 1961): 17, 20.

3599. "Personal Appearance No. 2: The Joe Harriott Quintet." Jazz News (September 24 1960): 16. Brief biographies of each of the groups members--Harriott, Shake Keane, Tommy Jones, Pat Smythe and Coleridge Goode.

3600. Race, Steve. "How Free is Free?" Jazz News (February 11 1961): 5. Discussion of Harriott's music.

3601. Scobie, Edward. "Musicians of the Caribbean 1: The Monk of Free-Form." Flamingo, Vol. 3, No. 2 (October 1963): 34-36.

3602. "This is Our Big Chance." Melody Maker (August 19 1961): 7.

3603. Wilmer, Valerie. "Joe Harriott, Jazz Abstractionist." down beat (September 10 1964): 12+.

3604. ________. "Pictures in Sound: Britain's most original alto saxist, Joe Harriott, is advancing the frontiers of jazz." Tropic (London), No. 8 (November 1960): 36-37.

Obituaries

3605. Crescendo International (February 1973): 40; (January 1974): 39.

3606. down beat (April 26 1973): 9-10.
3607. Jazz & Blues (March 1973): 17.
3608. Jazz Hot, No. 292 (March 1973): 21.
3609. Jazz Magazine, No. 208 (February 1973): 8.
3610. Jazz Podium (November 1972): 10.
3611. Melody Maker (January 6 1973): 5.
3612. Performing Right, No. 62 (November 1974): 13.

3613. Williams, Richard, et al. "'One of the few unique jazz voices nurtured by Britain has been stilled.'" Melody Maker (January 13 1973): 14.

HARRIS, BEAVER [William] (1936-) - Drums

3614. Carles, Philippe, and Jean-Louis Comolli. Free Jazz, Black Power. 2nd ed. Paris: Editions Galilee, 1979, p. 406.

3615. Carr, Ian. "Harris, Beaver." In Jazz: The Essential Companion. New York: Prentice Hall Press, 1988.

3616. Claghorn, Charles Eugene. Biographical Dictionary of Jazz. Englewood Cliffs, NJ: Prentice-Hall, 1982.

3617. Dictionnaire du Jazz, eds. Philippe Carles, et al. Paris: Laffont, 1988.

3618. Feather, Leonard, and Ira Gitler. The Encyclopedia of Jazz in the Seventies. New York: Horizon Press, 1976.

3619. The New Grove Dictionary of Jazz. London: Macmillan Press, 1988.

3620. Wilmer, Valerie. As Serious As Your Life. Westport, CT: Lawrence Hill & Co., 1981, p. 269-270.

Articles

3621. Case, Brian. "Beaver's Base." Melody Maker (October 6 1979): 57+. [Interview]

3622. Feehan, Gene. "Black Baseball to Black Music." down beat (March 15 1973): 18-21. [Interview]

3623. Freeman, L. Sharon. "The 360o of Beaver Harris." Jazz Spotlite News (February/March 1980): 12-13. [Interview]

3624. Hazell, Ed. "Portraits: Beaver Harris." Modern Drummer (November 1989): 50-53. [Interview]

3625. Kleiss, P. "Beaver Harris." Jazz Podium (July 1979): 19.

3626. Rouy, Gerard, and Thierry Trombert. "Beaver Harris." Jazz Magazine, No. 243 (April 1976): 14-15. [Interview]

3627. Rusch, Bob. "Beaver Harris: Stories." Cadence, Vol. 9, No. 2-4 (1983).

3628. Steiner, Ken. "The 360o Music Experience." Coda, No. 175 (October 1980): 10-14. [Interview]

3629. Welch, Jane. "Different Drummers: A Composite Profile." down beat (March 19 1970): 19, 37.

3630. Wilmer, Valerie. "Attica Blues." Melody Maker (August 19 1972): 16. Conversation with Harris, Archie Shepp and attorney William Kunstler.

3631. ________. "Eager Beaver of the Drums." Melody Maker (December 2 1967).

3632. ________. "Full Circle." Time Out (May 11-17 1979).

HARRIS, CRAIG (1954-) - Trombone

3633. Baraka, Amiri (LeRoi Jones), and Amina Baraka. The Music; reflections on jazz and blues. New York: Morrow, 1987, pp. 217-220. Reprint of the liner notes to Harris's India Navigation lp "Aboriginal Affairs."

3634. Dictionnaire du Jazz, eds. Philippe Carles, et al. Paris: Laffont, 1988.

3635. The New Grove Dictionary of Jazz. London: Macmillan Press, 1988.

Articles

3636. Chenard, Marc. "The Many Slides of Craig Harris." Coda, No. 211 (Dec 86/Jan 87): 8-11. [Interview]

3637. Davis, Francis. "If It Sounds Good, It Is Good." High Fidelity (October 1985): 75-77. [Interview]

3638. Endress, Gudrun. "Craig Harris." Jazz Podium (June 1987): 3-7. [Interview]

3639. Jeske, Lee. "Profile: Craig Harris." down beat (April 1983): 44-45.

3640. Pareles, Jon. "Craig Harris's Horn Helps Keep Up Jazz Heritage." New York Times (July 22 1983): C4.

3641. Rusch, Bob. "Craig Harris: interview." Cadence, Vol. 14, No. 4 (April 1988): 16-26, 74; No. 5 (May 1988): 16-24, 88.

3642. Scherman, Tony. "Fingers to the 'Bone: Trombonist/ composer Craig Harris tries to break out in Cold Sweat." Musician (September 1990): 20, 22, 24.

HAUGE, HERMAN (Great Britain) - Reeds

See # 1229

HELIAS, MARK (1950-) - Bass

3643. Dictionnaire du Jazz, eds. Philippe Carles, et al. Paris: Laffont, 1988.

3644. The New Grove Dictionary of Jazz. London: Macmillan Press, 1988.

Articles

3645. Carles, Philippe, and Christian Gauffre. "Les Harmonies d'Helias." Jazz Magazine, No. 320 (July/August 1983): 30-31, 73-74. [Interview]

3646. Rusch, Bob. "Mark Helias." Cadence, Vol. 14, No. 8 (August 1988): 5-26, 72. [Interview]

3647. Whitehead, Kevin. "Profile: Mark Helias." down beat (September 1988): 48-49.

HEMINGWAY, GERRY (1955-) - Percussion

See also # 492-494

3648. Dictionnaire du Jazz, eds. Philippe Carles, et al. Paris: Laffont, 1988.

3649. Lock, Graham. "Gerry Hemingway, Percussion." In Forces in Motion: The Music and Thought of Anthony Braxton. New York: Da Capo Press, 1989, pp. 252-264.

Articles

3650. Blumenthal, Bob. "Fascinatin' Rhythms: Notes and paradiddles from the underground." Boston Phoenix (July 3 1987): Sec. 3, p. 10.

3651. Jazzjaarboek (Amsterdam), Vol. 7 (1988): 79-90. [Interview]

3652. Laskin, David LL. "The Heart of the Improviser." Ear (March 1989): 43.

3653. Mandel, Howard. "Profile: Gerry Hemingway." down beat (August 1989): 50-51.

HEMPHILL, JULIUS (1940-) - Alto Saxophone

See also # 6943-6957

3654. Vuijsje, Bert. De Nieuwe Jazz. Baarn: Bosch & Keuning, 1978, pp. 203-209. [Interview]

Biographical Dictionaries

3655. Berry, Lemuel, Jr. Biographical Dictionary of Black Musicians and Music Educators. Guthrie, OK: Educational Book Publishers, 1978.

3656. Carles, Philippe, and Jean-Louis Comolli. Free Jazz, Black Power. 2nd ed. Paris: Editions Galilee, 1979, p. 406.

3657. Carr, Ian. "Hemphill, Julius." In Jazz: The Essential Companion. New York: Prentice Hall Press, 1988.

3658. Claghorn, Charles Eugene. Biographical Dictionary of Jazz. Englewood Cliffs, NJ: Prentice-Hall, 1982.

3659. Dictionnaire du Jazz, eds. Philippe Carles, et al. Paris: Laffont, 1988.

3660. Feather, Leonard, and Ira Gitler. The Encyclopedia of Jazz in the Seventies. New York: Horizon Press, 1976.

3661. The Penguin Encyclopedia of Popular Music, ed. Donald Clarke. New York: Viking, 1989.

3662. Such, David G. "Hemphill, Julius." In The New Grove Dictionary of Jazz. London: Macmillan Press, 1988.

3663. Wilmer, Valerie. As Serious As Your Life. Westport, CT: Lawrence Hill & Co., 1981, p. 270.

Articles

3664. Ardonceau, Pierre-Henri. "Julius Hemphill." Jazz Magazine, No. 289 (September 1980): 18.

3665. Case, Brian. "I heard it through the hardware store." New Musical Express (July 16 1977): 24. [Interview]

3666. Charlton, Hannah. "Breaking Out of Uniform." Melody Maker (December 6 1980): 23. [Interview]

3667. Cole, William. "Julius Hemphill." Saxophone Journal, Vol. 12, No. 1 (1987): 26-31.

3668. Cook, Richard. "Julius Hemphill. A New York Conversation." Wire, No. 49 (March 1988): 40-41, 43, 45. [Interview]

3669. Dutilh, Alex. "L'Iteneraire de Julius Hemphill." Jazz Hot, No. 374/75 (Summer 1980): 42-45, 53.

3670. Frank, Ellen. "Musical Mates: Julius Hemphill/Ursula Oppens." Ear (February 1990): 22. [Profile]

3671. Jackson, D. "Profile: Julius Hemphill; Oliver Lake." down beat (June 19 1975): 32.

3672. "Jazz Lives in New York." Rolling Stone, No. 248 (September 22 1977): 20+.

3673. Jenkins, M. "On the Scene-U.S.A.: A Saxophone Opera." Jazz Forum, No. 120 (1989): 17-18. Report on Hemphill's jazz opera "Long Tongues."

3674. Pelliciotti, Giacomo. "Spirit of Saint Louis." Jazz Magazine, No. 309 (July/August 1982): 50-52. [Interview]

3675. Riggins, Roger. "An Introduction to Julius Hemphill." Coda, No. 150 (August-September 1976): 24.

3676. Rouy, Gerard. "Julius Hemphill." Jazz Magazine, No. 263 (March/April 1978): 16.

3677. Schoemaker, Bill. "Blindfold Test: Julius Hemphill." down beat (June 1989): 43.

3678. ________. "Julius Hemphill and the Theater of Sound." down beat (February 1986): 20-22.

3679. Smith, Bill, and David Lee. "Julius Hemphill." Coda, No. 161 (June 1978): 4-10. [Interview]

3680. Smith, Miyoshi. "Julius Hemphill." Cadence, Vol. 14, No. 6 (June 1988): 10-17, 32. [Interview]

3681. Stern, Chip. "The Hard Blues of Julius Hemphill." Musician, Player and Listener, No. 25 (June-July 1980): 44-49.

3682. Ware, Celestine. "Julius Hemphill x Two." Jazz Spotlite News, Vol. 2, No. 2 (1980-81): 54+.

Newspaper Articles

3683. Crouch, Stanley. "Riffs: Hemphill and Lewis: Two Novelist Musicians." Village Voice (November 28 1977): 61.

3684. Joyce, Mike. "Julius Hemphill, Making the Sax Sing." Washington Post (September 27 1989).

3685. Kaplan, Fred. "Hemphill and the Cellist of Choice." City Paper [Washington, D.C.] (November 10 1988).

3686. Raether, K. "Obscurity? It's in the eye of the beholder." Albuquerque Tribune (January 4 1985): 3.

3687. Sandow, Gregory. "Music: But Is It Art?" Village Voice (March 4 1981): 63.

3688. Watrous, Peter. "Using a Saxophone Opera to Recount Black Culture." New York Times (December 6 1990): C17, C19. Preview of the New York premiere of Hemphill's "Long Tongues."

Concert Reviews

3689. "Caught: Julius Hemphill." down beat (January 15 1976): 40+.

3690. Himes, Geoffrey. "Sax: Peaking In 'Tongues'." Washington Post (September 29 1989). Review of debut performance at Washington's Warner Theatre of Hemphill's opera "Long Tongues."

3691. Litweiler, John. "Caught in the Act: Oliver Lake/Julius Hemphill, AACM, Chicago." down beat (June 12 1969): 34-35.

3692. Pareles, John. "Tour With Saxophones Through Black History." New York Times (December 8 1990): 19. Review of "Long Tongues."

3693. Tepper, Henry. "Eareviews: Julius Hemphill." Ear, Vol. 12, No. 7 (October 1987): 27.

HENDERSON, ERROL (1941-) - Bass

3694. Carles, Philippe, and Jean-Louis Comolli. Free Jazz, Black Power. 2nd ed. Paris: Editions Galilee, 1979, p. 407.

3695. Wilmer, Valerie. As Serious As Your Life. Westport, CT: Lawrence Hill & Co., 1981, p. 270.

HIGGINS, BILLY (1936-) - Drums

See also # 69

3696. Wilmer, Valerie. "A Lesson in Lovemaking." Jazz People. Indianapolis: Bobbs-Merrill, 1970. [Reprint of # 3717]

Biographical Dictionaries

3697. Claghorn, Charles Eugene. Biographical Dictionary of American Music. West Nyack, NY: Parker Pub. Co., 1973.

3698. _________. Biographical Dictionary of Jazz. Englewood Cliffs, NJ: Prentice-Hall, 1982.

3699. Dictionnaire du Jazz, eds. Philippe Carles, et al. Paris: Laffont, 1988.

3700. Feather, Leonard. The Encyclopedia of Jazz. Rev. ed. New York: Horizon Press, 1960.

3701. _________. The Encyclopedia of the Jazz in the Sixties. New York: Horizon Press, 1966.

3702. ________, and Ira Gitler. The Encyclopedia of Jazz in the Seventies. New York: Horizon Press, 1976.

3703. The Penguin Encyclopedia of Popular Music, ed. Donald Clarke. New York: Viking, 1989.

3704. Priestley, Brian. "Higgins, Billy." In Jazz: The Essential Companion. New York: Prentice Hall Press, 1988.

3705. Reclams Jazzfuhrer. 2nd, rev. ed. Stuttgart: Reclam, 1977.

3706. Tenot, Frank. Dictionnaire du Jazz. Paris: Larousse, 1967.

3707. Ullman, Michael. "Higgins, Billy." In The New Grove Dictionary of Jazz. London: Macmillan Press, 1988.

Articles

3708. Bennett, Karen. "Time on his Hands." Wire, No. 72 (February 1990): 16-18, 72.

3709. Bernstein, Charles M. "The Traditional Roots of Billy Higgins." Modern Drummer (February 1983): 20-23, 74-75. [Interview]

3710. Case, Brian. "Sizzle in a big mystery: Higgins investigated." New Musical Express (January 31 1976): 28-29, 41. [Interview]

3711. Daverat, Xavier. "Billy Higgins: 'la batterie c'est l'infini.'" Jazz Magazine, No. 383 (June 1989): 55. [Interview]

3712. "Dico Disco & Co." Jazz Magazine, No. 298 (June 1981): 43. Biographical sketch.

3713. Hildebrand, Lee. "Jazzman Billy Higgins: He's had time for everyone but himself." San Francisco Chronicle/Datebook (October 5 1986).

3714. Howlett, M., and D. Roustain. "Billy Higgins: Autour de Minuit." Jazz Magazine, No. 348 (March 1986): 15. [Interview]

3715. Ioakimidis, Demetre. "Voici Billy Higgins au Confluent de Trois Courants." Jazz Hot, No. 197 (April 1964): 30-32.

3716. Levi, Titus. "Billy Higgins." Option (November/December 1986): 47-48. [Interview]

3717. Wilmer, Valerie. "Billy Higgins--drum love." down beat (March 21 1968): 27+. [Reprinted in # 3696]

3718. ________. "Billy Higgins is born again." Melody Maker (September 4 1971): 18.

HILL, ANDREW (1937-) (Haiti/U.S.) - Piano

See also # 695, 705

3719. Berry, Lemuel, Jr. Biographical Dictionary of Black Musicians and Music Educators. Guthrie, OK: Educational Book Publishers, 1978, p. 248.

3720. Case, Brian, and Stan Britt. The Harmony Illustrated Encyclopedia of Jazz. 3rd. ed. New York: Harmony Books, 1987.

3721. Claghorn, Charles Eugene. Biographical Dictionary of American Music. West Nyack, NY: Parker Pub. Co., 1973.

3722. _________. Biographical Dictionary of Jazz. Englewood Cliffs, NJ: Prentice-Hall, 1982.

3723. Dictionnaire du Jazz, eds. Philippe Carles, et al. Paris: Laffont, 1988.

3724. Feather, Leonard. The Encyclopedia of Jazz in the Sixties. New York: Horizon Press, 1966.

3725. _________, and Ira Gitler. The Encyclopedia of Jazz in the Seventies. New York: Horizon Press, 1976.

3726. Hazell, Ed. "Hill, Andrew." In The New Grove Dictionary of Jazz. London: Macmillan Press, 1988.

3727. McRae, Barry. "Andrew Hill." In The Jazz Handbook. Harlow, Essex, Eng.: Longman, 1987, pp. 196-197.

3728. The Penguin Encyclopedia of Popular Music, ed. Donald Clarke. New York: Viking, 1989.

3729. Priestley, Brian. "Hill, Andrew." In Jazz: The Essential Companion. New York: Prentice Hall Press, 1988.

3730. Reclams Jazzfuhrer. 2nd, rev. ed. Stuttgart: Reclam, 1977.

3731. Southern, Eileen. Biographical Dictionary of Afro-American and African Musicians. Westport, CT: Greenwood Press, 1982.

3732. Tenot, Frank. Dictionnaire du Jazz. Paris: Larousse, 1967.

3733. Who's Who Among Black Americans. 6th ed. 1990/91. Detroit: Gale Research, 1990.

Articles

3734. Berg, Chuck. "Andrew Hill: innovative enigma." down beat (March 10 1977): 16-17, 45. [Interview]

3735. Bizot, J. F. "Hill, l'homme d'Haiti." Jazz Magazine, No. 138 (January 1967): 39-43.

3736. Bratton, Elliot. "ThoughtsDanceInFourViews (Reflections on the Sound of Andrew Hill)." Coda, No. 234 (October/November 1990): 8-11. [Interview/review]

3737. Crouch, Stanley. "Andrew Hill's Alternative Avant-Garde." Village Voice (October 30 1984): 93-94.

3738. Dutilh, Alex. "Andrew Hill - la periode bleue." Jazz Hot, No. 321 (November 1975): 16-18.

3739. Feather, Leonard. "Blindfold Test: Andrew Hill." down beat (January 14 1965): 30-31.

3740. Heckman, Don. "Roots, Culture and Economics." down beat (May 5 1966): 19-21. [Interview]

3741. Hill, Andrew. "Send Money." Jazz (New York), Vol. 5, No. 8 (August 1966): 11.

3742. "His Own Man." BMI (April 1972): 18-19.

3743. Ioakimidis, Demetre. "Andrew Hill et sa revolution tranquille." Jazz Hot, No. 218 (March 1966): 20-23.

3744. Jeske, Lee. "The Eternal Spirit of Andrew Hill: Out of the Out-of-Print and Back on Blue Note." Cash Box (November 4 1989): 7+. [Interview]

3745. Lewis, David. "Andrew Hill." Coda, No. 213 (April/May 1987): 30-31. [Interview]

3746. Litweiler, John. "Andrew Hill and two others." Jazz Monthly (October 1967): 28+. [Concert review]

3747. Mandel, Howard. "Andrew Hill: Second Coming." Wire, No. 73 (March 1990): 14-16. [Interview]

3748. Riggins, Roger. "Andrew Hill: Quiet Pioneer." down beat (January 18 1973): 14.

3749. Rusch, Bob. "Andrew Hill: Interview." Cadence, Vol. 1, No. 10 (September 1976): 3-4.

3750. Twelftree, Alan. "Andrew Hill." Melody Maker (August 2 1969): 20.

3751. Watrous, Peter. "60's Jazz Innovator Returns from End of an Era." New York Times (January 28 1989).

3752. Wilmer, Valerie. "Andrew takes in some country air." Melody Maker (January 15 1972): 14.

HOGGARD, JAY (1954-) - Vibraphone

3753. Baraka, Amiri (LeRoi Jones), and Amina Baraka. The Music: reflections on jazz and blues. New York: Morrow, 1987, pp. 221-228. Reprint of the liner notes to two of Hoggard's Indian Navigation lps--"Solo Album" and "Mystic Winds."

Biographical Dictionaries

3754. Case, Brian, and Stan Britt. The Harmony Illustrated Encyclopedia of Jazz. 3rd. ed. New York: Harmony Books, 1987.

3755. Dictionnaire du Jazz, eds. Philippe Carles, et al. Paris: Laffont, 1988.

3756. Wild, David. "Hoggard, Jay." In The New Grove Dictionary of Jazz. London: Macmillan Press, 1988.

Articles

3757. Jeske, Lee. "Jay Hoggard: Banking on the Vibes." Down Beat (December 1982): 26-28.

3758. Solothurnmann, Jurg. "Jay Hoggard." Jazz Forum, No. 77 (1982): 40-43. [Interview]

3759. Stern, Chip. "Faces: Jay Hoggard." Musician, Player and Listener, No. 16 (January-February 1979): 13.

3760. Thompson, Scott H. "Jay Hoggard: A Fresh Voice on Vibes." Jazz Times (July 1990): 13.

HOLDER, FRANK (Guyana/Great Britain) - Vocal/Bongos/Congas

3761. Wilmer, Valerie. "Musicians of the Caribbean 4: The Versatile Frank Holder." Flamingo (March 1964): 33-35. Profile of the percussionist who played in British saxophonist Joe Harriott's early ensembles.

HOLLAND, DAVE (1946-) (Great Britain/U.S.) - Bass

See also 1977-1981

3762. Carr, Ian. "Holland, Dave." In Jazz: The Essential Companion. New York: Prentice Hall Press, 1988.

3763. Case, Brian, and Stan Britt. The Harmony Illustrated Encyclopedia of Jazz. 3rd. ed. New York: Harmony Books, 1987.

3764. Claghorn, Charles Eugene. Biographical Dictionary of Jazz. Englewood Cliffs, NJ: Prentice-Hall, 1982.

3765. Dictionnaire du Jazz, eds. Philippe Carles, et al. Paris: Laffont, 1988.

3766. Feather, Leonard, and Ira Gitler. The Encyclopedia of Jazz in the Seventies. New York: Horizon Press, 1976.

3767. Hazell, Ed. "Holland, Dave." In The New Grove Dictionary of Jazz. London: Macmillan Press, 1988.

3768. Jost, Ekkehard. "Dave Holland." In Jazzmusiker: Materialen zur Soziologie der Afro-Amerikanischen Musik. Frankfurt am Main: Ullstein, 1982, pp. 134-155.

3769. The Penguin Encyclopedia of Popular Music, ed. Donald Clarke. New York: Viking, 1989.

Articles

3770. "Dave Holland/Sam Rivers." Radio Free Jazz (February 1977): 12-13.

3771. Endress, Gudrun. "Emanzipierter Bass: Dave Holland." Jazz Podium (November 1973): 20-23.

3772. Feather, Leonard. "Blindfold Test." down beat (December 26 1968): 36.

3773. Goddet, Laurent. "Dave Holland--la liberte dans la simplicite." Jazz Hot, No. 321 (November 1975): 8-12. [Interview]

3774. Gourse, Leslie. "David Holland: Miles Ahead." Jazz Times (April 1989): 16+.

3775. Jenkins, Willard, Jr. "Dave Holland: jumpin' back in." Jazz Times (November 1984): 12+. [Interview]

3776. Jones, Max. "Holland: respect for tradition." Melody Maker (July 20 1974): 56. [Interview]

3777. Lee, David. "David Holland - Seeds of Time." Coda, No. 206 (February/March 1986): 18-19.

3778. Lock, Graham. "David Holland." Wire, No. 50 (April 1988):46-49. [Interview]

3779. Mandel, Howard. "Dave Holland: Creative Collaborator." down beat (October 1989): 20-23.

3780. Negre, M. P. "Holland at Home." Jazz Magazine, No. 316 (March 1983): 40-43.

3781. Primack, Bret. "Dave Holland: diverse and dedicated." down beat (May 18 1978): 18-20, 46.

3782. Smith, Bill. "Dave Holland: Jazz Educator." Coda, No. 229 (Dec 1989-Jan 1990): 4-6. [Interview]

3783. _________. "Song for the Newborn." Coda (March/April 1973): 2-4. [Interview]

3784. Sommer, Jeff. "The Bass is My Life." Jazz (Basel), No. 2 (1982).

3785. Summers, Russ. "Dave Holland." Option (May/June 1989): 52-57.

3786. Turi, G. "Dave Holland: future in the past." Jazz Forum, No. 112 (1988): 36-40. [Interview]

3787. Williams, Richard. "After Miles: a Circle of friends." Melody Maker (November 28 1970): 32.

3788. Wright, C., and Mark Gilbert. "Dave Holland: from rags to Bitches' and beyond." Jazz Journal International (January 1986): 16-17.

HONSINGER, TRISTAN - Cello

3789. Ansell, Kenneth. "Tristan Honsinger." Impetus (London), No. 6 (1977): 245-246. [Interview]

3790. Danson, Peter. "Tristan Honsinger." Coda, No. 190 (June 1983): 9-11. [Interview]

3791. van der Berg, Erik. "Tristan Honsinger: 'Ik hoor bij geen enkele scene'." Jazzjaarboek (Amsterdam), Vol. 5 (1986): 41-48. [Interview]

HOPKINS, FRED (1947-) - Bass

See also # 760-773

3792. Carles, Philippe, and Jean-Louis Comolli. Free Jazz, Black Power. 2nd ed. Paris: Editions Galilee, 1979, p. 407.

3793. Claghorn, Charles Eugene. Biographical Dictionary of Jazz. Englewood Cliffs, NJ: Prentice-Hall, 1982.

3794. Dictionnaire du Jazz, eds. Philippe Carles, et al. Paris: Laffont, 1988.

3795. The New Grove Dictionary of Jazz. London: Macmillan Press, 1988.

3796. Wilmer, Valerie. As Serious As Your Life. Westport, CT: Lawrence Hill & Co., 1981, p. 283.

Articles

3797. Lee, David. "Fred Hopkins." Coda, No. 196 (June 1984): 23-26. [Interview]

3798. Trombert, Thierry. "Fred Hopkins." Jazz Magazine, No. 255 (June 1977): 20-21.

3799. Van Trikt, Ludwig. "Fred Hopkins: a short talk." Cadence, Vol. 11, No. 8 (August 1985): 17-19.

HOVE, FRED VAN (1937-) (Belgium) - Drums

3800. Carles, Philippe, and Jean-Louis Comolli. Free Jazz, Black Power. 2nd ed. Paris: Editions Galilee, 1979, pp. 452-453.

3801. Iannapollo, Robert J. "Van Hove, Fred." In The New Grove Dictionary of Jazz. London: Macmillan Press, 1988.

3802. Noglik, Bert. "Fred van Hove." In Jazzwerkstatt International. Berlin: Verlag Neue Musik, 1981, pp. 47-64.

3803. "Van Hove, Fred." In Dictionnaire du Jazz, eds. Philippe Carles, et al. Paris: Laffont, 1988.

Articles

3804. Leroy, Jean-Luc. "Propos de et sur Fred van Hove." Jazz 360o (Sierre, Switzerland), No. 56 (February 1983): 4-6.

3805. Maertens, Guido. "Fred van Hove." Jazz 360o, No. 18 (May 1979): 2-5. [Interview]

3806. Rouy, Gerard. "Belgique: Fred van Hove." Jazz Magazine, No. 220 (1974): 24+.

3807. _________. "Fred van Hove: une force s'est manifestee parmi nous..." Jazz Magazine, No. 262 (February 1978): 35. [Interview]

3808. _________. "Fred van Hove: an interview." Musics (London), No. 18 (July 1978): 14-15.

3809. Schoemaker, Bill. "Fred van Hove ... Belgium." Coda, No. 180 (October 1981): 12-14. [Interview]

Discographies

3810. Cerutti, Gustave. Fred Van Hove Discography, 1968-1983 (on records). Sierre, Switzerland: G. Cerutti (8, ave. du Marche, CH-3960, Sierre), 1984.

HOWARD, NOAH (1943-) - Alto Saxophone

See also # 598-601

3811. Carles, Philippe, and Jean-Louis Comolli. Free Jazz, Black Power. 2nd ed. Paris: Editions Galilee, 1979, p. 407.

3812. Claghorn, Charles Eugene. Biographical Dictionary of Jazz. Englewood Cliffs, NJ: Prentice-Hall, 1982.

3813. Dictionnaire du Jazz, eds. Philippe Carles, et al. Paris: Laffont, 1988.

3814. Feather, Leonard, and Ira Gitler. The Encyclopedia of Jazz in the Seventies. New York: Horizon Press, 1976.

3815. The New Grove Dictionary of Jazz. London: Macmillan Press, 1988.

3816. Wilmer, Valerie. As Serious As Your Life. Westport, CT: Lawrence Hill & Co., 1981, p. 270.

Articles

3817. Case, Brian. "If music be a baby's cry, read on..." New Musical Express (December 7 1974): 44-45. [Interview]

3818. Positif, Francois. "The Noah Howard-Frank Wright Quartet." Jazz Hot, No. 257 (January 1970): 18-22. [Interview]

3819. Rock, Henry. "Noah Howard interview." Cadence, Vol. 2, No. 12 (July 1977): 3+.

3820. Terlizzi, Roberto. "Noah Howard." Coda (April 1976): 10-12. [Interview]

3821. Williams, Richard. "Noah: a child of the avant-garde." Melody Maker (August 28 1971): 14.

3822. Wilmer, Valerie. "Caught in the Act." down beat (December 21 1972): 37-38. [Concert review]

3823. ________. "Noah; feeling for his roots." Melody Maker (May 1 1971): 26.

HUFF, LIGHT HENRY

See # 3094-3096

HUMAN ARTS ENSEMBLE

3824. Constant, Denis. "Human Arts Ensemble." Jazz Magazine, No. 269 (October 1978): 12.

3825. Dutilh, Alex. "Human Arts Ensemble, a Trois." Jazz Hot, No. 356/7 (December 1978/January 1979): 54.

3826. Smith, Will. "Record Reviews: Whisper of Dharma / Poem of Gratitude." down beat (March 28 1974): 29. Review of two HAE lps on the group's own Universal Justice label.

HUTCHERSON, BOBBY (1941-) - Vibraphone

See also # 695

3827. Carles, Philippe, and Jean Louis Comolli. Free Jazz, Black Power. 2nd ed. Paris: Editions Galilee, 1979, p. 408.

3828. Claghorn, Charles Eugene. Biographical Dictionary of American Music. West Nyack, NY: Parker Pub. Co., 1973.

3829. Feather, Leonard. The Encyclopedia of Jazz in the Sixties. New York: Horizon Books, 1966.

3830. ________, and Ira Gitler. The Encyclopedia of Jazz in the Seventies. New York: Horizon Books, 1976.

3831. Jeske, Lee. "Hutcherson, Bobby." In The New Grove Dictionary of Jazz. London: Macmillan Press, 1988.

3832. Wilmer, Valerie. As Serious As Your Life. Westport: Lawrence Hill & Co., 1981, p. 270.

Articles

3833. "About the Vibes: Bobby Hutcherson Talking." Crescendo International (April 1971): 24.

3834. "Bobby sans Hobby." Jazz Magazine, No. 158 (September 1968): 37-39. [Interview]

3835. Bourne, Michael. "Bobby Hutcherson, a Natural Player." down beat (March 14 1974): 18, 36. [Interview]

3836. Darroch, Lynn. "Bobby Hutcherson: Tradition's Adventurous Edge." Jazz Times (August 1985): 12-13. [Interview]

3837. Gerber, Alain. "Bobby a la Pointe?" Jazz Magazine, No. 151 (February 1968): 49+.

3838. Ginibre, Jean Louis, and Philippe Carles. "Dictionnaire du Vibraphone." Jazz Magazine, No. 151 (February 1968): 41-42. Biographical sketch.

3839. Ioakimidis, Demetre. "Bravo, vibra Bobby!" Jazz Hot, No. 121 (June 1966): 16-19, 36. [Interview]

3840. Kronzek, Allen Z. "Black to the Woodshed: Bobby Hutcherson." down beat (March 10 1966): 16-17.

3841. Underwood, Lee. "Bobby Hutcherson: Cruisin' Down Highway One." down beat (April 19 1979): 14-16. [Interview]

3842. Wilmer, Valerie. "New Boss Man in the Bags Mould." Melody Maker (September 16 1967): 8.

Discographies

3843. Wilbraham, Roy J. "Discography: Bobby Hutcherson." Jazz Monthly (February 1967): 26-28.

INSTANT COMPOSERS POOL

See also # 360

3844. Dictionnaire du Jazz, eds. Philippe Carles, et al. Paris: Laffont, 1988.

Articles

3845. "Caught in the Act." Melody Maker (December 15 1973): 58. [Concert review]

3846. Goddet, Laurent. "Instant Composers Pool." Jazz Hot, No. 284 (June 1972): 18-20.

3847. "Records: Instant Composers Pool." Jazz Forum, No. 15 (1972): 102-103.

3848. Rouy, Gerard. "Fete tranquille pour I.C.P." Jazz Magazine, No. 259 (November 1973): 28-29.

3849. Smith, Will. "I.C.P. rides again." Jazz & Pop (August 1971): 30-32.

3850. Tepperman, Barry. "ICP." Coda, Vol. 10, No. 7 (1972): 11-14.

3851. Tra, Gijs. "Instant Composers Pool: a decade of musical and political innovation." Key Notes (Amsterdam), No. 7 (June 1978): 7-9.

INTERFACE

3852. Berg, Chuck. "Caught." down beat (January 13 1977): 38. [Concert review]

3853. _________. "Record Reviews: Interface." down beat (February 22 1979): 28.

3854. Palmer, Robert. "Interface, Jazz Band, Evolves Over a Year." New York Times (June 5 1977): 62. [Concert review]

3855. Schulte, Thomas. "John Fischer's European Interface." Jazz Podium (August 1983): 18.

IZENSON, DAVID (1932-1979) - Bass

See also # 2021, 2292, 2297, 2303

3856. Carles, Philippe, and Jean-Louis Comolli. Free Jazz, Black Power. 2nd ed. Paris: Editions Galilee, 1979, pp. 408-409.

3857. Carr, Ian. "Izenson, David." In Jazz: The Essential Companion. New York: Prentice Hall Press, 1988.

3858. Claghorn, Charles Eugene. Biographical Dictionary of American Music. West Nyack, NY: Parker Pub. Co., 1973.

3859. _________. Biographical Dictionary of Jazz. Englewood Cliffs, NJ: Prentice-Hall, 1982.

3860. Dictionnaire du Jazz, eds. Philippe Carles, et al. Paris: Laffont, 1988.

3861. Feather, Leonard. The Encyclopedia of Jazz in the Sixties. New York: Horizon Press, 1966.

3862. _________, and Ira Gitler. The Encyclopedia of Jazz in the Seventies. New York: Horizon Press, 1976.

3863. Reclams Jazzfuhrer. 2nd, rev. ed. Stuttgart: Reclam, 1977.

3864. Voigt, John. "Izenson, David." In The New Grove Dictionary of Jazz. London: Macmillan Press, 1988.

3865. Tenot, Frank. Dictionnaire du Jazz. Paris: Larousse, 1967.

3866. Wilmer, Valerie. As Serious As Your Life. Westport, CT: Lawrence Hill & Co., 1981, p. 270.

Articles

3867. Dawbarn, Bob. "Seven Steps to Jazz." Melody Maker (December 17 1966): 8. Biographical sketch.

3868. Houston, Bob. "Izenson." Melody Maker (May 21 1966): 6.

3869. "Izenson: Keeping up on bass with Ornette." Melody Maker (August 28 1965): 6.

3870. Smith, Arnold Jay. "Izenson dedicates opera." down beat (March 27 1975): 9.

3871. Wilmer, Valerie. "David Izenson and the Hazards of Virtuosity." down beat (June 2 1966): 18-19.

Obituaries

3872. Cadence (December 1979): 70.

3873. down beat (December 1979): 13.

3874. International Society of Bassists' Newsletter, Vol. 6, No. 2 (1979): 595.

3875. Melody Maker (November 3 1979): 44.

3876. Trombert, Thierry. "Quelques mots d'Izenson." Jazz Magazine, No. 281 (December 1979): 50+.

JACKSON, AMBROSE - Trumpet

3877. Gros-Claude, P. "Ambrose Jackson: un Afro Americain a Paris." Jazz Magazine, No. 199 (April 1972): 27-29. [Interview]

3878. Merrell, Charles. "Big Band Concert Review: Ambrose Jackson." Radio Free Jazz (January 1977): 12. Review of an performance by a Jackson-led big band at the New York loft Environ. Also offers information on Jackson's past and present musical activities.

3879. "People in Paris: Ambrose Jackson." Essence (October 1970): 52-53.

JACKSON, JOHN SHENOY (1923-) - Trumpet

3880. Carles, Philippe, and Jean-Louis Comolli. Free Jazz, Black Power. 2nd ed. Paris: Editions Galilee, 1979, p. 409.

3881. Dictionnaire du Jazz, eds. Philippe Carles, et al. Paris: Laffont, 1988.

3882. Wilmer, Valerie. As Serious As Your Life. Westport, CT: Lawrence Hill & Co., 1981, p. 271.

JACKSON, MICHAEL GREGORY (1953-) - Guitar

See also # 702

3883. Dictionnaire du Jazz, eds. Philippe Carles, et al. Paris: Laffont, 1988.

3884. Rinzler, Paul. "Jackson, Michael Gregory." In The New Grove Dictionary of Jazz. London: Macmillan Press, 1988.

Articles

3885. Lozaw, T. "Michael Gregory on the Rocks." Creem (April 1984): 15-16.

3886. Mulhern, Tom. "Michael Gregory Jackson: a Jazz-rock career with an Avant-garde foundation." Guitar Player (October 1980): 30-34. [Profile]

3887. Palmer, Robert. "Michael Gregory Jackson's Future Funk." Rolling Stone (November 1 1979): 22.

3888. Rusch, Bob. "Michael G. Jackson interview." Cadence (June 1977): 6.

3889. Safane, Clifford Jay. "Michael Gregory Jackson: avant heads for the center." down beat (March 1980): 29-30, 62.

3890. Skovgaard, Ib. "Structures et Couleurs: Michael Gregory Jackson." Jazz Hot, No. 366 (October 1979): 18-21. [Interview]

3891. Sullivan, J. "Formerly Michael Jackson: Michael Gregory plays the name game." Record (February 1984): 7.

3892. Ward, Ed. "Michael Gregory Jackson: heart in the wrong place." Village Voice (January 28 1979): 61-62.

3893. Zabor, Rafi. "Faces: Michael Gregory Jackson." Musician, Player and Listener, No. 24 (April-May 1980): 32-33.

JACKSON, RONALD SHANNON (1940-) - Drums

See also # 2857, 4380

3894. Weinstein, Norman. A Night in Tunisia: Imaginations of Africa in Jazz. Metuchen, NJ: Scarecrow Press, 1991. Includes a chapter on Jackson.

Biographical Dictionaries

3895. Case, Brian, and Stan Britt. The Harmony Illustrated Encyclopedia of Jazz. 3rd ed. New York: Harmony Books, 1987.

3896. Dictionnaire du Jazz, eds. Philippe Carles, et al. Paris: Laffont, 1988.

3897. Hazell, Ed. "Jackson, Ronald Shannon." In The New Grove Dictionary of Jazz. London: Macmillan Press, 1988.

3898. Priestley, Brian. "Jackson, Ronald Shannon." In Jazz: The Essential Companion. New York: Prentice Hall Press, 1988.

3899. Who's Who in Entertainment. 1st ed. 1989-1990.

3900. Wilmer, Valerie. As Serious As Your Life. Westport, CT: Lawrence Hill & Co., 1981, p. 283.

Articles

3901. Barber, Lynden. "The Mandancer." Melody Maker (April 30 1983): 8-9. [Interview]

3902. Coleman, Mukami Ireri. "Ronald Shannon Jackson." Jazz Echo, No. 43 (March 1980): 1, 24. [Interview]

3903. Cook, Richard. "Breaking the Dance Code." New Musical Express (March 19 1983): 14. [Interview]

3904. Doherty, Charles. "Decoding the Society." down beat (August 1982): 24-25.

3905. Giddins, Gary. "Transcending the Limits with Old Fashioned Swing." Esquire (March 1982): 102-104.

3906. Lake, Steve. "Ronald Shannon Jackson: this music is a life experience." Jazz Forum, No. 116 (1989): 34-37. [Interview]

3907. Macnie, Jim. "Ronald Shannon Jackson." Coda, No. 196 (June 1984): 10-11. [Interview]

3908. Mandel, Howard. "Blindfold Test." down beat (January 1983): 46+.

3909. Natalacchi, Giorgio. "Deciphering the Funk." Black Music and Jazz Review [London] (October 1982): 23.

3910. Palmer, Don. "Faces: Ronald Shannon Jackson." Musician, No. 53 (March 1983): 33.

3911. Pareles, Jon. "Ronald Shannon Jackson and Poly-Everything." Village Voice (July 1 1981): 67-68.

3912. Solothurnmann, Jurg. "Ronald Shannon Jackson: jazz from 10 worlds." Jazz Forum, No. 75 (1982): 40-44. [Interview]

3913. Stern, Chip. "Ronald Shannon Jackson's rhythms of life." Modern Drummer (March 1984): 14-17. [Interview]

3914. Wilmer, Valerie. "Ronald Shannon Jackson: A Shaman for the '80s." down beat (August 1982): 22+. [Interview]

3915. _________. "Ronald Shannonn Jackson - Texas Blues." Jazz Magazine, No. 299 (July-August 1981): 42-44. [Interview]

3916. _________. "Time On His Hands." City Limits (March 11-17 1983).

3917. Woodard, Josef. "Jazz and the Abstract Truth: Drummer Ronald Shannon Jackson's Triumph of the Spirit." Option (November/December 1989): 46-51.

3918. Zabor, Rafi, and David Breskin. "Ronald Shannon Jackson: The Future of Jazz Drumming." Musician, Player and Listener, No. 33 (June 1981): 60-66, 68, 70. [Interview]

JAMAL, KHAN (1946-) - Vibraphone

3919. Carles, Philippe, and Jean-Louis Comolli. Free Jazz, Black Power. 2nd ed. Paris: Editions Galilee, 1979, p. 409.

3920. Claghorn, Charles Eugene. Biographical Dictionary of Jazz. Englewood Cliffs, NJ: Prentice-Hall, 1982.

3921. Dictionnaire du Jazz, eds. Philippe Carles, et al. Paris: Laffont, 1988.

3922. Feather, Leonard, and Ira Gitler. The Encyclopedia of Jazz in the Seventies. New York: Horizon Press, 1976.

3923. Iannapollo, Robert J. "Jamal, Khan." In The New Grove Dictionary of Jazz. London: Macmillan Press, 1988.

3924. Wilmer, Valerie. As Serious As Your Life. Westport, CT: Lawrence Hill & Co., 1981, p. 271.

Articles

3925. Futrick, Gerard. "Khan Jamal." Coda, No. 196 (June 1984): 27-28. [Interview]

3926. Gauffre, Christian. "N'Oubliez pas Philadelphie." Jazz Magazine, No. 276 (June 1979): 17-18. [Interview]

3927. Hollenberg, David. "Profile: Khan Jamal." down beat (June 21 1979): 50, 52.

3928. Iannapollo, Robert. "Khan Jamal." Option, Issue J (1986).

3929. Van Trikt, Ludwig. "Khan Jamal." Cadence, Vol. 13, No. 3 (March 1987): 5-10, 69. [Interview]

3930. "Warren Khan Jamal." Jazz World Index, No. 46 (August 1981): 3.

3931. Wilmer, Val. "Tickling the Tubes." Time Out [London] (May 25-31 1979).

JAMI, HAKIM (1940-) - Bass

See also # 69

3932. Carles, Philippe, and Jean-Louis Comolli. Free Jazz, Black Power. 2nd ed. Paris: Editions Galilee, 1979, p. 410.

3933. Wilmer, Valerie. As Serious As Your Life. Westport, CT: Lawrence Hill & Co., 1981, p. 271.

3934. ________. "Orbiting the Sun." Melody Maker (October 21 1972): 18.

JARMAN, JOSEPH (1937-) - Reeds

See also # 436-437, 914-965

3935. Litweiler, John. "Leo Smith, Anthony Braxton, Joseph Jarman, and Roscoe Mitchell." In The Freedom Principle: Jazz After 1958. New York: William Morrow, 1984, pp. 265-286.

Biographical Dictionaries

3936. Carles, Philippe, and Jean-Louis Comolli. Free Jazz, Black Power. 2nd ed. Paris: Editions Galilee, 1979, p. 410.

3937. Carr, Ian. "Jarman, Joseph." In Jazz: The Essential Companion. New York: Prentice Hall Press, 1988.

3938. Claghorn, Charles Eugene. Biographical Dictionary of Jazz. Englewood Cliffs, NJ: Prentice-Hall, 1982.

3939. Dictionnaire du Jazz, eds. Philippe Carles, et al. Paris: Laffont, 1988.

3940. Feather, Leonard, and Ira Gitler. The Encyclopedia of Jazz in the Seventies. New York: Horizon Press, 1976.

3941. Kernfeld, Barry. "Jarman, Joseph." In The New Grove Dictionary of Jazz. London: Macmillan Press, 1988.

3942. Southern, Eileen. Biographical Dictionary of Afro-American and African Musicians. Westport, CT: Greenwood Press, 1982.

3943. Who's Who in Entertainment. 1st ed. 1989-1990.

3944. Wilmer, Valerie. As Serious As Your Life. Westport, CT: Lawrence Hill & Co., 1981, p. 271.

Articles

3945. Carles, Philippe. "Joseph Jarman." Jazz Magazine, No. 215 (September 1973): 38-39. [Interview]

3946. Case, Brian. "Jarman: Dreaming of the Masters." Melody Maker (April 18 1979): 44+.

3947. Henderson, Bill. "Jarman Lesson." Black Music and Jazz Review, Vol. 2, No. 2 (May 1979): 18-19, 47. [Interview]

3948. Kostakis, Peter, and Art Lange. "An Interview with Joseph Jarman." Brilliant Corners: A Magazine of the Arts (Chicago), No. 8 (Winter 1978): 92-115.

3949. Lange, Art, and Peter Kostakis. "Joseph Jarman." Coda, No. 158 (November/December 1977): 2-4.

3950. Litweiler, John B. "There Won't Be Any More Music." Down Beat's Music, Vol. 17 (1972): 23-26, 37. [Interview]

3951. Rusch, Bob. "Joseph Jarman: interview." Cadence, Vol. 5, No. 5 (May 1979): 3-6.

3952. Tepperman, Barry. "Further Soundings from the A.A.C.M. - Some Notes." Pieces of Jazz (1971): 19-22.

3953. Wilmer, Valerie. "Rainy Day in the Windy City." Melody Maker (September 23 1972): 24.

Concert Reviews

3954. Litweiler, John. "Caught in the Act: Joseph Jarman, Hyde Park Art Center, Chicago." down beat (January 23 1969): 35-36.

3955. Mandel, Howard. Caught: Joseph Jarman, University of Chicago." down beat (March 24 1977): 33.

3956. Quinn, Bill. "Caught in the Act." down beat (March 9 1967): 27-28.

3957. Welding, Pete. "Caught in the Act." down beat (January 13 1966): 35-36. Review of a Joseph Jarman-John Cage concert held at Chicago's Harper Theater.

Record Reviews

3958. Kart, Larry. "Record Reviews: As If It Were the Seasons." down beat (March 6 1969): 25-27.

3959. Pekar, Harvey. "Record Reviews: Song For." down beat (May 16 1968): 30.

JARVIS, CLIFFORD (1941-) - Drums

3960. Carles, Philippe, and Jean-Louis Comolli. Free Jazz, Black Power. 2nd ed. Paris: Editions Galilee, 1979, p. 410.

3961. Carr, Ian. "Jarvis, Clifford." In Jazz: The Essential Companion. New York: Prentice Hall Press, 1988.

3962. Claghorn, Charles Eugene. Biographical Dictionary of Jazz. Englewood Cliffs, NJ: Prentice-Hall, 1982.

3963. Dictionnaire du Jazz, eds. Philippe Carles, et al. Paris: Laffont, 1988.

3964. Feather, Leonard, and Ira Gitler. The Encyclopedia of Jazz in the Seventies. New York: Horizon Press, 1976.

3965. The New Grove Dictionary of Jazz. London: Macmillan Press, 1988.

3966. Wilmer, Valerie. As Serious As Your Life. Westport, CT: Lawrence Hill & Co., 1981, p. 271.

Articles

3967. Welch, Jane. "Different Drummers: a composite profile." down beat (March 19 1970): 18-19.

3968. Wilmer, Valerie. "From Ra's drummer to cabbie." Melody Maker (February 24 1973): 44.

JAUME, ANDRE (1940-) (France) - Reeds

3969. Carles, Philippe, and Jean-Louis Comolli. Free Jazz, Black Power. 2nd ed. Paris: Editions Galilee, 1979, p. 411.

3970. Dictionnaire du Jazz, eds. Philippe Carles, et al. Paris: Laffont, 1988.

3971. Laplace, Michel. "Jaume, Andre." In The New Grove Dictionary of Jazz. London: Macmillan Press, 1988.

Articles

3972. Aguetai, C. "Andre Jaume." Jazz Magazine, No. 289 (September 1980): 16-17.

2973. Brun, Jean-Paul. "Quand Jaume s'Ecoute." Jazz Magazine, No. 341 (July-August 1985): 32-33. [Interview]

3974. Carles, Philippe. "Andre Jaume a l'Ecoute." Jazz Magazine, No. 281 (December 1979): 52+.

3975. Chenard, Marc. "Andre Jaume: Short Talk." Cadence (November 1990): 21-25, 91.

3976. Chesnel, J. "Jaume: on ne souffle pas." Jazz Magazine, No. 365 (1987): 24-25. [Interview]

3977. Jaume, Andre. "Choisir une Clarinette." Jazz Magazine, No. 286 (May 1980): 34-35. [Interview]

3978. Litterst, Gerhard. "Blick auf die Franzoesische Szene: Andre Jaume--le sax animilier." Jazz Podium (June 1981): 13-15.

3979. Tarting, Christian. "Andre Jaume et la Langue de l'Oc." Jazz Magazine, No. 305 (March 1982): 38-39; No. 306 (April 1982): 40. [Interview]

JAZZ PASSENGERS

3980. Chapin, Gary Parker. "The Jazz Passengers: A Match of Two Half's." Wire, No. 74 (April 1990): 26-28.

3981. __________. "Opposites Attract: Cultures Collide When the Jazz Passengers Play." Option, No. 33 (July/August 1990): 44-47.

3982. Mandel, Howard. "Jazz Passengers." down beat (June 1990): 13.

3983. Milkowski, Bill. "How many Jazz Passengers can you fit in a Volkswawgen?" Pulse! [Tower Records] (September 1990).

3984. Watrous, Peter. "Blending Jazz with Theater In a New Form of Vaudeville." New York Times (December 13 1990): C15, C17. Preview of Roy Nathanson's music/theatre piece "Jazz Passengers in Egypt."

JAZZ WARRIORS (Great Britain)

See also # 5595

3985. Sinker, Mark. "Into Battle." New Musical Express (September 19 1987): 11.

3986. _________. "Jazz Warriors: life during wartime." Wire, No. 76 (June 1990): 34-37.

JENKINS, LEROY (1932-   ) - Violin

3987. Carles, Philippe, and Jean-Louis Comolli. Free Jazz, Black Power. 2nd ed. Paris: Editions Galilee, 1979, p. 411.

3988. Carr, Ian. "Jenkins, Leroy." In Jazz: The Essential Companion. New York: Prentice Hall Press, 1988.

3989. Case, Brian, and Stan Britt. The Harmony Illustrated Encyclopedia of Jazz. 3rd ed. New York: Harmony Books, 1987.

3990. Claghorn, Charles Eugene. Biographical Dictionary of Jazz. Englewood Cliffs, NJ: Prentice-Hall, 1982.

3991. Dictionnaire du Jazz, eds. Philippe Carles, et al. Paris: Laffont, 1988.

3992. Feather, Leonard, and Ira Gitler. The Encyclopedia of Jazz in the Seventies. New York: Horizon Press, 1976.

3993. Gridley, Mark C. "Jenkins, Leroy." In The New Grove Dictionary of American Music. London: Macmillan Press, 1986.

3994. _________. "Jenkins, Leroy." In The New Grove Dictionary of Jazz. London: Macmillan Press, 1988.

3995. Horne, Aaron. Woodwind Music of Black Composers. New York: Greenwood Press, 1990, p. 32.

3996. McRae, Barry. "Leroy Jenkins." In The Jazz Handbook. Harlow, Essex, Eng.: Longman, 1987, pp. 199-200.

3997. Southern, Eileen. Biographical Dictionary of Afro-American and African Musicians. Westport, CT: Greenwood Press, 1982.

3998. Who's Who in Entertainment. 1st ed. 1989-1990.

3999. Wilmer, Valerie. As Serious As Your Life. Westport, CT: Lawrence Hill & Co., 1981, p. 271-272.

Articles

4000. Ayobami, Ms. "Leroy Jenkins." Jazz Spotlite News (February/March 1980): 7.

4001. Birnbaum, Larry. "Leroy Jenkins: Space Minds, New Worlds, Survival of America." Ear (Dec 1989/Jan 1990): 34-39.

4002. Blumenthal, Bob. "Leroy Jenkins: Violinist of the New Music." down beat (March 1982): 20-22, 70.

4003. Bryant, Christina. "Interview with Leroy Jenkins." Jazz Echo, No. 45 (Winter 1981): 1, 12-13.

4004. Case, Brian. "Leroy Lays It." New Musical Express (July 29 1978): 31. [Interview]

4005. Giddins, Gary. "Leroy Jenkins's Territorial Imperative." Village Voice (April 24 1978): 68.

4006. Jeske, Lee. "Blindfold Test." down beat (December 1980): 47.

4007. Kostakis, Peter. "Bon Soi, Catgut Jump and Horsehair Stomp: A Note on Leroy Jenkins." Brilliant Corners: A Magazine of the Arts (Chicago), No. 8 (Winter 1978): 77-84.

4008. "Leroy Jenkins." Jazz Echo, Vol. 9, No. 42 (1979): 11.

4009. McRae, Barry. "Leroy Jenkins." Jazz Journal International (July 1980): 28-29.

4010. Palmer, Robert. "Jazz: Leroy Jenkins' New Music for Septets." Rolling Stone (November 27 1980): 39.

4011. Primack, Bret. "Leroy Jenkins: Gut-Plucking Revolutionary." down beat (November 16 1978): 23-24+.

4012. Sabien, Randy. "Leroy Jenkins." Jazz String Newsletter (October/December 1982): 7-18. [Interview]

4013. Schoemaker, Bill. "Leroy Jenkins." Coda, No. 174 (August 1980): 4-5.

4014. Stern, Chip. "Black, Brown and Beige." Musician, Player and Listener, No. 18 (May 15-July 1979): 45-47.

4015. Ullman, Michael. "Leroy Jenkins." The New Republic (May 24 1980): 25-27.

4016. Weber, Mark. "Leroy Jenkins." Option: Music Alternatives (May/June 1987): 44-46.

4017. Wilmer, Valerie. "Fiddling with Change." Time Out (July 7-13 1978): 17.

4018. ________. "Jenkins Fights for Survival." Melody Maker (July 31 1971): 12.

JENNY-CLARK, JEAN-FRANCOIS (1944-) (France) - Bass

4019. Carles, Philippe, and Jean-Louis Comolli. Free Jazz, Black Power. 2nd ed. Paris: Editions Galilee, 1979, pp. 411-412.

4020. Clergeat, Andre. "Jenny-Clark, Jean-Francois." In The New Grove Dictionary of Jazz. London: Macmillan Press, 1988.

4021. Dictionnaire du Jazz, eds. Philippe Carles, et al. Paris: Laffont, 1988.

Articles

4022. Carles, Philippe, and Alain Gerber. "Pieges pour Jenny Clark." Jazz Magazine, No. 174 (January 1970): 30+.

4023. Dutilh, Alex, and P. Cardat. "Portrait of Jenny Clark." Jazz Hot, No. 301 (January 1974): 6-9.

4024. "Jenny Clark Romano: sanctification interdite." Jazz Magazine, No. 262 (February 1978): 27. [Interview]

4025. Litterst, Gerhard. "Grenzgaenger: Michel Portal und Jean-Francois Jenny-Clark." Jazz Podium (February 1981): 18-23.

4026. Matthyssens, X. "J.F.: Souvenirs de Faces." Jazz Magazine, No. 375 (Octobre 1988): 42-43. [Interview]

4027. "7 [sept] noms; voici les nouveau-nes du jazz francais!: J-F Jenny Clark." Jazz Magazine, No. 117 (April 1965): 31-32.

JOHNSON, DEWEY (1939-) - Trumpet

4028. Carles, Philippe, and Jean-Louis Comolli. Free Jazz, Black Power. 2nd ed. Paris: Editions Galilee, 1979, p. 412.

4029. Dictionnaire du Jazz, eds. Philippe Carles, et al. Paris: Laffont, 1988.

4030. Wilmer, Valerie. As Serious As Your Life. Westport, CT: Lawrence Hill & Co., 1981, p. 272.

JOHNSON, OLIVER (1944-) - Drums

4031. Carles, Philippe, and Jean-Louis Comolli. Free Jazz, Black Power. 2nd ed. Paris: Editions Galilee, 1979, pp. 412-413.

4032. "Les Paradoxes de TOK." Jazz Magazine, No. 283 (February 1980): 68. Profile of the TOK trio consisting of Mais Takashi (piano), Oliver Johnson (drums) and Kent Carter (bass).

JOHNSON, REGGIE [Reginald Volney] (1940-) - Bass

4033. Carles, Philippe, and Jean-Louis Comolli. Free Jazz, Black Power. 2nd ed. Paris: Editions Galilee, 1979, p. 413.

4034. Claghorn, Charles Eugene. Biographical Dictionary of American Music. West Nyack, NY: Parker Pub. Co., 1973.

4035. ________. Biographical Dictionary of Jazz. Englewood Cliffs, NJ: Prentice-Hall, 1982.

4036. Dictionnaire du Jazz, eds. Philippe Carles, et al. Paris: Laffont, 1988.

4037. Feather, Leonard. The Encyclopedia of Jazz in the Sixties. New York: Horizon Press, 1966.

4038. Reclams Jazzfuhrer. 2nd, rev. ed. Stuttgart: Reclam, 1977.

4039. Voigt, John. "Johnson, Reggie." In The New Grove Dictionary of Jazz. London: Macmillan Press, 1988.

4040. Wilmer, Valerie. As Serious As Your Life. Westport, CT: Lawrence Hill & Co., 1981, p. 272.

JONES, ARTHUR - Alto Saxophone

4041. Carles, Philippe, and Jean-Louis Comolli. Free Jazz, Black Power. 2nd ed. Paris: Editions Galilee, 1979, p. 413.

4042. "Les Nouvelles Tetes de la Nouvelle Musique." Jazz Magazine, No. 171 (October 1969): 23.

4043. Wilmer, Valerie. As Serious As Your Life. Westport, CT: Lawrence Hill & Co., 1981, p. 272.

JONES, ELVIN (1927-) - Drums

See also # 2461, 2491, 2592

4044. Endress, Gudrun. "Elvin Jones." In Jazz Podium. Stuttgart: Deutsche Verlags-Anstalt, 1980, pp. 96-103. [German text]

4045. Hunt, David C. "Elvin Jones: The Rhythmic Energy of Contemporary Drumming." In The Black Giants, eds. Pauline Rivelli and Robert Levin. New York: The World Publishing Company, 1970, pp. 51-55.

4046. Taylor, Arthur. "Elvin Jones." In Notes and Tones. New York: Perigee Books, 1982, pp. 219-229. [Interview]

Biographical Dictionaries

4047. Baker's Biographical Dictionary of Musicians. 7th ed. revised by Nicolas Slonimsky. New York: Schirmer Books, 1984.

4048. Berry, Lemuel, Jr. Biographical Dictionary of Black Musicians and Music Educators. Guthrie, OK: Educational Book Publishers, 1978.

4049. Case, Brian, and Stan Britt. The Harmony Illustrated Encyclopedia of Jazz. 3rd ed. New York: Harmony Books, 1987.

4050. Claghorn, Charles Eugene. Biographical Dictionary of American Music. West Nyack, NY: Parker Pub. Co., 1973.

4051. ________. Biographical Dictionary of Jazz. Englewood Cliffs, NJ: Prentice-Hall, 1982.

4052. Dictionnaire du Jazz, eds. Philippe Carles, et al. Paris: Laffont, 1988.

4053. Feather, Leonard. The Encyclopedia of Jazz in the Sixties. New York: Horizon Press, 1966.

4054. ________, and Ira Gitler. The Encyclopedia of Jazz in the Seventies. New York: Horizon Press, 1976.

4055. The Penguin Encyclopedia of Popular Music, ed. Donald Clarke. New York: Viking, 1989.

4056. Priestley, Brian. "Jones, Elvin." In Jazz: The Essential Companion. New York: Prentice Hall Press, 1988.

4057. Reclams Jazzfuhrer. 2nd, rev. ed. Stuttgart: Reclam, 1977.

4058. Southern, Eileen. Biographical Dictionary of Afro-American and African Musicians. Westport, CT: Greenwood Press, 1982.

4059. Tenot, Frank. Dictionnaire du Jazz. Paris: Larousse, 1967.

4060. Who's Who in Entertainment. 1st ed. 1989-1990.

4061. Wilmer, Valerie. As Serious As Your Life. Westport, CT: Lawrence Hill & Co., 1981, p. 272.

4062. Wilson, Olly. "Jones, Elvin." In The New Grove Dictionary of Jazz. London: Macmillan Press, 1988.

Articles

4063. Ansell, Derek. "Elvin Jones." Jazz Journal International (September 1989): 6-7.

4064. "L'Apport d'Elvin." Jazz Magazine, No. 120 (July 1965): 44-48.

4065. Balliett, Whitney. "Profiles." New Yorker (May 18 1968): 45+.

4066. Bravos, A. G. "An Interview with Elvin Jones." Percussive Notes, Vol. 21, No. 2 (1983): 40-45.

4067. Bravos, T. "An Interview with Elvin Jones." Percussive Notes, Vol. 18, No. 3 (1980): 35.

4068. Brow, J. "Elvin Jones." Jazz Monthly (May 1962): 16-17.

4069. Case, Brian. "Elvin, out of the barnyard." Melody Maker (October 4 1980): 443.

4070. _________. "This is the surgeon who pared the flab." New Musical Express (June 21 1975): 26-27. [Interview]

4071. Dallas, Karl. "Drums: Elvin Jones." Acoustic Music (London), No. 28 (July 1980): 16, 18, 20. [Interview]

4072. DeMichael, Don. "The Sixth Man." down beat (March 28 1963): 16-17, 44. [Profile]

4073. "Elvin: a Jones few drummers can keep up with." Melody Maker (February 19 1966): 11.

4074. "Elvin Jones." Jazz Magazine, No. 234 (July 1975): 22-23. [Interview]

4075. Feather, Leonard. "Blindfold Test." down beat (October 12 1972): 33.

4076. _________. "Blindfold Test." down beat (November 17 1966): 38.

4077. _________. "Elvin Jones." Melody Maker (October 29 1966): 10.

4078. _________. "Man of Many Parts." Melody Maker (July 8 1972): 30.

4079. Gibson, M. "Elvin Jones." Jazz Journal (July 1961): 13+.

4080. Gitler, Ira. "Playing the Truth: Elvin Jones." down beat (October 2 1969): 12+.

4081. Goldman, Albert. "Elvin Jones's Kinesthetic Trip." Life (February 6 1970): 12.

4082. Hart, H. "Elvin Jones: a different drummer." down beat (March 20 1969): 20-21.

4083. Hennessey, Mike. "The Emancipation of Elvin Jones." down beat (March 24 1966): 23-25.

4084. Howland, Harold. "Elvin Jones." Modern Drummer (August/September 1979): 14-17. [Interview]

4085. Hunt, David C. "Elvin Jones: the rhythmic energy of contemporary drumming." Jazz & Pop (March 1970): 20-23.

4086. James, S. "Elvin!" Jazz, Vol. 2 (July-August 1963): 11+.

4087. Jaspar, Bobby. "Elvin Jones and Philly Joe Jones." The Jazz Review, Vol. 2 (February 1959): 6-8.

4088. "John Coltrane's drummer Elvin Jones talks to Jazz News." Jazz News (November 22 1961): 11.

4089. Jones, Elvin. "Drummers Discourse; on film acting, drum styles and the future." Crescendo International (February 1973): 21-22.

4090. Joyce, Mike. "Elvin Jones: interview." Cadence, Vol. 7, No. 2 (February 1981): 9-12.

4091. Kettle, Rupert. "Re: Elvin Jones." down beat (August 11 1966): 17-19.

4092. Kofsky, Frank. "Elvin Jones--Part I: Rhythmic Innovator." Journal of Jazz Studies, Vol. 4, No. 1 (1976): 3-24.

4093. ________. "Elvin Jones: Rhythmic Displacement in the Art of Elvin Jones." Journal of Jazz Studies, Vol. 4, No. 2 (1977): 11-32.

4094. ________. "Elvin Jones." Journal of Jazz Studies, Vol. 5, No. 1 (1978): 81-90. [Interview]

4095. ________. "Elvin Jones." Jazz & Pop (November 1968): 18-23. [Interview]

4096. Lattes, P. "Elvin...!" Jazz Hot, No. 193 (December 1963): 22-25.

4097. Mattingly, Rick. "Elvin." Modern Drummer (December 1982): 88-89. [Interview]

4098. Nolan, Herb. "Blindfold Test." down beat (March 27 1975): 25.

4099. ________. "'I Play Drums, That's Just What I Do'--Elvin Jones." down beat (November 8 1973): 18+. [Interview]

4100. ________. "No Concession Man: Elvin Jones." down beat (May 19 1977): 21+. [Interview]

4101. ________. "Rhythmic Pulsemaster: Elvin Jones." down beat (December 15 1977): 13-14. [Interview]

4102. Shera, M. "Elvin Jones." Jazz Journal (January 1971): 22-23.

4103. Tomkins, Les. "Coltrane and I Played without Preparation." Crescendo International, Vol. 9, No. 3 (1970): 10+. [Interview]

4104. ________. "A Conversation on Drums: Elvin Jones." Crescendo International (November 1974): 22-23.

4105. ________. "Group Discussion: Elvin Jones Quartet." Crescendo International (August 1975): 6-9.

4106. ________, and J. Tagford. "A Drum talk-in with Elvin Jones." Crescendo International (October 1974): 22+.

4107. Welch, Chris. "Elvin Jones." Melody Maker (December 16 1972). [Interview]

4108. Wilmer, Valerie. "Elvin Talk: an interview with Elvin Jones." down beat (March 16 1972): 14-15.

4109. ________. "Gunslinging Across the Rio Grande." Melody Maker (July 11 1970): 14.

4110. Zondek, S. "Elvin Jones." Jazz Forum, No. 21 (February 1973): 36-37.

Media Materials

4111. Different Drummer. Dir., Ed Gray. 30 minute documentary. Includes footage of Jones's 1979 quartet--Pat La Barbara, Ryo Kawasaki and David Williams, along with a discussion of Jones' approach to rhythm and the trap set. Of particular interest is a clip of the classic Coltrane quartet in full flight. [Available from Rhapsody Films, Inc., P.O. Box 179, New York, NY 10014. Tel. 212/243-0152]

JONES, LEONARD (1943-) - Bass

4112. Carles, Philippe, and Jean-Louis Comolli. Free Jazz, Black Power. 2nd ed. Paris: Editions Galilee, 1979, p. 413.

4113. Dictionnaire du Jazz, eds. Philippe Carles, et al. Paris: Laffont, 1988.

4114. Wilmer, Valerie. As Serious As Your Life. Westport, CT: Lawrence Hill & Co., 1981, p. 272.

JONES, NORRIS

See Sirone

JORDAN, LEWIS (1946-) - Alto Saxophone

See also # 6697-6699

4115. Coda, No. 163 (October 1978): 28. Biographical sketch.

KALAPARUSHA

See McIntyre, Maurice

KEANE, SHAKE (1927-) (St. Vincent/G. Britain) - Trumpet

4116. Berry, Lemuel, Jr. Biographical Dictionary of Black Musicians and Music Educators. Guthrie, OK: Educational Book Publishers, 1978, p 258.

4117. Carr, Ian. "Keane, Shake." In Jazz: The Essential Companion. New York: Prentice Hall Press, 1988.

4118. Feather, Leonard. The Encyclopedia of Jazz in the Sixties. New York: Horizon Press, 1966.

4119. Reclams Jazzfuhrer. 2nd, rev. ed. Stuttgart: Reclam, 1977.

Articles

4120. Grime, Kitty. "Star Sideman: Shake Keane." Jazz News (January 31 1962): 8-9.

4121. Harrison, Max. "David Mack and Serial Jazz: A Choice of Routes?" Jazz Monthly (October 1965): 14-15.

4122. James, C. "Shake Keane all over." Melody Maker (January 20 1973): 14.

4123. Morgan, Alun. "Shake Keane." Jazz Monthly (December 6 1975): 26-27.

4124. Pixley, Dick. "Musicians of the Caribbean 3: Shake Keane." Flamingo [London] (February 1964): 9-11.

4125. Wilmer, Valerie. "Caught in the Act." Melody Maker (April 12 1969): 6. [Concert review]

4126. ________. "Shake Keane: Burning 'Speare." Wire, No. 68 (October 1989): 44-45. [Interview]

KENYATTA, ROBIN (1942-) - Alto Saxophone

4127. Carles, Philippe, and Jean-Louis Comolli. Free Jazz, Black Power. 2nd ed. Paris: Editions Galilee, 1979, pp. 413-414.

4128. Dictionnaire du Jazz, eds. Philippe Carles, et al. Paris: Laffont, 1988.

4129. The New Grove Dictionary of Jazz. London: Macmillan Press, 1988.

4130. Southern, Eileen. Biographical Dictionary of Afro-American and African Musicians. Westport, CT: Greenwood Press, 1982.

4131. Wilmer, Valerie. As Serious As Your Life. Westport, CT: Lawrence Hill & Co., 1981, p. 272.

Articles

4132. Carles, Philippe. "Qui es-tu Kenyatta? un saxophoniste qui reve de decouvrir l'Afrique." Jazz Magazine, No. 172 (November 1969): 38+. [Interview]

4133. ________. "Pieges pour Kenyatta." Jazz Magazine, No. 197 (February 1972): 22-23.

4134. Cuscuna, Michael. "The New Voice of Robin Kenyatta." Jazz & Pop (August 1968): 44-46.

4135. Goddet, Laurent, and P. Cressant. "Robin Kenyatta." Jazz Hot, No. 269 (February 1971): 6-9. [Interview]

4136. "Jazz Talk: Kenyatta, Evans." BMI (January 1972): 10-11.

4137. "Kenyatta's journey: the jazzman moveth." Soul (January 7 1974): 11.

4138. "Robin returns from Africa." down beat (November 2 1978): 13.

4139. Sharpe, Lynn. "The Robin Flies." Encore (May 1974): 58.

4140. Silver, Esther. "People: Robin Kenyatta." Essence (December 1970): 57.

4141. Townley, Ray. "Robin's Roost." down beat (April 25 1974): 20.

4142. "Until and Beyond: an interview with Robin Kenyatta." Coda, Vol. 8, No. 9 (September/October 1968): 10-12.

4143. Wilmer, Valerie. "Kenyatta: the sound out there." Melody Maker (February 27 1971): 12.

4144. _________. "Robin Kenyatta and the gypsy life." down beat (July 20 1972): 13, 48.

4145. Wilson, John S. "Caught in the Act." down beat (March 21 1968): 40. [Concert review]

KONDO, TOSHINORI (1948-) (Japan) - Trumpet

4146. Dictionnaire du Jazz, eds. Philippe Carles, et al. Paris: Laffont, 1988.

Articles

4147. Ansell, Kenneth. "Russell/Turner/Kondo." Jazz Journal International (August 1980): 24-25. [Interview]

4148. Charlton, Hannah. "Toshinori Kondo: l'amour d'un art martial." Jazz Magazine, No. 322 (October 1983): 56-57. [Interview]

4149. Cook, Richard. "Toshinori Kondo: A Heavy Metal Piston." Wire, No. 36 (February 1987): 18-20.

KOWALD, PETER (1944-) (W. Germany) - Bass

See also # 511, 614, 616

4150. Iannapollo, Robert J. "Kowald, Peter." In The New Grove Dictionary of Jazz. London: Macmillan Press, 1988.

4151. Noglik, Bert. "Peter Kowald." In Jazzwerkstatt International. Berlin: Verlag Neue Musik, 1981, pp. 427-446. [Interview]

Articles

4152. Carr, J. "One bass hit." Jazz Journal International (October 1978): 52.

4153. Chenard, Marc. "Peter Kowald - A Global Musician." Coda, No. 206 (February/March 1986): 22-23.

4154. Dutilh, Alex. "Hans Reichel, Peter Kowald: pas de conversation." Jazz Hot, No. 368 (1979-80): 51.

4155. Noglik, Bert. "Laudatio fur Peter Kowald." Jazz (Basel), Nr. 6 (1984?).

4156. Ogan, Bernd. "Free Jazz - Multilateral: Smith-Kowald-Sommer." Jazz Podium (October 1980): 24-25.

4157. Pareles, Jon. "Jazz: Peter Kowald Quartet." New York Times (June 4 1984). [Concert review]

KUEHN, JOACHIM (1944-) - Piano

See also # 323

4158. Carles, Philippe, and Jean Louis Comolli. Free Jazz, Black Power. 2nd ed. Paris: Editions Galilee, 1979, p. 414.

4159. Claghorn, Charles Eugene. Biographical Dictionary of Jazz. Englewood Cliffs, NJ: Prentice-Hall, 1982.

4160. Dean, Roger T. "Joachim Kuehn." In The New Grove Dictionary of Jazz. London: Macmillan, 1988.

4161. Feather, Leonard, and Ira Gitler. The Encyclopedia of Jazz in the Seventies. New York: Horizon Books, 1976.

Articles

4162. Czajkowski, Sylwester. "Five Years After." Jazz Forum, No. 29 (June 1975): 38-41. [Interview]

4163. Dutilh, Alex, and Alain Tercinet. "Joachim Kuehn Interview." Jazz Hot, No. 306 (June 1974): 20-22.

4164. Ginibre, Jean-Louis. "Joachim, un des Kuehn." Jazz Magazine, No. 162 (January 1969): 28-31. [Interview]

4165. "Kuehn et son frere." Jazz Magazine, No. 230 (February 1975): 20-21. [Interview]

4166. Serra, P. "Joachim Kuehn." Jazz Hot, No. 255 (November 1969): 17-19. [Interview]

4167. Tercinet, Alain. "Joachim Kuehn." Jazz Hot, No. 273 (june 1971): 4-8.

4168. Wilmer, Valerie. "Joachim Kuehn in a Trance." Melody Maker (January 16 1971): 14.

KUHN, STEVE (1938-) - Piano

See also # 144

4169. Claghorn, Charles Eugene. Biographical Dictionary of American Music. West Nyack, NY: Parker Pub. Co., 1973.

4170. Feather, Leonard. The Encyclopedia of Jazz in the Sixties. New York: Horizon Press, 1966.

4171. ________, and Ira Gitler. The Encyclopedia of Jazz in the Seventies. New York: Horizon Press, 1976.

4172. Lyons, Leonard. "Steve Kuhn." In The Great Jazz Pianists. New York: Morrow, 1983, pp. 229-234.

4173. Rinzler, Paul. "Kuhn, Steve." In The New Grove Dictionary of Jazz. London: Macmillan Press, 1988.

Articles

4174. Doerschuk, Bob. "Steve Kuhn: on playing standards and the death of free-form jazz." Keyboard Magazine (April 1988): 48-50.

4175. Gerber, Alain. "La calme revolte de Steve Kuhn." Jazz Magazine, No. 144 (July 1967): 24+.

4176. ________. "Steve entre Bill et Cecil." Jazz Magazine, No. 165 (April 1979): 11.

4177. Ginibre, Jean Louis. "Pieges pour Steve Kuhn." Jazz Magazine, No. 167 (June 1969): 28-29.

4178. Jones, Max. "Kuhn; let the listener make up his own mind." Melody Maker (March 11 1967): 13.

4179. Lyons, Len. "Steve Kuhn: from Harvard to Coltrane to Sweden and back." Contemporary Keyboard (March 1979): 14, 57.

4180. Riker, Don. "Steve Kuhn: now in season." Jazz (New York), Vol. 4, No. 11 (December 1965): 8-10.

4181. Williams, Martin. "Steve Kuhn - Piano." down beat (February 8 1968): 22-23.

4182. Zabor, Rafi. "Steve Kuhn and Sheila Jordan." Musician, Player and Listener, No. 27 (September-October 1980): 24+.

KURYOKHIN, SERGEY (1954-) (Russia) - Piano

4183. Feigin, Leo. "The Ways of Freedom (Sergey Kuryokhin's Interview)." In Russian Jazz, New Identity, ed. Leo Feigin. London: Quartet Books, 1985, pp. 98-111.

4184. Ojakaar, Walter. "Kuryokhin, Sergey." In The New Grove Dictionary of Jazz. London: Macmillan Press, 1988.

Articles

4185. Benson, Michael R. "Uncivil Engineering: Sergey Kuryokhin and his Popular Mechanics give performance art a Soviet twist." Interview (December 1988): 182-183, 195.

4186. Boulay, S. "On the Scene-U.S.A.: Kuryokhin's Arrival." Jazz Forum, No. 118 (1989): 13-14.

4187. Doerschuk, Bob. "Sergey Kuryokhin: a controversial improviser thrives despite Soviet bureaucracy." Keyboard Magazine (July 1987): 98+.

4188. Duffill, Graham. "The Contemporary Music Club Leningrad 1982." The Wire, No. 7 (Summer 1984): 13. Impressionistic report on a Kuryokhin concert in Leningrad.

4189. ________. "Russian Free Jazz - Sergey Kuryokhin Interview." OP, issue R (July/August 1983): 45-47.

4190. ________. "Serguey Kuryokhin: un regard de l'interieur." Jazz Hot, No. 405 (November 1983): 20. [Interview]

4191. Fish, Mike. "Sergei Kuryokhin: Crazy they call him..." Wire, No. 62 (April 1989): 34-35.

4192. Khan, Alexander. "Sergey Kuryokhin: interview." Cadence, Vol. 9, No. 2 (February 1983): 10-14, 24.

4193. Mandel, Howard. "Sergey Kuryokhin: The Russian Martian Arrives." down beat (April 1989): 26-28.

4194. Meilicke, Joerg. "Sergej Kurjokhin." Jazzthetik, Vol. 2, No. 12 (December 1988): 8-11.

4195. Minor, William. "Sergey Kuryokhin - Pop Mechanics." Coda, No. 231 (April/May 1990): 20-23.

4196. Petrochenkov, Alexander. "Sergei Kuryokhin: the search for freedom." Jazz Forum, No. 82 (1983): 45-47. [Interview]

4197. Sandow, Gregory. "Sergey Kuryokhin; Leningrad Downtown." Village Voice (July 29 1986).

LACY, STEVE [Steven Lackritz] (1934-) - Soprano Saxophone

Works in English

4198. Davis, Francis. "An American in Paris." In Outcats: Jazz Composers, Instrumentalists, and Singers. New York: Oxford University Press, 1990, pp. 100-107. [Reprint of # 4222]

4199. Lacy, Bobbie. "Introducing Steve Lacy." In Jazz Panorama; from the pages of the Jazz Review. New York: Crowell, 1962, pp. 268-272. [Reprint of # 4233]

4200. Preiss, Clifford, comp. The Steve Lacy Festival Handbook. New York: WKCR-FM (208 Ferris Booth Hall, Columbia University, New York City 10027), 1982. 61p.

Biographical Dictionaries

4201. Carr, Ian. "Lacy, Steve." In Jazz: The Essential Companion. New York: Prentice Hall Press, 1988.

4202. Case, Brian, and Stan Britt. The Harmony Illustrated Encyclopedia of Jazz. 3rd ed. New York: Harmony Books, 1987.

4203. Claghorn, Charles Eugene. Biographical Dictionary of American Music. West Nyack, NY: Parker Pub. Co., 1973.

4204. _________. Biographical Dictionary of Jazz. Englewood Cliffs, NJ: Prentice-Hall, 1982.

4205. Feather, Leonard. The Encyclopedia of Jazz in the Sixties. New York: Horizon Press, 1966.

4206. _________, and Ira Gitler. The Encyclopedia of Jazz in the Seventies. New York: Horizon Press, 1976.

4207. Kernfeld, Barry. "Lacy, Steve." In The New Grove Dictionary of American Music. London: Macmillan Press, 1986.

4208. _________, and H. L. Lindenmaier. "Lacy, Steve." In The New Grove Dictionary of Jazz. London: Macmillan Press, 1988.

4209. McRae, Barry. "Steve Lacy." In The Jazz Handbook. Harlow, Essex, Eng.: Longman, 1987, pp. 202-203.

4210. The Penguin Encyclopedia of Popular Music, ed. Donald Clarke. New York: Viking, 1989.

4211. Wilmer, Valerie. As Serious As Your Life. Westport, CT: Lawrence Hill & Co., 1981, p. 272.

Articles

4212. Ansell, Kenneth. "Steve Lacy." Impetus (London), No. 6 (1977): 254-255. [Interview w/discography]

4213. Balliett, Whitney. "New York Notes." New Yorker (February 21 1977): 101-102. [Concert review]

4214. Breskin, David. "Faces: Steve Lacy." Musician, Player & Listener, No. 31 (March 1981): 40-41.

4215. Burwell, Paul, and David Toop. "I'm Not Much of a Hoofer Myself..." Musics (London), No. 12 (May 1977): 4-9. [Interview]

4216. Case, Brian. "The spark, the gap, the leap." Melody Maker (April 7 1979): 53. [Interview]

4217. ________. "Steve Lacy." The Wire, No. 1 (Summer 1982): 6-7.

4218. Cook, Richard. "A Duck is Calling Your Name: Some Thoughts on Steve Lacy and the Art of Going Solo on Soprano." The Wire, No. 19 (1985).

4219. Cordle, Owen. "Steve Lacy." Jazz Times (December 1987): 11. [Interview]

4220. Danson, Peter. "Steve Lacy." Coda (August 1984): 13-15. [Interview]

4221. Davidson, Martin. "The Great Big Beautiful Sounds of Steve Lacy." Into Jazz (London), Vol. 1, No. 4 (May 1974).

4222. Davis, Francis. "An American in Paris: the soprano saxophonist Steve Lacy has always gone his own way." The Atlantic (November 1989): 120+. [Reprinted in # 4198]

4223. Fish, Mike. "Steve Lacy: Wail of the Times." Wire, No. 74 (April 1990): 8.

4224. France, C., and B. France. "Steve Lacy: interview." Cadence, Vol. 4, No. 12 (December 1978): 3+.

4225. Gamble, Peter. "Steve Lacy." Jazz Journal International (November 1990): 12-13. [Interview]

4226. Gervais, Raymond, and Yves Bouliane. "Interview with Steve Lacy." Trans. from the French by Effie Mihopolous. Brilliant Corners: A Magazine of the Arts (Chicago), No. 5 (Spring 1977): 77-112. [Orig. pub. in Parachute [Montreal] (Autumn 1976)]

4227. Gitler, Ira. "Focus on Steve Lacy." down beat (March 2 1961): 15, 46.

4228. Griggs, Steve. "Steve Lacy's solo on Skippy - a soprano saxophone transcription." down beat (December 1987): 60+.

4229. Harrison, Max. "Musicians Talking: Steve Lacy." Jazz Monthly (March 1966): 7-14. [Interview w/discography]

4230. Jeske, Lee. "Prolific Steve Lacy and his Poly-Free Bag." down beat (May 1980): 20-23. [Interview]

4231. Johnson, Tom. "An American in Paris." Village Voice (March 9 1982): 74. [Interview]

4232. Kostakis, Peter. "Up a Lacy river." down beat (May 1987): 30. Survey of recent Lacy lps.

4233. Lacy, Bobbie. "Introducing Steve Lacy." Jazz Review, Vol. 2 (September 1959): 22-25. [Reprinted in # 4199]

4234. Lacy, Steve. "My Favorite Thing." Metronome (December 1961): 24-25.

4235. "The Land of Monk." down beat (October 10 1963): 14-15. [Profile]

4236. Lange, Art. "Record & CD Reviews: Lacy & Co." down beat (October 1989): 32. Survey of recent recordings by Lacy.

4237. Lock, Graham. "The Five Colours Blind You, the Five Notes Deafen You." New Musical Express (January 22 1983): 10-11. [Interview]

4238. McRae, Barry. "Avant Courier." Jazz Journal International (April 1981): 24-25.

4239. Palmer, Robert. "A Rare Visit from Mr. Soprano Sax." New York Times (January 28 1977).

4240. ________. "Steve Lacy: Taming the Soprano Sax." Rolling Stone (March 5 1981): 53.

4241. Parry, Roger. "Futurities: Steve Lacy's lyrics." Coda, No. 216 (October-November 1987): 22-24. [Interview]

4242. "Steve Lacy." Melody Maker (August 21 1965): 27.

4243. "Steve Lacy: the man who explained it to Coltrane." Melody Maker (July 24 1965): 6.

4244. Terlizzi, Roberto. "The Steve Lacy Interview." Coda, No. 153 (January-February 1977): 8-11.

4245. Weinstein, Norman. "Was That a Real Creeley Poem, Or Did You Swing That Tune Yourself?" Noh Quarter, Vol. 1, No. 3 (Summer 1986): 11-16. Review essay on Lacy's "Futurities" lp.

4246. Weiss, Jason. "Steve Lacy: in search of the way." Jazz Forum, No. 69 (1981): 35-39. [Interview]

4247. Welburn, Ron. "An Interview with Steve Lacy." The Grackle, Vol. 1, No. 3 (Autumn 1976): 7-15.

4248. Whitehead, Kevin. "Steve Lacy: the interview." down beat (December 1987): 24+.

4249. "Why Some Men Leave Home." down beat (June 17 1965): 15. Lacy gives his reasons for wanting to move to Europe.

4250. Wilmer, Valerie. "Lacy-thinking aloud." Melody Maker (March 16 1974): 47. [Interview]

4251. ________. "Steve Lacy: Birth Pains." Melody Maker (January 9 1971): 14.

4252. Zwerin, Michael. "Jazz Journal: Scuffling." Village Voice (June 15 1967): 21-22. [Profile]

Works in French, German and Italian

4253. Carles, Philippe, and Jean-Louis Comolli. Free Jazz, Black Power. 2nd ed. Paris: Editions Galilee, 1979, pp. 414-415.

4254. Dictionnaire du Jazz, eds. Philippe Carles, et al. Paris: Laffont, 1988.

4255. Reclams Jazzfuhrer. 2nd, rev. ed. Stuttgart: Reclam, 1977.

4256. Reda, Jacques. Anthologie des Musiciens de Jazz. Paris: Stock, 1981, pp. 325-326.

4257. Tenot, Frank. Dictionnaire du Jazz. Paris: Larousse, 1967.

Articles

4258. Arcangeli, Stefano. "Intervista con Steve Lacy." Musica Jazz, Vol. 33, No. 1 (1977): 20-22. [Interview]

4259. Bailey, Derek. "Derek Bailey im Gespraech mit Steve Lacy." Jazz Podium (March 1986): 16-18.

4260. Balli, Enrico. "Steve Lacy." Musica Jazz (January 1960): 25.

4261. Carles, Philippe. "Fidele Lacy." Jazz Magazine, No. 121 (August 1965): 12-17. [Interview]

4262. _________. "Lacy: les arts et les lettres." Jazz Magazine, No. 381 (April 1989): 29. [Interview]

4263. Constant, Denis. "Lacy toujours Fidele." Jazz Magazine, No. 184 (December 1970): 13-14.

4264. Dalla Bona, Giuseppe. "Steve Lacy: la geometria del disordine." Musica Jazz (February 1986): 16-21.

4265. Dutilh, Alex. "Steve Lacy." Jazz Hot, No. 288 (November 1972): 23.

4266. Endress, Gudrun. "Poly-free musik: Interview mit Steve Lacy." Jazz Podium (November 1986): 6-9.

4267. Gros-Claude, P. "Steve Lacy parle." Jazz Magazine, No. 186 (February 1971): 16-17.

4268. Hardy, Alain-Rene. "Steve Lacy--face a face." Jazz Magazine, No. 246 (August 1976): 14-15. [Interview]

4269. _________, and P. Quinsac. "Steve Lacy: evidences et reflexions." Jazz Magazine, No. 243 (April 1976): 20-23. [Interview]

4270. Lattes, P. "Un Soprano Discret." Jazz Hot, No. 211 (July-August 1965): 35-37. [Interview]

4271. Leroy, Jean-Luc. "Interview: Steve Lacy." Jazz 360o (Sierre, Switzerland), No. 55 (January 1983): 2-6.

4272. ________. "Steve Lacy." Jazz 360o, No. 46 (March 1982): 8-14.

4273. "Lettre de Steve." Jazz Magazine, No. 149 (December 1967): 26.

4274. "Le Non Lassant Lacy." Jazz Magazine, No. 172 (November 1969): 11+.

4275. Prevost, Xavier. "Steve Lacy Geant Meconnu?" Jazz Magazine, No. 310 (September 1982): 45. [Interview]

4276. Rouy, Gerard. "Lacy: Albert, Sonny, Cecil et les autres." Jazz Magazine, No. 367 (Dec 1987-Jan 1988): 48-49. [Interview]

4277. ________. "Lacy: 'Thelonious Monk et Moi.'" Jazz Magazine, No. 368 (February 1988): 32-33. [Interview]

4278. ________. "Lacy the Last." Jazz Magazine, No. 369 (March 1988): 32-35. [Interview]

4279. ________. "Steve Lacy: la solitude du souffleur de fond." Jazz Magazine, No. 366 (1987): 36-38. [Interview]

4280. "Steve Lacy Individualista Insobornable." Qu'artica Jazz (Barcelona), No. 15/16 (Autumn 1983).

4281. "Steve Lacy Interview." Jazz Podium (January 1966): 8-11.

4282. Weiss, Jason. "Steve Lacy et Brion Gysin." Jazz Magazine, No. 300 (September 1981): 22-23. [Interview]

4283. Westin, L. "Steve Lacy: 'man maaste lita paa sin musik!'" Orkester Journalen (January 1983): 13-16.

Discographies

4284. Lindenmaier, H. L. 25 Years of Fish Horn Recording: the Steve Lacy discography, 1954-1979. Freiburg, West Germany: Jazz Realities, 1982. 66p.

4285. Maertens, Guido, and Gustave Cerutti. Discographie de Steve Lacy 1954-Octobre 1979. Revised and updated ed. Sierre, Switzerland: Jazz 360o (c/o G. Cerutti, Ave. du Marche 8, CH-3960, Sierre), 1982. 32p. (Orig. 1980)

Media Materials

4286. Lift the Bandstand (198?). Documentary. [Available from Rhapsody Films, P.O. Box 179, New York, NY 10014. Tel. 212/243-0152]

LA FARO, SCOTT (1936-1961) - Bass

4287. Roggeman, Willy. "Scott LaFaro." In Free en Andere Jazz-Essays. The Hague: Van Ditmar, 1969, pp. 123-127. [Dutch text]

4288. Williams, Martin. "Introducing Scott La Faro." In Jazz Panorama; from the pages of the Jazz Review. New York: Crowell, 1962, pp. 278-280.

Biographical Dictionaries

4289. Claghorn, Charles Eugene. Biographical Dictionary of American Music. West Nyack, NY: Parker Pub. Co., 1973.

4290. ________. Biographical Dictionary of Jazz. Englewood Cliffs, NJ: Prentice-Hall, 1982.

4291. Dictionnaire du Jazz, eds. Philippe Carles, et al. Paris: Laffont, 1988.

4292. Feather, Leonard. The Encyclopedia of Jazz. Rev. ed. New York: Horizon Press, 1960.

4293. ________. The Encyclopedia of Jazz in the Sixties. New York: Horizon Press, 1966.

4294. Kernfeld, Barry. "La Faro, Scott." In The New Grove Dictionary of American Music. London: Macmillan Press, 1986.

4295. ________. "La Faro, Scott." In The New Grove Dictionary of Jazz. London: Macmillan Press, 1988.

4296. The Penguin Encyclopedia of Popular Music, ed. Donald Clarke. New York: Viking, 1989.

4297. Priestley, Brian. "La Faro, Scott." In Jazz: The Essential Companion. New York: Prentice Hall Press, 1988.

4298. Reclams Jazzfuhrer. 2nd, rev. ed. Stuttgart: Reclam, 1977.

4299. Reda, Jacques. Anthologie des Musiciens de Jazz. Paris: Stock, 1981, pp. 327-328.

4300. Tenot, Frank. Dictionnaire du Jazz. Paris: Larousse, 1967.

Articles

4301. "Annuaire biographique de la contrebasse." Jazz Magazine, No. 9 (May 1963): 26. Biographical sketch.

4302. Binchet, J. P. "Le Phare La Faro." Jazz Magazine, No. 153 (April 1968): 20-23.

4303. Charlesworth, B. "The Flying Scott." Jazz Journal International (June 1989): 16-17.

4304. Hunt, David C. "The Contemporary Approach to Jazz Bass." Jazz & Pop (August 1969): 18-20.

4305. Kopel, G. "Wilbur Ware et Scott La Faro." Jazz Magazine, No. 6 (December 1959): 16-17.

4306. Levitt, Al. "Du Temps de La Faro." Jazz Magazine, No. 283 (February 1980): 38-39, 64-66; No. 285 (April 1980): 42, 68.

4307. Pekar, Harvey. "The Development of Modern Bass." down beat (October 11 1962): 21.

4308. Williams, Martin. "Introducing Scott La Faro." The Jazz Review (August 1960): 16-17.

Obituaries

4309. down beat (August 17 1961): 13.
4310. Jazz Magazine, No. 7 (September 1961): 16.
4311. Metronome (September 1961): 1.

LAKE, OLIVER (1942-) - Reeds

See also # 6943-6957

4312. Jost, Ekkehard. "Oliver Lake." In Jazzmusiker: Materialen zur Soziologie der Afro-Amerikanischen Musik. Frankfurt am Main: Ullstein, 1982, pp. 129-134.

Biographical Dictionaries

4313. Anderson, Ruth. Contemporary American Composers: a biographical dictionary. 2nd ed. Boston, MA: G.K. Hall, 1982.

4314. ASCAP Biographical Dictionary. 4th ed. New York: R.R. Bowker, 1980.

4315. Carles, Philippe, and Jean-Louis Comolli. Free Jazz, Black Power. 2nd ed. Paris: Editions Galilee, 1979, p. 415.

4316. Carr, Ian. "Lake, Oliver." In Jazz: The Essential Companion. New York: Prentice Hall Press, 1988.

4317. Claghorn, Charles Eugene. Biographical Dictionary of Jazz. Englewood Cliffs, NJ: Prentice-Hall, 1982.

4318. Dictionnaire du Jazz, eds. Philippe Carles, et al. Paris: Laffont, 1988.

4319. Feather, Leonard, and Ira Gitler. The Encyclopedia of Jazz in the Seventies. New York: Horizon Press, 1976.

4320. Kernfeld, Barry. "Lake, Oliver." In The New Grove Dictionary of American Music. London: Macmillan Press, 1986.

4321. ________. "Lake, Oliver." In The New Grove Dictionary of Jazz. London: Macmillan Press, 1988.

4322. McRae, Barry. "Oliver Lake." In The Jazz Handbook. Harlow, Essex, Eng.: Longman, 1987, pp. 239-240.

4323. The Penguin Encyclopedia of Popular Music, ed. Donald Clarke. New York: Viking, 1989, p. 681.

4324. Southern, Eileen. Biographical Dictionary of Afro-American and African Musicicians. Westport, CT: Greenwood Press, 1982.

4325. Who's Who of American Music: Classical, ed. Jacques Cattell Press. 2nd ed. New York: R.R. Bowker, 1985.

4326. Wilmer, Valerie. As Serious As Your Life. Westport, CT: Lawrence Hill & Co., 1981, p. 273.

Articles

4327. "Birthday Pace of Lake." down beat (November 16 1978): 13.

4328. Blum, Joe. "Oliver Lake: A Virtuoso Marriage of Avant-Garde Jazz and Reggae-Funk Dance." Musician, No. 49 (November 1982): 27-28, 30, 32, 34, 36. [Interview]

4329. Bouchard, Fred. "Blindfold Test." down beat (March 1983): 45.

4330. Brisset, B. "Lake/Carrol/Fabiano." Jazz Hot, No. 307 (July-August 1974): 31-32.

4331. Charlton, Hannah. "Breaking Out of Uniform." Melody Maker (December 6 1980): 23.

4332. Engelhardt, J. "Oliver Lake." Jazz Podium (June 1981): 23.

4333. Giddins, Gary. "Oliver Lake Seeks the Right Time." Village Voice (September 25 1978): 94, 96.

4334. Goldman, Vivien. "Oliver Lake." Melody Maker (June 9 1979): 64.

4335. Henderson, Bill. "Lake Air Waves." Black Music and Jazz Review (London), Vol. 2, No. 6 (September 1979): 18-19. [Interview]

4336. Jackson, D. "Profile: Julius Hemphill; Oliver Lake." down beat (June 19 1975): 33.

4337. Kan, A. "Oliver Lake: Moving On." Jazz Forum, No. 115 (1988): 40-44. [Interview]

4338. Litweiler, John. "Caught in the Act: Oliver Lake/Julius Hemphill, AACM, Chicago." down beat (June 12 1969): 34-35. [Concert review]

4339. McRae, Barry. "Avant Courier: Beyond the Mainstream." Jazz Journal International (February 1980): 25-26. [Profile]

4340. Mandel, Howard. "Riffs & Licks: How Hip the Stroll." Village Voice (September 17 1985): 69+.

4341. Milkowski, Bill. "Oliver Lake: Sax in the Hip Pocket." down beat (May 1983): 22-24.

4342. Palmer, Robert. "Oliver Lake's Eclectic Light Orchestra." Rolling Stone (November 2 1978): 36.

4343. Rusch, Bob. "Speaking with Oliver Lake." Cadence, Vol. 2, No. 5 (September 1977): 3-6, 12.

4344. Smith, Bill. "The Oliver Lake Interview." Coda (May 1976): 2-4+.

4345. ________. "Oliver Lake: Jump Up." Coda, No. 193 (December 1983): 8-9. [Interview]

4346. ________. "Oliver Lake: Passin' Thru." Coda, No. 233 (August/September 1990): 10-12.

4347. Tagliaferri, Enrico, and Giampiero Gallina. "Intervista con Oliver Lake." Musica Jazz, Vol. 33, No. 12 (1977): 6-8.

4348. Wilmer, Valerie. "Lake-Side Developments." Melody Maker (March 6 1976): 42. [Interview]

4349. Zipkin, Michael. "Blindfold Test: Oliver Lake." down beat (August 9 1979): 45.

LANCASTER, BYARD [William] (1942-) - Reeds

4350. Carles, Philippe, and Jean-Louis Comolli. Free Jazz, Black Power. 2nd ed. Paris: Editions Galilee, 1979, p. 415-416.

4351. Claghorn, Charles Eugene. Biographical Dictionary of Jazz. Englewood Cliffs, NJ: Prentice-Hall, 1982.

4352. Dictionnaire du Jazz, eds. Philippe Carles, et al. Paris: Laffont, 1988.

4353. Feather, Leonard, and Ira Gitler. The Encyclopedia of Jazz in the Seventies. New York: Horizon Press, 1976.

4354. Such, David G. "Lancaster, Byard." In The New Grove Dictionary of Jazz. London: Macmillan Press, 1988.

4355. Wilmer, Valerie. As Serious As Your Life. Westport, CT: Lawrence Hill & Co., 1981, p. 273.

Articles

4356. Futrick, Gerard. "Byard Lancaster." Coda, No. 194 (February 1984): 4-6. [Interview]

4357. Jeske, Lee. "Profile: Byard Lancaster." down beat (January 1981): 50

4358. Karp, Sid. "Byard Lancaster." Coda, Vol. 9, No. 3-4 (December 1969): 11-13. [Profile]

4359. "On the Bandstand." Jazz Forum, No. 44 (1976): 36-37.

4360. "The Questionnaire." Cadence (January 1991): 28, 33, 91. Compilation of biographical information submitted by Lancaster to Cadence editor Bob Rusch.

4361. Rusch, Bob. "Byard Lancaster: interview." Cadence, Vol. 6, No. 3 (March 1980): 5-9.

4362. Szwed, John. "Byard Lancaster." Jazz & Pop (April-May 1969): 58-62.

4363. Wilmer, Valerie. "Everybody is a Star." Melody Maker (January 1 1972): 12.

Discographies

4364. Hames, Mike. Albert Ayler, Sunny Murray, Cecil Taylor, Byard Lancaster, Kenneth Terroade on disc and tape. Ferndown, Eng.: Hames (16 Pinewood Road, Ferndown, Dorset BH22 9RW), 1983. 61p.

LASHA, PRINCE [W. B. Lawsha] (1930-) - Alto Saxophone

See also # 695-696

4365. Berry, Lemuel, Jr. Biographical Dictionary of Black Musicians and Music Educators. Guthrie, OK: Educational Book Publishers, 1978, p. 261.

4366. Carles, Philippe, and Jean-Louis Comolli. Free Jazz, Black Power. 2nd ed. Paris: Editions Galilee, 1979, p. 416.

4367. Claghorn, Charles Eugene. Biographical Dictionary of American Music. West Nyack, NY: Parker Pub. Co., 1973.

4368. _________. Biographical Dictionary of Jazz. Englewood Cliffs, NJ: Prentice-Hall, 1982.

4369. Dictionnaire du Jazz, eds. Philippe Carles, et al. Paris: Laffont, 1988.

4370. Feather, Leonard. The Encyclopedia of Jazz in the Sixties. New York: Horizon Press, 1966.

4371. The New Grove Dictionary of Jazz. London: Macmillan Press, 1988.

4372. The Penguin Encyclopedia of Popular Music, ed. Donald Clarke. New York: Viking, 1989, pp. 684-685.

4373. Wilmer, Valerie. As Serious As Your Life. Westport, CT: Lawrence Hill & Co., 1981, p. 273.

Articles

4374. "Off on the Search for Perfect Sounds." Melody Maker (January 8 1966): 6.

4375. Romero, Enrico. "Prince Lawsha: a short talk." Cadence, Vol. 7, No. 6 (June 1981): 10-11.

4376. Tynan, John. "Take Five." down beat (April 11 1963): 40. [Profile]

4377. Wilmer, Valerie. "Prince Lasha." Jazz Journal (June 1966): 27. [Interview]

LASHLEY, LESTER (1935-) - Trombone/Bass/Cello

See also # 706

4378. Carles, Philippe, and Jean-Louis Comolli. Free Jazz, Black Power. 2nd ed. Paris: Editions Galilee, 1979, p. 416.

4379. Wilmer, Valerie. As Serious As Your Life. Westport, CT: Lawrence Hill & Co., 1981, p. 273.

LAST EXIT

4380. Lake, Steve. "Last Exit: The Living End." Wire, No. 29 (July 1986): 22-23, 25. Interview with the group--Peter Broetzmann, Ronald Shannon Jackson, Bill Laswell and Sonny Sharrock.

LASWELL, BILL - Guitar

See # 4380

LEADERS, THE (formed 1984)

4381. The New Grove Dictionary of Jazz. London: Macmillan Press, 1988.

Articles

4382. Balliett, Whitney. "Jazz." New Yorker (June 23 1986): 94-95.

4383. Detro, J. "The Leaders." Jazz Times (May 1989): 18-19. [Interview]

4384. Giddins, Gary. "Weatherbird: Leaders in the Pack." Village Voice (June 10 1986): 66.

4385. Woodard, Josef. "Riffs: The Leaders." down beat (January 1987): 14.

Media Materials

4386. Jazz in Paris 1988. 54 min. [Available from Rhapsody Films, Dept. A, Box 179, New York, NY 10014. Tel. 212/243-0152; Or, Stash Records, 611 Broadway, Suite 411, NYC 10012]

LEE, JEANNE (1939-) - Vocal

See also # 694

4387. Carles, Philippe, and Jean-Louis Comolli. Free Jazz, Black Power. 2nd ed. Paris: Editions Galilee, 1979, p. 416.

4388. Claghorn, Charles Eugene. Biographical Dictionary of American Music. West Nyack, NY: Parker Pub. Co., 1973.

4389. ________. Biographical Dictionary of Jazz. Englewood Cliffs, NJ: Prentice-Hall, 1982.

4390. Dictionnaire du Jazz, eds. Philippe Carles, et al. Paris: Laffont, 1988.

4391. Feather, Leonard. The Encyclopedia of Jazz in the Sixties. New York: Horizon Press, 1966.

4392. Reclams Jazzfuhrer. 2nd, rev. ed. Stuttgart: Reclam, 1977.

4393. Scheinin, Richard. "Lee, Jeanne." In The New Grove Dictionary of Jazz. London: Macmillan Press, 1988.

4394. Wilmer, Valerie. As Serious As Your Life. Westport, CT: Lawrence Hill & Co., 1981, p. 283.

Articles

4395. Belgrave, B. "Jeanne Lee et Ran Blake." Jazz Hot, No. 189 (July-August 1963): 12+.

4396. Buchter-Romer, Ute. "New Vocal Jazz." Jazz Research Papers, Vol. 9 (1989): 48-53.

4397. Coss, Bill. "The Agonies of Exploration: Jeanne Lee and Ran Blake." down beat (September 13 1962): 18.

4398. Foote, Lona. "Meet the Composer." Ear, Vol. 13, No. 3 (May 1988): 28-29.

4399. Geiger, Annette. "Jeanne Lee." Jazz (Basel), No. 5 (1983).

4400. Hicks, Robert. "Voices with Vision: Jeanne Lee, Terry Jenoure and Amina Claudine Myers." Option, No. 34 (Sept/Oct 1990): 74-79.

4401. "Jeanne Lee, Ran Blake find success in Europe." down beat (July 18 1963): 9-10.

4402. Riggins, Roger. "Jeanne Lee and Gunter Hampel." Coda, No. 164 (February 1979): 6-9.

4403. Shange, Ntozake. "Jean Lee/she sings..." Village Voice (April 29 1981): 77.

4404. Williams, Martin. "With Blake and Lee in Europe." down beat (May 7 1964): 14-17.

LEFLORE, FLOYD - Trumpet

4405. Carles, Philippe, and Jean-Louis Comolli. Free Jazz, Black Power. 2nd ed. Paris: Editions Galilee, 1979, p. 416.

4406. Wilmer, Valerie. As Serious As Your Life. Westport, CT: Lawrence Hill & Co., 1981, p. 273.

LEVIN, MARC (1942-) - Trumpet

4407. Claghorn, Charles Eugene. Biographical Dictionary of Jazz. Englewood Cliffs, NJ: Prentice-Hall, 1982.

4408. Dictionnaire du Jazz, eds. Philippe Carles, et al. Paris: Laffont, 1988.

4409. The New Grove Dictionary of Jazz. London: Macmillan Press, 1988.

Articles

4410. Baggenaes, Roland. "Marc Levin." Coda, No. 145 (March 1976): 2-4. [Interview]

4411. Rusch, Bob. "Marc Levin: interview." Cadence, Vol. 4, No. 11 (November 1978): 8-13.

LEWIS, ART (1938-) - Drums

See also # 69

4412. Carles, Philippe, and Jean-Louis Comolli. Free Jazz, Black Power. 2nd ed. Paris: Editions Galilee, 1979, p. 417.

4413. Wilmer, Valerie. As Serious As Your Life. Westport, CT: Lawrence Hill & Co., 1981, p. 273.

4414. _________. "Art's Class." Melody Maker (September 2 1972): 26.

LEWIS, BILL (1927-) - Vibraphone

4415. Woessner, Russell. "Philly's Long March Jazz School." down beat (November 1979): 16.

4416. _________. "Profile: Bill Lewis." down beat (July 1981): 54-55.

LEWIS, GEORGE (1952-) - Trombone/Computers

See also # 697, 707

4417. Endress, Gudrun. "George Lewis." In Jazz Podium. Stuttgart: Deutsche Verlags-Anstalt, 1980, pp. 204-211.

Biographical Dictionaries

4418. Carles, Philippe, and Jean-Louis Comolli. Free Jazz, Black Power. 2nd ed. Paris: Editions Galilee, 1979, p. 417.

4419. Carr, Ian. "Lewis, George." In Jazz: The Essential Companion. New York: Prentice Hall Press, 1988.

4420. Dictionnaire du Jazz, eds. Philippe Carles, et al. Paris: Laffont, 1988.

4421. Passy, Charles. "Lewis, George (ii)." In The New Grove Dictionary of American Music. London: Macmillan Press, 1986.

4422. ________, and David Wild. "Lewis, George (ii)." In The New Grove Dictionary of Jazz. London: Macmillan Press, 1988.

4423. The Penguin Encyclopedia of Popular Music, ed. Donald Clarke. New York: Viking, 1989.

4424. Wilmer, Valerie. As Serious As Your Life. Westport, CT: Lawrence Hill & Co., 1981, p. 283.

Articles

4425. Case, Brian. "Elbowing the No Risk Zone." New Musical Express (August 12 1978): 29. [Interview]

4426. De Muth, Jerry. "Anthony Braxton--George Lewis." Cadence, Vol. 2, No. 2 (December 1976): 3+.

4427. "Ein Stern Geht auf Der Posaunist George Lewis." Jazz Podium (juni 1978): 4-9.

4428. Flicker, Chris. "George Lewis: pas une revolution mais une mutation." Jazz Magazine, No. 266 (July/August 1978): 38-40.

4429. Foote, Lona. "Meet the Composer: George Lewis." Ear: New Music News, Vol. 13, No. 1 (March 1988): 30-31.

4430. Litweiler, John B. "Profile: George Lewis." down beat (August 11 1977): 36-38.

4431. Smith, Bill. "George Lewis: a conversation." Coda, No. 155 (May/June 1977): 2-13.

4432. Tinder, Cliff. "Faces: George Lewis." Musician, Player, and Listener, No. 36 (September-October 1981): 47.

LINCOLN, ABBEY [aka Aminata Moseka]

4433. Clouzet, J., and Jean Wagner. "12 heures avec Abbey Lincoln." Jazz Magazine, No. 104 (March 1964): 24-29.

4434. Gardner, Barbara. "Metamorphosis: Abbey Lincoln." down beat (September 14 1961): 18-20. [Interview]

4435. Kofsky, Frank. "Abbey Lincoln." Radio Free Jazz, Vol. 18, No. 2 (1977): 11, 14. See also response from Dan Morgenstern (March 1977): 2.

4436. Polillo, Arrigo. "Max + Abbey = Protesta." Musica Jazz (February 1964): 15-17.

4437. "Racial Prejudice in Jazz: A Panel Discussion." down beat (March 15 1962): 20-26; (March 29 1962): 22-25. The first part of this article includes a reprint of Ira Gitler's Nov. 9 1961 db review of Abbey Lincoln's lp "Straight Ahead" which was the spark for the discussion. Panelists include Abbey Lincoln, Max Roach, Lalo Schifrin, Don Ellis, Ira Gitler, Don De Michael, Nat Hentoff and Bill Coss.

4438. "The Revolt of Abbey Lincoln." Sepia (October 1961): 29-31.

4439. Rivelli, Pauline. "Abbey Lincoln." Jazz (New York), Vol. 4, No. 7 (July 1965): 8-12. [Interview]

4440. Smith, Bill. "Abbey Lincoln Talks with Bill Smith." Coda, No. 170 (December 1979): 12-16. [Interview]

4441. Smith, Charles Edward. "Record Reviews: Straight Ahead." Metronome (September 1961): 29.

4442. Vander, M., and G. Rovere. "Max et Abbey." Jazz Hot, No. 232 (June 1967): 18-23. [Interview]

4443. Vercelli, Gary G. "Profile: Aminata Moseka/Abbey Lincoln." down beat (September 6 1979): 42-44.

4444. Watson, Patrick. "Abbey Lincoln." Coda (April/May 1965): 6-8. [Interview]

4445. Wilson, John S. "Miss Lincoln Sizes Up Women's Place in Jazz." New York Times (June 17 1983).

LINDBERG, JOHN (1959-   ) - Bass

See also # 6107-6108

4446. Dictionnaire du Jazz, eds. Philippe Carles, et al. Paris: Laffont, 1988.

4447. The New Grove Dictionary of Jazz. London: Macmillan Press, 1988.

Articles

4448. Boija, S. "Bassisten John Lindberg: 'frihet och tradition'." Orkester Journalen (November 1989): 18-20. [Interview]

4449. Bouchet, Jean-Luc, and Jerome Reese. "Contrebasse au Present." Jazz Hot, No. 398 (February/March 1983): 28-30, 50. [Interview]

LISSACK, SELWYN (South Africa/UK) - Drums

4450. Williams, Richard. "Jazz Records: Facets of the Universe." Melody Maker (January 9 1971): 18. [Record review]

4451. Wilmer, Valerie. "Strong Words from Selwyn." Melody Maker (November 29 1969): 10. [Interview]

LITTLE, BOOKER (1938-1961) - Trumpet

4452. Berry, Lemuel, Jr. Biographical Dictionary of Black Musicians and Music Educators. Guthrie, OK: Educational Book Publishers, 1978, p. 262.

4453. Case, Brian, and Stan Britt. The Harmony Illustrated Encyclopedia of Jazz. 3rd ed. New York: Harmony Books, 1987.

4454. Claghorn, Charles Eugene. Biographical Dictionary of American Music. West Nyack, NY: Parker Pub. Co., 1973.

4455. ________. Biographical Dictionary of Jazz. Englewood Cliffs, NJ: Prentice-Hall, 1982.

4456. Dictionnaire du Jazz, eds. Philippe Carles, et al. Paris: Laffont, 1988.

4457. Feather, Leonard. The Encyclopedia of Jazz in the Sixties. New York: Horizon Press, 1966.

4458. The Penguin Encyclopedia of Popular Music, ed. Donald Clarke. New York: Viking, 1989, p. 710.

4459. Priestley, Brian. "Little, Booker." In Jazz: The Essential Companion. New York: Prentice Hall Press, 1988.

4460. Reclams Jazzfuhrer. 2nd, rev. ed. Stuttgart: Reclam, 1977.

4461. Tenot, Frank. Dictionnaire du Jazz. Paris: Larousse, 1967.

4462. Wild, David. "Little, Booker." In The New Grove Dictionary of Jazz. London: Macmillan Press, 1988.

Articles

4463. Futterman, Steve. "A case of neglect: trumpeter Booker Little: artistry in the shadows, recordings out of print." High Fidelity (February 1987): 68-69.

4464. Hamilton, Andy. "Little Big Horn." Wire, No. 55 (September 1988): 38-39, 41-42.

4465. Hunt, David C. "The Unheralded Brilliance of Booker Little." Jazz & Pop (February 1969): 40-42.

4466. Kerschbaumer, Franz. "Booker Little: seine Improvisations- und Kompositionstechnik." Jazz Research/Jazzforschung, Vol. 14 (1982): 9-60. [English summary]

Obituaries

4467. "Booker Little." Jazz Magazine, No. 8 (January 1962): 13.

4468. Hentoff, Nat. "Booker Little." Metronome (December 1961): 11.

4469. Levin, Robert. "Booker Little." Metronome (October 1961): 32-34.

4470. "A talent cut down--a promise unfilled." down beat (November 9 1961): 11.

4471. Variety (October 11 1961): 79.

Discography

4472. Monti, Pierre-Andre. Booker Little discography. Sierre: Jazz 360o (c/o G. Cerutti, 8, ave. du Marche, CH-3960, Sierre, Switzerland), 1983. 16p.

LOGAN, GIUSEPPI (1935-) - Reeds

See also # 288, 695, 698

4473. Carles, Philippe, and Jean-Louis Comolli. Free Jazz, Black Power. 2nd ed. Paris: Editions Galilee, 1979, pp. 417-418.

4474. Claghorn, Charles Eugene. Biographical Dictionary of American Music. West Nyack, NY: Parker Pub. Co., 1973.

4475. ________. Biographical Dictionary of Jazz. Englewood Cliffs, NJ: Prentice-Hall, 1982.

4476. Dictionnaire du Jazz, eds. Philippe Carles, et al. Paris: Laffont, 1988.

4477. Feather, Leonard. The Encyclopedia of Jazz in the Sixties. New York: Horizon Press, 1966.

4478. The New Grove Dictionary of Jazz. London: Macmillan Press, 1988.

4479. Reclams Jazzfuhrer. 2nd, rev. ed. Stuttgart: Reclam, 1977.

4480. Wilmer, Valerie. As Serious As Your Life. Westport, CT: Lawrence Hill & Co., 1981, p. 273-274.

Articles

4481. Lequime, M. "Giuseppi Logan." Jazz Hot, No. 287 (October 1972): 11-13.

4482. Morgenstern, Dan. "Caught in the Act." down beat (July 15 1965): 12. [Concert review]

LONDON JAZZ COMPOSERS ORCHESTRA (formed 1970)

4483. Adams, Simon. "London Jazz Composers Orchestra." In The New Grove Dictionary of Jazz. London: Macmillan Press, 1988.

4484. Claghorn, Charles Eugene. Biographical Dictionary of Jazz. Englewood Cliffs, NJ: Prentice-Hall, 1982, p. 353.

Concert Reviews

4485. Jack, Adrian. "Modern." Music and Musicians (February 1974): 44+.

4486. Jones, Max. "It's all at the Co-op." Melody Maker (October 2 1971): 26.

4487. Unwin, R. "Caught in the Act." Melody Maker (April 29 1972): 30.

4488. Williams, Richard. "Caught in the Act." Melody Maker (May 8 1971): 32.

LOVENS, PAUL (1949-) (W. Germany) - Drums

4489. Carles, Philippe, and Jean-Louis Comolli. Free Jazz, Black Power. 2nd ed. Paris: Editions Galilee, 1979, p. 418.

4490. Carr, Ian. "Lovens, Paul." In Jazz: The Essential Companion. New York: Prentice Hall Press, 1988.

4491. Iannapollo, Robert J. "Lovens, Paul." In The New Grove Dictionary of Jazz. London: Macmillan Press, 1988.

Articles

4492. Cook, Richard. "Paul Lytton and Paul Lovens: The Inclined Sticks." Wire, No. 34/35 (Dec 1986/Jan 1987): 32-34.

4493. Rouy, Gerard. "Paul Lovens, le tambour du Globe Unity." Jazz Magazine, No. 272 (February 1979): 49-50, 68. [Interview]

4494. Thiem, Michael. "Paul Lovens: so offen wie moglich improvisieren." Jazz Podium, Vol. 26, No. 3 (1977): 12-13. [Interview]

LOWE, FRANK (1943-   ) - Tenor Saxophone

See also # 69

4495. Carles, Philippe, and Jean-Louis Comolli. Free Jazz, Black Power. 2nd ed. Paris: Editions Galilee, 1979, p. 418.

4496. Case, Brian, and Stan Britt. The Harmony Illustrated Encyclopedia of Jazz. 3rd ed. New York: Harmony Books, 1987.

4497. Claghorn, Charles Eugene. Biographical Dictionary of Jazz. Englewood Cliffs, NJ: Prentice-Hall, 1982.

4498. Dictionnaire du Jazz, eds. Philippe Carles, et al. Paris: Laffont, 1988.

4499. Feather, Leonard, and Ira Gitler. The Encyclopedia of Jazz in the Seventies. New York: Horizon Press, 1976.

4500. The Penguin Encyclopedia of Popular Music, ed. Donald Clarke. New York: Viking, 1989.

4501. Such, David G. "Lowe, Frank." In The New Grove Dictionary of Jazz. London: Macmillan Press, 1988.

4502. Wilmer, Valerie. As Serious As Your Life. Westport, CT: Lawrence Hill & Co., 1981, p. 274.

Articles

4503. Case, Brian. "Jazz: Lowe and Behold." Melody Maker (January 16 1982): 23-24. [Interview]

4504. Herson, J., and Bret Primack. "Profile: Frank Lowe." down beat (July 12 1979): 40.

4505. Macnie, Jim. "Frank Lowe." Coda, No. 209 (August/September 1986): 18-20. [Interview]

4506. ________. "Riffs: Frank Lowe." down beat (March 1986): 14.

4507. Palmer, Bob. "Frank Lowe: chasin' the Trane out of Memphis." down beat (October 10 1974): 18+.

4508. Rusch, Bob. "Frank Lowe: Interview." Cadence, Vol. 8, No. 1 (January 1982): 5-8, 90.

4509. Safane, Clifford Jay. "Frank Lowe." Coda, No. 163 (October 1978): 12-13. [Interview]

4510. Wilmer, Valerie. "Lowe: A Breath of Rhythm." Melody Maker (December 23 1972): 41.

4511. ________. "Lowe Profile." City Limits [London] (October 16-22 1981).

LYONS, JIMMY (1933-1986) - Alto Saxophone

4512. Levin, Robert. "The Emergence of Jimmy Lyons." In Music and Politics. New York: The World Publishing Co., 1970, pp. 87-92.

4513. Vuijsje, Bert. De Nieuwe Jazz. Baarn: Bosch & Keuning, 1978, pp. 125-133. [Interview]

Biographical Dictionaries

4514. Berry, Lemuel, Jr. Biographical Dictionary of Black Musicians and Music Educators. Guthrie, OK: Educational Book Publishers, 1978, p. 263.

4515. Carles, Philippe, and Jean-Louis Comolli. Free Jazz, Black Power. 2nd ed. Paris: Editions Galilee, 1979, p. 419.

4516. Carr, Ian. "Lyons, Jimmy." In Jazz: The Essential Companion. New York: Prentice Hall Press, 1988.

4517. Claghorn, Charles Eugene. Biographical Dictionary of American Music. West Nyack, NY: Parker Pub. Co., 1973.

4518. _________. Biographical Dictionary of Jazz. Englewood Cliffs, NJ: Prentice-Hall, 1982.

4519. Dictionnaire du Jazz, eds. Philippe Carles, et al. Paris: Laffont, 1988.

4520. Feather, Leonard. The Encyclopedia of Jazz in the Sixties. New York: Horizon Press, 1966.

4521. _________, and Ira Gitler. The Encyclopedia of Jazz in the Seventies. New York: Horizon Press, 1976.

4522. Hazell, Ed. "Lyons, Jimmy." In The New Grove Dictionary of Jazz. London: Macmillan Press, 1988.

4523. The Penguin Encyclopedia of Popular Music, ed. Donald Clarke. New York: Viking, 1989.

4524. Reclams Jazzfuhrer. 2nd, rev. ed. Stuttgart: Reclam, 1977.

4525. Wilmer, Valerie. As Serious As Your Life. Westport, CT: Lawrence Hill & Co., 1981, p. 274.

Articles

4526. Case, Brian. "The Man Who Keeps on Stretching." New Musical Express (September 6 1975): 22-23. [Interview]

4527. "Dictionnaire de l'Alto." Jazz Magazine, No. 137 (December 1966): 45. Biographical sketch.

4528. Giddins, Gary. "Jimmy Lyons: A Sideman's Self." Village Voice (December 18 1978): 94, 96.

4529. Lattanzi, Guglielmo, and Dino Giannasi. "Due chiacchiere con Andrew Cyrille e Jimmy Lyons." Musica Jazz (December 1975): 18-19, 48. [Interview]

4530. Litweiler, John B. "Profile: Jimmy Lyons." down beat (January 16 1975): 34.

4531. Rusch, Bob. "Jimmy Lyons: interview." Cadence, Vol. 4, No. 10 (October 1978): 23-24, 26-28.

4532. Wilmer, Valerie. "In the Lyons Den..." Melody Maker (May 15 1971): 32.

Obituaries

4533. Auerbach, Brian. "Words on the Passing of Jimmy Lyons." Coda, No. 209 (August/September 1986): 7.

4534. Crouch, Stanley. "Jimmy Lyons: 1931-1986." Village Voice (August 19 1986): 3.

4535. Jazz Forum, No. 102 (1986): 18.

4536. Jazz Magazine, No. 352 (July-August 1986): 9.

4537. Mandel, Howard. "Jimmy Lyons, 1932-1986." down beat (August 1986): 12.

LYTTON, PAUL (Great Britain) - Drums

4538. Carles, Philippe, and Jean-Louis Comolli. Free Jazz, Black Power. 2nd ed. Paris: Editions Galilee, 1979, p. 419.

4539. Jazz Now: the Jazz Centre Society Guide, ed. Roger Cotterrell. London: Quartet Books, 1976, pp. 145-146.

4540. New/Rediscovered Musical Instruments, ed. David Toop. London: Quartz/Mirliton, 1974, pp. 16-17. Designs and photos for instruments created by Paul Lytton.

Articles

4541. "Caught in the Act." Melody Maker (July 12 1975): 44. [Concert review]

4542. Charlton, Hannah. "Skinning Back on a Low Grade." Melody Maker (November 8 1980): 50. [Interview]

4543. Cook, Richard. "Paul Lytton and Paul Lovens: The Inclined Sticks." Wire, No. 34/35 (Dec 1986/Jan 1987): 32-34.

4544. Goddet, Laurent. "Une Musique de l'Eclatement--Evan Parker/Paul Lytton." Jazz Hot, No. 327 (May 1976): 16-21. [Interview]

MCBEE, CECIL (1935-) - Bass

See also # 4381-4386

4545. Baraka, Amiri (LeRoi Jones), and Amina Baraka. The Music; reflections on jazz and blues. New York: Morrow, 1987, pp. 214-216. Reprint of the liner notes to McBee's India Navigation lp "Flying Out."

Biographical Dictionaries

4546. Claghorn, Charles Eugene. Biographical Dictionary of Jazz. Englewood Cliffs, NJ: Prentice-Hall, 1982.

4547. Dictionnaire du Jazz, eds. Philippe Carles, et al. Paris: Laffont, 1988.

4548. Feather, Leonard, and Ira Gitler. The Encyclopedia of Jazz in the Seventies. New York: Horizon Press, 1976.

4549. Hazell, Ed. "McBee, Cecil." In The New Grove Dictionary of Jazz. London: Macmillan Press, 1988.

4550. The Penguin Encyclopedia of Popular Music, ed. Donald Clarke. New York: Viking, 1989.

4551. Priestley, Brian. "McBee, Cecil." In Jazz: The Essential Companion. New York: Prentice Hall Press, 1988.

4552. Wilmer, Valerie. As Serious As Your Life. Westport, CT: Lawrence Hill & Co., 1981, p. 274.

Articles

4553. Gourse, Leslie. "Cecil McBee." Jazz Times (March 1989): 31.

4554. Kuhl, Chris. "Cecil McBee, Chico Freeman: interview." Cadence, Vol. 9, No. 6 (June 1983): 5-8, 12.

4555. West, Hollie. "Cecil McBee: reflections." Jazz Times (March 1982): 10-11. [Interview]

McCALL, STEVE (1933-1989) - Drums

See also # 760-773

4556. Jost, Ekkehard. "Steve McCall." In Jazzmusiker: Materialen zur Soziologie der Afro-Amerikanischen Musik. Frankfurt am Main: Ullstein, 1982, pp. 114-123.

Biographical Dictionaries

4557. Carles, Philippe, and Jean-Louis Comolli. Free Jazz, Black Power. 2nd ed. Paris: Editions Galilee, 1979, pp. 419-420.

4558. Dictionnaire du Jazz, eds. Philippe Carles, et al. Paris: Laffont, 1988.

4559. Mandel, Howard. "McCall, Steve." In The New Grove Dictionary of Jazz. London: Macmillan Press, 1988.

4560. Wilmer, Valerie. As Serious As Your Life. Westport, CT: Lawrence Hill & Co., 1981, p. 274.

Articles

4561. Dublin, Larry. "Steve McCall." Coda, No. 182 (February 1982): 4-6. [Interview]

4562. Terlizzi, Roberto. "Steve McCall." Coda, No. 134 (December 1974): 6-7.

4563. Whitehead, Kevin. "Steve McCall: Interview." Cadence, Vol. 8, No. 7 (July 1982): 11-14, 27.

Obituaries

4564. Arts Midwest Jazzletter, Vol. 7, No. 3 (Fall 1989): 15. Cites cause of death as "fatal stroke."

4565. Ear (July-August 1989): 27.
4566. Coda, No. 227 (August/September 1989): 27.
4567. down beat (August 1989): 13.
4568. Jazz Forum, No. 119 (1989): 37.
4569. Jazz Magazine, No. 384 (July-August 1989): 4.
4570. Jazz Podium (November 1989): 49.
4571. Jazz Times (September 1989): 4.

MCDANIELS, RUDY

See Tacuma, Jamaladeen

MCGREGOR, CHRIS (1936-1990) (South Africa) - Piano/Bandleader

See also # 705, 1741-1747

4572. Carles, Philippe, and Jean-Louis Comolli. Free Jazz, Black Power. 2nd ed. Paris: Editions Galilee, 1979, p. 420.

4573. Carr, Ian. "McGregor, Chris." In Jazz: The Essential Companion. New York: Prentice Hall Press, 1988.

4574. Case, Brian, and Stan Britt. The Harmony Illustrated Encyclopedia of Jazz. 3rd ed. New York: Harmony Books, 1987.

4575. De Ledesma, Charles. "McGregor, Chris." In The New Grove Dictionary of Jazz. London: Macmillan Press, 1988.

4576. Dictionnaire du Jazz, eds. Philippe Carles, et al. Paris: Laffont, 1988.

4577. Jazz Now: the Jazz Centre Society Guide, ed. Roger Cotterrell. London: Quartet Books, 1976, pp. 146-147.

4578. McRae, Barry. "Chris McGregor." In The Jazz Handbook. Harlow, Essex, Eng.: Longman, 1987, pp. 204-205.

Articles

4579. Aime, B. "McGregor: j'ai essaye d'oublier l'Afrique du Sud." Jazz Magazine, No. 384 (July-August 1989): 16-17. [Interview]

4580. Bird, Christopher. "Caught in the Act: McGregor." Melody Maker (January 14 1967): 12. [Concert review]

4581. ________. "McGregor: The New Boss Man from Cape Town." Melody Maker (July 15 1967): 6. [Profile]

4582. ________. "McGregor Ork." Melody Maker (July 1 1967): 4. [Concert review]

4583. "Blue Notes: a hard struggle." Melody Maker (March 26 1966): 10.

4584. Buda, E., and Serge Loupien. "Chris McGregor." Jazz Hot, No. 320 (October 1975): 14-15. [Interview]

4585. Constant, Denis. "McGregor: un souffle qui vient d'Afrique." Jazz Magazine, No. 209 (March 1973): 16-19. [Interview]

4586. Cotterrell, Roger. "Chris McGregor: African Roots." Jazz Forum, No. 46 (1977): 40-43.

4587. de Ledesma, Charles. "Chris McGregor." Wire, No. 12 (February 1985): 37-38.

4588. "He Plays Coloured to Play Jazz." Drum (June 1963): 27.

4589. Illingworth, Dave. "Jazz in Britain: Chris McGregor Group." Jazz Journal (May 1968): 30-32. [Profile]

4590. Jones, Colin. "'Very Urgent'." Pieces of Jazz, No. 6 (1969): 9-11.

4591. Koopmans, Rudy. "Chris McGregor: The Breath of the Brotherhood." Jazz Nu (Amsterdam), Vol. 3, No. 9 (June 1981): 395-398. [Profile]

4592. Latxague, Robert. "Chris McGregor: Le Second Souffle." Jazz Magazine, No. 297 (May 1981): 22-23, 47. [Interview]

4593. Lock, Graham. "Chris McGregor: An African Way of Swing." The Wire, No. 12 (February 1985): 40-43. [Interview]

4594. Naidoo, G. R. "A Blow on the Beach." Drum (June 1964): 36-39.

4595. Rouy, Gerard. "Chris McGregor pianiste et paysan." Jazz Magazine, No. 245 (June-July 1976): 22-23.

4596. Smith, Bill. "Chris McGregor: Letters from a Friend." Coda, Vol. 8, No. 6 (March/April 1968): 2-7.

4597. Tomkins, Les. "Chris McGregor feels free." Crescendo International (August 1978): 14, 38.

4598. Wilmer, Valerie. "Chris: for me, a piano is a drum with melody." Melody Maker (April 10 1971): 12. [Interview]

4599. _________. "Chris McGregor: Now's the Time." Melody Maker (May 30 1970): 8. [Interview]

4600. _________. "McGregor: taking care of business." Melody Maker (June 10 1972): 18. [Interview]

4601. _________. "McGregor to the Rescue." Melody Maker (March 8 1969): 6. [Concert review]

4602. _________. "McGregor's Mission." Jazzbeat, Vol. 2, No. 10 (October 1965): 20-21.

Obituaries

4603. Atkins, Ronald. "African Jazz on White Keys." The Guardian (May 30 1990).

4604. Boyd, Joe. "Chris McGregor." The Independent (July 7 1990).

4605. "Chris McGregor." The Times [London] (May 30 1990).

4606. "Final Bar: Chris McGregor." down beat (October 1990): 11.

4607. Loupien, Serge. "McGregor Sans Laisser d'Adresse." Liberation (May 29 1990): 39-40.

4608. McRae, Barry. "Obituaries: Chris McGregor." Jazz Journal International (July 1990): 26-27.

4609. Voce, Steve. "Chris McGregor." The Independent (May 28 1990).

4610. Wilmer, Val. "Chris McGregor 1936-1990." Wire, No. 77 (July 1990): 28-29, 64. [Memorial/Obit]

MCINTYRE, KEN (1931-) - Reeds

See also # 612, 696

4611. Ullman, Michael. "Ken McIntyre." In Jazz Lives. Washington, D.C.: New Republic Books, 1980, pp. 153-162.

Biographical Dictionaries

4612. Carles, Philippe, and Jean-Louis Comolli. Free Jazz, Black Power. 2nd ed. Paris: Editions Galilee, 1979, p. 420.

4613. Carr, Ian. "McIntyre, Ken." In Jazz: The Essential Companion. New York: Prentice Hall Press, 1988.

4614. Claghorn, Charles Eugene. Biographical Dictionary of American Music. West Nyack, NY: Parker Pub. Co., 1973.

4615. ________. Biographical Dictionary of Jazz. Englewood Cliffs, NJ: Prentice-Hall, 1982.

4616. Dictionnaire du Jazz, eds. Philippe Carles, et al. Paris: Laffont, 1988.

4617. Feather, Leonard. The Encyclopedia of Jazz in the Sixties. New York: Horizon Press, 1966.

4618. ________, and Ira Gitler. The Encyclopedia of Jazz in the Seventies. New York: Horizon Press, 1976.

4619. Southern, Eileen. Biographical Dictionary of Afro-American and African Musicians. Westport, CT: Greenwood Press, 1982.

4620. Such, David G. "McIntyre, Ken." In The New Grove Dictionary of Jazz. London: Macmillan Press, 1988.

4621. Wilmer, Valerie. As Serious As Your Life. Westport, CT: Lawrence Hill & Co., 1981, p. 274.

Articles

4622. Case, Brian. "Days with Dolphy." Melody Maker (June 23 1979): 57.

4623. "Dictionnaire de l'Alto." Jazz Magazine, No. 137 (December 1966): 46. Biographical sketch.

4624. Goddet, Laurent. "Ken McIntyre parle." Jazz Hot, No. 272 (May 1971): 12-13.

4625. Heckman, Don. "Ken McIntyre: A Musician's Philosophy." down beat (November 7 1963): 18-19.

4626. Rusch, Bob. "Ken McIntyre." Cadence, Vol. 14, No. 11 (November 1988): 5-17. [Interview]

4627. Wettley, Ruediger. "Ken McIntyre - der dritte im bunde." Jazz Podium (January 1966): 18-19.

MCINTYRE, MAURICE [Benford] [aka Kalaparusha Ahrah Difda] (1936-) - Tenor Saxophone

4628. Carles, Philippe, and Jean-Louis Comolli. Free Jazz, Black Power. 2nd ed. Paris: Editions Galilee, 1979, pp. 420-421.

4629. Dictionnaire du Jazz, eds. Philippe Carles, et al. Paris: Laffont, 1988.

4630. Hazell, Ed. "McIntyre, Kalaparusha Maurice." In The New Grove Dictionary of Jazz. London: Macmillan Press, 1988.

Articles

4631. Litweiler, John B. "Caught in the Act: Kalaparusha and the Light." down beat (July 18 1974): 38. [Concert review]

4632. Marmande, Francois. "Kalaparusha, alias Maurice McIntyre." Jazz Magazine, No. 260 (December 1977): 32-33. [Interview]

4633. Rusch, Bob. "Kalaparusha Maurice McIntyre: Interview." Cadence, Vol. 8, No. 10 (October 1982): 5-8.

MCLEOD, ALICE

See Coltrane, Alice

MCPHEE, JOE (1939-) - Reeds

4634. Carles, Philippe, and Jean-Louis Comolli. Free Jazz, Black Power. 2nd ed. Paris: Editions Galilee, 1979, p. 421.

4635. Case, Brian, and Stan Britt. The Harmony Illustrated Encyclopedia of Jazz. 3rd ed. New York: Harmony Books, 1987.

4636. Dictionnaire du Jazz, eds. Philippe Carles, et al. Paris: Laffont, 1988.

4637. The New Grove Dictionary of Jazz. London: Macmillan Press, 1988.

Articles

4638. Daubresse, J. P. "Joe McPhee." Jazz Hot, No. 329 (July-August 1976): 30-31.

4639. Davison, Paul. "Profile: Joe McPhee." down beat (October 1981): 58-59.

4640. Derradji, Saddri. "Joe McPhee." Jazz, Blues & Co. (Paris), No. 17 (May/June 1978): 6-7. [Interview]

4641. "Joe McPhee." Jazz Hot, No. 321 (November 1975): 22.

4642. McRae, Barry. "Avant Courier: Beyond the Mainstream." Jazz Journal International (February 1980): 25-26. [Profile]

4643. "On the Bandstand: Joe McPhee." Jazz Forum, No. 46 (1977): 25-26.

4644. Riggins, Roger. "Joe McPhee: Sound Sculptor." Jazz Forum, No. 83 (1983): 36-39. [Interview]

4645. Rusch, Bob. "Rapping with Joe McPhee." Cadence, Vol. 2, No. 3/4 (January 1977): 3-5, 9. [Interview]

4646. Smith, Bill. "Joe McPhee - Visitation." Coda, No. 201 (April/May 1985): 16-18. [Interview]

4647. "Les Voix de Joe McPhee: autoportrait d'un saxophoniste/ trompettiste." Jazz Magazine, No. 254 (mai 1977): 14-17, 49-50. [Interview]

4648. Zufferey, Maurice. "Entretien avec Joe McPhee." Jazz 360o (Sierre, Switzerland), No. 27 (April 1980): 2-6.

Discographies

4649. Cerutti, Gustave. Joe McPhee Discography. Sierre: Jazz 360o (c/o Cerutti, 8, ave. du Marche, CH-3960, Sierre, Switzerland), 1983. 12p.

4650. "Discographie de Joe McPhee." Jazz 360o, No. 9 (June 1978): 4-6.

MADDOX, PAUL

See AkLaff, Pheeroan

MALFATTI, RADU (1943-) (Austria) - Trombone

4651. Carles, Philippe, and Jean-Louis Comolli. Free Jazz, Black Power. 2nd ed. Paris: Editions Galilee, 1979, p. 421.

4652. Jazz Now: the Jazz Centre Society Guide, ed. Roger Cotterrell. London: Quartet Books, 1976, p. 148.

4653. Noglik, Bert. "Radu Malfatti." In Jazzwerkstatt International. Berlin: Verlag Neue Musik, 1981, pp. 128-149. [Interview]

Articles

4654. Lobko, Sonia. "Interview: Radu Malfatti." Jazz 360o (Sierre, Switzerland), No. 54 (December 1982): 2-6.

4655. Rouy, Gerard. "Radu Malfatti." Jazz Magazine, No. 266-267 (July-August 1978): 40-42. [Interview]

MANGELSDORFF, ALBERT (1928-) (W. Germany) - Trombone

See also # 323, 343, 697, 3341

4656. Berendt, Joachim Ernst. "Wiederentdecken, was Jazz in Wirklichkeit ist Gespraech mit Albert Mangelsdorff." In Ein Fenster aus Jazz. Frankfurt am Main: S. Fischer, 1977, pp. 59-72.

4657. Noglik, Bert. "Albert Mangelsdorff." In Jazzwerkstatt International. Berlin: Verlag Neue Musik, 1981, pp. 65-84. [Interview]

4658. Noll, Dietrich J. "Aspekte der Klangflachenimprovisation II: Albert Mangelsdorff." In Zur Improvisation im Deutschen Free Jazz. Hamburg: Verlag der Musikalienhandlung Wagner, 1977, pp. 55-74.

Biographical Dictionaries

4659. Berendt, Joachim-Ernst, and Wolfram Knauer. "Mangelsdorff, Albert." In The New Grove Dictionary of Jazz. London: Macmillan Press, 1988.

4660. Carles, Philippe, and Jean-Louis Comolli. Free Jazz, Black Power. 2nd ed. Paris: Editions Galilee, 1979, p. 421.

4661. Carr, Ian. "Mangelsdorff, Albert." In Jazz: The Essential Companion. New York: Prentice Hall Press, 1988.

4662. Claghorn, Charles Eugene. Biographical Dictionary of Jazz. Englewood Cliffs, NJ: Prentice-Hall, 1982.

4663. Dictionnaire du Jazz, eds. Philippe Carles, et al. Paris: Laffont, 1988.

4664. Feather, Leonard. The Encyclopedia of Jazz. New ed. New York: Horizon Press, 1960.

4665. ________. The Encyclopedia of Jazz in the Sixties. New York: Horizon Press, 1966.

4666. ________, and Ira Gitler. The Encyclopedia of Jazz in the Seventies. New York: Horizon Press, 1976.

4667. The Penguin Encyclopedia of Popular Music, ed. Donald Clarke. New York: Viking, 1989.

4668. Reclams Jazzfuhrer. 2nd, rev. ed. Stuttgart: Reclam, 1977.

Articles

4669. "Albert Mangelsdorff." Jazz Magazine, No. 234 (July 1975): 14. [Interview]

4670. "Albert Mangelsdorff." Crescendo International (September 1983): 6. [Interview]

4671. "Albert Mangelsdorff: trombonist extraordinaire." Jazz Journal International (May 1978): MS xiii-xiv.

4672. Berendt, Joachim Ernst. "Albert Mangelsdorff." Jazz Forum, Vol. 7, No. 21 (1973): 41-45. [Interview]

4673. ________. "Albert Mangelsdorff." Jazz Hot, No. 339/340 (July-August 1977): 20-22. [Interview]

4674. ________. "Albert Mangelsdorff: big noise from Frankfurt." down beat (February 10 1977): 16+. [Interview]

4675. Broussard, G. L. "Multitalented Multiphonic Albert Manglesdorff [sic]." Journal of the International Trombone Association, Vol. 17, No. 3 (1989): 14-18.

4676. "Caught!" down beat (February 8 1979): 41-42. [Concert review]

4677. Dunstheimer, Jona. "Albert Mangelsdorff." Le Jazzophone, No. 12 (1982): 30-32. [Interview]

4678. Endress, Gudrun. "Albert Mangelsdorff." Jazz Podium (May 1989): 3+. [Interview]

4679. Everett, T. "Albert Mangelsdorff: interview." Cadence, Vol. 3, No. 4/5 (October 1977): 10+.

4680. Lake, Steve. "The Stunning Art of Albert Mangelsdorff." Melody Maker (April 17 1976): 39+.

4681. Noglik, Bert. "Albert Mangelsdorff: 30 years in jazz." Jazz Forum, No. 69 (1981): 32-35. [Interview]

4682. Rouy, Gerard. "Albert Mangelsdorff: des voix en coulisse." Jazz Magazine, No. 315 (February 1983): 38-40. [Interview]

4683. Sandner, Wolfgang. "Jazz Portraet: Albert Mangelsdorff." HiFi-Stereophonie (July 1977): 814-818.

4684. Smith, Bill. "Albert Mangelsdorff." Coda, No. 168 (August 1979): 4-10. [Interview]

4685. Tomkins, Les. "A Meeting with Mumps: John Surman and Albert Mangelsdorff." Crescendo International (January 1978): 23+; (February 1978): 14-15. [Interview]

4686. "Zwischen Solo und Ensemble: Albert Mangelsdorff." Jazz Podium (February 1977): 10-13. [Interview]

MANTLER, MICHAEL (1943-) - Trumpet

See also # 575, 1342, 1353

4687. Carles, Philippe, and Jean-Louis Comolli. Free Jazz, Black Power. 2nd ed. Paris: Editions Galilee, 1979, pp. 421-422.

4688. Carr, Ian. "Mantler, Mike." In Jazz: The Essential Companion. New York: Prentice Hall Press, 1988.

4689. Case, Brian, and Stan Britt. The Harmony Illustrated Encyclopedia of Jazz. 3rd ed. New York: Harmony Books, 1987.

4690. Claghorn, Charles Eugene. Biographical Dictionary of American Music. West Nyack, NY: Parker Pub. Co., 1973.

4691. ________. Biographical Dictionary of Jazz. Englewood Cliffs, NJ: Prentice-Hall, 1982.

4692. Dictionnaire du Jazz, eds. Philippe Carles, et al. Paris: Laffont, 1988.

4693. Feather, Leonard, and Ira Gitler. The Encyclopedia of Jazz in the Seventies. New York: Horizon Press, 1976.

4694. Reclams Jazzfuhrer. 2nd, rev. ed. Stuttgart: Reclam, 1977.

4695. Theroux, Gary. "Mantler, Mike." In The New Grove Dictionary of Jazz. London: Macmillan Press, 1988.

4696. Wilmer, Valerie. As Serious As Your Life. Westport, CT: Lawrence Hill & Co., 1981, p. 274.

Articles

4697. Carey, Joe. "The High-Watt Energy of Mike Mantler." down beat (November 1983): 17-19.

4698. Case, Brian. "Avant garde on the escalator." New Musical Express (October 26 1974): 40-41. [Interview]

4699. Knox, Keith. "Mantler/Bley Quintet." Jazz Monthly (February 1967): 8-9.

4700. Levi, Titus. "Under the Volcano: a conversation with Carla Bley, Steve Swallow, Mike Mantler and Jack Cumming." Coda, No. 212 (February/March 1987): 4-5.

4701. Rahn, Eckart. "Mike Mantler Interview." Jazz Podium (March 1966): 75.

4702. Smith, Bill. "An Interview with Carla Bley and Mike Mantler." Coda, Vol. 10, No. 9 (1972): 11-14.

4703. Thompson, Keith G. "Carla Bley and Mike Mantler - A Unique Combination." Pieces of Jazz (1970): 48-52.

4704. Van Der Mei, Elizabeth. "Mike Mantler." Jazz Hot, No. 245 (December 1968): 35-39. [Interview]

4705. Witherden, Barry. "Michael Mantler." Wire, No. 58/59 (Dec 1988/Jan 1989): 32-33.

MARSHALL, JAMES - Reeds

4706. "Tape Talk: Illuminations." Cadence, Vol. 11 (November 1985): 64.

4707. Wilmer, Valerie. As Serious As Your Life. Westport, CT: Lawrence Hill & Co., 1981, pp. 274-275.

MARTIN, STU (1938-1980) - Drums

4708. Dictionnaire du Jazz, eds. Philippe Carles, et al. Paris: Laffont, 1988.

Articles

4709. "Americans in Europe." Jazz Forum, No. 19 (October 1972): 91-92.

4710. Byrczek, Jan, and Roman Kowal. "The Trio--Surman Phillips Martin." Jazz Forum, No. 13/14 (Autumn/Winter 1971): 62-63, 72-74. [Interview]

4711. Cullaz, Maurice. "John Surman, Barre Phillips, Stu Martin--interview." Jazz Hot, No. 259 (March 1970): 16-19.

4712. Czajkowski, Sylwester. "Face to Face with the Monster --Stu Martin at Chodzica." Jazz Forum, No. 26 (December 1973): 45-48.

Obituaries

4713. "Final Bar: Stu Martin." down beat (December 1980): 14.

4714. Jazz Magazine, No. 288 (July-August 1980): 10.

4715. "Stu Martin dies in France." Melody Maker (June 28 1980): 33.

MASLAK, KESHAVAN (1948-) - Reeds

4716. Dictionnaire du Jazz, eds. Philippe Carles, et al. Paris: Laffont, 1988.

Articles

4717. Coppens, George. "Keshavan Maslak." Coda, No. 177 (February 1981): 10-13. [Interview]

4718. Davis, Francis. "Keshavan." down beat (August 1982): 54. [Profile]

4719. Szwed, John F. "Riffs: Is It R & B?" Village Voice (September 28 1982): 86. [Profile]

MASSEY, CAL (1928-1972) - Trumpet/Composer/Arranger

See also # 69

4720. Claghorn, Charles Eugene. Biographical Dictionary of Jazz. Englewood Cliffs, NJ: Prentice-Hall, 1982.

4721. Dictionnaire du Jazz, eds. Philippe Carles, et al. Paris: Laffont, 1988.

4722. Feather, Leonard, and Ira Gitler. The Encyclopedia of Jazz in the Seventies. New York: Horizon Press, 1976.

4723. Jaffe, Andrew. "Massey, Cal." In The New Grove Dictionary of Jazz. London: Macmillan Press, 1988.

4724. Priestley, Brian. "Massey, Cal." In Jazz: The Essential Companion. New York: Prentice Hall Press, 1988.

Articles

4725. Mandel, Howard. "Caught." down beat (September 1985): 55. Review of a tribute to Cal Massey.

4726. Positif, Francois. "Cal Massey--quarante deux ans, trompette." Jazz Hot, No. 264 (September 1970): 22-23. [Interview]

4727. Welch, Jane. "Cal Massey's Odyssey." down beat (February 4 1971): 20, 33.

Obituaries

4728. down beat (December 7 1972): 9-10.
4729. International Musician (February 1973): 18+.
4730. Jazz Hot, No. 289 (December 1972): 26.
4731. Jazz Magazine, No. 206 (December 1972): 5.
4732. Jazz Podium (January 1973): 7.
4733. Melody Maker (November 11 1972): 4.

MELFORD, MYRA - Piano

See also # 701

4734. McElfresh, Suzanne. "Riffs: Myra Melford." Down Beat (October 1990): 13.

MENGELBERG, MISHA (1935-) (Ukraine/Netherlands) - Piano

See also # 360

4735. Vuijsje, Bert. De Nieuwe Jazz. Baarn: Bosch & Keuning, 1978, pp. 155-165. [Interview]

Biographical Dictionaries

4736. Baker's Biographical Dictionary of Musicians. 7th ed. revised by Nicolas Slonimsky. New York: Schirmer Books, 1984.

4737. Carles, Philippe, and Jean-Louis Comolli. Free Jazz, Black Power. 2nd ed. Paris: Editions Galilee, 1979, p. 422.

4738. Dictionnaire du Jazz, eds. Philippe Carles, et al. Paris: Laffont, 1988.

4739. The New Grove Dictionary of Jazz. London: Macmillan Press, 1988.

Articles

4740. Ansell, Kenneth. "Misha Mengelberg." Impetus (London), No. 6 (1977): 266-268. [Interview]

4741. Koopmans, Rudy. "Composers' Voice Special: Misha Mengelberg." Key Notes (Amsterdam), No. 16 (1982): 34-35.

4742. _________. "On Music and Politics -- Activism of five Dutch composers: Louis Andriessen, Reinbert de Leeuw, Misha Mengelberg, Peter Schat, Jan van Vlijmen." Key Notes (Amsterdam), No. 4 (1976): 19-36.

4743. _________. "The Retarded Clockmaker." Key Notes, No. 1 (1975): 19-31. Analysis of the musics of Willem Breuker and Misha Mengelberg.

4744. Mengelberg, Misha. "Choir of Preservation: teaching of music." Collusion (London), No. 1 (August 1981): 34-36.

4745. Rouy, Gerard. "Misha Mengelberg: '...comme des chiens de garde.'" Jazz Magazine, No. 295 (March 1981): 30-31. [Interview]

4746. Schwager, Walter. "Misha Mengelberg - Off Minor." Coda, No. 220 (June/July 1988): 12-14. [Interview]

4747. Sinker, Mark. "Misha Mengelberg: Cool in the Pool." Wire, No. 56 (October 1988): 14-16.

4748. Witts, Dick. "On Misha Mengelberg, on Louis Andriessen..." Musics (London), No. 18 (July 1978): 8-11. [Interview]

MILLER, HARRY (1941-1983) (South Africa) - Bass

4749. Carles, Philippe, and Jean-Louis Comolli. Free Jazz, Black Power. 2nd ed. Paris: Editions Galilee, 1979, pp. 422-423.

4750. Carr, Ian. "Miller, Harry." In Jazz: The Essential Companion. New York: Prentice Hall Press, 1988.

4751. Case, Brian, and Stan Britt. The Harmony Illustrated Encyclopedia of Jazz. 3rd ed. New York: Harmony Books, 1987.

4752. De Ledesma, Charles. "Miller, Harry." In The New Grove Dictionary of Jazz. London: Macmillan Press, 1988.

4753. Jazz Now: the Jazz Centre Society Guide, ed. Roger Cotterrell. London: Quartet Books, 1976, p. 150.

Articles

4754. Bussy, Pascal. "Harry Miller et Ogun Records." ATEM (France), No. 11 (January 1978): 9-11. [Interview]

4755. _________, and Kenneth Ansell. "Harry Miller." Impetus (London), No. 8 (1978): 361-366. [Interview]

4756. Constant, Denis. "Harry Miller: le tropique d'Ogun." Jazz Magazine, No. 239 (December 1975): 19-20.

4757. Cotterrell, Roger. "This Music Doesn't Die Tommorrow: it lives forever." Jazz Forum, No. 52 (1978): 40-42. [Interview]

4758. de Ledesma, Charles. "Harry Miller." Wire, No. 12 (February 1985): 28-30.

4759. Dyani, Johnny. "On the Scene - Republic of South Africa: Memories of Harry." Jazz Forum, No. 87 (1984): 23.

4760. Hyder, Ken. "Miller's Travels." Melody Maker (February 24 1973): 18.

4761. McRae, Barry. "Jazz in Britain: Isipingo at the Phoenix." Jazz Journal (December 1971): 18. [Concert review]

4762. May, Chris. "Harry Miller." Black Music, Vol. 4, No. 38 (January 1977): 15. Profile of the South African bassist.

Obituaries

4763. Cadence (February 1984): 75.
4764. Coda (April 1984): 36.
4765. down beat (April 1984): 13.
4766. Jazz Forum, No. 86 (1984): 18.
4767. Jazz Magazine, No. 326 (February 1984): 8.
4768. Jazz Podium (April 1984): 33.
4769. Melody Maker (Jan 7 1984): 18; (Jan 21 1984): 19.
4770. Wire, No. 6 (Spring 1984): 8.

MINTON, PHIL (Great Britain) - Vocals

4771. Ansell, Kenneth. "Phil Minton and Roger Turner: Out of Cold Storage." The Wire, No. 12 (February 1985): 15-19.

MITCHELL, J. R. (1940-) - Drums

4772. Carles, Philippe, and Jean-Louis Comolli. Free Jazz, Black Power. 2nd ed. Paris: Editions Galilee, 1979, p. 423.

4773. Wilmer, Valerie. As Serious As Your Life. Westport, CT: Lawrence Hill & Co., 1981, p. 275.

MITCHELL, ROSCOE (1940-) - Reeds

See also # 417, 436, 707, 914-965

4774. Litweiler, John. "Leo Smith, Anthony Braxton, Joseph Jarman, and Roscoe Mitchell." In The Freedom Principle: Jazz After 1958. New York: William Morrow, 1984, pp. 265-286.

Biographical Dictionaries

4775. ASCAP Biographical Dictionary. 4th ed. New York: R.R. Bowker, 1980.

4776. Carles, Philippe, and Jean-Louis Comolli. Free Jazz, Black Power. 2nd ed. Paris: Editions Galilee, 1979, p. 423.

4777. Carr, Ian. "Mitchell, Roscoe." In Jazz: The Essential Companion. New York: Prentice Hall Press, 1988.

4778. Claghorn, Charles Eugene. Biographical Dictionary of Jazz. Englewood Cliffs, NJ: Prentice-Hall, 1982.

4779. Dictionnaire du Jazz, eds. Philippe Carles, et al. Paris: Laffont, 1988.

4780. Feather, Leonard, and Ira Gitler. The Encyclopedia of Jazz in the Seventies. New York: Horizon Press, 1976.

4781. Holly, Ellistine Perkins, comp. Biographies of Black Composers and Songwriters: A Supplementary Textbook. Dubuque, IA: Wm. C. Brown Publishers, 1990, pp. 32-33.

4782. Horne, Aaron. Woodwind Music of Black Composers. New York: Greenwood Press, 1990, pp. 44-45.

4783. Kernfeld, Barry. "Mitchell, Roscoe." In The New Grove Dictionary of Jazz. London: Macmillan Press, 1988.

4784. The Penguin Encyclopedia of Popular Music, ed. Donald Clarke. New York: Viking, 1989.

4785. Reda, Jacques. Anthologie des Musiciens de Jazz. Paris: Stock, 1981, pp. 340-341.

4786. Southern, Eileen. Biographical Dictionary of Afro-American and African Musicians. Westport, CT: Greenwood Press, 1982.

4787. Who's Who in Entertainment. 1st ed. 1989-1990.

4788. Wilmer, Valerie. As Serious As Your Life. Westport, CT: Lawrence Hill & Co., 1981, p. 275.

Articles

4789. Baker, Paul. "Roscoe Mitchell: The Next Step." Coda, No. 228 (October/November 1989): 18-21. [Interview]

4790. Case, Brian. "All-round Expanding Personality." Melody Maker (June 2 1979): 22. [Interview]

4791. Conley, George W. "Roscoe Mitchell: A fresh new art is born, and the message is impact." Melody Maker (August 30 1969): 10.

4792. Davis, Francis. "Roscoe Mitchell: The Art Ensemble Sage Saxist Brings Order Out of Improvisatory Chaos." Musician, No. 62 (December 1983): 26, 28, 30, 32, 34. [Interview]

4793. Lake, Steve. "Muhal Richard Abrams / Leo Smith / Roscoe Mitchell." Melody Maker (January 1 1977): 22.

4794. Litweiler, John B. "There Won't Be Any More Music." Down Beat's Music, Vol. 17 (1972): 23-26, 37. [Interview]

4795. Maino, Francesco. "Roscoe Mitchell: a short talk." Cadence, Vol. 8, No. 11 (November 1982): 11, 30.

4796. Martin, Terry. "Blowing Out in Chicago - Roscoe Mitchell." down beat (April 6 1967): 20-21, 47-49.

4797. Palmer, Robert. "The Innovative Jazz Arsenal of Roscoe Mitchell." New York Times (February 26 1977).

4798. Smith, Bill. "Roscoe Mitchell Interview." Coda, No. 141 (September 1975): 2-10.

4799. Tepperman, Barry. "A Third Generation in Chicago - Roscoe Mitchell and the A.A.C.M." Pieces of Jazz (1970): 48-52.

4800. Wilmer, Valerie. "AACM, the Peaceful Revolution." Melody Maker (April 11 1970): 8, 10. Discussion of the Art Ensemble of Chicago.

Concert Reviews

4801. Litweiler, John B. "Andrew Hill and two others." Jazz Monthly (October 1967): 28, 30. Review of concerts by Andrew Hill and Roscoe Mitchell/Wilbur Ware at the University of Chicago.

4802. _________. "Caught in the Act." down beat (December 15 1966): 38.

4803. _________. "Caught in the Act: Roscoe Mitchell, University of Chicago." down beat (July 25 1968): 29-32.

4804. Martin, Terry. "Caught in the Act: Roscoe Mitchell Art Ensemble, University of Chicago." down beat (September 7 1967): 28-29.

4805. Welding, Pete. "Caught in the Act." down beat (May 19 1966): 44.

Record Reviews

4806. Kart, Larry. "Record Reviews: Congliptious." down beat (February 6 1969): 26-27.

4807. Mathieu, Bill. "Record Reviews: Sound." down beat (June 15 1967): 34-35.

4808. Schoemaker, Bill. "Roscoe Mitchell." Coda, No. 185 (August 1982): 14-15. Review essay on four recent Mitchell recordings.

MOFFETT, CHARLES MACK (1929-) - Drums

See also # 2021, 2292, 2297, 2303

4809. Carles, Philippe, and Jean-Louis Comolli. Free Jazz, Black Power. 2nd ed. Paris: Editions Galilee, 1979, p. 424.

4810. Claghorn, Charles Eugene. Biographical Dictionary of Jazz. Englewood Cliffs, NJ: Prentice-Hall, 1982.

4811. Dictionnaire du Jazz, eds. Philippe Carles, et al. Paris: Laffont, 1988.

4812. Feather, Leonard. The Encyclopedia of Jazz in the Sixties. New York: Horizon Press, 1966.

4813. ________, and Ira Gitler. The Encyclopedia of Jazz in the Seventies. New York: Horizon Press, 1976.

4814. The New Grove Dictionary of Jazz. London: Macmillan Press, 1988.

4815. Priestley, Brian. "Moffett, Charles." In Jazz: The Essential Companion. New York: Prentice Hall Press, 1988.

4816. Wilmer, Valerie. As Serious As Your Life. Westport, CT: Lawrence Hill & Co., 1981, p. 275.

Articles

4817. Coppens, George. "Charles Moffett." Coda, No. 191 (August 1983): 12-15. [Interview]

4818. Giddins, Gary. "The Moffett Family: Prodigal Kids." Village Voice (July 23 1979): 51-52.

4819. Houston, Bob. "Moffett, drum discovery from deep in the heart of Texas." Melody Maker (April 23 1966): 8.

4820. "Talent's All In The Family Moffett." down beat (March 8 1979): 12.

4821. Wilmer, Valerie. "Charles Moffett: Gettin' Out There." down beat (May 4 1967): 18-19, 43.

MOHOLO, LOUIS (1940-) (South Africa) - Drums

4822. Carles, Philippe, and Jean-Louis Comolli. Free Jazz, Black Power. 2nd ed. Paris: Editions Galilee, 1979, p. 424.

4823. Carr, Ian. "Moholo, Louis." In Jazz: The Essential Companion. New York: Prentice Hall Press, 1988.

4824. de Ledesma, Charles. "Moholo, Louis T." In The New Grove Dictionary of Jazz. New York: Grove's Dictionaries of Music, 1988.

4825. Dictionnaire du Jazz, eds. Philippe Carles, et al. Paris: Laffont, 1988.

4826. Jazz Now: the Jazz Centre Society Guide, ed. Roger Cotterrell. London: Quartet Books, 1976, p. 151.

Articles

4827. de Ledesma, Charles. "Louis Moholo." Wire, No. 12 (February 1985): 34.

4828. "Jazz News: Viva Moholo!" Melody Maker (November 13 1982): 32. Announcement of Moholo's planned move to Zimbabwe.

4829. Lake, Steve. "Rhythmic Organization." Black Music and Jazz Review, Vol. 1, No. 2 (May 1978): 18-19. [Interview]

4830. Rouy, Gerard. "Louis Moholo, le Rhythme de Souffle." Jazz Magazine, No. 239 (December 1975): 20-23.

4831. Wilmer, Valerie. "Freedom is Just Another Word; Louis Moholo talks to Valerie Wilmer." Melody Maker (March 3 1973): 50.

4832. ________. "Hear My Heart's Vibrations." Melody Maker (June 20 1970): 10. [Interview]

Concert Reviews

4833. Harvey, Dave. "Caught in the Act: Moholo." Melody Maker (September 5 1970): 22.

4834. ________. "Caught in the Act: Moholo." Melody Maker (August 15 1970): 21.

4835. Wilmer, Valerie. "Rocking Good Time with Moholo." Melody Maker (January 2 1971): 18.

MONCUR, GRACHAN III (1937-) - Trombone

See also # 706

4836. Berry, Lemuel, Jr. Biographical Dictionary of Black Musicians and Music Educators. Guthrie, OK: Educational Book Publishers, 1978, p. 267.

4837. Carles, Philippe, and Jean-Louis Comolli. Free Jazz, Black Power. 2nd ed. Paris: Editions Galilee, 1979, p. 424.

4838. Case, Brian, and Stan Britt. The Harmony Illustrated Encyclopedia of Jazz. 3rd ed. New York: Harmony Books, 1987.

4839. Claghorn, Charles Eugene. Biographical Dictionary of American Music. West Nyack, NY: Parker Pub. Co., 1973.

4840. ________. Biographical Dictionary of Jazz. Englewood Cliffs, NJ: Prentice-Hall, 1982.

4841. Dictionnaire du Jazz, eds. Philippe Carles, et al. Paris: Laffont, 1988.

4842. Feather, Leonard. The Encyclopedia of Jazz in the Sixties. New York: Horizon Press, 1966.

4843. ________, and Ira Gitler. The Encyclopedia of Jazz in the Seventies. New York: Horizon Press, 1976.

4844. Hazell, Ed. "Moncur, Grachan, III." In The New Grove Dictionary of Jazz. London: Macmillan Press, 1988.

4845. The Penguin Encyclopedia of Popular Music, ed. Donald Clarke. New York: Viking, 1989.

4846. Priestley, Brian. "Moncur, Grachan." In Jazz: The Essential Companion. New York: Prentice Hall Press, 1988.

4847. Reclams Jazzfuhrer. 2nd, rev. ed. Stuttgart: Reclam, 1977.

4848. Tenot, Frank. Dictionnaire du Jazz. Paris: Larousse, 1967.

4849. Wilmer, Valerie. As Serious As Your Life. Westport, CT: Lawrence Hill & Co., 1981, p. 275.

Articles

4850. Bright, George. "Getting Into It--Grachan Moncur III." down beat (January 28 1965): 14-15.

4851. Cohen, Elaine. "The Evolution of Grachan Moncur III." Coda, No. 215 (August-September 1987): 4-6. [Interview]

4852. Endress, Gudrun. "Grachan Moncur Interview." Jazz Podium (November/December 1967): 314-316.

4853. "The Evolution of Grachan Moncur." Jazzbeat (June 1965): 21.

4854. Ioakimidis, Demetre. "Grachan Moncur 3." Jazz Hot, No. 203 (November 1964): 26+.

4855. Lake, Steve. "Grachan: 'I'm Ready for Stardom'." Melody Maker (July 24 1976): 36. [Interview]

4856. "The Method Trombonist." Melody Maker (May 15 1965): 6.

4857. "Seven Steps to Jazz." Melody Maker (March 26 1966): 10. Biographical sketch.

4858. Tepperman, Barry. "Rudd, Moncur and some other stuff." Coda (July/August 1971): 8-11.

4859. Twelftree, Alan. "Grachan Moncur III on record." Melody Maker (October 24 1970): 14.

4860. Wilmer, Valerie. "Grachan Moncur 3rd." Jazz Monthly (July 1965): 20-23. [Interview]

MOONDOC, JEMEEL (1951-) - Alto Saxophone/Bandleader

4861. Dictionnaire du Jazz, eds. Philippe Carles, et al. Paris: Laffont, 1988.

Articles

4862. Hills, Henry. "Jemeel Moondoc." Coda, No. 174 (August 1980): 6-8. [Interview]

4863. "Jemeel Moondoc." Jazz Echo, Vol. 9, No. 42 (1979): 11+.

4864. Jeske, Lee. "Profile: Jemeel Moondoc." down beat (March 1982): 56-57.

4865. Rusch, Bob. "Jemeel Moondoc: interview." Cadence, Vol. 7, No. 11 (November 1981): 10-13.

MOORE, DON (1932-) - Bass

See also # 5065-5067

4866. Carles, Philippe, and Jean-Louis Comolli. Free Jazz, Black Power. 2nd ed. Paris: Editions Galilee, 1979, pp. 424-425.

4867. The New Grove Dictionary of Jazz. London: Macmillan Press, 1988.

4868. Wilmer, Valerie. As Serious As Your Life. Westport, CT: Lawrence Hill & Co., 1981, p. 275.

MORRIS, BUTCH [Lawrence] (1947-) - Trumpet/Arranger

4869. The New Grove Dictionary of Jazz. London: Macmillan Press, 1988.

Articles

4870. Briancon, Pierre. "Lawrence 'Butch' Morris." Jazz, Blues and Co. (Paris), No. 7 (February-March 1977): 4-5.

4871. Chenard, Marc. "Butch Morris '... so locked into the tradition.'" Coda, No. 227 (August/September 1989): 28-29.

4872. Ilic, Dave. "Butch Morris: Batons in the Belfry." The Wire, No. 63 (May 1989): 44-46.

4873. Levi, Titus. "Freedom of Expression: Butch Morris." OPtion (July/August 1986): 44-47. [Interview]

4874. Mandel, Howard. "Butch Morris: Conducting the New Tradition." down beat (October 1986): 26-28, 61.

4875. _________. "The Young Bloods--A New Generation in Jazz: The Conductor's Vocabulary." Village Voice (June 25 1985): 72+. [Interview]

4876. Pareles, Jon. "Morris Tests the Limits of Improvisation." New York Times (July 26 1985): C19.

4877. Riggins, Roger. "Butch Morris." Coda, No. 157 (September/October 1977): 12-13. [Interview]

4878. Samuelson, Andra. "Music Toys and Boxes: the play's the thing." Ear (Dec 1989/Jan 1990): 24-30. Photo essay on Morris's "music machines."

4879. Smith, Miyoshi. "Lawrence 'Butch' Morris." Cadence, Vol. 15, No. 7 (July 1989): 13-18. [Interview]

4880. Solothurnmann, Jurg. "Butch Morris: 'I'm not in a hurry'." Jazz Forum, No. 103 (1986): 32-37. [Interview]

4881. Tate, Greg. "Superconductor Butch Morris." Village Voice (November 14 1989): 89.

4882. Tuynman, Carol. "Lawrence D. (Butch) Morris: Composer on the Podium." Ear: New Music News, Vol. 13, No. 9 (December 1988-January 1989): 22-23.

4883. Wagner, C. "Lawrence Butch Morris." Jazz Podium, Vol. 35 (October 1986): 20-22.

4884. Watrous, Peter. "Butch Morris." Musician, No. 91 (May 1986): 17-18, 20, 22.

MORRIS, WILBER (1937-) - Bass

4885. Hazell, Ed. "Wilber Morris." Cadence (February 1988): 16-20. [Interview]

MOSES, J. C. (1936-1977) - Drums

See also # 5065-5067

4886. Carles, Philippe, and Jean-Louis Comolli. Free Jazz, Black Power. 2nd ed. Paris: Editions Galilee, 1979, p. 425.

4887. Dictionnaire du Jazz, eds. Philippe Carles, et al. Paris: Laffont, 1988.

4888. The New Grove Dictionary of Jazz. London: Macmillan Press, 1988.

4889. Wilmer, Valerie. As Serious As Your Life. Westport, CT: Lawrence Hill & Co., 1981, pp. 275-276.

MOTIAN, PAUL [Stephen] (1931-) - Drums

4890. Braman, Chuck. "Motian, Paul." In The New Grove Dictionary of Jazz. London: Macmillan Press, 1988.

4891. Claghorn, Charles Eugene. Biographical Dictionary of American Music. West Nyack, NY: Parker Pub. Co., 1973.

4892. _________. Biographical Dictionary of Jazz. Englewood Cliffs, NJ: Prentice-Hall, 1982.

4893. Dictionnaire du Jazz, eds. Philippe Carles, et al. Paris: Laffont, 1988.

4894. Feather, Leonard. The Encyclopedia of Jazz. New ed. New York: Horizon Press, 1960.

4895. _________. The Encyclopedia of Jazz in the Sixties. New York: Horizon Press, 1966.

4896. ________, and Ira Gitler. The Encyclopedia of Jazz in the Seventies. New York: Horizon Press, 1976.

4897. The Penguin Encyclopedia of Popular Music, ed. Donald Clarke. New York: Viking, 1989.

4898. Priestley, Brian. "Motian, Paul." In Jazz: The Essential Companion. New York: Prentice Hall Press, 1988.

4899. Reclams Jazzfuhrer. 2nd, rev. ed. Stuttgart: Reclam, 1977.

Articles

4900. Blum, Joe. "Paul Motian: conversation with a drummer." Jazz Times (October 1987): 15.

4901. Cotta, S. "La grande oreille de Paul Motian." Le Monde de la Musique, No. 61 (1983): 68+.

4902. Fish, Scott Kevin. "Paul Motian: drawing from tradition." Modern Drummer (April/May 1980): 16-19. [Interview]

4903. Flicker, Chris. "Paul Motian ou l'amour des formes." Jazz Magazine, No. 273 (March 1979): 26-27. [Interview]

4904. Henkels, Michael. "Paul Motian: 'I'd like to bring back the art of playing the drum set.'" Jazz Forum, No. 56 (1978): 30-32.

4905. Lake, Steve. "Paul Motian." The Wire, No. 25 (1986).

4906. Mandel, Howard. "Poetry in Motian." down beat (May 1986): 23+. [Interview]

4907. Soutif, Daniel. "Motion + Emotion = Motian." Jazz Magazine, No. 323 (November 1983): 24-27, 51. [Interview]

MOYE, FAMOUDOU DON (1946-) - Drums

See also # 914-965, 2858, 4381-4386

4908. ASCAP Biographical Dictionary. 4th ed. New York: R.R. Bowker, 1980.

4909. Carles, Philippe, and Jean-Louis Comolli. Free Jazz, Black Power. 2nd ed. Paris: Editions Galilee, 1979, p. 425.

4910. Carr, Ian. "Moye, Don." In Jazz: The Essential Companion. New York: Prentice Hall Press, 1988.

4911. Claghorn, Charles Eugene. Biographical Dictionary of Jazz. Englewood Cliffs, NJ: Prentice-Hall, 1982.

4912. Dictionnaire du Jazz, eds. Philippe Carles, et al. Paris: Laffont, 1988.

4913. Feather, Leonard, and Ira Gitler. The Encyclopedia of Jazz in the Seventies. New York: Horizon Press, 1976.

4914. Kernfeld, Barry. "Moye, Don." In The New Grove Dictionary of Jazz. London: Macmillan Press, 1988.

4915. Wilmer, Valerie. As Serious As Your Life. Westport, CT: Lawrence Hill & Co., 1981, p. 276.

Articles

4916. Be-Bop and Beyond, Vol. 2, No. 1 (January/February 1984). [Interview]

4917. Case, Brian. "Dressing Up to Play." Melody Maker (August 30 1980): 13. [Interview]

4918. "Famadou Don Moye." Son! (Abymes, Guadeloupe), No. 3 (1984): 23. Report on Don Moye's trip to Guadeloupe to learn the local "gwo-ka" rhythm.

4919. Henderson, Bill. "Don Moye: Sun Drummer." Black Music and Jazz Review, Vol. 2, No. 5 (August 1979): 24-25. [Interview]

4920. Kunze, Katrin A. "Don Moye." Jazzthetik, Vol. 4, No. 10 (October 1990): 13-15.

4921. Litweiler, John B. "There Won't Be Any More Music." Down Beat's Music, Vol. 17 (1972): 23-26, 37. [Interview]

4922. Mattingly, Rick. "Famoudou Don Moye: Drawing on Tradition." Modern Drummer (April 1981): 14+. [Interview]

4923. Rouy, Gerard. "Don Moye: battre et se battre." Jazz Magazine, No. 362 (1987): 48-49.

4924. Rusch, Bob. "Don Moye: interview." Cadence, Vol. 5, No. 10 (October 1979): 14, 16-18.

MURRAY, DAVID (1955-) - Tenor Saxophone/Bass Clarinet

4925. Vuijsje, Bert. De Nieuwe Jazz. Baarn: Bosch & Keuning, 1978, pp. 210-221. [Interview]

Biographical Dictionaries

4926. ASCAP Biographical Dictionary. 4th ed. New York: R.R. Bowker, 1980.

4927. Carles, Philippe, and Jean-Louis Comolli. Free Jazz, Black Power. 2nd ed. Paris: Editions Galilee, 1979, p. 426.

4928. Carr, Ian. "Murray, David." In Jazz: The Essential Companion. New York: Prentice Hall Press, 1988.

4929. Case, Brian, and Stan Britt. The Harmony Illustrated Encyclopedia of Jazz. 3rd ed. New York: Harmony Books, 1987.

4930. Claghorn, Charles Eugene. Biographical Dictionary of Jazz. Englewood Cliffs, NJ: Prentice-Hall, 1982.

4931. Dictionnaire du Jazz, eds. Philippe Carles, et al. Paris: Laffont, 1988.

4932. Feather, Leonard, and Ira Gitler. The Encyclopedia of Jazz in the Seventies. New York: Horizon Press, 1976.

4933. Kernfeld, Barry. "Murray, David." In The New Grove Dictionary of Jazz. London: Macmillan Press, 1988.

4934. McRae, Barry. "David Murray." In The Jazz Handbook. Harlow, Essex, Eng.: Longman, 1987, p. 244.

4935. The Penguin Encyclopedia of Popular Music, ed. Donald Clarke. New York: Viking, 1989.

4936. Who's Who Among Black Americans. 6th ed. 1990/91. Detroit: Gale Research, 1990.

4937. Wilmer, Valerie. As Serious As Your Life. Westport, CT: Lawrence Hill & Co., 1981, p. 283.

Articles

4938. Berendt, Joachim Ernst. "David Murray and Wynton Marsalis." Jazz Podium (October 1989): 3-7.

4939. Case, Brian. "David Murray: Low Class Conspirator." Black Music and Jazz Review (London), Vol. 1, No. 1 (April 1978): 16-19. [Interview]

4940. _________. "New Far-Outnesses at Changes Bar." New Musical Express (June 18 1977): 18-19. [Interview]

4941. _________. "Success is Swallowing Your Mouthpiece." New Musical Express (May 13 1978): 38-39. [Interview]

4942. Danson, Peter. "David Murray." Coda, No. 201 (April 1985): 7-10. [Interview]

4943. Davis, Francis. "David Murray: Tenor Energy." Down Beat (June 1983): 24-26.

4944. Giddins, Gary. "Sax on Demand." Vanity Fair, Vol. 46 (September 1983): 24+.

4945. Goddet, Laurent. "David Murray." Jazz Hot, No. 343 (November 1977): 11-15.

4946. Herrington, Tony. "I'm David Murray!" The Wire, No. 67 (September 1989): 30-31, 34-35. [Interview]

4947. Johnson, David. "Beyond the Mainstream: New Faces." Jazz Journal International (March 1980): 25.

4948. Johnson, Herschel. "The New Generation and the Arts: Genius of many young blacks enriches cultures of America and the world." Ebony (August 1978): 148-149. [Profile]

4949. Lange, Art. "Murray's Steps." down beat (August 1990): 41. Round-up of recent and reissued Murray recordings.

4950. McRae, Barry. "David Murray: A Progress Report." Jazz Journal International (September 1980): 27-28.

4951. Mandel, Howard. "David Murray: Searching for the Sound." down beat (October 1985): 26-28.

4952. Miller, Jim. "Playing with Fire; A New Generation of Jazz Experimentalists is Bringing Formal Complexity and Daredevil Energy to its Music." Newsweek (November 28 1983): 99-101.

4953. Occhiogrosso, Peter. "Profile: Stanley Crouch and David Murray." down beat (March 25 1976): 38-39.

4954. Palmer, Don. "David Murray." Musician, Player and Listener, No. 38 (December 1981): 68, 70, 120-121.

4955. Riggins, Roger. "Caught: David Murray Trio." down beat (March 11 1976): 34, 42. [Concert review]

4956. ________. "David Murray." Jazz Magazine, No. 255 (June 1977): 16-17. [Interview]

4957. Santoro, Gene. "David Murray." The Nation (April 25 1987): 554+.

4958. Schilling, Grant. "David Murray's Tenor: 'I just keep playing'." Option (March/April 1986): 43-44. [Interview]

4959. Watrous, Peter. "David Murray: The Monster Tenor Awaits His Moment." Musician, No. 85 (November 1985): 23-24, 26, 112.

4960. White, William D. "David Murray." Cadence, Vol. 15, No. 5 (May 1989): 5-8, 10. [Interview]

4961. Wilmer, Valerie. "Safety First Murray." Melody Maker (August 19 1978). [Concert review]

Newspaper Articles

4962. Giddins, Gary. "David Murray: Beautiful Beauty." Village Voice (July 28 1975): 94-95.

4963. ________. "David Murray is Too So Great." Village Voice (February 28 1977): 47.

4964. ________. "David Murray: The Complete Tenor Saxophonist." Village Voice (August 28 1990): 59-60.

4965. Israel, Stephen. "Freeman and Murray: New Jazz Wave Flows from Lofts." The Villager (December 22 1977): 19, 24.

Discographies

4966. Cerrutti, Gustave. "Discographie: David Murray." Jazz 360o (Switzerland), No. 39 (June/July 1981): 5-11.

MURRAY, DEIDRE - Cello

4967. Be-Bop and Beyond, Vol. 3, No. 4 (August/September 1985). [Interview]

4968. Demetz, Bettina. "New Faces: Deidre Murray." Ear, Vol. 12, No. 7 (October 1987): 22.

MURRAY, SUNNY [James Marcellus Arthur] (1937-) - Drums

See also # 181, 288, 543, 700, 1469

4969. Jones, LeRoi. "Sonny's Time Now." In Black Music. New York: Morrow Paperback Editions, 1967, pp. 177-179.

4970. Levin, Robert. "Going Outside." In Music and Politics, eds. John Sinclair and Robert Levin. New York: World Publishing Co., 1971, pp.71-77.

4971. ________. "Sunny Murray: The Continuous Crackling of Glass." In The Black Giants, ed. Pauline Rivelli and Robert Levin. New York: The World Publishing Co., 1970. [Reprint of # 4999]

4972. Vuijsje, Bert. De Nieuwe Jazz. Baarn: Bosch & Keuning, 1978, pp. 104-111. [Interview]

4973. Weinstein, Norman. A Night in Tunisia: Imaginations of Africa in Jazz. Metuchen, NJ: Scarecrow Press, 1991. Includes a chapter on Murray.

4974. Wilmer, Valerie. As Serious As Your Life. Westport, CT: Lawrence Hill & Co., 1981, pp. 159-164, 276.

Biographical Dictionaries

4975. Carles, Philippe, and Jean-Louis Comolli. Free Jazz, Black Power. 2nd ed. Paris: Editions Galilee, 1979, p. 426.

4976. Case, Brian, and Stan Britt. The Harmony Illustrated Encyclopedia of Jazz. 3rd ed. New York: Harmony Books, 1987.

4977. Claghorn, Charles Eugene. Biographical Dictionary of American Music. West Nyack, NY: Parker Pub. Co., 1973.

4978. ________. Biographical Dictionary of Jazz. Englewood Cliffs, NJ: Prentice-Hall, 1982.

4979. Dictionnaire du Jazz, eds. Philippe Carles, et al. Paris: Laffont, 1988.

4980. Feather, Leonard. The Encyclopedia of Jazz in the Sixties. New York: Horizon Press, 1966.

4981. ________, and Ira Gitler. The Encyclopedia of Jazz in the Seventies. New York: Horizon Press, 1976.

4982. The Penguin Encyclopedia of Popular Music, ed. Donald Clarke. New York: Viking, 1989.

4983. Priestley, Brian. "Murray, Sunny." In Jazz: The Essential Companion. New York: Prentice Hall Press, 1988.

4984. Reclams Jazzfuhrer. 2nd, rev. ed. Stuttgart: Reclam, 1977.

4985. Tenot, Frank. Dictionnaire du Jazz. Paris: Larousse, 1967.

4986. Ullman, Michael. "Murray, Sunny." In The New Grove Dictionary of American Music. London: Macmillan Press, 1986.

4987. ________. "Murray, Sunny." In The New Grove Dictionary of Jazz. London: Macmillan Press, 1988.

Articles

4988. Case, Brian. "Father of the Free." New Musical Express (July 2 1977): 20-21. [Interview]

4989. ________. "Jazz: When Sunny Gets Blue." Melody Maker (November 8 1980): 32. [Interview]

4990. Cooke, Jack. "New York Nouvelle Vague 3." Jazz Monthly (August 1965): 14-17. Discussion of new jazz drumming focusing on Tony Williams and Sunny Murray.

4991. ________. "New York Nouvelle Vague 8: Sunny Murray." Jazz Monthly (November 1967): 13.

4992. ________. "Sonny Murray in Paris." Jazz & Blues, Vol. 2 (January 1973): 16-18.

4993. Cullaz, Maurice. "Sunny Murray Parle." Jazz Hot, No. 274 (July 1971): 48.

4994. Davis, S. "Caught." down beat (April 8 1976): 37-38. [Interview]

4995. Flicker, Chris, and Thierry Trombert. "Sunny Murray." Jazz Magazine, No. 255 (June 1977): 22-23. [Interview]

4996. Francard, P. Blanc, and Francis Pinguet. "Sunny Murray." Jazz Hot, No. 245 (December 1968): 24-27.

4997. Gros-Claude, R. "Sunny Murray: le tambour 71." Jazz Magazine, No. 189 (May 1971): 12+.

4998. Jones, LeRoi. "Strong Voices in Today's Black Music." down beat (February 10 1966): 48.

4999. Levin, Robert. "Sunny Murray: the continuous crackling of glass." Jazz & Pop (April-May 1969): 52-55. [Reprinted in # 4971]

5000. "Le Retour de Murray." Jazz Magazine, No. 210 (April 1973): 19.

5001. Weinstein, Norman. "Sunny Murray: The Creation of Time." Village Voice/Jazz Special (August 30 1988): 24-25.

5002. Welch, Chris. "Sunny Causes a Storm." Melody Maker (October 26 1968): 12.

5003. Weston, Spencer. "Sunny Murray: interview." Cadence, Vol. 5, No. 6 (June 1979): 14-16, 18.

5004. Wilmer, Valerie. "Controlled Freedom is the Thing This Year." down beat (March 23 1967): 16-17. [Interview]

5005. _________. "A Legend in His Own Time." Time Out [London] (September 14-20 1979).

5006. _________. "Murray, Drummer Blowing the Fuses." Melody Maker (November 5 1966): 10.

5007. _________. "A Sacrifice for Freedom." Melody Maker (November 2 1968).

Discographies

5008. Hames, Mike. Albert Ayler, Sunny Murray, Cecil Taylor, Byard Lancaster, Kenneth Terroade on disc and tape. Ferndown, Eng.: Hames (16 Pinewood Road, Ferndown, Dorset BH22 9RW), 1983. 61p.

MUSIC IMPROVISATION COMPANY (Great Britain)

5009. "Jazz Albums: Music Improvisation Company: 1968-1971." Melody Maker (January 1 1977): 17.

5010. Williams, Richard. "Bringing Emotion Back to Free Music." Melody Maker (February 13 1971): 12.

MYERS, AMINA CLAUDINE (c.1943-) - Piano

See also # 694

5011. Case, Brian, and Stan Britt. The Harmony Illustrated Encyclopedia of Jazz. 3rd ed. New York: Harmony Books, 1987.

5012. Dictionnaire du Jazz, eds. Philippe Carles, et al. Paris: Laffont, 1988.

5013. Handy, D. Antoinette. Black Women in American Bands and Orchestras. Metuchen, NJ: Scarecrow Press, 1981, pp. 195-196.

5014. The New Grove Dictionary of Jazz. London: Macmillan Press, 1988.

5015. Wilmer, Valerie. As Serious As Your Life. Westport, CT: Lawrence Hill & Co., 1981, p. 284.

Articles

5016. "Dico Disco & Co." Jazz Magazine, No. 298 (June 1981): 51. Biographical sketch.

5017. Gourse, Leslie. "Amina Claudine Myers." Jazz Times (January 1990): 7.

5018. Hicks, Robert. "Voices with Vision: Jeanne Lee, Terry Jenoure and Amina Claudine Myers." Option, No. 34 (Sept/Oct 1990): 74-79.

5019. Palmer, Don. "Hands and Voices: Amina Claudine Myers." Musician, Player and Listener, No. 41 (March 1982): 24, 26, 28.

5020. "'Rhythmus und Feeling sind das wichtigste in Meiner Musik' - Amina Claudine Myers." Jazz Podium (October 1983): 12-13.

5021. Stein, Stephanie. "Amina Claudine Myers: Invitation to the Song." down beat (March 1989): 27-28.

5022. Wilmer, Valerie. "Amina Claudine Myers." Coda, No. 169 (October 1979): 4-6. [Interview]

5023. _________. "Amina Myers: Piano Roles." Melody Maker (March 10 1979): 38, 47. [Interview]

5024. _________. "Amina ou l'A.A.C.M. au Feminin." Jazz Magazine, No. 288 (July-August 1980): 24-25. [Interview]

NAUGHTON, BOBBY (1944-) - Vibraphone

See also # 492-496

5025. Claghorn, Charles Eugene. Biographical Dictionary of Jazz. Englewood Cliffs, NJ: Prentice-Hall, 1982.

5026. Dean, Roger T. "Naughton, Bobby." In The New Grove Dictionary of Jazz. London: Macmillan Press, 1988.

5027. Dictionnaire du Jazz, eds. Philippe Carles, et al. Paris: Laffont, 1988.

5028. Feather, Leonard, and Ira Gitler. The Encyclopedia of Jazz in the Seventies. New York: Horizon Press, 1976.

Articles

5029. Cameron, Alan. "Music: The New Haunts of Vibes." New Haven Advocate (February 9 1977).

5030. Frazer, Vernon, and Barry Tepperman. "Record Reviews: The Haunt." Coda, No. 156 (July/August 1977): 18-19.

5031. Hazell, Ed. "Bobby Naughton." Coda, No. 185 (August 1982): 7-11. [Interview]

5032. McNally, Owen. "Naughton Masters Challenge as Vibist." Hartford Courant (August 7 1978). [Concert review]

5033. ________. "Vibraphonist Brings Fresh Expressions." Hartford Courant (November 1 1976): 43. [Concert review]

5034. Waz, Joe. "Bobby Naughton: the mission of the small label." Jazz Forum, No. 52 (1978): 37-39.

NEIDLINGER, BUELL (1936-) - Bass

5035. Carles, Philippe, and Jean-Louis Comolli. Free Jazz, Black Power. 2nd ed. Paris: Editions Galilee, 1979, pp. 426-427.

5036. Claghorn, Charles Eugene. Biographical Dictionary of American Music. West Nyack, NY: Parker Pub. Co., 1973.

5037. ________. Biographical Dictionary of Jazz. Englewood Cliffs, NJ: Prentice-Hall, 1982.

5038. Dictionnaire du Jazz, eds. Philippe Carles, et al. Paris: Laffont, 1988.

5039. Feather, Leonard. The Encyclopedia of Jazz. New ed. New York: Horizon Press, 1960.

5040. ________. The Encyclopedia of Jazz in the Sixties. New York: Horizon Press, 1966.

5041. ________, and Ira Gitler. The Encyclopedia of Jazz in the Seventies. New York: Horizon Press, 1976.

5042. Kernfeld, Barry. "Neidlinger, Buell." In The New Grove Dictionary of Jazz. London: Macmillan Press, 1988.

5043. The Penguin Encyclopedia of Popular Music, ed. Donald Clarke. New York: Viking, 1989.

5044. Reclams Jazzfuhrer. 2nd, rev. ed. Stuttgart: Reclam, 1977.

5045. Wilmer, Valerie. As Serious As Your Life. Westport, CT: Lawrence Hill & Co., 1981, p. 276.

Articles

5046. "Chords and Discords: Hot Wind From Texas." down beat (October 24 1963): 6. Neidlinger letter to db criticizing the state of jazz criticism; followed by a response by Dan Morgenstern (December 5 1963): 8, 10; and a follow up response by Neidlinger (February 13 1964): 6, 8.

5047. Heineman, Alan. "The Many Sides of Buell Neidlinger." Down Beat's Music '72, Vol. 17 (1972): 13-15, 36. [Interview]

5048. Rusch, Bob. "Buell Neidlinger: interview." Cadence, Vol. 12, No. 6 (June 1986): 5-21, 66.

5049. Stewart, Zan. "Buell Neidlinger." down beat (June 1981): 21-23, 60. [Interview]

5050. Underwood, Lee. "Profile: Buell Neidlinger." down beat (April 10 1975): 28-29.

5051. Weiss, Jason. "Buell Neidlinger." Coda, No. 188 (February 1983): 8-12. [Interview]

5052. Yanow, Scott. "Buell Neidlinger." down beat (April 1988): 15.

NEIL, AL (1924-) (Canada) - Piano

5053. Miller, Mark, and Bob Smith. "Neil, Al." In Encyclopedia of Music in Canada, eds. Helmut Kallmann, et al. Toronto: University of Toronto Press, 1981, pp. 671-672.

Articles

5054. Baker, Richard. "Record Reviews: Canadian New Music." Coda, No. 153 (January/February 1977): 16.

5055. Lemon, Sandy. "Al Neil: Music and Life." Coda, Vol. 7, No. 11 (Dec 1966-Jan 1967): 8-11. [Interview]

5056. Norris, John. "Jazz in Canada." International Musician (January 1967): 12.

5057. Smith, Bill. "Sacred and Profane: Al Neil Talks to Bill Smith." Coda (January/February 1970): 10-12.

NEW YORK ART QUARTET

5058. Claghorn, Charles Eugene. Biographical Dictionary of Jazz. Englewood Cliffs, NJ: Prentice-Hall, 1982, p. 358.

5059. Dictionnaire du Jazz, eds. Philippe Carles, et al. Paris: Laffont, 1988.

5060. The New Grove Dictionary of Jazz. London: Macmillan Press, 1988.

Articles

5061. Berton, Ralph. "Caught in the Act." down beat (September 9 1965): 22. [Concert review]

5062. Cooke, Jack. "New York Nouvelle Vague, 5: the New York Art Quartet." Jazz Monthly (November 1966): 2-4.

5063. Mathieu, Bill. "Record Reviews: Mohawk." down beat (January 12 1967): 32-33.

5064. __________. "Record Reviews: New York Art Quartet." down beat (November 18 1965): 30.

NEW YORK CONTEMPORARY FIVE

See also # 695, 2895, 2956

5065. Claghorn, Charles Eugene. Biographical Dictionary of Jazz. Englewood Cliffs, NJ: Prentice-Hall, 1982, p. 358.

5066. Dictionnaire du Jazz, eds. Philippe Carles, et al. Paris: Laffont, 1988.

5067. The New Grove Dictionary of Jazz. London: Macmillan Press, 1988.

NEWTON, JAMES (1953-) - Flute

See also # 707

5068. Carles, Philippe, and Jean-Louis Comolli. Free Jazz, Black Power. 2nd ed. Paris: Editions Galilee, 1979, p. 427.

5069. Carr, Ian. "Newton, James." In Jazz: The Essential Companion. New York: Prentice Hall Press, 1988.

5070. Dictionnaire du Jazz, eds. Philippe Carles, et al. Paris: Laffont, 1988.

5071. Kernfeld, Barry. "Newton, James." In The New Grove Dictionary of Jazz. London: Macmillan Press, 1988.

5072. Wilmer, Valerie. As Serious As Your Life. Westport, CT: Lawrence Hill & Co., 1981, p. 284.

Articles

5073. Be-Bop and Beyond, Vol. 1, No. 5 (September/October 1983). [Interview]

5074. Blum, Joe, and Jock Baird. "James Newton: Mystery Roots and the Solo Flute." Musician, Player & Listener, No. 46 (August 1982): 65-66, 68.

5075. Buchanan, Steve. "A Conversation with James Newton." The Grackle, No. 5 (1979): 16-19.

5076. Case, Brian. "The Funker Who Found His Right Voice." Melody Maker (June 30 1979): 46.

5077. Coppens, George. "James Newton." Coda, No. 162 (August 1978): 4-8.

5078. "Dico Disco & Co." Jazz Magazine, No. 298 (June 1981): 51. Biographical sketch.

5079. Dutilh, Alex. "James Newton: L'Apres Dolphy." Jazz Hot, No. 367 (November 1979): 8-14. [Interview]

5080. Endress, Gudrun. "James Newton." Jazz Podium (April 1984): 6-9. [Interview]

5081. Feather, Leonard. "Blindfold Test: James Newton." down beat (January 1981): 51.

5082. Giddins, Gary. "Jazz Out of School: In Search of a Text." Village Voice (February 19 1979): 58.

5083. Hershon, R. "James Newton: Learning from Other Cultures." Jazz Journal International (June 1986): 14-15.

5084. "High-flutin' Newton." Vogue (March 1984): 126.

5085. "James Newton Interview." Cadence, Vol. 6, No. 8 (August 1980): 5-7, 18.

5086. Jeske, Lee. "James Newton." down beat (April 1983): 24-26.

5087. Levenson, Jeff. "The Body and Soul of Flutist James Newton." Hot House (New York), Vol. 3, No. 4 (May 1984): 14-15.

5088. Lindenmaier, H. Lukas. "James Newton: a short talk." Cadence, Vol. 6, No. 2 (February 1980): 5-6.

5089. Loupien, Serge, and Gerard Rouy. "L'Unique Amour de James Newton." Jazz Magazine, No. 277 (July/August 1979): 36-37, 64. [Interview]

5090. Miller, Jim. "Playing with Fire; A New Generation of Jazz Experimentalists is Bringing Formal Complexity and Daredevil Energy to its Music." Newsweek (November 28 1983): 99-101.

5091. Safane, Clifford Jay. "Profile: James Newton." down beat (March 1980): 54-55.

5092. Townsend, Lee. "James Newton: Young Lion." Jazz Times (December 1982): 10-11. [Interview]

NEWTON, LAUREN - Vocals

5093. Buchter-Romer, Ute. "Lauren Newton." Jazz Podium (June 1986): 33.

5094. _________. "New Vocal Jazz." Jazz Research Papers, Vol. 9 (1989): 48-53.

5095. Endress, Gudrun. "Neue Toene von Lauren Newton." Jazz Podium (July 1978): 4-6.

5096. Giddins, Gary. "Weatherbird: From bop-ba-du-zet to chiki-tiki-da." Village Voice (July 5 1983): 77.

5097. Jaenichen, Lothar. "Stimme als Instrument: Lauren Newton." Jazz Podium (February 1983): 10-12.

NICOLS, MAGGIE (1948-) (Great Britain) - Vocals

5098. Carr, Ian. "Nicols, Maggie." In Jazz: The Essential Companion. New York: Prentice Hall Press, 1988.

5099. Dictionnaire du Jazz, eds. Philippe Carles, et al. Paris: Laffont, 1988.

5100. Jazz Now: the Jazz Centre Society Guide, ed. Roger Cotterrell. London: Quartet Books, 1976, p. 152.

5101. The New Grove Dictionary of Jazz. London: Macmillan Press, 1988.

Articles

5102. Charlton, Hannah. "Maggie Nichols: liberating women's music." Jazz Forum, No. 76 (1982): 40-43. [Interview]

5103. Hyder, Ken. "Maggie: speed is the essence." Melody Maker (September 8 1973): 47.

5104. Ilic, Dave. "Maggie Nicols: Living Out Your Contradictions." The Wire, No. 24 (February 1986): 22-23, 27.

5105. Loupien, Serge. "La Voix Quotidienne de Maggie Nicols." Jazz Magazine, No. 288 (July-August 1980): 46-47. [Interview]

5106. "Maggie's Music." Melody Maker (September 27 1969): 8.

5107. May, S. "Maggie's Mix." Jazz Journal International (May 1985): 13. [Interview]

5108. Tarting, Claude. "Maggie Nichols." Diapason-Harmonie, No. 331 (October 1987): 37.

5109. Williams, Richard. "Maggie Helps Herself." Melody Maker (April 22 1972): 34.

NIX, BERN - Guitar

5110. Nix, Bern. "Guest Editorial: Great Art, Sad Profession." Guitar Player (January 1988): 8.

OCHS, LARRY - Reeds

See # 5625-5638

OLD AND NEW DREAMS

5111. Claghorn, Charles Eugene. Biographical Dictionary of Jazz. Englewood Cliffs, NJ: Prentice-Hall, 1982, p. 359.

5112. Dictionnaire du Jazz, eds. Philippe Carles, et al. Paris: Laffont, 1988.

Articles

5113. Blumenthal, Bob. "Children of Ornette Coleman; Cross Country Tour of Old and New Dreams." Rolling Stone (May 31 1979): 24.

5114. Giddins, Gary. "Riffs: Old and New Dreams Change the Century." Village Voice (April 2 1979): 57.

5115. Silvert, Conrad. "Old and New Dreams." down beat (June 1980): 16+. [Interview]

5116. Wilmer, Val. "The Discreet [sic] Charm of Blowing Free." Time Out [London] (May 9-15 1980): 14-15.

OSBORNE, MIKE (1941-) (Great Britain) - Alto Sax/Clarinet

5117. Carles, Philippe, and Jean-Louis Comolli. Free Jazz, Black Power. 2nd ed. Paris: Editions Galilee, 1979, p. 428.

5118. Carr, Ian. "Osborne, Mike." In Jazz: The Essential Companion. New York: Prentice Hall Press, 1988.

5119. Case, Brian, and Stan Britt. The Harmony Illustrated Encyclopedia of Jazz. 3rd ed. New York: Harmony Books, 1987.

5120. Gilbert, Mark. "Osborne, Mike." In The New Grove Dictionary of Jazz. London: Macmillan Press, 1988.

5121. Jazz Now: the Jazz Centre Society Guide, ed. Roger Cotterrell. London: Quartet Books, 1976.

Articles

5122. Hyder, Ken. "Ossie's back in the swim." Melody Maker (May 19 1973): 56.

5123. Walters, M. "Fresh Music from Osborne." Sounds (February 6 1971): 12.

5124. Williams, Richard. "Mike - underrated but undefeated." Melody Maker (January 3 1970): 8.

5125. _________. "Partners in Rhythm." Melody Maker (May 6 1972): 22.

5126. Wilmer, Valerie. "Mike Osborne and His Trio." Jazz Forum, No. 13/14 (Autumn/Winter 1971): 78-79.

5127. Witherden, Barry. "Outlines." Wire, No. 77 (July 1990): 61, 63. [Profile]

OWENS, JIMMY (1943-) - Trumpet

5128. Jost, Ekkehard. Jazzmusiker: Materialien zur Soziologie der Afro-Amerikanischen Musik. Frankfurt am Main: Ullstein, 1982, pp. 97-109.

5129. Underwood, Lee. "Jimmy Owens: Creating the Business Legacy." down beat (October 19 1978): 15-16+.

OXLEY, TONY (1938-) (Great Britain) - Drums

5130. Noglik, Bert. "Tony Oxley." In Jazzwerkstatt International. Berlin: Verlag Neue Musik, 1981, pp. 447-467.

Biographical Dictionaries

5131. Carles, Philippe, and Jean-Louis Comolli. Free Jazz, Black Power. 2nd ed. Paris: Editions Galilee, 1979, p. 428.

5132. Carr, Ian. "Oxley, Tony." In Jazz: The Essential Companion. New York: Prentice Hall Press, 1988.

5133. Claghorn, Charles Eugene. Biographical Dictionary of Jazz. Englewood Cliffs, NJ: Prentice-Hall, 1982.

5134. Dictionnaire du Jazz, eds. Philippe Carles, et al. Paris: Laffont, 1988.

5135. Feather, Leonard. The Encyclopedia of Jazz in the Seventies. New York: Horizon Press, 1976.

5136. Gilbert, Mark. "Oxley, Tony." In The New Grove Dictionary of Jazz. London: Macmillan Press, 1988.

5137. Jazz Now: the Jazz Centre Society Guide, ed. Roger Cotterrell. London: Quartet Books, 1976, pp. 153-154.

Articles

5138. Dawbarn, Bob. "Caught in the Act." Melody Maker (September 27 1969): 15. [Concert review]

5139. ________. "Oxley, drummer at the storm centre." Melody Maker (August 10 1968): 8.

5140. Endress, Gudrun. "Tony Oxley." Jazz Podium (April 1986): 10-12. [Interview]

5141. Houston, Bob. "Tony's Big Break, At Last." Melody Maker (April 26 1969): 8.

5142. Hyder, Ken. "Oxley in Control." Melody Maker (February 16 1974): 56.

5143. McRae, Barry. "Dying with my boots on." Jazz Journal International (July 1978): 41.

5144. "New Thinking on Drums." Melody Maker (March 1 1969): 19.

5145. "Practise like a pianist." Melody Maker (November 23 1968): 20.

5146. Priestley, Brian. "Tony Oxley: A Drum Celebration." The Wire, No. 32 (October 1986): 22-24.

5147. Williams, Richard. "Electric Tony Oxley." Melody Maker (September 5 1970): 14.

5148. _________. "Forget the Thick Drummer Myth." Melody Maker (March 7 1970): 12.

5149. _________. "Riley, Oxley and the new music." Melody Maker (November 29 1969): 10.

PAPADIMITRIOU, SAKIS (1940-) (Greece) - Piano

5150. Dictionnaire du Jazz, eds. Philippe Carles, et al. Paris: Laffont, 1988.

Articles

5151. Jaume, Andre. "Sakis's Moods." Jazz Magazine, No. 330 (June 1984): 10. Saxophonist Jaume talks about his experience playing with Papadimitriou.

5152. Papadimitriou, Sakis. "Chance Music, Performers and Improvisation." Jazz Forum, No. 29 (June 1974): 48-49.

PARKER, ERROL [Raph Schecroun] (1930-) (Algeria/US) - Piano/Drums

5153. Davis, Francis. "A School of One." In Outcats: Jazz Composers, Instrumentalists, and Singers. New York: Oxford University Press, 1990, pp. 53-58. [Reprint of # 5155]

Articles

5154. "Ah! Sahara, Sahara, Sahara; ou, La revolution d'Errol Parker." Jazz Magazine, No. 390 (February 1990): 44-47. [Interview]

5155. Davis, Francis. "Music: A School of One." Village Voice (January 5 1988): 77. [Reprinted in # 5153]

5156. "Errol Parker." Swinging Newsletter, Vol. 8, No. 36 (1978): 2.

5157. Fox, Ted. "Success Story: Self-Made Records." Jazz Magazine (Northport, NY), Vol. 2, No. 4 (1978): 48-55. Includes a discussion of Parker's Sahara Records label.

5158. Franklin, D. "An Original...Errol Parker." Jazz Times (May 1989): 12.

5159. Futrick, Gerard. "The Errol Parker Experience." Coda, No. 232 (June/July 1990): 8-9. [Interview]

5160. Jeske, Lee. "Profile: Errol Parker." down beat (August 1981): 53.

5161. Lee, R. M. "Europeans in America: Errol Parker." Jazz Forum, No. 26 (December 1973): 49-50.

5162. McAffee, James. "The Errol Parker Experience." Jazz Spotlite News (April/May 1980): 12-13. [Interview]

5163. Mack, Gerald. "North African Jazz: Errol Parker Interviewed." Be-bop and Beyond, Vol. 5, No. 3 (Fall 1987): 15-18.

5164. McRae, Barry. "Errol Parker: An appraisal of the Algerian-born pianist and drummer." Jazz Journal International (August 1990): 8-9.

5165. Mialy, Louis-Victor. "Errol Parker: un Americain bien de chez nous." Jazz Hot, No. 384 (May 1981): 26-30. [Interview]

5166. Parker, Errol. "Errol Parker's Experience." down beat (July 1980): 8, 72. Response to a down beat record review.

5167. _________. "How to Produce Your Own Record." Jazz Echo, Vol. 9, No. 42 (1979): 15.

5168. Rusch, Bob. "Errol Parker: Interview." Cadence, Vol. 11, No. 12 (December 1985): 8-22, 30, 90.

5169. Wood, Wendy. "Errol Parker: interview." Cadence, Vol. 6, No. 1 (August 1980): 8-12.

PARKER, EVAN (1944-) (Great Britain) - Reeds

5170. Carr, Ian. "Evan Parker." In Music Outside. London: Latimer New Dimensions, 1973, pp. 68-89.

5171. New/Rediscovered Musical Instruments, ed. David Toop. London: Quartz/Mirliton, 1974, pp. 13-15. Designs and photos of instruments created by Evan Parker.

5172. Noglik, Bert. "Evan Parker." In Jazzwerkstatt International. Berlin: Verlag Neue Musik, 1981, pp. 9-28. [Interview]

Biographical Dictionaries

5173. Carles, Philippe, and Jean-Louis Comolli. Free Jazz, Black Power. 2nd ed. Paris: Editions Galilee, 1979, p. 429.

5174. Carr, Ian. "Parker, Evan." In Jazz: The Essential Companion. New York: Prentice Hall Press, 1988.

5175. Case, Brian, and Stan Britt. The Harmony Illustrated Encyclopedia of Jazz. 3rd ed. New York: Harmony Books, 1987.

5176. Claghorn, Charles Eugene. Biographical Dictionary of Jazz. Englewood Cliffs, NJ: Prentice-Hall, 1982.

5177. Dictionnaire du Jazz, eds. Philippe Carles, et al. Paris: Laffont, 1988.

5178. Feather, Leonard, and Ira Gitler. The Encyclopedia of Jazz in the Seventies. New York: Horizon Press, 1976.

5179. Gilbert, Mark. "Parker, Evan." In The New Grove Dictionary of Jazz. London: Macmillan Press, 1988.

5180. Jazz Now: the Jazz Centre Society Guide, ed. Roger Cotterrell. London: Quartet Books, 1976, pp. 154-155.

5181. McRae, Barry. "Evan Parker." In The Jazz Handbook. Harlow, Essex, Eng.: Longman, 1987, pp. 244-245.

Articles

5182. Ansell, Kenneth. "Evan Parker." Impetus (London), No. 6 (1977): 255-259. [Interview w/discography]

5183. Case, Brian. "If it's too easy it ain't music." New Musical Express (November 12 1977): 58-59. [Interview]

5184. Cook, Richard. "The Magnificent Evan." New Musical Express (February 9 1985): 6-7. [Interview]

5185. Dallas, Karl. "Improvisations." Melody Maker (June 26 1976): 41. [Interview]

5186. "Evan Parker d'une Musique a l'Autre." Jazz Magazine, No. 284 (March 1980): 32+. [Interview]

5187. Goddet, Laurent. "Une Musique de l'Eclatement--Evan Parker/Paul Lytton." Jazz Hot, No. 327 (May 1976): 16-21. [Interview]

5188. Hyder, Ken. "Evan for Free." Melody Maker (October 20 1973): 59.

5189. Johnson, Tom. "Evan Parker's Free Sax." Village Voice (November 19 1980): 82, 86.

5190. Keegan, P. "Evan Parker: the breath and breadth of the saxophone." down beat (April 1987): 26-28. [Interview]

5191. Kopf, Biba. "Evan Parker: Working Against the Normal." Wire, No. 27 (May 1986): 32-33, 35, 48.

5192. Lake, Steve. "Evan Parker." Jazz Forum, No. 51 (1978): 38-41. [Interview w/discography]

5193. McRae, Barry. "Evan Parker: Moving Forward with Tradition." Jazz Journal International (January 1985): 10-11.

5194. Paton, Maureen. "Jazzscene: solo Parker." Melody Maker (November 19 1977): 50.

5195. Rouy, Gerard. "Evan Parker: le message des anches." Jazz Magazine, No. 282 (January 1980): 22+. [Interview]

5196. Rusch, Bob. "Evan Parker: interview." Cadence, Vol. 5, No. 4 (April 1979): 8-11.

5197. Schonfield, Victor. "Evan, from Time to Time." Melody Maker (March 29 1969): 12.

5198. ________. "Total Improvisation." IT (London), No. 53 (March 28-April 10 1969): 15. [Interview]

5199. Summers, Russ. "Sax Obsessed: Evan Parker's 'Obscure Hobby.'" Option, No. 32 (May/June 1990): 58-61. [Interview]

5200. Tarting, Claude. "Evan Parker." Diapason-Harmonie (May 1988): 40.

5201. Terlizzi, Roberto. "Evan Parker." Coda, No. 167 (June 1979): 2-3. [Interview]

Discographies

5202. Cerutti, Gustave, and Riccardo Bergerone. Evan Parker Discography (on Records and Cassettes), 1968-1983. 2nd ed. rev. and enl. Sierre: Jazz 360o (c/o Cerutti, 8, ave. du Marche, CH-3960, Sierre, Switzerland), 1985(?). (Orig. 1981)

PARKER, WILLIAM (1952-) - Bass

5203. Carles, Philippe, and Jean-Louis Comolli. Free Jazz, Black Power. 2nd ed. Paris: Editions Galilee, 1979, p. 429.

5204. Wilmer, Valerie. As Serious As Your Life. Westport, CT: Lawrence Hill & Co., 1981, p. 276.

Articles

5205. Hazell, Ed. "William Parker - Sound Unity." Coda, No. 206 (February/March 1986): 24-26. [Interview]

5206. Riggins, Roger. "The Avantgarde Today: An Interview with William Parker." New Observations, No. 65 (March 1989): 21-23.

5207. Rusch, Bob. "William Parker." Cadence (December 1990): 5-16, 77. [Interview]

PARRAN, J. D. (1948-) - Reeds

5208. Carles, Philippe, and Jean-Louis Comolli. Free Jazz, Black Power. 2nd ed. Paris: Editions Galilee, 1979, p. 429.

5209. Dictionnaire du Jazz, eds. Philippe Carles, et al. Paris: Laffont, 1988.

5210. Marshall, Gregory J. "Profile: J.D. Parran." down beat (July 14 1977): 23-24.

PATRICK, PAT (1929-) - Baritone Saxophone

5211. Carles, Philippe, and Jean-Louis Comolli. Free Jazz, Black Power. 2nd ed. Paris: Editions Galilee, 1979, pp. 429-430.

5212. Dictionnaire du Jazz, eds. Philippe Carles, et al. Paris: Laffont, 1988.

5213. The New Grove Dictionary of Jazz. London: Macmillan Press, 1988.

5214. Wilmer, Valerie. As Serious As Your Life. Westport, CT: Lawrence Hill & Co., 1981, pp. 276-277.

Articles

5215. Cullaz, Maurice. "Pat Patrick." Jazz Hot, No. 330 (September 1976): 34-35.

5216. "Dictionnaire du Baryton." Jazz Magazine, No. 143 (June 1967): 38-39. Biographical sketch.

5217. Fiofori, Tam. "Pat's Rhythm Thing." Melody Maker (April 10 1971): 28.

5218. _________. "Les Premiers Satellites." Jazz Magazine, No. 196 (January 1972): 21-23.

5219. "L'Impossible Liberte; Entretien avec Sun Ra, John Gilmore, Marshall Allen et Pat Patrick." Jazz Magazine, No. 196 (January 1972): 10-13.

5220. Schaap, Phil. "Pat Patrick." Jazz Magazine, No. 306 (April 1982): 18-19.

PATTERSON, RAYMOND

See Ali, Muhammad

PATTERSON, ROBERT, JR.

See Ali, Rashied

PAVONE, MARIO - Bass

See also # 492-496

5221. Frazer, Vernon. "Mario Pavone." Coda, No. 190 (June 1983): 14-16. [Interview]

5222. _________. "Master of His Own Music: Mario Pavone gives himself and other non-mainstream jazz musicians a chance to record their music." The Hartford Advocate (June 19 1989): 32. Profile of Pavone and his record label, Alacra.

PEACOCK, GARY (1935-) - Bass

See also # 703

5223. Endress, Gudrun. "Gary Peacock." In Jazz Podium. Stuttgart: Deutsche Verlags-Anstalt, 1980, pp. 196-203.

Biographical Dictionaries

5224. Carles, Philippe, and Jean-Louis Comolli. Free Jazz, Black Power. 2nd ed. Paris: Editions Galilee, 1979, p. 430.

5225. Carr, Ian. "Peacock, Gary." In Jazz: The Essential Companion. New York: Prentice Hall Press, 1988.

5226. Claghorn, Charles Eugene. Biographical Dictionary of American Music. West Nyack, NY: Parker Pub. Co., 1973.

5227. ________. Biographical Dictionary of Jazz. Englewood Cliffs, NJ: Prentice-Hall, 1982.

5228. Dictionnaire du Jazz, eds. Philippe Carles, et al. Paris: Laffont, 1988.

5229. Feather, Leonard. The Encyclopedia of Jazz in the Sixties. New York: Horizon Press, 1966.

5230. The Penguin Encyclopedia of Popular Music, ed. Donald Clarke. New York: Viking, 1989.

5231. Reclams Jazzfuhrer. 2nd, rev. ed. Stuttgart: Reclam, 1977.

5232. Tenot, Frank. Dictionnaire du Jazz. Paris: Larousse, 1967.

5233. Ullman, Michael. "Peacock, Gary." In The New Grove Dictionary of American Music. London: Macmillan Press, 1986.

5234. ________. "Peacock, Gary." In The New Grove Dictionary of Jazz. London: Macmillan Press, 1988.

5235. Wilmer, Valerie. As Serious As Your Life. Westport, CT: Lawrence Hill & Co., 1981, p. 277.

Articles

5236. "Annuaire biographique de la contrebasse." Jazz Magazine, No. 9 (May 1963): 27. Biographical sketch.

5237. "Gary Peacock." Jazz Podium (September 1977): 14-17.

5238. Ginibre, Jean-Louis, and Philippe Carles. "Dictionairre de la Contrbasse." Jazz Magazine, No. 166 (May 1969): 51. Biographical sketch.

5239. Goddet, Laurent. "Gary le Magnifique." Jazz Hot, No. 338 (June 1977): 8-15.

5240. Lequime, M. "Gary Peacock." Jazz Hot, No. 290 (January 1973): 14-17.

5241. Quersin, Benoit. "Les Horizons de Peacock." Jazz Magazine, No. 114 (January 1965): 24-31. [Interview]

5242. Solomon, Mark. "Bassist Peacock into Zen, est and ECM." down beat (May 17 1979): 9.

5243. Williams, Martin. "Gary Peacock, the beauties of intuition." down beat (June 6 1963): 16-17.

PEPPER, JIM - Tenor Saxophone

5244. Gschwendner, Willie. "Marty Cook's New Jazz and Jim Pepper." Jazz Podium (May 1986): 24-25.

5245. Heckman, Don. "Jim Pepper talks to Don Heckman." Jazz & Pop (April-May 1969): 41-43.

PERRY, FRANK (1948-) (Great Britain) - Percussion

See also # 343

5246. Carles, Philippe, and Jean-Louis Comolli. Free Jazz, Black Power. 2nd ed. Paris: Editions Galilee, 1979, p. 431.

Articles

5247. Lake, Steve. "Sanctified Sound." Melody Maker (April 23 1977): 28. [Interview]

5248. Williams, Richard. "Caught in the Act." Melody Maker (May 13 1972): 58. [Concert review]

PETERSON, HANNIBAL MARVIN (1948-) - Trumpet

5249. Case, Brian, and Stan Britt. The Harmony Illustrated Encyclopedia of Jazz. 3rd ed. New York: Harmony Books, 1987.

5250. Dictionnaire du Jazz, eds. Philippe Carles, et al. Paris: Laffont, 1988.

5251. Feather, Leonard, and Ira Gitler. The Encyclopedia of Jazz in the Seventies. New York: Horizon Press, 1976.

5252. Kernfeld, Barry. "Peterson, Hannibal Marvin." In The New Grove Dictionary of Jazz. London: Macmillan Press, 1988.

5253. Wilmer, Valerie. As Serious As Your Life. Westport, CT: Lawrence Hill & Co., 1981, p. 269.

Articles

5254. Giddins, Gary. "Weatherbird: Out of Africa." Village Voice (December 18 1990): 94.

5255. Goddet, Laurent. "Interview: Hannibal." Jazz Hot, No. 304 (April 1974): 11-13.

5256. "Marvin Hannibal Peterson." Jazz Forum, No. 45 (1977): 23-24.

5257. Primack, Bret J. "Spotlight: Hannibal." down beat (September 8 1977): 24, 26.

5258. Wilmer, Valerie. "Hannibal the Great." Melody Maker (March 18 1978): 44. [Interview]

PETROWSKY, ERNST-LUDWIG (1933-) (E. Germany) - Reeds

5259. Dictionnaire du Jazz, eds. Philippe Carles, et al. Paris: Laffont, 1988.

5260. Noglik, Bert. "Ernst-Ludwig Petrowsky." In Jazzwerkstatt International. Berlin: Verlag Neue Musik, 1981. [Interview]

5261. ________. "Petrowsky, Ernst-Ludwig." In The New Grove Dictionary of Jazz. London: Macmillan Press, 1988.

5262. ________, and Heinz-Jurgen Lindner. "Ernst-Ludwig Petrowsky." In Jazz im Gesprach. Berlin: Verlag Neue Musik, 1978, pp. 117-139.

Articles

5263. Corbett, John. "Ernst-Ludwig Petrowsky: interview." Cadence, Vol. 15, No. 9 (September 1989): 16-18, 20.

5264. "Eurojazz personalities." Jazz Forum, No. 27 (February 1974): 67-69.

5265. Kalwa, J. "Die Jazz-Musiker sind keine Aussenseiter." Neue Musikzeitung, Vol. 27, No. 5 (1978): 12. [Interview]

5266. Kumpf, Hans. "Ernst Ludwig Petrowsky." Jazz Podium (January 1981): 14-16.

5267. Noglik, Bert. "Ernst Ludwig Petrowsky." Jazz Podium (January 1984): 33.

PHILLIPS, BARRE (1934-) - Bass

5268. Anderson, Ruth. Contemporary American Composers: a biographical dictionary. 2nd ed. Boston, MA: G.K. Hall, 1982.

5269. Carles, Philippe, and Jean-Louis Comolli. Free Jazz, Black Power. 2nd ed. Paris: Editions Galilee, 1979, p. 431.

5270. Claghorn, Charles Eugene. Biographical Dictionary of American Music. West Nyack, NY: Parker Pub. Co., 1973.

5271. ________. Biographical Dictionary of Jazz. Englewood Cliffs, NJ: Prentice-Hall, 1982.

5272. Dictionnaire du Jazz, eds. Philippe Carles, et al. Paris: Laffont, 1988.

5273. Feather, Leonard. The Encyclopedia of Jazz in the Sixties. New York: Horizon Press, 1966.

5274. Voigt, John. "Phillips, Barre." In The New Grove Dictionary of Jazz. London: Macmillan Press, 1988.

5275. Wilmer, Valerie. As Serious As Your Life. Westport, CT: Lawrence Hill & Co., 1981, p. 277.

Articles

5276. Buhrdorf, Uwe. "Barre Phillips." Jazzthetik, Vol. 4, No. 11 (November 1990): 12-17.

5277. Byrczek, Jan, and Roman Kowal. "The Trio--Surman Phillips Martin." Jazz Forum, No. 13/14 (Autumn/Winter 1971): 62-63, 72-74.

5278. Carles, Philippe. "Barre Phillips: la basse et le reste." Jazz Magazine, No. 239 (December 1975): 34-35. [Interview]

5279. Cullaz, Maurice. "John Surman, Barre Phillips, Stu Martin--interview." Jazz Hot, No. 259 (March 1970): 16-19.

5280. Ginibre, Jean Louis. "Phillips c'est plus pur." Jazz Magazine, No. 166 (May 1969): 63-65. [Interview]

5281. "Pieges pour Barre." Jazz Magazine, No. 179 (June 1970): 28-29.

5282. Schoukroun, Guy. "Phillips a la Barre." Jazz Magazine, No. 296 (April 1981): 26-29, 52. [Interview]

5283. Smith, Bill. "Barre Phillips." Coda, No. 198 (October 1984): 19-23. [Interview]

5284. Summers, Russ. "The Jazz Fest Circuit: Barre Phillips, Maarten Altena and Pierre Dorge in Vancouver." Option, No. 36 (January/February 1991): 44-49.

5285. Terrones, G. "Barre Phillips." Jazz Hot, No. 260 (April 1970): 20-23. [Interview]

5286. Williams, Richard. "Barre: playing his birth." Melody Maker (March 21 1970): 8.

5287. Wilmer, Valerie. "Barre blasts off at 'cold' British." Melody Maker (April 12 1969): 8.

PINE, COURTNEY (1964-) (Great Britain) - Tenor Saxophone

5288. Adams, Simon. "Pine, Courtney." In The New Grove Dictionary of Jazz. London: Macmillan Press, 1988.

5289. Carr, Ian. "Pine, Courtney." In Jazz: The Essential Companion. New York: Prentice Hall Press, 1988.

5290. Case, Brian, and Stan Britt. The Harmony Illustrated Encyclopedia of Jazz. 3rd ed. New York: Harmony Books, 1987.

5291. Dictionnaire du Jazz, eds. Philippe Carles, et al. Paris: Laffont, 1988.

5292. McRae, Barry. "Courtney Pine." In The Jazz Handbook. Harlow, Essex, Eng.: Longman, 1987, pp. 245-246.

5293. The Penguin Encyclopedia of Popular Music, ed. Donald Clarke. New York: Viking, 1989.

Articles

5294. Coleman, Nick. "Needle-Sharp." New Musical Express (January 25 1986): 4. [Profile]

5295. Cook, Richard. "The Main Man: Courtney Pine." Wire, No. 46/47 (Dec 1987/Jan 1988): 40-41, 45-47, 49.

5296. Gauffre, Christian. "Pas trop star Courtney Pine." Jazz Magazine, No. 361 (1987): 22-23. [Interview]

5297. Hennessey, Mike. "The Ascent of Courtney Pine." Jazz Times (June 1988): 20-22. [Interview]

5298. Herrington, Tony. "Locking Horns." Wire (November 1989): 33, 36-37. [Interview]

5299. Hewitt, Paolo. "On the Trail of the Courtney Pine." New Musical Express (October 18 1986): 30-31, 57.

5300. Laret, J. "Courtney Pine...voix nouvelle." Jazz Magazine, No. 354 (October 1986): 39. [Interview]

5301. Levenson, Jeff. "Courtney Pine: pursuing a song of destiny." down beat (September 1988): 20-22. [Interview]

5302. Nicholson, Stuart. "Young Turks: Courtney Pine." The Wire, No. 25 (March 1986): 31-32.

5303. Okri, Ben. "Gifted...and Black." New Statesman (October 17 1986): 36.

5304. "Shrink Rap." Melody Maker (December 13 1986): 12. [Interview]

5305. Stubbs, D. "Blowing Hot." Melody Maker (November 15 1986): 12. [Interview]

5306. Summers, Russ. "England Swings and Courtney Pine is Living Proof." Option, No. 34 (Sept/Oct 1990): 58-61.

5307. Testa, Bart. "New British Jazz Warrior." Macleans (May 30 1988): 55.

Newspaper Articles

5308. Case, Brian. "A Cool Blast of Pine." Sunday Times Magazine [London] (August 3 1986): 34-35.

5309. Emerson, Bo. "Courtney Pine Has All the Chops, Now He's Learning to Blow American." Atlanta Constitution (March 23 1990): D-3.

5310. Giddins, Gary. "Courtney Pine; The Empire Strikes Back." Village Voice (May 17 1988): 90.

5311. Tesser, Neil. "Splendid Isolation." Chicago Tribune (March 25 1990): Sec. 13, p. 24. [Profile]

PLIMLEY, PAUL (1953-) (Canada) - Piano

5312. Lewis, Scott. "Paul Plimley - Out into the World." Coda, No. 231 (April/May 1990): 10-11. [Interview]

5313. Miller, Mark. "Paul Plimley." In Boogie, Pete & the Senator: Canadian Musicians in Jazz: the eighties. Toronto: Nightwood Editions, 1987, pp. 219-225.

POPE, ODEAN (1938-) - Tenor Saxophone

5314. Davis, Francis. "The Philadelphia Story." In Outcats: Jazz Composers, Instrumentalists, and Singers. New York: Oxford University Press, 1990, pp. 107-110. [Profile]

5315. Dictionnaire du Jazz, eds. Philippe Carles, et al. Paris: Laffont, 1988.

5316. The New Grove Dictionary of Jazz. London: Macmillan Press, 1988.

Articles

5317. Stern, Chip. "Odean Pope: students and teachers: tracing forgotten tenor traditions." Musician, No. 65 (March 1984): 26+. [Interview]

5318. Van Trikt, Ludwig. "Odean Pope." Cadence, Vol. 15, No. 2 (February 1989): 5-11. [Interview]

5319. Woessner, Russell. "Profile: Odean Pope." down beat (March 1983): 46-47.

PORTAL, MICHEL (1935-) (France) - Reeds

5320. Carles, Philippe, and Jean-Louis Comolli. Free Jazz, Black Power. 2nd ed. Paris: Editions Galilee, 1979, pp. 431-432.

5321. Carr, Ian. "Portal, Michel." In Jazz: The Essential Companion. New York: Prentice Hall Press, 1988.

5322. Dictionnaire du Jazz, eds. Philippe Carles, et al. Paris: Laffont, 1988.

5323. Feather, Leonard, and Ira Gitler. The Encyclopedia of Jazz in the Seventies. New York: Horizon Press, 1976.

5324. Laplace, Michel. "Portal, Michel." In The New Grove Dictionary of Jazz. London: Macmillan Press, 1988.

Articles

5325. Buin, Yves. "Michel Portal: un choix courageux." Jazz Hot, No. 218 (March 1966): 18-19. [Interview]

5326. Buzelin, Jean. "Michel Portal." Jazz Hot, No. 318 (July-August 1975): 24-25.

5327. Carles, Philippe, and Francis Marmande. "Michel Portal ou la parole au present." Jazz Magazine, No. 210 (April 1973): 10+. [Interview]

5328. Constant, P. "Michel Portal." Jazz Hot, No. 241 (May-July 1968): 14-16. [Interview]

5329. Delmas, J., and M. Lequime. "Portal en long, Portal en travers." Jazz Hot, No. 296 (July-August 1973): 8+. [Interview]

5330. Gerber, Alain. "Michel Portal--chant et contrechant." Jazz Magazine, No. 240 (January 1976): 12+. [Interview]

5331. "Instants de Michel Portal." Jazz Magazine, No. 298 (June 1981): 54-57. Photo essay.

5332. Kumpf, Hans. "Musique Commune: Michel Portal." Jazz Podium (April 1973): 24-26.

5333. Laverdure, Michel. "Michel Portal." Jazz Magazine, No. 282 (January 1980): 16.

5334. Litterst, Gerhard. "Grenzgaenger: Michel Portal und Jean-Francois Jenny-Clark." Jazz Podium (February 1981): 18-23.

5335. Loupien, Serge. "Michel Portal." Jazz Magazine, No. 283 (February 1980): 13.

5336. Marmande, Francis. "Michel Portal: 'voulez-vous jouer avec moi?'" Jazz Magazine, No. 350 (May 1986): 18-21. [Interview]

5337. "Michel Portal: une interview a faire vous-memes." Jazz Magazine, No. 262 (February 1978): 16.

5338. "Michel Portal face a face." Jazz Magazine, No. 290 (October 1980): 46-47.

5339. Rossi, P. L. "Michel polyvalent Portal." Jazz Magazine, No. 142 (May 1967): 24. [Interview]

5340. Soutif, Daniel. "Michel Portal: Le prix de la musique." Jazz Magazine, No. 329 (May 1984): 51.

POTTS, STEVE (1945-) - Alto Saxophone

5341. Carles, Philippe, and Jean-Louis Comolli. Free Jazz, Black Power. 2nd ed. Paris: Editions Galilee, 1979, p. 432.

5342. Dictionnaire du Jazz, eds. Philippe Carles, et al. Paris: Laffont, 1988.

5343. "Encyclopedie permanente Jazzmag." Jazz Magazine, No. 389 (January 1990): 43-44.

POZAR, CLEVE F. (1941-) - Percussion

5344. Anderson, Ruth. Contemporary American Composers: a biographical dictionary. 2nd ed. Boston, MA: G.K. Hall, 1982.

PREVOST, EDDIE (Great Britain) - Drums

See also # 876-889

5345. Prevost, Eddie. "Improvisation: Music for an Occasion." British Journal of Music Education, Vol. 2, No. 2 (1985): 177-186.

5346. Schonfield, Victor. "We're Not Interested in Music." Melody Maker (June 5 1971): 28. [Interview]

5347. Welch, Chris. "Caught in the Act." Melody Maker (March 4 1972): 42. [Concert review]

PRIESTER, JULIAN (1935-) - Trombone

5348. Carr, Ian. "Priester, Julian." In Jazz: The Essential Companion. New York: Prentice Hall Press, 1988.

5349. Claghorn, Charles Eugene. Biographical Dictionary of Jazz. Englewood Cliffs, NJ: Prentice-Hall, 1982.

5350. Dictionnaire du Jazz, eds. Philippe Carles, et al. Paris: Laffont, 1988.

5351. Feather, Leonard. The Encyclopedia of Jazz. New ed. New York: Horizon Press, 1960.

5352. ________, and Ira Gitler. The Encyclopedia of Jazz in the Seventies. New York: Horizon Press, 1976.

5353. Reclams Jazzfuhrer. 2nd, rev. ed. Stuttgart: Reclam, 1977.

5354. Wild, David. "Priester, Julian." In The New Grove Dictionary of Jazz. London: Macmillan Press, 1988.

Articles

5355. Chadbourne, Eugene. "Wandering Spirit Song." Coda (December 1974).

5356. Crooks, Mack. "Julian Priester: Interview." Cadence, Vol. 4, No. 1 (April 1978): 12-15, 20.

PUKWANA, DUDU (1938-1990) (South Africa/UK) - Alto Sax

See also # 69

5357. Carr, Ian. "Pukwana, Dudu." In Jazz: The Essential Companion. New York: Prentice Hall Press, 1988.

5358. de Ledesma, Charles. "Pukwana, Dudu." In The New Grove Dictionary of Jazz. London: Macmillan Press, 1988.

5359. Dictionnaire du Jazz, eds. Philippe Carles, et al. Paris: Laffont, 1988.

5360. Jazz Now: the Jazz Centre Society Guide, ed. Roger Cotterrell. London: Quartet Books, 1976, pp. 157-158.

5361. The Penguin Encyclopedia of Popular Music, ed. Donald Clarke. New York: Viking, 1989, pp. 947-948.

Articles

5362. de Ledesma, Charles. "Dudu Pukwana." Wire, No. 12 (February 1985): 30-31.

5363. Latxague, Robert, and M. Jurado. "Dudu: Change de Cap." Jazz Magazine, No. 319 (June 1983): 30-31. [Interview]

5364. Litterst, Gerhard. "Musik aus Afrika: Klange aus der Elektronischen Buschtrommel." Jazz Podium (November 1987): 14. Biographical sketch.

5365. May, Chris. "Dudu Pukwana: King of Afro Rock." Black Music, Vol. 3, No. 27 (February 1976): 40-41, 53.

5366. _________. "Home Is Where the Music Is." Black Music and Jazz Review [London] (April 1981): 16-17.

5367. Williams, Richard. "Caught in the Act." Melody Maker (April 18 1970): 12. [Concert review]

5368. Wilmer, Valerie. "Assegai, Spearhead of the African Sound." Melody Maker (February 6 1971): 35.

5369. _________. "On the School Trip." The Independent (June 27 1990).

5370. _________. "Pukwana." Melody Maker (September 26 1970): 32.

Obituaries

5371. "Dudu Pukwana." The Times [London] (July 4 1990).

5372. "Final Bar: Dudu Pukwana." down beat (October 1990): 11.

5373. Fordham, John. "Honks from a Rain Barrell." The Guardian (July 3 1990): 39.

5374. Gilbert, Mark. "Obituaries: Dudu Pukwana." Jazz Journal International (October 1990): 25.

5375. Mokone, Moji. "Dudu Pukwana." The Independent (July 9 1990).

5376. Voce, Steve. "Dudu Pukwana." The Independent (July 3 1990).

5377. Wilmer, Valerie. "Dudu Pukwana." The Independent (July 14 1990).

PULLEN, DON (1944-) - Piano

See also # 187, 698, 705

5378. Carles, Philippe, and Jean-Louis Comolli. Free Jazz, Black Power. 2nd ed. Paris: Editions Galilee, 1979, p. 432.

5379. Case, Brian, and Stan Britt. The Harmony Illustrated Encyclopedia of Jazz. 3rd ed. New York: Harmony Books, 1987.

5380. Claghorn, Charles Eugene. Biographical Dictionary of Jazz. Englewood Cliffs, NJ: Prentice-Hall, 1982.

5381. Dictionnaire du Jazz, eds. Philippe Carles, et al. Paris: Laffont, 1988.

5382. Feather, Leonard, and Ira Gitler. The Encyclopedia of Jazz in the Seventies. New York: Horizon Press, 1976.

5383. Kernfeld, Barry. "Pullen, Don." In The New Grove Dictionary of Jazz. London: Macmillan Press, 1988.

5384. McRae, Barry. "Don Pullen." In The Jazz Handbook. Harlow, Essex, Eng.: Longman, 1987, pp. 208-209.

5385. The Penguin Encyclopedia of Popular Music, ed. Donald Clarke. New York: Viking, 1989.

5386. Priestley, Brian. "Pullen, Don." In Jazz: The Essential Companion. New York: Prentice Hall Press, 1988.

5387. Who's Who in Entertainment. 1st ed. 1989-1990.

5388. Wilmer, Valerie. As Serious As Your Life. Westport, CT: Lawrence Hill & Co., 1981, p. 277.

Articles

5389. Case, Brian. "New Far-Outnesses at Changes Bar." New Musical Express (June 18 1977): 18-19. [Interview]

5390. Davis, Michael. "Don Pullen: Mingus sideman, club organist, solo pianist." Keyboard (September 1982): 42-52. [Interview]

5391. Frazer, Vernon. "Don Pullen: an interview." Coda, No. 151 (October-November 1976): 2+.

5392. Gamble, Pete. "Don Pullen." Jazz Journal International (June 1980): 28. [Profile]

5393. Giddins, Gary. "Don Pullen: Pumping Calluses." Village Voice (December 19 1989): 82.

5394. Goddet, Laurent. "Free Blues: Don Pullen." Jazz Hot, No. 331 (October 1976): 15-18. [Interview]

5395. Gourse, Leslie. "Don Pullen." Jazz Times (November 1989): 21, 29.

5396. Graves, Milford, and Don Pullen. "Black Music." Liberator (New York), Vol. 7, No. 1 (January 1967): 20. Statement on the independent label SRP (Self Reliance Program), co-founded by Graves and Pullen.

5397. Macnie, Jim. "Don Pullen: a romantic avant-gardist plays the whole piano." Musician, No. 96 (October 1986): 19+. [Interview]

5398. Mandel, Howard. "Blindfold Test: Don Pullen." down beat (November 1989): 43.

5399. _________. "Don Pullen: Piano Inside and Out." down beat (June 1985): 20+. [Interview]

5400. Milkowski, Bill. "Reap the Whirlwind: Don Pullen finds a trio's company for his New Beginning." Pulse! [Tower Records magazine] (November 1989): 67.

5401. Smith, Arnold Jay. "Profile: Don Pullen." down beat (July 14 1977): 17-18.

5402. Smith, Bill. "Don Pullen." Coda (November/December 1970): 40-43.

5403. Steiner, Ken. "The 360o Music Experience." Coda, No. 175 (October 1980): 10-14. [Interview]

5404. Thebault, Yves. "Un Don peu paisible." Jazz Magazine, No. 289 (September 1980): 64+. [Interview]

5405. Watrous, Peter. "Don Pullen, Making Sense of Jazz's Radical 60's." New York Times (July 16 1989).

5406. Whitehead, Kevin. "Don Pullen: Reconciling Opposites." down beat (November 1989): 26-28. [Interview]

5407. Wilmer, Valerie. "Pullen: Echoes of the Sixties." Melody Maker (March 25 1978): 39.

Record Reviews

5408. Jones, LeRoi. "Apple Cores: A Few Notes on the Avant-Garde." down beat (January 26 1967): 10. Review of Pullen-Milford Graves duo lp recorded live at Yale University.

5409. Mathieu, Bill. "Record Reviews: Milford Graves-Don Pullen Duo." down beat (April 20 1967): 36, 38, 40. Review of live lp recorded at Yale University.

5410. _________. "Record Reviews: Nommo." down beat (November 14 1968): 22. Review of the Don Pullen/Milford Graves duo lp "Nommo."

Discographies

5411. Luzzi, Mario. "Discografia: Don Pullen." Musica Jazz, Vol. 33, No. 4 (1977): 15-16.

PURCELL, JOHN (1951-) - Reeds

5412. Dictionnaire du Jazz, eds. Philippe Carles, et al. Paris: Laffont, 1988.

5413. Jeske, Lee. "Profile: John Purcell." down beat (December 1983): 54-55.

QUATUOR DE JAZZ LIBRE DU QUEBEC (ca 1963-1974) (Canada)

5414. Menard, Denise, and Mark Miller. "Quatuor de Jazz Libre du Quebec." In Encyclopedia of Music in Canada, eds. Helmut Kallmann, et al. Toronto/Buffalo: University of Toronto Press, 1981, p. 784.

QUAYE, TERRI (Great Britain) - Percussion

5415. Case, Brian. "The Drums Say: 'Women get a raw deal.'" New Musical Express (October 8 1977): 26-27. Interview with conga player Terri Quaye.

RAGIN, HUGH (1951-) - Trumpet

5416. Hazell, Ed. "Hugh Ragin: The Metaphysical Question." Coda, No. 215 (August/September 1987): 24-25.

RASKIN, JON - Reeds

See # 5625-5638

RAVA, ENRICO (1943-) (Italy) - Trumpet

5417. Jost, Ekkehard. "Enrico Rava." In Jazzmusiker: Materialen zur Soziologie der Afro-Amerikanischen Musik. Frankfurt am Main: Ullstein, 1982, pp. 155-168.

Biographical Dictionaries

5418. Carles, Philippe, and Jean-Louis Comolli. Free Jazz, Black Power. 2nd ed. Paris: Editions Galilee, 1979, p. 432-433.

5419. Carr, Ian. "Rava, Enrico." In Jazz: The Essential Companion. New York: Prentice Hall Press, 1988.

5420. Dictionnaire du Jazz, eds. Philippe Carles, et al. Paris: Laffont, 1988.

5421. Feather, Leonard, and Ira Gitler. The Encyclopedia of Jazz in the Seventies. New York: Horizon Press, 1976.

5422. The New Grove Dictionary of Jazz. London: Macmillan Press, 1988.

Articles

5423. Carles, Philippe. "Ravis du Nouveau Rava." Jazz Magazine, No. 333 (November 1984): 24-25. [Interview]

5424. Cuscuna, Michael. "Enrico Rava: 'The Real Music Comes from the People'." down beat (April 11 1974): 15, 34.

5425. "Dico Disco & Co." Jazz Magazine, No. 298 (June 1981): 52. Biographical sketch.

5426. Endress, Gudrun. "Enrico Rava." Jazz Podium (July 1988): 12-15. [Interview]

5427. Le Bec, Jean-Yves. "Enrico Rava: 'maintenant je joue pour...'" Jazz Magazine, No. 388 (December 1989): 22-24. [Interview]

5428. Luzzi, Mario. "Enrico Rava." Coda, No. 160 (April 1978): 24-26. [Interview]

5429. Mandel, Howard. "Enrico Rava: Italian on the Up Swing." down beat (February 9 1978): 16-17.

5430. Rouy, Gerard. "Enrico Rava." Jazz Magazine, No. 215 (September 1973): 44-47. [Interview]

5431. Rozek, M. "Faces; Enrico Rava." Musician, Player and Listener, No. 19 (July-August 1979): 26-27.

5432. Solothurnmann, Jurg. "Die Aktionen und Provokationen des Ernico Rava." Jazz (Basel), Nr. 3 (1984). [Interview]

5433. ________. "Enrico Rava: 'Jazz is Everywhere.'" Jazz Forum, No. 92 (1985): 36-41. [Interview]

5434. Soutif, Daniel. "Enrico Rava entre New York et l'Italie." Jazz Magazine, No. 252 (February-March 1977): 14+.

REDMAN, DEWEY [Walter] (1931-) - Tenor Saxophone

See also # 69, 5111-5116

5435. Carles, Philippe, and Jean-Louis Comolli. Free Jazz, Black Power. 2nd ed. Paris: Editions Galilee, 1979, p. 433.

5436. Carr, Ian. "Redman, Dewey." In Jazz: The Essential Companion. New York: Prentice Hall Press, 1988.

5437. Case, Brian, and Stan Britt. The Harmony Illustrated Encyclopedia of Jazz. 3rd ed. New York: Harmony Books, 1987.

5438. Claghorn, Charles Eugene. Biographical Dictionary of Jazz. Englewood Cliffs, NJ: Prentice-Hall, 1982.

5439. Dictionnaire du Jazz, eds. Philippe Carles, et al. Paris: Laffont, 1988.

5440. Feather, Leonard, and Ira Gitler. The Encyclopedia of Jazz in the Seventies. New York: Horizon Press, 1976.

5441. Kernfeld, Barry. "Redman, Dewey." In The New Grove Dictionary of American Music. London: Macmillan Press, 1986.

5442. ________. "Redman, Dewey." In The New Grove Dictionary of Jazz. London: Macmillan Press, 1988.

5443. The Penguin Encyclopedia of Popular Music, ed. Donald Clarke. New York: Viking, 1989.

5444. Southern, Eileen. Biographical Dictionary of Afro-American and African Musicians. Westport, CT: Greenwood Press, 1982.

5445. Wilmer, Valerie. As Serious As Your Life. Westport, CT: Lawrence Hill & Co., 1981, p. 277.

Articles

5446. Crouch, Stanley. "Dewey Redman." Village Voice (August 13 1985): 31.

5447. "Dewey's sax blows a changing tune." Soul (September 30 1974): 10.

5448. "Dico Disco & Co." Jazz Magazine, No. 298 (June 1981): 52, 60. Biographical sketch.

5449. Henderson, Bill. "Dewey Redman into the spotlight." Black Music and Jazz Review, Vol. 1, No. 4 (July 1978): 10-13.

5450. Litweiler, John. "Dewey Redman: Coincidentals." down beat (November 6 1975): 14+. [Interview]

5451. Mandel, Howard. "Dewey Redman: Nobody's Foil." down beat (February 1983): 18+. [Interview]

5452. Mathieson, Kenny. "Dewey Redman: New Music, Old Dreams." Wire, No. 32 (October 1986): 10, 64.

5453. Pareles, Jon. "Pop/Jazz: Redman, A Tenor Sax Player Who Bloomed Late." New York Times (November 26 1982).

5454. Positif, Francois. "Dewey Redman, l'homme qui chante en jouant du Tenor." Jazz Hot, No. 279 (January 1972): 10-14. [Interview]

5455. Riggins, Roger. "Dewey Redman." Coda, No. 171 (February 1980): 28-29. [Interview]

5456. Whitehead, Kevin. "Dewey Redman: setting out on his own." Jazz Times (October 1983): 6-7.

5457. Wilmer, Val. "Singing Through the Horn." Time Out [London] (May 28-June 1 1978).

5458. ________. "Song of Dewey." Melody Maker (November 13 1971): 26.

REICHEL, HANS (1949-) (W. Germany) - Guitar

See also # 702

5459. Carles, Philippe, and Jean-Louis Comolli. Free Jazz, Black Power. 2nd ed. Paris: Editions Galilee, 1979, p. 433.

5460. Dictionnaire du Jazz, eds. Philippe Carles, et al. Paris: Laffont, 1988.

Articles

5461. Buzelin, Jean and Francoise. "Hans Reichel, Rudiger Carl: deux nouvelles voix de la N.M.E." Jazz Hot, No. 359 (March 1979): 22-25. [Interview]

5462. Dery, Mark. "Forging a new guitar vocabulary: Peter Cusack, Hans Reichel, David Fulton, Davey Williams." Guitar Player (July 1988): 52, 56, 58, 61, 64.

5463. Dutilh, Alex. "Hans Reichel, Peter Kowald: pas de conversation." Jazz Hot, No. 368 (1979-80): 51.

5464. Froese, D. H. "Schnapsglas in der Hand: Gitarrist Hans Reichel." Jazz Podium (February 1973): 22-23.

5465. "Hans Reichel." Jazz Podium (April 1972): 114.

5466. Rouy, Gerard. "Hans Reichel ou les mains libres." Jazz Magazine, No. 253 (April 1977): 21.

REID, BOB [Robert] - Bass

5467. Carles, Philippe, and Jean-Louis Comolli. Free Jazz, Black Power. 2nd ed. Paris: Editions Galilee, 1979, p. 433.

5468. Wilmer, Valerie. As Serious As Your Life. Westport, CT: Lawrence Hill & Co., 1981, p. 277.

5469. ________. "Now Reid On." Melody Maker (April 15 1972): 42. [Interview]

REID, STEVE (1944-) - Drums

5470. Carles, Philippe, and Jean-Louis Comolli. Free Jazz, Black Power. 2nd ed. Paris: Editions Galilee, 1979, pp. 433-434.

5471. Dictionnaire du Jazz, eds. Philippe Carles, et al. Paris: Laffont, 1988.

5472. Wilmer, Valerie. As Serious As Your Life. Westport, CT: Lawrence Hill & Co., 1981, p. 278.

Articles

5473. "On the Bandstand: Steve Reid." Jazz Forum, No. 48 (1977): 24-25.

5474. Reid, Steve. "Mustevic ou les musiques de Steve Reid." Jazz Magazine, No. 290 (October 1980): 52-53, 62.

REVOLUTIONARY ENSEMBLE

See also # 69

5475. Claghorn, Charles Eugene. Biographical Dictionary of American Music. West Nyack, NY: Parker Pub. Co., 1973.

5476. ________. Biographical Dictionary of Jazz. Englewood Cliffs, NJ: Prentice-Hall, 1982, p. 364.

5477. Kernfeld, Barry. "Revolutionary Ensemble." In The New Grove Dictionary of American Music. London: Macmillan Press, 1986.

5478. ________. "Revolutionary Ensemble." In The New Grove Dictionary of Jazz. London: Macmillan Press, 1988.

5479. Southern, Eileen. Biographical Dictionary of Afro-American and African Musicians. Westport, CT: Greenwood Press, 1982.

Articles

5480. Jenkins, Leroy. "The Only Way." down beat (March 15 1973): 10. Open letter from a member of the Revolutionary Ensemble urging musicians to form collectives to gain greater control over their music.

5481. Occhiogrosso, Peter. "U.S. News: End of era as Revolutionary Ensemble splits." Melody Maker (January 21 1978): 6.

5482. "Revolutionary Ensemble dissolves." down beat (December 15 1977): 11.

5483. "The Revolutionary Ensemble wants to be heard." down beat (November 8 1973): 13-14.

5484. Riggins, Roger. "Caught in the Act: Revolutionary Ensemble, Artists' House." down beat (October 26 1972): 34. [Concert review]

5485. ________. "The Revolutionary Ensemble." down beat (November 22 1973): 15, 42.

5486. Williams, Patrick. "Revolutionary Ensemble." Jazz 360o (Sierre, Switzerland), No. 28 (May 1980): 4-6.

5487. Wilmer, Valerie. "Caught in the Act: Revolutionary Ensemble." Melody Maker (August 5 1972). [Concert review]

Discographies

5488. "Discographie du Revolutionary Ensemble." Jazz 360o (Sierre, Switzerland), No. 28 (May 1980): 6-7.

REYSEGER, ERNST (The Netherlands) - Cello

5489. Mathieson, Kenny. "The Importance of Being Ernst." Wire, No. 67 (September 1989): 14-16. [Interview]

5490. Smith, Bill. "Ernst Reyseger." Coda, No. 191 (August 1983): 18-19. [Interview]

5491. van der Berg, Erik. "Ernst Reijseger, cellist." Jazzjaarboek (Amsterdam), Vol. 2 (1983): 62-71. [Interview]

RHAMES, ARTHUR - Tenor Saxophone/Piano/Guitar

5492. Crouch, Stanley. "Riffs: Arthur Rhames Takes the Coltrane." Village Voice (June 17 1981): 64-65.

5493. "Dico Disco & Co." Jazz Magazine, No. 298 (June 1981): 60. Biographical sketch.

5494. McRae, Barry. "Beyond the Mainstream: A Nightingale Sang." Jazz Journal International (May 1980): 27-28.

5495. Reid, Vernon. "Unknown Greats: Cardiac Guitar." Guitar Player (March 1989): 44, 46.

5496. Youngblood, James. "A Blast of Arthur Rhames." Guitar World (May 1981): 14, 17.

RIGBY, JOE (1940-) - Reeds

5497. Carles, Philippe, and Jean-Louis Comolli. Free Jazz, Black Power. 2nd ed. Paris: Editions Galilee, 1979, p. 434.

5498. Wilmer, Valerie. As Serious As Your Life. Westport, CT: Lawrence Hill & Co., 1981, p. 278.

RILEY, HOWARD (1943-) (Great Britain) - Piano

5499. Carles, Philippe, and Jean-Louis Comolli. Free Jazz, Black Power. 2nd ed. Paris: Editions Galilee, 1979, p. 434.

5500. Carr, Ian. "Riley, Howard." In Jazz: The Essential Companion. New York: Prentice Hall Press, 1988.

5501. Claghorn, Charles Eugene. Biographical Dictionary of Jazz. Englewood Cliffs, NJ: Prentice-Hall, 1982.

5502. Feather, Leonard, and Ira Gitler. The Encyclopedia of Jazz in the Seventies. New York: Horizon Press, 1976.

5503. Hazell, Ed. "Riley, Howard." In The New Grove Dictionary of Jazz. London: Macmillan Press, 1988.

5504. International Who's Who in Music and Musicians' Directory. 12th ed. 1990/91.

5505. Jazz Now: the Jazz Centre Society Guide, ed. Roger Cotterrell. London: Quartet Books, 1976, pp. 161-162.

Articles

5506. Ansell, Kenneth. "Howard Riley and His Music." Jazz Journal International (October 1980): 20-21.

5507. Barry, M. "Howard Riley and 'Non-jazz.'" Contact, No. 14 (1976): 12.

5508. Case, Brian. "Confrontation with the Insidious Forces of Industry." New Musical Express (February 25 1978): 42-43. [Interview]

5509. Dawbarn, Bob. "The trouble with people who listen with their feet." Melody Maker (June 28 1969): 8.

5510. Fordham, John. "Life of Riley." Melody Maker (December 22 1973): 19.

5511. "Howard Riley." Music and Musicians (February 1976): 18+.

5512. Ilic, Dave. "Howard Riley." The Wire, No. 5 (Autumn 1983): 7, 9.

5513. Lake, Steve. "Life of Riley." Melody Maker (October 16 1976): 48. [Interview]

5514. Lee, R. M. "The Music of Howard Riley; a progress report." Jazz Forum, No. 15 (1972): 82-83.

5515. Parker, Chris. "The Freedom Attitude." The Wire, No. 67 (September 1989): 36-37.

5516. Riley, Howard. "'But you can't teach improvisation'--the challenge of jazz and improvised music." Music in Education, Vol. 39, No. 373 (1975): 112-113.

5517. ________. "Contemporary Improvised Music, technical and aesthetic features." The Music Review, Vol. 33, No. 2 (1972): 218-221.

5518. "Riley's Progress." Melody Maker (June 10 1972): 42.

5519. Smith, Arnold Jay. "Profile: Howard Riley." down beat (February 10 1977): 33.

5520. Walsh, A. "Riley: opening up new ideas." Melody Maker (May 4 1968): 8.

5521. Williams, Richard. "Howard helps make jazz legitimate." Melody Maker (May 9 1970): 14.

5522. _________. "Riley: Creating despite the Establishment." Melody Maker (August 14 1971): 2.

5523. _________. "Riley, Oxley and the new music." Melody Maker (November 29 1969): 10.

5524. Witherden, Barry. "Conversation Pieces." Jazz Monthly (April 1969): 8-10.

RIVERS, SAM (1923-) - Tenor/Soprano Sax/Flute/Piano

See also # 604, 677-689, 3770

5525. Jost, Ekkehard. "Sam Rivers." In Jazzmusiker: Materialen zur Soziologie der Afro-Amerikanischen Musik. Frankfurt am Main: Ullstein, 1982, pp. 77-85.

5526. Ullman, Michael. "Sam Rivers." In Jazz Lives. Washington, D.C.: New Republic Books, 1980, pp. 131-140.

5527. Vuijsje, Bert. De Nieuwe Jazz. Baarn: Bosch & Keuning, 1978, pp. 178-190. [Interview]

Biographical Dictionaries

5528. Carles, Philippe, and Jean-Louis Comolli. Free Jazz, Black Power. 2nd ed. Paris: Editions Galilee, 1979, p. 434.

5529. Carr, Ian. "Rivers, Sam." In Jazz: The Essential Companion. New York: Prentice Hall Press, 1988.

5530. Case, Brian, and Stan Britt. The Harmony Illustrated Encyclopedia of Jazz. 3rd ed. New York: Harmony Books, 1987.

5531. Claghorn, Charles Eugene. Biographical Dictionary of Jazz. Englewood Cliffs, NJ: Prentice-Hall, 1982.

5532. Dictionnaire du Jazz, eds. Philippe Carles, et al. Paris: Laffont, 1988.

5533. Dobbins, Bill. "Rivers, Sam." In The New Grove Dictionary of American Music. London: Macmillan Press, 1986.

5534. _________. "Rivers, Sam." In The New Grove Dictionary of Jazz. London: Macmillan Press, 1988.

5535. Feather, Leonard. The Encyclopedia of Jazz in the Sixties. New York: Horizon Press, 1966.

5536. _________, and Ira Gitler. The Encyclopedia of Jazz in the Seventies. New York: Horizon Press, 1976.

5537. Jacobi, Hugh William. Contemporary American Composers: based at American Colleges and universities. Paradise, CA: Paradise Arts Publisher, 1975.

5538. McRae, Barry. "Sam Rivers." In The Jazz Handbook. Harlow, Essex, Eng.: Longman, 1987, pp. 246-247.

5539. The Penguin Encyclopedia of Popular Music, ed. Donald Clarke. New York: Viking, 1989.

5540. Southern, Eileen. Biographical Dictionary of Afro-American and African Musicians. Westport, CT: Greenwood Press, 1982.

5541. Wilmer, Valerie. As Serious As Your Life. Westport, CT: Lawrence Hill & Co., 1981, p. 278.

Articles

5542. Bazurro, Alberto. "La Parabola Artistica di Sam Rivers." Musica Jazz, Vol. 38, No. 6 (June 1982): 18-25. [Profile]

5543. Brower, W. A. "Sam Rivers: Warlord of the Lofts." down beat (November 16 1978): 21-22, 39, 47-49.

5544. Cunniff, Joe. "Riffs: Sam Rivers." down beat (March 1990): 15. [Profile]

5545. Fayenz, Franco. "Sam Rivers: Il Volto e la Maschera." Discoteca-Alta Fedelta (Milano) (October 1977): 26-31. [Interview]

5546. Gans, Charles J. "Sam Rivers: A Determined Survivor." Jazz Forum, No. 54 (1978): 29-32, 42.

5547. Johnson, David. "Play it Again, Sam!" Jazz Journal International [London] (December 1978): 6-8. [Profile]

5548. Lyons, Len. "Sam Rivers: Avant-Garde Jazz Pianist and Multi-Instrumentalist." Contemporary Keyboard (June 1978): 16, 36-38.

5549. Mackinnon, Angus. "That Ol' Sam Rivers." New Musical Express (March 14 1981): 26-27, 57. [Interview]

5550. Marmande, Francis and Isabelle. "Sam Rivers." Jazz Magazine, No. 255 (June 1977): 14-15. [Interview]

5551. Minor, William. "Sam Rivers: As Time Goes By." Coda, No. 224 (February/March 1989): 12-13.

5552. Ogan, Bernd. "Sam Rivers." Jazz Podium (May 1982): 35-36.

5553. Palmer, Bob. "Sam Rivers: An Artist on an Empty Stage." down beat (February 13 1975): 12-13, 33.

5554. "Rivers' Music Flows: He's A One-Man Band." Soul, No. 8 (January 21 1974): 11.

5555. Rouy, Gerard. "Sam Rivers: La Recherche de la Perfection." Jazz Magazine, No. 213 (July 1973): 8-11.

5556. Turner, Marcus. "Sam Rivers." Coda, No. 185 (August 1982): 4-6.

5557. Ullman, Michael. "Sam Rivers." New Republic (December 2 1978): 25+.

5558. Wilmer, Val. "Raising the Roof." Time Out [London] (January 9-15 1981).

Concert Reviews

5559. Davis, Peter G. "Solomon and Sheba Provide Inspiration for Harlem Opera." New York Times (June 25 1973).

5560. Hazziezah. "Sam Rivers: Making a Powerful Musical Statement." New York Amsterdam News (February 5 1977): B-2.

5561. Reitz, Rosetta. "Riffs." Village Voice (May 3 1973): 51-52.

5562. ________. "Riffs." Village Voice (June 14 1973): 58, 60. Review of Rivers' opera "Solomon and Sheba."

Discographies

5563. Luzzi, Mario. "Discografia Completa di Sam Rivers." Musica Jazz (Milano), Vol. 38, No. 6 (June 1982): 60-61.

ROACH, MAX (1925-) - Drums

See also # 532

Works in English

5564. Crawford, Marc. "The Drummer Most Likely to Succeed." down beat (March 30 1961): 20-21.

5565. Griffith, Pat. "The Evolution of Max Roach." down beat (March 16 1972): 16-17.

5566. Kuhl, Chris. "Max Roach: interview." Cadence, Vol. 8, No. 7 (July 1982): 5-7.

5567. "No 'Freedom Now' in South Africa." down beat (June 21 1962): 11. Report on the banning of the Freedom Now Suite in South Africa.

5568. "Racial Prejudice in Jazz: A Panel Discussion." down beat (March 15 1962): 20-26; (March 29 1962): 22-25. The first part of this article includes a reprint of Ira Gitler's Nov. 9 1961 db review of Abbey Lincoln's "Straight Ahead" lp which acted as the spark for the discussion. Panel participants include Abbey Lincoln, Max Roach, Lalo Schifrin, Don Ellis, Ira Gitler, Don De Michael, Nat Hentoff and Bill Coss.

5569. Runcie, John. "Max Roach: militant black artist." Jazz Journal International (May 1980): 20-21.

5570. Rusch, Bob. "Max Roach: interview." Cadence, Vol. 5, No. 6 (June 1979): 3-8, 24.

5571. Williams, Richard. "Black People Have Always Been Militant." Melody Maker (July 3 1971): 12.

Works in French and Italian

5572. Clouzet, J., and Jean Wagner. "30 Questions a Max." Jazz Magazine, No. 114 (January 1965): 18-23. [Interview]

5573. Lattes, P. "Le Manifeste; an interview de Max." Jazz Hot, No. 195 (February 1964): 24-26.

5574. "Max Roach--musique e(s)t politique." Jazz Magazine, No. 238 (November 1975): 20-21. [Interview]

5575. "My Taylor is Roach." Jazz Magazine, No. 332 (September-October 1984): 36-39. [Interview]

5576. Pellicciotti, Giacomo. "Braxton et Roach: ensemble a Alassio." Jazz Magazine, No. 270 (November-December 1978): 32-35.

5577. Polillo, Arrigo. "Max + Abbey = Protesta." Musica Jazz (February 1964): 15-17.

5578. Vander, M., and G. Rovere. "Max et Abbey." Jazz Hot, No. 232 (June 1967): 18-23. [Interview]

5579. Wagner, Jean. "Le souffle de la violence." Jazz Magazine, No. 104 (March 1964): 18-23.

Concert Reviews

5580. Giddins, Gary. "Riffs: Roach and Taylor Charge in Unison." Village Voice (December 31 1979): 81. Review of Roach/Cecil Taylor duo concert.

5581. Palmer, Robert. "The Taylor-Roach Duo Concert." New York Times (December 17 1979).

5582. Pareles, Jon. "A Pair of Opposites in a Reunion." New York Times (December 13 1989): C25. Review of Roach/Cecil Taylor reunion concert.

Record Reviews

5583. Cooke, Jack. "We Insist! The Max Roach Group Today and The Freedom New Suite." Jazz Monthly (July 1962): 3-8.

5584. DeGange, Stephen. "Freedom Now: The That Max Roach Built." Freedomways, Vol. 21, No. 1 (1981): 41-45.

5585. DeMichael, Don. "In Review: We Insist! Freedom Now Suite." down beat (March 30 1961): 30.

5586. Lock, Graham. "Great Recordings: Max Roach - We Insist! Freedom Now Suite." Wire, No. 12 (February 1985): 45.

5587. Tepperman, Barry. "Record Reviews: We Insist!--Freedom Now Suite." Coda, No. 146 (April 1976): 15-16.

5588. Tronchot, J. "La 'Freedom Now Suite' du Concert Max Roach: un message lourd et riche." Jazz Hot, No. 195 (February 1964): 7-8.

5589. Welding, Pete. "Record Reviews: Percussion Bitter Sweet." down beat (January 4 1962): 30. Dismissed as "another of the tedious essays in race-consciousness" produced by Max Roach.

5590. White, Ted. "Record Reviews: We Insist!" Metronome (May 1961): 34-35.

ROBERTS, HANK - Cello

5591. Endress, Gudrun. "Hank Roberts." Jazz Podium (November 1988): 10-15. [Interview]

5592. Lake, Steve. "Hank Roberts." Wire, No. 52 (June 1988): 18-19.

5593. Rosenbaum, Joshua. "Improvisations: Hank Roberts." Strings, Vol. V, No. 2 (Sept/Oct 1990): 36, 38, 40, 42. [Interview]

5594. Santoro, Gene. "Music: Tim Berne, Bill Frisell, Hank Roberts." The Nation (April 2 1988): 474-476. Discussion of recent recordings by Roberts, Berne and Frisell.

ROBINSON, ORPHY (1960-) (Great Britain) - Vibraphone

See also # 3985-3986

5595. Watson, Ben. "Orphic Rites." The Wire, No. 63 (May 1989): 24-27. Interview with the vibraphonist of the British ensemble the Jazz Warriors.

ROBINSON, PERRY (1938-) - Clarinet

5596. Carles, Philippe, and Jean-Louis Comolli. Free Jazz, Black Power. 2nd ed. Paris: Editions Galilee, 1979, pp. 434-435.

5597. Carr, Ian. "Robinson, Perry." In Jazz: The Essential Companion. New York: Prentice Hall Press, 1988.

5598. Dictionnaire du Jazz, eds. Philippe Carles, et al. Paris: Laffont, 1988.

5599. Feather, Leonard, and Ira Gitler. The Encyclopedia of Jazz in the Seventies. New York: Horizon Press, 1976.

5600. Wild, David. "Robinson, Perry." In The New Grove Dictionary of Jazz. London: Macmillan Press, 1988.

Articles

5601. Endress, Gudrun. "Der Magier der Klarinette: Perry Robinson." Jazz Podium (July 1972): 228-230.

5602. Palmer, Bob. "Perry Robinson: clarinet energy." down beat (October 12 1972): 16. [Interview]

5603. "Perry Robinson: The Trailblazing Jazz Clarinetist." OP, Issue R (July/August 1983): 32-33.

ROLLINS, SONNY [Theodore Walter] (1929-) - Tenor Sax

See also # 2073, 2425, 2484, 2554

5604. "Free Jazz a l'Olympia avec Sonny Rollins." Jazz Hot, No. 184 (February 1963): 6-7.

5605. Hadlock, Dick. "La 'Freedom Suite' de Sonny Rollins." Jazz Hot, No. 26 (July-August 1960): 24-26.

5606. ________. "Sonny Rollins' Freedom Suite." The Jazz Review, Vol. 2, No. 4 (May 1959): 10-11.

ROMANO, ALDO (1941-) (Italy) - Drums

5607. Carles, Philippe, and Jean-Louis Comolli. Free Jazz, Black Power. 2nd ed. Paris: Editions Galilee, 1979, p. 435.

5608. Carr, Ian. "Romano, Aldo." In Jazz: The Essential Companion. New York: Prentice Hall Press, 1988.

5609. Clergeat, Andre. "Romano, Aldo." In The New Grove Dictionary of Jazz. London: Macmillan Press, 1988.

5610. Dictionnaire du Jazz, eds. Philippe Carles, et al. Paris: Laffont, 1988.

Articles

5611. Byrczek, Jan. "Eurojazz personalities." Jazz Forum, No. 15 (1972): 116-117.

5612. Carles, Philippe. "Pieges pour Aldo." Jazz Magazine, No. 175 (February 1970): 32+.

5613. ________, and Y. Delubac. "Aldo Romano: une valeur en hausse." Jazz Magazine, No. 155 (June 1968): 16+.

5614. "Jenny Clark Romano: sanctification interdite." Jazz Magazine, No. 262 (February 1978): 27. [Interview]

5615. "7 [sept] noms; voici les nouveau-nes du jazz francais!: Aldo Romano." Jazz Magazine, No. 117 (April 1965): 33-34.

5616. Soutif, Daniel. "Aldo Romano." Jazz Magazine, No. 286 (May 1980): 18-19.

5617. ________. "Une Musique pour la Rue: Aldo Romano." Jazz Magazine, No. 287 (June 1980): 40+. [Interview]

5618. "Total Issue: vers quoi?" Jazz Magazine, No. 192 (September 1971): 12+.

ROSEWOMAN, MICHELE (1953-) - Piano

5619. Davis, Francis. "Outchicks." In Outcats: Jazz Composers, Instrumentalists, and Singers. New York: Oxford University Press, 1990, pp. 122-128. Discussion of Rosewoman's "Quintessence" lp.

5620. Dictionnaire du Jazz, eds. Philippe Carles, et al. Paris: Laffont, 1988.

Articles

5621. Blum, Joe. "Michele Rosewoman: Cross-Cultural Consciousness." Jazz Times (September 1990): 7, 26. [Interview]

5622. Endress, Gudrun. "Michele Rosewoman, New Yor-uba." Jazz Podium (July 1985): 7-9. [Interview]

5623. Stein, Stephanie. "Riffs: Michele Rosewoman." down beat (September 1989): 15.

ROSS, BRANDON - Guitar

5624. McElfresh, Suzanne. "Brandon Ross: Jazz Warrior." Ear (April 1990): 32-37.

ROVA SAXOPHONE QUARTET

5625. Dictionnaire du Jazz, eds. Philippe Carles, et al. Paris: Laffont, 1988.

5626. Shere, Charles. "Rova Saxophone Quartet." In The New Grove Dictionary of American Music. London: Macmillan Press, 1986.

Articles

5627. Besecker, Bill. "Jazz Red Hot & Cool." Coda, No. 196 (June 1984): 5-9. Interview with Rova member Larry Ochs re: Rova's tour of Russia and Eastern Europe.

5628. Charlton, Hannah. "There's Art in the Sax." Melody Maker (January 31 1981): 12. [Interview]

5629. Emerson, Bo. "Rova Saxophone Quartet Likes Being in 'Dangerous Territory'." Atlanta Constitution (September 14 1989): B-3. [Profile]

5630. Gaudynski, Thomas. "Rova Sax Quartet Interview." OP (Los Angeles, CA), issue R (July-August 1983): 48-51.

5631. Goldberg, Michael. "ROVA Saxophone Quartet Wants You to Wake Up." down beat (January 1981): 23-25.

5632. Kahn, Alexander. "Rova." Jazzthetik, Vol. 4, No. 5 (May 1990): 12-17. Interview with Larry Ochs.

5633. Kleinert, G. "Disziplin der Improvisation: Anthony Braxton und Rova." Jazz Podium (March 1989): 12-15. [Interview]

5634. Lawrence, Anne R. "Rova is very saxy." Ear, Vol. 12, No. 2 (April 1987): 12.

5635. Means, Loren. "The Rova Saxophone Quartet." Coda, No. 167 (June 1979): 12-13. [Profile]

5636. Rodefer, Stephen. "News: Saxophone Diplomacy." down beat (November 1983): 11. Note on Rova's tour of Russia and Eastern Europe.

5637. Romero, Enrico, and Lorenzo Pallini. "Rova Interview." Cadence, Vol. 8, No. 2 (February 1982): 5-7, 20.

5638. "The Rova Saxophone Quartet." Coda, No. 167 (June 1979): 12-13. [Profile]

RUDD, ROSWELL (1935-) - Trombone

See also # 695, 697, 706, 5058-5064

5639. Carles, Philippe, and Jean-Louis Comolli. Free Jazz, Black Power. 2nd ed. Paris: Editions Galilee, 1979, p. 435.

5640. Carr, Ian. "Rudd, Roswell." In Jazz: The Essential Companion. New York: Prentice Hall Press, 1988.

5641. Case, Brian, and Stan Britt. The Harmony Illustrated Encyclopedia of Jazz. 3rd ed. New York: Harmony Books, 1987.

5642. Claghorn, Charles Eugene. Biographical Dictionary of Jazz. Englewood Cliffs, NJ: Prentice-Hall, 1982.

5643. Dictionnaire du Jazz, eds. Philippe Carles, et al. Paris: Laffont, 1988.

5644. Feather, Leonard. The Encyclopedia of Jazz in the Sixties. New York: Horizon Press, 1966.

5645. _________, and Ira Gitler. The Encyclopedia of Jazz in the Seventies. New York: Horizon Press, 1976.

5646. Jeske, Lee. "Rudd, Roswell." In The New Grove Dictionary of American Music. London: Macmillan Press, 1986.

5647. _________. "Rudd, Roswell." In The New Grove Dictionary of Jazz. London: Macmillan Press, 1988.

5648. McRae, Barry. "Roswell Rudd." In The Jazz Handbook. Harlow, Essex, Eng.: Longman, 1987, pp. 209-210.

5649. The Penguin Encyclopedia of Popular Music, ed. Donald Clarke. New York: Viking, 1989.

5650. Reclams Jazzfuhrer. 2nd, rev. ed. Stuttgart: Reclam, 1977.

5651. Wilmer, Valerie. As Serious As Your Life. Westport, CT: Lawrence Hill & Co., 1981, p. 278.

Articles

5652. Constant, Denis. "Roswell le Rude." Jazz Magazine, No. 179 (June 1970): 36-9+.

5653. Danson, Peter. "Roswell Rudd." Coda, No. 183 (April 1982): 4-9.

5654. Heckman, Don. "Roswell Rudd." down beat (January 30 1964): 14-15. [Profile]

5655. McRae, Barry. "Roswell Rudd - All the Way from Dixie." Jazz Journal (May 1975): 20-22.

5656. Primack, Bret. "Roswell Rudd: Transmission from the Soul." down beat (October 5 1978): 24+.

5657. "Rudd en Quelques Mots." Jazz Magazine, No. 207 (January 1973): 4.

5658. Rudd, Roswell. "Some Quartertones Around the Drone - the Universality of the Blues." down beat (January 25 1968): 22+.

5659. Tepperman, Barry. "Rudd, Moncur and Some Other Stuff." Coda (July/August 1971): 8-11.

5660. Wilmer, Valerie. "Trad Trombone in Outer Space." Melody Maker (November 11 1967): 8.

5661. Wilson, John S. "Jazz Envelops 'Village' Church." New York Times (March 2 1968). [Concert review]

RUEGG, MATHIAS (1952-) (Switzerland) - Bandleader

See also # 6706-6715

5662. Coudert, Francoise Marie. "Mathias Ruegg: entre blues et Brahms." Jazz Magazine, No. 381 (April 1989): 38-39. [Interview]

5663. The Penguin Encyclopedia of Popular Music, ed. Donald Clarke. New York: Viking, 1989.

5664. Priestley, Brian. "Ruegg, Mathias." In Jazz: The Essential Companion. New York: Prentice Hall Press, 1988.

RUSSELL, JOHN (Great Britain) - Guitar

See also # 1229

5665. Ansell, Kenneth. "Russell/Turner/Kondo." Jazz Journal International (August 1980): 24-25. [Interview]

5666. Sinker, Mark. "John Russell: Hammer Very Quietly." Wire, No. 33 (November 1986): 12.

RUTHERFORD, PAUL (1940-) (Great Britain) - Trombone

See also # 706

5667. Noglik, Bert. "Paul Rutherford." In Jazzwerkstatt International. Berlin: Verlag Neue Musik, 1981, pp. 346-361. [Interview]

Biographical Dictionaries

5668. Adams, Simon. "Rutherford, Paul." In The New Grove Dictionary of Jazz. London: Macmillan Press, 1988.

5669. Carles, Philippe, and Jean-Louis Comolli. Free Jazz, Black Power. 2nd ed. Paris: Editions Galilee, 1979, p. 435.

5670. Carr, Ian. "Rutherford, Paul." In Jazz: The Essential Companion. New York: Prentice Hall Press, 1988.

5671. Dictionnaire du Jazz, eds. Philippe Carles, et al. Paris: Laffont, 1988.

5672. Jazz Now: the Jazz Centre Society Guide, ed. Roger Cotterrell. London: Quartet Books, 1976, p. 165.

5673. McRae, Barry. "Paul Rutherford." In The Jazz Handbook. Harlow, Essex, Eng.: Longman, 1987, pp. 210-211.

Articles

5674. Ansell, Kenneth. "Paul Rutherford." Impetus (London), No. 6 (1977): 264-266. [Interview]

5675. Bailey, Derek. "Soundcheck: Derek Bailey Discusses the Improvising of Paul Rutherford." The Wire, No. 36 (1987).

5676. Brown, Ron. "Paul Rutherford." Jazz Journal (March 1973): 4-6. [Interview]

5677. Carles, Philippe. "Ici Londres: Paul Rutherford." Jazz Magazine, No. 273 (March 1979): 30-31, 68, 70. [Interview]

5678. "Caught in the Act." Melody Maker (July 12 1975): 44. [Concert review]

5679. Davidson, Martin. "Blows against the empire." Melody Maker (March 24 1973): 46.

5680. "Heroes." Melody Maker (October 4 1986): 28. Discussion of the various influences on Rutherford's style.

5681. Ilic, Dave. "Paul Rutherford." The Wire, No. 3 (Spring 1983): 6-7.

5682. Lake, Steve. "Red Brassman." Melody Maker (April 30 1977): 40+. [Interview]

5683. Lee, David. "The Gentle Harm of the Bourgeoisie: Paul Rutherford in Canada." Coda, No. 215 (August/September 1987): 7-9. [Interview]

5684. "Paul Rutherford." Journal of the International Trombone Association, Vol. 13, No. 2 (1985): 17. Biographical sketch.

5685. Williams, Richard. "Iskra--putting space into the new music." Melody Maker (November 21 1970): 28.

5686. ________. "This should be the year for..." Melody Maker (January 3 1970): 13.

5687. ________. "Trombone Pioneer." Melody Maker (January 17 1970): 8.

SAMS, GEORGE (1948-) - Trumpet

See also # 6697-6699

5688. Coda, No. 163 (October 1978): 27-28. Biographical sketch.

5689. Cohen, Elaine. "George Sams..." Coda, No. 164/5 (February 1979): 57.

SANDERS, PHAROAH [Farrell] (1940-) - Tenor Saxophone

See also # 40, 286, 474, 695, 699

5690. "Pharoah Sanders." In The Black Giants, eds. Pauline Rivelli and Robert Levin. New York: The World Publishing Co., 1970, pp. 47-50. [Interview]

5691. Roggeman, Willy. "Pharoah Sanders." In Free en Andere Jazz-Essays. The Hague: Van Ditmar, 1969, pp. 109-112. [Dutch text]

5692. Vuijsje, Bert. De Nieuwe Jazz. Baarn: Bosch & Keuning, 1978, pp. 114-119. [Interview]

5693. Williams, Martin. "Pharoah's Tale." In Jazz Masters in Transition, 1957-1969. New York: Macmillan, 1970.

Biographical Dictionaries

5694. Carles, Philippe, and Jean-Louis Comolli. Free Jazz, Black Power. 2nd ed. Paris: Editions Galilee, 1979, p. 436.

5695. Carr, Ian. "Sanders, Pharoah." In Jazz: The Essential Companion. New York: Prentice Hall Press, 1988.

5696. Case, Brian, and Stan Britt. The Harmony Illustrated Encyclopedia of Jazz. 3rd ed. New York: Harmony Books, 1987.

5697. Claghorn, Charles Eugene. Biographical Dictionary of Jazz. Englewood Cliffs, NJ: Prentice-Hall, 1982.

5698. Dictionnaire du Jazz, eds. Philippe Carles, et al. Paris: Laffont, 1988.

5699. Feather, Leonard. The Encyclopedia of Jazz in the Sixties. New York: Horizon Press, 1966.

5700. _________, and Ira Gitler. The Encyclopedia of Jazz in the Seventies. New York: Horizon Press, 1976.

5701. Kernfeld, Barry. "Sanders, Pharoah." In The New Grove Dictionary of American Music. London: Macmillan Press, 1986.

5702. _________. "Sanders, Farrell." In The New Grove Dictionary of Jazz. London: Macmillan Press, 1988.

5703. McRae, Barry. "Pharoah Sanders." In The Jazz Handbook. Harlow, Essex, Eng.: Longman, 1987, pp. 211-212.

5704. The Penguin Encyclopedia of Popular Music, ed. Donald Clarke. New York: Viking, 1989.

5705. Reclams Jazzfuhrer. 2nd, rev. ed. Stuttgart: Reclam, 1977.

5706. Southern, Eileen. Biographical Dictionary of Afro-American and African Musicians. Westport, CT: Greenwood Press, 1982.

5707. Wilmer, Valerie. As Serious As Your Life. Westport, CT: Lawrence Hill & Co., 1981, pp. 278-279.

Articles

5708. Blum, Joe. "Pharaoh Sanders: a free-jazz flower child blooms in a new age." Musician, No. 50 (December 1982): 36, 38, 40, 42, 44-45, 113.

5709. Case, Brian. "Pharoah Sanders has been here and gone." New Musical Express (June 22 1974): 36-37. [Interview]

5710. Dallas, Karl. "Jazz: Pharoah Sanders." Melody Maker (June 28 1980): 26. [Interview]

5711. Gerber, Alain. "Les Terres de Pharoah." Jazz Magazine, No. 161 (December 1968): 46+.

5712. Giddins, Gary. "Pharoah Sanders goes secular." Village Voice (April 11 1977): 53.

5713. Hentoff, Nat. "Pharoah Sanders." BMI (June 1971): 7.

5714. Kemper, Peter. "Zwischen Mythos und Logos: Pharoah Sanders." Jazz Podium (December 1979): 6-12.

5715. Lena, A., and Daniel Berger. "Pharoah Sanders." Jazz Hot, No. 246 (January 1969): 20-23.

5716. May, Chris. "In the Land of Pharoah." Black Music and Jazz Review, Vol. 1, No. 2 (May 1978): 14-15.

5717. Palmer, Bob. "Pharoah Sanders." Rolling Stone (April 30 1970): 44, 46.

5718. "Pharoah Sanders." Jazz & Pop (February 1970): 30-32. [Interview] [Reprinted in # 5690]

5719. Randolph, S. "A good look at Pharoah Sanders." Jazz Monthly (March 1970): 2-6.

5720. Rosenthal, David. "New Jazz from New York." Jazz Journal (July 1965): 10-12. Discussion of Sanders, Archie Shepp and John Tchicai.

5721. Setterberg, Fred. "Pharoah Sanders - Two Decades in Pursuit of the Musical Truth." Coda, No. 228 (October/ November 1989): 8-10. [Interview] [Reprinted from Image Magazine]

5722. Tanter, L. "The Evolution of Pharoah Sanders." Soul (July 23 1973): 6.

5723. Tepperman, Barry. "Pharoah Sanders...Some Casual Impressions." Pieces of Jazz (1970): 22-26, 60. Includes a lengthy discography.

5724. Van der Mei, Elizabeth. "Les Confessions de Pharoah." Jazz Hot, No. 239 (March 1968): 17-24.

5725. ________. "Far Out Pharoah." Jazz Magazine, No. 152 (March 1968): 22+. [Interview]

5726. ________. "Pharoah Sanders: A Philosophical Conversation." Coda, Vol. 8, No. 2 (June/July 1967): 2-6.

5727. Welch, Jane. "Pharoah Sanders: 'I Play for the Creator'." down beat (May 13 1971): 15+.

5728. Williams, Martin. "Pharoah's Tale." down beat (May 16 1968): 21-22.

5729. Wilmer, Val. "Rights and Rituals." Time Out [London] (June 27-July 3 1980).

SARBIB, SAHEB - Bass

5730. Devoghelaere, Mon. "Saheb Sarbib: halfweg tussen Mingus - Sun Ra." Swingtime (Belgium), No. 19 (maart 1977): 7-8. [Interview]

5731. Rusch, Bob. "Saheb Sarbib: interview." Cadence, Vol. 7, No. 10 (December 1981): 8-10, 44.

5732. "Saheb Sarbib." Jazz Hot, No. 321 (November 1975): 22.

SCHLIPPENBACH, ALEXANDER VON (1938-) (W. Germany) - Piano

See also # 323, 343, 511, 3341

5733. Noglik, Bert. "Alex von Schlippenbach." In Jazzwerkstatt International. Berlin: Verlag Neue Musik, 1981, pp. 97-127. [Interview]

Biographical Dictionaries

5734. Carles, Philippe, and Jean-Louis Comolli. Free Jazz, Black Power. 2nd ed. Paris: Editions Galilee, 1979, pp. 453-454.

5735. Carr, Ian. "Von Schlippenbach, Alexander." In Jazz: The Essential Companion. New York: Prentice Hall Press, 1988.

5736. Claghorn, Charles Eugene. "Von Schlippenbach, Alexander." In Biographical Dictionary of Jazz. Englewood Cliffs, NJ: Prentice-Hall, 1982.

5737. Dictionnaire du Jazz, eds. Philippe Carles, et al. Paris: Laffont, 1988.

5738. Feather, Leonard, and Ira Gitler. "Von Schlippenbach, Alexander." In The Encyclopedia of Jazz in the Seventies. New York: Horizon Press, 1976.

5739. Noglik, Bert. "Schlippenbach, Alexander von." In The New Grove Dictionary of Jazz. London: Macmillan Press, 1988.

Articles

5740. "Alex Schlippenbach." Jazz Magazine, No. 234 (July 1975): 15-17.

5741. Cook, Richard. "Alex von Schlippenbach: The Indispensable Focus." Wire, No. 30 (August 1986): 10-11, 48.

5742. Lake, Steve. "Centre of the Globe." Melody Maker (February 2 1974): 53. [Interview]

5743. Schlippenbach, Alex von. "Free Jazz." Neue Zeitschrift fur Musik (May/June 1979): 244-249.

5744. Storb, Ilse. "Fragen an Alexander von Schlippenbach." Jazz Podium (October 1978): 4-7. [Interview]

5745. "Swinging News: West Berlin; Schlippenbach's new effort." Jazz Forum, No. 48 (1977): 12.

5746. Thiem, Michael. "Alexander von Schlippenbach." Jazz Forum, No. 77 (1982): 44-47. [Interview]

5747. Williams, Richard. "Re-thinking big band music." Melody Maker (June 13 1970): 16.

SCHOENENBERG, DETLEF (1944-) (W. Germany) - Drums

5748. Carles, Philippe, and Jean-Louis Comolli. Free Jazz, Black Power. 2nd ed. Paris: Editions Galilee, 1979, p. 436.

5749. Noglik, Bert. "Detlef Schoenenberg." In Jazzwerkstatt International. Berlin: Verlag Neue Musik, 1981, pp. 150-172. [Interview]

Articles

5750. Christmann, Gunter, and Detlef Schoenenberg. "Nur alte Ahnungen von einer freien Musik." Neue Musikzeitung, Vol. 27, No. 2 (1978): 12.

5751. Froese, D. H. "Das Free Jazz Duo Schoenenberg-Christmann: We Play." Jazz Podium (May 1973): 22-23.

5752. Panke, Werner. "Christmann-Schoenenberg duo." Coda, No. 154 (March-April 1977): 10-11.

5753. ________. "Gunter Christman and Detlef Schonenberg: plunged into musical risks." Jazz Forum, No. 48 (1977): 43-45. [Profile]

5754. Schipper, E. "Wie heisst das Stueck? Christmann-Schoenenberg Duo." Jazz Podium (May 1977): 12-14.

SCHOOF, MANFRED (1936-) (W. Germany) - Trumpet

5755. Carles, Philippe, and Jean-Louis Comolli. Free Jazz, Black Power. 2nd ed. Paris: Editions Galilee, 1979, p. 436.

5756. Carr, Ian. "Schoof, Manfred." In Jazz: The Essential Companion. New York: Prentice Hall Press, 1988.

5757. Claghorn, Charles Eugene. Biographical Dictionary of Jazz. Englewood Cliffs, NJ: Prentice-Hall, 1982.

5758. Dictionnaire du Jazz, eds. Philippe Carles, et al. Paris: Laffont, 1988.

5759. Feather, Leonard, and Ira Gitler. The Encyclopedia of Jazz in the Seventies. New York: Horizon Press, 1976.

5760. Iannapollo, Robert J. "Schoof, Manfred." In The New Grove Dictionary of Jazz. London: Macmillan Press, 1988.

5761. Reclams Jazzfuhrer. 2nd, rev. ed. Stuttgart: Reclam, 1977.

Articles

5762. Endress, Gudrun. "Free Jazz, aber auch Klangliches, Farbiges, Schoenes im althergebrachten Sinn; Manfred Schoof Orchester." Jazz Podium (January 1984): 6-9. [Interview]

5763. Kumpf, Hans. "Der Komponist Manfred Schoof--Plattendokumente aus den Jahren 1965-1969." Jazz Podium (January 1973): 21.

5764. ________. "Der Komponist Manfred Schoof--Plattendokumente aus den Jahren 1970-1972." Jazz Podium (April 1973): 28-29.

5765. "On the Scene: G.D.R.--Schoof on tour (Orchestra)." Jazz Forum, No. 86 (1984): 16-17.

5766. Reichelt, Rolf. "Manfred Schoof: beyond free jazz." Jazz Forum, No. 61 (1979): 40-43. [Interview]

5767. Storb, Ilse. "Fragen an Manfred Schoof." Jazz Podium (July 1978): 11-13.

5768. Williams, Richard. "Schoof: apostle of the new music." Melody Maker (March 14 1970): 12.

SCHWEIZER, IRENE (1941-) (Switzerland) - Piano

See also # 3131-3133

5769. Carles, Philippe, and Jean-Louis Comolli. Free Jazz, Black Power. 2nd ed. Paris: Editions Galilee, 1979, p. 436.

5770. Dictionnaire du Jazz, eds. Philippe Carles, et al. Paris: Laffont, 1988.

5771. Noglik, Bert. "Irene Schweizer." In Jazzwerkstatt International. Berlin: Verlag Neue Musik, 1981, pp. 298-314. [Interview]

5772. ________. "Schweizer, Irene." In The New Grove Dictionary of Jazz. London: Macmillan Press, 1988.

Articles

5773. Caflisch, E. "Jobs zum Ueberleben: Irene Schweizer." Jazz Podium (October 1976): 13-15.

5774. Charlton, Hannah. "Collective Impressions." Melody Maker (September 13 1980): 30. [Interview]

5775. Chenard, Marc. "Irene Schweizer." Coda, No. 222 (October/November 1988): 11-13. [Interview]

5776. Geiger, Annette. "Irene Schweizer in New York rund ums Sound-Unity-Festival." Jazz (Basel), Nr. 4 (1984). [Interview]

5777. Lock, Graham. "Irene Schweizer: An Ear for Freedom." The Wire, No. 11 (January 1985): 12-13.

5778. Noglik, Bert. "Irene Schweizer: uncompromising continuity." Jazz Forum, No. 65 (1980): 34-36. [Interview]

5779. Ogilvie, Bertrand. "Le Bal d'Irene." Jazz Magazine, No. 371 (May 1988): 27-28. [Interview]

5780. Rouy, Gerard. "Irene Schweizer." Jazz Magazine, No. 235 (August 1975): 16-17. [Interview]

5781. Rusch, Bob. "Irene Schweizer Interview." Cadence (January 1991): 5-12, 23, 27.

5782. Solothurnmann, Jurg. "Irene Schweizer." Jazz Forum, No. 17 (June 1972): 61-64.

Discographies

5783. Cerutti, Gustave. "Discographie: Irene Schweizer." Jazz 360o, No. 33 (December 1980): 6-9.

SHARROCK, LINDA (1939-) - Vocals

See also # 694

5784. Carles, Philippe, and Jean-Louis Comolli. Free Jazz, Black Power. 2nd ed. Paris: Editions Galilee, 1979, p. 437.

5785. Claghorn, Charles Eugene. Biographical Dictionary of Jazz. Englewood Cliffs, NJ: Prentice-Hall, 1982.

5786. Feather, Leonard, and Ira Gitler. The Encyclopedia of Jazz in the Seventies. New York: Horizon Press, 1976.

5787. Wilmer, Valerie. As Serious As Your Life. Westport, CT: Lawrence Hill & Co., 1981, p. 279.

SHARROCK, SONNY [Warren Harding] (1940-) - Guitar

See also # 702, 4380

5788. Vuijsje, Bert. De Nieuwe Jazz. Baarn: Bosch & Keuning, 1978, pp. 134-145. [Interview]

Biographical Dictionaries

5789. Carles, Philippe, and Jean-Louis Comolli. Free Jazz, Black Power. 2nd ed. Paris: Editions Galilee, 1979, p. 436.

5790. Carr, Ian. "Sharrock, Sonny." In Jazz: The Essential Companion. New York: Prentice Hall Press, 1988.

5791. Claghorn, Charles Eugene. Biographical Dictionary of Jazz. Englewood Cliffs, NJ: Prentice-Hall, 1982.

5792. Dictionnaire du Jazz, eds. Philippe Carles, et al. Paris: Laffont, 1988.

5793. Feather, Leonard, and Ira Gitler. The Encyclopedia of Jazz in the Seventies. New York: Horizon Press, 1976.

5794. Iannapollo, Robert J. "Sharrock, Sonny." In The New Grove Dictionary of Jazz. London: Macmillan Press, 1988.

5795. McRae, Barry. "Sonny Sharrock." In The Jazz Handbook. Harlow, Essex, Eng.: Longman, 1987, pp. 248-249.

5796. Reclams Jazzfuhrer. 2nd, rev. ed. Stuttgart: Reclam, 1977.

5797. Wilmer, Valerie. As Serious As Your Life. Westport, CT: Lawrence Hill & Co., 1981, p. 279.

Articles

5798. Bisceglia, J., and Jean-Louis Ginibre. "Sharrock--La dent dure et les dents longues." Jazz Magazine, No. 180 (July-August 1970): 34+. [Interview]

5799. Bourne, Mike. "Sonny Sharrock's Story." down beat (June 11 1970): 16-18, 25. [Interview]

5800. Dery, Mark, and Henry Kaiser. "Sonny Sharrock: the leading American free-jazz guitar exponent." Guitar Player (February 1990): 70+. [Interview]

5801. Drozdowski, Ted. "Sonny Sharrock: learning to win friends and alienate people with the father of the free guitar." Musician, No. 119 (September 1988): 60-62. [Interview]

5802. Endress, Gudrun. "Sonny Sharrock." Jazz Hot, No. 247 (February 1969): 28-31. [Interview] [Reprinted from Jazz Podium]

5803. Hill, D. "Sonny Sharrock--Free Improvisation: an innovator's view." Guitar Player (February 1989): 101-102.

5804. Lake, Steve. "Sonny Sharrock." Jazz Forum, No. 108 (1987): 30-32. [Interview]

5805. Ratliff, Ben. "Sonny Sharrock: Seize the Rainbow." Coda, No. 234 (Oct/Nov 1990): 21-23. [Interview]

5806. Sinker, Mark. "Sonny Sharrock - Melvin Gibbs: New York is Now." Wire, No. 73 (March 1990): 22, 26.

5807. Trombert, Thierry, and Paul Alessandrini. "La Dent Dur." Jazz Hot, No. 276 (October 1971): 13-15. [Interview]

5808. Walters, M. "A Guitarist with No Time for Chords and All That Jazz." Melody Maker (November 30 1968): 22.

5809. Williams, Richard. "Like no other guitarist ever born." Melody Maker (June 27 1970): 24.

5810. Wilmer, Valerie. "The State of Sonny." Melody Maker (October 9 1971): 32.

SHAW, CHARLES BOBO (1947-) - Drums

5811. Carles, Philippe, and Jean-Louis Comolli. Free Jazz, Black Power. 2nd ed. Paris: Editions Galilee, 1979, pp. 437-438.

5812. Dictionnaire du Jazz, eds. Philippe Carles, et al. Paris: Laffont, 1988.

5813. The New Grove Dictionary of Jazz. London: Macmillan Press, 1988.

5814. Wilmer, Valerie. As Serious As Your Life. Westport, CT: Lawrence Hill & Co., 1981, p. 279.

Articles

5815. Amiard, Barnard. "West B'way Blues." Jazz Magazine, No. 261 (January 1978): 8-9.

5816. Rensen, Jan, and Rinus van der Heijden. "Bobo Shaw and the Human Arts Ensemble/Association." Jazz/Press (Holland), No. 52 (June 1978): 10-11.

SHEPP, ARCHIE [Vernon] (1937-) - Tenor Saxophone

See also # 58, 69, 121, 144, 181, 518, 543, 695, 2565, 5065-5067

Works in English

5817. "Archie Vernon Shepp." In The Black Composer Speaks, eds. David N. Baker, Lida N. Belt, and Herman C. Hudson. Metuchen, NJ: The Scarecrow Press, 1978, pp. 290-312.

5818. Hentoff, Nat. "Archie Shepp: The Way Ahead." In The Black Giants, eds. Pauline Rivelli and Robert Levin. New York: The World Publishing Co., 1970, pp. 118-121.

5819. Jones, LeRoi. "Four for Trane." In Black Music. New York: Morrow Paperback Editions, 1967, pp. 156-161.

5820. _________. "New Tenor Archie Shepp Talking." In Black Music. New York: Morrow, 1967, pp. 145-155.

5821. Jost, Ekkehard. "Archie Shepp." In Free Jazz. Graz: Universal Edition, 1974, pp. 105-120.

5822. Natambu, Kofi. "Archie Shepp: We Must Move Toward a Critique of American Culture." In Cultures in Contention, eds. Douglas Kahn and Diane Neumaier. Seattle: The Real Comet Press, 1985, pp. 166-171. [Reprinted from Solid Ground: A New World Journal [Detroit] (September 1981)].

5823. Putschoegl, Gerard. "Black Music--Key Force in Afro-American Culture: Archie Shepp on Oral Tradition and Black Culture." In History and Tradition in Afro-American Culture, ed. Gunter H. Lenz. Frankfurt/New York: Campus, 1984, pp. 262-276

5824. Shepp, Archie. "Innovations in Jazz." In History and Tradition in Afro-American Culture, ed. Gunter H. Lenz. Frankfurt/New York: Campus, 1984, pp. 256-261.

5825. Weinstein, Norman. A Night in Tunisia: Imaginations of Africa in Jazz. Metuchen, NJ: Scarecrow Press, 1991. Includes a chapter on Shepp.

5826. Wilmer, Valerie. "The Fire This Time." In Jazz People. New York: Bobbs-Merrill, 1970, pp. 155-162.

Biographical Dictionaries

5827. Berry, Lemuel, Jr. Biographical Dictionary of Black Musicians and Music Educators. Guthrie, OK: Educational Book Publishers, 1978.

5828. Carr, Ian. "Shepp, Archie." In Jazz: The Essential Companion. New York: Prentice Hall Press, 1988.

5829. Case, Brian, and Stan Britt. The Harmony Illustrated Encyclopedia of Jazz. 3rd ed. New York: Harmony Books, 1987.

5830. Claghorn, Charles Eugene. Biographical Dictionary of American Music. West Nyack, NY: Parker Pub. Co., 1973.

5831. ________. Biographical Dictionary of Jazz. Englewood Cliffs, NJ: Prentice-Hall, 1982.

5832. Feather, Leonard. The Encyclopedia of Jazz in the Sixties. New York: Horizon Press, 1966.

5833. ________, and Ira Gitler. The Encyclopedia of Jazz in the Seventies. New York: Horizon Press, 1976.

5834. Kernfeld, Barry. "Shepp, Archie." In The New Grove Dictionary of American Music. London: Macmillan Press, 1986.

5835. ________. "Shepp, Archie." In The New Grove Dictionary Jazz. London: Macmillan Press, 1988.

5836. McRae, Barry. "Archie Shepp." In The Jazz Handbook. Harlow, Essex, Eng.: Longman, 1987, pp. 212-213.

5837. The Penguin Encyclopedia of Popular Music, ed. Donald Clarke. New York: Viking, 1989.

5838. Southern, Eileen. Biographical Dictionary of Afro-American and African Musicians. Westport, CT: Greenwood Press, 1982.

5839. Wilmer, Valerie. As Serious As Your Life. Westport, CT: Lawrence Hill & Co., 1981, p. 279.

Dissertations

5840. Hardin, Christopher L. "Black Professional Musicians in Higher Education: A Study Based on in-depth interviews." Dissertation (Ed.D.) University of Massachusetts, 1987.

Articles

5841. "Archie Shepp." Melody Maker (August 7 1965): 6.

5842. "At Home." BMI (April 1966): 10-11.

5843. Bird, Christopher. "Shepp Opens and No One Shouts 'Rubbish'." Melody Maker (November 18 1967): 6.

5844. Bouchard, Fred. "Blindfold Test." down beat (September 1983): 49.

5845. Cooke, Jack. "New York Nouvelle Vague 4: Archie Shepp." Jazz Monthly (June 1966): 2-9.

5846. Dallas, Karl. "Jazz: The Sounds of Change." Melody Maker (November 21 1981): 32. [Interview]

5847. "Dico Disco & Co." Jazz Magazine, No. 298 (June 1981): 60. Biographical sketch.

5848. Feather, Leonard. "Archie Shepp: Some of My Best Friends Are White." Melody Maker (April 30 1966): 6.

5849. _________. "Blindfold Test." down beat (May 5 1966): 36; (May 19 1966): 40-41.

5850. _________. "Shepp: Look Forward in Anger." Music Maker [London] (October 1966): 25+.

5851. Freedman, Samuel. "Archie Shepp: Embracing the Jazz Ritual." down beat (April 1982): 22-25. [Interview]

5852. Gans, Charles J. "Archie Shepp: in the tradition." Jazz Forum, No. 93 (1985): 36-42. [Interview]

5853. Heckman, Don. "Archie Shepp." BMI: The Many Worlds of Music (May 1967): 22.

5854. Hentoff, Nat. "Archie Shepp, the way ahead." Jazz & Pop (June 1968): 16-17.

5855. Hunt, David C. "Coleman, Coltrane and Shepp: the need for an educated audience." Jazz & Pop (October 1968): 18-21.

5856. Jones, LeRoi. "Voice From the Avant-Garde: Archie Shepp." down beat (January 14 1965): 18, 36.

5857. Levin, Robert. "The Third World. Archie Shepp: A Period of Reflection." Jazz & Pop (November 1970): 12.

5858. _________. "The Third World. Archie Shepp II." Jazz & Pop (December 1970): 12.

5859. Litweiler, John. "Archie Shepp: An Old Schoolmaster in a Brown Suit." down beat (November 7 1974): 15+. [Interview]

5860. Lock, Graham. "Let My Notes Be Bullets." New Musical Express (March 5 1983): 20-21. [Interview]

5861. Long, David. "Archie Shepp--Jazz Playwright." Jazz (New York), Vol. 5, No. 1 (January 1966): 26.

5862. McRae, Barry. "Archie Shepp." Jazz Journal (January 1968): 34-35.

5863. _________. "Avant Courier. No. 21: Things Have Got To Change." Jazz Journal (February 1974): 26+.

5864. ________. "The Traditionalism of Archie Shepp." Jazz Journal 28 (September 1975): 14-16.

5865. Neal, Lawrence P. "A Conversation with Archie Shepp." Liberator (New York), Vol. V, No. 11 (November 1965): 24-25.

5866. Patterson, Michael. "A Profile-Interview: Archie Shepp." Black World (November 1973): 58-61.

5867. Primack, Bret. "Archie Shepp: Back to Schooldays." down beat (December 21 1978): 27+. [Interview]

5868. Richmond, Norman. "The Political Thought of Archie Shepp." Fuse (Toronto), Vol. V, No. 10 (January-March 1982): 330-336.

5869. Rock, Henry. "Looking at Mr. Shepp." Jazz Spotlite News (Fall 1980/Winter 1981): 45, 48.

5870. Rosenthal, David. "New Jazz from New York." Jazz Journal (July 1965): 10-12. Discussion of Sanders, Archie Shepp and John Tchicai.

5871. Runcie, John. "'American Negro Music is Very Political, Whites Don't Want to Accept This'." Melody Maker (September 21 1974): 30.

5872. ________. "Archie Shepp." Jazz Journal International (April 1980): 28-29.

5873. Rusch, Bob. "Archie Shepp: interview." Cadence, Vol. 5, No. 3 (March 1979): 3-6.

5874. Sanderson, Rita, and Barry McRae. "Archie Shepp." The Wire, No. 3 (Spring 1983): 16-19. [Interview]

5875. Shepp, Archie. "An Artist Speaks Bluntly." down beat (December 16 1965): 11+.

5876. ________. "Fortunes Unattended: Notes on the History of Black American Music." Lightworks, No. 10 (Fall 1978): 47-49.

5877. ________. "On Jazz." Jazz (New York), Vol. 4, No. 8 (August 1965): 24.

5878. ________. "On Pugilism." Jazz (New York), Vol. 5, No. 7 (1966): 7.

5879. ________. "A View From the Inside." Down Beat's Music '66, Vol. 11 (1966): 39-42, 44.

5880. "Shepp Gets Staff Post at New York State U." down beat (February 6 1969): 10.

5881. Smith, Bill. "Archie Shepp: four for Trane." Coda, No. 204 (October/November 1985): 20-22. [Interview]

5882. Smith, Miyoshi. "Archie Shepp interview." Cadence, Vol. 15, No. 8 (August 1989): 5-12.

5883. Spellman, A. B. "Introducing Archie Shepp." Metronome (November 1961): 26.

5884. Stepien, B., and Norman Richmond. "Archie Shepp." Coda, No. 171 (February 1980): 4-11.

5885. Walden, Daniel. "Black Music and Cultural Nationalism: The Maturation of Archie Shepp." Negro American Literature Forum, Vol. 5, No. 4 (Winter 1971): 150-153.

5886. Walker, Malcolm. "Archie Shepp." Jazz Monthly (June 1966): 30-31.

5887. Williams, Martin. "The Problematic Mr. Shepp." Saturday Review (November 12 1966): 90.

5888. Wilmer, Valerie. "Attica Blues." Melody Maker (August 19 1972): 16. Conversation with Shepp, Beaver Harris and attorney William Kunstler.

5889. _________. "Shepp the Teacher." Melody Maker (October 16 1971): 14.

5890. _________. "The Tenorist Playwright Who Speaks for Black Expressionism." Melody Maker (October 14 1967): 18.

Newspaper Articles

5891. Crouch, Stanley. "Archie Shepp's Neoclassicist Dilemma." Village Voice (February 3 1982): 63-64.

5892. Giddins, Gary. "Archie Shepp without Rhetoric." Village Voice (November 27 1977): 88-89.

5893. Roberts, Jim. "Jazz is Dead." New Haven Advocate (May 19, 1982): 3, 14. [Interview]

5894. Shepp, Archie. "Black Power and Black Jazz." The New York Times (November 26 1967): Sec. 13, p. 1, 4.

Works in French, German, Dutch and Italian

5895. Fayenz, Franco. "Archie Shepp." In Il Jazz dal Mito All' avanguardia. Milano: Sapere, 1970, pp. 441-483.

5896. Roggeman, Willy. "Archie Shepp." In Free en Andere Jazz-Essays. The Hague: Van Ditmar, 1969, pp. 89-96. [Dutch text]

5897. Vuijsje, Bert. De Nieuwe Jazz. Baarn: Bosch & Keuning, 1978, pp. 56-66. [Interview]

Biographical Dictionaries

5898. Carles, Philippe, and Jean-Louis Comolli. Free Jazz, Black Power. 2nd ed. Paris: Editions Galilee, 1979, p. 438-439.

5899. Dictionnaire du Jazz, eds. Philippe Carles, et al. Paris: Laffont, 1988.

5900. Reclams Jazzfuhrer. 2nd, rev. ed. Stuttgart: Reclam, 1977.

5901. Reda, Jacques. Anthologie des Musiciens de Jazz. Paris: Stock, 1981, pp. 334-336.

5902. Tenot, Frank. Dictionnaire du Jazz. Paris: Larousse, 1967.

Articles

5903. "Archie Me'connu." Jazz Magazine, No. 119 (June 1965): 50-55.

5904. Boujut, Michel. "Shepp en Six Questions." Jazz Magazine, No. 279 (October 1979): 34+. [Interview]

5905. Carles, Philippe. "Shepp sans Prevision." Jazz Magazine, No. 150 (January 1968): 14-15.

5906. Endress, Gudrun. "Archie Shepp Interview." Jazz Podium (May 1966): 122-126.

5907. Evers, M. "C'est Shepp que J'Aime." Jazz Hot, No. 236 (November 1967): 19.

5908. Goddet, Laurent. "Archie Shepp: le lien." Jazz Hot, No. 320 (October 1975): 4-9. [Interview]

5909. Kemper, Peter. "Archie Shepp: Zur Sensibilitat eines traditionsbewussten Avantgardisten." Jazz Podium (mai 1979): 4-9; (juni 1979): 9-11.

5910. Naura, M. "Der Schrei Mienes Volkes." Jazz Podium (March 1975): 4+.

5911. ________. "Unsere Musik war fuer die Schwarzen immer relevant." Jazz Podium (February 1975): 4-6. [Interview]

5912. Pellicciotti, Giacomo. "Archie Shepp." Jazz Magazine, No. 243 (April 1976): 16+. [Interview]

5913. Positif, Francois, and Guy Kopelowicz. "Archie Shepp ou la Maree qui Monte." Jazz Hot, No. 210 (June 1965): 22-26; No. 211 (July-August 1965): 38-41.

5914. Putschoegl, Gerhard. "Zur Schluesselfunktion der Musik in der Afro-Amerikanischen Kultur: Archie Shepp ueber die Musiktradition der Schwarzen Amerikaner." Jazz Research/Jazzforschung, No. 18 (1986): 67-86. [English summary]

5915. Reese, Jerome. "Archie Shepp ou la Memoire du Peuple Noir." Jazz Hot, No. 390 (December 1981): 10-13. [Interview]

5916. Schiozzi, Bruno. "Questo e Archie Shepp." Musica Jazz (November 1965): 17-18.

5917. Schmidt-Joos, Siegfried. "Archie Shepp; free jazz fuer Mr. Charlie." Musikalische Jugend, Vol. 17, No. 6 (1968-69): 26.

5918. "Shepp le Rebele." Jazz Magazine, No. 125 (December 1965): 78-81.

5919. Sidran, Ben. "Shepp: des sons pour le dire." Jazz Magazine, No. 365 (1987): 36-39; No. 366 (1987): 28-30. [Interview]

5920. Sundin, B. "Archie Shepp-Bill Dixon Quartet." Orkester Journalen (September 1962): 12-13.

Concert Reviews

5921. Cuscuna, Michael. "Caught in the Act." down beat (June 13 1968): 40-41.

5922. Gallagher, J. "Caught in the Act." down beat (July 24 1969): 26.

5923. Hardy, J. W. "Caught in the Act." down beat (July 14 1966): 30.

5924. Hoefer, George. "Caught in the Act: Bill-Dixon-Archie Shepp." down beat (March 14 1963): 36. Review of a Judson Hall concert.

5925. Jones, LeRoi. "Archie Shepp Live." Jazz (New York), Vol. 4, No. 1 (January 1965): 8-9.

5926. Mathieu, Bill. "Caught in the Act." down beat (May 5 1966): 36.

5927. Sinclair, John. "Cecil Taylor, John Coltrane, and Archie Shepp at the Down Beat Festival, Chicago, 8/15/65." Change (Detroit), No. 1 (Fall/Winter 1965): 34-38.

Record Reviews

5928. Bethune, C. "L'ABC de Shepp." Jazz Magazine, No. 341 (July-August 1985): 34-37; No. 342 (September 1985): 22-25; No. 344 (November 1985): 32-35. Discussion of Shepp's Impulse recordings.

5929. Cooke, Jack. "New York Nouvelle Vague 2." Jazz Monthly (April 1965): 29-30. Discussion of Archie Shepp-Bill Dixon Quartet lp.

5930. Fero, Charles. "Sounds Recalled: Archie Shepp/Bill Dixon Quartet." Sounds & Fury (April 1966): 64. Review of the Savoy lp of the same name.

5931. Gitler, Ira. "Record Reviews: Mama Too Tight." down beat (November 30 1967): 30-31.

5932. Mathieu, Bill. "Record Reviews: Archie Shepp-Bill Dixon Quartet." down beat (September 26 1963): 35.

5933. ________. "Record Reviews: Four for Trane." down beat (April 8 1965): 31-32.

5934. Quinn, Bill. "Record Reviews: Live in San Francisco." down beat (January 26 1967): 30.

5935. Spellman, A. B. "Archie Shepp/Bill Dixon Quartet." Kulchur, No. 11 (Autumn 1963): 94-95. Review of Savoy lp.

5936. Welding, Pete. "Record Reviews: Bill Dixon 7-tette/Archie Shepp and the New York Contemporary 5." down beat (October 8 1964): 27-28.

Discographies

5937. Cerutti, Gustave, and Guido Maertens. Discographie: Archie Shepp 1960-1980. Sierre: Jazz 360o (c/o Cerutti, 8, ave. du Marche, CH-3960, Sierre, Switzerland), 1982. 24p.

5938. Rissi, Mathias. Archie Shepp: Discography. Adliswil, Switzerland: The Author (Haldenstr. 23, CH-8134 Adliswil), 1977. 21p.

Media Materials

5939. Archie Shepp: I Am Jazz...It's My Life (1984). 52 min. Dir. by Frank Cassenti. [Available from Rhapsody Films, P.O. Box 179, New York, NY 10014. Tel. 212/243-0152]

5940. Imagine the Sound (1981). 91 min. Directed by Ron Mann. Documentary on the life and music of Archie Shepp, Bill Dixon, Cecil Taylor and Paul Bley. [For distribution information contact: Bill Smith, c/o Coda Publications, Box 87, Station J, Toronto, Ontario M4J 4X8, Canada]

SHIPP, MATHEW - Piano

5941. Griepenburg, Anne M. "New Faces: Mathew Shipp." Ear (March 1989): 66.

SHORTER, ALAN (1931-) - Trumpet

5942. Carles, Philippe, and Jean-Louis Comolli. Free Jazz, Black Power. 2nd ed. Paris: Editions Galilee, 1979, p. 439.

5943. Dictionnaire du Jazz, eds. Philippe Carles, et al. Paris: Laffont, 1988.

Articles

5944. Berger, Daniel, and A. Corneau. "Allan [sic] Shorter et le monstre magnetique." Jazz Magazine, No. 232 (June 1967): 24-25. [Interview]

5945. Shorter, Alan. "Call and Response: Letters." Cadence (November 1976): 8.

5946. ________. "Vivre la New Music." Jazz Magazine, No. 219 (February 1974): 10-11.

5947. Williams, Richard. "'Everybody is a Leader'; flugelhornist Alan Shorter talks to Richard Williams." Melody Maker (May 1 1971): 18.

SILVA, ALAN (1939-) (Bermuda/U.S.) - Bass

5948. Carles, Philippe, and Jean-Louis Comolli. Free Jazz, Black Power. 2nd ed. Paris: Editions Galilee, 1979, p. 439-440.

5949. Clergeat, Andre. "Silva, Alan." In The New Grove Dictionary of Jazz. London: Macmillan Press, 1988.

5950. Dictionnaire du Jazz, eds. Philippe Carles, et al. Paris: Laffont, 1988.

5951. Wilmer, Valerie. As Serious As Your Life. Westport, CT: Lawrence Hill & Co., 1981, p. 279.

Articles

5952. Arnaud, Gerald. "L'I.A.C.P.: entretien avec Alan Silva." Jazz Hot, No. 397 (January 1983): 35-36.

5953. Bisceglia, J. "Alan Silva: un sideman et ses leaders." Jazz Magazine, No. 182 (Octobre 1970): 32-35. [Interview]

5954. Carles, Philippe. "Alan Silva ou le Triangle des Bermudes." Jazz Magazine, No. 280 (November 1979): 38+. [Interview]

5955. ________, and Serge Loupien. "Les Ecoles d'Alan Silva." Jazz Magazine, No. 278 (September 1979): 50+. [Interview]

5956. Caux, Daniel. "Alan Silva a Paris." Jazz Hot, No. 249 (April 1969): 9.

5957. ________. "Un Rayonnant Silva." Jazz Hot, No. 250 (May 1969): 6-7.

5958. ________, and M. Chiari. "Alan Silva de la contrebasse au violon." Jazz Hot, No. 247 (February 1969): 21-23. [Interview]

5959. Damian, J. M. "Silva Viole Royan." Jazz Magazine, No. 189 (May 1971): 18-19.

5960. Griffiths, Pat. "The Silva Lining." Melody Maker (May 15 1971): 32.

5961. Gros-Claude, P., and Philippe Carles. "Communication Celestrielle." Jazz Magazine, No. 186 (February 1971): 9+.

5962. Wilmer, Valerie. "Silva: Making History." Melody Maker (April 5 1975): 41.

SIMMONS, SONNY (1933-) - Alto Saxophone

See also # 695-696

5963. Carles, Philippe, and Jean-Louis Comolli. Free Jazz, Black Power. 2nd ed. Paris: Editions Galilee, 1979, p. 440.

5964. Claghorn, Charles Eugene. Biographical Dictionary of Jazz. Englewood Cliffs, NJ: Prentice-Hall, 1982.

5965. Dictionnaire du Jazz, eds. Philippe Carles, et al. Paris: Laffont, 1988.

5966. Feather, Leonard. The Encyclopedia of Jazz in the Sixties. New York: Horizon Press, 1966.

5967. ________, and Ira Gitler. The Encyclopedia of Jazz in the Seventies. New York: Horizon Press, 1976.

5968. Wild, David. "Simmons, Sonny." In The New Grove Dictionary of Jazz. London: Macmillan Press, 1988.

5969. Wilmer, Valerie. As Serious As Your Life. Westport, CT: Lawrence Hill & Co., 1981, p. 279.

Articles

5970. "Dictionnaire de l'Alto." Jazz Magazine, No. 137 (December 1966): 49. Biographical sketch.

5971. Feather, Leonard. "Blindfold Test." down beat (May 16 1968): 33.

5972. Hunt, David C. "Sonny Simmons." Jazz & Pop (May 1971): 20-21.

5973. James, Michael. "Some Interesting Contemporaries." Jazz & Blues (January 1973): 13. Discussion of Simmons' Contemporary lp.

5974. Russell, R. "Sonny Simmons." Jazz Hot, No. 267 (December 1970): 16-17.

5975. Tynan, John. "Take Five." down beat (April 11 1963): 40. [Profile]

SIRONE [Norris Jones] (1940-) - Bass

5976. Carles, Philippe, and Jean-Louis Comolli. Free Jazz, Black Power. 2nd ed. Paris: Editions Galilee, 1979, p. 440.

5977. Claghorn, Charles Eugene. Biographical Dictionary of Jazz. Englewood Cliffs, NJ: Prentice-Hall, 1982.

5978. Dictionnaire du Jazz, eds. Philippe Carles, et al. Paris: Laffont, 1988.

5979. Feather, Leonard, and Ira Gitler. The Encyclopedia of Jazz in the Seventies. New York: Horizon Press, 1976.

5980. The New Grove Dictionary of Jazz. London: Macmillan Press, 1988.

5981. Southern, Eileen. Biographical Dictionary of Afro-American and African Musicians. Westport, CT: Greenwood Press, 1982.

5982. Wilmer, Valerie. As Serious As Your Life. Westport, CT: Lawrence Hill & Co., 1981, p. 280.

Articles

5983. "Sirone: 'Amerika braucht eine Revolte!'" Jazzthetik, Vol. 4, No. 11 (November 1990): 18-21.

5984. Wilmer, Valerie. "Sirone is one hell of a dirty bass player." Melody Maker (July 15 1972): 44.

SKIDMORE, ALAN (1942-) (Great Britain) - Tenor Saxophone

5985. Carles, Philippe, and Jean-Louis Comolli. Free Jazz, Black Power. 2nd ed. Paris: Editions Galilee, 1979, p. 440.

5986. Carr, Ian. "Skidmore, Alan." In Jazz: The Essential Companion. New York: Prentice Hall Press, 1988.

5987. Gilbert, Mark. "Skidmore, Alan." In The New Grove Dictionary of Jazz. London: Macmillan Press, 1988.

5988. Jazz Now: the Jazz Centre Society Guide, ed. Roger Cotterrell. London: Quartet Books, 1976, p. 167.

Articles

5989. Dawbarn, Bob. "We've been here before baby." Melody Maker (July 12 1969): 10.

5990. Henshaw, L. "Alan follows in dad's footsteps." Melody Maker (March 15 1969): 11.

SMITH, BILL (1938-) (Great Britain/Canada) - Reeds

5991. Miller, Mark. "Bill Smith." In Boogie, Pete & the Senator: Canadian Musicians in Jazz: the Eighties. Toronto: Nightwood Editions, 1987, pp. 232-240.

5992. ________. "Smith, Bill." In Encyclopedia of Music in Canada, eds. Helmut Kallmann, et al. Toronto/Buffalo: University of Toronto Press, 1981, pp. 874-875.

5993. Smith, Bill. Imagine the Sound No. 5: The Book: Photographs and Writings. Toronto: Nightwood Editions, 1985. 196p.

Articles

5994. Miller, Mark. "A New Kind of Jazz Moves In." The Canadian Composer, No. 144 (October 1979): 16-23. [Interview]

SMITH, LEO (1941-) - Trumpet

5995. Litweiler, John. "Leo Smith, Anthony Braxton, Joseph Jarman, and Roscoe Mitchell." In The Freedom Principle: Jazz After 1958. New York: William Morrow, 1984, pp. 265-286.

5996. Smith, Leo. Notes (8 Pieces) Source A New World Music: Creative Music. New Haven, CT: the Author, 1973. Unpaged.

Biographical Dictionaries

5997. Carles, Philippe, and Jean-Louis Comolli. Free Jazz, Black Power. 2nd ed. Paris: Editions Galilee, 1979, p. 441.

5998. Claghorn, Charles Eugene. Biographical Dictionary of Jazz. Englewood Cliffs, NJ: Prentice-Hall, 1982.

5999. Dictionnaire du Jazz, eds. Philippe Carles, et al. Paris: Laffont, 1988.

6000. Feather, Leonard, and Ira Gitler. The Encyclopedia of Jazz in the Seventies. New York: Horizon Press, 1976.

6001. Kernfeld, Barry. "Smith, Leo." In The New Grove Dictionary of Jazz. London: Macmillan Press, 1988.

6002. The Penguin Encyclopedia of Popular Music, ed. Donald Clarke. New York: Viking, 1989.

6003. Southern, Eileen. Biographical Dictionary of Afro-American and African Musicians. Westport, CT: Greenwood Press, 1982.

6004. Wilmer, Valerie. As Serious As Your Life. Westport, CT: Lawrence Hill & Co., 1981, p. 280.

Articles

6005. Ansell, Keith. "Leo Smith." Impetus (London), No. 6 (1977): 259-260. [Interview]

6006. Arcangelli, Stefano. "Parla Leo Smith." Musica Jazz, Vol. 33, No. 8/9 (1977): 26-29. [Interview]

6007. Birnbaum, Larry. "Meet the Composer: Wadada Leo Smith." Ear: New Music News, Vol. 13, No. 5 (July-August 1988): 22-25.

6008. "Dico Disco & Co." Jazz Magazine, No. 298 (June 1981): 64. Biographical sketch.

6009. Giddins, Gary. "Theory and Practice in Leo Smith." Village Voice (May 17 1976): 98.

6010. Lake, Steve. "Bound for Glory: Muhal Richard Abrams, Leo Smith, Roscoe Mitchell." Melody Maker (January 1 1977): 22.

6011. Lieb, Elliott. "Leo Smith's World Music: Jazz Meets Jah." OPtion (January/February 1986): 42-43. [Interview]

6012. Ness, Bob. "Profile: Leo Smith." down beat (October 7 1976): 36-37.

6013. Occhiogrosso, Peter. "Brassy Horn and a Metal Arsenal." Soho Weekly News (August 21 1975): 31. [Concert review]

6014. Ogan, Bernd. "Free Jazz - Multilateral: Smith-Kowald-Sommer." Jazz Podium (October 1980): 24-25.

6015. Palmer, Robert. "Jazz: Leo Smith's Avant-Garde Delta Blues." Rolling Stone (July 10 1980): 26.

6016. Rouy, Gerard. "L'Esthetique Noire selon Leo Smith: Du Blues aux Musique de l'A.A.C.M. de Chicago." Jazz Magazine, No. 277 (July/August 1979): 10-11, 63. [Interview]

6017. ________. "Leo Smith: Pour la Musique Creative." Jazz Magazine, No. 278 (September 1979): 80-81, 106.

6018. Rusch, Bob. "Leo Smith: Interview." Cadence, Vol. 3, No. 10 (February 1978): 29-30+.

6019. Smith, Bill. "Leo Smith." Coda, No. 143 (November 1975): 2-9.

6020. ________. "Leo Smith: Rastafari." Coda, No. 192 (October 1983): 4-8.

6021. Smith, Leo. "Lecture/Workshop May 27th 1978." Musics (London), No. 18 (July 1978): Supplement p.II-III.

6022. ________. "(M1) American Music." Black Perspective in Music, Vol. 2, No. 2 (Fall 1974): 111-116.

6023. ________. "Thoughts of an Improvisor." Jazz Forum, Vol. 23 (June 1973): 43.

6024. Thompson, Robert Farris. "Mambo Minkisi: the Mind and Music of Leo Smith." Coda, No. 143 (November 1975). Review of Smith's notes (8 pieces) (# 5996).

6025. Weinstein, Norman. "Reggae or Not: Jazz Goes Dread?" down beat (March 1987): 63. Discussion of Smith's embrace of rastafarianism and reggae in his 1980s music.

6026. Wilmer, Valerie. "Caught in the Act: Leo Smith." Melody Maker (November 5 1977). [Concert review]

6027. ________. "Leo, Lion of the Trumpet." Melody Maker (June 11 1977): 28.

6028. _________. "Leo Smith: Aware of the Hazards." Melody Maker (September 11 1971): 32.

Discographies

6029. Cerutti, Gustave. "Discographie de Leo Smith." Jazz 360o (Sierre, Switzerland), No. 24 (January 1980): 7-13.

SMITH, ROGER (Great Britain) - Guitar

6030. Case, Brian. "Let's Hear it from the Cool Front Room." New Musical Express (March 11 1978): 34-35. [Interview]

SMITH, WARREN (1934-) - Percussion

6031. Carles, Philippe, and Jean-Louis Comolli. Free Jazz, Black Power. 2nd ed. Paris: Editions Galilee, 1979, p. 441.

6032. Claghorn, Charles Eugene. Biographical Dictionary of Jazz. Englewood Cliffs, NJ: Prentice-Hall, 1982.

6033. Dictionnaire du Jazz, eds. Philippe Carles, et al. Paris: Laffont, 1988.

6034. Feather, Leonard, and Ira Gitler. The Encyclopedia of Jazz in the Seventies. New York: Horizon Press, 1976.

6035. Hazell, Ed. "Smith, Warren, (Jr.) (ii)." In The New Grove Dictionary of Jazz. London: Macmillan Press, 1988.

6036. Southern, Eileen. Biographical Dictionary of Afro-American and African Musicians. Westport, CT: Greenwood Press, 1982.

6037. Wilmer, Valerie. As Serious As Your Life. Westport, CT: Lawrence Hill & Co., 1981, p. 280.

Articles

6038. Hazell, Ed. "Warren Smith." Coda, No. 211 (December 1986/January 1987): 18-19. [Interview]

6039. Rusch, Bob, and H. Ryan. "Warren Smith." Cadence, Vol. 14, No. 3 (March 1988): 5-19, 89. [Interview]

6040. Smith, Arnold Jay. "Profile: Warren Smith." Down Beat (June 5 1975): 30-31.

SMYTHE, PAT (d.1983) (Great Britain) - Piano

See also # 3599

6041. "Last Chorus." Crescendo International (February-March 1984): 25. Obituary for the pianist best known for his work with saxophonist Joe Harriott.

6042. "Round and About: Remembering Pat." Crescendo International (October-November 1983): 2-3. Report on a benefit/memorial concert for Smythe.

6043. Wilmer, Valerie. "Breaking with the Law." Jazz News (September 24 1960): 5. [Interview]

SOLOMON, DAVID (Great Britain) - Drums

See # 1229

SOMMER, GUNTER "BABY" (1943-) (E. Germany) - Drums

6044. Carles, Philippe, and Jean-Louis Comolli. Free Jazz, Black Power. 2nd ed. Paris: Editions Galilee, 1979, p. 441.

6045. Dictionnaire du Jazz, eds. Philippe Carles, et al. Paris: Laffont, 1988.

6046. Noglik, Bert. "Gunter Sommer." In Jazz im Gesprach. Berlin: Verlag Neue Musik, 1978, pp. 169-184.

6047. ________. "Gunter Sommer." In Jazzwerkstatt International. Berlin: Verlag Neue Musik, 1981, pp. 315-345. [Interview]

6048. ________. "Sommer, Gunter." In The New Grove Dictionary of Jazz. London: Macmillan Press, 1988.

Articles

6049. Charlton, Hannah. "Snapshots of East Germany." Melody Maker (September 19 1981): 21. [Interview]

6050. "Dico Disco & Co." Jazz Magazine, No. 298 (June 1981): 64. Biographical sketch.

6051. "Guenter Baby Sommer and Crams Percussion Staff." Jazz Podium (May 1987): 12-14.

6052. Martin, D. "Gunter Sommer: la liberte venue de l'Est." Jazz Magazine, No. 376 (November 1988): 18-19. [Interview]

6053. Ogan, Bernd. "Free Jazz - Multilateral: Smith-Kowald-Sommer." Jazz Podium (October 1980): 24-25.

6054. Reichelt, Rolf. "Gunter Sommer: Baby Comes of Age." Jazz Forum, No. 67 (1980): 47-49. [Interview]

SPONTANEOUS MUSIC ENSEMBLE (formed 1965) (Great Britain)

6055. Adams, Simon. "Spontaneous Music Ensemble." In The New Grove Dictionary of Jazz. London: Macmillan Press, 1988.

6056. Case, Brian, and Stan Britt. The Harmony Illustrated Encyclopedia of Jazz. 3rd ed. New York: Harmony Books, 1987.

6057. Claghorn, Charles Eugene. Biographical Dictionary of Jazz. Englewood Cliffs, NJ: Prentice-Hall, 1982, p. 369.

6058. McRae, Barry. "Spontaneous Music Ensemble." In The Jazz Handbook. Harlow, Essex, Eng.: Longman, 1987, pp. 213-214.

Articles

6059. Parry, Roger. "Spontaneous Music Ensemble." Coda, No. 218 (February/March 1988): 22-24. Discussion of SME's recorded works.

6060. Paton, Maureen. "SME." Melody Maker (June 11 1977): 39.

6061. Schonfield, Victor. "Caught in the Act: Spontaneous Music Ensemble/Derek Bailey, Little Theatre Club." down beat (January 11 1968): 41. [Concert review]

6062. Williams, Richard. "SME on Record." Melody Maker (March 7 1970): 8.

Concert Reviews

6063. "Caught in the Act." Melody Maker (February 22 1969): 6.

6064. "Caught in the Act." Melody Maker (November 1 1969): 6.

6065. McRae, Barry. "Jazz in Britain." Jazz Journal (September 1967): 22. Review of a Little Theatre Club performance.

6066. Schonfield, Victor. "Caught in the Act." down beat (January 11 1968): 41.

6067. ________. "Caught in the Act." Melody Maker (September 14 1968): 6.

6068. ________. "Caught in the Act." Melody Maker (February 11 1967): 15.

6069. ________. "Caught in the Act." Melody Maker (September 23 1967): 4.

6070. Williams, Richard. "Caught in the Act." Melody Maker (January 31 1970): 6.

STANKO, TOMASZ (1942-) (Poland) - Trumpet

6071. Carr, Ian. "Stanko, Tomasz." In Jazz: The Essential Companion. New York: Prentice Hall Press, 1988.

6072. Claghorn, Charles Eugene. Biographical Dictionary of Jazz. Englewood Cliffs, NJ: Prentice-Hall, 1982.

6073. Dictionnaire du Jazz, eds. Philippe Carles, et al. Paris: Laffont, 1988.

6074. Feather, Leonard, and Ira Gitler. The Encyclopedia of Jazz in the Seventies. New York: Horizon Press, 1976.

6075. Noglik, Bert. "Stanko, Tomasz." In The New Grove Dictionary of Jazz. London: Macmillan Press, 1988.

Articles

6076. Byrczek, Jan, and Barbara Czajkowska. "On Free Jazz - Stanko, Trzaskowski, Wroblewski." Jazz Forum, No. 13/14 (Autumn/ Winter 1971): 70-71, 80.

6077. Czyz, K. "Tomasz Stanko: hat-trick." Jazz Forum, No. 33 (January 1975): 41-43.

6078. Kowal, Roman. "Tomasz Stanko--jazz is the message." Jazz Forum, No. 18 (August 1972): 51-53.

6079. "Stanko quintet disbanded." Jazz Forum, No. 27 (February 1974): 25.

STEVENS, JOHN (Great Britain) (1940-) - Drums

See also # 344, 867-875, 6055-6070

6080. Carr, Ian. "John Stevens and Trevor Watts - The Spontaneous Music Ensemble." In Music Outside. London: Latimer New Dimensions, 1973, pp. 39-54.

6081. Stevens, John. Search and Reflect. London: Community Music (1 Hoxton Square, London N16 NU), 1985. 112p.

Biographical Dictionaries

6082. Carles, Philippe, and Jean-Louis Comolli. Free Jazz, Black Power. 2nd ed. Paris: Editions Galilee, 1979, p. 442.

6083. Carr, Ian. "Stevens, John." In Jazz: The Essential Companion. New York: Prentice Hall Press, 1988.

6084. Hazell, Ed. "Stevens, John." In The New Grove Dictionary of Jazz. London: Macmillan Press, 1988.

6085. Jazz Now: the Jazz Centre Society Guide, ed. Roger Cotterrell. London: Quartet Books, 1976, p. 170.

6086. The Penguin Encyclopedia of Popular Music, ed. Donald Clarke. New York: Viking, 1989.

Articles

6087. Blake, David. "4 to the Bar." Melody Maker (March 24 1979): 52-53; (June 23 1979): 52. [Interview]

6088. Case, Brian. "Digestible Wig Bubbles Explained." New Musical Express (August 23 1975): 24-25. [Interview]

6089. Hyder, Ken. "Best of British. - No. 3: John Stevens." Jazz Journal International (April 1978): 35.

6090. ________. "Stevens: searching for space to play." Melody Maker (March 17 1973): 52.

6091. Lake, Steve. "Stevens: up, up, and away." Melody Maker (October 30 1976): 33. [Interview]

6092. Paton, Maureen. "Away Day." Melody Maker (June 18 1977): 32. [Interview]

6093. Shand, John. "John Stevens: free jazz pioneer." Jazz (Sydney), No. 11 (October 1982): 24-25. [Interview]

6094. "Stevens: Ring in the New Wave (British)." Melody Maker (January 8 1966): 6.

6095. Turner, Andrew. "John Stevens: Spontaneous Music." The Wire, No. 1 (Summer 1982): 30-31; No. 2 (Winter 1982/83): 30-31. [Interview]

6096. Welch, Chris. "Stevens; a sadder but wiser avant gardist." Melody Maker (February 18 1967): 8.

6097. Williams, Richard. "John Finds a Place for Amateurs." Melody Maker (May 16 1970): 8.

6098. ________. "Stevens: getting in a jam." Melody Maker (July 22 1972): 14.

6099. ________. "Total Honesty is John's Motivation." Melody Maker (March 27 1971): 12.

6100. Wilmer, Valerie. "Caught in the Act: John Stevens." Melody Maker (August 10 1974). [Concert review]

6101. ________. "Freedom Sweet." Melody Maker (February 10 1979): 32. [Interview]

STEWART, BOB (1945-) - Tuba

6102. Carr, Ian. "Stewart, Bob." In Jazz: The Essential Companion. New York: Prentice Hall Press, 1988.

Articles

6103. Case, Brian. "Tuba, or Not Tuba?" Melody Maker (January 9 1982): 23. [Interview]

6104. Jeske, Lee. "Profile: Bob Stewart." down beat (December 1980): 48, 50.

6105. Whitehead, Kevin. "Bob Stewart Interview." Cadence (October 1990): 9-15.

6106. ________. "Riffs: Bob Stewart." down beat (October 1989): 14.

STRING TRIO OF NEW YORK (formed 1977)

6107. Whitehead, Kevin. "String Trio of New York: a decade of perseverance." down beat (November 1987): 26-28. [Interview]

Media Materials

6108. Built By Hand: The String Trio of New York (1988). 30 min. [Available from Rhapsody Films, Box 179, New York, NY 10014. Tel. 212/243-0152; or, Stash Records, 611 Broadway, Suite 411, New York, NY 10012. Tel. 1-800-666-JASS]

STUBBLEFIELD, JOHN (1945-) - Tenor Saxophone

6109. Carles, Philippe, and Jean-Louis Comolli. Free Jazz, Black Power. 2nd ed. Paris: Editions Galilee, 1979, p. 442.

6110. Dictionnaire du Jazz, eds. Philippe Carles, et al. Paris: Laffont, 1988.

6111. The New Grove Dictionary of Jazz. London: Macmillan Press, 1988.

6112. Wilmer, Valerie. As Serious As Your Life. Westport, CT: Lawrence Hill & Co., 1981, p. 280.

Articles

6113. Endress, Gudrun. "Bushman." Jazz Podium (November 1987): 6-10. [Interview]

6114. Leymarie, Isabelle. "John Stubblefield: 'l'A.A.C.M. m'a sauve la vie'." Jazz Magazine, No. 346 (1986): 34+. [Interview]

6115. Smith, Arnold Jay. "Profile: John Stubblefield." down beat (January 29 1976): 30.

SUDLER, MONNETTE (1952-) - Guitar

See also # 694

6116. Carles, Philippe, and Jean-Louis Comolli. Free Jazz, Black Power. 2nd ed. Paris: Editions Galilee, 1979, p. 442.

6117. Dictionnaire du Jazz, eds. Philippe Carles, et al. Paris: Laffont, 1988.

6118. Wilmer, Valerie. As Serious As Your Life. Westport, CT: Lawrence Hill & Co., 1981, p. 280.

Articles

6119. Grass, Randall F. "Profile: Monnette Sudler." down beat (January 1981): 50-52.

6120. Hasson, Bill. "Monnette Sudler at the Hershey Hotel, Philadelphia, PA." Jazz Times (May 1990): 36. Report on Sudler's recent activities.

6121. "Monette Sudler." Jazz Magazine, No. 235 (August 1975): 17.

6122. Shapiro, Jill. "Monette Sudler: Contemporary Jazz Stylist." Guitar Player (February 1980): 92, 94, 96. [Interview]

SUN RA [aka Herman 'Sonny' Blount/Sonny Bourke/Harman Lee] (c.1914-) - Piano/Synthesizers/Bandleader

See also # 276, 695, 698, 700, 705

Works in English

6123. Sun Ra; souvenir booklet of the 1970 tour. London: Music Now, 1970. 16p. Includes statements and poems by Sun Ra selected from published and unpublished material. [Held by the Black Arts Research Center (# 7085)]

Books with Sections on Sun Ra

6124. Jost, Ekkehard. "Sun Ra." In Free Jazz. Graz: Universal Edition, 1974, pp. 180-199. Formal analysis of Sun Ra's recordings.

6125. Litweiler, John. "The Free Jazz Underground and Sun Ra." In The Freedom Principle: Jazz After 1958. New York: Morrow, 1984, pp. 129-150.

6126. Lyons, Leonard. "Sun Ra." In The Great Jazz Pianists. New York: Morrow, 1983, pp. 83-92. [Interview]

6127. Rusch, Robert. "Sun Ra." In Jazz Talk: The Cadence Interviews. Secaucus, NJ: Lyle Stuart, 1985. [Reprint of # 6169]

6128. Wilmer, Valerie. "Sun Ra - Pictures of Infinity." In As Serious As Your Life. Westport, CT: Lawrence Hill & Co., 1981, pp. 74-92. See also, p. 281.

Biographical Dictionaries

6129. Case, Brian, and Stan Britt. The Harmony Illustrated Encyclopedia of Jazz. 3rd ed. New York: Harmony Books, 1987.

6130. Claghorn, Charles Eugene. Biographical Dictionary of Jazz. Englewood Cliffs, NJ: Prentice-Hall, 1982.

6131. Dickow, Robert. "Sun Ra." In The New Grove Dictionary of American Music. London: Macmillan Press, 1986.

6132. _________. "Sun Ra." In The New Grove Dictionary of Jazz. London: Macmillan Press, 1988.

6133. Feather, Leonard. The Encyclopedia of Jazz in the Sixties. New York: Horizon Press, 1966.

6134. _________, and Ira Gitler. The Encyclopedia of Jazz in the Seventies. New York: Horizon Press, 1976.

6135. McRae, Barry. "Sun Ra." In The Jazz Handbook. Harlow, Essex, Eng.: Longman, 1987, pp. 214-216.

6136. The Penguin Encyclopedia of Popular Music, ed. Donald Clarke. New York: Viking, 1989.

6137. Priestley, Brian. "Sun Ra." In Jazz: The Essential Companion. New York: Prentice Hall Press, 1988.

6138. Southern, Eileen. Biographical Dictionary of Afro-American and African Musicians. Westport, CT: Greenwood Press, 1982.

6139. Who's Who in Entertainment. 1st ed. 1989-1990.

Articles

6140. Barber, Lynden. "The Joy of Life." Melody Maker (November 19 1983): 30-31. [Interview]

6141. Burks, J. "Sun Ra." Rolling Stone (April 19 1969): 16-18.

6142. Chenard, Marc. "Sun Ra - Swing and a Myth." Coda, No. 231 (April/May 1990): 24-25.

6143. Cohen, S. "Faces; Sun Ra." Musician, Player and Listener, No. 19 (July-August 1979): 27.

6144. Farris, John. "Space is the Place." Spin (April 1989): 98+.

6145. Fiofori, Tam. "The Illusion of Sun Ra." Liberator (New York), Vol. 7, No. 12 (December 1967): 12-15.

6146. _________. "Moog Modulations: a symposium." down beat (July 23 1970): 34+.

6147. _________. "Sun Ra's African Roots." Melody Maker (February 12 1972): 32.

6148. _________. "Space Age Music: The Music of Sun Ra." Negro Digest (January 1970): 23-28.

6149. _________. "The Space Age Music of Sun Ra." Jazz & Pop (January 1968): 17-19.

6150. _________. "Sun Ra's Space Odyssey." down beat (May 14 1970): 14-17.

6151. Fleming, Robert. "Sun Ra's Soul Food Music." Encore American and Worldwide News (April 16 1979): 40-41.

6152. Franckling, Ken. "Sun Ra." Jazz Times (April 1988): 23. [Interview]

6153. "From Under the Pyramid." Jazz Journal (July 1970): 17.

6154. Gill, Andy. "Space is the Place." New Musical Express (August 7 1982): 24-26. [Interview]

6155. Gleason, Ralph J. "Perspectives: Sun Ra will be on the jukes." Rolling Stone (March 30 1972): 30.

6156. Jensen, J. R. "An Entirely New Reality." Jazz Forum, No. 32 (December 1974): 37. [Interview]

6157. Johnson, Brooks. "Toms and Tomming: A Contemporary Report." down beat (June 16 1966): 24, 44.

6158. Levenson, Jeff. "The Celestial Connection: Sun Ra." Hot House, Vol. 4, No. 11 (November 1985): 14.

6159. Lock, Graham. "Along Came Ra!" The Wire (London), No. 6 (Spring 1984): 2-3, 5-6.

6160. Lyons, Len. "Sun Ra: Interstellar Prophet of Jazz." Contemporary Keyboard (December 1978): 16+.

6161. Macnie, Jim. "Sun Ra Has Landed." Musician, No. 99 (January 1987): 60-63. [Interview]

6162. McRae, Barry. "Avant Courier." Jazz Journal (December 1972): 20-21.

6163. _________. "Sun Ra." Jazz Journal (August 1966): 15-16.

6164. Mandel, Howard. "John Cage Meets Sun Ra. Coney Island of the Minds." Ear, Vol. 11, No. 1 (August/September 1986): 20-21.

6165. _________. "Sun Ra: Space Relations." Ear (June 1990): 22-23.

6166. Primack, Bret. "Captain Angelic: Sun Ra." Down Beat (May 4 1978): 14+. [Interview]

6167. Reid, John L. "It's After the End of the World." Coda, No. 231 (April/May 1990): 30-32. [Interview]

6168. Rodrigues, D. A. "Sun Ra's Prophecy." Jazz Forum (December 1974): 35-37.

6169. Rusch, Bob. "Sun Ra: interview." Cadence, Vol. 4, No. 4 (June 1978): 3+. [Reprinted in # 6127]

6170. Sale, Bryan. "Sun Ra." Option (March-April 1987): 54-57.

6171. Schonfield, Victor. "Humanity/Sun Ra." Jazz Monthly (November 1970): 7.

6172. Shore, Michael. "Sun Ra." Musician, Player and Listener, No. 24 (April-May 1980): 49-51, 66.

6173. Sinclair, John. "Words from Sun Ra." Vibrations (New York), Vol. 1, No. 1 (July 1967): 16-19, 21.

6174. Sun Ra. "Humanity." Jazz Monthly, No. 189 (November 1970): 6-7.

6175. _________. "My Music is Words." The Cricket: Black Music in Evolution (Newark, NJ), No. 1 (1968?): 4-11.

6176. "Sun Ra." Jazz Times (September 1987): 21.

6177. "Sun Ra." Re Search (San Francisco), No. 1 (1980): 15.

6178. "Sun Ra: A Change of Laws." Soul (February 18 1974): 10.

6179. "Sun Ra and Europe's Space Music Scene." Rolling Stone (January 21 1971): 36-37.

6180. "Sun Ra reveals his cosmic music." Soul (July 9 1973): 11.

6181. "Sun Ra's Duality." Melody Maker (February 5 1972): 28.

6182. Theis, Rich. "Sun Ra." OP, Issue S (October-November 1983): 48-51.

6183. Thomas, J. C. "Sun Ra's Space Probe." down beat (June 13 1968): 19-20.

6184. Townley, Ray. "Sun Ra." down beat (December 20 1973): 18+.

6185. White, Charles. "The People Are the Instrument: Interview with Sun Ra." Lightworks (Ann Arbor, MI), No. 11/12 (Fall 1979): 16-18.

6186. Williams, Richard. "Sun Ra was into 'space music' 15 years before Pink Floyd." Melody Maker (September 4 1976): 13.

6187. Wilmer, Valerie. "Sun Ra." Melody Maker (October 29 1966): 8. [Interview]

6188. _________. "Sun Ra - In Search of Space." Melody Maker (November 4 1972): 48.

Newspaper Articles

6189. Crouch, Stanley. "Riffs: Last of the Great Bandleaders." Village Voice (June 1 1982): 65.

6190. Fiofori, Tam. "The Space Music of Sun Ra and His Space Arkestra." IT (London), No. 59 (July 4-17 1969): 18.

6191. Shore, Michael. "Calling Planet Earth." Soho Weekly News (July 19 1979): 48-49.

6192. Wilson, John S. "Sun Ra: 'I'm Talking About Cosmic Things.'" New York Times (April 7 1968): Sec. 2, pp. 1, 18.

6193. Zwerin, Michael. Sun Ra interview. Village Voice (August 15 1965).

Works in French, German and Dutch

6194. Berendt, Joachim Ernst. "Sun Ra und sein Schwarzer Kosmos." In Ein Fenster aus Jazz. Frankfurt am Main: S. Fischer, 1977, pp. 107-114.

6195. Vuijsje, Bert. De Nieuwe Jazz. Baarn: Bosch & Keuning, 1978, pp. 67-79. [Interview]

Biographical Dictionaries

6196. Carles, Philippe, and Jean-Louis Comolli. Free Jazz, Black Power. 2nd ed. Paris: Editions Galilee, 1979, pp. 442-445.

6197. Dictionnaire du Jazz, eds. Philippe Carles, et al. Paris: Laffont, 1988.

6198. Reclams Jazzfuhrer. 2nd, rev. ed. Stuttgart: Reclam, 1977.

6199. Reda, Jacques. Anthologie des Musiciens de Jazz. Paris: Stock, 1981, pp. 182-183.

Articles

6200. Buzelin, Jean. "Sun Ra and his Intergalactic Orchestra." Jazz Hot, No. 330 (Septembe 1976): 42-43.

6201. Carles, Philippe. "L'Opera Cosmique de Sun Ra." Jazz Magazine, No. 159 (October 1968): 26+.

6202. _________. "'Il sera temps d'edifier la maison noire...' Sun Ra." Jazz Magazine, No. 217 (December 1973): 24-26.

6203. _________, et. al. "Dossier Sun Ra." Jazz Magazine, No. 196 (January 1972): 9-23.

6204. _________, and Daniel Soutif. "Sun Ra and his Arkestra." Jazz Magazine, No. 216 (October-November 1973): 60.

6205. Caux, Daniel. "Free Jazz." Chroniques de l'Art Vivant (Paris), No. 7 (Janvier 1970): 30. Includes a brief personal statement by Sun Ra.

6206. _________. "The Strange World of Sun Ra." Chroniques de L'Art Vivant, No. 16 (Decembre 1970): 32-33.

6207. Cullaz, Maurice. "Sun Ra." Jazz Hot, No. 265 (October 1970): 30-31; No. 266 (November 1970): 22-24. [Interview]

6208. Cutler, Chris. "Sun Ra: Das Reich des Blitzes." Rock Session, Vol. 7 (1983): 57-88.

6209. "Dico Disco & Co." Jazz Magazine, No. 298 (June 1981): 64. Biographical sketch.

6210. Fiofori, Tam. "Sun Ra." Orkester Journalen (October 1971): 6+. [Interview]

6211. ________. "Sun Ra et l'Extension Intergalactique." Jazz Magazine, No. 185 (January 1971): 20+.

6212. Goddet, Laurent. "A propos de Sun Ra." Jazz Hot, No. 266 (November 1970): 28.

6213. "L'Impossible Liberte; Entretien avec Sun Ra, John Gilmore, Marshall Allen et Pat Patrick." Jazz Magazine, No. 196 (January 1972): 10-13.

6214. Noames, Jean-Louis. "Visite au Dieu Soleil." Jazz Magazine, No. 125 (December 1965): 70-77.

6215. "Les Nuits de Sun Ra." Jazz Magazine, No. 190 (June-July 1971): 36-37.

6216. Positif, Francois. "Sun Ra Existe: je l'ai rencontre." Jazz Hot, No. 298 (October 1973): 31.

6217. "Un Soir au Chatelet. Compte rendua plusieurs voix." Jazz Magazine, No. 196 (January 1972): 14-17. Roundtable discussion of Sun Ra's music by a panel of French critics.

6218. "Le Soleil dans sa Maison." Jazz Magazine, No. 322 (Octobre 1983): 20-23.

6219. Soutif, Daniel. "Sun Ra: un beau soleil sous le bonnet." Claviers, No. 1 (May 1981): 40-46, 90. [Interview]

6220. "Sun Ra et l'Odyssee Spatiale." Jazz Magazine, No. 185 (January 1971): 26+. [Interview]

6221. Tercinet, Alain. "Le soleil n'a pas brille pour nous ou comment je n'ai pas entendu Sun Ra." Jazz Hot, No. 267 (December 1970): 9.

Concert Reviews

6222. Brecht, Stefan S. "Sun Ra." Evergreen Review (May 1968): 88, 90. Review of a performance at the New York club Slugs.

6223. "Caught in the Act." down beat (April 2 1970): 30.

6224. Gleason, Ralph J. "Sun Ra's Astro-Infinity Arkestra." New York Post (December 31 1968).

6225. "In the Press." BMI (April 1967): 10. Excerpts from a New York Times review by John S. Wilson on a Sun Ra concert at Slugs.

6226. "Sun Ra and His Disney Odyssey Arkestra." Variety (March 1 1989): 70.

6227. Wilson, John S. "'Space Age Jazz' Lacks Boosters. Cosmic Group Fails to Orbit with Rhythmic Propulsion." New York Times (February 19 1962).

6228. ________. "Sun Ra Presents Multimedia Trip. Leads Arkestra in Museum of Art 'Composers' Series." New York Times (February 5 1971).

6229. ________. "Sun Ra's Arkestra Plays Continuously for Over 2 Hours." New York Times (February 23 1970).

6230. Zwerin, Michael. "Jazz Journal: One For Two." Village Voice (May 25 1967): 17. Concert at Slugs.

Record Reviews

6231. McRae, Barry. "Avant Courier: Another Look at Sun Ra." Jazz Journal (December 1975): 14+.

6232. Pekar, Harvey. "Sun Ra." Coda, No. 139 (June/July 1975): 2-8.

6233. Vein, Julian. "Sun Ra on Saturn and Savoy." Jazz Journal (November 1967): 19, 22.

Discographies

6234. Buzelin, Jean, and Alain Rene Hardy. "Disco Sun Ra." Jazz Hot, No. 361 (May 1979): 15-18; No. 362 (June 1979): 23-25. [Part 1: 1953-1970; Part 2: 1971-1978]

6235. Fluckiger, Otto. "Discography of Sun Ra." Jazz Statistics, No. 21 (March 1961): 4-6; additions and corrections from Michael Vogler, No. 22 (June 1961): 6.

6236. Geerken, Hartmut. Chronological Discography of the Acoustic Works of Sun Ra, 1956-1981. Athens, Greece: Geerken (P.O. Box 1022 (Omonia), Athens, Greece), 1982. 21p.

6237. Stahl, Tilman. Sun Ra Materialen = Sun Ra Materials. Rev. and enl. ed. Freudenberg, W. Germany: T. Stahl (Romershagenerstr. 27, 5905 Freudenberg), 1987. (looseleaf). (Orig. 1983) [German and English text]

Media Materials

6238. The Cry of Jazz (1959). Features an appearance by Sun Ra and the Arkestra.

6239. Bland, Edward. "On 'The Cry of Jazz.'" Film Culture (Summer 1960): 28-32.

6240. "The Death of Jazz." down beat (April 30 1959): 13. Review of "The Cry of Jazz."

6241. Mystery, Mr. Ra (1984). 51 min. Dir. by Frank Cassenti. [Available from Rhapsody Films, Box 179, New York, NY 10014. Tel. 212/243-0152; Or, Stash Records, 611 Broadwy, Suite 411, New York, NY 10012. Tel. 1-800-666-JASS]

6242. Sun Ra: A Joyful Noise. Directed by Robert Mugge. 60 min., color. [Available from Rhapsody Films, P.O. Box 179, New York, NY 10014. Tel. 212/243-0152]

SURMAN, JOHN (1945-) (Great Britain) - Reeds

6243. Fox, Charles. "Common Market Jazzman." In The Jazz Scene. London: Hamlyn, 1972, pp. 86-89.

Biographical Dictionaries

6244. Carr, Ian. "Surman, John." In Jazz: The Essential Companion. New York: Prentice Hall Press, 1988.

6245. Case, Brian, and Stan Britt. The Harmony Illustrated Encyclopedia of Jazz. 3rd ed. New York: Harmony Books, 1987.

6246. Claghorn, Charles Eugene. Biographical Dictionary of Jazz. Englewood Cliffs, NJ: Prentice-Hall, 1982.

6247. Dictionnaire du Jazz, eds. Philippe Carles, et al. Paris: Laffont, 1988.

6248. Feather, Leonard, and Ira Gitler. The Encyclopedia of Jazz in the Seventies. New York: Horizon Press, 1976.

6249. Jazz Now: the Jazz Centre Society Guide, ed. Roger Cotterrell. London: Quartet Books, 1976, p. 172.

6250. McRae, Barry. "John Surman." In The Jazz Handbook. Harlow, Essex, Eng.: Longman, 1987, pp. 216-217.

6251. The New Grove Dictionary of Jazz. London: Macmillan Press, 1988.

6252. The Penguin Encyclopedia of Popular Music, ed. Donald Clarke. New York: Viking, 1989.

Articles

6253. Bird, Christopher. "John Surman." Melody Maker (December 9 1967): 4.

6254. Byrczek, Jan, and Roman Kowal. "The Trio--Surman Phillips Martin." Jazz Forum, No. 13/14 (Autumn/Winter 1971): 62-63, 72-74.

6255. Cotterrell, Roger. "John Surman: Perpetual Motion." Jazz Forum, No. 76 (1982): 25+.

6256. Cullaz, Maurice. "John Surman, Barre Phillips, Stu Martin--interview." Jazz Hot, No. 259 (March 1970): 16-19.

6257. Danson, Peter. "John Surman." Coda, No. 189 (April 1983): 12-13. [Interview]

6258. Gourse, Leslie. "John Surman." down beat (December 1985): 25-27. [Interview]

6259. Henshaw, L. "Now Surman Joins the British Jazz Brain Drain." Melody Maker (June 14 1969): 10.

6260. King, M. C. "British jazzmen: John Surman." Jazz Journal (January 1971): 6.

6261. Lock, Graham. "Save the Wail." The Wire, No. 14 (April 1985): 34-35, 37.

6262. McRae, Barry. "Upon Reflection." Jazz Journal International (July 1989): 14-17.

6263. Paton, Maureen. "Surman on the Mount." Melody Maker (April 22 1978): 52. [Interview]

6264. Priestley, Brian. "John Surman." Jazz Monthly (March 1970): 30.

6265. Rouy, Gerard. "Ici Londres: John Surman." Jazz Magazine, No. 273 (March 1979): 32-33.

6266. Schonfield, Victor. "World class baritone from the west country." Melody Maker (August 12 1967): 6.

6267. Tomkins, Les. "A Meeting with Mumps: John Surman and Albert Mangelsdorff." Crescendo International (January 1978): 23+; (February 1978): 14-15. [Interview]

6268. Williams, Richard. "Surman for Today." Melody Maker (April 28 1973): 25.

6269. ________. "Surman: the happy wanderer." Melody Maker (March 14 1970): 8.

6270. Witherden, Barry. "John Surman: no profit in his own country." Wire, No. 76 (June 1990): 20-23.

6271. "World Class." Melody Maker (February 24 1968): 22.

TACUMA, JAMALADEEN [Rudy McDaniel] (1956-) - Bass

6272. Case, Brian, and Stan Britt. The Harmony Illustrated Encyclopedia of Jazz. 3rd ed. New York: Harmony Books, 1987.

6273. Dictionnaire du Jazz, eds. Philippe Carles, et al. Paris: Laffont, 1988.

6274. Milkowski, Bill. "Tacuma, Jamaladeen." In The New Grove Dictionary of Jazz. London: Macmillan Press, 1988.

Articles

6275. Gans, Charles J. "Jamaladeen Tacuma: 21st century electrical bass guitarist." Jazz Forum, No. 80 (1983): 52-57. [Interview]

6276. Lake, Steve. "A Renaissance Man for All Seasons." The Wire (London), No. 21 (November 1985): 18-19, 21.

6277. May, Chris. "Full Bass Ahead." Black Music and Jazz Review [London] (November 1983): 20-22.

6278. Milkowski, Bill. "Jamaladeen Tacuma." down beat (June 1985): 14-15.

6279. ________, and Chip Stern. "Jamaladeen Tacuma: breaking bass barriers." Guitar Player (May 1983): 76-85. [Interview]

6280. Tate, Gregory. "The Sons of Ornette: Jamaladeen Tacuma, Blood Ulmer and The Future of Harmolodics." Musician, No. 51 (January 1983): 62-64, 66.

6281. Tinder, Cliff. "Jamaladeen Tacuma: electric bass in the harmolodic pocket." down beat (April 1982): 19-21, 71. [Interview]

TAPSCOTT, HORACE (1934-) - Piano/Bandleader

See also # 187

6282. Carles, Philippe, and Jean-Louis Comolli. Free Jazz, Black Power. 2nd ed. Paris: Editions Galilee, 1979, pp. 445-446.

6283. Claghorn, Charles Eugene. Biographical Dictionary of Jazz. Englewood Cliffs, NJ: Prentice-Hall, 1982.

6284. Dictionnaire du Jazz, eds. Philippe Carles, et al. Paris: Laffont, 1988.

6285. Feather, Leonard, and Ira Gitler. The Encyclopedia of Jazz in the Seventies. New York: Horizon Press, 1976.

6286. The New Grove Dictionary of Jazz. London: Macmillan Press, 1988.

6287. Southern, Eileen. Biographical Dictionary of Afro-American and African Musicians. Westport, CT: Greenwood Press, 1982.

Articles

6288. Cohen, Elaine. "Horace Tapscott Alive and Well in L.A." Jazz World, Vol. 14, No. 59 (1984).

6289. ________. "Horace Tapscott Talking: A Legacy to Pass On." Cadence, Vol. 10, No. 7 (July 1984): 8-10+; No. 8 (August 1984): 12-14.

6290. Crouch, Stanley. "Black Song West." The Cricket: Black Music in Evolution (Newark, NJ), No. 4 (1971): 21-27. Profile of Horace Tapscott and the Community Cultural Orchestra.

6291. Ginibre, Jean-Louis. "April in LA." Jazz Magazine, No. 288 (July/August 1980): 66. On the Pan-African People's Arkestra.

6292. Keller, David. "Horace Tapscott." Jazz Times (October 1982): 8-9.

6293. Kofsky, Frank. "Horace Tapscott." Jazz & Pop (December 1969): 16-18. [Interview]

6294. Levi, Titus. "Pianist Horace Tapscott: Keeping It Lit." OPtion (September/October 1986): 37-38. [Interview]

6295. Lock, Graham. "Check." Wire, No. 19 (September 1985): 53. Review of Tapscott's lp "The Tapscott Sessions."

6296. Meyner, Stephan. "Horace Tapscott." Jazz Podium (November 1982): 26-7. [Profile]

6297. Mitchell, Rico. "Horace Tapscott." down beat (January 1988): 13.

6298. "Quiet West Coast Giant Reawakens." down beat (December 21 1978): 13.

6299. Stewart, Zan. "Horace Tapscott." Musician, Player and Listener, No. 21 (November 1979): 54-7. [Interview]

6300. Vercelli, Gary. "Horace Tapscott." Radio Free Jazz, Vol. 19, No. 5 (May 1978): 17-18. [Profile]

6301. Weiss, Jason. "Horace Tapscott: L'Autre West Coast." Jazz Magazine, No. 321 (September 1983): 28-29, 50. [Interview]

6302. _________. "Horace Tapscott: Music for the People." Jazz Forum, No. 83 (1983): 24-29. [Interview]

6303. Williams, J. "Tapscott Taps Out a New System." Billboard (April 10 1976): 22.

Newspaper Articles

6304. Blumenthal, Bob. "Ode to Horace: Tapscott and the silver age of jazz." Boston Phoenix (July 3 1984). [Concert review]

6305. Burk, Greg. "Heh-heh: Horace Tapscott in the Heart of It." L.A. Weekly (July 28-August 3 1989): 49.

6306. Keller, David. "Horace Tapscott's Musical Ark." Los Angeles Reader, Vol. 4, No. 36 (July 2 1982).

6307. Snowden, Don. "Horace Tapscott: In the Shadow of a Crusade." Los Angeles Times (August 30 1980): Part II, p. 10.

6308. Stokes, W. Royal. "Nurturing the Jazz Craft." Washington Post (April 5 1986).

TARASOV, VLADIMIR (1947-) (Russia) - Drums

See also # 3210-3238

6309. Ojakaar, Walter. "Tarasov, Vladimir." In The New Grove Dictionary of Jazz. London: Macmillan Press, 1988.

TAYLOR, CECIL [Percival] (1933-)

See also # 69, 181, 282, 543, 554, 695, 703, 705, 6769

Works in English

6310. Various Authors. Cecil Taylor in Berlin '88. Berlin: Free Music Production (Behaimstrasse 4, 1000 Berlin 10, Germany), 1990. 188p. Book accompanying an 11-CD box set of Taylor duos and solos.

Books with Sections on Cecil Taylor

6311. Davis, Francis. "The Cantos of Cecil Taylor." In Outcats. New York: Oxford University Press, 1990, pp. 42-45.

6312. Giddins, Gary. "The Avant-Gardist Who Came In from the Cold." In Riding on a Blue Note. New York: Oxford University Press, 1981, pp. 274-296.

6313. Goldberg, Joe. "Cecil Taylor." In Jazz Masters of the Fifties. New York: Da Capo Press, 1983, pp. 213-227. (Reprint of 1965 ed.)

6314. Jost, Ekkehard. "Cecil Taylor." In Free Jazz. Graz: Universal Edition, 1974, pp. 66-83.

6315. Litweiler, John. "Cecil Taylor." In The Freedom Principle. New York: Morrow, 1984, pp. 200-221.

6316. Lyons, Leonard. "Cecil Taylor." In The Great Jazz Pianists. New York: Morrow, 1983, pp. 301-311.

6317. Rusch, Robert. "Cecil Taylor." In Jazz Talk: The Cadence Interviews. Secaucus, NJ: Lyle Stuart, 1984, pp. 49-60.

6318. Spellman, A. B. "Cecil Taylor." In Four Lives in the Bebop Business. New York: Pantheon Books, 1966, pp. 3-76.

6319. Wilmer, Valerie. "Cecil Taylor - Eighty-Eight Tuned Drums." In As Serious As Your Life. Westport, CT: Lawrence Hill & Co., 1981, pp. 45-59. See also, p. 281.

6320. ________. "Each Man His Own Academy." In Jazz People. New York: Bobbs-Merrill, 1970, pp. 23-30.

Biographical Dictionaries

6321. Baker's Biographical Dictionary of Musicians. 7th ed. revised by Nicolas Slonimsky. New York: Schirmer Books, 1984.

6322. Berry, Lemuel, Jr. Biographical Dictionary of Black Musicians and Music Educators. Guthrie, OK: Educational Book Publishers, 1978.

6323. Carr, Ian. "Taylor, Cecil." In Jazz: The Essential Companion. New York: Prentice Hall Press, 1988.

6324. Case, Brian, and Stan Britt. The Harmony Illustrated Encyclopedia of Jazz. 3rd ed. New York: Harmony Books, 1987.

6325. Claghorn, Charles Eugene. Biographical Dictionary of Jazz. Englewood Cliffs, NJ: Prentice-Hall, 1982.

6326. Dobbins, Bill. "Taylor, Cecil (Percival)." In The New Grove Dictionary of American Music. London: Macmillan Press, 1986.

6327. ________. "Taylor, Cecil Percival." In The New Grove Dictionary of Jazz. London: Macmillan Press, 1988.

6328. Feather, Leonard. The Encyclopedia of Jazz in the Sixties. New York: Horizon Press, 1966.

6329. ________, and Ira Gitler. The Encyclopedia of Jazz in the Seventies. New York: Horizon Press, 1976.

6330. McRae, Barry. "Cecil Taylor." In The Jazz Handbook. Harlow, Essex, Eng.: Longman, 1987, pp. 217-219.

6331. The Penguin Encyclopedia of Popular Music, ed. Donald Clarke. New York: Viking, 1989.

6332. Southern, Eileen. Biographical Dictionary of Afro-American and African Musicians. Westport, CT: Greenwood Press, 1982.

6333. Who's Who in Entertainment. 1st ed. 1989-1990.

Articles

6334. Balliett, Whitney. "Jazz: Cecil." New Yorker (May 5 1986): 106+. [Profile]

6335. Beckett, Alan. "Motifs: Cecil Taylor." New Left Review, No. 23 (January-February 1964): 89-91.

6336. Blumenthal, Bob. "Cecil Taylor: Unfettered and Alive." Rolling Stone (June 28 1979): 36.

6337. Brasz, Marc. "Unit Structure: Cecil Taylor: Apotheosis of." Boss (New York), No. 2 (Spring 1967): 56-61.

6338. Buholzer, Meinrad. "Cecil Taylor: Interview." Cadence, Vol. 10, No. 12 (December 1984): 5-9.

6339. Case, Brian. "Into the Hot Jazz." Melody Maker (October 5 1985): 41. [Interview]

6340. ________. "Ladies and Gentlemen, Please Adjust Your Re-Entry Goggles." New Musical Express (June 7 1975): 34-35. [Profile]

6341. _________. "Two Slices for the Piano Athlete." New Musical Express (September 20 1975): 31. [Interview]

6342. "Cecil Taylor attacked on street; wrist broken." down beat (August 27 1964): 8-9.

6343. Coss, Bill. "Cecil Taylor's Struggle for Existence; Portrait of the artist as a coiled spring." down beat (October 26 1961): 19-21.

6344. Darter, Tom. "Piano Giants of Jazz: Cecil Taylor." Contemporary Keyboard (May 1981): 56-57.

6345. Doerschuk, Bob. "Cecil Taylor: In the Eye of the Hurricane." Keyboard, Vol. 11, No. 1 (1985): 38+.

6346. Durfee, Roy. "Cecil Taylor in Santa Fe." Coda, No. 220 (June/July 1988): 10-11. Report on a C.T. workshop in Santa Fe, New Mexico.

6347. Easter, Gilbert. "So, What is Jazz?; a mainstream view of the avant-garde." Jazz & Blues (June 1972): 25.

6348. Figi, J. B. "Cecil Taylor: African Code, Black Methodology." down beat (April 10 1975): 12+. [Interview]

6349. Goldberg, Joe. "Cecil Taylor and the New Tradition." Saturday Review (February 9 1963): 42-43.

6350. Griffith, Pat. "Cecil speaks." Melody Maker (April 3 1971): 12. [Interview]

6351. Gushee, Larry. "Cecil Taylor." Jazz Review, Vol. 3 (June 1960): 28+.

6352. Hentoff, Nat. "Cecil Taylor." BMI (May 1965): 18. [Biography]

6353. _________. Interview with Cecil Taylor. Status (November 1965).

6354. _________. "The Persistent Challenge of Cecil Taylor." down beat (February 25 1965): 16, 40.

6355. Jazz 360o (Sierre, Switzerland), No. 22 (November 1979). Special Cecil Taylor issue.

6356. Jeske, Lee. "Cecil Taylor Expanded Unit." down beat (June 1982): 59.

6357. _________. "Max and Cecil: Percussive Pianist Meets Melodic Drummer." down beat (April 1980): 16-19, 60, 71. [Interview]

6358. Litweiler, John. "Needs and Acts; Cecil Taylor in Wisconsin." down beat (October 14 1971): 16+.

6359. Lock, Graham. "Out to Lunch with a Jazz Eccentric." New Musical Express (June 18 1983): 16-18. [Interview]

6360. Lynch, Kevin. "Cecil Taylor and the Poetics of Living." down beat (November 1986): 22-24, 67.

6361. Lyons, Len. "Cecil Taylor." Contemporary Keyboard (January 1979): 26+. [Interview]

6362. Macnie, Jim. "Piano Summit: Cecil Taylor meets Ahmad Jamal." Musician (May 1990): 28-31, 34-36, 38-39. [Interview]

6363. McRae, Barry. "Avant Courier: excursions on a wobbly rail." Jazz Journal (December 1974): 14+.

6364. Mathieson, Kenny. "Cecil Taylor: Striking the Note." Wire, No. 46/47 (December 1987-January 1988): 57-59, 66. [Interview]

6365. Miller, Mark. "Cecil Taylor; Musician Poet Dancer." Coda, No. 220 (June/July 1988): 4-6. [Reprinted from Banff Letters (1986)]

6366. Priestley, Brian. "Florescent Stripper." Wire, No. 82/83 (Dec 90/Jan 1991): 24-26, 74. [Interview]

6367. Quinn, Bill. "Cecil Taylor's alternative auditory architecture." Radio Free Jazz (February 1978): 8-10.

6368. Rothbart, Peter. "Cecil Taylor Unit at the Creative Music Studio: Orchestrating the Collective Unconscious." down beat (April 1980): 17, 20-21.

6369. Runcie, John. "Cecil Taylor's Artistic Triumph." Black Music and Jazz Review, Vol. 2, No. 2 (May 1979): 22-23.

6370. ________. "The Hard Times and Artistic Triumph of Cecil Taylor." Jazz Journal International (February 1980): 28-29. [Interview]

6371. Rusch, Bob. "Cecil Taylor: interview." Cadence, Vol. 4, No. 1 (April 1978): 3-6, 11.

6372. Russell, Charlie L. "Has Jazz Lost Its Roots." Liberator (New York), Vol. IV, No. 8 (August 1964): 4-7. [Interview]

6373. Santoro, Gene. "Cecil Taylor: An American Romantic." down beat (June 1990): 16-18. [Interview]

6374. Smith, Bill. "Unit Structures: Cecil Taylor in Conversation." Coda (March 1975): 2-8. [Interview]

6375. Spellman, A. B. "Genesis of the New Music - II: Cecil Taylor." Evergreen Review (April 1967): 72-73, 107.

6376. Summers, Russ. "Cecil Taylor." Option (July/August 1989): 70-73. [Interview]

6377. "Taylor, Cecil." Current Biography 1986.

6378. Tomkins, Les. "Anatomy of the Avant-Garde: Cecil Taylor." Crescendo International (October 1975): 22-23.

6379. Webb, Mary Lou. "Cecil Taylor." Different Drummer, Vol. 1, No. 4 (January 1974): 8-9.

6380. White, Ted. "Cecil Taylor: the danger of style." Metronome (September 1960): 36-37.

6381. Williams, Martin. "The Trials of Cecil Taylor." Saturday Review (March 11 1967): 120.

6382. Williams, Richard. "Cecil Taylor's music made people nervous and still does." Melody Maker (December 11 1976): 14.

6383. ________. "For Cecil Taylor, it's just beginning." Melody Maker (November 8 1969): 12.

6384. ________. "Stoking the Fires of Controversy?" Melody Maker (October 25 1969): 9.

6385. Wilmer, Val. "In the Key of Life." City Limits [London] (November 13-19 1981): 53.

6386. Wise, D. "Cecil Taylor: Why I Don't Call My Music Jazz." Melody Maker (December 31 1966): 6.

Newspaper Articles

6387. "Cecil Taylor: The Space of 61 Years Danced Through." Village Voice/Voice Jazz Special (June 26 1990). Special section devoted to Taylor. Edited by Gary Giddins. Includes essays by Richard Cook, Norman Weinstein, and Ekkehard Jost.

6388. Crouch, Stanley. "Riffs: Cecil Taylor: Pitfalls of the Primitive." Village Voice (March 30 1982): 59.

6389. Giddins, Gary. "A Benign Hell." Village Voice (November 27 1984): 100, 132.

6390. ________. "Cecil Taylor: An American Master Brings the Voodoo Home." Village Voice (April 28 1975): 124-125.

6391. ________. "Pick a Card, Any Card." Village Voice (March 12 1979): 70.

6392. Mandel, Howard. "Improvisations and Innovations. Cecil Taylor's Piano Passion." Washington Post (November 25 1984): G1, G6-G7. [Interview]

Works in French, German, Dutch and Italian

6393. Buholzer, Meinrad, Abi S. Rosenthal, and Val Wilmer. Auf der Suche nach Cecil Taylor. Hofheim, Germany: Wolke Verlag; Tel Aviv, Israel: JAS Publikationen, 1990. 166p.

6394. Roggeman, Willy. "Cecil Taylor." In Free en Andere Jazz-Essays. The Hague: Van Ditmar, 1969, pp. 73-80. [Dutch text]

6395. Vuijsje, Bert. De Nieuwe Jazz. Baarn: Bosch & Keuning, 1978, pp. 38-55. [Interview]

Biographical Dictionaries

6396. Carles, Philippe, and Jean-Louis Comolli. Free Jazz, Black Power. 2nd ed. Paris: Editions Galilee, 1979, pp. 446-450.

6397. Dictionnaire du Jazz, eds. Philippe Carles, et al. Paris: Laffont, 1988.

6398. Reclams Jazzfuhrer. 2nd, rev. ed. Stuttgart: Reclam, 1977.

6399. Reda, Jacques. Anthologie des Musiciens de Jazz. Paris: Stock, 1981, pp. 323-324.

6400. Tenot, Frank. Dictionnaire du Jazz. Paris: Larousse, 1967.

Articles

6401. Arrigoni, A. "Qual cosa sta cambiando." Musica Jazz (June 1960): 17-21.

6402. Balli, Enrico. "Cecil Taylor." Musica Jazz (March 1960): 26. [Biography]

6403. Berger, Daniel. "Cecil Taylor a la Trace." Jazz Hot, No. 227 (January 1967): 15-19; No. 228 (February 1967): 15-21.

6404. Binchet, P. "Portrait: Cecil Taylor." Jazz Magazine, No. 9 (November 1963): 45-47.

6405. Caux, Daniel, et Philippe Gras. "Cecil Taylor: Interview Exclusive." Chroniques de L'Art Vivant, No. 7 (janvier 1970): 26-28.

6406. "Cecil: a la ville comme a la scene." Jazz Magazine, No. 294 (February 1981): 30+. Photo essay.

6407. "Cecil Taylor." Jazz Magazine, No. 234 (July 1975): 26+. [Interview]

6408. "Cecil Taylor a Paris." Jazz Magazine, No. 138 (January 1967): 32-37.

6409. Delorme, Michel. "Cecil Taylor a la Face de Droit." Jazz Hot, No. 227 (January 1967): 5.

6410. "Dico Disco & Co." Jazz Magazine, No. 298 (June 1981): 64. Biographical sketch.

6411. Echenoz, J. "Ce que je sais de Cecil Taylor." Jazz Hot, No. 296 (July-August 1973): 18-19.

6412. Endress, Gudrun. "Cecil Taylor Interview." Jazz Podium (July 1966): 176-179.

6413. Griffith, Pat. "Taylor raconte octobre et la suite." Jazz Magazine, No. 188 (April 1971): 26-29. [Interview]

6414. Hofstein, F., et Denis Constant. "Cecil a Saint-Paul." Jazz Magazine, No. 169-170 (September 1969): 10-11.

6415. Jalard, Michel-Claude. "Trois Apotres du Discontinu." Jazz Magazine, No. 6 (December 1960): 42+.

6416. Le Bris, M. "Interview." Jazz Hot, No. 248 (March 1969): 20-22.

6417. "My Taylor is Roach." Jazz Magazine, No. 332 (September-October 1984): 36-39. [Interview]

6418. Paudras, Francis. "Cecil Taylor." Jazz Hot, No. 206 (February 1965): 24-26.

6419. Pinguet, Francis. "Cecil Taylor le Solitaire." Jazz Hot, No. 248 (March 1969): 14-19.

6420. _________, et Maurice Cullaz. "Cecil Taylor: deux nuits a la Fondation Maeght." Jazz Hot, No. 253 (September 1969): 11-14.

6421. "Le Systeme Taylor." Jazz Magazine, No. 125 (December 1965): 32-38.

6422. Werner, L. "Cecil Taylor." Orkester Journalen (October 1962): 10-11. [Biography]

6423. _________. "Cecil Taylor Stimulerande." Orkester Journalen (November 1962): 16.

Concert Reviews

6424. Albertson, Chris. "Caught in the Act: Cecil Taylor, Slugs." down beat (April 16 1970): 28.

6425. Balliett, Whitney. "Jazz Concerts." New Yorker (March 14 1959): 88+.

6426. _________. "Jazz Concerts: Performance of the New Thing at Town Hall." New Yorker (March 20 1965): 175-176.

6427. _________. "Jazz Concerts." New Yorker (June 6 1977): 122, 127. Review of Mary Lou Williams/Cecil Taylor concert.

6428. Blevins, Brian. "Taylor Triumphs in Nice." Melody Maker (August 16 1969): 6. Review of Taylor performance in Saint-Paul de Vence, France at La Fondation Maeght.

6429. Boyd, Herb. "Caught in the Act: Cecil Taylor, Ibo Cultural Center, Detroit." down beat (February 3 1972): 28-29.

6430. Brasz, Marc. "Cecil Taylor at Town Hall." Liberator (New York), Vol. 6, No. 8 (August 1966): 20-21.

6431. Giddins, Gary. "Caught in the Act: Cecil Taylor, Metropolitan Museum of Art." down beat (June 22 1972): 30.

6432. Hofstein, F., and Denis Constant. "Cecil a Saint-Paul." Jazz Magazine, No. 169-170 (September 1969): 10-11.

6433. Jones, LeRoi. "Caught in the Act: John Coltrane-Cecil Taylor-Art Blakey." down beat (February 27 1964): 34. Review of a New Year's eve concert at New York's Philharmonic Hall. Of particular note was the appearance of Albert Ayler with C.T.'s group.

6434. Morgenstern, Dan. "Caught in the Act." down beat (July 28 1966): 24.

6435. Norris, John. "Caught in the Act." down beat (May 30 1968): 34.

6436. Piazza, I. "Williams-Taylor Concert." Jazz Magazine (Northport, NY), Vol. 1, No. 4 (1977): 14+.

6437. Positif, Francois. "New York in Jazz Time." Jazz Hot (December 1960): 23-24. Comments on a Cecil Taylor performance at the New York club the Showplace.

6438. Sinclair, John. "Cecil Taylor, John Coltrane, and Archie Shepp at the Down Beat Festival, Chicago, 8/15/65." Change (Detroit), No. 1 (Fall/Winter 1965): 34-38.

6439. Smith, Arnold Jay. "Caught: Mary Lou Williams/Cecil Taylor, Carnegie Hall." down beat (July 14 1977): 54, 56.

6440. Williams, Martin. "Caught in the Act." down beat (May 6 1965): 36.

6441. _________. "Caught in the Act." down beat (May 1 1969): 38.

Newspaper Reviews

6442. Crouch, Stanley. "'Eatin' Rain in Space': Mikhail Baryshnikov Meets Cecil Taylor." Soho Weekly News (August 16 1979): 8-9.

6443. Giddins, Gary. "Cecil and Misha's Entangling Alliance." Village Voice (September 3 1979): 68-69.

6444. _________. "Mary Lou and Cecil Shake Hands." Village Voice (April 25 1977). Review of Mary Lou Williams/Cecil Taylor duo concert.

6445. _________. "Riffs: Roach and Taylor Charge in Unison." Village Voice (December 31 1979): 58.

6446. Johnson, Tom. "Cecil Taylor, Expressionist." Village Voice (June 30 1975): 101.

6447. Occhiogrosso, Peter. "When Pianos Collide." Soho Weekly News (May 5 1977): 42. Review of Mary Lou Williams/Cecil Taylor concert.

6448. Palmer, Robert. "Jazz: The Taylor-Roach Duo Concert." New York Times (December 17 1979).

6449. Pareles, Jon. "A Pair of Opposites in a Reunion." New York Times (December 13 1989): C25. Review of CT/Max Roach reunion concert.

6450. Taylor, J. R. "Concerts Disconcerting." Village Voice (January 24 1974): 52.

6451. Wilson, John S. "Taylor, Jazz Pianist, Plays in Town Hall." New York Times (September 20 1966).

Record Reviews

6452. Atkins, Ronald. "Jazz Piano: Present and Future." Jazz Monthly, Vol. 8 (September 1962): 10-11.

6453. Balleras, Jon. "Record Reviews: Spring of Two Blue-J's." down beat (April 11 1974): 18.

6454. Balliett, Whitney. "Jazz Records." New Yorker (October 21 1961): 168-172.

6455. Berg, Chuck. "Record Reviews: Embraced." down beat (December 7 1978): 29. Review of the recording from the Mary Lou Williams/Cecil Taylor concert.

6456. Giddins, Gary. "Cecil Taylor: Record of the Year." Village Voice (January 9 1990): 61. Review of Free Music Production's 11 CD set "Cecil Taylor in Berlin '88".

6457. ________. "Pick a Card, Any Card." Village Voice (March 12 1979): 70. Review of the New World lp "The Cecil Taylor Unit."

6458. James, Michael. "Some Interesting Contemporaries." Jazz & Blues (January 1973): 13. Discussion of Taylor's Contemporary lps.

6459. Kofsky, Frank. "In Review: The World of Cecil Taylor." down beat (March 30 1961): 40, 42.

6460. Litweiler, John B. "Jazz: Cecil Taylor Live at the Cafe Montmartre." Kulchur, No. 15 (Autumn 1964): 96-98.

6461. Mathieu, Bill. "Record Reviews: Live at the Cafe Montmartre." down beat (April 9 1964): 29.

6462. Milkowski, Bill. "Cecil Taylor Boxed in Berlin." Pulse! (September 1990): 17, 19. Description of the 11-CD Free Music Production collection of C.T. solos and duos.

6463. Quinn, Bill. "Record Reviews: Unit Structures." down beat (February 23 1967): 31-32.

6464. Schuller, Gunther. "Cecil Taylor." Jazz Review, Vol. 2 (January 1959): 28-31.

6465. Smith, Will. "Record Reviews: Indent." down beat (October 25 1973): 18.

6466. Tolley, Trevor. "The Early World of Cecil Taylor." Coda, No. 234 (Oct/Nov 1990): 34-37. Review of "The Complete Candid Recordings of Cecil Taylor and Buell Neidlinger."

Discographies

6467. Hames, Mike. Albert Ayler, Sunny Murray, Cecil Taylor, Byard Lancaster, Kenneth Terroade on disc and tape. Ferndown, Eng.: Hames (16 Pinewood Road, Ferndown, Dorset BH22 9RW), 1983. 61p.

Media Materials

6468. Imagine the Sound (1981). 91 min. Directed by Ron Mann. Documentary on the life and musics of Archie Shepp, Bill Dixon, Cecil Taylor and Paul Bley. [For distribution information contact: Bill Smith, c/o Coda Publications, Box 87, Station J, Toronto, Ontario M4J 4X8, Canada]

6469. Marian McPartland's Piano Jazz: Cecil Taylor (Audiotape). 60 minutes. Includes a tribute to Jimmy Lyons and a duet with Marian McPartland on "Get Out of Town." [Available from National Public Radio, Cassette Publishing, 2025 M Street, N.W., Washington, D.C. 20036. Tel. 800/253-0808]

TCHICAI, JOHN (1936-) (Denmark) - Alto Saxophone

See also # 543, 695-696, 5058-5067

6470. Noglik, Bert. "John Tchicai." In Jazzwerkstatt International. Berlin: Verlag Neue Musik, 1981, pp. 399-413. [Interview]

6471. Roggeman, Willy. "John Tchicai." In Free en Andere Jazz-Essays. The Hague: Van Ditmar, 1969, pp. 97-101. [Dutch text]

6472. Tchicai, John. Advice to Improvisers: Compositions and Exercises for All Instruments. Copenhagen: Edition Wilhelm Hansen, 1989(?). 43p.

Biographical Dictionaries

6473. Carles, Philippe, and Jean-Louis Comolli. Free Jazz, Black Power. 2nd ed. Paris: Editions Galilee, 1979, p. 450.

6474. Claghorn, Charles Eugene. Biographical Dictionary of Jazz. Englewood Cliffs, NJ: Prentice-Hall, 1982.

6475. Dictionnaire du Jazz, eds. Philippe Carles. Paris: Laffont, 1988.

6476. Feather, Leonard. The Encyclopedia of Jazz in the Sixties. New York: Horizon Press, 1966.

6477. Matthiessen, Ole, and Erik Wiedemann. "Tchicai, John." In The New Grove Dictionary of Jazz. London: Macmillan Press, 1988.

6478. Priestley, Brian. "Tchicai, John." In Jazz: The Essential Companion. New York: Prentice Hall Press, 1988.

6479. Reclams Jazzfuhrer. 2nd, rev. ed. Stuttgart: Reclam, 1977.

6480. Southern, Eileen. Biographical Dictionary of Afro-American and African Musicians. Westport, CT: Greenwood Press, 1982.

6481. Tenot, Frank. Dictionnaire du Jazz. Paris: Larousse, 1967.

6482. Wilmer, Valerie. As Serious As Your Life. Westport, CT: Lawrence Hill & Co., 1981, p. 281.

Articles

6483. Baggenaes, Roland. "John Tchicai." Coda, No. 221 (August/September 1988): 16-17.

6484. Barnett, Anthony. "John Tchicai, Of Three Continents." Jazz Monthly (October 1968): 2-6.

6485. Caloum, M. "John Tchicai: Jours Tranquille a Copenhague." Jazz Magazine, No. 189 (May 1971): 26-29. [Interview]

6486. Carles, Philippe. "Tchicai et la Lune Vide." Jazz Magazine, No. 188 (April 1971): 8-9.

6487. Comolli, Jean-Louis. "Tchicai sans Chique." Jazz Magazine, No. 137 (December 1966): 28-31. [Interview]

6488. "Danes Vote Tchicai 'Jazzman of the Year.'" Variety (February 19 1969): 64.

6489. "Dictionnaire de l'Alto." Jazz Magazine, No. 137 (December 1966): 50. Biographical sketch.

6490. Dixon, F. "Sorting Out the Good from the Bad." Melody Maker (October 12 1968): 12.

6491. Farne, Libero. "John Tchicai." Musica Jazz (August/September 1979): 16-19.

6492. Fiofori, Tam. "Meditating with Tchicai." Melody Maker (March 25 1972): 16.

6493. Flicker, Chris, and G. Noel. "Je m'Appelle John Tchicai." Jazz Hot, No. 272 (May 1971): 9-11.

6494. Lake, Steve. "Tchicai's Return." Melody Maker (January 22 1977): 32.

6495. "Lettre de Tchicai." Jazz Magazine, No. 139 (February 1967): 19.

6496. McRae, Barry. "Jazz in Britain." Jazz Journal (April 1969): 13-14.

6497. Morgenstern, Dan. "John Tchicai: A Calm Member of the Avant-Garde." down beat (February 10 1966): 20, 49.

6498. Pullman, Peter. "John Tchicai: The Danish Connection." Village Voice (August 28 1990): 71. [Profile]

6499. Raben, Erik. "John Tchicai, Dansk Avantgardist med Fairg." Orkester Journalen (February 1970): 8-9. [Interview]

6500. Rosenthal, David. "New Jazz from New York." Jazz Journal (July 1965): 10-12. Discussion of Tchicai, Pharoah Sanders, and Archie Shepp.

6501. Rouy, Gerard. "John Tchicai: Musique et Yoga." Jazz Magazine, No. 249 (November 1976): 14-15.

6502. _________. "John Tchicai: Jour Tranquille a Copenhague." Jazz Magazine, No. 286 (May 1980): 26-28. [Interview]

6503. Simmons, D. "London Music." Musical Opinion (November 1968): 64.

6504. Thomsen, C. B. "John Tchicai, Uppmarksammad Avantgarde-Musiker." Orkester Journalen (September 1965): 14.

6505. Wilmer, Valerie. "Caught in Act." down beat (December 12 1968): 33. [Concert review]

6506. _________. "Tchicai in Full Control." Melody Maker (October 12 1968): 8.

6507. Williams, Richard. "It Must Be Good - It's Danish!" Melody Maker (November 22 1969): 8.

6508. Zufferey, Maurice. "Interview: John Tchicai." Jazz 360o (Sierre, Switzerland), No. 58 (April 1983): 2-7.

Discographies

6509. Cerrutti, Gustave. John Tchicai Discography (on records) 1962-1985. 3rd ed. rev. and enl. Sierre, Switzerland: Jazz 360o (c/o G. Cerutti, 8, avenue du Marche, 3960 Sierre, Switzerland), 1982. (Orig. 1979)

6510. Hames, Mike. John Tchicai on Disc and Tape. London: Mike Hames (16 Pinewood Road, Ferndown, Wimborne, Dorset BH22 9RW England), 198?.

TERROADE, KENNETH (1944-) (Jamaica) - Tenor Saxophone

See also # 69

6511. Carles, Philippe, and Jean-Louis Comolli. Free Jazz, Black Power. 2nd ed. Paris: Editions Galilee, 1979, p. 451.

6512. Wilmer, Valerie. As Serious As Your Life. Westport, CT: Lawrence Hill & Co., 1981, p. 281.

Articles

6513. "L'Homme de la Jamaique." Jazz Magazine, No. 169-170 (September 1969): 14-15.

6514. "Ken Terroade: a name to watch." Melody Maker (October 11 1969): 8.

6515. McRae, Barry. "Kenneth Terroade at the Kensington." Jazz Journal (November 1969): 26-27. [Concert review]

6516. Renaud, J. "Free Jazz au Gill's Club." Jazz Hot, No. 251 (June 1969): 12. [Concert review]

6517. Wilmer, Valerie. "Growing Day by Day." Melody Maker (June 13 1970): 16.

Discographies

6518. Hames, Mike. Albert Ayler, Sunny Murray, Cecil Taylor, Byard Lancaster, Kenneth Terroade on disc and tape. Ferndown, Eng.: Hames (16 Pinewood Road, Ferndown, Dorset BH22 9RW), 1983. 61p.

THOMAS, LUTHER - Alto Saxophone

6519. Shore, Michael. "Bop Gettin' Ready to Funk." Soho Weekly News (January 24 1980): 34.

THORNTON, CLIFFORD (1936-) - Trumpet/Valve-Trombone

6520. Carles, Philippe, and Jean-Louis Comolli. Free Jazz, Black Power. 2nd ed. Paris: Editions Galilee, 1979, p. 451.

6521. Claghorn, Charles Eugene. Biographical Dictionary of Jazz. Englewood Cliffs, NJ: Prentice-Hall, 1982.

6522. Dictionnaire du Jazz, eds. Philippe Carles, et al. Paris: Laffont, 1988.

6523. Feather, Leonard, and Ira Gitler. The Encyclopedia of Jazz in the Seventies. New York: Horizon Press, 1976.

6524. The New Grove Dictionary of Jazz. London: Macmillan Press, 1988.

6525. Who's Who Among Black Americans. 6th ed. 1990/91.

6526. Wilmer, Valerie. As Serious As Your Life. Westport, CT: Lawrence Hill & Co., 1981, p. 281-282.

Articles

6527. Carles, Philippe. "Clifford Thornton: pour l'exemple." Jazz Magazine, No. 208 (February 1973): 14+. [Interview]

6528. "Clifford Thornton." Jazz Hot, No. 336 (April 1977): 34.

6529. Constant, Denis. "Clifford Thornton - l'enseignement, la musique et l'Afrique." Jazz Magazine, No. 262 (February 1978): 40-43. [Interview]

6530. "France bars Thornton as Panther 'suspect'." down beat (April 29 1971): 8-9.

6531. "On the Bandstand: Clifford Thornton." Jazz Forum, No. 46 (1977): 26.

6532. Palmer, Robert. "Clifford Thornton: flowers in the Gardens of Harlem." down beat (June 19 1975): 19+.

6533. Solothurnmann, Jurg. "Clifford Thornton: a creative sense of tradition." Jazz Forum, No. 59 (1979): 28-33. [Interview]

6534. Welch, Jane. "Caught in the Act: Clifford Thornton New Art Ensemble/Jayne Cortez/Rashied Ali Quartet." down beat (October 1 1970): 27-28. [Concert review]

6535. Wilmer, Valerie. "Clifford Thornton." Jazz & Blues, Vol. 2 (May 1972): 12-13.

6536. _________. "Thornton's Black Studies." Melody Maker (January 29 1972): 12.

THREADGILL, HENRY (1944-   ) - Reeds

See also # 417, 760-773

6537. Davis, Francis. "Positively Charged." In Outcats: Jazz Composers, Instrumentalists, and Singers. New York: Oxford University Press, 1990, pp. 59-62.

Biographical Dictionaries

6538. Carles, Philippe, and Jean-Louis Comolli. Free Jazz, Black Power. 2nd ed. Paris: Editions Galilee, 1979, p. 452.

6539. Carr, Ian. "Threadgill, Henry." In Jazz: The Essential Companion. New York: Prentice Hall Press, 1988.

6540. Claghorn, Charles Eugene. Biographical Dictionary of Jazz. Englewood Cliffs, NJ: Prentice-Hall, 1982.

6541. Dictionnaire du Jazz, eds. Philippe Carles, et al. Paris: Laffont, 1988.

6542. McRae, Barry. "Henry Threadgill." In The Jazz Handbook. Harlow, Essex, Eng.: Longman, 1987, pp. 249-250.

6543. Mandel, Howard. "Threadgill, Henry." In The New Grove Dictionary of Jazz. London: Macmillan Press, 1988.

6544. The Penguin Encyclopedia of Popular Music, ed. Donald Clarke. New York: Viking, 1989.

6545. Wilmer, Valerie. As Serious As Your Life. Westport, CT: Lawrence Hill & Co., 1981, p. 282.

Articles

6546. Birnbaum, Larry. "Meet the Composer: Henry Threadgill." EAR: New Music News, Vol. 12, No. 7 (October 1987): 16-18.

6547. Blum, Joe. "Henry Threadgill: Beyond Air." Jazz Times (September 1983): 10-12. [Interview]

6548. Buchanan, Steve. "Interview...Henry Threadgill." Be-Bop and Beyond, Vol. 4, No. 2 (March/April 1986): 21-22.

6549. Butler, Paul. "Henry Threadgill: Riddles of a Chicago Alchemist." Wire (April 1989): 24-27.

6550. Case, Brian. "Jazz: Air on a Hubcap." Melody Maker (October 3 1981): 28-29. [Interview]

6551. Kalbacher, Gene. "Theatrical Music: Henry Threadgill." Hot House, Vol. 4, No. 9 (September 1985): 14-15.

6552. Litweiler, John. "Rags to Switches." Chicago Tribune (June 4 1989): Sec. 13, p. 26. [Profile]

6553. Lock, Graham. "Henry Threadgill: Riddles of a Chicago Alchemist." Wire Magazine (April 1989): 25-27.

6554. Lynch, Kevin. "Henry Threadgill: Composer, Bandleader, and Alchemist." down beat (February 1988): 20-22.

6555. Mandel, Howard. "Henry Threadgill: Music to Make the Sun Come Up." down beat (July 1985): 26-28, 47.

6556. Pareles, Jon. "Big Ideas Take a Back Seat to a Good Time." New York Times (December 6 1987): Sec. 2, pp. 27, 33.

6557. ________. "Henry Threadgill Follows Through." Village Voice (May 28 1979): 59-60, 62.

6558. Santoro, Gene. "Henry Threadgill." The Nation (July 18 1987): 65-68.

6559. Smith, Miyoshi. "Henry Threadgill." Cadence, Vol. 14, No. 10 (October 1988): 25-28. [Interview]

6560. Van Trikt, Ludwig. "Henry Threadgill." Cadence, Vol. 11, No. 9 (September 1985): 5+. [Interview]

6561. Vries, Renze de. "Henry Threadgill, Subject to Change." Jazzjaarboek (Amsterdam), Vol. 5 (1986): 76-83.

6562. Woodard, Josef. "Henry Threadgill." Musician, No. 99 (January 1987): 56-58, 70, 91, 98. [Interview]

6563. Zabor, Rafi. "Faces: Henry Threadgill." Musician, Player and Listener, No. 28 (November 1980): 36-37.

TIPPETT, KEITH (1947-) (Great Britain) - Piano

See also # 344, 867-875

6564. Gilbert, Mark. "Tippett, Keith." In The New Grove Dictionary of Jazz. London: Macmillan, 1988.

6565. Jazz Now: the Jazz Centre Society Guide, ed. Roger Cotterrell. London: Quartet Books, 1976.

Articles

6566. Ansell, Keith. "No Gossip from the Mujician." The Wire, No. 2 (1982).

TOLLIVER, CHARLES (1942-) - Trumpet

6567. Taylor, Arthur. "Charles Tolliver." In Notes and Tones. New York: Perigee Books, 1982, pp. 76-82. 1970 interview.

Biographical Dictionaries

6568. Case, Brian, and Stan Britt. The Harmony Illustrated Encyclopedia of Jazz. 3rd ed. New York: Harmony Books, 1987.

6569. Claghorn, Charles Eugene. Biographical Dictionary of Jazz. Englewood Cliffs, NJ: Prentice-Hall, 1982.

6570. Dictionnaire du Jazz, eds. Philippe Carles, et al. Paris: Laffont, 1988.

6571. Feather, Leonard. The Encyclopedia of Jazz in the Sixties. New York: Horizon Press, 1966.

6572. _________, and Ira Gitler. The Encyclopedia of Jazz in the Seventies. New York: Horizon Press, 1976.

6573. Kernfeld, Barry. "Tolliver, Charles." In The New Grove Dictionary of Jazz. London: Macmillan Press, 1988.

6574. The Penguin Encyclopedia of Popular Music, ed. Donald Clarke. New York: Viking, 1989.

6575. Reclams Jazzfuhrer. 2nd, rev. ed. Stuttgart: Reclam, 1977.

Articles

6576. Case, Brian. "Conserving the Lip." New Musical Express (July 12 1975): 26-27. [Interview]

6577. Luzzi, Mario. "Tolliver Dice la Sua." Musica Jazz, Vol. 34, No. 6 (June 1978): 11-14.

6578. Westin, Anita. "Musik och Politik gar inte i Hop: Charles Tolliver." Orkester Journalen, Vol. 46, No. 2 (February 1978): 10-11.

6579. Williams, Richard. "Tolliver's Travels." Melody Maker (September 2 1972): 18.

6580. Wilmer, Valerie. "Music Inc--Making it Alone." Melody Maker (October 10 1970): 18.

6581. _________. "Tolliver - ignoring the freedom bandwagon." Melody Maker (November 30 1968): 23.

6582. _________. "Tolliver's Five Year Plan." Melody Maker (May 24 1975): 44.

6583. _________. "What Charles Tolliver Can Use." down beat (February 20 1969): 16-17.

TURNER, ROGER (Great Britain) - Percussion

6584. Ansell, Kenneth. "Phil Minton and Roger Turner: Out of Cold Storage." The Wire, No. 12 (February 1985): 15-19.

6585. _________. "Russell/Turner/Kondo." Jazz Journal International (August 1980): 24-25. [Interview]

TUSQUES, FRANCOIS (1938-) (France) - Piano

6586. Carles, Philippe, and Jean-Louis Comolli. Free Jazz, Black Power. 2nd ed. Paris: Editions Galilee, 1979, p. 452.

6587. Dictionnaire du Jazz, eds. Philippe Carles, et al. Paris: Laffont, 1988.

Articles

6588. Carles, Philippe. "Tusques: d'ou viennent lessons justes?" Jazz Magazine, No. 202 (July 1972): 22+. [Interview]

6589. Constant, Denis. "Free sans cri." Jazz Magazine, No. 177 (April 1970): 14.

6590. "Francois Tusques." Chroniques de L'Art Vivant, No. 21 (Juin 1971): 30.

6591. Le Bris, M. "Francois Tusques." Jazz Hot, No. 247 (February 1969): 32-33. [Interview]

6592. Lecomte, Henry. "Tusques: une 'fusion' a la Francaise." Jazz Hot, No. 383 (April 1981): 38-39. [Interview]

6593. Loupien, Serge. "Francois Tusques: pour une nouvelle musique bretonne." Jazz Magazine, No. 280 (November 1979): 30-31, 62-63.

6594. "7 [sept] noms; voici les nouveau-nes du jazz francais!" Jazz Magazine, No. 117 (April 1965): 39-40.

6595. Tusques, Francois. "Pour une nouvelle musique bretonne." Jazz Magazine, No. 280 (November 1979): 30+.

6596. ________. "Un soir autour d'Ayler." Jazz Magazine, No. 193 (October 1971): 5-6.

6597. "Tusques parle." Jazz Magazine, No. 185 (January 1971): 18-19. [Interview]

TYLER, CHARLES (1941-) - Alto Saxophone

See also # 663

6598. Jost, Ekkehard. "Charles Tyler." In Jazzmusiker: Materialen zur Soziologie der Afro-Amerikanischen Musik. Frankfurt am Main: Ullstein, 1982, pp. 123-129.

Biographical Dictionaries

6599. Carles, Philippe, and Jean-Louis Comolli. Free Jazz, Black Power. 2nd ed. Paris: Editions Galilee, 1979, p. 452.

6600. Dictionnaire du Jazz, eds. Philippe Carles, et al. Paris: Laffont, 1988.

6601. The Penguin Encyclopedia of Popular Music, ed. Donald Clarke. New York: Viking, 1989.

6602. Such, David G. "Tyler, Charles." In The New Grove Dictionary of Jazz. London: Macmillan Press, 1988.

6603. Wilmer, Valerie. As Serious As Your Life. Westport, CT: Lawrence Hill & Co., 1981, p. 282.

Articles

6604. "Dictionnaire de l'Alto." Jazz Magazine, No. 137 (December 1966): 51. Biographical sketch.

6605. Flicker, Chris. "Charles Tyler." Jazz Magazine, No. 255 (June 1977): 18-19. [Interview]

6606. Gauffre, Christian, and J. Sorano. "Gros Plan." Jazz Magazine, No. 344 (November 1985): 26-27. [Interview]

6607. Litweiler, John. "Profile: Charles Tyler." down beat (May 1984): 56, 59, 62.

6608. Occhiogrosso, Peter. "Up from Under." Soho Weekly News (March 11 1976): 36. [Concert review]

6609. Safane, Clifford J. "Charles Tyler: The Saga of a Saxophonist." Music Journal [New York] (September/October 1979): 18-19.

6610. Weinstein, Norman. "Charles Tyler's Saga of the Outlaws: Jazz at the Threshold of a Shootout." Noh Quarter, Vol. 2, No. 3 (Summer 1987): 40-44.

TYNER, McCOY [Alfred] [aka Sulaimon Saud] (1938-) - Piano

See also # 2461, 2491, 2592

6611. Berendt, Joachim Ernst. "McCoy Tyner - Echoes of a Friend." In Ein Fenster aus Jazz. Frankfurt am Main: S. Fischer, 1977, pp. 73-79.

6612. Feather, Leonard. The Passion for Jazz. New York: Horizon Press, 1980, pp. 126-130.

6613. Kofsky, Frank. "McCoy Tyner: An Interview." In Black Nationalism and the Revolution in Music. New York: Pathfinder Press, 1970, pp. 207-219.

6614. Lyons, Leonard. "McCoy Tyner." In The Great Jazz Pianists. New York: Morrow, 1983, pp. 235-248.

6615. Vuijsje, Bert. De Nieuwe Jazz. Baarn: Bosch & Keuning, 1978, pp. 120-124. [Interview]

Biographical Dictionaries

6616. Carr, Ian. "Tyner, McCoy." In Jazz: The Essential Companion. New York: Prentice Hall Press, 1988.

6617. Case, Brian, and Stan Britt. The Harmony Illustrated Encyclopedia of Jazz. 3rd ed. New York: Harmony Books, 1987.

6618. Claghorn, Charles Eugene. Biographical Dictionary of Jazz. Englewood Cliffs, NJ: Prentice-Hall, 1982.

6619. Dictionnaire du Jazz, eds. Philippe Carles, et al. Paris: Laffont, 1988.

6620. Dobbins, Bill. "Tyner, McCoy." In The New Grove Dictionary of American Music. London: Macmillan Press, 1986.

6621. _________. "Tyner, McCoy." In The New Grove Dictionary of Jazz. London: Macmillan Press, 1988.

6622. Feather, Leonard. The Encyclopedia of Jazz in the Sixties. New York: Horizon Press, 1966.

6623. _________, and Ira Gitler. The Encyclopedia of Jazz in the Seventies. New York: Horizon Press, 1976.

6624. McRae, Barry. "McCoy Tyner." In The Jazz Handbook. Harlow, Essex, Eng.: Longman, 1987, p. 250.

6625. The Penguin Encyclopedia of Popular Music, ed. Donald Clarke. New York: Viking, 1989.

6626. Southern, Eileen. Biographical Dictionary of Afro-American and African Musicians. Westport, CT: Greenwood Press, 1982.

6627. Tenot, Frank. Dictionnaire du Jazz. Paris: Larousse, 1967.

6628. Who's Who Among Black Americans. 6th ed. 1990/91. Detroit: Gale Research, 1990.

6629. Who's Who in Entertainment. 1st ed. 1989-1990.

6630. Wilmer, Valerie. As Serious As Your Life. Westport, CT: Lawrence Hill & Co., 1981, p. 282.

Articles

6631. Bashier, A. "McCoy Tyner." Jazz Journal (December 1966): 29-30.

6632. "The Black Scholar Interviews: McCoy Tyner." The Black Scholar, Vol. 2 (October 1970): 40-46.

6633. Bourne, Michael. "McCoy Tyner." down beat (December 8 1973): 14-15.

6634. Brodowski, Pawel. "McCoy Tyner: outburst of energy." Jazz Forum, No. 33 (January 1975): 38-40.

6635. Case, Brian. "Doctor McCoy Tyner, I presume..." New Musical Express (September 28 1974): 40-41. [Interview]

6636. _________. "Let's hear it for the sanctity of organic interaction." New Musical Express (July 10 1976): 33. [Interview]

6637. _________. "This time, really the real McCoy." New Musical Express (November 13 1976): 46. [Interview]

6638. Coleman, Ray. "The Real McCoy." Melody Maker (July 18 1964): 6.

6639. Dance, Stanley. "Tyner Talk." down beat (October 24 1963): 18-19. [Interview]

6640. Danson, Peter. "McCoy Tyner - USA." Coda, No. 180 (October 1981): 4-7. [Interview]

6641. "Dico Disco & Co." Jazz Magazine, No. 298 (June 1981): 68. Biographical sketch.

6642. Diliberto, John. "McCoy Tyner: Piano Visionary." down beat (February 1984): 20-22.

6643. Doerschuk, Bob. "McCoy Tyner." Keyboard Magazine (August 1981): 28+. [Interview]

6644. Feather, Leonard. "Piano Giants of Jazz: McCoy Tyner." Contemporary Keyboard (August 1978): 54-55.

6645. Franckling, Ken. "McCoy Tyner." Jazz Times (November 1989): 24-25.

6646. Gerber, Alain. "Tyner: l'ombre apres la lumiere." Jazz Magazine, No. 177 (April 1970): 20+.

6647. Hoefer, George. "The Hot Box." down beat (January 21 1960): 42.

6648. Ioakimidis, Demetre. "A l'ombre de Coltrane." Jazz Hot, No. 217 (February 1966): 20+.

6649. "JP Gespraech mit McCoy Tyner." Jazz Podium (February 1986): 10-13.

6650. Keepnews, Orrin. "Orrin Keepnews: producing McCoy Tyner." Keyboard Magazine (August 1981): 38+.

6651. Kohanov, Linda. "Following the release of his second in a trilogy of solo Blue Note albums, John Coltrane's one-time pianist takes time to sum up the real McCoy Tyner." Pulse! [Tower Records] (December 1990): 64-65. [Interview]

6652. Lake, Steve. "Tyner: Fly with the Wind." Melody Maker (November 27 1976): 44+. [Interview]

6653. Lyons, Len. "McCoy Tyner: Tyner in Transition." down beat (October 20 1977): 12+. [Interview]

6654. "McCoy Tyner." Jazz Hot, No. 311 (December 1974): 8+. [Interview]

6655. "Piano Stylists Talking: McCoy Tyner on technique and influence." Crescendo International, Vol. 24, No. 2 (1987): 20.

6656. Rinzler, Paul. "McCoy Tyner: style and syntax." Annual Review of Jazz Studies (1983): 109-149.

6657. Rock, Henry. "Profiling McCoy Tyner." Jazz Spotlite News, Vol. 2, No. 3 (1981): 10.

6658. Rusch, Bob. "McCoy Tyner: interview." Cadence, Vol. 10, No. 1 (January 1984): 5-10.

6659. Stewart, Zan. "Tyner." Musician, Player and Listener, No. 10 (December 15 1977/January 30 1978): 26-29. [Interview]

6660. Thompson, Vern. "McCoy Tyner." Different Drummer, Vol. 1, No. 11 (September 1974): 15-17.

6661. Underwood, Lee. "McCoy Tyner: savant of the astral latitudes." down beat (September 11 1975): 12+.

6662. Watson, Philip. "Surreal McCoy." Wire, No. 77 (July 1990): 34-37. [Interview]

6663. Wild, David. "McCoy Tyner: The Jubilant Experience of the Classic Quartet; John Coltrane Quartet, 1961-1965." down beat (July 12 1979): 18+. [Interview]

6664. Wilmer, Valerie. "Tyner--keeping it clean." Melody Maker (September 8 1973): 16.

6665. ________. "When You Lose an 'Elder Brother'." Melody Maker (August 19 1967): 8. Interview following the death of John Coltrane.

6666. Zabor, Rafi. "Giants in Transition: McCoy Tyner/ Freddie Hubbard." Musician, Player and Listener, No. 13 (July-August 1978): 20+.

Discographies

6667. Gardner, Mark. "McCoy Tyner; a discography." Jazz Journal (August 1967): 34; (September 1967): 26-28.

Media Materials

6668. Marian McPartland's Piano Jazz, No. 43: McCoy Tyner (Audiotape). 60 min. Composer-pianist McCoy Tyner discusses his career with interviewer Marian McPartland, and also plays selected songs. [Held by the Rodgers & Hammerstein Collection at Lincoln Center (# 7097)]

ULMER, JAMES "BLOOD" (1942-) - Guitar

6669. Carr, Ian. "Ulmer, James Blood." In Jazz: The Essential Companion. New York: Prentice Hall Press, 1988.

6670. Case, Brian, and Stan Britt. The Harmony Illustrated Encyclopedia of Jazz. 3rd ed. New York: Harmony Books, 1987.

6671. Claghorn, Charles Eugene. Biographical Dictionary of Jazz. Englewood Cliffs, NJ: Prentice-Hall, 1982.,

6672. Dictionnaire du Jazz, eds. Philippe Carles, et al. Paris: Laffont, 1988.

6673. Kernfeld, Barry. "Ulmer, James Blood." In The New Grove Dictionary of Jazz. London: Macmillan Press, 1988.

6674. The Penguin Encyclopedia of Popular Music, ed. Donald Clarke. New York: Viking, 1989.

Articles

6675. Barber, Lynden. "Blood Lines." Melody Maker (January 10 1981): 9. [Interview]

6676. ________. "Blood Transfusions." Melody Maker (July 23 1983): 10+. [Interview]

6677. Caux, Beatrice. "James Blood Ulmer: les contes du capitaine Blood." Jazz Hot, No. 388 (February 1981): 34-35. [Interview]

6678. Cook, Richard. "Jazz Gets a Blood Transfusion." New Musical Express (November 28 1981): 22-23. [Interview]

6679. "Dico Disco & Co." Jazz Magazine, No. 298 (June 1981): 68. Biographical sketch.

6680. Goldman, Vivien. "The Adventures of Captain Blood." New Musical Express (October 25 1980): 24-25, 60. [Interview]

6681. Lake, Steve. "Blood: off the tracks." The Wire, No. 22 (December 1985): 24-25.

6682. Loupias, Bernard. "James Blood Ulmer: un sang nouveau pour nos sillons?" Jazz Magazine, No. 294 (February 1981): 34-35, 46.

6683. May, Chris. "Four on the Floor is a Hook-Up." Black Music and Jazz Review, Vol. 3, No. 10 (February 1981): 20-23.

6684. Palmer, Don. "James Blood Ulmer." Musician, Player and Listener, No. 44 (June 1982): 30.

6685. Palmer, Robert. "Futuristic Jazz-Funk of James Ulmer." Rolling Stone (June 12 1980): 23.

6686. Reinert, D. "James Blood Ulmer: Ich spiele nur Gitarre." Jazz Podium (April 1986): 16-17. [Interview]

6687. Safane, Clifford Jay. "Harmolodic Diatonic Funk of James Blood Ulmer." down beat (October 1980): 22+.

6688. Stern, Chip. "Blood Ulmer and Punk Jazz." Musician, Player and Listener, No. 20 (September-October 1979): 44-46, 38.

6689. Tate, Gregory. "The Sons of Ornette: Jamaladeen Tacuma, Blood Ulmer and The Future of Harmolodics." Musician, No. 51 (January 1983): 62-64, 66.

6690. Woodlief, Mark. "From Harmolodics to the Blues Disease: James Blood Ulmer's Got it Bad." Option, No. 32 (May/June 1990): 38-41. [Interview]

6691. Zwerin, Mike. "James Blood Ulmer: a step forward in jazz." Jazz Forum, No. 75 (1982): 37-39. [Interview]

Newspaper Articles

6692. Crouch, Stanley. "Riffs: Blood Ulmer's Orchestral Guitar." Village Voice (June 5 1978): 45.

6693. Giddins, Gary, and Robert Christgau. "Riffs: Blood Ulmer in/con/trans fusion." Village Voice (June 25 1979): 53.

6694. Litweiler, John. "Free Spirit, Free Jazz." Chicago Tribune (March 21 1990): Sec. 5, p. 3. [Profile]

6695. Stern, Chip. "Licks: Blood's Hookup." Village Voice (August 13 1979): 63+.

6696. Tate, Gregory. "Knee Deep in Blood Ulmer." Village Voice (November 18-24 1981): 77.

UNITED FRONT

6697. Auerbach, Brian. "United Front." down beat (February 1986): 45-47.

6698. Rizy, Helmut. "United Front: die ganze tradition der schwarzen musik." Jazz Podium (April 1983): 21-24. [Interview]

Media Materials

6699. Outside in Sight: The Music of United Front. Produced and Directed by Greg Chapnick and Sharon Wood. 30 min., color. [Available from Rhapsody Films, Inc., P.O. Box 179, New York, NY 10014. Tel. 212/243-0152]

VAN HOVE, FRED

See Hove, Fred van

VAN REGTEREN ALTENA, MAARTEN

See Altena, Maarten

VESALA, EDWARD (1945-) (Finland) - Drums

6700. Claghorn, Charles Eugene. Biographical Dictionary of Jazz. Englewood Cliffs, NJ: Prentice-Hall, 1982.

6701. Dictionnaire du Jazz, eds. Philippe Carles, et al. Paris: Laffont, 1988.

6702. Gronow, Pekka. "Vesala, Edward." In The New Grove Dictionary of Jazz. London: Macmillan Press, 1988.

6703. Vuorela, Jari-Pekka. "Edward Vesala." In Finnish Jazz. 3rd rev. ed. Helsinki: Foundation for the Promotion of Finnish Music Information Centre, 1986, pp. 46-47.

Articles

6704. Sermila, Jarmo. "Edward's thoughts--interview with Edward Vesala." Jazz Forum, No. 28 (April 1974): 46-48.

6705. Vaehaesilta, T. "Edward Vesala: a drummer from the North." Jazz Forum, No. 92 (1985): 30-35. [Interview]

VIENNA ART ORCHESTRA

6706. Dictionnaire du Jazz, eds. Philippe Carles, et al. Paris: Laffont, 1988.

6707. Schulz, Klaus. "Vienna Art Orchestra." In The New Grove Dictionary of Jazz. London: Macmillan Press, 1988.

Articles

6708. Ansell, Kenneth. "Vienna Art Orchestra: A Notion in Perpetual Motion." The Wire, No. 24 (February 1986): 24-25.

6709. Buholzer, Meinrad. "Jazz et Satie: Vienna Art." Jazz Magazine, No. 335 (January 1985): 27-29. [Interview]

6710. Davis, Francis. "Vienna Art Orchestra: variations on a big band theme." down beat (February 1985): 26-28.

6711. Hollenstein, Harold. "Le Wiener Art Orchester." Jazz 360o (Sierre, Switzerland), No. 35 (February 1981): 3-5.

6712. Kuehn, G. "Das Wiener Art Orchester." Jazz Podium (December 1980): 18-19.

6713. Schulte, Klaus. "Austria: Vienna Art Orchestra." Jazz Forum, No. 71 (1981): 11.

6714. Solothurnmann, Jurg. "Mathias Ruegg and Vienna Art Orchestra." Jazz Forum, No. 79 (1982): 30-36. [Interview]

6715. _________, and Gudrun Endress. "Vienna Art Orchestra." Jazz Podium (October 1982): 4-11. Interview with VAO's leader Mathias Ruegg.

VITET, BERNARD (1934-) (France) - Trumpet

6716. Carles, Philippe, and Jean-Louis Comolli. Free Jazz, Black Power. 2nd ed. Paris: Editions Galilee, 1979, p. 453.

6717. Dictionnaire du Jazz, eds. Philippe Carles, et al. Paris: Laffont, 1988.

Articles

6718. Lecomte, Henri. "Le souffle continu." Jazz Hot, No. 394 (April 1982): 27-30. [Interview]

6719. Rossi, P. L. "Un homme libre." Jazz Magazine, No. 114 (January 1965): 40-44. [Interview]

VOIGHT, ANDREW - Reeds

See # 5625-5638

VON SCHLIPPENBACH, ALEXANDER

See Schlippenbach, Alexander von

WADUD, ABDUL [Ronald DeVaughn] (1947-) - Cello

6720. Claghorn, Charles Eugene. Biographical Dictionary of Jazz. Englewood Cliffs, NJ: Prentice-Hall, 1982.

6721. Dictionnaire du Jazz, eds. Philippe Carles. Paris: Laffont, 1988.

6722. Hazell, Ed. "Wadud, Abdul." In The New Grove Dictionary of Jazz. London: Macmillan Press, 1988.

Articles

6723. "Dico Disco & Co." Jazz Magazine, No. 298 (June 1981): 69. Biographical sketch.

6724. Jeske, Lee. "Profile: Abdul Wadud." down beat (November 1982): 52-53.

6725. Lee, David. "Abdul Wadud." Coda, No. 176 (December 1980): 8-13. [Interview]

WALDRON, MAL (1926-) - Piano

6726. Case, Brian, and Stan Britt. The Harmony Illustrated Encyclopedia of Jazz. 3rd ed. New York: Harmony Books, 1987.

6727. Claghorn, Charles Eugene. Biographical Dictionary of Jazz. Englewood Cliffs, NJ: Prentice-Hall, 1982.

6728. Dictionnaire du Jazz, eds. Philippe Carles, et al. Paris: Laffont, 1988.

6729. Doerschuk, Bob. "Waldron, Mal." In The New Grove Dictionary of Jazz. London: Macmillan Press, 1988.

6730. Feather, Leonard. The Encyclopedia of Jazz. New ed. New York: Horizon Press, 1960.

6731. _________. The Encyclopedia of Jazz in the Sixties. New York: Horizon Press, 1966.

6732. _________, and Ira Gitler. The Encyclopedia of Jazz in the Seventies. New York: Horizon Press, 1976.

6733. The Penguin Encyclopedia of Popular Music, ed. Donald Clarke. New York: Viking, 1989.

6734. Priestley, Brian. "Waldron, Mal." In Jazz: The Essential Companion. New York: Prentice Hall Press, 1988.

6735. Reclams Jazzfuhrer. 2nd, rev. ed. Stuttgart: Reclam, 1977.

Articles

6736. Be-Bop and Beyond, Vol. 2, No. 4 (July/August 1984). [Interview]

6737. Baggenaes, Roland. "Mal Waldron." Coda, No. 153 (January-February 1977): 2-3. [Interview]

6738. Blumenthal, Bob. "Mal Waldron." down beat (April 1981): 28-30. [Interview]

6739. Case, Brian. "Pianist Gasses Twenty Before Concert." New Musical Express (November 22 1975): 32-33. [Interview]

6740. Cohen, Elaine. "Mal Waldron: a profile." Coda, No. 192 (October 1983): 26-27.

6741. Cullaz, Maurice. "Mal Waldron." Jazz Hot, No. 251 (June 1969): 20-21. [Interview]

6742. Cutler, Howard. "Mal Waldron." Cadence, Vol. 14, No. 5 (May 1988): 5-15, 88. [Interview]

6743. Darroch, Lynn. "Mal Waldron: 'Nothing Limits Me Now.'" Jazz Times (April 1985): 12-14. [Interview]

6744. Doerschuk, Bob. "Mal Waldron: Life on the Borderline." Keyboard Magazine, Vol. 10, No. 7 (1984): 42.

6745. Feather, Leonard. "Blindfold Test: Mal Waldron." down beat (November 1981): 51.

6746. Gitler, Ira. "Mal Content on the Content." Radio Free Jazz (May 1976): 5-6.

6747. Glassman, Marc. "Mal Waldron." Coda, No. 223 (December 1988/January 1989): 10-13.

6748. Goddet, Laurent. "Mal Waldron." Orkester Journalen (April 1970): 8. [Interview]

6749. Lauder, Cliff. "Mal Waldron: further pursuance of the quest." Jazz Spotlite News (Fall/Winter 1981-Spring/Summer 1982): 41.

6750. Lock, Graham. "Mal Waldron: Waltzing with Fire." New Musical Express (December 17 1983): 20-21. [Interview]

6751. Mackey, Nathaniel, and Herman Gray. "A Conversation with Pianist/Composer Mal Waldron." Jazz Spotlite News (Fall 1980/Winter 1981): 18-21.

6752. Maher, Jack. "Mal Waldron/versatile young swinger." Metronome (April 1959): 16.

6753. "Mal Waldron." Melody Maker (February 28 1959): 5.

6754. Palmer, Don. "Jazz Pianist as Prince of Darkness and Earl of Emotion." Musician, No. 76 (February 1985): 25+.

6755. Pussiau, Jean-Jacques. "Mal Waldron." Jazz Magazine, No. 258 (October 1977): 22. [Interview]

6756. Su, Alice. "Mal Waldron: 'Then I Heard Charlie Parker and Sold My Saxophone'." Jazz (Basel), Nr. 3 (1983).

6757. Weber, Horst. "Mal Waldron." Jazz Forum, No. 19 (October 1972): 63-64. [Interview]

6758. Whitehead, Kevin. "Mal Waldron: interview." Cadence, Vol. 6, No. 10 (October 1980): 5-8, 32.

6759. Wilson, T. "Waldron--an exile in Ireland." Melody Maker (March 28 1970): 8.

Discographies

6760. Mathiesen, Anders. Mal Waldron: A Black Artist. Denmark: A. Mathiesen (Broendsteds Alle 4, Ck-1803 FRB C, Denmark), 1989. 182p.

WARD, CARLOS (1940-) (Panama/U.S.) - Alto Saxophone

6761. Claghorn, Charles Eugene. Biographical Dictionary of Jazz. Englewood Cliffs, NJ: Prentice-Hall, 1982.

6762. Dictionnaire du Jazz, eds. Philippe Carles, et al. Paris: Laffont, 1988.

6763. Feather, Leonard, and Ira Gitler. The Encyclopedia of Jazz in the Seventies. New York: Horizon Press, 1976.

6764. Wild, David. "Ward, Carlos." In The New Grove Dictionary of Jazz. London: Macmillan Press, 1988.

Articles

6765. Gabel, Lars. "Carlos Ward: expressway to creative truth." down beat (July 17 1975): 17, 39.

6766. Smith, Bill. "Carlos Ward - A Love Supreme." Coda, No. 202 (June/July 1985): 24-26. [Interview]

WARE, DAVID (1949-) - Tenor Saxophone

6767. Dictionnaire du Jazz, eds. Philippe Carles, et al. Paris: Laffont, 1988.

6768. The New Grove Dictionary of Jazz. London: Macmillan Press, 1988.

Articles

6769. Case, Brian. "Aw, come on! Doncha feel just a tiny bit scared of Cecil?" New Musical Express (August 21 1976): 33. [Interview]

6770. Crouch, Stanley. "Jazz in the Lofts: New Directions." Soho Weekly News (January 15 1976): 35, 38. [Concert review]

6771. Gbezo, Vital T. "David S. Ware: du silence a la musique." L'Independant du Jazz (Paris), No. 17 (January 1979).

6772. Quist, Jean. "David S. Ware at 12." Jazz Nu (May 1982): 342-344. [Interview]

6773. Rusch, Bob. "David Ware: interview." Cadence, Vol. 6, No. 1 (January 1980): 5-7, 15-16.

WARFORD, RITA - Vocals

See # 694

WATERS, PATTY - Vocals

6774. Weinstein, Norman. "Patty Waters and the Rephrasing of the Siren's Song." Noh Quarter, Vol. 2, No. 2 (Spring 1987): 45-53.

WATTS, MARZETTE (1938-) - Tenor Saxophone

6775. Anderson, Ruth. Contemporary American Composers: a biographical dictionary. 2nd ed. Boston, MA: G.K. Hall, 1982.

WATTS, TREVOR (1939-) (Great Britain) - Tenor Saxophone

See also # 867-875, 6055-6070

6776. Carr, Ian. "John Stevens and Trevor Watts - The Spontaneous Music Ensemble." In Music Outside. London: Latimer New Dimensions, 1973, pp. 39-54.

Biographical Dictionaries

6777. Adams, Simon. "Watts, Trevor." In The New Grove Dictionary of Jazz. London: Macmillan Press, 1988.

6778. Carles, Philippe, and Jean-Louis Comolli. Free Jazz, Black Power. 2nd ed. Paris: Editions Galilee, 1979, pp. 454.

6779. Carr, Ian. "Watts, Trevor." In Jazz: The Essential Companion. New York: Prentice Hall Press, 1988.

6780. Case, Brian, and Stan Britt. The Harmony Illustrated Encyclopedia of Jazz. 3rd ed. New York: Harmony Books, 1987.

6781. Claghorn, Charles Eugene. Biographical Dictionary of Jazz. Englewood Cliffs, NJ: Prentice-Hall, 1982.

6782. Feather, Leonard, and Ira Gitler. The Encyclopedia of Jazz in the Seventies. New York: Horizon Press, 1976.

6783. Jazz Now: the Jazz Centre Society Guide, ed. Roger Cotterrell. London: Quartet Books, 1976, pp. 178-179.

Articles

6784. Ansell, Kenneth. "Closer to the Music of Trevor Watts." Jazz Journal International (July 1980): 30-31. [Interview]

6785. ________. "In Phase with Trevor Watts' Moire Music." The Wire, No. 9 (1984): 36+.

6786. Davidson, Martin. "Watts: rhythm is the essence." Melody Maker (January 27 1973): 43.

6787. Johnston, Mike. "Trevor Watts." Coda, No. 185 (August 1982): 12-13. [Interview]

6788. "The Questionnaire." Cadence (January 1990): 33-34, 62. Biographical sketch made up of information supplied by Watts to Cadence editor Bob Rusch.

6789. Schonfield, Victor. "Out of SME and on the right road now." Melody Maker (December 16 1967): 6.

6790. Yason, T. "Watts: finding our lost rhythm." Melody Maker (April 24 1971): 12.

WESTBROOK, MIKE (1936-) (Great Britain) - Bandleader

6791. Carr, Ian. "Mike Westbrook." In Music Outside. London: Latimer New Dimensions, 1973, pp. 15-38.

Biographical Dictionaries

6792. Carles, Philippe, and Jean-Louis Comolli. Free Jazz, Black Power. 2nd ed. Paris: Editions Galilee, 1979, p. 454.

6793. Carr, Ian. "Westbrook, Mike." In Jazz: The Essential Companion. New York: Prentice Hall Press, 1988.

6794. Case, Brian, and Stan Britt. The Harmony Illustrated Encyclopedia of Jazz. 3rd ed. New York: Harmony Books, 1987.

6795. Claghorn, Charles Eugene. Biographical Dictionary of Jazz. Englewood Cliffs, NJ: Prentice-Hall, 1982.

6796. Dictionnaire du Jazz, eds. Philippe Carles, et al. Paris: Laffont, 1988.

6797. Feather, Leonard. The Encyclopedia of Jazz in the Sixties. New York: Horizon Press, 1966.

6798. ________, and Ira Gitler. The Encyclopedia of Jazz in the Seventies. New York: Horizon Press, 1976.

6799. Fox, Charles, and Digby Fairweather. "Westbrook, Mike." In The New Grove Dictionary of Jazz. London: Macmillan Press, 1988.

6800. Jazz Now: the Jazz Centre Society Guide, ed. Roger Cotterrell. London: Quartet Books, 1976, pp. 179-180.

6801. McRae, Barry. "Mike Westbrook." In The Jazz Handbook. Harlow, Essex, Eng.: Longman, 1987, pp. 222-223.

6802. The Penguin Encyclopedia of Popular Music, ed. Donald Clarke. New York: Viking, 1989.

6803. Reclams Jazzfuhrer. 2nd, rev. ed. Stuttgart: Reclam, 1977.

Articles

6804. Bird, Christopher. "The Paradox of Westy." Melody Maker (May 17 1969): 8.

6805. Case, Brian. "Warehouse of the Western World." Melody Maker (February 17 1979): 24. [Interview]

6806. Cotterrell, Roger. "Mike Westbrook: taking music to the people." Jazz Forum, No 39 (1976): 38-41. [Interview]

6807. Dallas, Karl. "Present Use of the Past Tense." Melody Maker (June 13 1981): 28-29. [Interview]

6808. ________. "Westbrook: discipline of the 'Citadel'." Melody Maker (July 19 1975): 42. [Interview]

6809. ________. "Westbrook's Voices." Melody Maker (February 20 1982): 23. [Interview]

6810. "Dico Disco & Co." Jazz Magazine, No. 298 (June 1981): 70. Biographical sketch.

6811. Duncan, Andy. "Mike Westbrook." Impetus (London), No. 4 (1977): 169-172; No. 5 (1977): 205-206. [Interview]

6812. Houston, Bob. "Westbrook, Wild Man from the West Country." Melody Maker (May 14 1966): 9.

6813. Lock, Graham. "Sweet Thunder." The Wire, No. 14 (April 1985): 10-13, 15.

6814. Loupien, Serge. "Mike Westbrook: 'j'ai oublie de m'enfermer dans un style'." Jazz Magazine, No. 275 (May 1979): 46-47, 62, 64. [Interview]

6815. Nguyen, Gerard, Xavier Beal, and Michel Lousquet. "Mike Westbrook." ATEM (France), No. 14 (December 1978): 16-17. [Interview]

6816. Parker, Chris. "Burning Bridges: Mike and Kate Westbrook Play Sad Songs for a Broken Europe." Wire, No. 46/47 (Dec 1987/Jan 1988): 28-30.

6817. Russell, P. "Plymouth Sound." Jazz Monthly (September 1965): 17-18.

6818. Shera, M. "Mike Westbrook and his orchestra." Jazz Journal (January 1966): 10-11.

6819. Sheridan, Chris. "Multi-Media Jazzman: Mike Westbrook." Jazz Journal International (May 1980): 30. [Profile]

6820. Tomkins, Les. "Mike Westbrook." Crescendo International, Vol. 8, No. 1 (1969): 8.

6821. Wilmer, Valerie. "Mike Westbrook: on being a composer." Jazz Forum, No. 12 (1971): 65-66.

6822. Zabor, Rafi. "Mike Westbrook plays William Blake's greatest hits." Musician, No. 58 (August 1983): 32-40, 97, 106.

Concert Reviews

6823. Dawbarn, Bob. "Caught in the Act." Melody Maker (Jun 1 1968): 6.

6824. Priestley, Brian. "Mike Westbrook 6tet." Jazz Monthly (September 1968): 26-27.

6825. Schonfield, Victor. "Caught in the Act." down beat (November 30 1967): 39.

6826. _________. "Caught in the Act." Melody Maker (August 19 1967): 4.

WHEELER, KENNY (1930-) (Canada/G. Britain) - Trumpet

6827. Miller, Mark. "Kenny Wheeler." In Boogie, Pete & the Senator: Canadian Musicians in Jazz: the Eighties. Toronto: Nightwood Editions, 1987, pp. 290-296.

Biographical Dictionaries

6828. Carles, Philippe, and Jean-Louis Comolli. Free Jazz, Black Power. 2nd ed. Paris: Editions Galilee, 1979, p. 454.

6829. Carr, Ian. "Wheeler, Kenny." In Jazz: The Essential Companion. New York: Prentice Hall Press, 1988.

6830. Case, Brian, and Stan Britt. The Harmony Illustrated Encyclopedia of Jazz. 3rd ed. New York: Harmony Books, 1987.

6831. Claghorn, Charles Eugene. Biographical Dictionary of Jazz. Englewood Cliffs, NJ: Prentice-Hall, 1982.

6832. Dictionnaire du Jazz, eds. Philippe Carles, et al. Paris: Laffont, 1988.

6833. Feather, Leonard, and Ira Gitler. The Encyclopedia of Jazz in the Seventies. New York: Horizon Press, 1976.

6834. Jazz Now: the Jazz Centre Society Guide, ed. Roger Cotterrell. London: Quartet Books, 1976, pp. 180-181.

6835. Kernfeld, Barry. "Wheeler, Kenny." In The New Grove Dictionary of Jazz. London: Macmillan Press, 1988.

6836. The Penguin Encyclopedia of Popular Music, ed. Donald Clarke. New York: Viking, 1989.

Articles

6837. Cotterrell, Roger. "Kenny Wheeler: Speaking softly but carrying a big horn." Jazz Forum, No. 57 (1979): 38-41. [Interview]

6838. Grime, Kitty. "Star Sideman: Kenny Wheeler." Jazz News (October 18 1961): 10-11.

6839. Husby, Per. "Kenny Wheeler: interview." Cadence, Vol. 7, No. 5 (May 1981): 12-18, 86-87.

6840. Lock, Graham. "Brass Menagerie." Wire, No. 72 (February 1990): 46-49.

6841. Miller, Mark. "Kenny Wheeler's Many Vehicles." down beat (April 1980): 22-24, 69.

6842. _________. "Profile: Kenny Wheeler." down beat (March 11 1976): 32.

6843. Priestley, Brian. "The little known side of Kenny Wheeler." Melody Maker (June 14 1969): 8.

6844. Remarc, V. "Kenny Wheeler." Coda, No. 163 (October 1978): 32-33.

6845. Sinker, Mark. "Subtle Survivor." New Statesman & Society (January 26 1990): 45-46.

6846. Smith, Bill. "Kenny Wheeler - Windmill Tilter." Coda, No. 207 (April/May 1986): 4-5. [Interview]

WHITE, ANDREW [Nathaniel III] (1942-) - Reeds

6847. White, Andrew. 24 Selected Essays, Vol. I & II. Washington, D.C.: Andrew's Music, 1989. 2 vols.

Biographical Dictionaries

6848. Berry, Lemuel, Jr. Biographical Dictionary of Black Musicians and Music Educators. Guthrie, OK: Educational Book Publishers, 1978.

6849. Claghorn, Charles Eugene. Biographical Dictionary of Jazz. Englewood Cliffs, NJ: Prentice-Hall, 1982.

6850. Dictionnaire du Jazz, eds. Philippe Carles, et al. Paris: Laffont, 1988.

6851. Feather, Leonard, and Ira Gitler. The Encyclopedia of Jazz in the Seventies. New York: Horizon Press, 1976.

6852. Hazell, Ed. "White, Andrew." In The New Grove Dictionary of Jazz. London: Macmillan Press, 1988.

6853. Holly, Ellistine Perkins, comp. Biographies of Black Composers and Songwriters: A Supplementary Textbook. Dubuque, IA: Wm. C. Brown Publishers, 1990, pp. 46, 72-73.

6854. Horne, Aaron. Woodwind Music of Black Composers. New York: Greenwood Press, 1990, pp. 63-64.

6855. International Who's Who in Music and Musicians' Directory. 11th ed. 1988.

6856. International Who's Who of Intellectuals. London: Eddison Press, 1981, Vols. 2/3.

6857. The Penguin Encyclopedia of Popular Music, ed. Donald Clarke. New York: Viking, 1989.

6858. Roach, Hildred. Black American Music: Past and Present. Malabar, FL: Krieger Pub. Co., 1985, Vol. 2, pp. 99-100.

6859. Southern, Eileen. Biographical Dictionary of Afro-American and African Musicians. Westport, CT: Greenwood Press, 1982.

Articles

6860. Dreyfus, Joel. "'A Fine Musician of Many Dimensions'." Washington Post (September 30 1975): B1, B4.

6861. Goddet, Laurent. "Interview: Andrew White." Jazz Hot, No. 304 (April 1974): 14+.

6862. Ingersoll, Chuck. "Andrew White." Different Drummer, Vol. 1, No. 11 (September 1974): 13-14.

6863. Joyce, Mike. "Spotlight: Saxophone Sound of Surprise." Washington Post (February 24 1986): D7. [Profile]

6864. McGinty, Doris E. "Conversation with Andrew White: Keeper of the 'Trane." The Black Perspective in Music, Vol. 12, No. 1 (Spring 1984): 80-97.

6865. Metalitz, Steve. "Andrew White: Working the Musical Mother Lode." Washington Review of the Arts, Vol. 1, No. 1 (May/July 1975): 9-10.

6866. Renninger, Christian. "'Andy's in the Basement'." Radio Free Jazz (July 1975): 10-12.

6867. Rusch, Bob. "Andrew White: interview." Cadence, Vol. 4, No. 4 (June 1978): 10-13, 23.

6868. __________. "Andrew White: Master Musician." Cadence, Vol. 1, No. 5 (May 1976): 9-11.

6869. __________. "Andrew White interview." Jazz Forum, No. 52 (1978): 33.

6870. _________. "Rusch on Record: Andrew White III - Independence and Imagination." Jazz Forum, No. 32 (December 1974): 60-61. [Record review]

6871. White, Andrew N. "Beware of Distributors; Invaluable tips for self-marketing records, cassettes, CDs." Sound Choice, No. 14 (Spring 1990): 39-41. Discussion of White's experiences recording and marketing his own label Andrew's Music.

6872. _________. "A Black Perspective of Black Jazz Saxophone." Saxophone Journal (Winter 1988): 26-29.

6873. _________. "How to Have a Jazz Band Part II: My Bands of the 1970s." Saxophone Journal (March-April 1989): 18-21.

6874. _________. "A Treatise on How to Use My Transcriptions and the Plight of Jazz Education." Jazz (Basel), Nr. 6 (1984?).

6875. _________. "What is the State of the Jazz Business?" Saxophone Journal (Spring 1988): 23-27.

Media Materials

6876. Andrew Video-Demo. 50 min. Video of Andrew White with big band and quartet. [Available from Andrew's Music, 4830 South Dakota Ave., N.E., Washington, D.C. 20017]

WHITECAGE, MARK - Alto Saxophone

6877. Besecker, Bill. "The Mark Whitecage Interview." Coda, No. 217 (December '87/January '88): 8-9.

WILEN, BARNEY [Bernard Jean] (1937-) (France) - Tenor

6878. Carles, Philippe, and Jean-Louis Comolli. Free Jazz, Black Power. 2nd ed. Paris: Editions Galilee, 1979, p. 455.

6879. Dictionnaire du Jazz, eds. Philippe Carles, et al. Paris: Laffont, 1988.

6880. Priestley, Brian. "Wilen, Barney." In Jazz: The Essential Companion. New York: Prentice Hall Press, 1988.

Articles

6881. Lapijover, Pierre. "Jazzman et Francais: Barney Wilen." Jazz Hot, No. 355 (November 1978): 30-35. [Interview]

6882. Pichol, Michel. "Monsieur le President..." Jazz Magazine, No. 305 (March 1982): 26-27. [Interview]

6883. Tarting, Claude. "Barney Wilen." Diapason-Harmonie, No. 327 (May 1987): 26.

WILKERSON, EDWARD - Reeds

See also # 3094-3096

6884. Davis, Francis. "Blowing in from Chicago." In Outcats: Jazz Composers, Instrumentalists, and Singers. New York: Oxford University Press, 1990, pp. 63-71. [Reprint of # 6886]

Articles

6885. Corbett, John. "Ed Wilkerson: Togetherness is Everything." Down Beat (April 1990): 22-23.

6886. Davis, Francis. "Blowing in from Chicago: Edward Wilkerson and his two jazz bands are set to arrive nationwide." The Atlantic (February 1989): 71-73. Discussion of Wilkerson's octet, 8 Bold Souls, and big band, Shadow Vignettes. [Reprinted in # 6884]

6887. _________. "Ed Wilkerson: Big Bands are Back...with a Difference." Musician, No. 95 (September 1986): 29-30. Profile of Wilkerson and his big band Shadow Vignettes.

6888. Kart, Larry. "The Edge of Stardom: Locale is Expanding for Edward Wilkerson Jr." Chicago Tribune (January 18 1987): Sect. 13, p. 10.

6889. Litweiler, John. "Blowin' in from Chicago, 1986." The Wire (London), No. 33 (November 1986): 22-24, 63. Profiles of Hal Russell and Ed Wilkerson.

6890. Sachs, Lloyd. "Bold Souls: a new generation is taking the reins at one of the country's most vital centers for jazz." Chicago (May 1989): 146, 151, 172, 176.

6891. Trimarchi, Michaeleen. "The Leading Edge: Ed Wilkerson, Jr." OPtion; Music Alternatives, No. 22 (September/October 1988): 56-59.

Media Materials

6892. Birth of a Notion: The Music of Edward Wilkerson, Jr. (199?). Director, Floyd Webb. [in post-production 6/90]

6893. Flesh, Metal, Wood (1982). Written, Produced and Directed by Floyd Webb. 10 minutes. 16mm b/w. Experimental film dealing with the spiritual nature of creative music with original soundtrack by Ed Wilkerson (tenor, ocarina, and percussion instruments) and Floyd Webb (bamboo flute, shakuhachi, glass bowls, and berimbau). [For distribution information contact: Floyd Webb, 213 W. Institute Place, Suite 207, Chicago, IL 60610. Tel. 312/509-2981]

6894. Honky Tonk Bud. Directed by Scott Laster. 11 minutes. A jazz-rap composition featuring the music of saxophonist/ composer/arranger, Edward Wilkerson. Stars John Toles-Bey as the Rap Narrator. [Available from Rhapsody Films, Inc., P.O. Box 179, New York, NY 10014. Tel. 212/243-0152]

WILSON, JOE LEE (1935-) - Vocals

See also # 671-676

6895. Carles, Philippe, and Jean-Louis Comolli. Free Jazz, Black Power. 2nd ed. Paris: Editions Galilee, 1979, p. 455.

6896. Claghorn, Charles Eugene. Biographical Dictionary of Jazz. Englewood Cliffs, NJ: Prentice-Hall, 1982.

6897. Dictionnaire du Jazz, eds. Philippe Carles, et al. Paris: Laffont, 1988.

6898. Feather, Leonard, and Ira Gitler. The Encyclopedia of Jazz in the Seventies. New York: Horizon Press, 1976.

6899. The New Grove Dictionary of Jazz. London: Macmillan Press, 1988.

6900. Wilmer, Valerie. As Serious As Your Life. Westport, CT: Lawrence Hill & Co., 1981, p. 282.

Articles

6901. Case, Brian. "Lower your jaw and go 'OMMMM'." New Musical Express (October 30 1976): 22. [Interview]

6902. Husby, Per. "Joe Lee Wilson: interview." Cadence, Vol. 8, No. 3 (March 1982): 14-17, 93.

6903. Kastin, David. "Profile: Joe Lee Wilson." down beat (February 24 1977): 34-36.

6904. Tomkins, Les. "Joe Lee Travels Hopefully." Crescendo International (August 1978): 15-16. [Interview]

6905. Wilmer, Valerie. "Joe Lee - 'Space' Singer." Melody Maker (August 28 1976): 28. [Interview]

6906. __________. "Joe Lee Wilson." Melody Maker (August 6 1977): 12. [Concert review]

6907. __________. "Joe Lee Wilson." Melody Maker (April 29 1978): 27. [Concert review]

WILSON, PHILLIP (1941-) - Drums

6908. Vuijsje, Bert. Jazzportretten. Amsterdam: Van Gennep, 1983, pp. 110-118. [Dutch text]

Biographical Dictionaries

6909. Carles, Philippe, and Jean-Louis Comolli. Free Jazz, Black Power. 2nd ed. Paris: Editions Galilee, 1979, p. 456.

6910. Claghorn, Charles Eugene. Biographical Dictionary of Jazz. Englewood Cliffs, NJ: Prentice-Hall, 1982.

6911. Dictionnaire du Jazz, eds. Philippe Carles, et al. Paris: Laffont, 1988.

6912. Feather, Leonard, and Ira Gitler. The Encyclopedia of Jazz in the Seventies. New York: Horizon Press, 1976.

6913. Hazell, Ed. "Wilson, Phillip." In The New Grove Dictionary of Jazz. London: Macmillan Press, 1988.

6914. Wilmer, Valerie. As Serious As Your Life. Westport, CT: Lawrence Hill & Co., 1981, p. 284.

Articles

6915. Case, Brian. "New Far-Outnesses at Changes Bar." New Musical Express (June 18 1977): 18-19. [Interview]

6916. "Philip Wilson ou la Batterie 'Expressive'." L'Independant du Jazz (Paris), No. 14 (January 1978): 8.

6917. Safane, Clifford Jay. "Spotlight: Phillip Wilson." down beat (September 8 1977): 22-23.

6918. Stern, Chip. "Beyond the Blues: Philip Wilson." Modern Drummer (October 1983): 16-19, 52-60. [Interview]

WINSTONE, NORMA (1941-) (Great Britain) - Vocals

6919. Carr, Ian. "Winstone, Norma." In Jazz: The Essential Companion. New York: Prentice Hall Press, 1988.

6920. Claghorn, Charles Eugene. Biographical Dictionary of Jazz. Englewood Cliffs, NJ: Prentice-Hall, 1982.

6921. Feather, Leonard, and Ira Gitler. The Encyclopedia of Jazz in the Seventies. New York: Horizon Press, 1976.

6922. Jazz Now: the Jazz Centre Society Guide, ed. Roger Cotterrell. London: Quartet Books, 1976, p. 182.

6923. Sheridan, Chris. "Winstone, Norma." In The New Grove Dictionary of Jazz. London: Macmillan Press, 1988.

Articles

6924. Bird, Christopher. "Not Enough of Norma." Melody Maker (April 15 1972): 57.

6925. Dawbarn, Bob. "Norma's Wisdom." Melody Maker (February 7 1970): 12.

6926. Gore-Humpries, Stephen, and Phillip Hanson. "Avant Courier: Norma Winstone." Jazz Journal International (August 1983): 10-11. [Interview]

6927. Henshaw, L. "Triumph for a Jazz Cinderella." Melody Maker (March 13 1971): 18.

6928. Jones, Max. "Norma." Melody Maker (November 5 1966): 8.

6929. Lock, Graham. "The Singing is the Song." The Wire, No. 15 (May 1985): 40-41.

6930. McIntosh, Adrian. "John Taylor and Norma Winstone: a jazz partnership." Jazz Forum, No. 59 (1979): 38-39, 45. [Interview]

6931. "Norma: new voice from the pubs of London." Melody Maker (March 5 1966): 6.

6932. Walsh, A. "Britain's Jazz Singers." Melody Maker (June 22 1968): 8.

6933. Wilmer, Valerie. "Norma Winstone: the human voice." Jazz Forum, No. 11 (Spring 1971): 54-55.

6934. Wooley, Stan. "Norma Winstone." Jazz Journal (July 1975): 4-6.

WORKMAN, REGGIE (1937-) - Bass

6935. Berry, Lemuel, Jr. Biographical Dictionary of Black Musicians and Music Educators. Guthrie, OK: Educational Book Publishers, 1978.

6936. Claghorn, Charles Eugene. Biographical Dictionary of Jazz. Englewood Cliffs, NJ: Prentice-Hall, 1982.

6937. Dictionnaire du Jazz, eds. Philippe Carles, et al. Paris: Laffont, 1988.

6938. Feather, Leonard. The Encyclopedia of Jazz in the Sixties. New York: Horizon Press, 1966.

6939. _________, and Ira Gitler. The Encyclopedia of Jazz in the Seventies. New York: Horizon Press, 1976.

6940. Gardner, Mark. "Workman, Reggie." In The New Grove Dictionary of Jazz. London: Macmillan Press, 1988.

6941. Reclams Jazzfuhrer. 2nd, rev. ed. Stuttgart: Reclam, 1977.

Articles

6942. Chapin, Gary Parker. "Reggie Workman: Educator on the Edge." Option, No. 34 (September/October 1990): 40-45, 129. [Interview]

WORLD SAXOPHONE QUARTET

6943. Carr, Ian. "World Saxophone Quartet." In Jazz: The Essential Companion. New York: Prentice Hall Press, 1988.

6944. Claghorn, Charles Eugene. Biographical Dictionary of Jazz. Englewood Cliffs, NJ: Prentice-Hall, 1982, p. 376.

6945. Dictionnaire du Jazz, eds. Philippe Carles, et al. Paris: Laffont, 1988.

6946. Gridley, Mark C. "World Saxophone Quartet." In The New Grove Dictionary of American Music. London: Macmillan Press, 1986.

6947. ________. "World Saxophone Quartet." In The New Grove Dictionary of Jazz. London: Macmillan Press, 1988.

Articles

6948. Cole, Bill. "The World Saxophone Quartet: A Unique Springboard." Saxophone Journal, Vol. 11, No. 1 (1986).

6949. Litweiler, John. "High, low points for jazz sax quartet." Chicago Tribune (January 22 1989): Sec. 5, p. 6.

6950. Macnie, Jim. "World Saxophone Quartet: Ruckus in the Avant Vernacular." Musician (December 1989): 46-50, 52, 54.

6951. Palmer, Robert. "Four Saxes in Search of an Audience." Rolling Stone, No. 311 (February 21 1980): 32.

6952. ________. "A Saxophone Foursome Comes Into its Own." New York Times (September 2 1979): 21.

6953. Safane, Clifford Jay. "The World Saxophone Quartet." down beat (October 1979): 26-29, 66.

6954. Santoro, Gene. "The World Saxophone Quartet: Building on a New Tradition." down beat (July 1989): 16-19.

6955. Stern, Chip. "Faces: World Saxophone Quartet." Musician, Player and Listener, No. 18 (May-July 1979): 29.

6956. Woodward, Richard B. "Four Saxmen, One Great Voice." New York Times Magazine (April 12 1987): 46-47, 72.

Media Materials

6957. Coming Into the World Saxophone Quartet. Video. 30 min. Produced by Anna Maria Horsford and Oz Scott.

WORRELL, LEWIS (1934-) - Bass

See also # 5058-5064

6958. Carles, Philippe, and Jean-Louis Comolli. Free Jazz, Black Power. 2nd ed. Paris: Editions Galilee, 1979, p. 456.

6959. Dictionnaire du Jazz, eds. Philippe Carles, et al. Paris: Laffont, 1988.

6960. Wilmer, Valerie. As Serious As Your Life. Westport, CT: Lawrence Hill & Co., 1981, p. 282.

WRIGHT, FRANK (1935-1990) - Tenor Saxophone

See also # 286, 698

6961. Carles, Philippe, and Jean-Louis Comolli. Free Jazz, Black Power. 2nd ed. Paris: Editions Galilee, 1979, pp. 457.

6962. Dictionnaire du Jazz, eds. Philippe Carles, et al. Paris: Laffont, 1988.

6963. The New Grove Dictionary of Jazz. London: Macmillan Press, 1988.

6964. Wilmer, Valerie. As Serious As Your Life. Westport, CT: Lawrence Hill & Co., 1981, p. 282.

Articles

6965. Carles, Philippe. "Wright is Right." Jazz Magazine, No. 173 (December 1969): 13.

6966. Heibel, V. "Meine Musik ist Universell Gueltig: Frank Wright." Jazz Podium (June 1975): 10-12.

6967. McRae, Barry. "Avant Courier: Frank Wright-Working On." Jazz Journal (August 1975): 12-13.

6968. Positif, Francois. "The Noah Howard-Frank Wright Quartet." Jazz Hot, No. 257 (January 1970): 18-22. [Interview]

6969. Wilmer, Valerie. "Caught in the Act." down beat (May 28 1970): 30. [Concert review]

6970. ________. "Caught in the Act." Melody Maker (April 4 1970): 6. [Concert review]

6971. ________. "Superman of the Tenor." Melody Maker (April 11 1970): 14.

Obituaries

6972. "Final Bar: Frank Wright." down beat (October 1990): 11.

6973. McRae, Barry. "Obituaries: Frank Wright." Jazz Journal International (August 1990): 21.

6974. Wilmer, Val. "Frank Wright." The Independent (June 21 1990).

YAMASHITA, YOSUKE (1942-) (Japan) - Piano

6975. Carles, Philippe, and Jean-Louis Comolli. Free Jazz, Black Power. 2nd ed. Paris: Editions Galilee, 1979, p. 457.

6976. Carr, Ian. "Yamashita, Yosuke." In Jazz: The Essential Companion. New York: Prentice Hall Press, 1988.

6977. Claghorn, Charles Eugene. Biographical Dictionary of Jazz. Englewood Cliffs, NJ: Prentice-Hall, 1982.

6978. Dictionnaire du Jazz, eds. Philippe Carles, et al. Paris: Laffont, 1988.

6979. Feather, Leonard, and Ira Gitler. The Encyclopedia of Jazz in the Seventies. New York: Horizon Press, 1976.

6980. Iwanami, Yozo. "Yamashita, Yosuke." In The New Grove Dictionary of Jazz. London: Macmillan Press, 1988.

Articles

6981. Doerschuk, Bob. "Conflict and Harmony at the Fringes of Jazz: avant-garde pianist Yosuke Yamashita." Keyboard Magazine (August 1985): 42-43. [Interview]

6982. Gribetz, Sid. "Yosuke Yamashita Live at Sweet Basil." Jazz Times (October 1990): 29. [Concert review]

6983. Hardy, Alain-Rene. "Le Piano Terrible de Yamashita." Jazz Magazine, No. 253 (April 1977): 18-19, 39-40.

6984. Prevost, Xavier. "Yamashita - un piano debride." Jazz Magazine, No. 354 (October 1986): 22. [Interview]

6985. Rensen, Jan. "Yosuke Yamashita." Jazz/Press (Holland), No. 41 (juli 1977): 3, 13. [Interview]

6986. Weber, Horst. "Yosuke Yamashita: power and speed." Jazz Forum, No. 32 (December 1974): 42-43. [Interview]

Appendix I

Reference Works

GENERAL WORKS

Computer Databases/CD ROMs

6987. Academic Index (1986-Feb 1990)
6988. General Periodicals Index (1986-Feb 1990)
6989. Magazine Index [May 1982-Dec 1990]
6990. MLA International Bibliography (1981-Sept 1989)
6991. National Newspaper Index (Sept. 1983-Feb 1990)
6992. RLIN (Research Libraries Information Network)
6993. UMI Newspaper Abstracts Ondisc (Jan 1988-April 1990)

Book, Newspaper and Periodical Indexes

Note: Dates in parentheses indicate years viewed by the author.

6994. Essay and General Literature Index [1900-1988]
6995. Humanities Index [1973-Sept. 1989]
6996. Index to Black Periodicals [1984-1988]
6997. Index to Periodical Articles by and About Blacks [1950-1983]
6998. Jazz Index [1977-1983]
6999. Music Index [1955-February 1990]
7000. Reader's Guide to Periodical Literature [1890-1988]

Journals

7001. American Visions [1986-April 1990]
7002. Black Creation [1970-1974/75]
7003. Black Music [scattered issues, Dec 1974-Mar 1978]
7004. Black Music and Jazz Review [March-July 1981]
7005. Brilliant Corners [1975-1979]
7006. Cadence [1976-Jan 1991]
7007. Chroniques de l'Art Vivant [Nov 1968-April 1975]
7008. Coda [1958-Dec 1990/Jan 1991]
7009. Cricket [1968?-1971?]
7010. Different Drummer [1973-1975]
7011. down beat [1960-Dec 1990]
7012. Down Beat's Music [1963-1973]
7013. Ear [May 1976-Dec 1990/Jan 1991]
7014. Ebony [1945-March 1990]

7015. Ebony Man [1986-Feb 1990]
7016. Encore American and Worldwide News [1972-1982]
7017. Essence [1970-Feb 1990]
7018. First World [1977-1980]
7019. Grackle [1977-1979]
7020. IT [1966-1973]
7021. Jazz Journal International [1990]
7022. Jazz News [Oct 1959-Dec 1963]
7023. Jazz Times [1990]
7024. Jazzforschung/Jazz Research [1969-1988]
7025. Jazzthetik [Jan-Nov 1990]
7026. Liberator [1961-1971]
7027. Musician [April 1982-December 1990]
7028. Musician, Player and Listener [Sept/Oct 1977-Mar 1982]
7029. New Musical Express [1974-Sept 1987]
7030. Notes [Sept 1979-Dec 1990]
7031. Option [March/April 1985-Nov/Dec 1990]
7032. Pieces of Jazz [1968-1971]
7033. Sepia [1952-53/1959-1981]
7034. Soho Weekly News [1973-1982]
7035. Village Voice [1959-1990]
7036. Wire [Summer 1983-Dec 90/Jan 1991]

Biographical Indexes

7037. Biography Index (1961-August 1990)

7038. The New York Times Obituaries Index 1858-1968. New York: New York Times/Arno Press, 1970.

7039. The New York Times Obituaries Index 1969-1978. New York: New York Times, 1980.

7040. Perry, Jeb H. Variety Obits: An Index to Obituaries in Variety, 1905-1978. Metuchen, NJ: Scarecrow Press, 1980.

7041. Spradling, Mary Mace. In Black and White. 3rd ed. Detroit: Gale, 1980. 2 vols. Bibliographic index to more than 15,000 Black individuals and groups.

7042. _________. In Black and White: Supplement. Detroit: Gale, 1985. 628p. Supplement to # 7041 with information on some 6,700 additional individuals and groups.

7043. Variety Obituaries, 1905-1986. New York: Garland Pub., 1986. 11 vols.

Dissertation and Theses Indexes

7044. Comprehensive Dissertations Index [1861-1988].
7045. Dissertations Abstracts International [1986-Nov 1990]
7046. Masters Abstracts [1962-Summer 1989].
7047. Master's Theses in the Arts and Social Sciences, No. 1-12 [1976-1988].

BIOGRAPHICAL DICTIONARIES and ENCYCLOPEDIAS

7048. Anderson, Ruth. Contemporary American Composers: a biographical dictionary. 2nd ed. Boston, MA: G.K. Hall, 1982. 578p.

7049. ASCAP Biographical Dictionary. 4th ed. New York: R.R. Bowker, 1980. 589p.

7050. Baker's Biographical Dictionary of Musicians. 7th ed. revised by Nicolas Slonimsky. New York: Schirmer Books, 1984. 2577p.

7051. Berry, Lemuel, Jr. Biographical Dictionary of Black Musicians and Music Educators. Guthrie, OK: Educational Book Publishers, 1978. 389p.

7052. Bohlander, Carlo, and Karl Heinz Holler. Reclams Jazzfuhrer. 2nd ed., rev. Stuttgart: Reclam, 1977. 996p.

7053. Carles, Philippe, Andre Clergeat, and Jean-Louis Comolli. Dictionnaire du Jazz. Paris: Robert Laffont, 1988. 1146p.

7054. _________, and Jean-Louis Comolli. Free Jazz, Black Power. 2nd ed. Paris: Editions Galilee, 1979, pp. 363-457.

7055. Carr, Ian, Digby Fairweather, and Brian Priestley. Jazz: The Essential Companion. New York: Prentice Hall Press, 1988. 562p.

7056. Case, Brian and Stan Britt. The Harmony Illustrated Encyclopedia of Jazz. 3rd ed. Rev. and updated by Chrissie Murray. New York: Harmony Books, 1987. 208p. [Orig. title: The Illustrated Encyclopedia of Jazz. London: Salamander Books, 1986].

7057. Claghorn, Charles Eugene. Biographical Dictionary of American Music. West Nyack, NY: Parker Pub. Co., 1973. 491p.

7058. _________. Biographical Dictionary of Jazz. Englewood Cliffs, NJ: Prentice-Hall, 1982. 377p.

7059. Feather, Leonard. The Encyclopedia of Jazz. Rev. ed. New York: Horizon Press, 1960. 527p.

7060. _________. The Encyclopedia of Jazz in the Sixties. New York: Horizon Press, 1966. 312p.

7061. _________, and Ira Gitler. The Encyclopedia of Jazz in the Seventies. New York: Horizon Press, 1976. 393p.

7062. Handy, D. Antoinette. Black Women in American Bands and Orchestras. Metuchen, NJ: Scarecrow Press, 1981. 319p.

7063. Holly, Ellistine Perkins. Biographies of Black Composers and Songwriters: A Supplementary Textbook. Dubuque, IA: Wm. C. Brown Publishers, 1990. 92p.

7064. Horne, Aaron. Woodwind Music of Black Composers. New York: Greenwood Press, 1990. 145p.

7065. Jacobi, Hugh William. Contemporary American Composers: based at American Colleges and universities. Paradise, CA: Paradise Arts Publisher, 1975. 240p.

7066. McRae, Barry. The Jazz Handbook. Harlow, Essex, Eng.: Longman, 1987; Boston: G.K. Hall, 1989. 272p.

7067. The New Grove Dictionary of American Music. London: Macmillan Press, 1986. 4 vols.

7068. The New Grove Dictionary of Jazz, ed. Barry Kernfeld. London: Macmillan Press, 1988. 2 vols.

7069. The Penguin Encyclopedia of Popular Music, ed. Donald Clarke. New York: Viking, 1989. 1378p.

7070. Roach, Hildred. Black American Music: Past and Present. Malabar, FL: Krieger Pub. Co., 1985. 2 vols.

7071. Southern, Eileen. Biographical Dictionary of Afro-American and African Musicians. Westport, CT: Greenwood Press, 1982. 478p.

7072. Tenot, Frank. Dictionnaire du Jazz. Paris: Larousse, 1967. 256p.

7073. Wilmer, Valerie. As Serious As Your Life: The Story of the New Jazz. Westport, CT: Lawrence Hill & Co., 1981, pp. 259-284.

BIBLIOGRAPHIES

7074. Carner, Gary. Jazz Performers: An Annotated Bibliography of Biographical Materials. New York: Greenwood Press, 1990. 384p.

7075. De Lerma, Dominique-Rene. Bibliography of Black Music. Westport, CT: Greenwood Press, 1981-1984. 4 vols.

DISCOGRAPHIES

7076. Bruyninckx, Walter. Progressive Jazz: Free-Third Stream Fusion. Mechelen, Belgium: 60 Years of Recorded Jazz Team, 1984- . 3 vols.

7077. ________. Sixty Years of Recorded Jazz 1917-1977. Mechelen, Belgium: W. Bruynincx, 198-?. 25 vols.

7078. McCarthy, Albert J., Alun Morgan, Paul Oliver and Max Harrison. Jazz on Record: A Critical Guide to the First 50 Years, 1917-1967. London: Hannover Books, 1968. 416p.

7079. Modern Jazz 1945-1970: The Essential Records. Compiled by Max Harrison, Alun Morgan, Ronald Atkins, Michael James and Jack Cooke. London: Aquarius Books, 1975. 140p.

7080. Raben, Erik. Discography of Free Jazz. Copenhagen: Karl Emil Knudsen, 1969. 38p.

7081. ________. Jazz Records 1942-80, a discography. Copenhagen: JazzMedia Aps, 1989.

FILMOGRAPHIES

7082. Hippenmeyer, Jean-Roland. Jazz zur Films (1917-1972). Yverdon, Switzerland: Thiele, 1973. 128p.

7083. Meeker, David. Jazz in the Movies. New Enlarged Edition. New York: Da Capo, 1982. 336p. Of the 3724 films listed in this filmography only 39 relate to Free Jazz. These are: 63, 94, 107, 142, 146, 149, 445, 461A, 492, 562, 698, 724, 778, 870, 1007, 1067, 1163, 1412, 1557, 1580, 1662-1663, 1665, 1672, 1714, 1921, 2065, 2162, 2216, 2317-2318, 2346, 2350, 2462, 2551, 2554, 3072, 3541 and 3629.

Appendix II

Archives and Research Centers

7084. "Libraries and Archives." In The New Grove Dictionary of Jazz. London: Macmillan Press, 1988.

7085. BLACK ARTS RESEARCH CENTER (30 Marion Street, Nyack, NY 10960. Tel. 914/358-2089). Director: John Gray. Archival resource center dedicated to the documentation, preservation and dissemination of the African cultural legacy. Holdings include some 1400 recordings, cassettes and videotapes, 500 books and journals, 300 clipping files and a 35,000+ entry computer database documenting Black activities in, and contributions to, music, dance, theatre, film, and traditional religion/healing of Africa and the African Diaspora.

7086. BRITISH LIBRARY NATIONAL SOUND ARCHIVE (29 Exhibition Road, London SW7 2AS. Tel. 01 589 6603). Contact: Chris Clark.

7087. Clark, Chris. "The Jazz Collection at the British Library National Sound Archive: a vital resource for the study of jazz in Europe." Jazzforschung, Vol. 21 (1989): 179-182.

7088. CHICAGO JAZZ ARCHIVE - JOSEPH REGENSTEIN LIBRARY - UNIVERSITY OF CHICAGO (1100 East 57th St., Chicago, IL 60637).

7089. JAZZ-BLUES-GOSPEL HALL OF FAME (Chicago Public Library Cultural Center, 78 East Washington St., 8th Fl., Chicago, IL 60602).

7090. Cunniff, Joe. "Jazz-Blues-Gospel Hall of Fame Announced." down beat (October 1989): 11.

7091. JAZZ-INSTITUT DARMSTADT (Kasinostrasse 3, D-1600 Darmstadt, Germany. Tel. (06151) 13-2877). Director: Dr. Wolfram Knauer.

7092. "Jazz Institute Opens in Darmstadt." CBMR Digest, Vol. 3, No. 3 (Fall 1990): 8.

7093. LIBRARY OF CONGRESS - MUSIC DIVISION (Washington, DC 20540)

7094. LIBRARY OF CONGRESS - MOTION PICTURE, BROADCASTING AND RECORDED SOUND DIVISION (Washington, DC 20540)

7095. Library of Congress Catalogs. Music and Phonorecords. 1953-72. Washington: Library of Congress.

7096. Library of Congress Catalogs. Music, Books on Music, and Sound Recordings. January/June 1973- . Washington: Library of Congress.

7097. NEW YORK PUBLIC LIBRARY - PERFORMING ARTS RESEARCH CENTER AT LINCOLN CENTER (111 Amsterdam Avenue, New York, NY 10023. Tel. Music Research Division: 212/870-1650; Recordings Research Division: 212/870-1663).

7098. CATNYP. Computer catalogue of the research libraries of the New York Public Library [1972-Sept 1990].

7099. Dictionary Catalog of the Music Collection. 2nd ed. Boston: G.K. Hall, 1982. 45 vols. Includes all works catalogued through 1971.

7100. Dictionary Catalog of the Music Collection, Supplement 1974. Boston: G.K. Hall, 1976. Continued by Bibliographic Guide to Music, 1975- .

7101. NEW YORK PUBLIC LIBRARY - SCHOMBURG CENTER FOR RESEARCH IN BLACK CULTURE (515 Lenox Avenue (at 135th St.), New York, NY 10037. Tel. 212/862-4000). Of particular interest is the Robert D. Rusch Collection of [the periodical literature of jazz] 1918-1972. 81 microfilm reels (Sc Micro R-912).

7102. New York Public Library. Schomburg Center for Research in Black Culture. Dictionary Catalog of the Schomburg Collection of Negro Literature and History. Boston: G.K. Hall, 1962. 9 vols.; First and Second Supplements (1969-1972). 6 vols. Continued by annual supplements under the title Bibliographic Guide to Black Studies.

7103. RUTGERS UNIVERSITY - INSTITUTE OF JAZZ STUDIES (135 Bradley Hall, Newark, NJ 07102. Tel. 201/648-5595). Director: Dan Morgenstern.

7104. Brodowski, Pawel. "This Music Will Survive." Jazz Forum, No. 111 (1988): 44-50.

7105. Deffaa, Chip. "Ad Lib: The Jazz Past Preserved." down beat (December 1984): 64.

Appendix III

List of Performers and Ensembles by Country

Argentina

Barbieri, Gato

Austria

Malfatti, Radu
Vienna Art Orchestra

Belgium

Fischer, John
Hove, Fred Van

Canada

Artists' Jazz Band
Broomer, Stuart
Dubin, Larry
Neil, Al
Plimley, Paul
Quatuor de Jazz Libre de Quebec
Smith, Bill
Wheeler, Kenny

Denmark

Doerge, Pierre
Tchicai, John

Finland

Aaltonen, Juhani
Vesala, Edward

France

Avenel, Jean-Jacques
Boni, Raymond
Chautemps, Jean-Louis

France (cont.)

Coursil, Jacques
Guerin, Beb
Jaume, Andre
Jenny-Clark, Jean-Francois
Portal, Michel
Tusques, Francois
Vitet, Bernard
Wilen, Barney

Germany

Bauer, Conrad
Berger, Karl
Broetzmann, Peter
Carl, Ruediger
Christmann, Gunter
Dauner, Wolfgang
Dudek, Gerd
Hampel, Gunter
Kowald, Peter
Kuhn, Joachim
Lovens, Paul
Mangelsdorff, Albert
Petrowsky, Ernst-Ludwig
Reichel, Hans
Schlippenbach, Alexander Von
Schoenenberg, Detlef
Schoof, Manfred
Sommer, Gunter "Baby"

Great Britain

Amalgam
AMM
Bailey, Derek
Beckett, Harry
Beresford/Coombes/Hauge/Russell/Solomon
Beresford, Steve

Great Britain (cont.)

Brotherhood of Breath
Coe, Tony
Company
Coombes, Nigel
Cooper, Lindsay
Coxhill, Lol
Dean, Elton
Feminist Improvising Group
Gare, Lou
Goode, Coleridge
Griffiths, Malcolm
Guy, Barry
Harriott, Joe
Holder, Frank
Holland, Dave
Jazz Warriors
Keane, Shake
London Jazz Composers Orchestra
Lytton, Paul
Minton, Phil
Music Improvisation Company
Nicols, Maggie
Osborne, Mike
Oxley, Tony
Parker, Evan
Perry, Frank
Pine, Courtney
Prevost, Eddie
Quaye, Terri
Riley, Howard
Robinson, Orphy
Russell, John
Rutherford, Paul
Skidmore, Alan
Smith, Roger
Smythe, Pat
Solomon, David
Spontaneous Music Ensemble
Stevens, John
Surman, John
Tippett, Keith
Turner, Roger
Watts, Trevor
Westbrook, Mike
Wheeler, Kenny
Winstone, Norma

Greece

Papadimitriou, Sakis

Italy

Gaslini, Giorgio
Rava, Enrico
Romano, Aldo

Jamaica

Terroade, Kenneth

Japan

Kondo, Toshinori
Yamashita, Yosuke

Netherlands

Altena, Maarten
Bennink, Han
Breuker, Willem
Cuypers, Leo
Instant Composers Pool
Mengelberg, Misha
Reyseger, Ernst

Poland

Stanko, Tomasz

Russia

Chekasin, Vladimir
Ganelin Trio
Ganelin, Vyacheslav
Kuryokhin, Sergey
Tarasov, Vladimir

South Africa

Beer, Ronnie
Dyani, Johnny
Feza, Mongezi
Lissack, Selwyn
McGregor, Chris
Miller, Harry
Moholo, Louis
Pukwana, Dudu

Switzerland

Aebi, Irene
Favre, Pierre
Ruegg, Mathias
Schweizer, Irene

United States

Abdullah, Ahmed
Aboriginal Music Society
Abrams, Muhal Richard
Ackley, Bruce
Air
akLaff, Pheeroan
Ali, Muhammad
Ali, Rashied

United States (cont.)

Allen, Byron
Allen, Geri
Allen, Marshall
Altschul, Barry
Anderson, Fred
Anderson, Ray
Art Ensemble of Chicago
Ayler, Albert
Ayler, Donald
Bang, Billy
Barker, Thurman
Batiste, Alvin
Berne, Tim
Black Music Infinity
Blackwell, Ed
Blank, Roger
Bley, Carla
Bley, Paul
Bloom, Jane Ira
Bluiett, Hamiet
Blythe, Arthur
Borca, Karen
Bourelly, Jean-Paul
Bowie, Joseph
Bowie, Lester
Boykins, Ronnie
Brackeen, Charles
Brackeen, Joanne
Bradford, Bobby
Braxton, Anthony
Brimfield, William
Brooks, Arthur
Brown, Marion
Burrell, Dave
Butler, Frank
Carroll, Baikida
Carter, John
Carter, Kent
Chancey, Vincent
Charles, Dennis
Cherry, Don
Christi, Ellen
Circle
Clark, Charles
Clay, James
Clayton, Jay
Cline, Alex
Cline, Nels
Cobbs, Call, Jr.
Cohran, Phil
Coleman, Denardo
Coleman, Ornette
Coleman, Steve
Colson, Adegoke Steve
Colson, Iqua
Coltrane, Alice
Coltrane, John

United States (cont.)

Cook, Marty
Cooper, Jerome
Corea, Chick
Cortez, Jayne
Cowell, Stanley
Creative Construction Company
Crispell, Marilyn
Cross, Earl
Crouch, Stanley
Cyrille, Andrew
Daniel, Ted
Dara, Olu
Davis, Anthony
Davis, Art
Davis, Charles
Davis, Richard
Davis, Steve
Decoding Society
Detroit Free Jazz
Dickerson, Walt
Dixon, Bill
Dolphy, Eric
Donald, Barbara
Doyle, Arthur
Dresser, Mark
Ehrlich, Marty
El-Zabar, Kahil
Emery, James
Ethnic Heritage Ensemble
Ewart, Douglas
Experimental Band
Eyges, David
Fasteau, Zusaan Kali
Favors, Malachi
Few, Bobby
Fielder, Alvin
Folwell, Bill
Freeman, Chico
Freeman, Earl
Friend, Becky
Frisell, Bill
Gaddy, Christopher
Gale, Eddie
Garrett, Donald Rafael
Garrison, Jimmy
Gayle, Charles
Gilmore, John
Golia, Vinny
Gomez, Eddie
Graves, Milford
Greene, Burton
Griffith, Earl
Grimes, Henry
Haden, Charlie
Harper, Billy
Harris, Beaver
Harris, Craig

United States (cont.)

Helias, Mark
Hemingway, Gerry
Hemphill, Julius
Higgins, Billy
Hill, Andrew
Hoggard, Jay
Honsinger, Tristan
Hopkins, Fred
Howard, Noah
Huff, Light Henry
Human Arts Ensemble
Hutcherson, Bobby
Izenson, David
Jackson, Ambrose
Jackson, John Shenoy
Jackson, Michael Gregory
Jackson, Ronald Shannon
Jamal, Khan
Jami, Hakim
Jarman, Joseph
Jarvis, Clifford
Jazz Passengers
Jenkins, Leroy
Johnson, Dewey
Johnson, Oliver
Johnson, Reggie
Jones, Arthur
Jones, Elvin
Jones, Leonard
Jordan, Lewis
Kenyatta, Robin
Kuhn, Steve
Lacy, Steve
La Faro, Scott
Lake, Oliver
Lancaster, Byard
Lasha, Prince
Lashley, Lester
Laswell, Bill
Leaders, The
Lee, Jeanne
LeFlore, Floyd
Levin, Marc
Lewis, Art
Lewis, Bill
Lewis, George
Lincoln, Abbey
Lindberg, John
Little, Booker
Logan, Giuseppi
Lowe, Frank
Lyons, Jimmy
McBee, Cecil
McCall, Steve
McIntyre, Ken
McIntyre, Maurice
McPhee, Joe

United States (cont.)

Mantler, Michael
Marshall, James
Martin, Stu
Maslak, Keshavan
Massey, Cal
Melford, Myra
Mitchell, J. R.
Mitchell, Roscoe
Moffett, Charles
Moncur, Grachan
Moondoc, Jemeel
Moore, Don
Morris, Butch
Morris, Wilber
Moses, J. C.
Motian, Paul
Moye, Famadou Don
Murray, David
Murray, Deirdre
Murray, Sunny
Myers, Amina Claudine
Naughton, Bobby
Neidlinger, Buell
New York Art Quartet
New York Contemporary Five
Newton, James
Nix, Bern
Ochs, Larry
Old and New Dreams
Owens, Jimmy
Parker, Errol
Parker, William
Parran, J. D.
Patrick, Pat
Pavone, Mario
Peacock, Gary
Pepper, Jim
Peterson, Hannibal Marvin
Phillips, Barre
Pope, Odean
Potts, Steve
Pozar, Cleve F.
Priester, Julian
Pullen, Don
Purcell, John
Ragin, Hugh
Raskin, Jon
Redman, Dewey
Reid, Bob
Reid, Steve
Revolutionary Ensemble
Rhames, Arthur
Rigby, Joe
Rivers, Sam
Roach, Max
Roberts, Hank
Robinson, Perry

United States (cont.)

Rollins, Sonny
Rosewoman, Michele
Ross, Brandon
Rova Saxophone Quartet
Rudd, Roswell
Sams, George
Sanders, Pharoah
Sarbib, Saheb
Sharrock, Linda
Sharrock, Sonny
Shaw, Charles Bobo
Shepp, Archie
Shipp, Mathew
Shorter, Alan
Silva, Alan
Simmons, Sonny
Sirone
Smith, Leo
Smith, Warren
Stewart, Bob
String Trio of NY
Stubblefield, John
Sudler, Monnette
Sun Ra
Tacuma, Jamaladeen
Tapscott, Horace
Taylor, Cecil
Thomas, Luther
Thornton, Clifford
Threadgill, Henry
Tolliver, Charles
Tyler, Charles
Tyner, McCoy
Ulmer, James Blood
United Front
Voight, Andrew
Wadud, Abdul
Waldron, Mal
Ward, Carlos
Ware, David
Warford, Rita
Waters, Patty
Watts, Marzette
White, Andrew N.
Whitecage, Mark
Wilkerson, Ed
Wilson, Joe Lee
Wilson, Phillip
Workman, Reggie
World Saxophone Quartet
Worrell, Lewis
Wright, Frank

Appendix IV

List of Performers by Instrument

Bass

Altena, Maarten
Avenel, Jean-Jacques
Boykins, Ronnie
Broomer, Stuart
Carter, Kent
Clark, Charles E.
Davis, Art
Davis, Richard
Davis, Steve
Dresser, Mark
Dyani, Johnny
Favors, Malachi
Freeman, Earl
Folwell, Bill
Garrett, Donald Rafael
Garrison, Jimmy
Gomez, Eddie
Goode, Coleridge
Grimes, Henry
Guerin, Beb
Guy, Barry
Haden, Charlie
Helias, Mark
Henderson, Errol
Holland, Dave
Hopkins, Fred
Izenson, David
Jami, Hakim
Jenny-Clark, Jean-Francois
Johnson, Reggie
Jones, Leonard
Kowald, Peter
LaFaro, Scott
Lashley, Lester
Lindberg, John
McBee, Cecil
Miller, Harry
Moore, Don
Morris, Wilber

Bass (cont.)

Neidlinger, Buell
Parker, William
Pavone, Mario
Peacock, Gary
Phillips, Barre
Reid, Bob
Sarbib, Saheb
Silva, Alan
Sirone
Tacuma, Jamaladeen
Workman, Reggie
Worrell, Lewis

Bass Clarinet

Dolphy, Eric
Doyle, Arthur
Garrett, Donald Rafael
Hampel, Gunter
Murray, David

Bassoon

Borca, Karen
Cooper, Lindsay

Cello

Eyges, David
Honsinger, Tristan
Lashley, Lester
Murray, Deirdre
Reyseger, Ernst
Roberts, Hank
Wadud, Abdul

Clarinet

Batiste, Alvin

Clarinet (cont.)

Carter, John
Coe, Tony
Osborne, Mike
Robinson, Perry

Drums/Percussion

akLaff, Pheeroan
Ali, Muhammad
Ali, Rashied
Altschul, Barry
Barker, Thurman
Bennink, Han
Blackwell, Ed
Blank, Roger
Butler, Frank
Charles, Dennis
Cline, Alex
Coleman, Denardo
Cooper, Jerome
Crouch, Stanley
Cyrille, Andrew
Dubin, Larry
El-Zabar, Kahil
Favre, Pierre
Fielder, Alvin
Graves, Milford
Harris, Beaver
Hemingway, Gerry
Higgins, Billy
Hove, Fred Van
Jackson, Ronald Shannon
Jarvis, Clifford
Johnson, Oliver
Jones, Elvin
Lewis, Art
Lissack, Selwyn
Lovens, Paul
Lytton, Paul
McCall, Steve
Martin, Stu
Mitchell, J. R.
Moffett, Charles
Moholo, Louis
Moses, J. C.
Motian, Paul
Moye, Famadou Don
Murray, Sunny
Oxley, Tony
Parker, Errol
Perry, Frank
Pozar, Cleve F.
Prevost, Eddie
Quaye, Terri
Reid, Steve
Roach, Max
Romano, Aldo

Drums/Percussion (cont.)

Schoenenberg, Detlef
Shaw, Charles Bobo
Smith, Warren
Sommer, Gunter "Baby"
Stevens, John
Tarasov, Vladimir
Turner, Roger
Vesala, Edward
Wilson, Phillip

French Horn

Chancey, Vincent

Guitar

Bailey, Derek
Boni, Raymond
Bourelly, Jean-Paul
Cline, Nels
Doerge, Pierre
Emery, James
Frisell, Bill
Jackson, Michael Gregory
Laswell, Bill
Nix, Bern
Reichel, Hans
Rhames, Arthur
Ross, Brandon
Russell, John
Sharrock, Sonny
Smith, Roger
Sudler, Monnette
Ulmer, James Blood

Piano

Abrams, Muhal Richard
Allen, Geri
Beresford, Steve
Bergman, Borah
Bley, Carla
Bley, Paul
Brackeen, Joanne
Broomer, Stuart
Burrell, Dave
Cobbs, Call, Jr.
Colson, Adegoke Steve
Coltrane, Alice
Corea, Chick
Cowell, Stanley
Crispell, Marilyn
Cuypers, Leo
Dauner, Wolfgang
Davis, Anthony
Fasteau, Zusaan Kali
Few, Bobby

Piano (cont.)

Fischer, John
Gaddy, Christopher
Ganelin, Vyacheslav
Gaslini, Giorgio
Greene, Burton
Hill, Andrew
Kuhn, Steve
Kuryokhin, Sergey
McGregor, Chris
Melford, Myra
Mengelberg, Misha
Myers, Amina Claudine
Neil, Al
Papadimitriou, Sakis
Parker, Errol
Plimley, Paul
Pullen, Don
Rhames, Arthur
Riley, Howard
Rivers, Sam
Rosewoman, Michele
Ruegg, Mathias
Schlippenbach, Alexander Von
Schweizer, Irene
Shipp, Mathew
Smythe, Pat
Sun Ra
Tapscott, Horace
Taylor, Cecil
Tippett, Keith
Tusques, Francois
Tyner, McCoy
Waldron, Mal
Westbrook, Mike
Yamashita, Yosuke

Reeds

Ackley, Bruce
Braxton, Anthony
Breuker, Willem
Carl, Ruediger
Chekasin, Vladimir
Dudek, Gerd
Ehrlich, Marty
Ewart, Douglas
Fasteau, Zusaan Kali
Golia, Vinny
Hauge, Herman
Jarman, Joseph
Jaume, Andre
Lancaster, Byard
Logan, Giuseppi
McPhee, Joe
Marshall, James
Maslak, Keshavan
Mitchell, Roscoe

Reeds (cont.)

Ochs, Larry
Parker, Evan
Parran, J. D.
Petrowsky, Ernst-Ludwig
Portal, Michel
Purcell, John
Raskin, Jon
Rigby, Joe
Rivers, Sam
Smith, Bill
Threadgill, Henry
Voight, Andrew
White, Andrew N.
Wilkerson, Ed

Alto Sax

Aaltonen, Juhani
Allen, Byron
Allen, Marshall
Beer, Ronnie
Berne, Tim
Blythe, Arthur
Brown, Marion
Coe, Tony
Coleman, Ornette
Coleman, Steve
Coxhill, Lol
Dean, Elton
Dolphy, Eric
Harriott, Joe
Hemphill, Julius
Howard, Noah
Jones, Arthur
Jordan, Lewis
Kenyatta, Robin
Lake, Oliver
Lasha, Prince
Lyons, Jimmy
McIntyre, Ken
Moondoc, Jemeel
Osborne, Mike
Potts, Steve
Pukwana, Dudu
Simmons, Sonny
Tchicai, John
Thomas, Luther
Tyler, Charles
Ward, Carlos
Whitecage, Mark

Baritone Sax

Bluiett, Hamiet
Davis, Charles
Patrick, Pat
Surman, John

Soprano Sax

Bloom, Jane Ira
Coltrane, John
Lacy, Steve

Tenor Sax

Aaltonen, Juhani
Anderson, Fred
Ayler, Albert
Barbieri, Gato
Beer, Ronnie
Brackeen, Charles
Broetzmann, Peter
Chautemps, Jean-Louis
Clay, James
Coltrane, John
Doyle, Arthur
Freeman, Chico
Gare, Lou
Gayle, Charles
Gilmore, John
Harper, Billy
Lowe, Frank
McIntyre, Maurice
Murray, David
Pepper, Jim
Pine, Courtney
Pope, Odean
Redman, Dewey
Rhames, Arthur
Rollins, Sonny
Sanders, Pharoah
Shepp, Archie
Skidmore, Alan
Stubblefield, John
Terroade, Kenneth
Ware, David
Watts, Marzette
Watts, Trevor
Wilen, Barney
Wright, Frank

Trombone

Anderson, Ray
Bauer, Conrad
Bowie, Joseph
Christmann, Gunter
Cook, Marty
Griffiths, Malcolm
Harris, Craig
Lashley, Lester
Lewis, George
Malfatti, Radu
Mangelsdorff, Albert
Moncur, Grachan III
Priester, Julian

Trombone (cont.)

Rudd, Roswell
Rutherford, Paul

Trumpet

Abdullah, Ahmed
Ayler, Donald
Beckett, Harry
Bowie, Lester
Bradford, Bobby
Brimfield, William
Brooks, Arthur
Carroll, Baikida
Cherry, Don
Cohran, Phil
Coleman, Ornette
Coursil, Jacques
Cross, Earl
Daniel, Ted
Dara, Olu
Dixon, Bill
Donald, Barbara
Feza, Mongezi
Gale, Eddie
Jackson, Ambrose
Jackson, John Shenoy
Johnson, Dewey
Keane, Shake
Kondo, Toshinori
LeFlore, Floyd
Levin, Marc
Little, Booker
Mantler, Michael
Massey, Cal
Morris, Butch
Owens, Jimmy
Peterson, Hannibal Marvin
Ragin, Hugh
Rava, Enrico
Sams, George
Schoof, Manfred
Shorter, Alan
Smith, Leo
Stanko, Tomasz
Thornton, Clifford
Tolliver, Charles
Vitet, Bernard
Wheeler, Kenny

Tuba

Stewart, Bob

Vibraphone

Berger, Karl
Dickerson, Walt

Vibraphone (cont.)

Griffith, Earl
Hampel, Gunter
Hoggard, Jay
Hutcherson, Bobby
Jamal, Khan
Lewis, Bill
Naughton, Bobby
Robinson, Orphy

Violin

Bang, Billy
Coleman, Ornette
Coombes, Nigel
Jenkins, Leroy

Vocals

Aebi, Irene
Christi, Ellen
Clayton, Jay
Colson, Iqua
Cortez, Jayne
Fasteau, Zusaan Kali
Holder, Frank
Lee, Jeanne
Lincoln, Abbey
Minton, Phil
Newton, Lauren
Nicols, Maggie
Sharrock, Linda
Warford, Rita
Waters, Patty
Wilson, Joe Lee
Winstone, Norma

Artist Index

A

B

Subject Index

Author Index

I

J

K

L

Q

R

Y

Z

About the Compiler

JOHN GRAY is currently director of the Black Arts Research Center, an archival resource center dedicated to the documentation, preservation and dissemination of the African cultural legacy. His previous publications include *African Music: A Bibliographical Guide to the Traditional, Popular, Art & Liturgical Musics of Sub-Saharan Africa*; *Blacks in Film and Television: A Pan-African Bibliography of Films, Filmmakers, and Performers*; *Black Theatre and Performance*; *Ashe, Traditional Religion and Healing in Sub-Saharan Africa and the Diaspora*; and *Blacks in Classical Music*, all published by Greenwood Press.